Ka
ke
gu
ru
i 9

Twin

⑨

K A K E G U R U I   T W I N

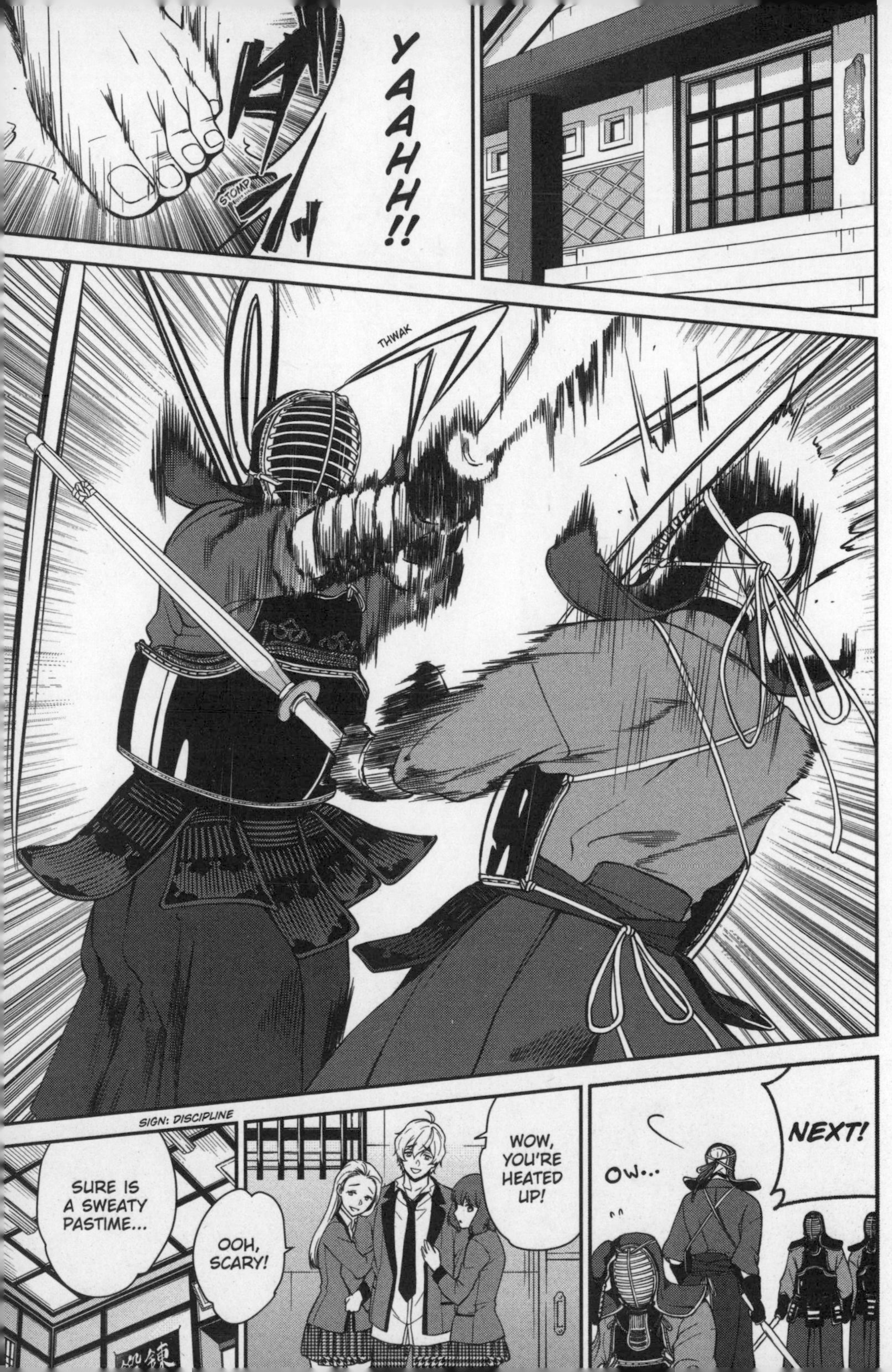
YAAHH!!
STOMP
THWAK
NEXT!
OW...
WOW, YOU'RE HEATED UP!
OOH, SCARY!
SIGN: DISCIPLINE
SURE IS A SWEATY PASTIME...

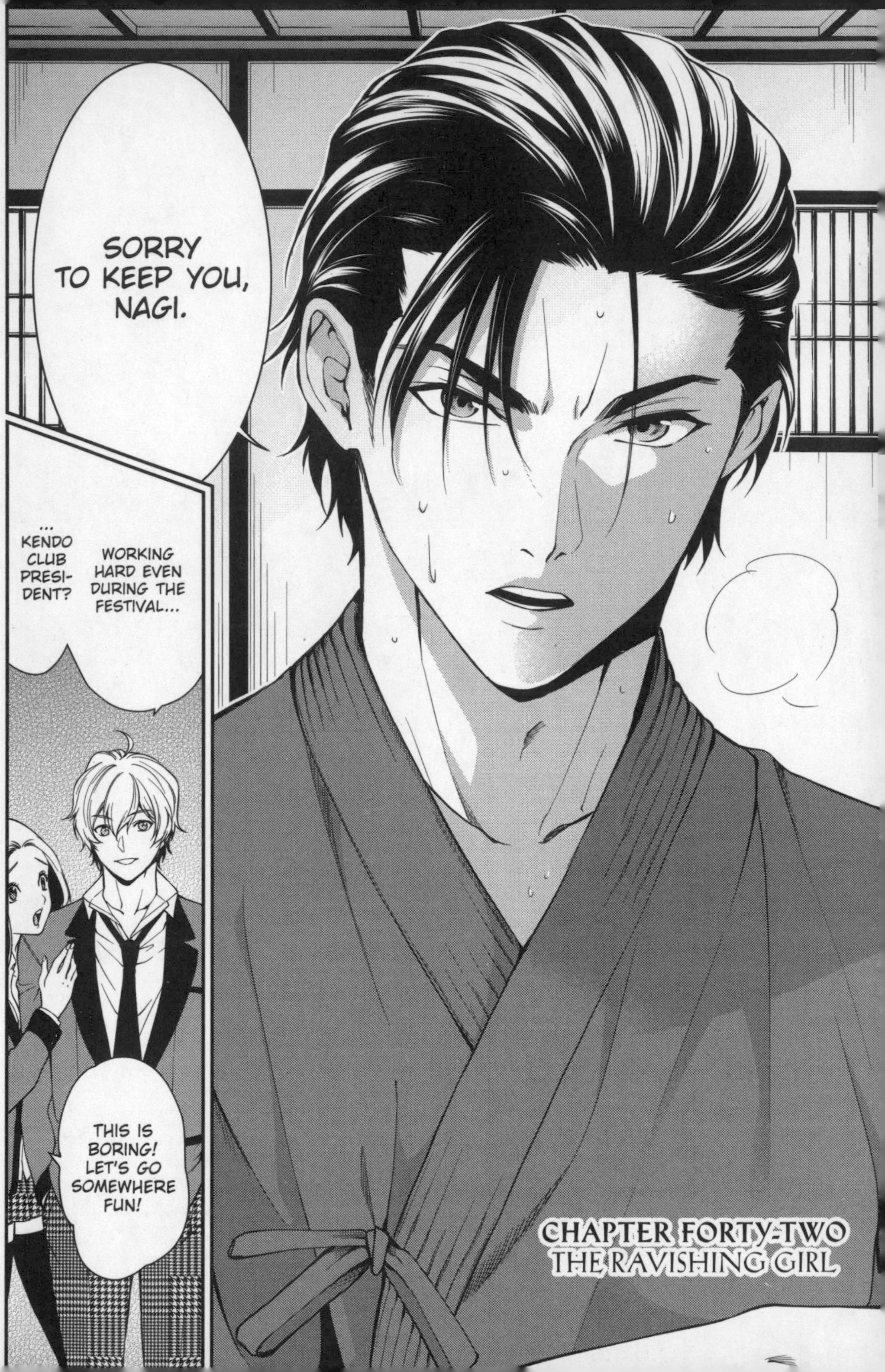
SORRY TO KEEP YOU, NAGI.
CHAPTER FORTY-TWO
THE RAVISHING GIRL
WORKING HARD EVEN DURING THE FESTIVAL...
...KENDO CLUB PRESIDENT?
THIS IS BORING! LET'S GO SOMEWHERE FUN!

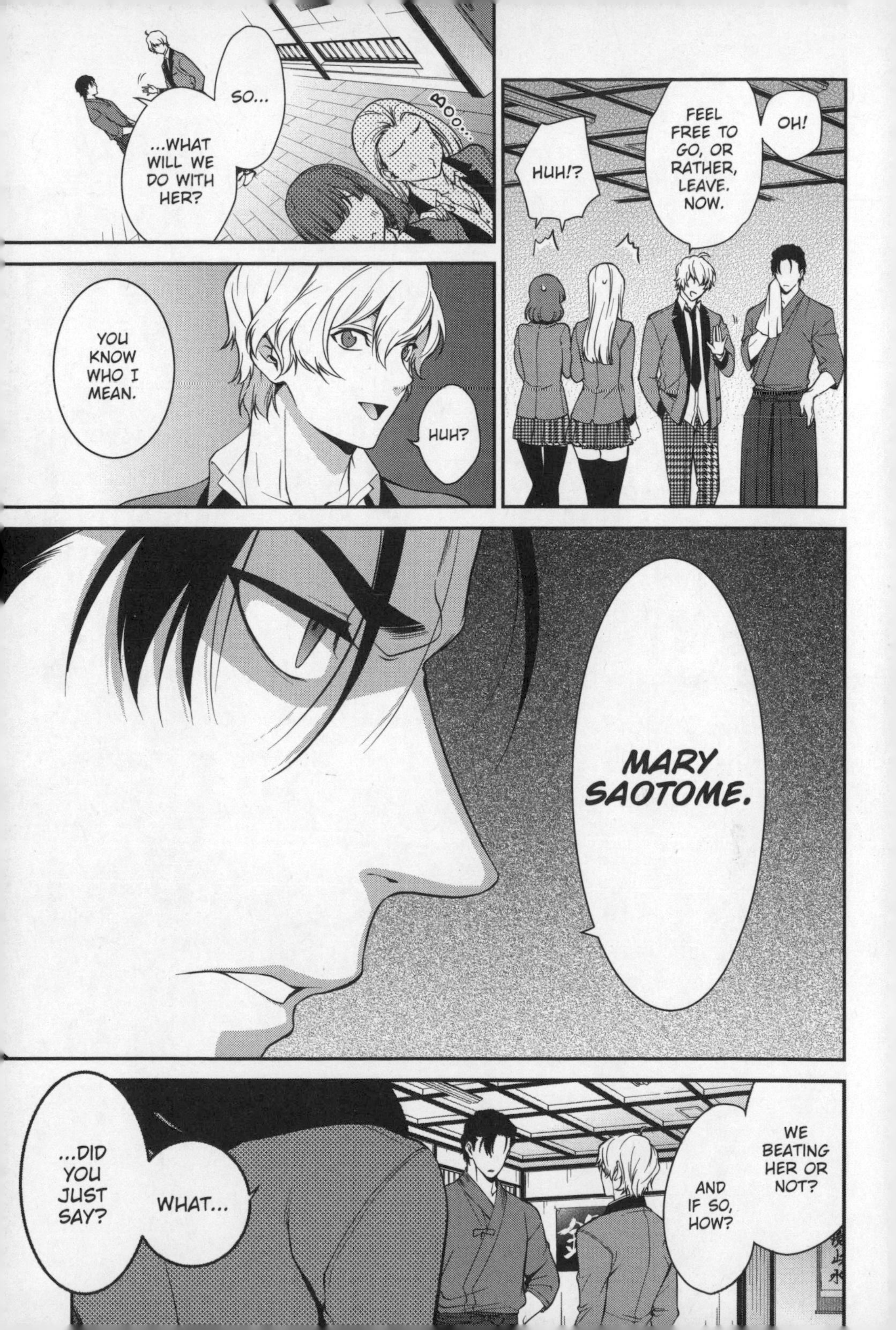
OH!
FEEL FREE TO GO, OR RATHER, LEAVE. NOW.
HUH!?
SO...
...WHAT WILL WE DO WITH HER?
BOO...
YOU KNOW WHO I MEAN.
HUH?
MARY SAOTOME.
WE BEATING HER OR NOT?
AND IF SO, HOW?
WHAT...
...DID YOU JUST SAY?

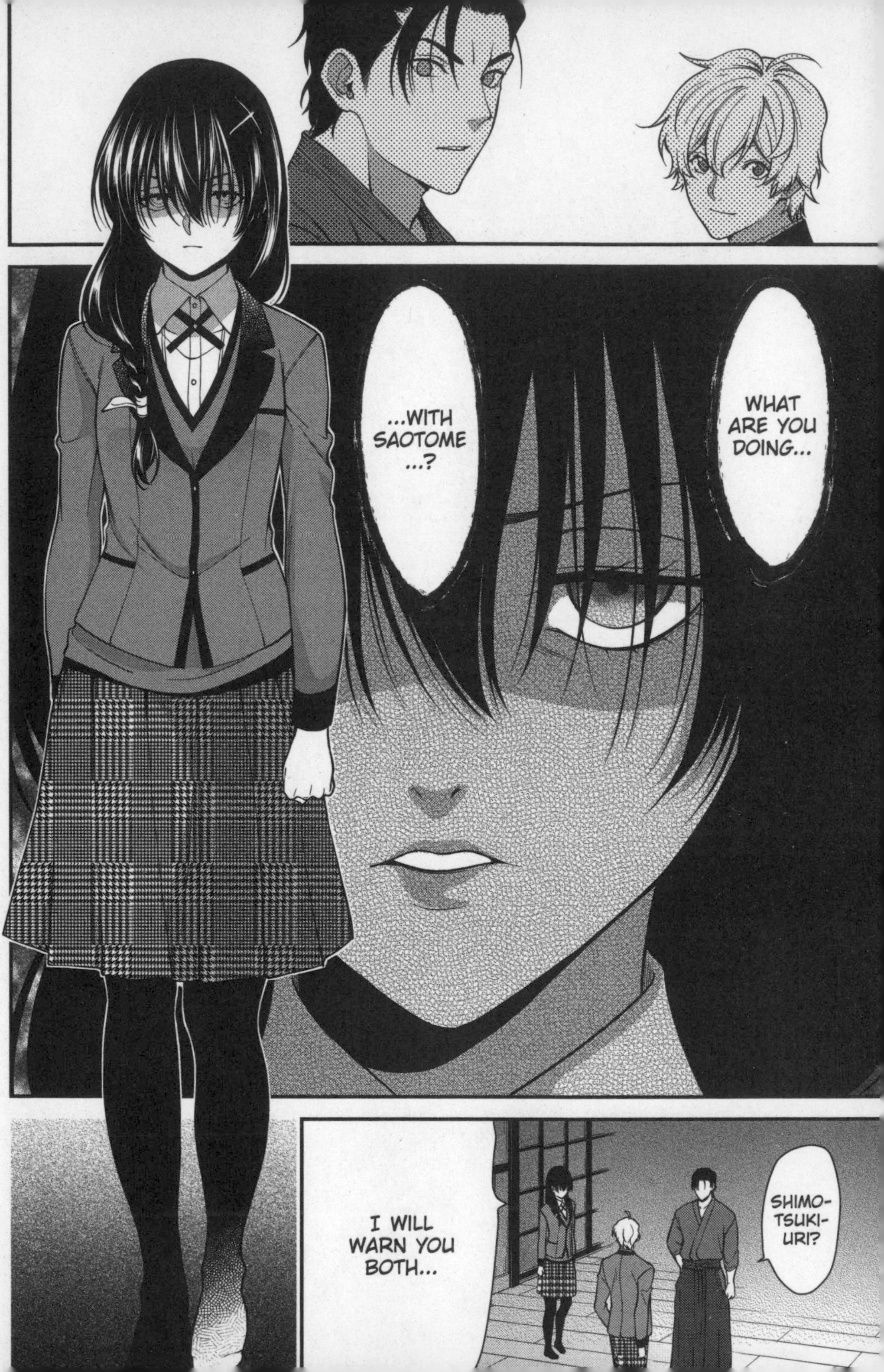
WHAT ARE YOU DOING...
...WITH SAOTOME ...?
SHIMO-TSUKI-URI?
I WILL WARN YOU BOTH...

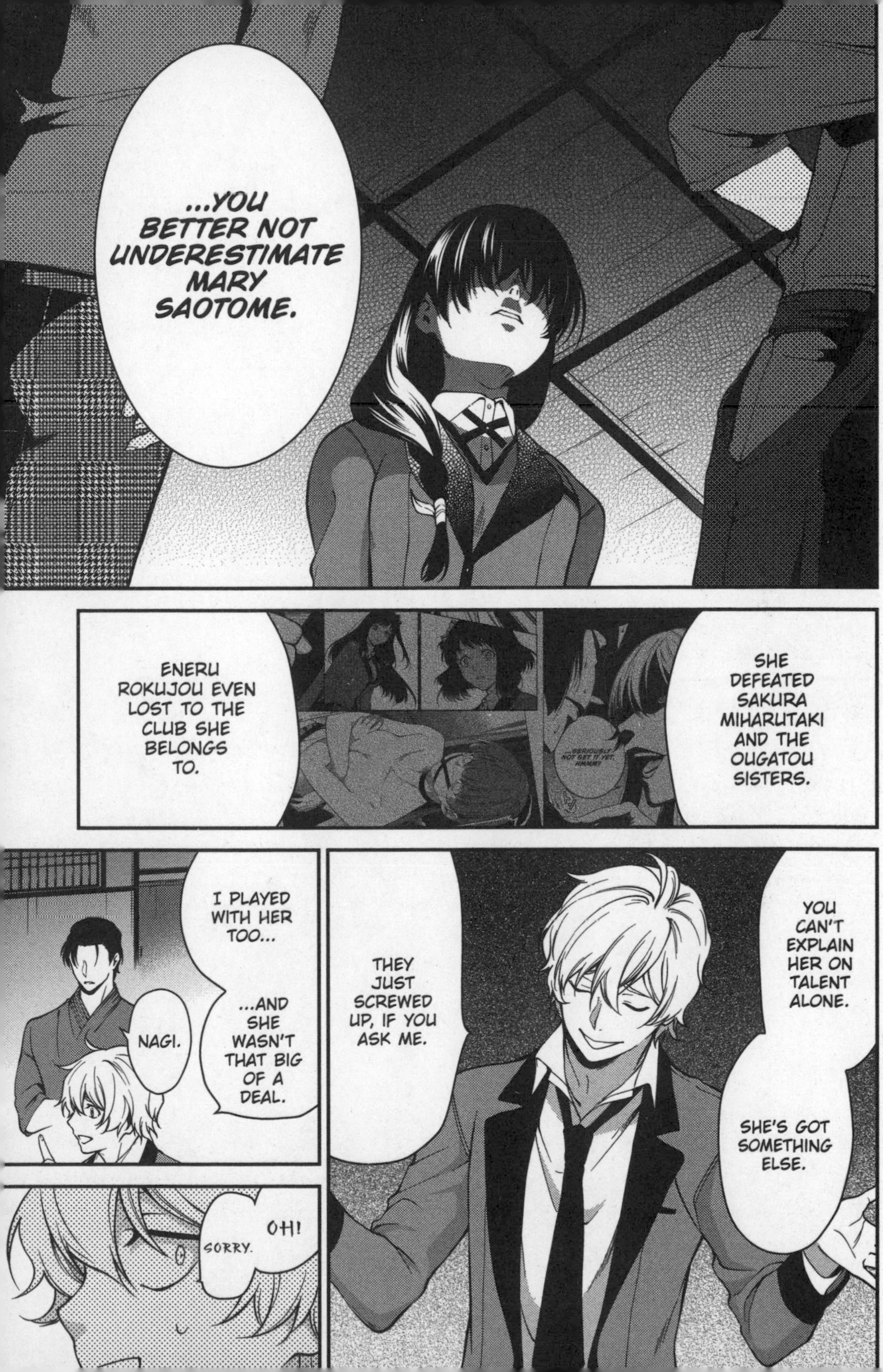
...YOU BETTER NOT UNDERESTIMATE MARY SAOTOME.
SHE DEFEATED SAKURA MIHARUTAKI AND THE OUGATOU SISTERS.
...SERIOUSLY NOT GET IT YET, HMM?
ENERU ROKUJOU EVEN LOST TO THE CLUB SHE BELONGS TO.
YOU CAN'T EXPLAIN HER ON TALENT ALONE.
SHE'S GOT SOMETHING ELSE.
THEY JUST SCREWED UP, IF YOU ASK ME.
I PLAYED WITH HER TOO...
...AND SHE WASN'T THAT BIG OF A DEAL.
NAGI.
OH!
SORRY.

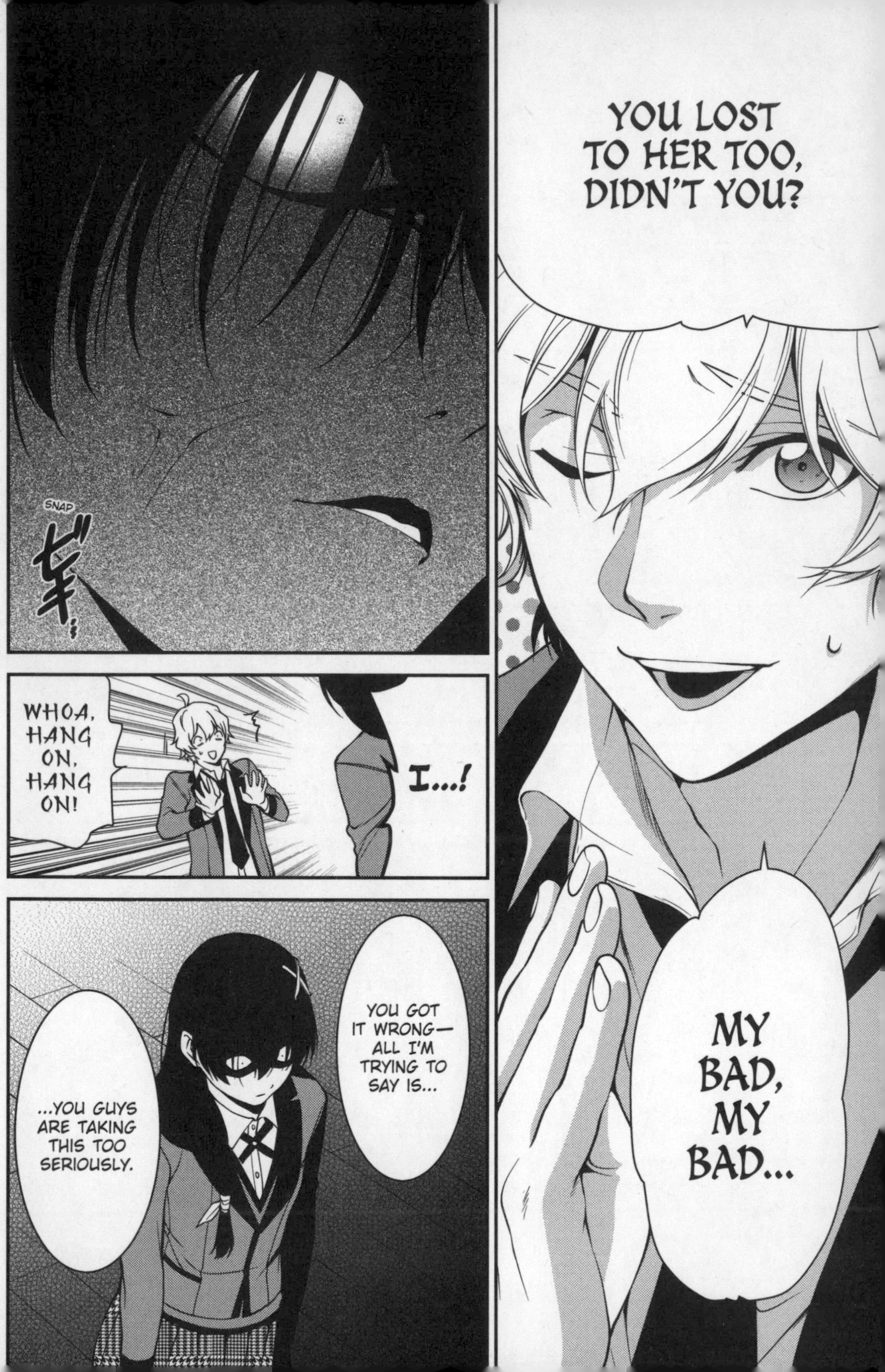
YOU LOST TO HER TOO, DIDN'T YOU?
MY BAD, MY BAD...
SNAP
ビキ
I...!
WHOA, HANG ON, HANG ON!
YOU GOT IT WRONG— ALL I'M TRYING TO SAY IS...
...YOU GUYS ARE TAKING THIS TOO SERIOUSLY.

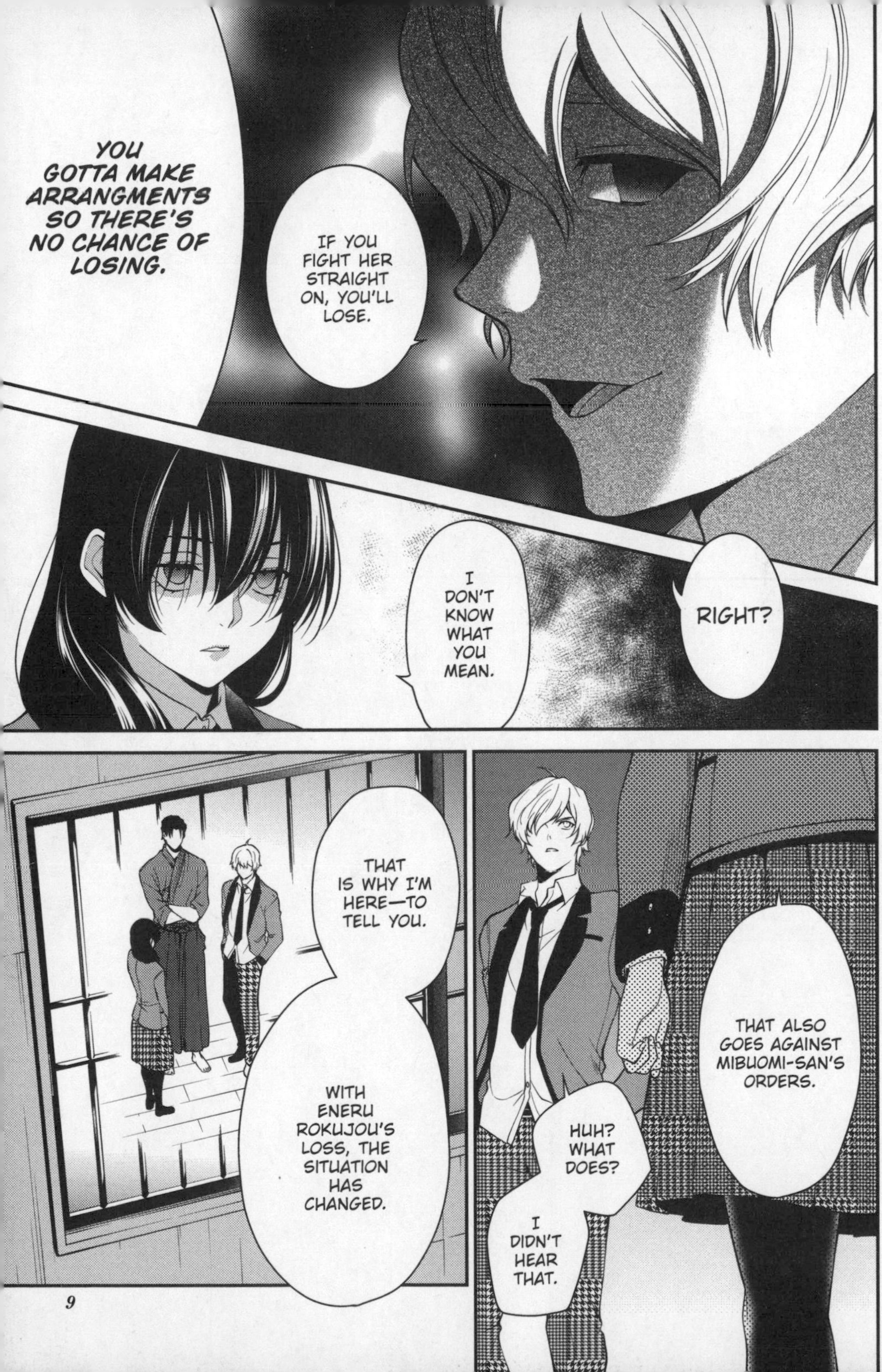
IF YOU FIGHT HER STRAIGHT ON, YOU'LL LOSE.
YOU GOTTA MAKE ARRANGMENTS SO THERE'S NO CHANCE OF LOSING.
RIGHT?
I DON'T KNOW WHAT YOU MEAN.
THAT ALSO GOES AGAINST MIBUOMI-SAN'S ORDERS.
HUH? WHAT DOES?
I DIDN'T HEAR THAT.
THAT IS WHY I'M HERE—TO TELL YOU.
WITH ENERU ROKUJOU'S LOSS, THE SITUATION HAS CHANGED.

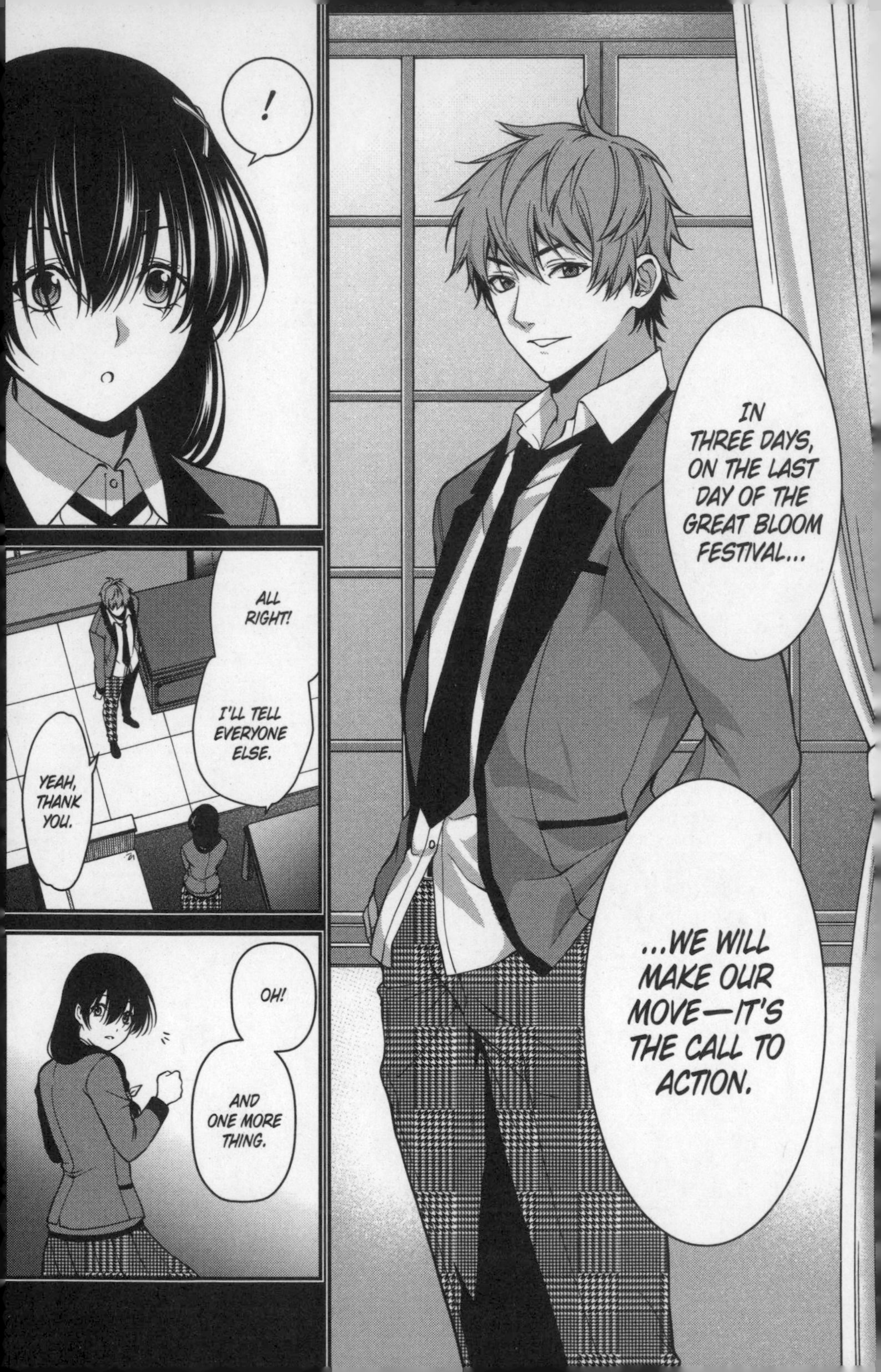
IN THREE DAYS, ON THE LAST DAY OF THE GREAT BLOOM FESTIVAL...
...WE WILL MAKE OUR MOVE—IT'S THE CALL TO ACTION.
!
ALL RIGHT!
I'LL TELL EVERYONE ELSE.
YEAH, THANK YOU.
OH!
AND ONE MORE THING.

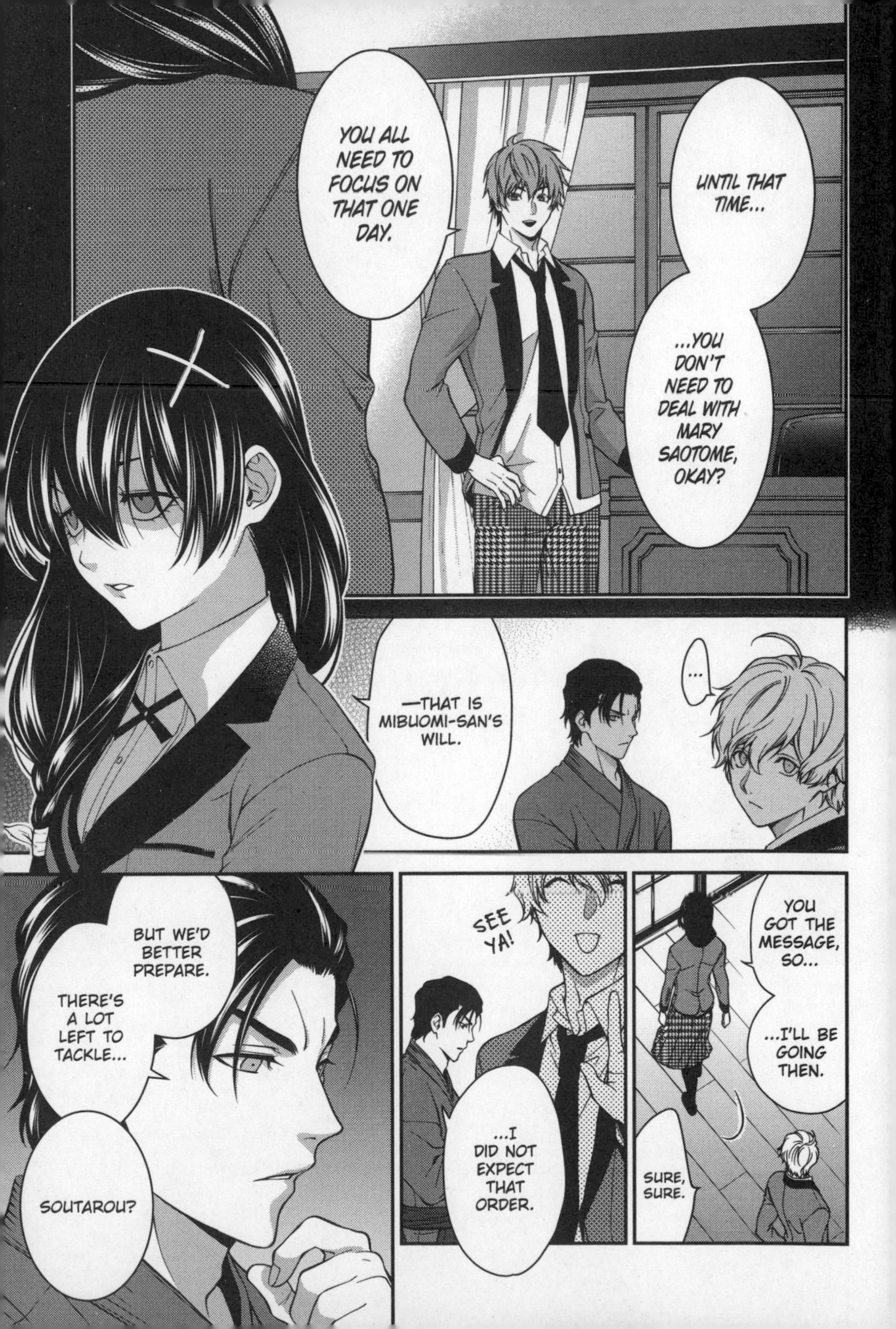
UNTIL THAT TIME...
...YOU DON'T NEED TO DEAL WITH MARY SAOTOME, OKAY?
YOU ALL NEED TO FOCUS ON THAT ONE DAY.
...
—THAT IS MIBUOMI-SAN'S WILL.
YOU GOT THE MESSAGE, SO...
...I'LL BE GOING THEN.
SURE, SURE.
SEE YA!
...I DID NOT EXPECT THAT ORDER.
BUT WE'D BETTER PREPARE.
THERE'S A LOT LEFT TO TACKLE...
SOUTAROU?

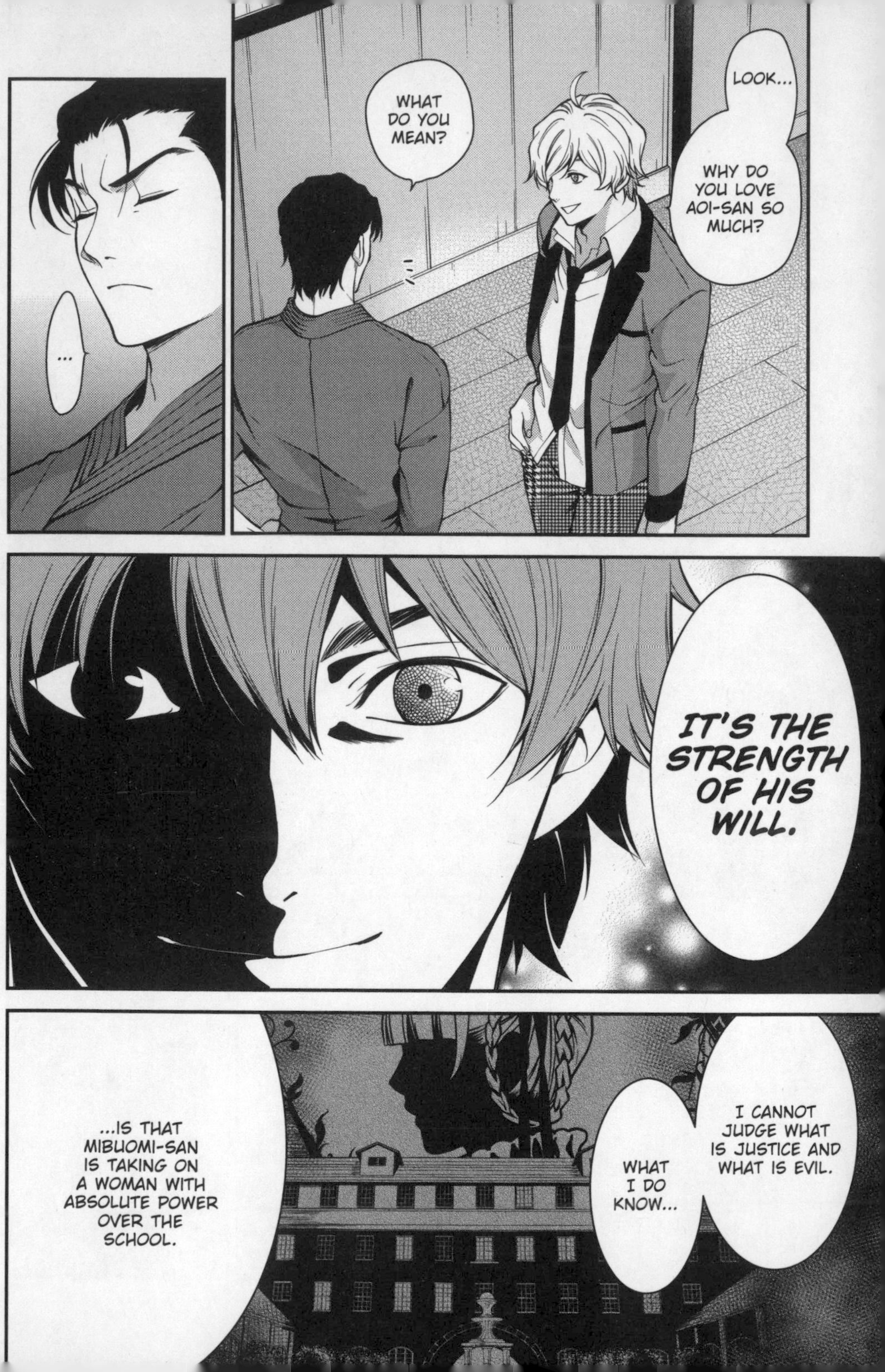
LOOK...
WHY DO YOU LOVE AOI-SAN SO MUCH?
WHAT DO YOU MEAN?
...
IT'S THE STRENGTH OF HIS WILL.
I CANNOT JUDGE WHAT IS JUSTICE AND WHAT IS EVIL.
WHAT I DO KNOW...
...IS THAT MIBUOMI-SAN IS TAKING ON A WOMAN WITH ABSOLUTE POWER OVER THE SCHOOL.

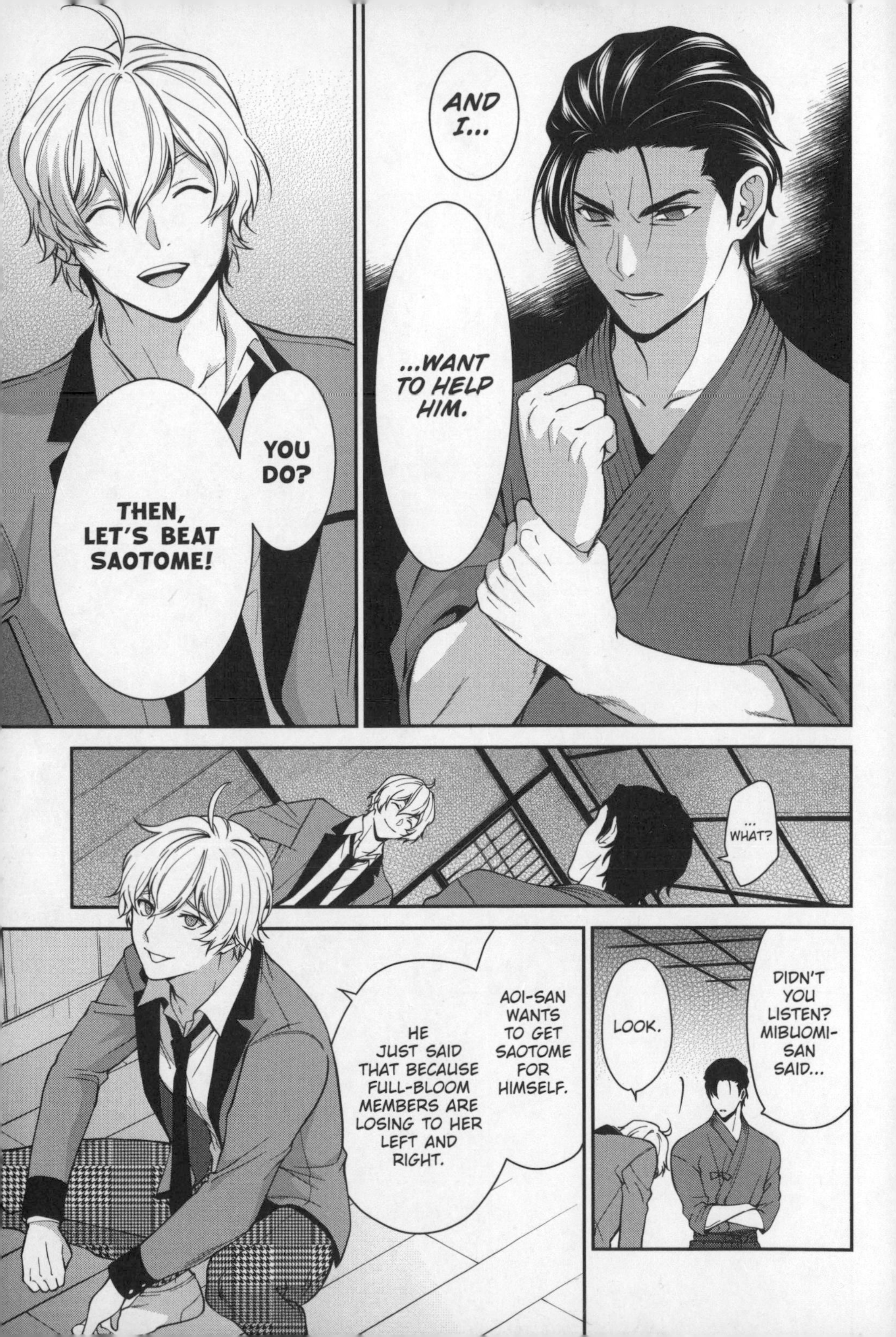
AND I...
...WANT TO HELP HIM.
YOU DO?
THEN, LET'S BEAT SAOTOME!
...WHAT?
DIDN'T YOU LISTEN? MIBUOMI-SAN SAID...
LOOK.
AOI-SAN WANTS TO GET SAOTOME FOR HIMSELF.
HE JUST SAID THAT BECAUSE FULL-BLOOM MEMBERS ARE LOSING TO HER LEFT AND RIGHT.

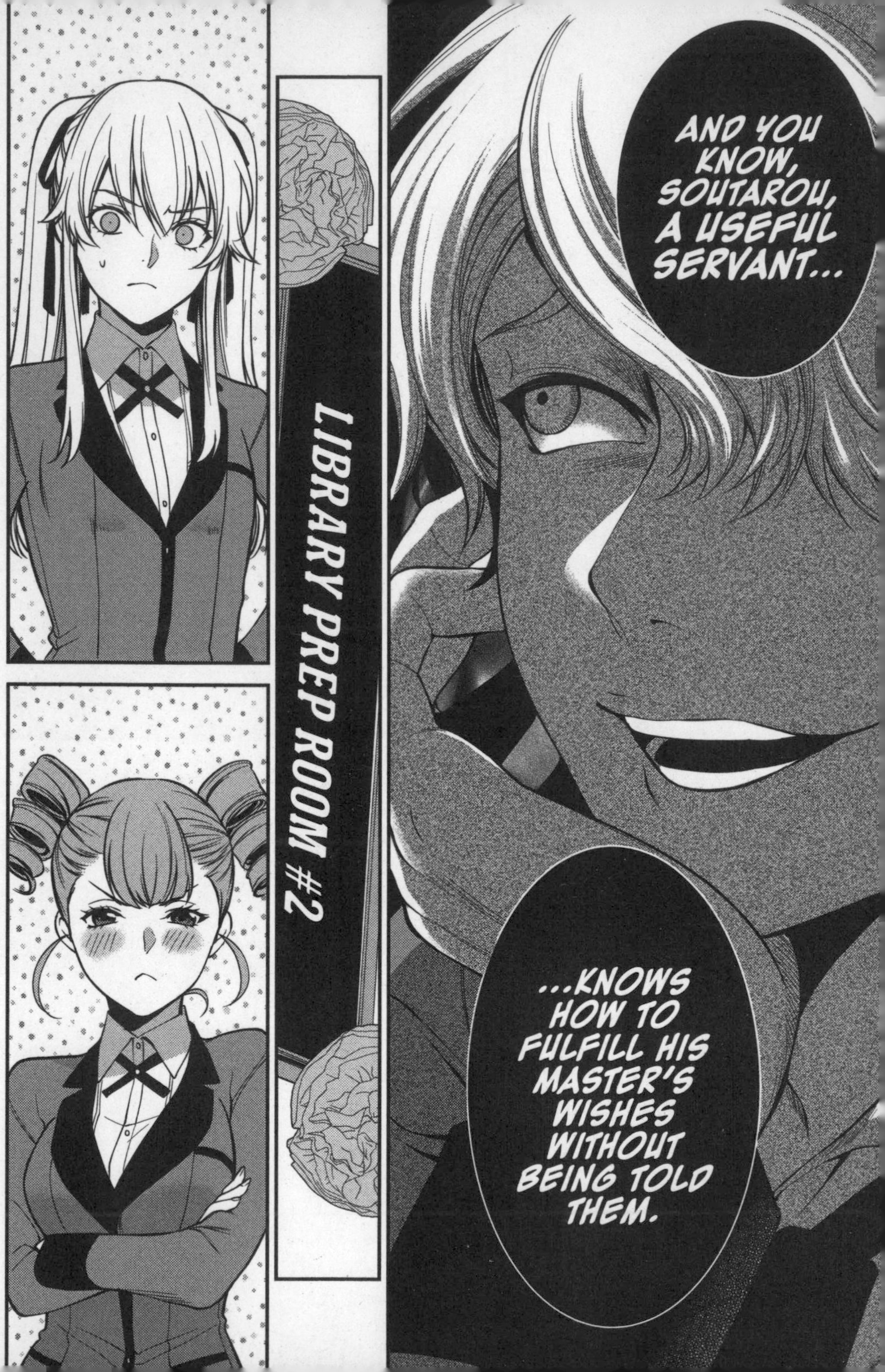
AND YOU KNOW, SOUTAROU, A USEFUL SERVANT...
...KNOWS HOW TO FULFILL HIS MASTER'S WISHES WITHOUT BEING TOLD THEM.
LIBRARY PREP ROOOM #2

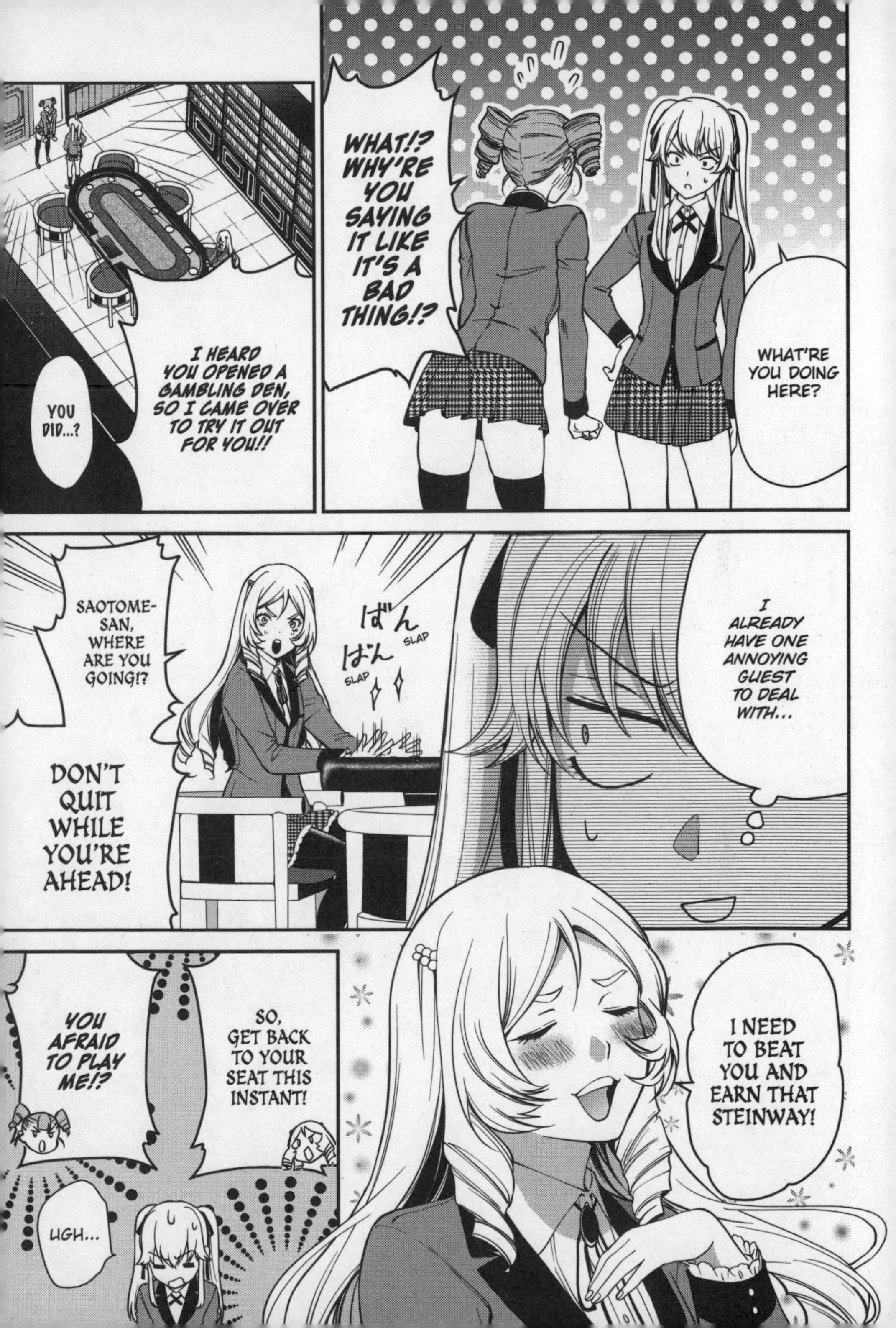
WHAT'RE YOU DOING HERE?
WHAT!? WHY'RE YOU SAYING IT LIKE IT'S A BAD THING!?
I HEARD YOU OPENED A GAMBLING DEN, SO I CAME OVER TO TRY IT OUT FOR YOU!!
YOU DID...?
I ALREADY HAVE ONE ANNOYING GUEST TO DEAL WITH...
SAOTOME-SAN, WHERE ARE YOU GOING!?
ばん
SLAP
ばん
SLAP
DON'T QUIT WHILE YOU'RE AHEAD!
I NEED TO BEAT YOU AND EARN THAT STEINWAY!
SO, GET BACK TO YOUR SEAT THIS INSTANT!
YOU AFRAID TO PLAY ME!?
UGH...

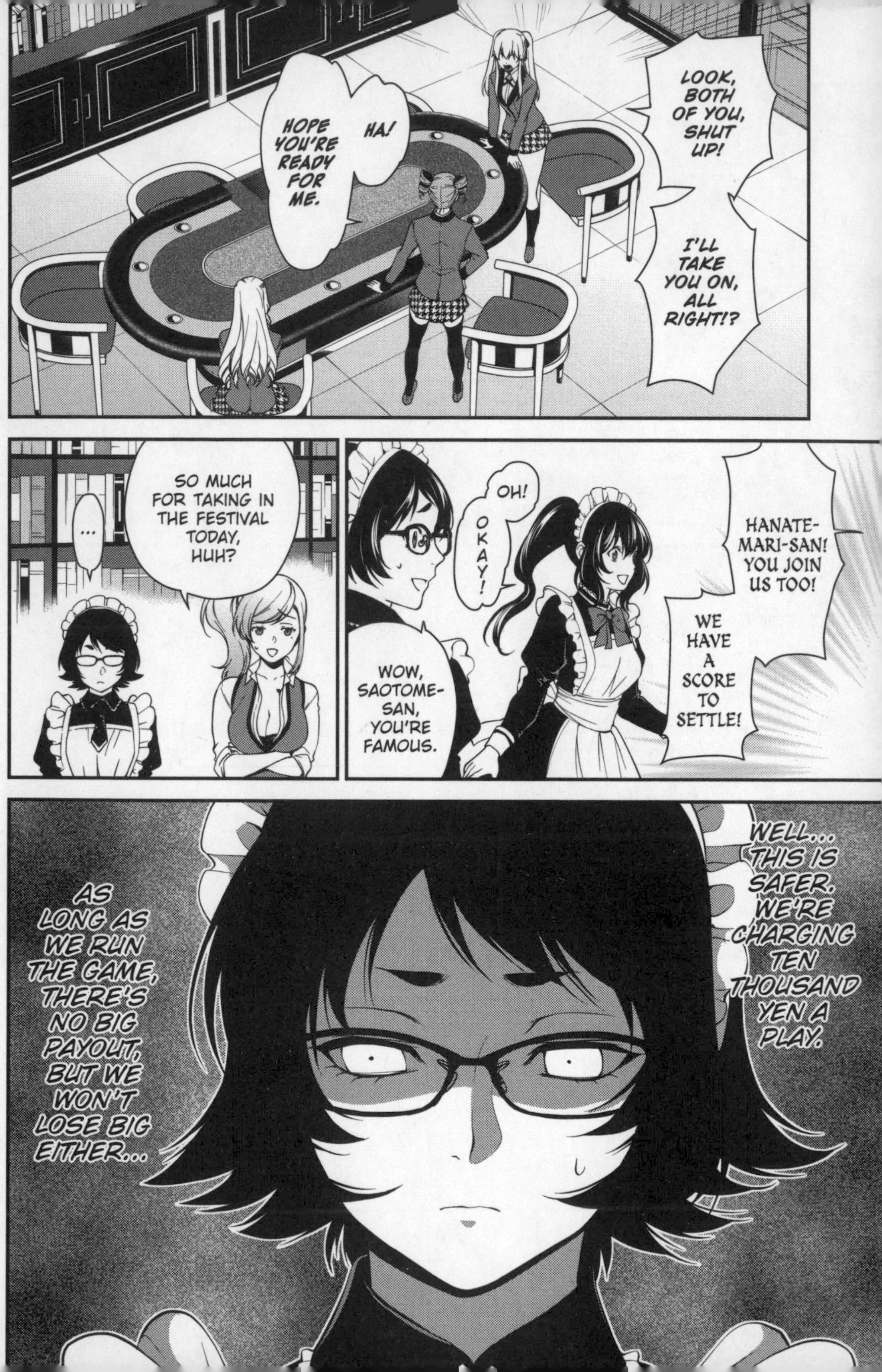
LOOK, BOTH OF YOU, SHUT UP!
I'LL TAKE YOU ON, ALL RIGHT!?
HA!
HOPE YOU'RE READY FOR ME.
HANATE-MARI-SAN! YOU JOIN US TOO!
WE HAVE A SCORE TO SETTLE!
OH!
OKAY!
WOW, SAOTOME-SAN, YOU'RE FAMOUS.
SO MUCH FOR TAKING IN THE FESTIVAL TODAY, HUH?
...
WELL... THIS IS SAFER. WE'RE CHARGING TEN THOUSAND YEN A PLAY.
AS LONG AS WE RUN THE GAME, THERE'S NO BIG PAYOUT, BUT WE WON'T LOSE BIG EITHER...

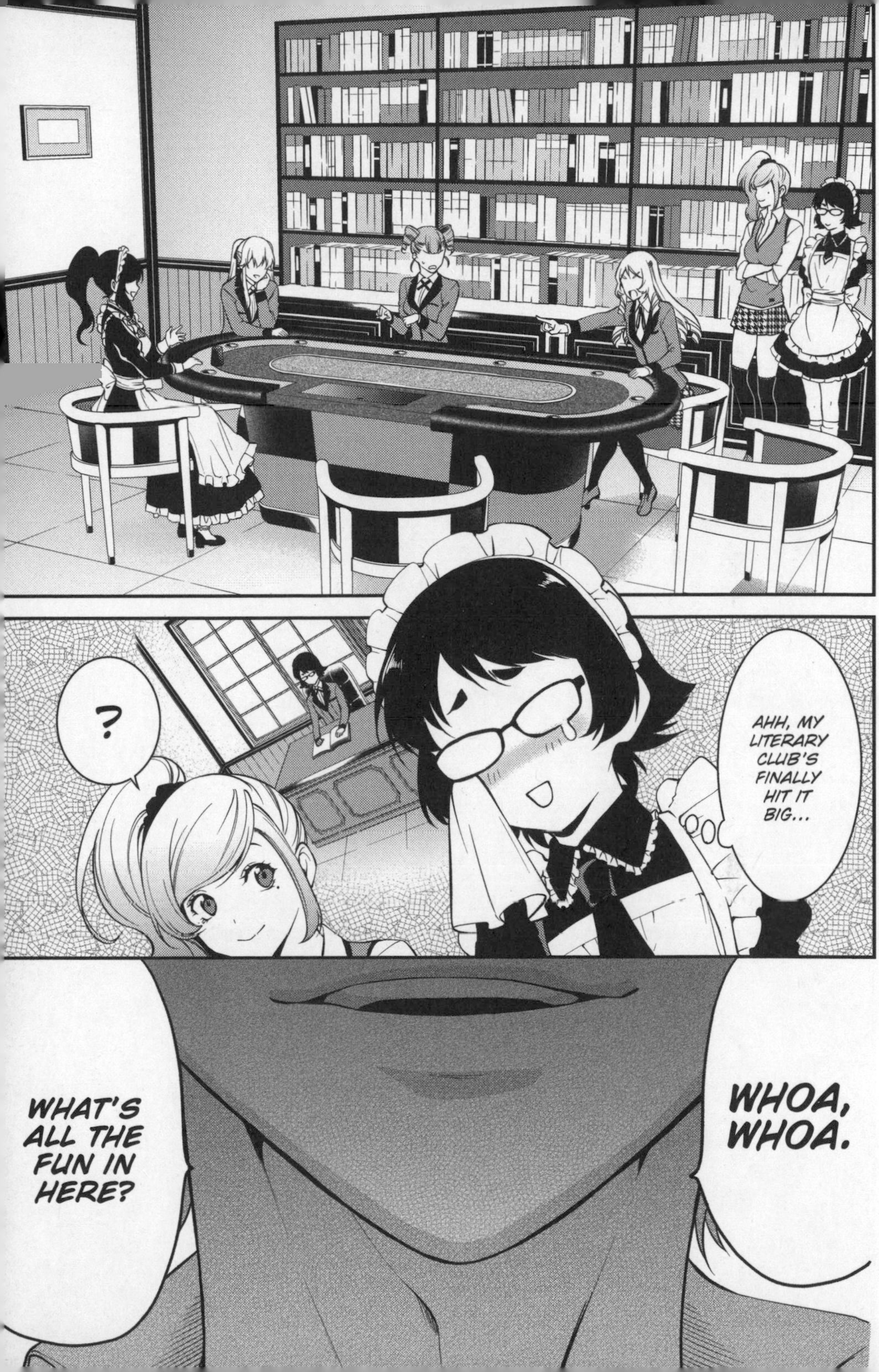
AHH, MY LITERARY CLUB'S FINALLY HIT IT BIG...
?
WHOA, WHOA.
WHAT'S ALL THE FUN IN HERE?

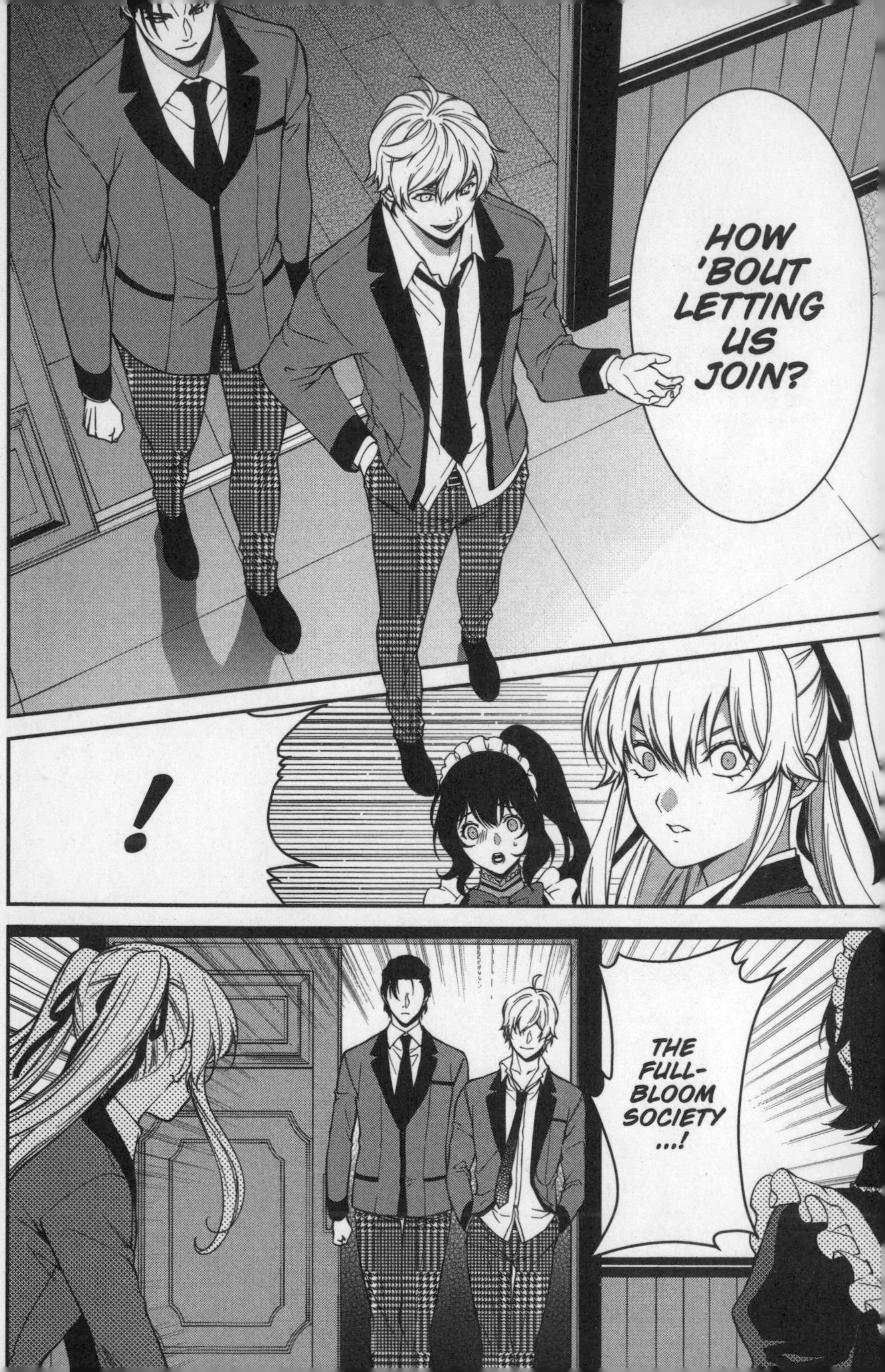
HOW 'BOUT LETTING US JOIN?
!
THE FULL-BLOOM SOCIETY ...!

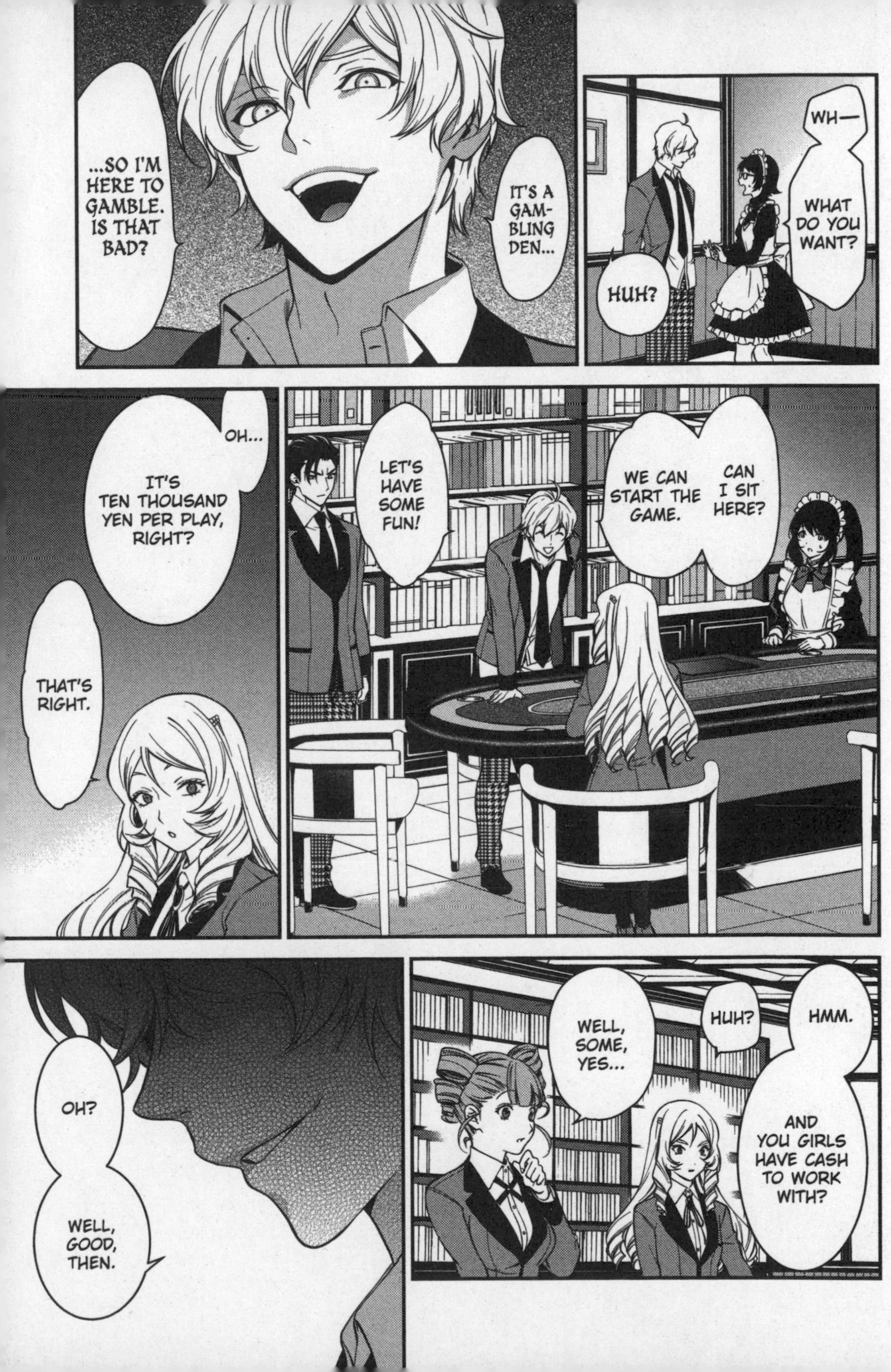
WH—
WHAT DO YOU WANT?
HUH?
IT'S A GAMBLING DEN...
...SO I'M HERE TO GAMBLE. IS THAT BAD?
CAN I SIT HERE?
WE CAN START THE GAME.
LET'S HAVE SOME FUN!
OH...
IT'S TEN THOUSAND YEN PER PLAY, RIGHT?
THAT'S RIGHT.
HMM.
AND YOU GIRLS HAVE CASH TO WORK WITH?
HUH?
WELL, SOME, YES...
OH?
WELL, GOOD, THEN.

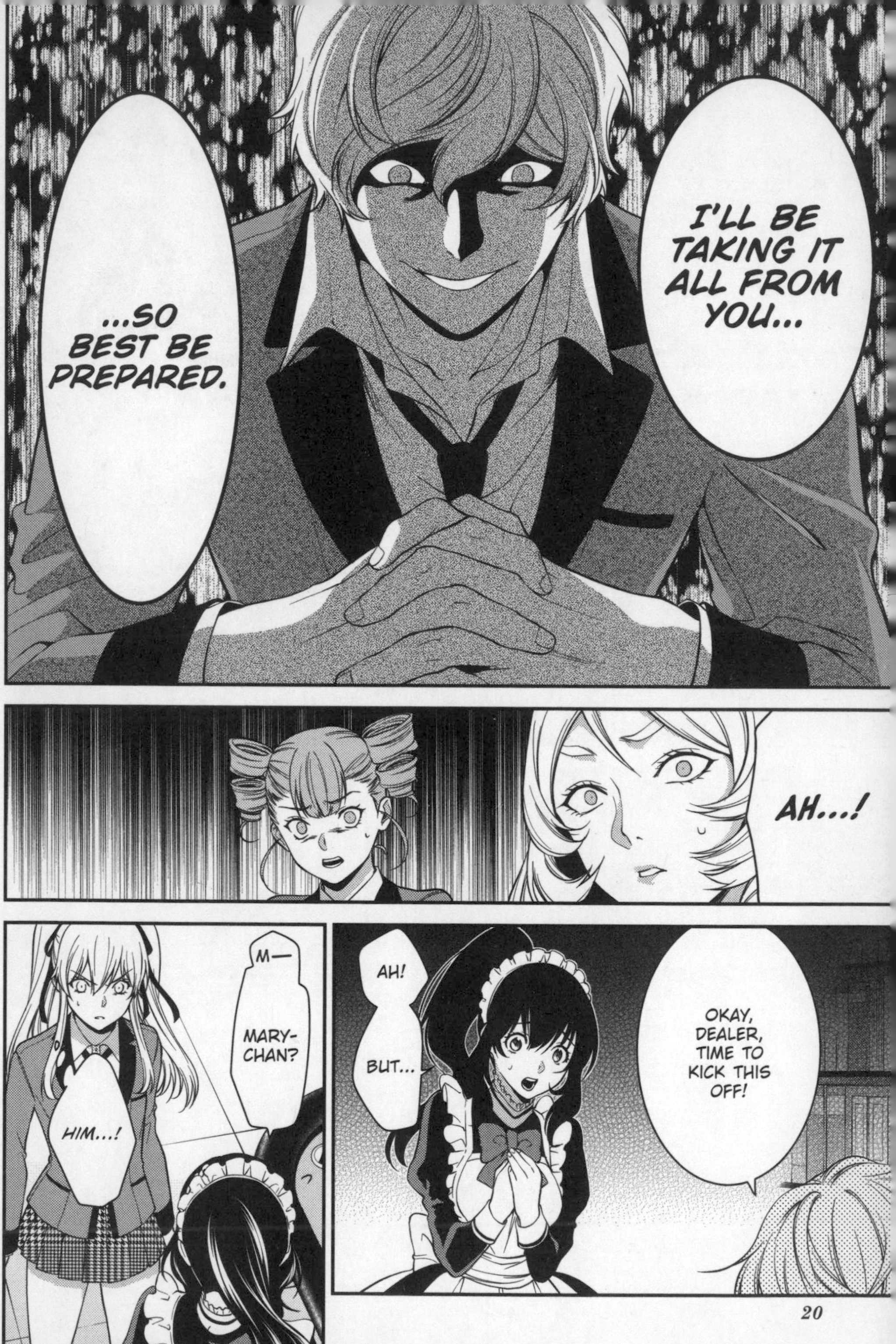
I'LL BE TAKING IT ALL FROM YOU...
...SO BEST BE PREPARED.
AH...!
OKAY, DEALER, TIME TO KICK THIS OFF!
AH!
BUT...
M—
MARY-CHAN?
HIM...!

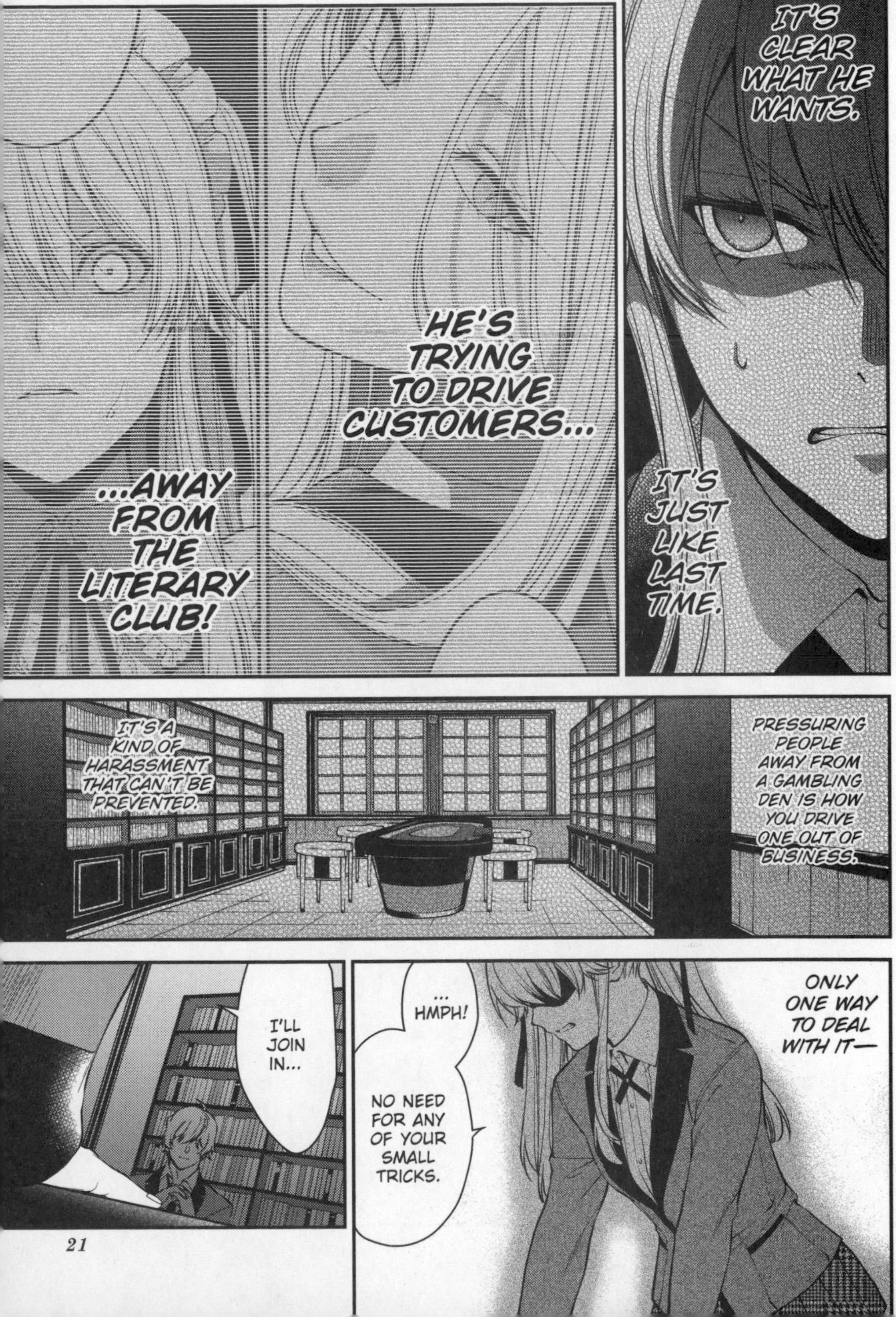
IT'S CLEAR WHAT HE WANTS.
IT'S JUST LIKE LAST TIME.
HE'S TRYING TO DRIVE CUSTOMERS...
...AWAY FROM THE LITERARY CLUB!
PRESSURING PEOPLE AWAY FROM A GAMBLING DEN IS HOW YOU DRIVE ONE OUT OF BUSINESS.
IT'S A KIND OF HARASSMENT THAT CAN'T BE PREVENTED.
ONLY ONE WAY TO DEAL WITH IT—
... HMPH!
NO NEED FOR ANY OF YOUR SMALL TRICKS.
I'LL JOIN IN...

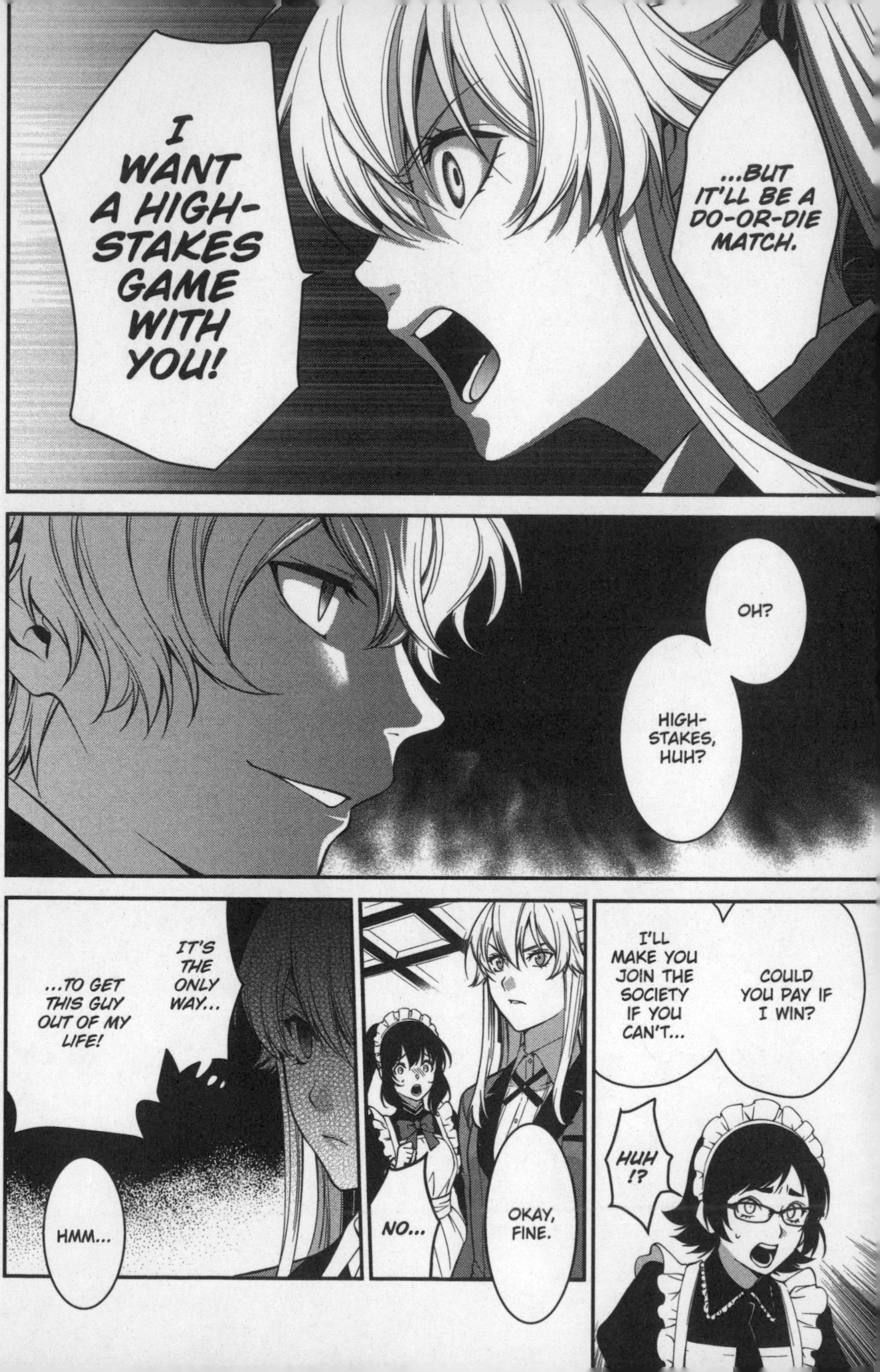
I WANT A HIGH-STAKES GAME WITH YOU!
...BUT IT'LL BE A DO-OR-DIE MATCH.
OH?
HIGH-STAKES, HUH?
COULD YOU PAY IF I WIN?
I'LL MAKE YOU JOIN THE SOCIETY IF YOU CAN'T...
HUH!?
OKAY, FINE.
NO...
IT'S THE ONLY WAY...
...TO GET THIS GUY OUT OF MY LIFE!
HMM...

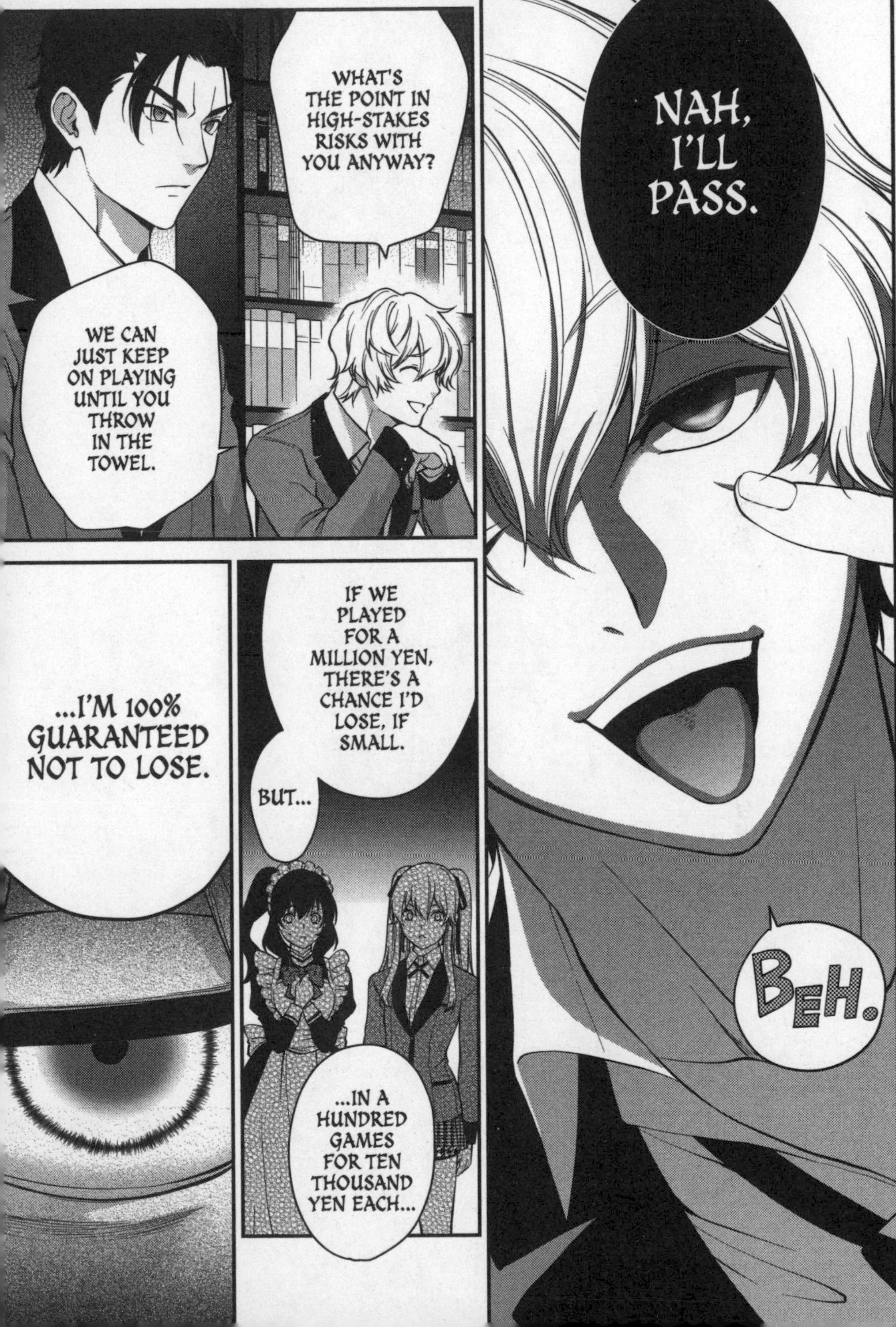
NAH, I'LL PASS.
BEH.
WHAT'S THE POINT IN HIGH-STAKES RISKS WITH YOU ANYWAY?
WE CAN JUST KEEP ON PLAYING UNTIL YOU THROW IN THE TOWEL.
IF WE PLAYED FOR A MILLION YEN, THERE'S A CHANCE I'D LOSE, IF SMALL.
BUT...
...IN A HUNDRED GAMES FOR TEN THOUSAND YEN EACH...
...I'M 100% GUARANTEED NOT TO LOSE.

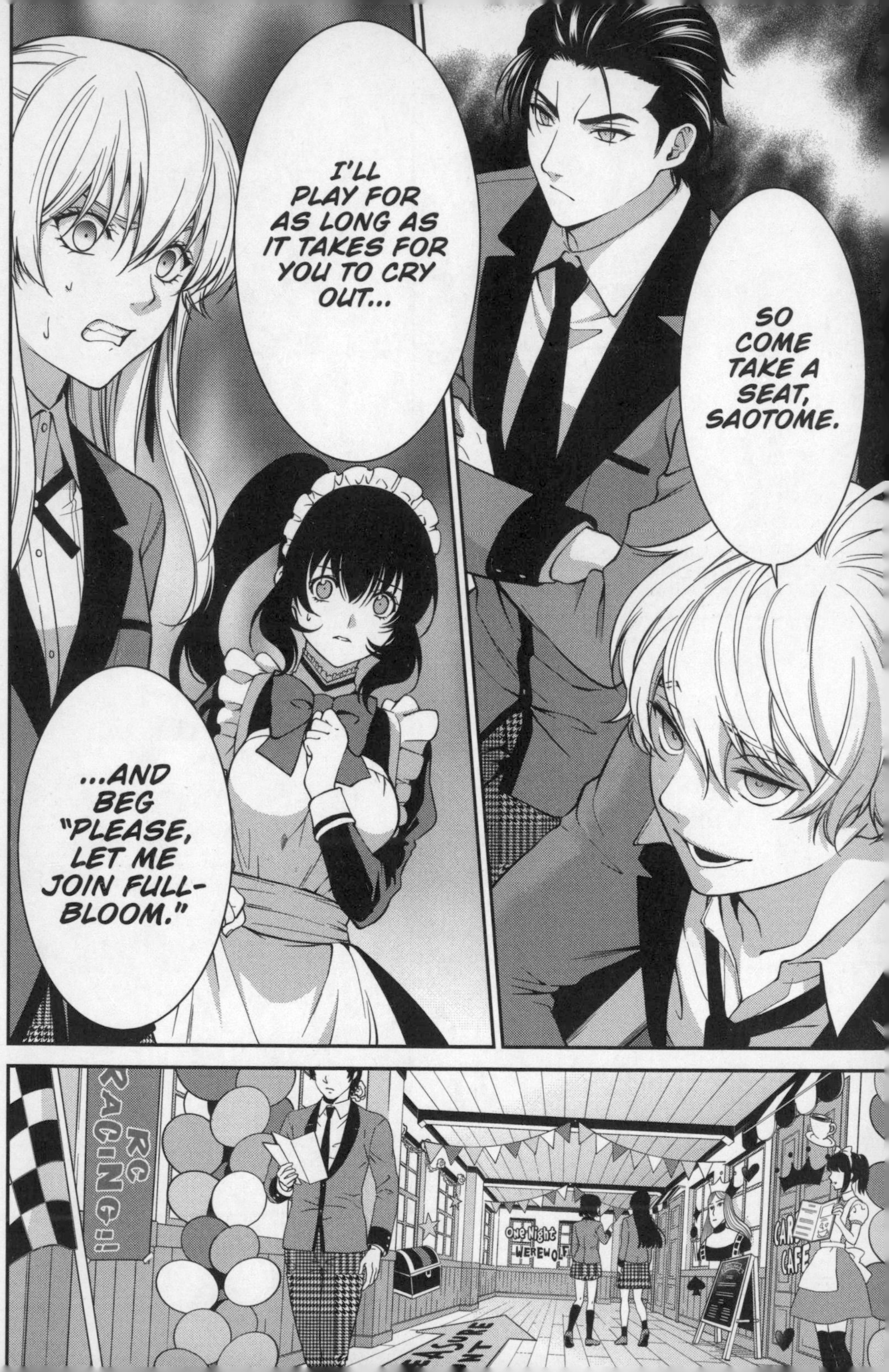
SO COME TAKE A SEAT, SAOTOME.
I'LL PLAY FOR AS LONG AS IT TAKES FOR YOU TO CRY OUT...
...AND BEG "PLEASE, LET ME JOIN FULL-BLOOM."
RC RACING!!
One Night WEREWOLF

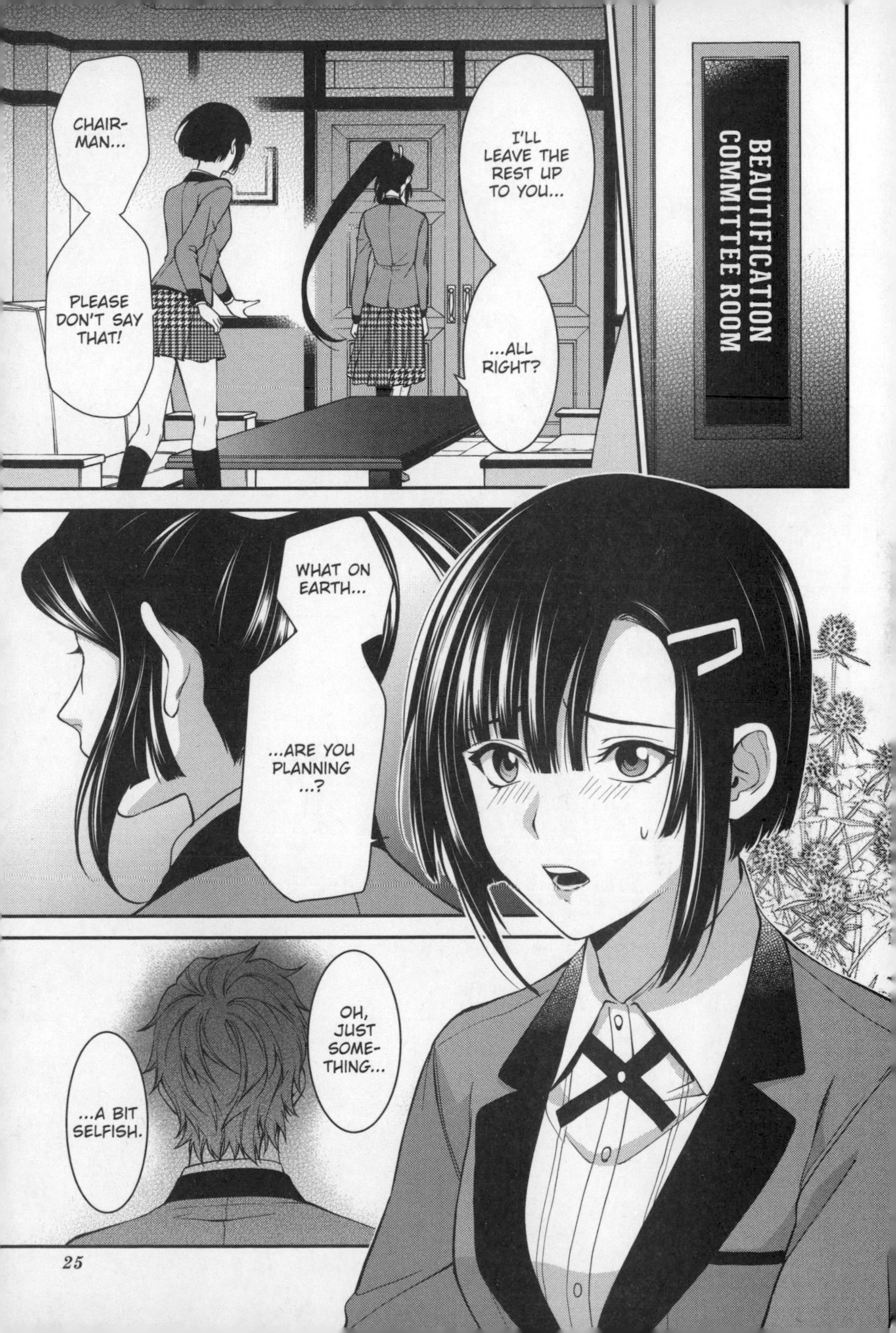
BEAUTIFICATION COMMITTEE ROOM
I'LL LEAVE THE REST UP TO YOU...
...ALL RIGHT?
CHAIR-MAN...
PLEASE DON'T SAY THAT!
WHAT ON EARTH...
...ARE YOU PLANNING ...?
OH, JUST SOME-THING...
...A BIT SELFISH.

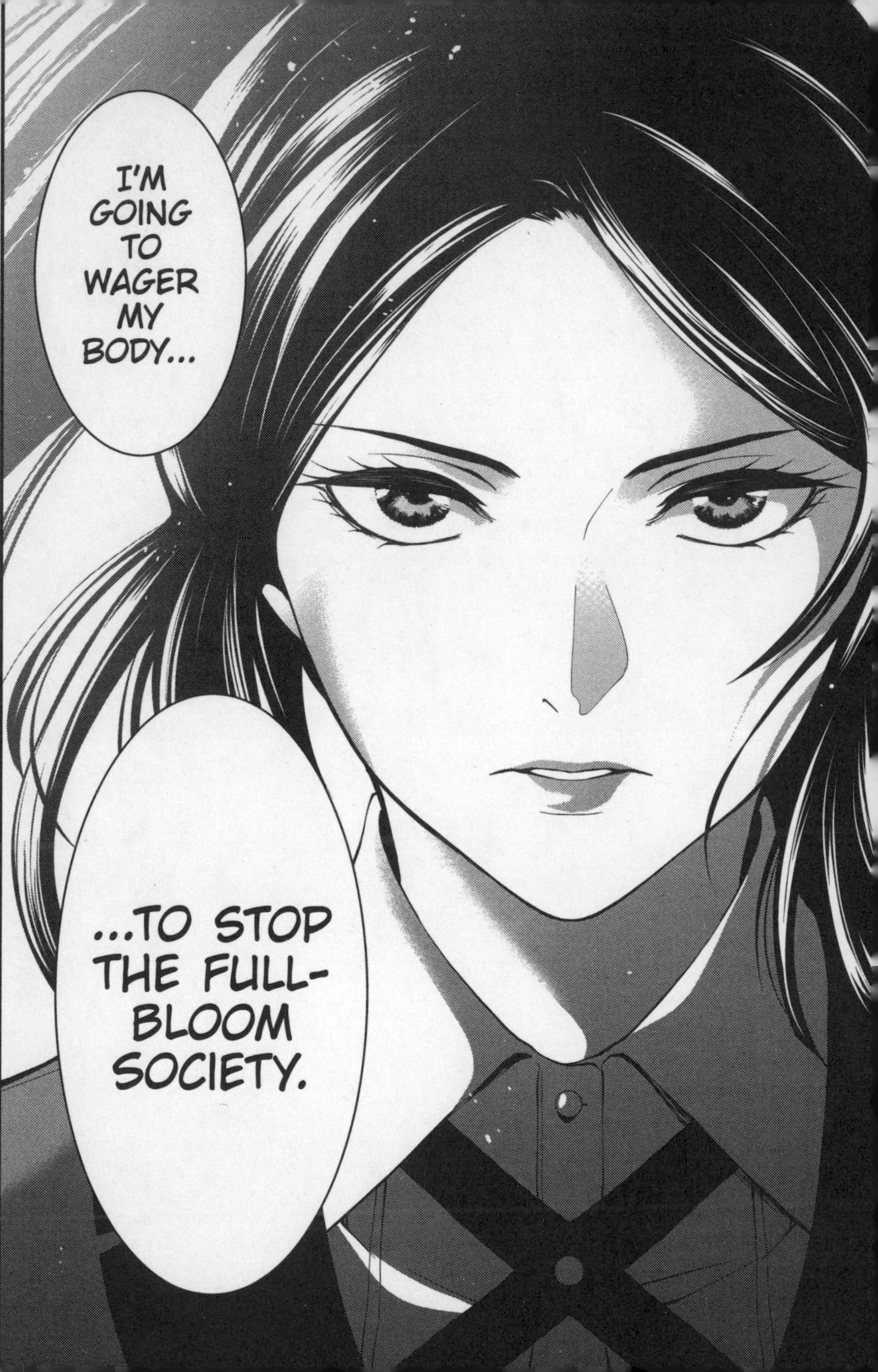
I'M GOING TO WAGER MY BODY...
...TO STOP THE FULL-BLOOM SOCIETY.

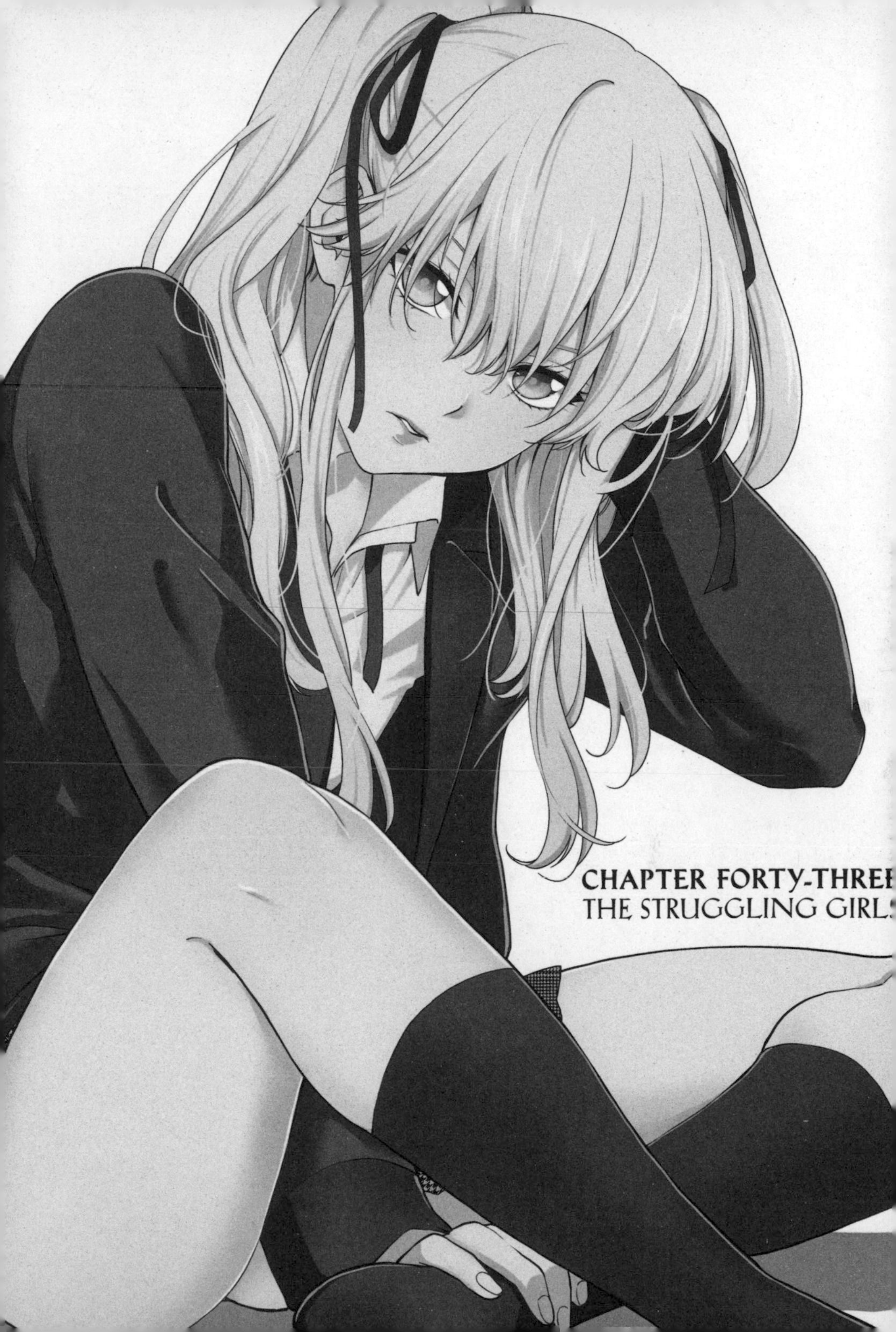

CHAPTER FORTY-THREE
THE STRUGGLING GIRLS

Kakegurui Twin

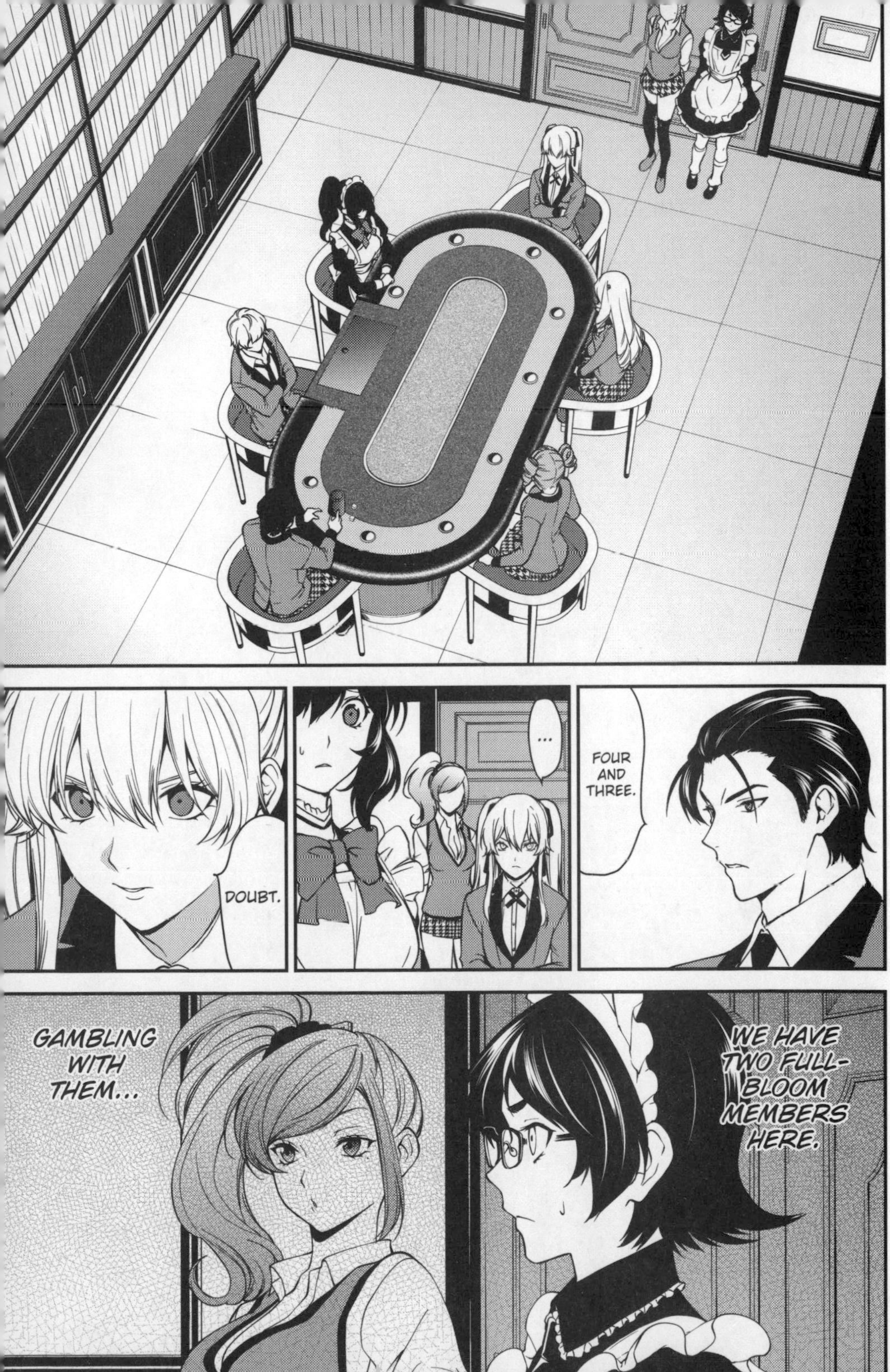
FOUR AND THREE.
...
DOUBT.
WE HAVE TWO FULL-BLOOM MEMBERS HERE.
GAMBLING WITH THEM...

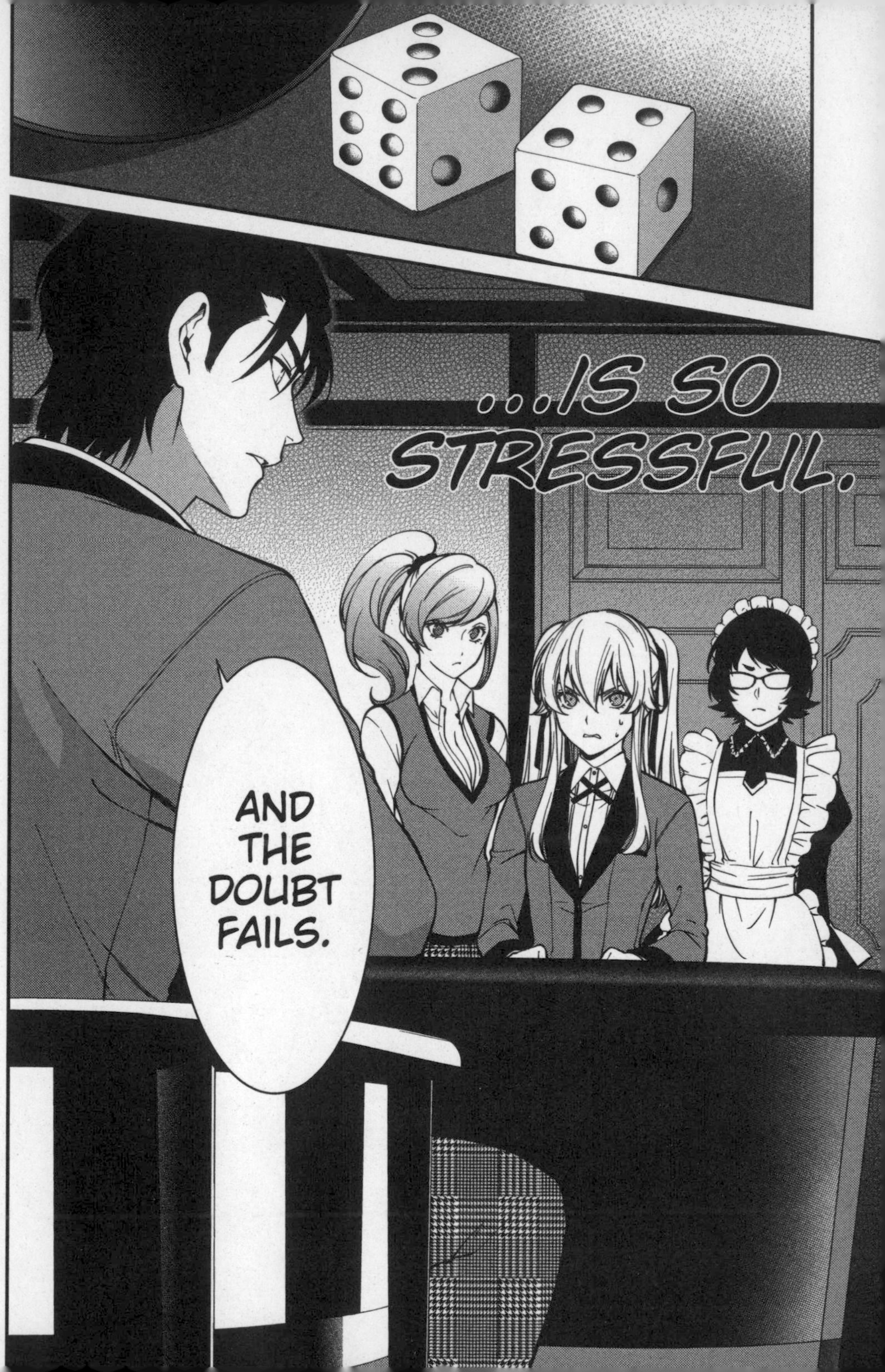
...IS SO STRESSFUL.
AND THE DOUBT FAILS.

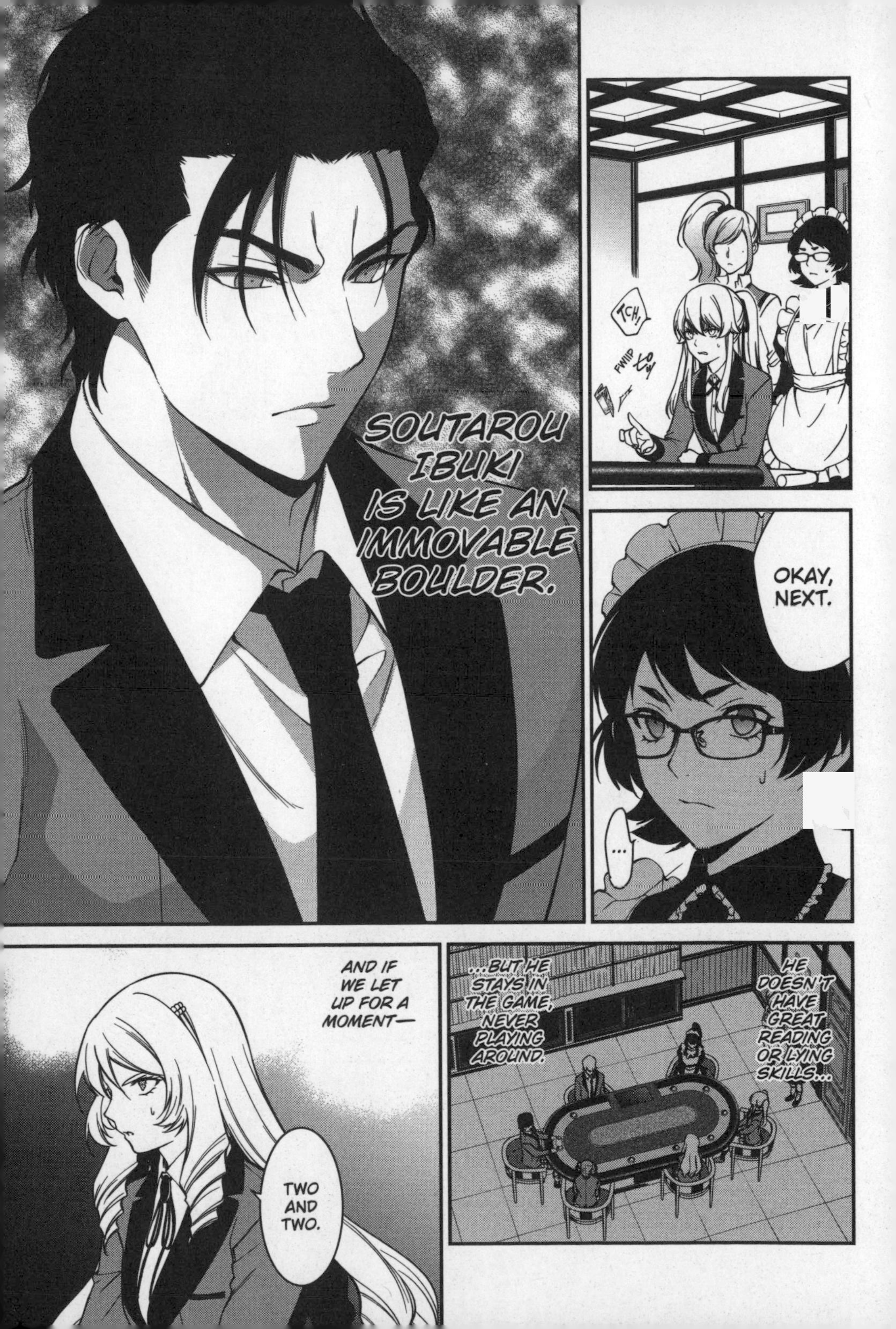
TCH!
FWIP
OKAY, NEXT.
...
SOUTAROU IBUKI IS LIKE AN IMMOVABLE BOULDER.
HE DOESN'T HAVE GREAT READING OR LYING SKILLS...
...BUT HE STAYS IN THE GAME, NEVER PLAYING AROUND.
AND IF WE LET UP FOR A MOMENT—
TWO AND TWO.

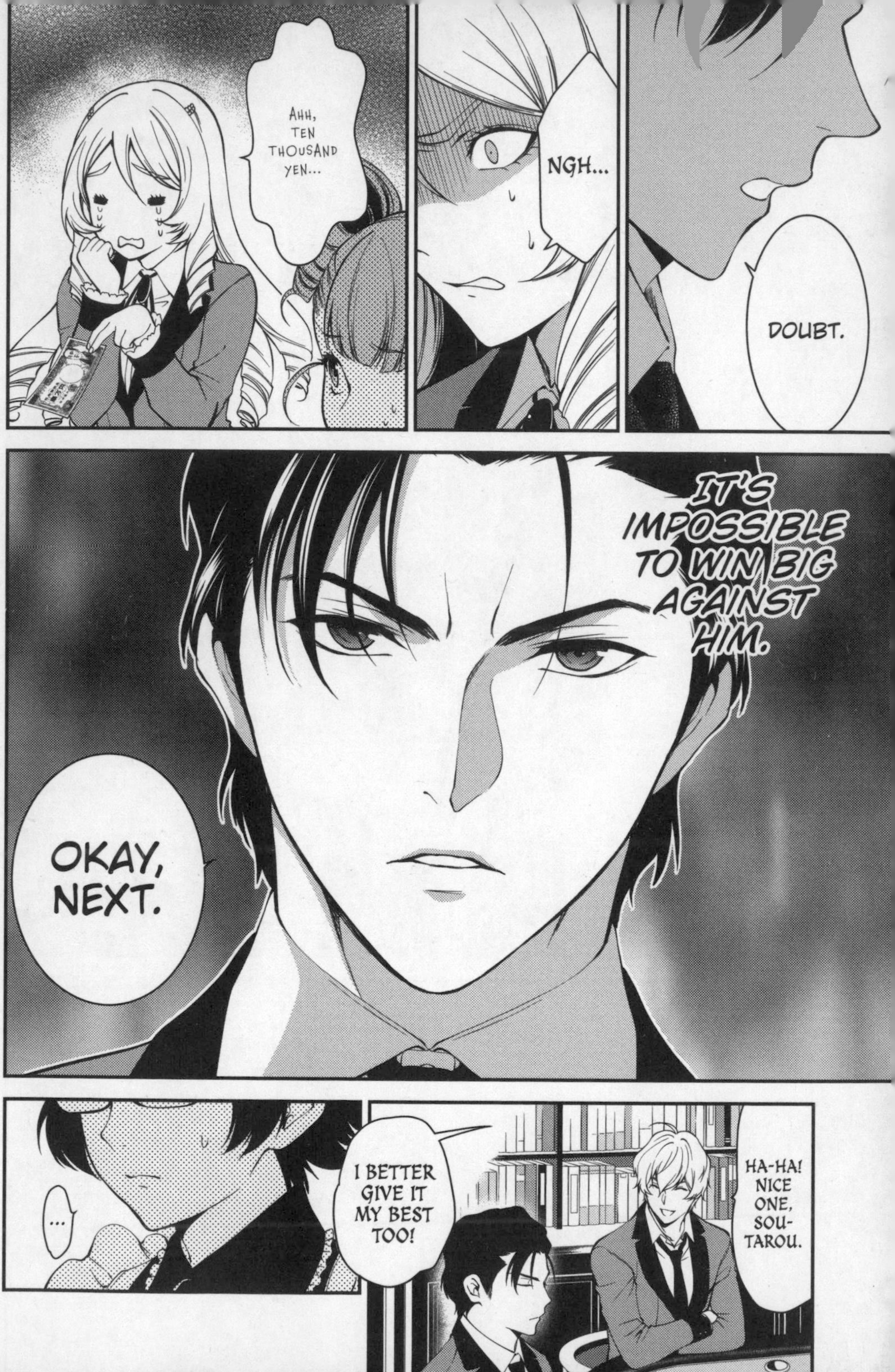
DOUBT.
NGH...
AHH, TEN THOUSAND YEN...
IT'S IMPOSSIBLE TO WIN BIG AGAINST HIM.
OKAY, NEXT.
HA-HA! NICE ONE, SOU-TAROU.
I BETTER GIVE IT MY BEST TOO!
...

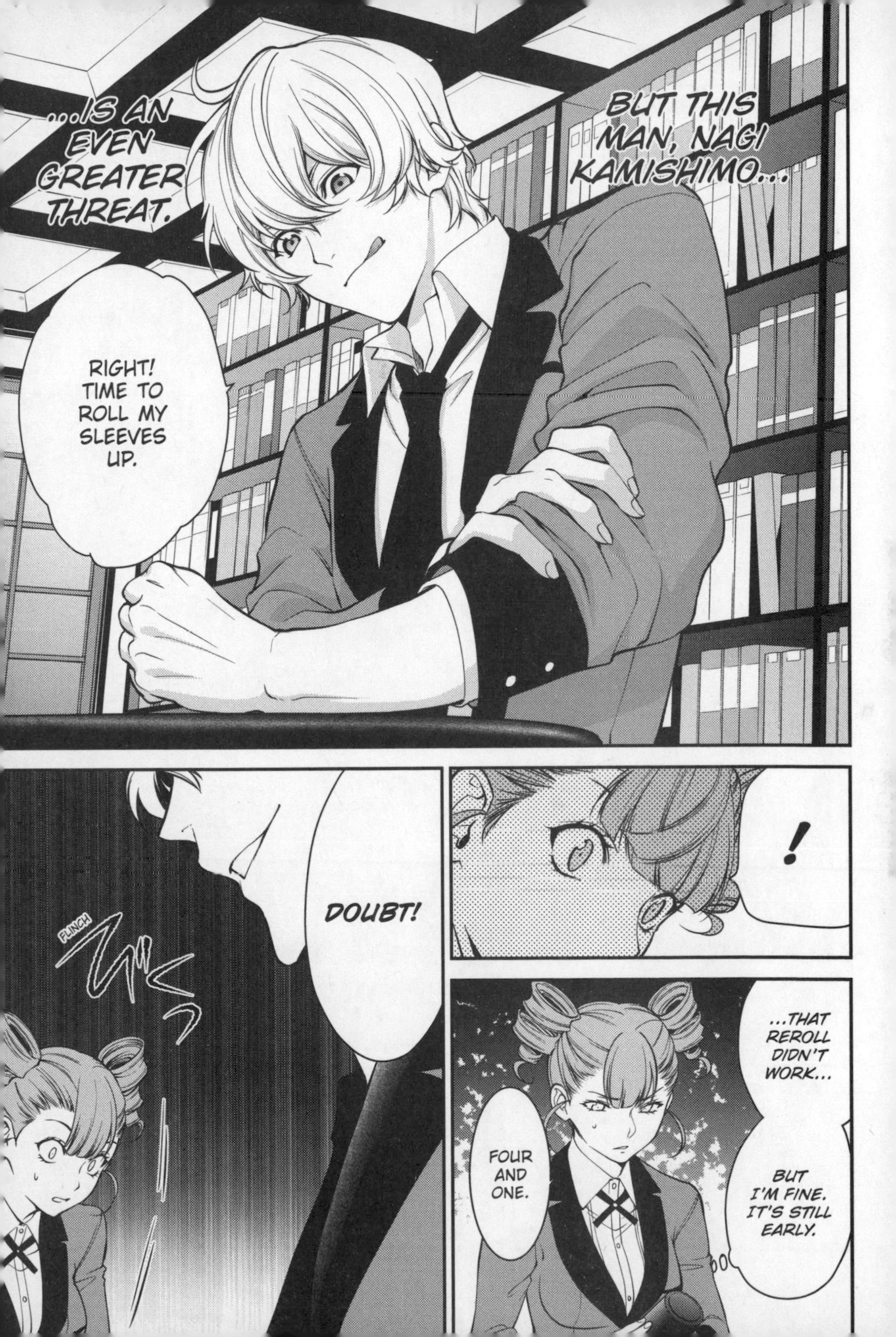
BUT THIS MAN, NAGI KAMISHIMO...
...IS AN EVEN GREATER THREAT.
RIGHT! TIME TO ROLL MY SLEEVES UP.
!
...THAT REROLL DIDN'T WORK...
BUT I'M FINE. IT'S STILL EARLY.
FOUR AND ONE.
DOUBT!
FLINCH

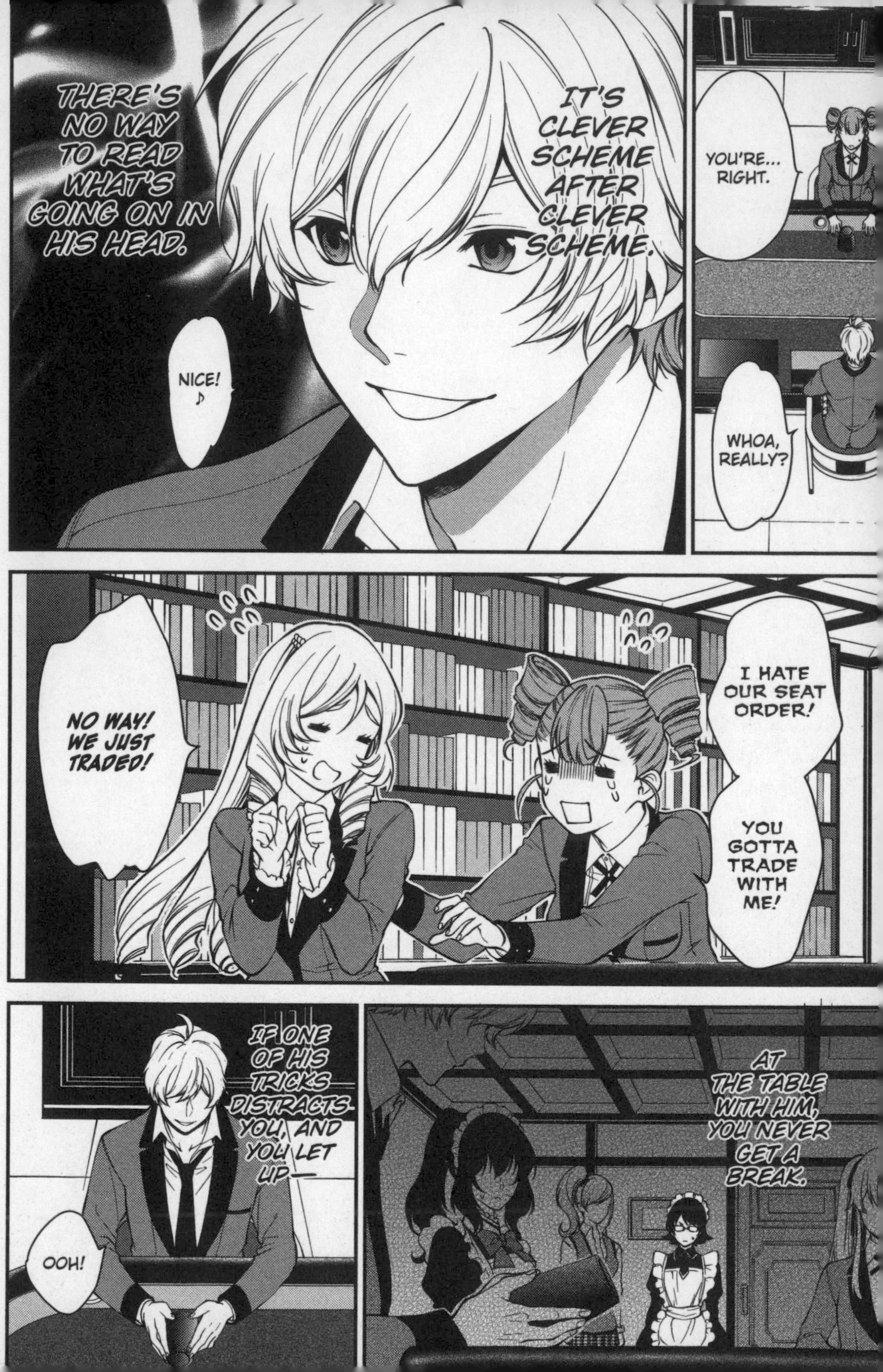
YOU'RE... RIGHT.
WHOA, REALLY?
IT'S CLEVER SCHEME AFTER CLEVER SCHEME.
THERE'S NO WAY TO READ WHAT'S GOING ON IN HIS HEAD.
NICE! ♪
I HATE OUR SEAT ORDER!
YOU GOTTA TRADE WITH ME!
NO WAY! WE JUST TRADED!
AT THE TABLE WITH HIM, YOU NEVER GET A BREAK.
IF ONE OF HIS TRICKS DISTRACTS YOU, AND YOU LET UP—
OOH!

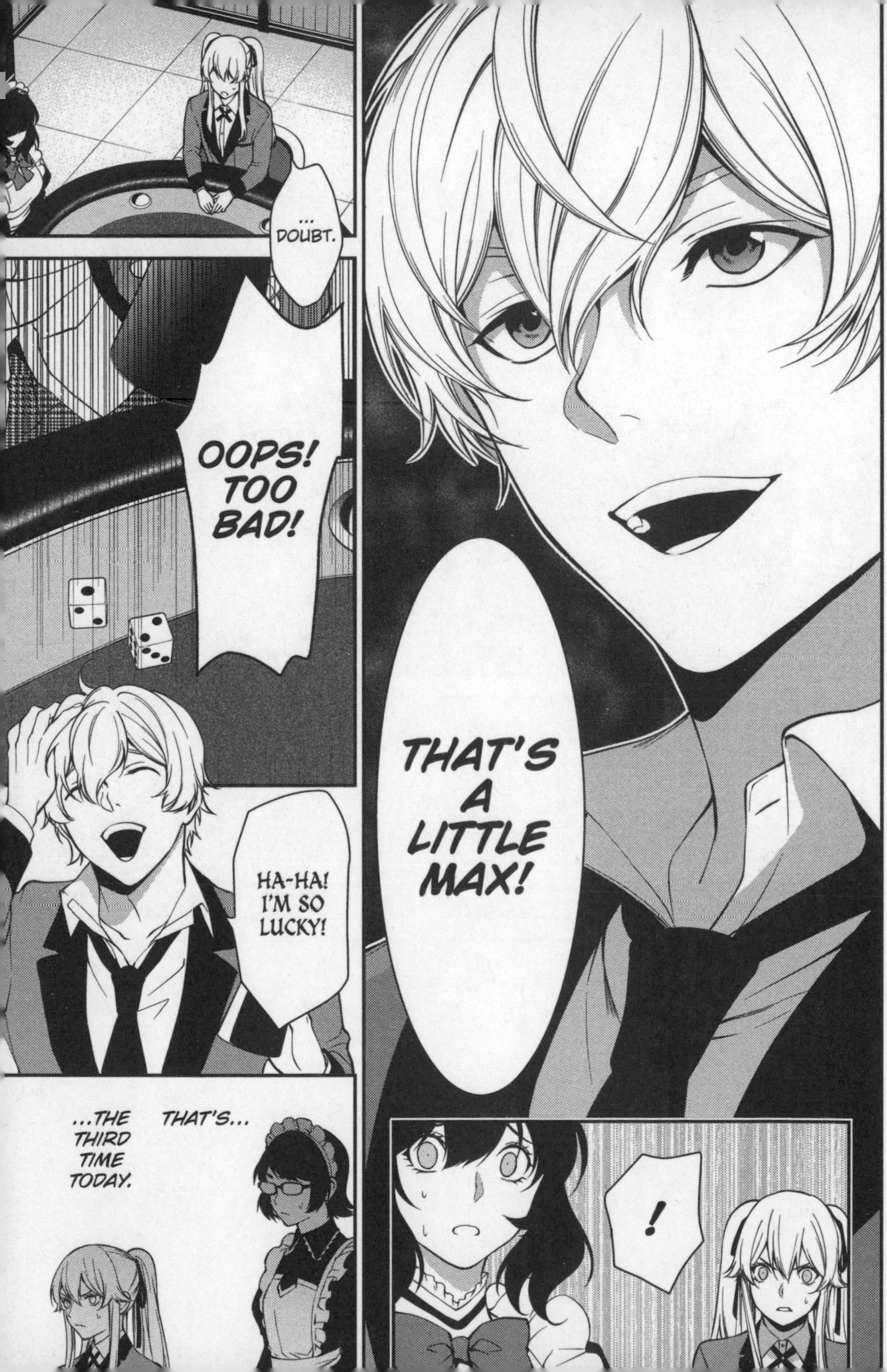
THAT'S A LITTLE MAX!
... DOUBT.
OOPS! TOO BAD!
HA-HA! I'M SO LUCKY!
!
THAT'S...
...THE THIRD TIME TODAY.

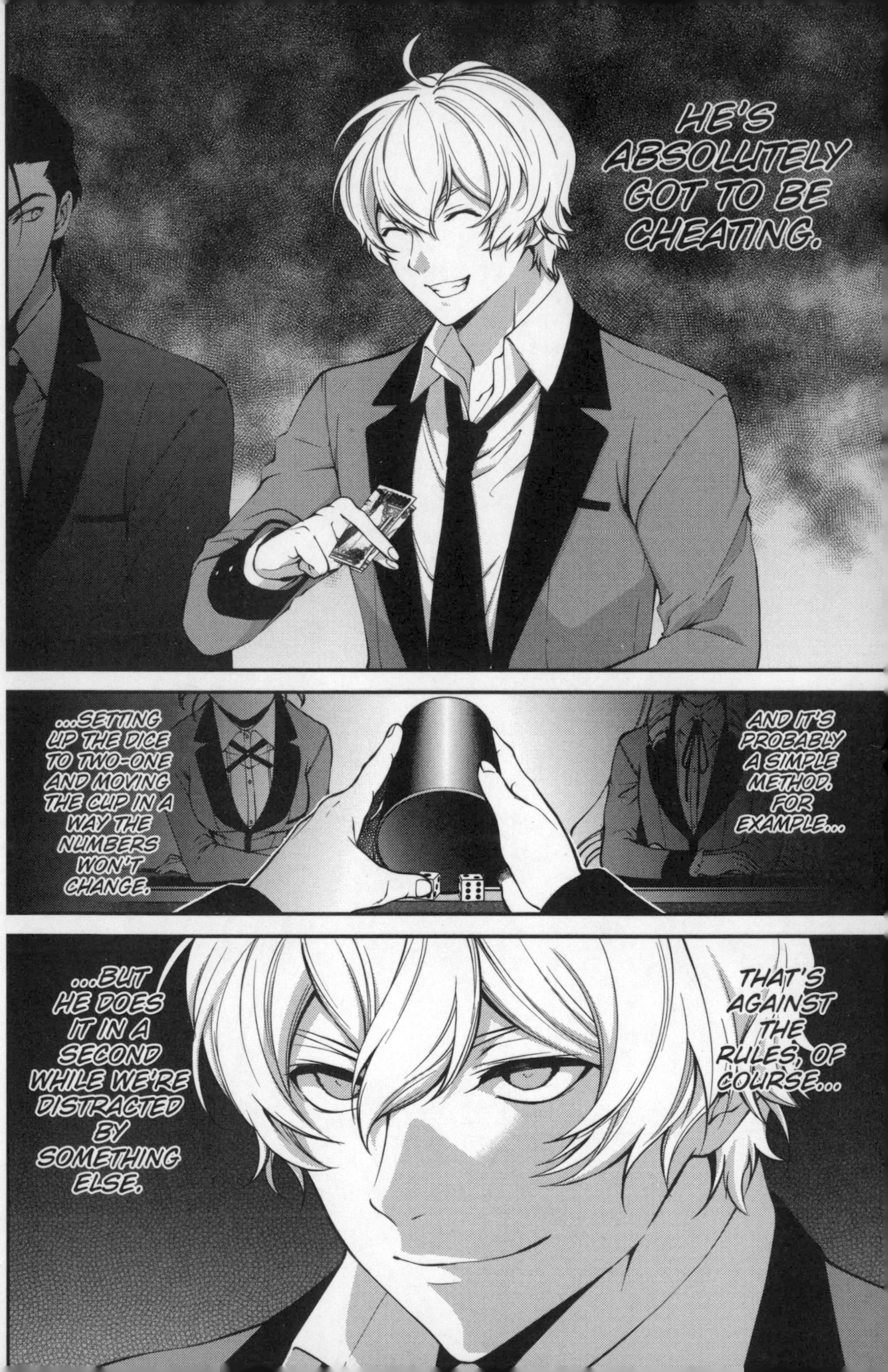
HE'S ABSOLUTELY GOT TO BE CHEATING.
AND IT'S PROBABLY A SIMPLE METHOD. FOR EXAMPLE...
...SETTING UP THE DICE TO TWO-ONE AND MOVING THE CUP IN A WAY THE NUMBERS WON'T CHANGE.
THAT'S AGAINST THE RULES, OF COURSE...
...BUT HE DOES IT IN A SECOND WHILE WE'RE DISTRACTED BY SOMETHING ELSE.

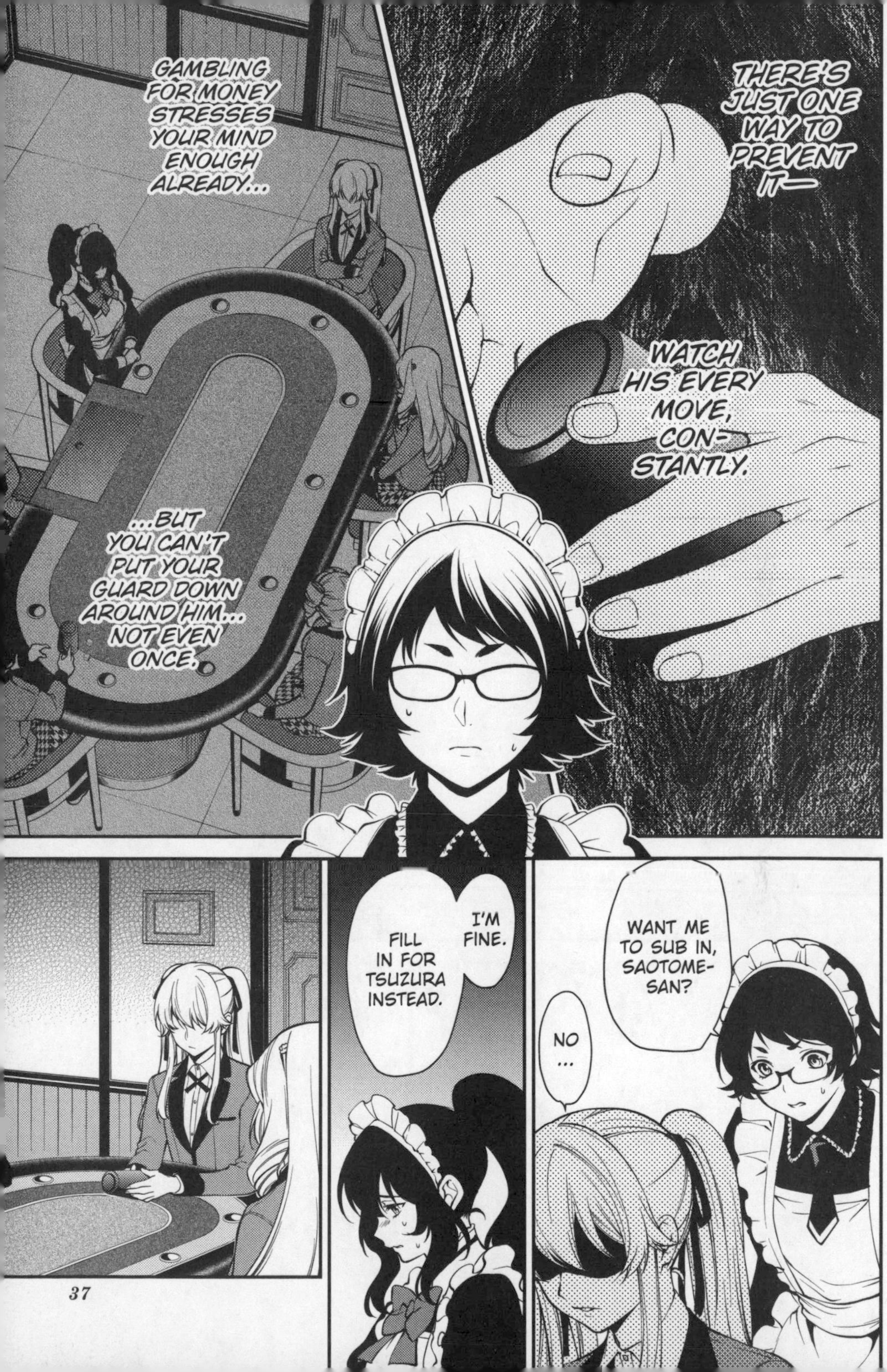
THERE'S JUST ONE WAY TO PREVENT IT—
WATCH HIS EVERY MOVE, CON-STANTLY.
GAMBLING FOR MONEY STRESSES YOUR MIND ENOUGH ALREADY...
...BUT YOU CAN'T PUT YOUR GUARD DOWN AROUND HIM... NOT EVEN ONCE.
WANT ME TO SUB IN, SAOTOME-SAN?
NO...
I'M FINE.
FILL IN FOR TSUZURA INSTEAD.

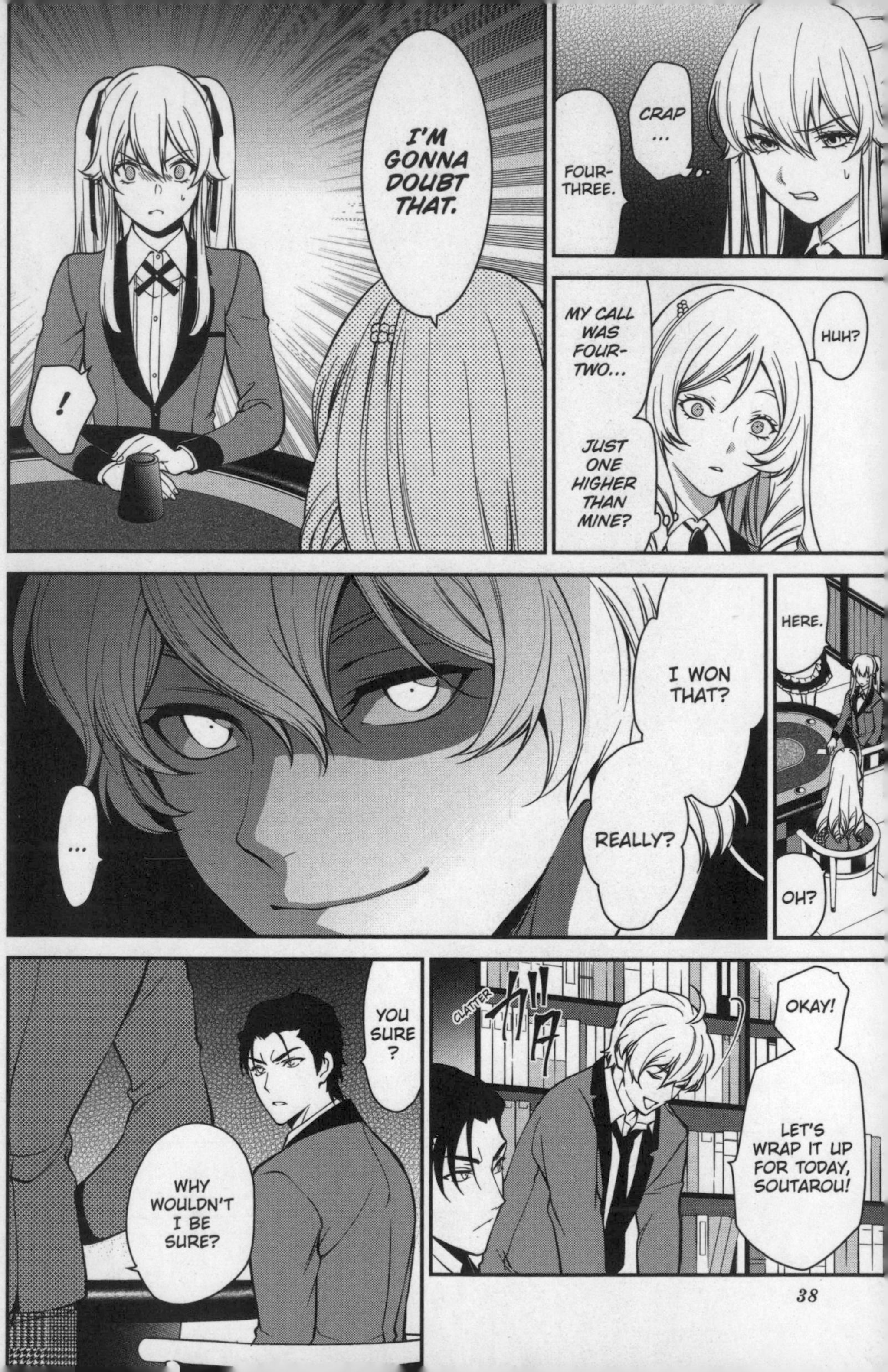
CRAP...
FOUR-THREE.
HUH?
MY CALL WAS FOUR-TWO...
JUST ONE HIGHER THAN MINE?
I'M GONNA DOUBT THAT.
!
HERE.
OH?
I WON THAT?
REALLY?
...
OKAY!
LET'S WRAP IT UP FOR TODAY, SOUTAROU!
CLATTER
YOU SURE?
WHY WOULDN'T I BE SURE?

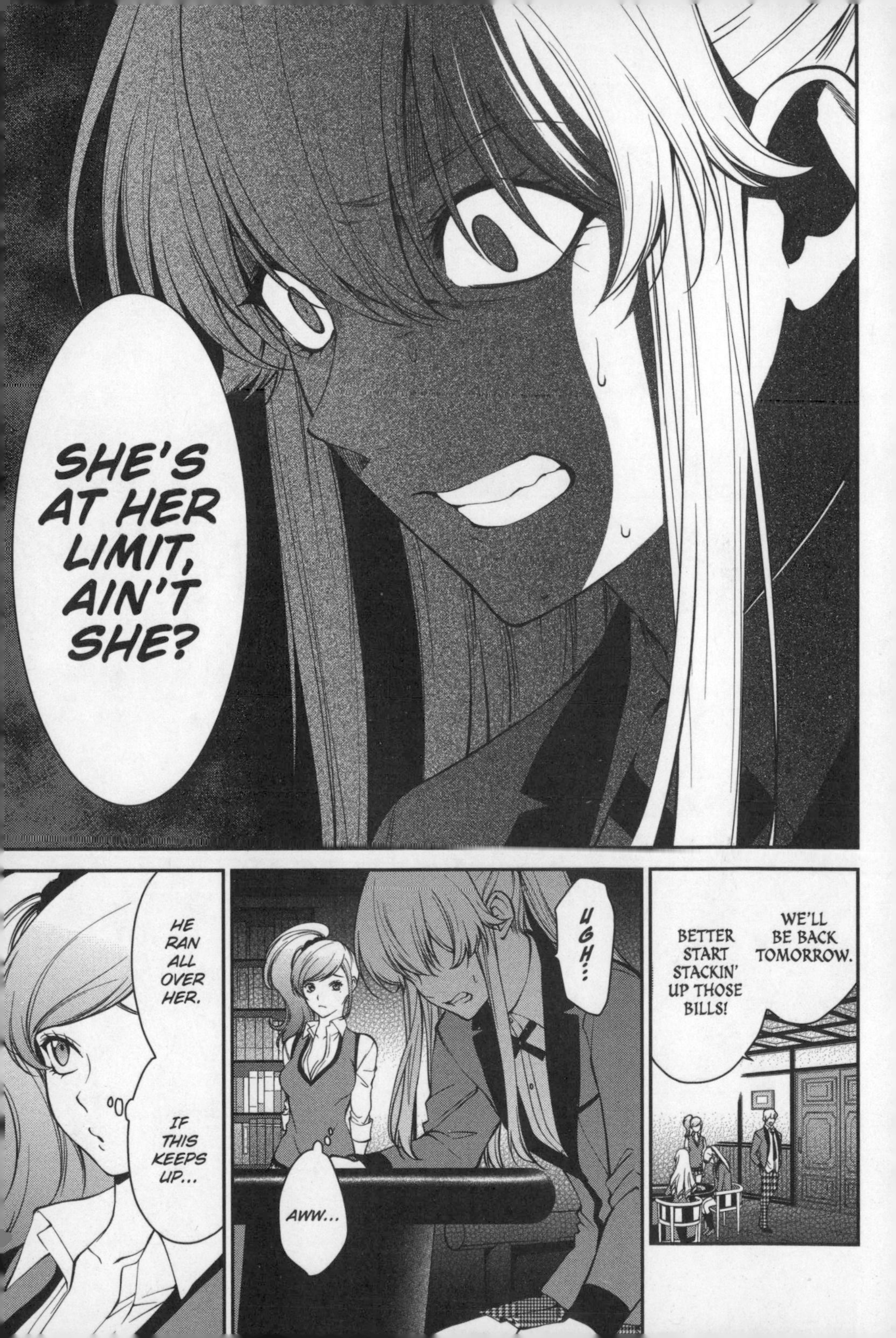
SHE'S AT HER LIMIT, AIN'T SHE?
WE'LL BE BACK TOMORROW.
BETTER START STACKIN' UP THOSE BILLS!
UGH...
AWW...
HE RAN ALL OVER HER.
IF THIS KEEPS UP...

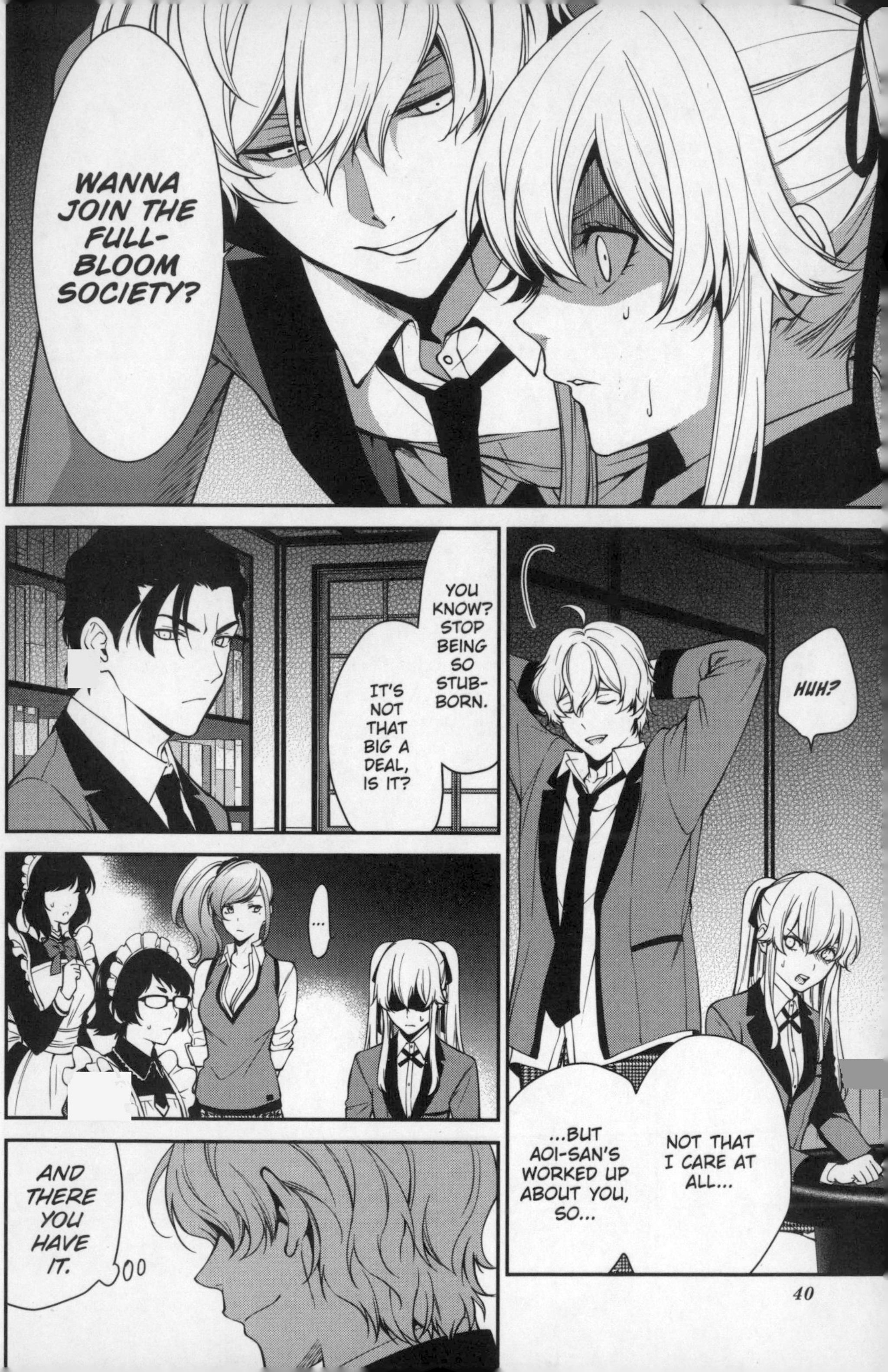
WANNA JOIN THE FULL-BLOOM SOCIETY?
HUH?
NOT THAT I CARE AT ALL...
...BUT AOI-SAN'S WORKED UP ABOUT YOU, SO...
YOU KNOW? STOP BEING SO STUBBORN.
IT'S NOT THAT BIG A DEAL, IS IT?
...
AND THERE YOU HAVE IT.

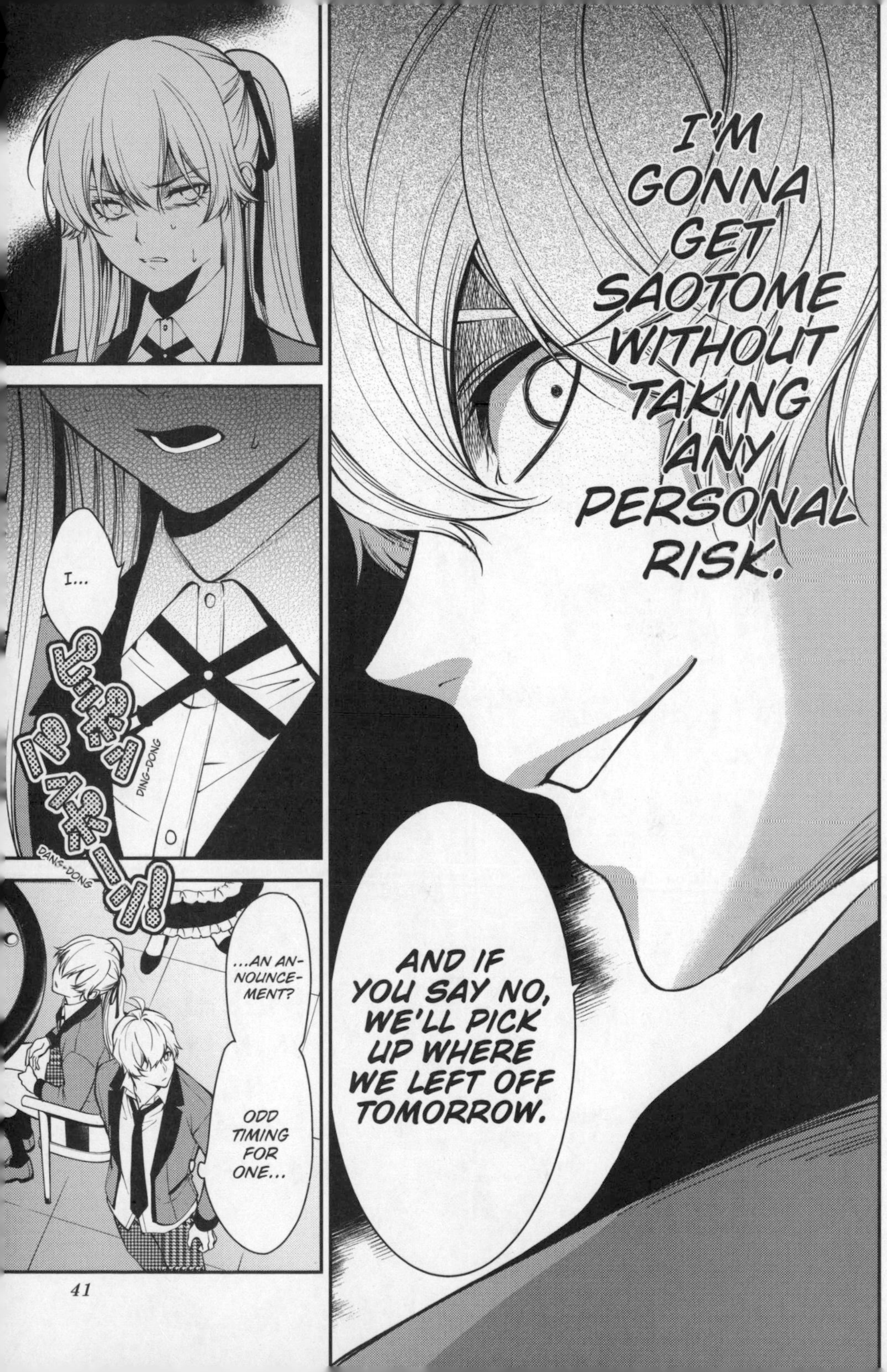
I'M GONNA GET SAOTOME WITHOUT TAKING ANY PERSONAL RISK.
AND IF YOU SAY NO, WE'LL PICK UP WHERE WE LEFT OFF TOMORROW.
I...
DING-DONG
DANG-DONG
...AN ANNOUNCEMENT?
ODD TIMING FOR ONE...

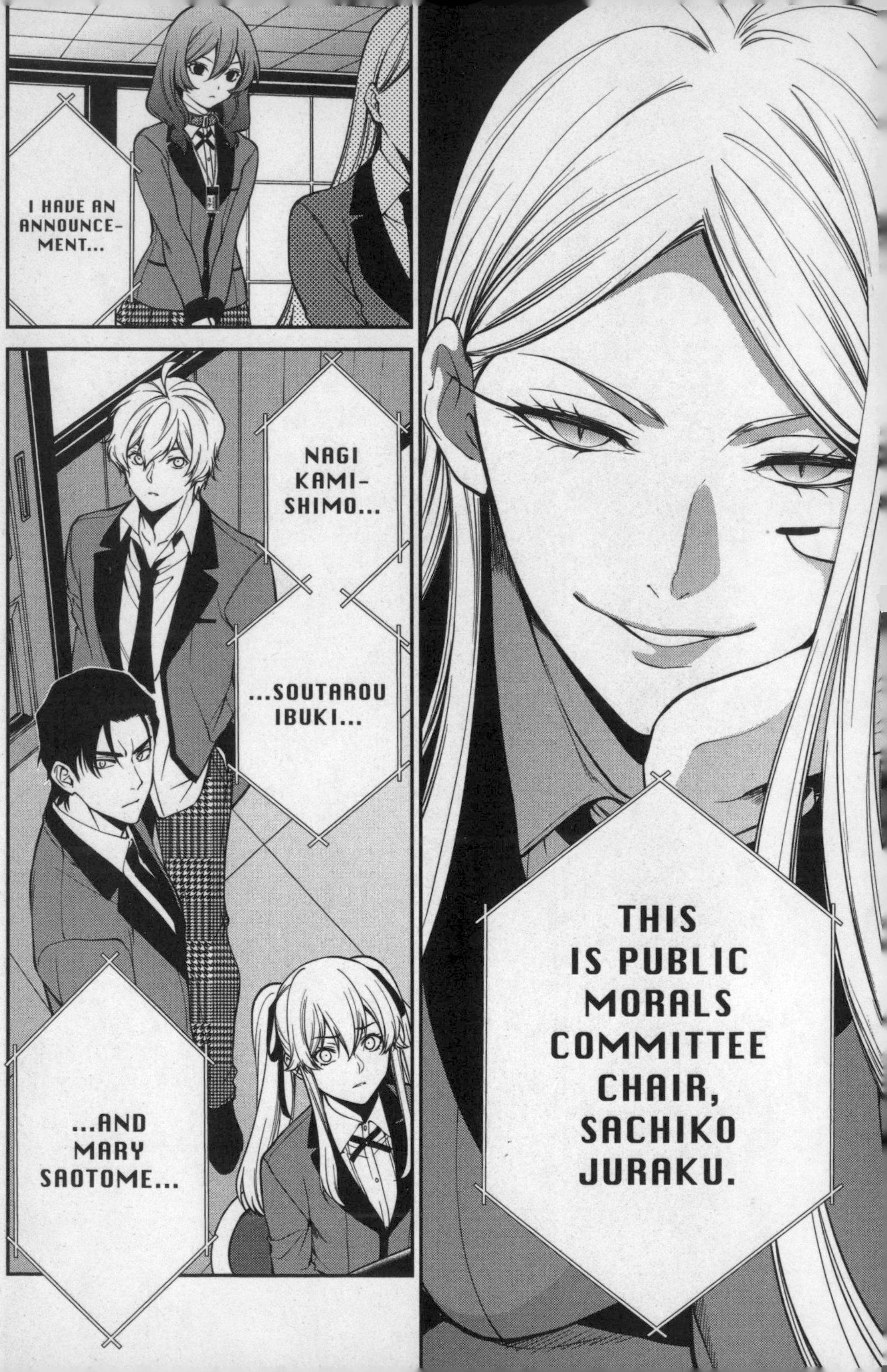
THIS IS PUBLIC MORALS COMMITTEE CHAIR, SACHIKO JURAKU.
I HAVE AN ANNOUNCEMENT...
NAGI KAMISHIMO...
...SOUTAROU IBUKI...
...AND MARY SAOTOME...

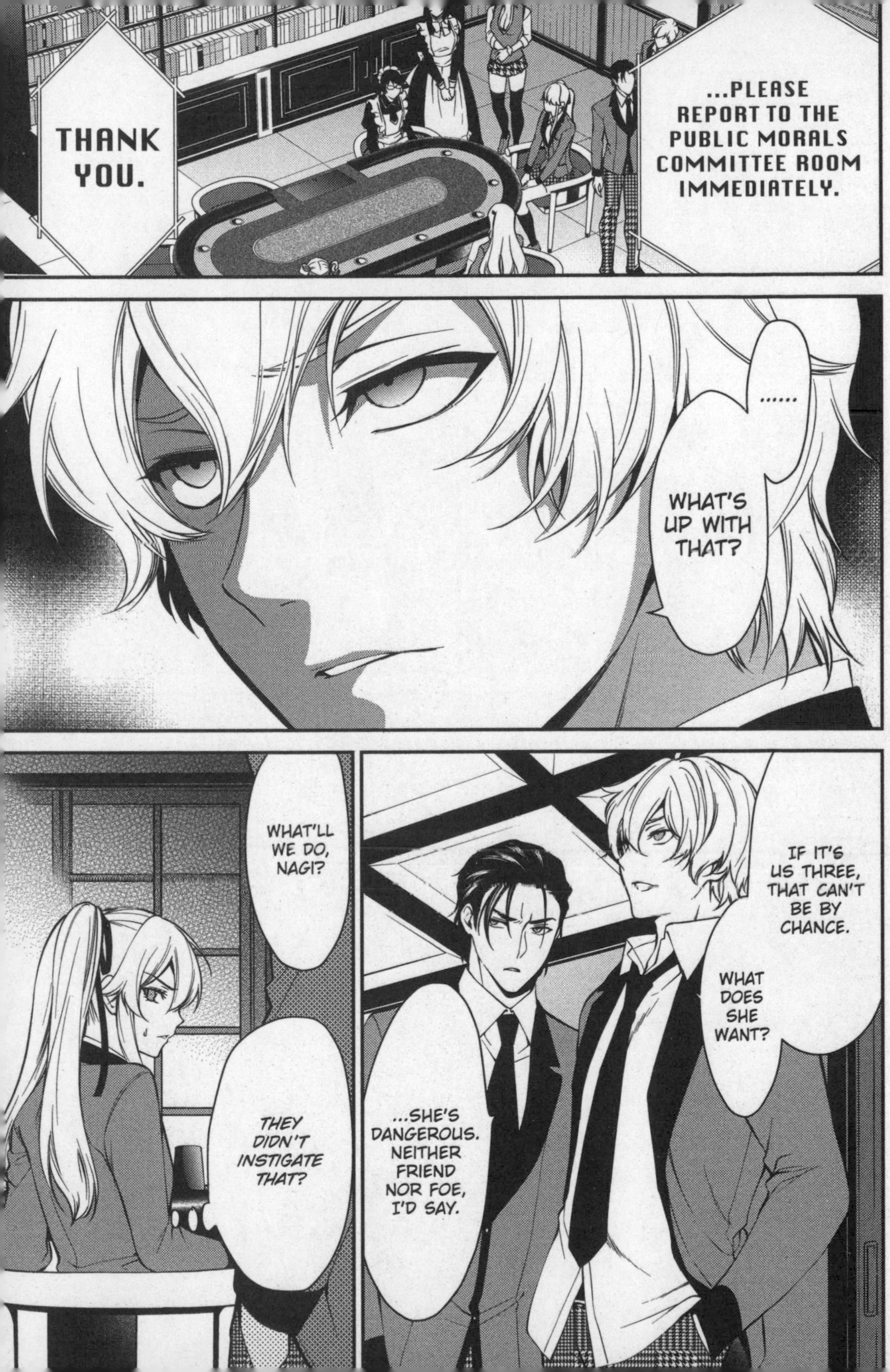
...PLEASE REPORT TO THE PUBLIC MORALS COMMITTEE ROOM IMMEDIATELY.
THANK YOU.
......
WHAT'S UP WITH THAT?
IF IT'S US THREE, THAT CAN'T BE BY CHANCE.
WHAT DOES SHE WANT?
...SHE'S DANGEROUS. NEITHER FRIEND NOR FOE, I'D SAY.
WHAT'LL WE DO, NAGI?
THEY DIDN'T INSTIGATE THAT?

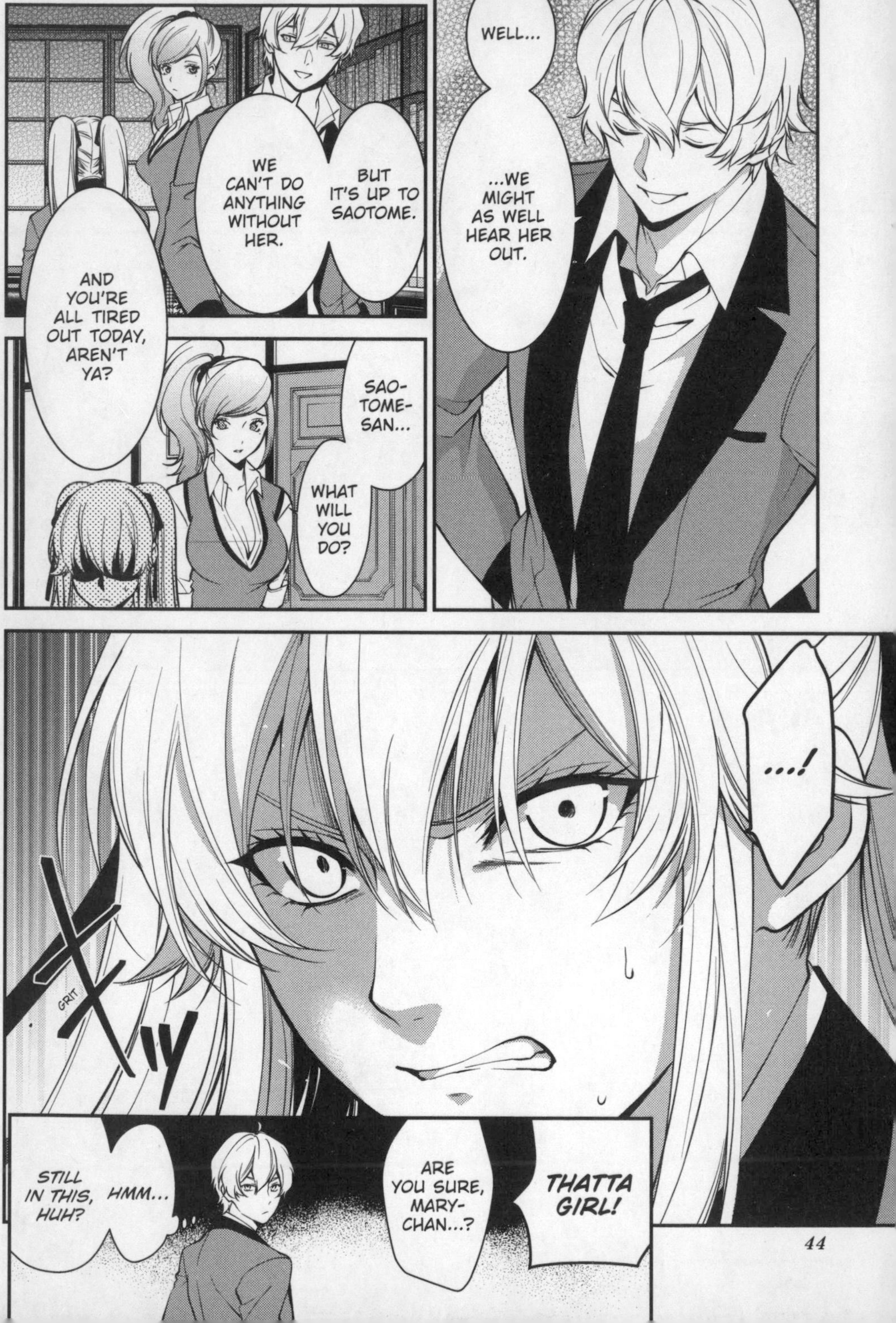
WELL...
...WE MIGHT AS WELL HEAR HER OUT.
BUT IT'S UP TO SAOTOME.
WE CAN'T DO ANYTHING WITHOUT HER.
AND YOU'RE ALL TIRED OUT TODAY, AREN'T YA?
SAO-TOME-SAN...
WHAT WILL YOU DO?
...!
GRIT
THATTA GIRL!
ARE YOU SURE, MARY-CHAN...?
HMM...
STILL IN THIS, HUH?

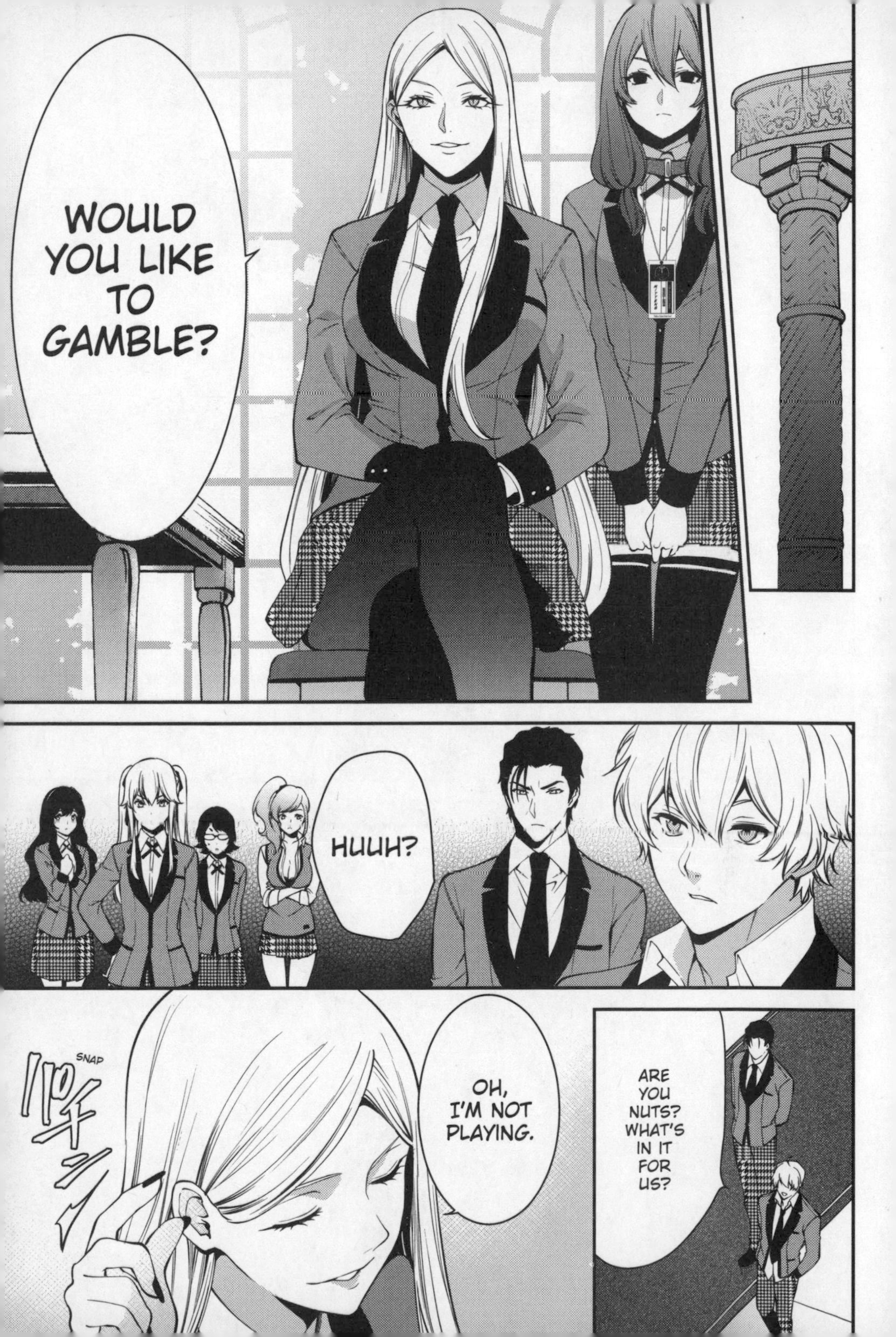
WOULD YOU LIKE TO GAMBLE?
HUUH?
ARE YOU NUTS? WHAT'S IN IT FOR US?
OH, I'M NOT PLAYING.
SNAP

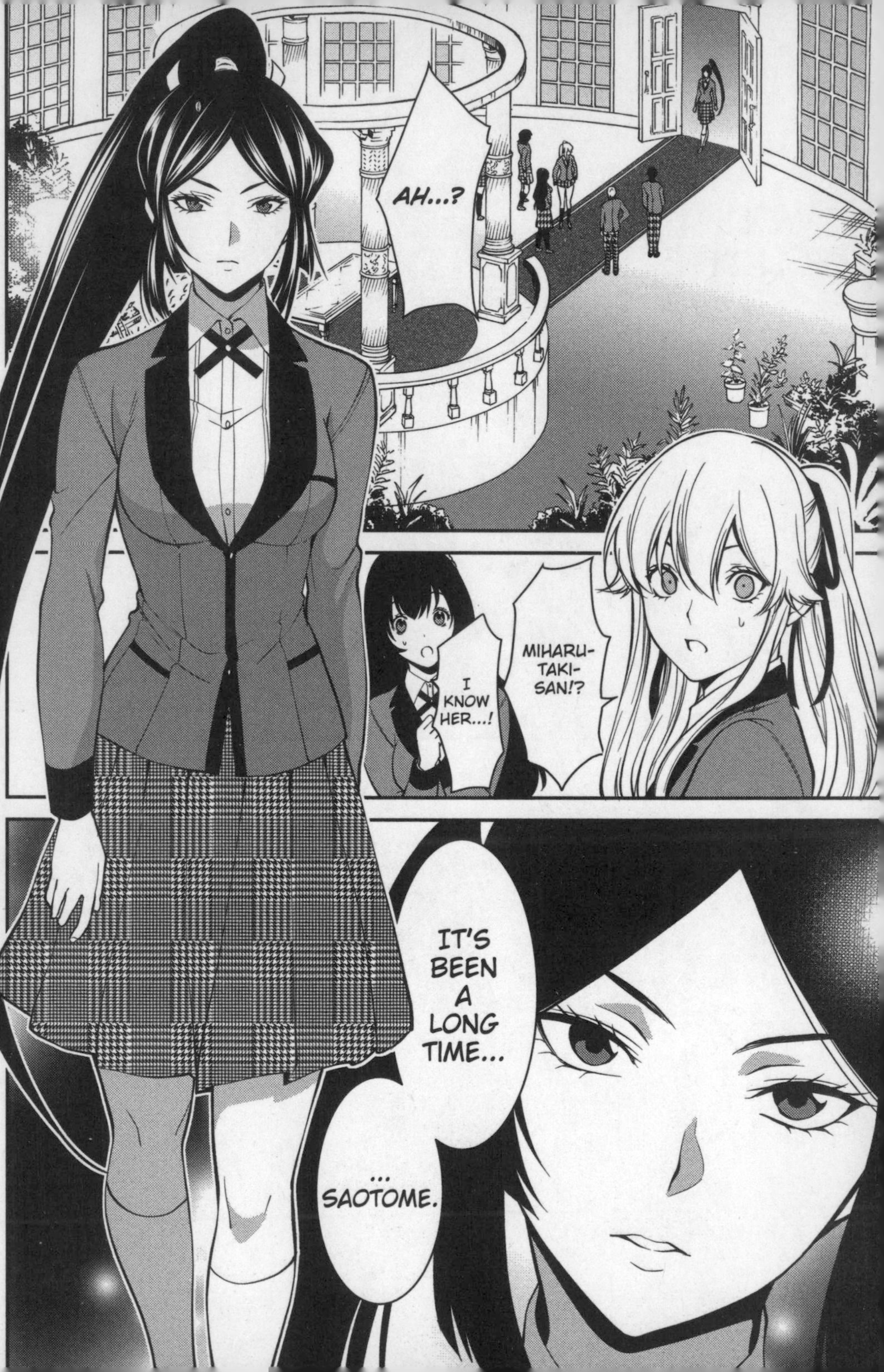
AH...?
MIHARU-TAKI-SAN!?
I KNOW HER...!
IT'S BEEN A LONG TIME...
... SAOTOME.

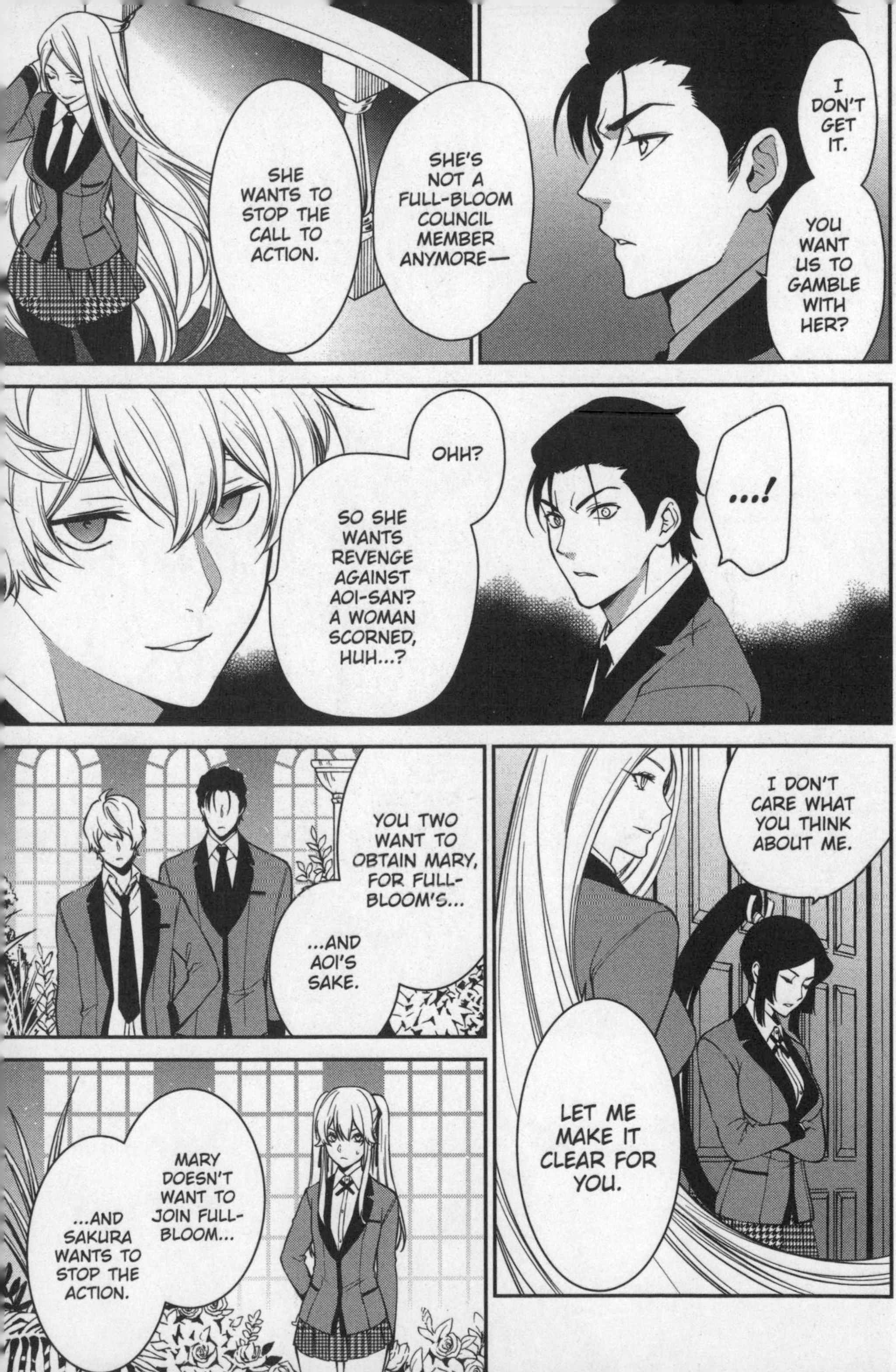
I DON'T GET IT.
YOU WANT US TO GAMBLE WITH HER?
SHE'S NOT A FULL-BLOOM COUNCIL MEMBER ANYMORE—
SHE WANTS TO STOP THE CALL TO ACTION.
...!
OHH?
SO SHE WANTS REVENGE AGAINST AOI-SAN? A WOMAN SCORNED, HUH...?
I DON'T CARE WHAT YOU THINK ABOUT ME.
LET ME MAKE IT CLEAR FOR YOU.
YOU TWO WANT TO OBTAIN MARY, FOR FULL-BLOOM'S...
...AND AOI'S SAKE.
MARY DOESN'T WANT TO JOIN FULL-BLOOM...
...AND SAKURA WANTS TO STOP THE ACTION.

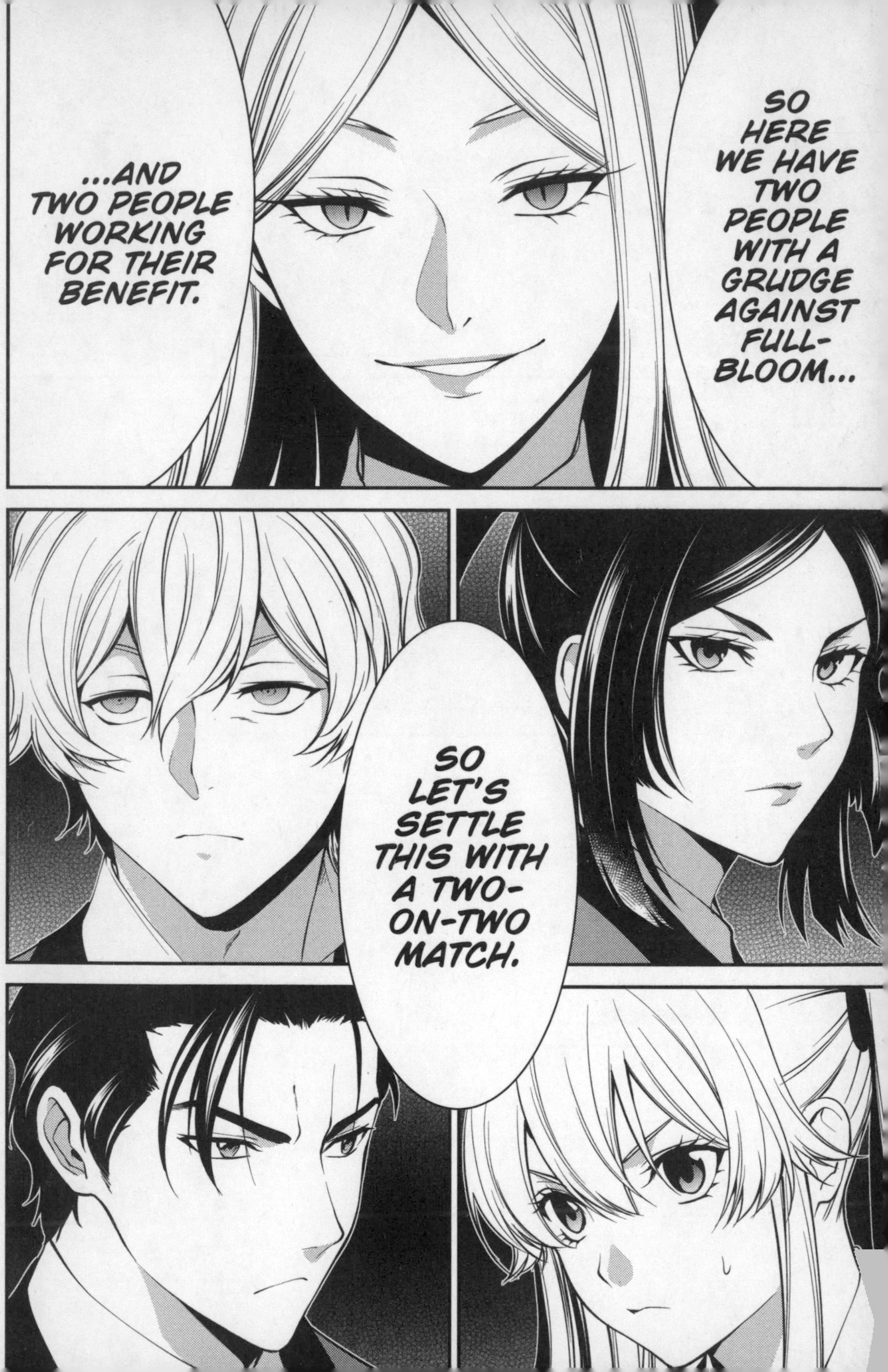
SO HERE WE HAVE TWO PEOPLE WITH A GRUDGE AGAINST FULL-BLOOM...
...AND TWO PEOPLE WORKING FOR THEIR BENEFIT.
SO LET'S SETTLE THIS WITH A TWO-ON-TWO MATCH.

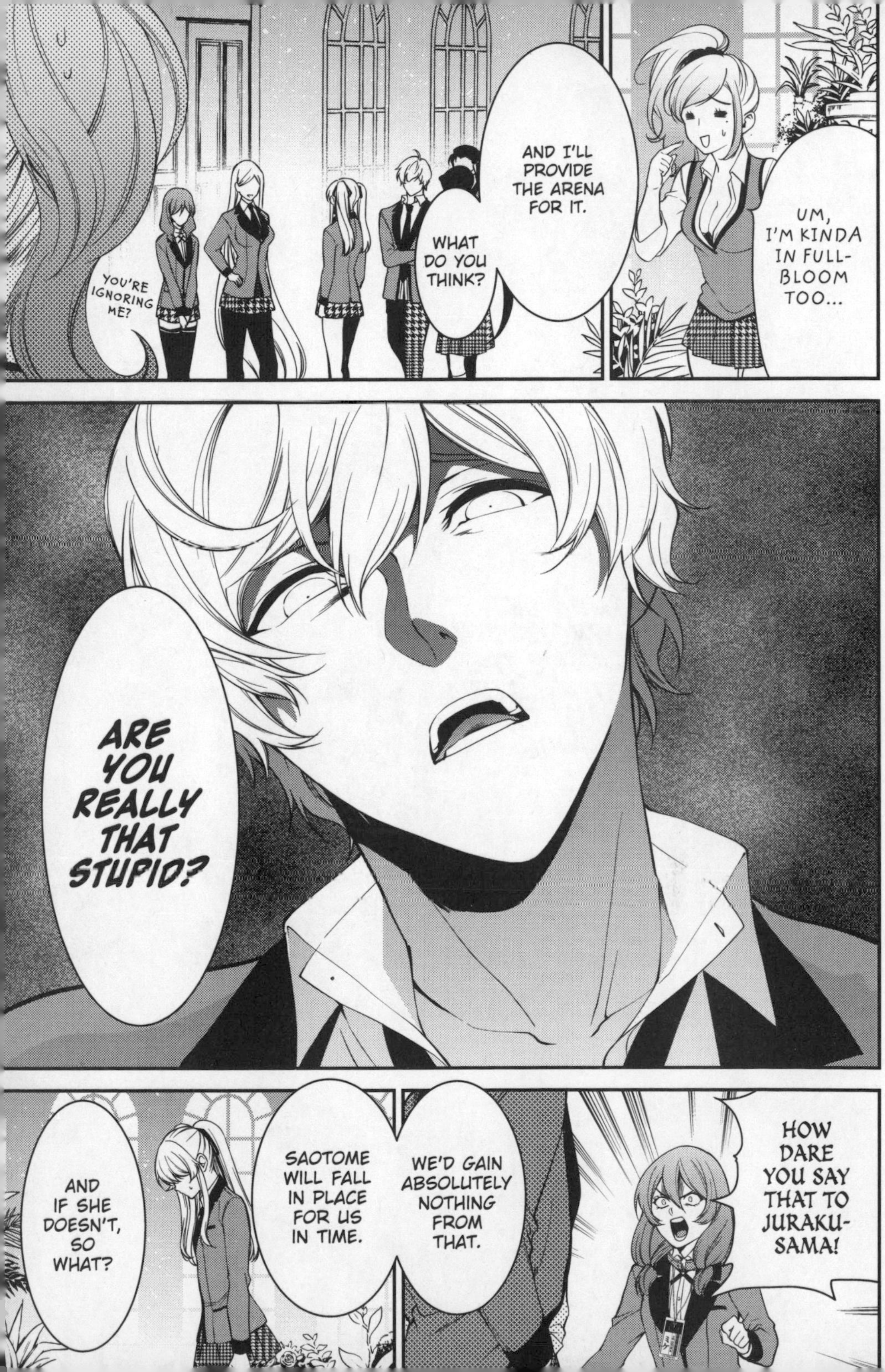
UM, I'M KINDA IN FULL-BLOOM TOO...
AND I'LL PROVIDE THE ARENA FOR IT.
WHAT DO YOU THINK?
YOU'RE IGNORING ME?
ARE YOU REALLY THAT STUPID?
HOW DARE YOU SAY THAT TO JURAKU-SAMA!
WE'D GAIN ABSOLUTELY NOTHING FROM THAT.
SAOTOME WILL FALL IN PLACE FOR US IN TIME.
AND IF SHE DOESN'T, SO WHAT?

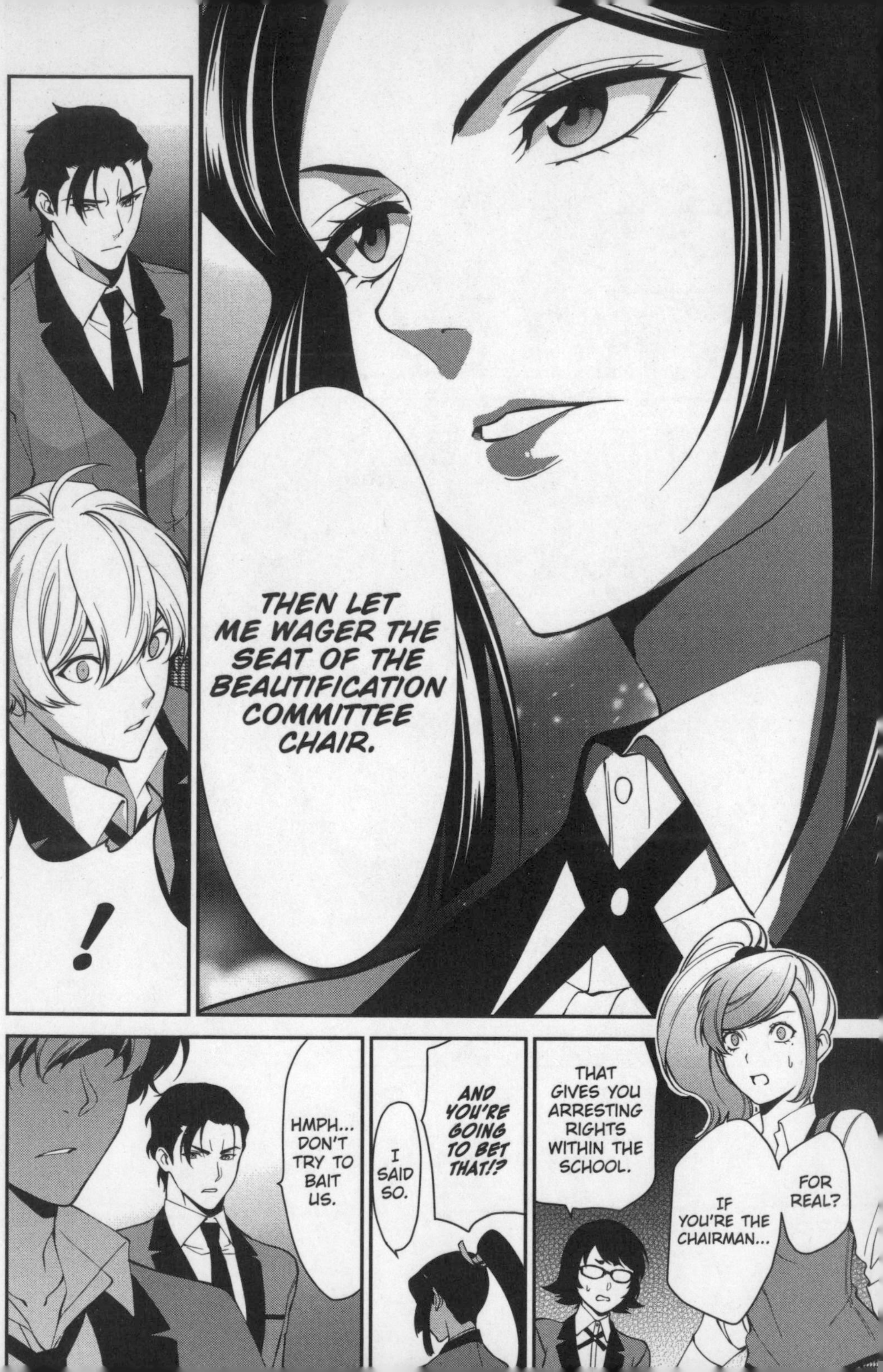
THEN LET ME WAGER THE SEAT OF THE BEAUTIFICATION COMMITTEE CHAIR.
!
FOR REAL?
IF YOU'RE THE CHAIRMAN...
THAT GIVES YOU ARRESTING RIGHTS WITHIN THE SCHOOL.
AND YOU'RE GOING TO BET THAT!?
I SAID SO.
HMPH... DON'T TRY TO BAIT US.

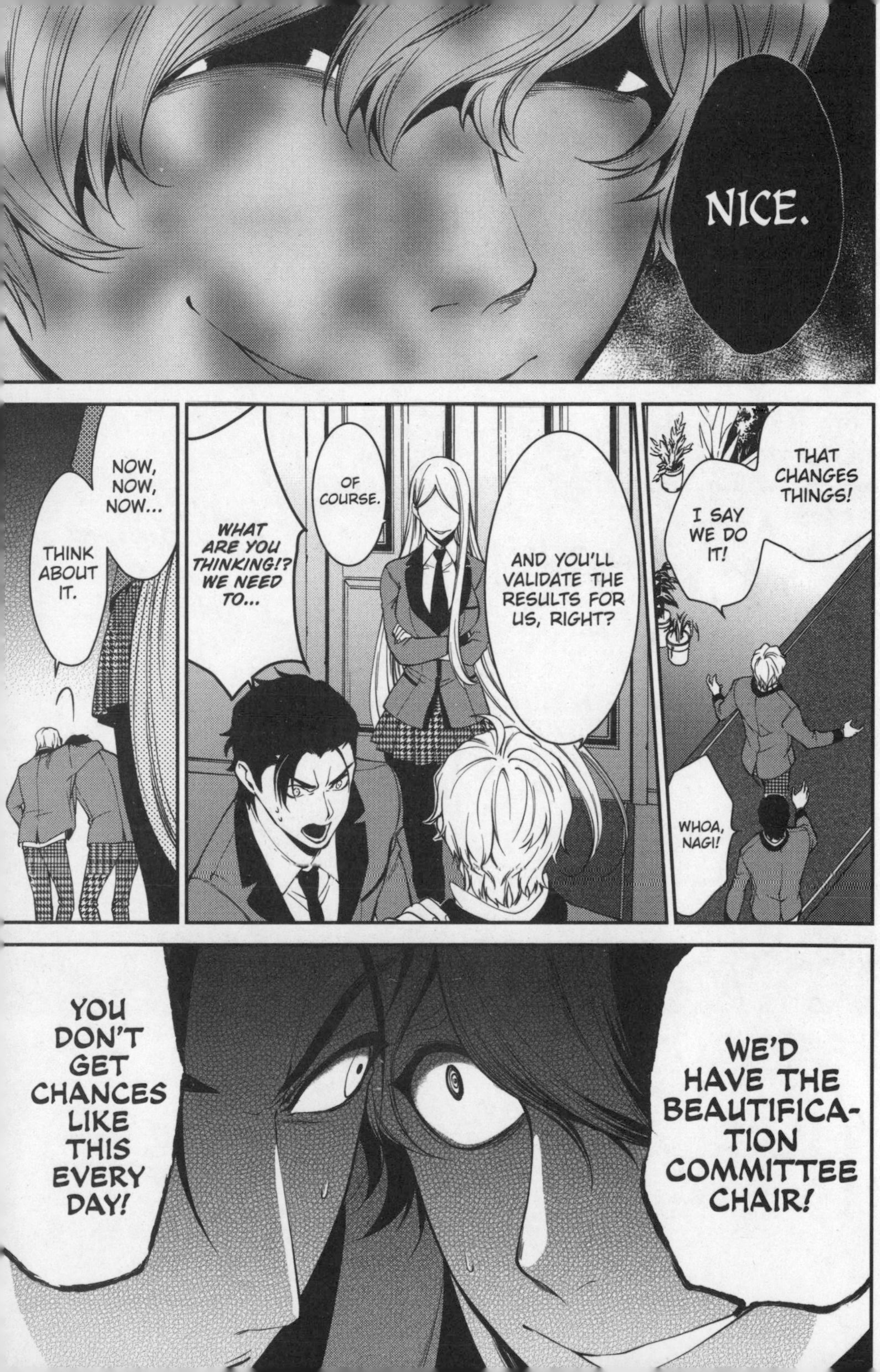
NICE.
THAT CHANGES THINGS!
I SAY WE DO IT!
WHOA, NAGI!
AND YOU'LL VALIDATE THE RESULTS FOR US, RIGHT?
OF COURSE.
WHAT ARE YOU THINKING!? WE NEED TO...
NOW, NOW, NOW...
THINK ABOUT IT.
WE'D HAVE THE BEAUTIFICA-TION COMMITTEE CHAIR!
YOU DON'T GET CHANCES LIKE THIS EVERY DAY!

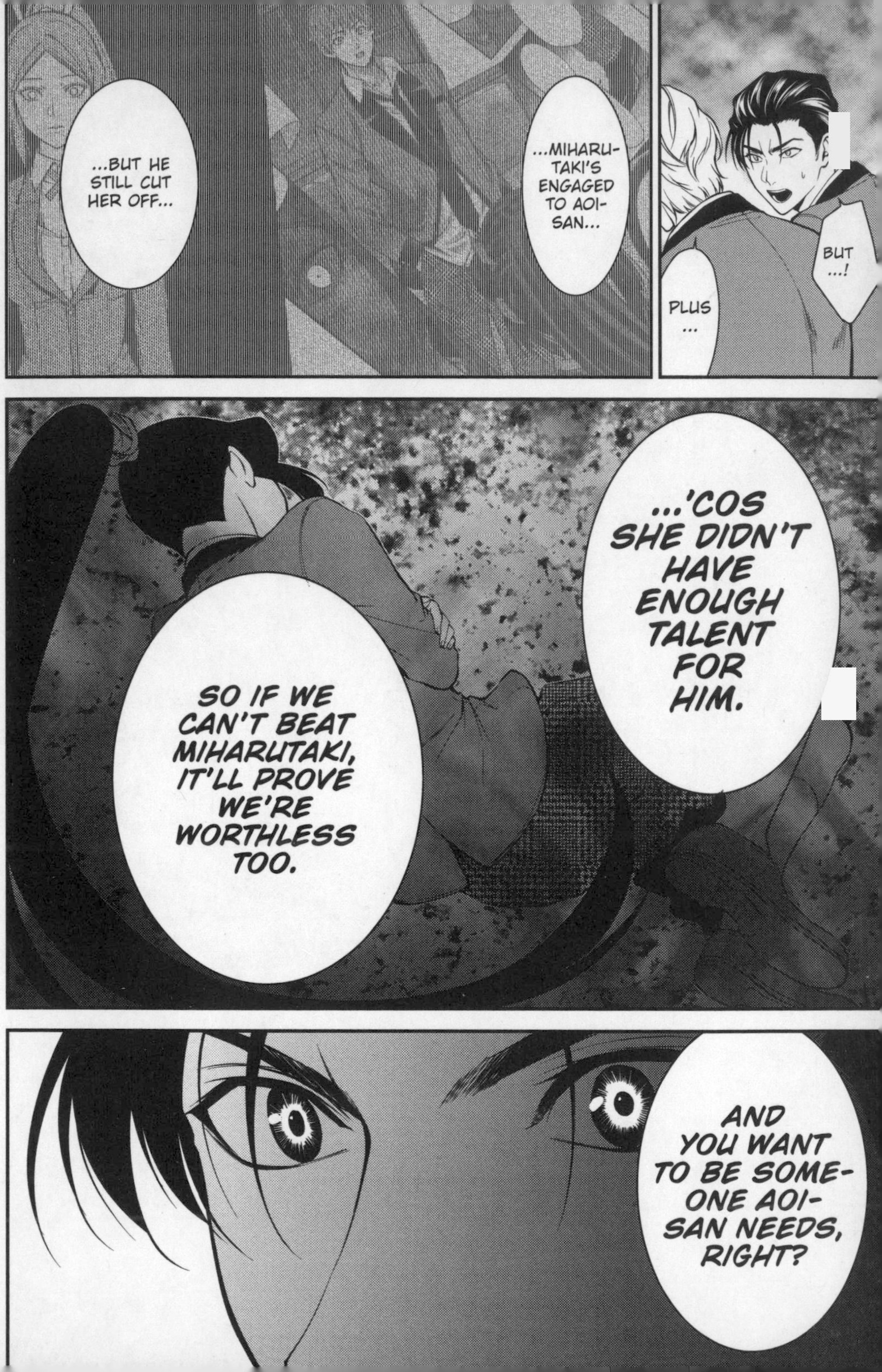
BUT ...!
PLUS ...
...MIHARU-TAKI'S ENGAGED TO AOI-SAN...
...BUT HE STILL CUT HER OFF...
...'COS SHE DIDN'T HAVE ENOUGH TALENT FOR HIM.
SO IF WE CAN'T BEAT MIHARUTAKI, IT'LL PROVE WE'RE WORTHLESS TOO.
AND YOU WANT TO BE SOME-ONE AOI-SAN NEEDS, RIGHT?

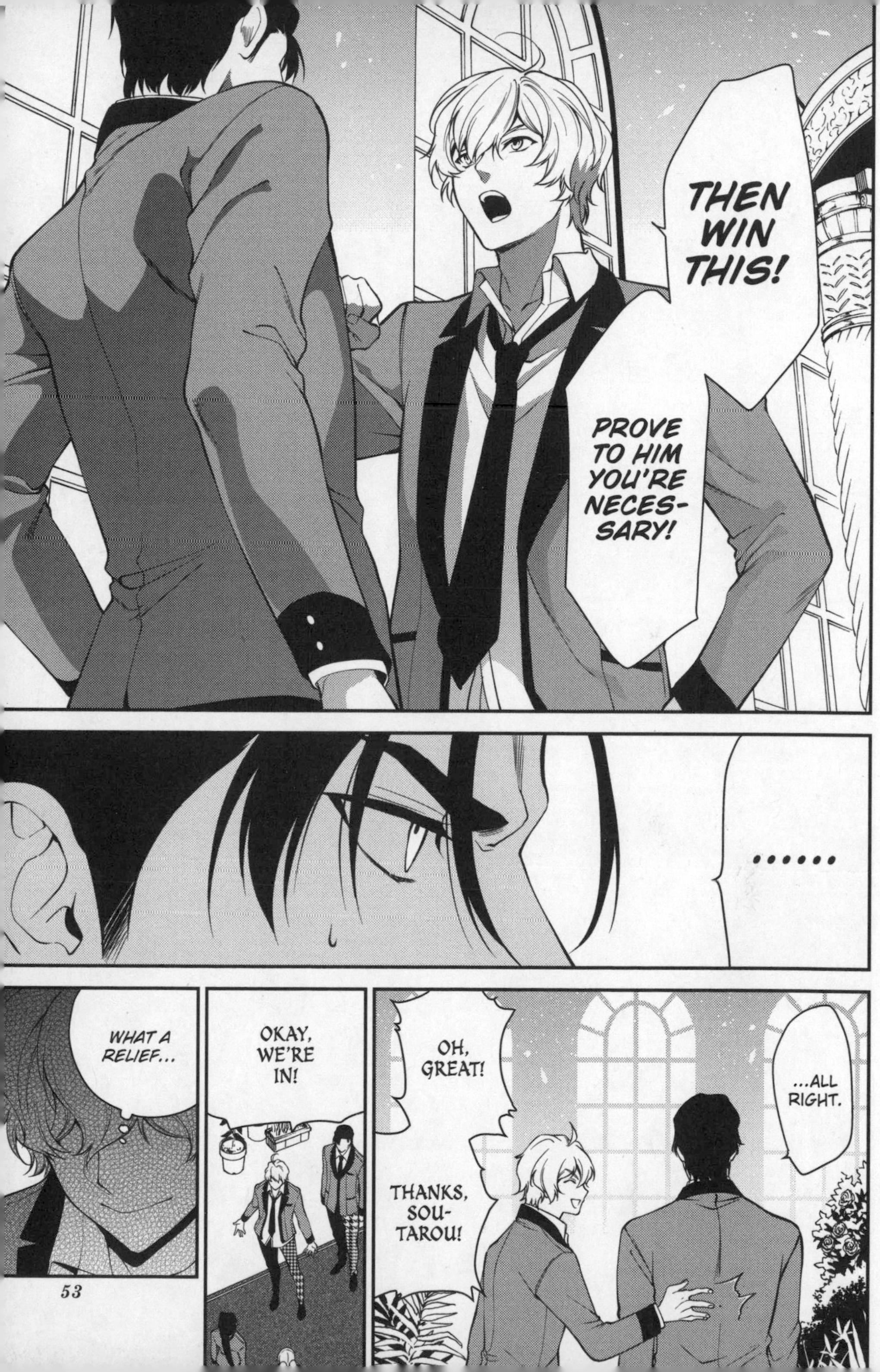
THEN WIN THIS!
PROVE TO HIM YOU'RE NECES-SARY!
......
...ALL RIGHT.
OH, GREAT!
THANKS, SOU-TAROU!
OKAY, WE'RE IN!
WHAT A RELIEF...

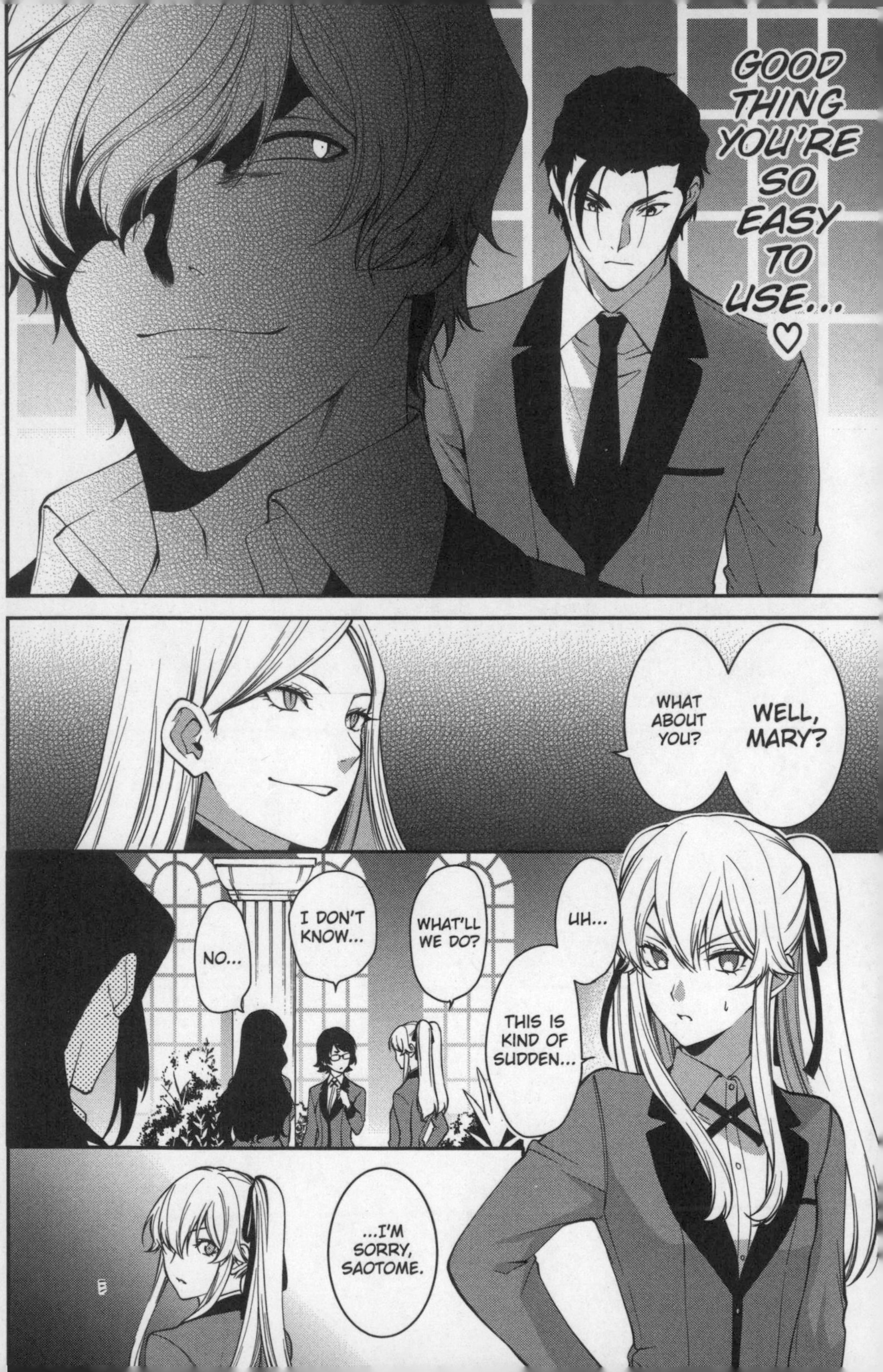
GOOD THING YOU'RE SO EASY TO USE... ♡
WELL, MARY?
WHAT ABOUT YOU?
UH...
THIS IS KIND OF SUDDEN...
WHAT'LL WE DO?
I DON'T KNOW...
NO...
...I'M SORRY, SAOTOME.

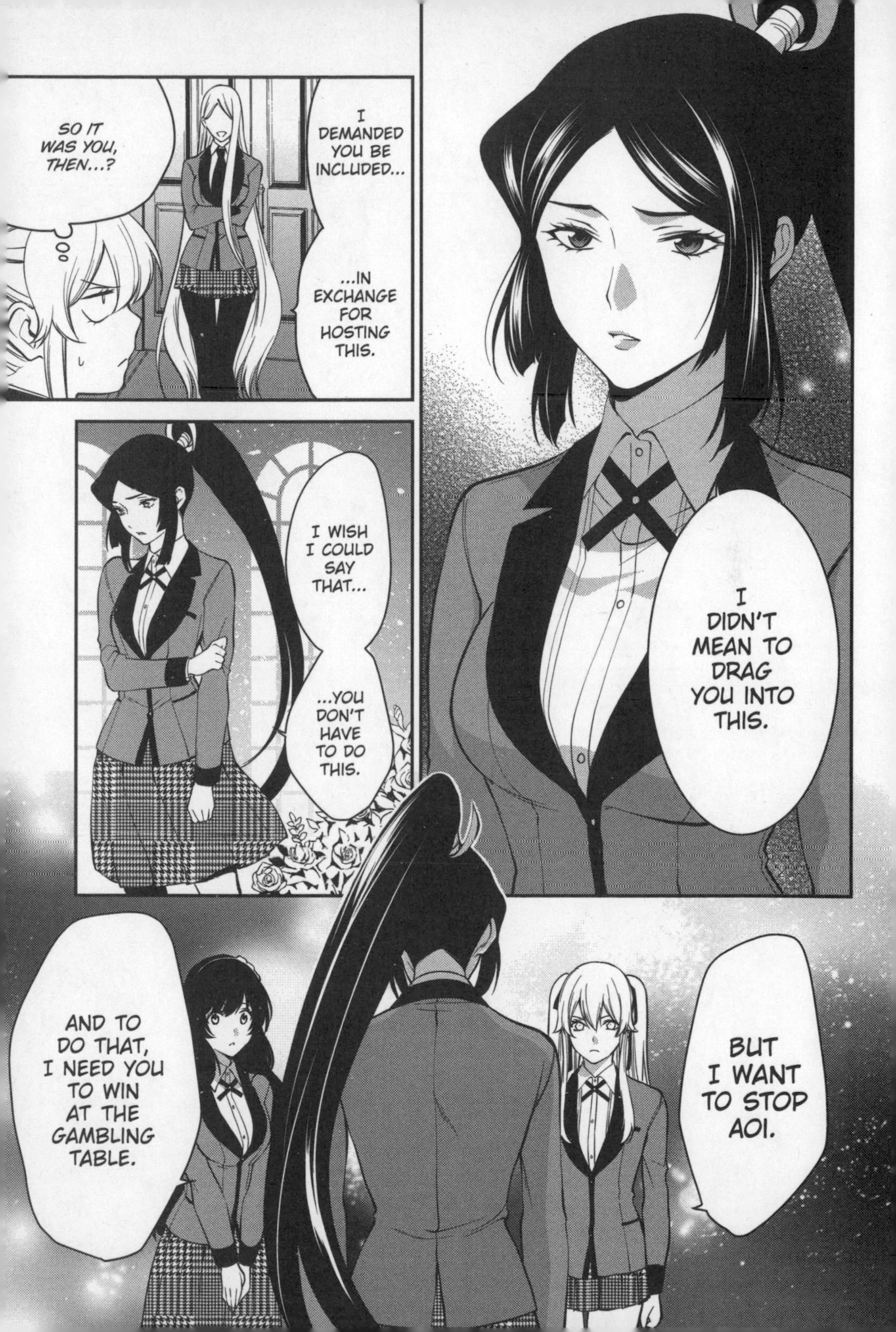
I DIDN'T MEAN TO DRAG YOU INTO THIS.
I DEMANDED YOU BE INCLUDED...
...IN EXCHANGE FOR HOSTING THIS.
SO IT WAS YOU, THEN...?
I WISH I COULD SAY THAT...
...YOU DON'T HAVE TO DO THIS.
BUT I WANT TO STOP AOI.
AND TO DO THAT, I NEED YOU TO WIN AT THE GAMBLING TABLE.

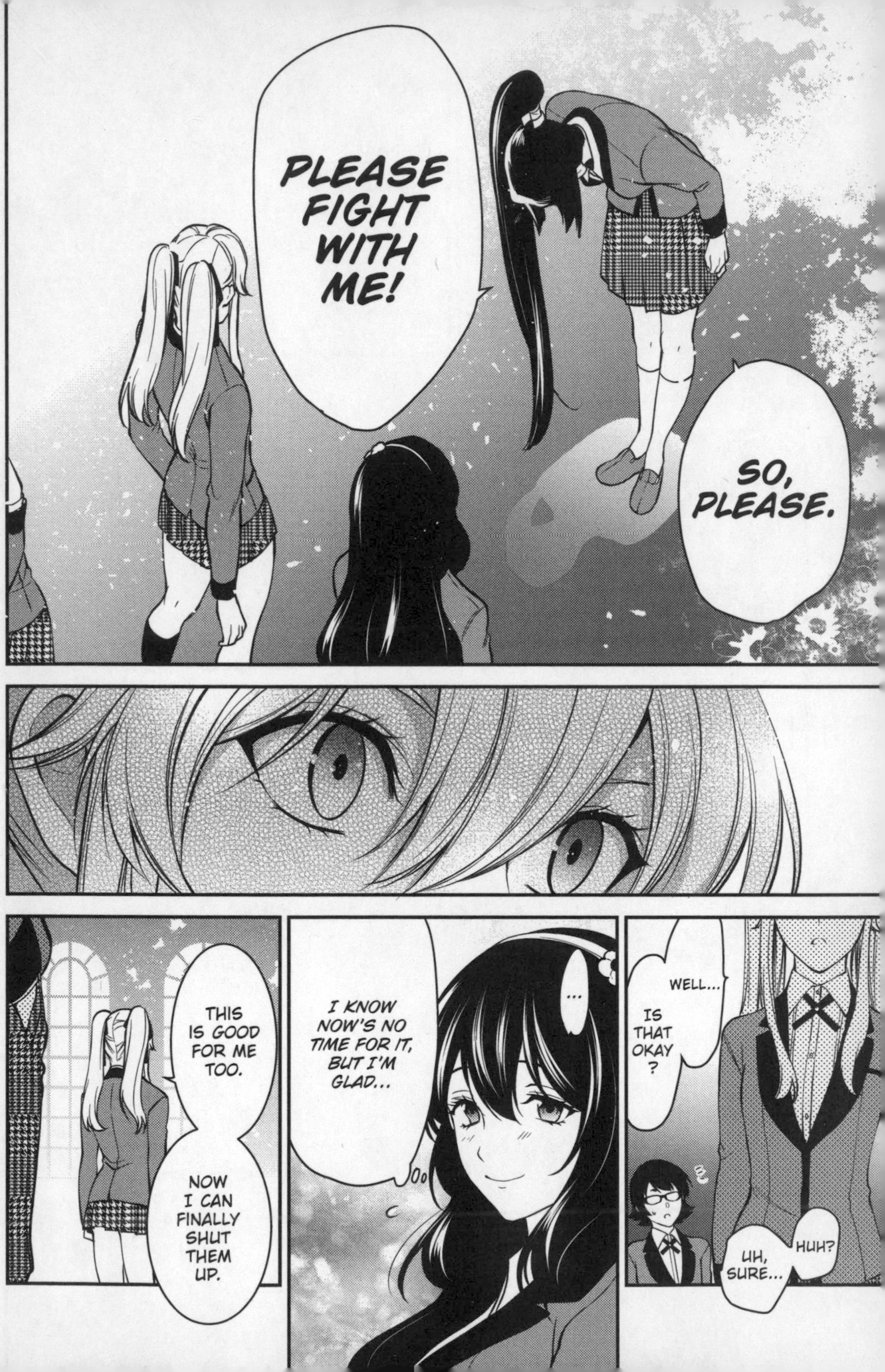
PLEASE FIGHT WITH ME!
SO, PLEASE.
WELL... IS THAT OKAY?
HUH?
UH, SURE...
...
I KNOW NOW'S NO TIME FOR IT, BUT I'M GLAD...
THIS IS GOOD FOR ME TOO.
NOW I CAN FINALLY SHUT THEM UP.

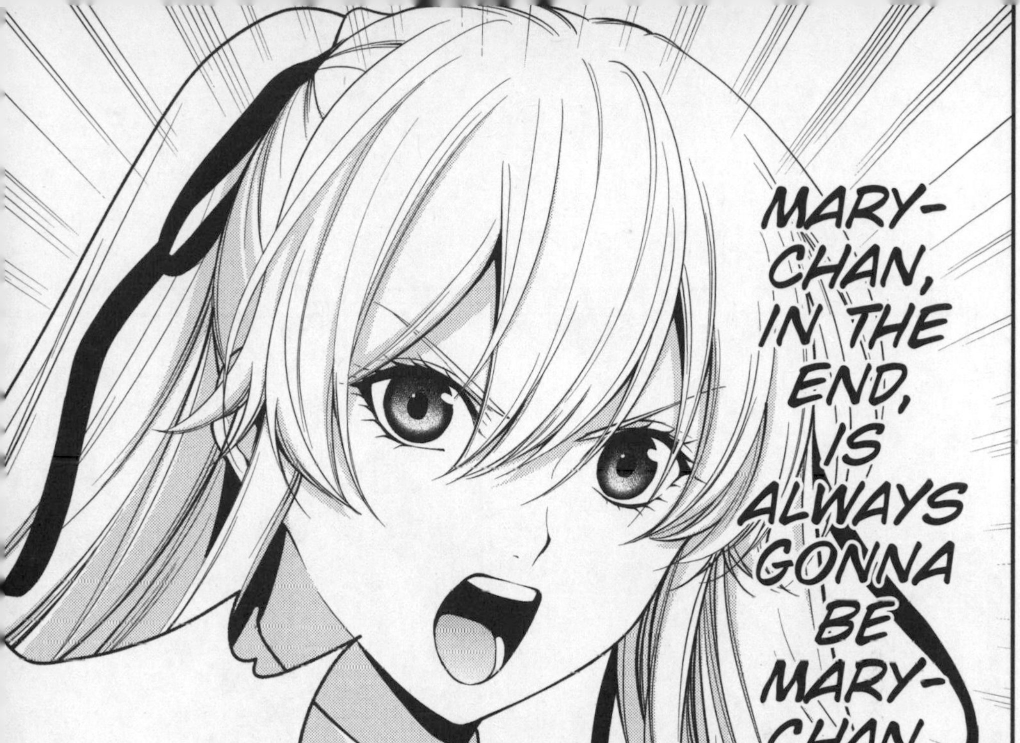
MARY-CHAN, IN THE END, IS ALWAYS GONNA BE MARY-CHAN.
I'LL ACCEPT YOUR CHALLENGE!
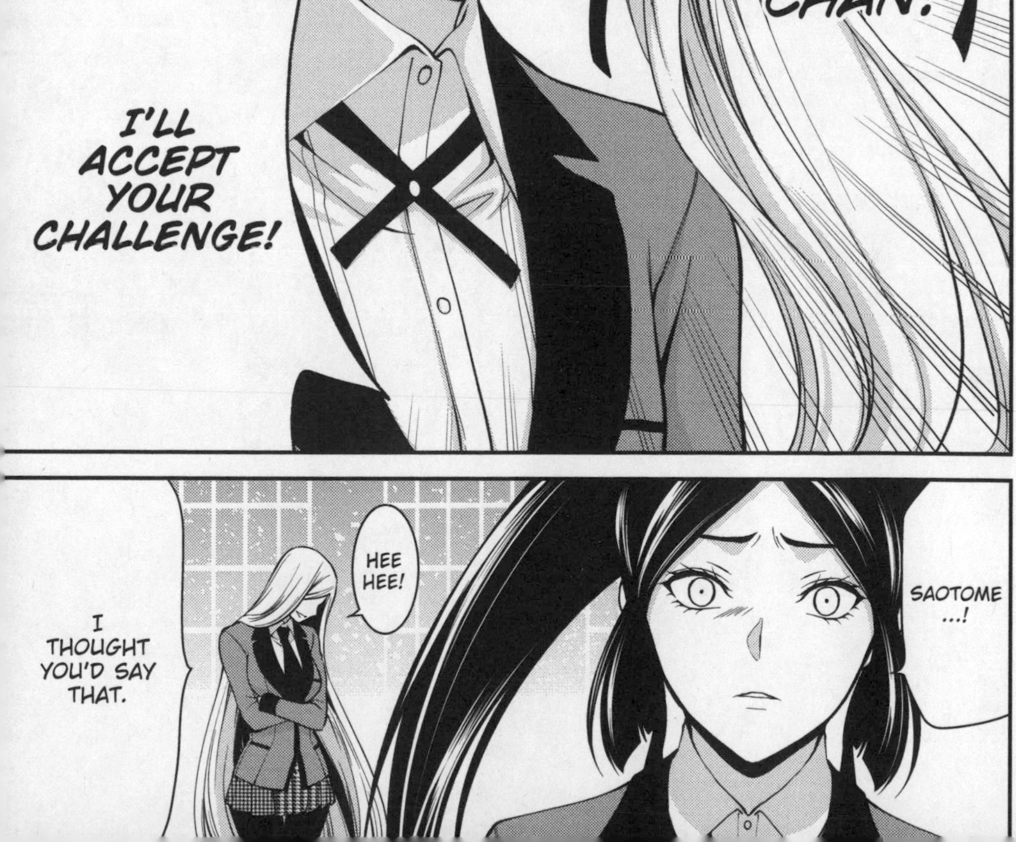
SAOTOME ...!
HEE HEE!
I THOUGHT YOU'D SAY THAT.

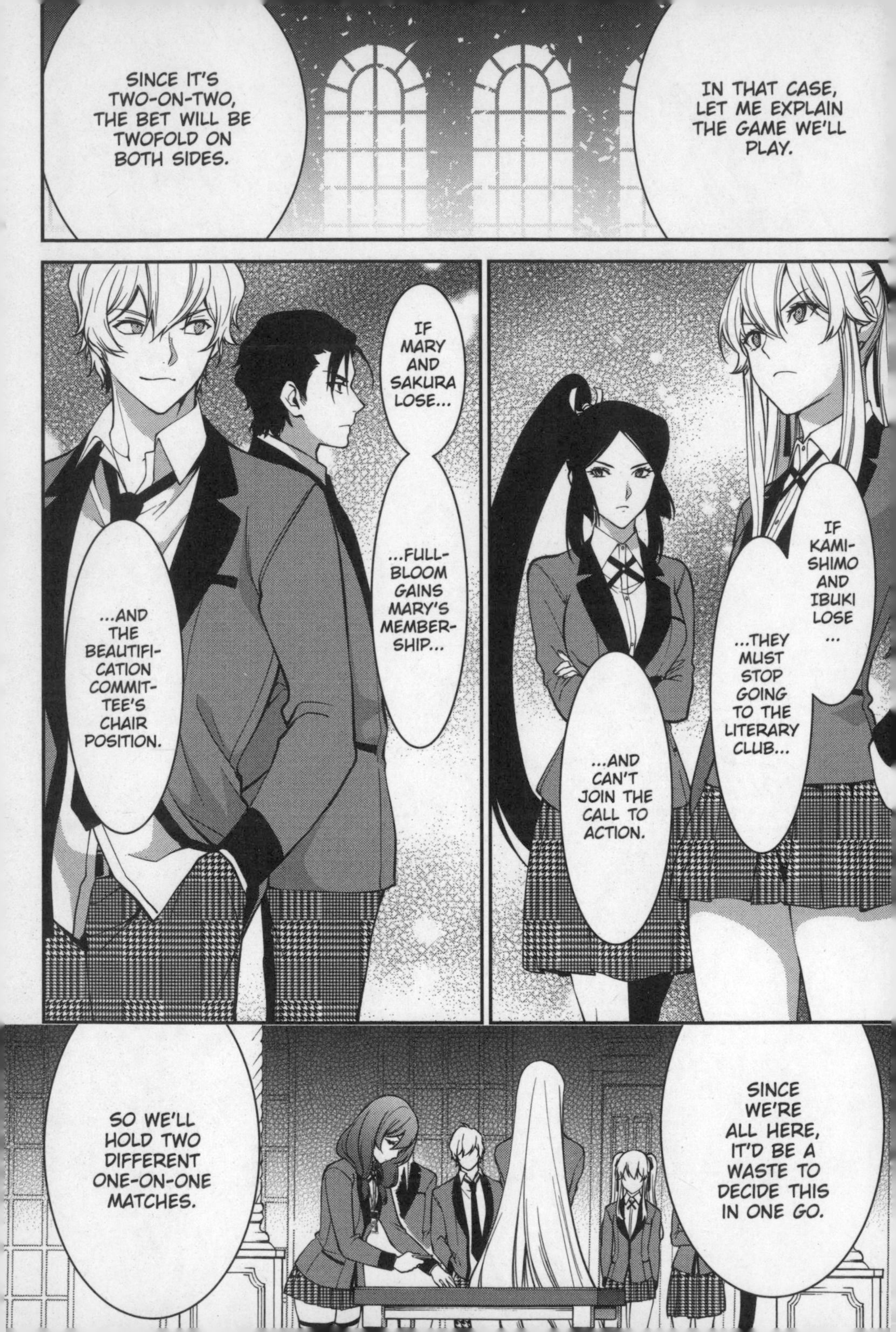
IN THAT CASE, LET ME EXPLAIN THE GAME WE'LL PLAY.
SINCE IT'S TWO-ON-TWO, THE BET WILL BE TWOFOLD ON BOTH SIDES.
IF KAMISHIMO AND IBUKI LOSE...
...THEY MUST STOP GOING TO THE LITERARY CLUB...
...AND CAN'T JOIN THE CALL TO ACTION.
IF MARY AND SAKURA LOSE...
...FULL-BLOOM GAINS MARY'S MEMBERSHIP...
...AND THE BEAUTIFICATION COMMITTEE'S CHAIR POSITION.
SINCE WE'RE ALL HERE, IT'D BE A WASTE TO DECIDE THIS IN ONE GO.
SO WE'LL HOLD TWO DIFFERENT ONE-ON-ONE MATCHES.

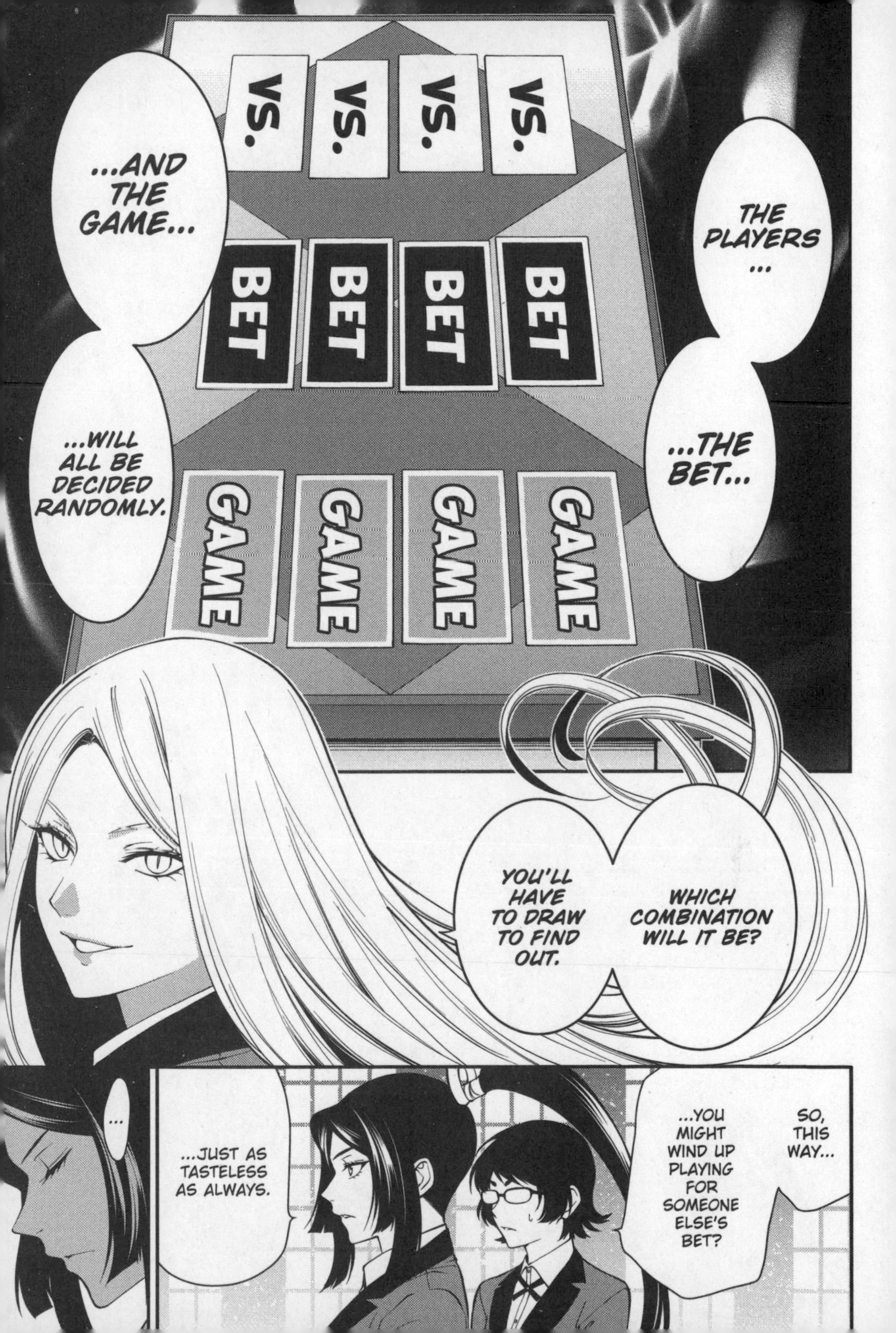
THE PLAYERS ...
...THE BET...
...AND THE GAME...
...WILL ALL BE DECIDED RANDOMLY.
VS.
VS.
VS.
VS.
BET
BET
BET
BET
GAME
GAME
GAME
GAME
WHICH COMBINATION WILL IT BE?
YOU'LL HAVE TO DRAW TO FIND OUT.
SO, THIS WAY...
...YOU MIGHT WIND UP PLAYING FOR SOMEONE ELSE'S BET?
...JUST AS TASTELESS AS ALWAYS.
...

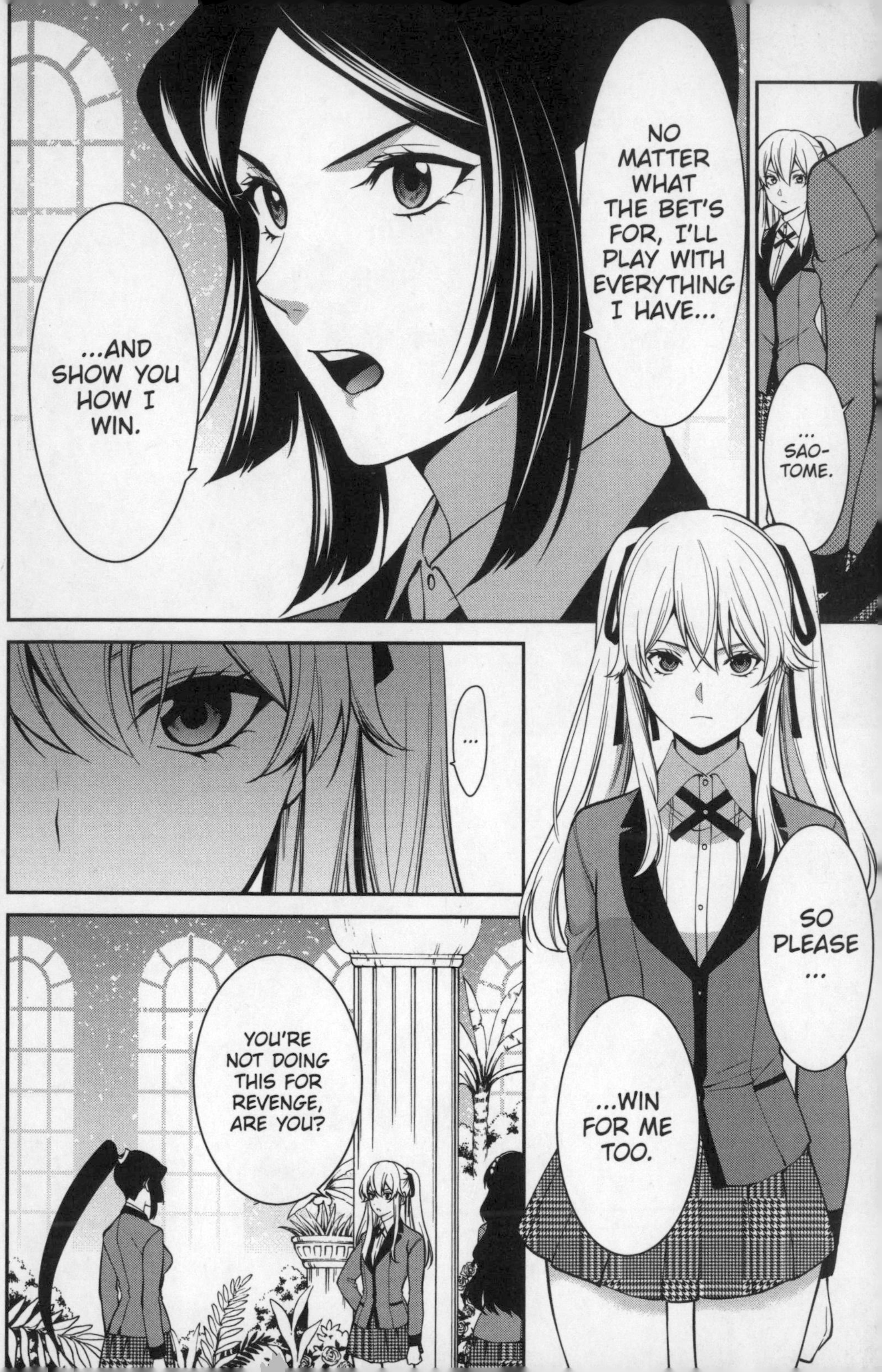

... SAO-TOME.
NO MATTER WHAT THE BET'S FOR, I'LL PLAY WITH EVERYTHING I HAVE...
...AND SHOW YOU HOW I WIN.
SO PLEASE ...
...WIN FOR ME TOO.
...
YOU'RE NOT DOING THIS FOR REVENGE, ARE YOU?

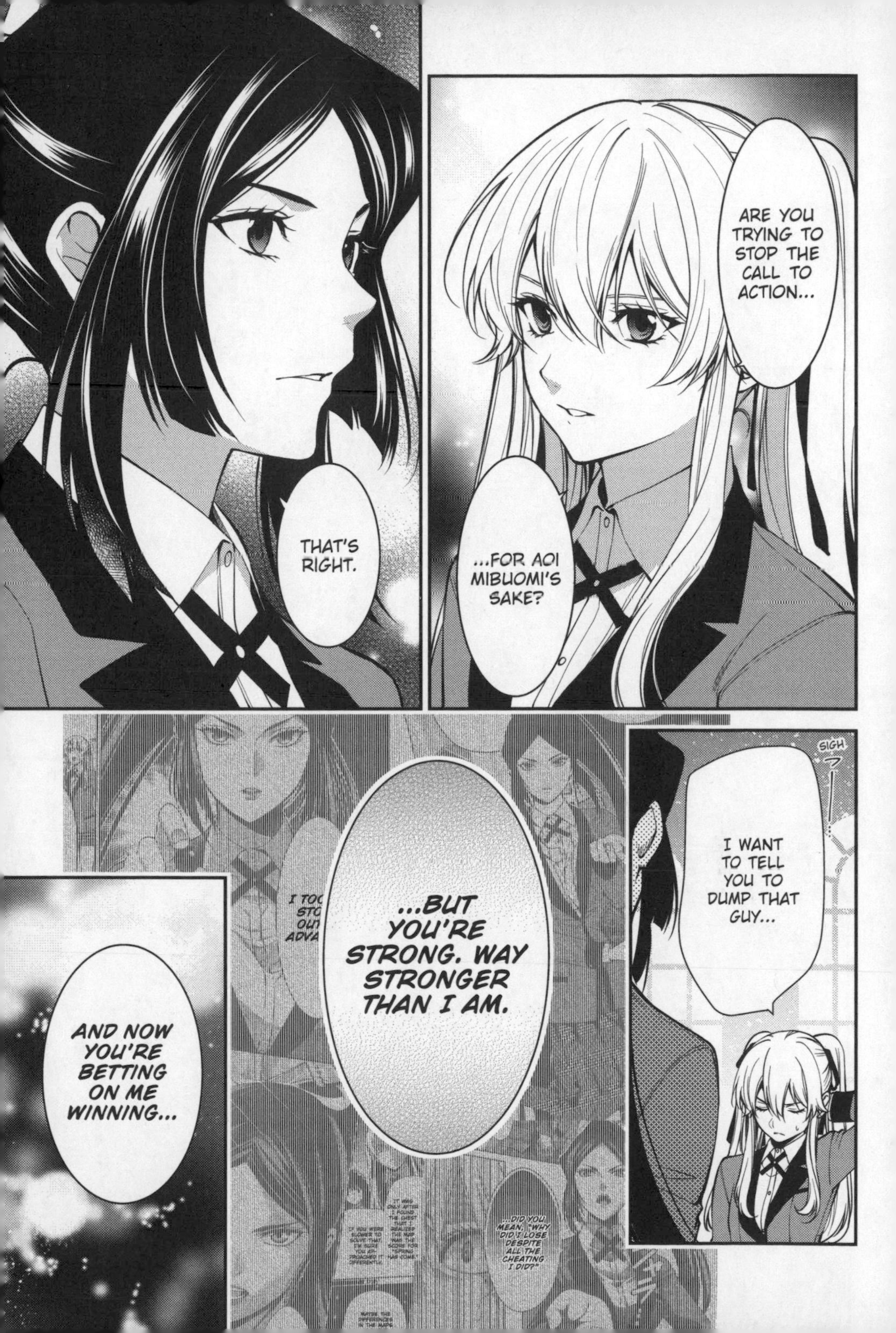
ARE YOU TRYING TO STOP THE CALL TO ACTION...
...FOR AOI MIBUOMI'S SAKE?
THAT'S RIGHT.
SIGH
I WANT TO TELL YOU TO DUMP THAT GUY...
...BUT YOU'RE STRONG. WAY STRONGER THAN I AM.
AND NOW YOU'RE BETTING ON ME WINNING...

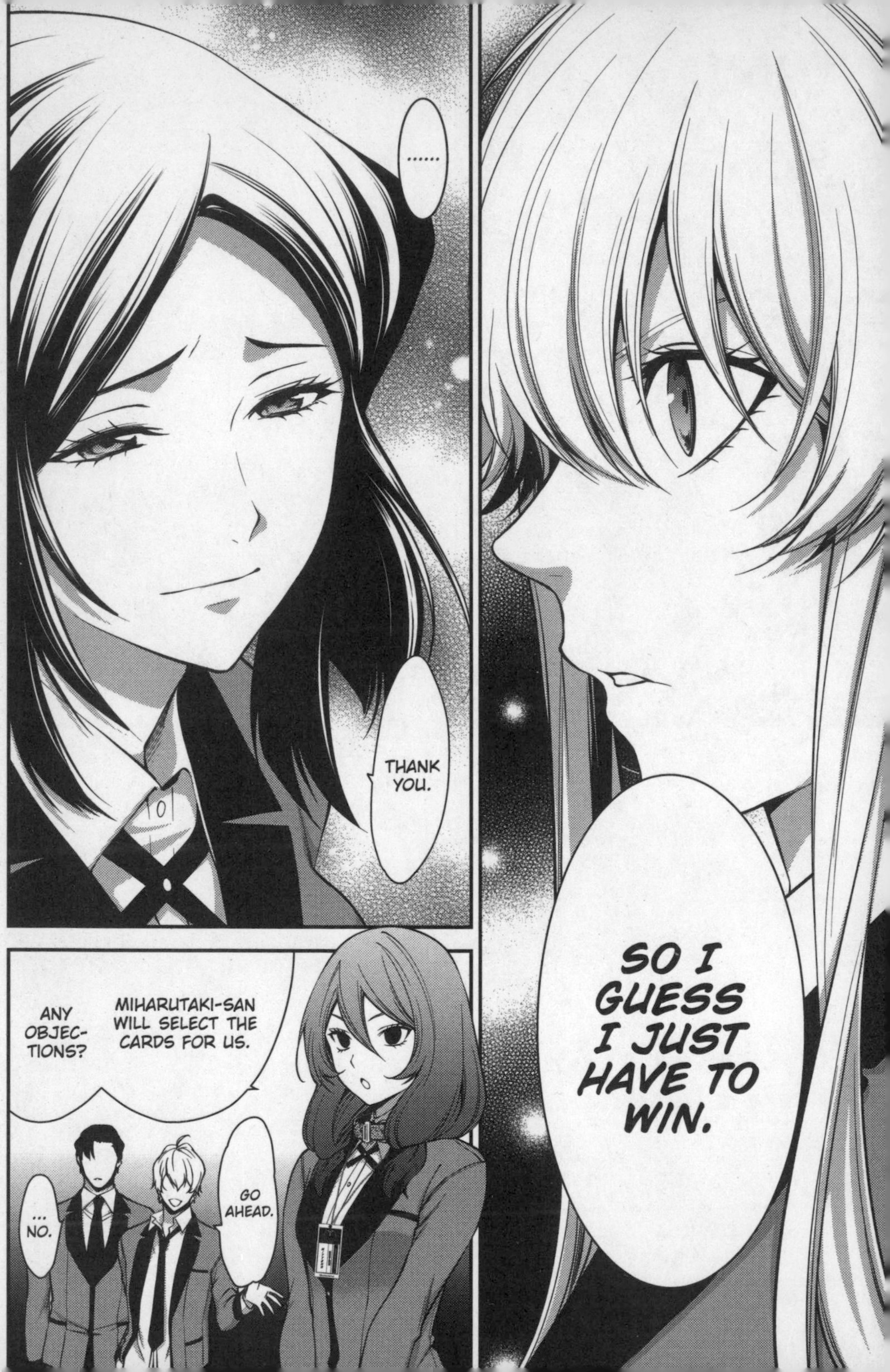
SO I GUESS I JUST HAVE TO WIN.
......
THANK YOU.
MIHARUTAKI-SAN WILL SELECT THE CARDS FOR US.
ANY OBJECTIONS?
GO AHEAD.
... NO.

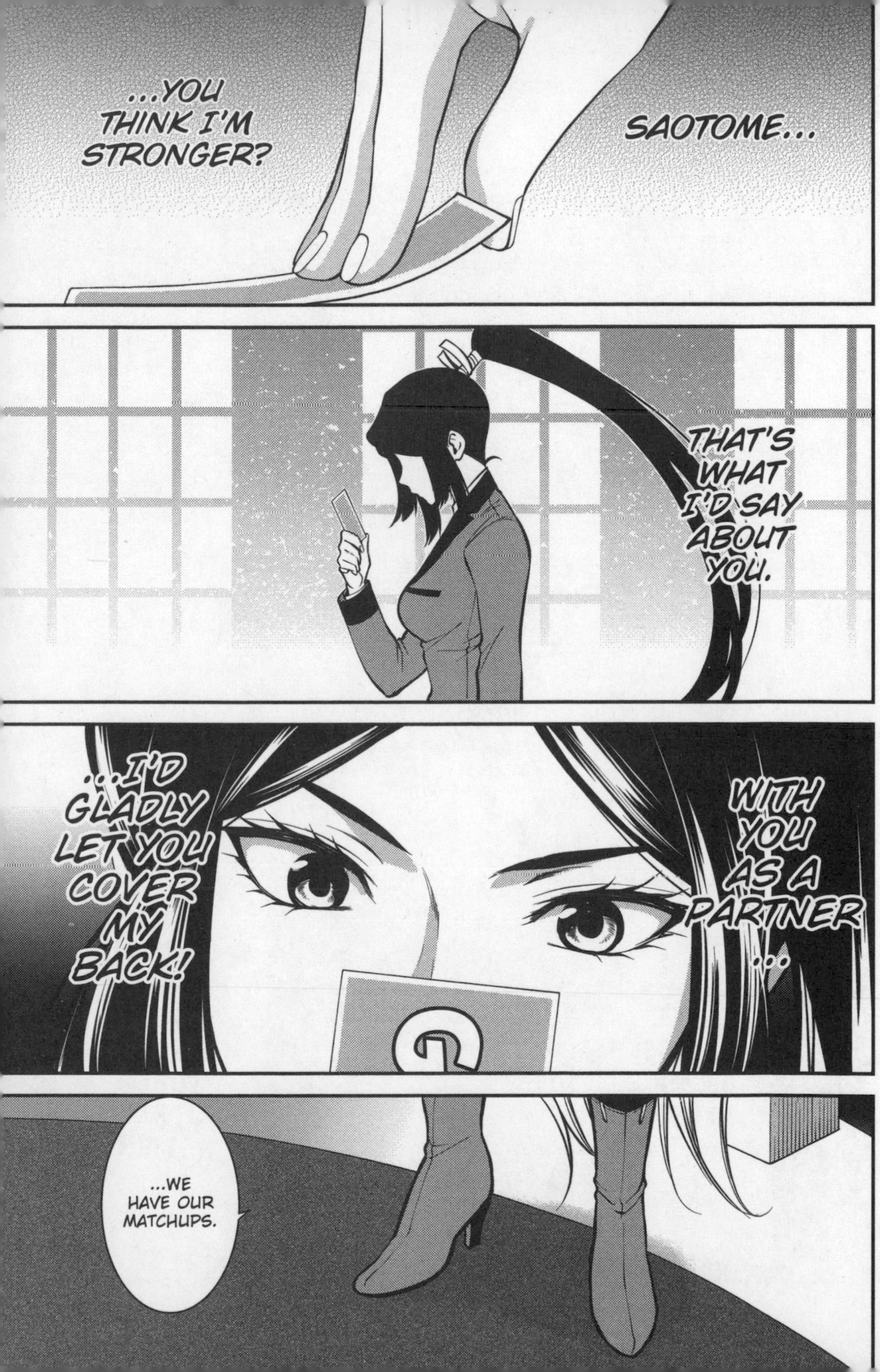
SAOTOME...
...YOU THINK I'M STRONGER?
THAT'S WHAT I'D SAY ABOUT YOU.
WITH YOU AS A PARTNER...
...I'D GLADLY LET YOU COVER MY BACK!
...WE HAVE OUR MATCHUPS.

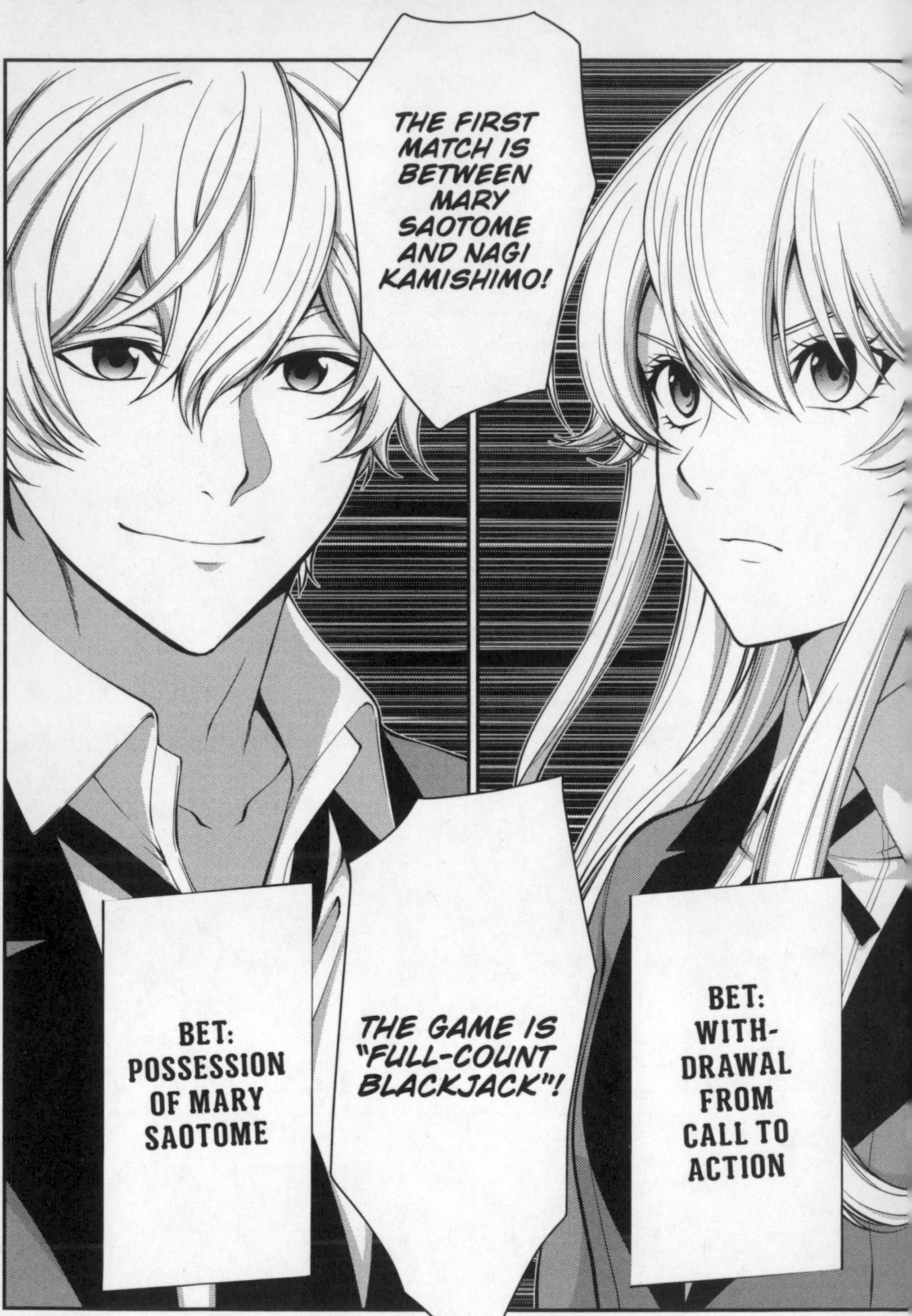
THE FIRST MATCH IS BETWEEN MARY SAOTOME AND NAGI KAMISHIMO!
BET: WITH-DRAWAL FROM CALL TO ACTION
THE GAME IS "FULL-COUNT BLACKJACK"!
BET: POSSESSION OF MARY SAOTOME

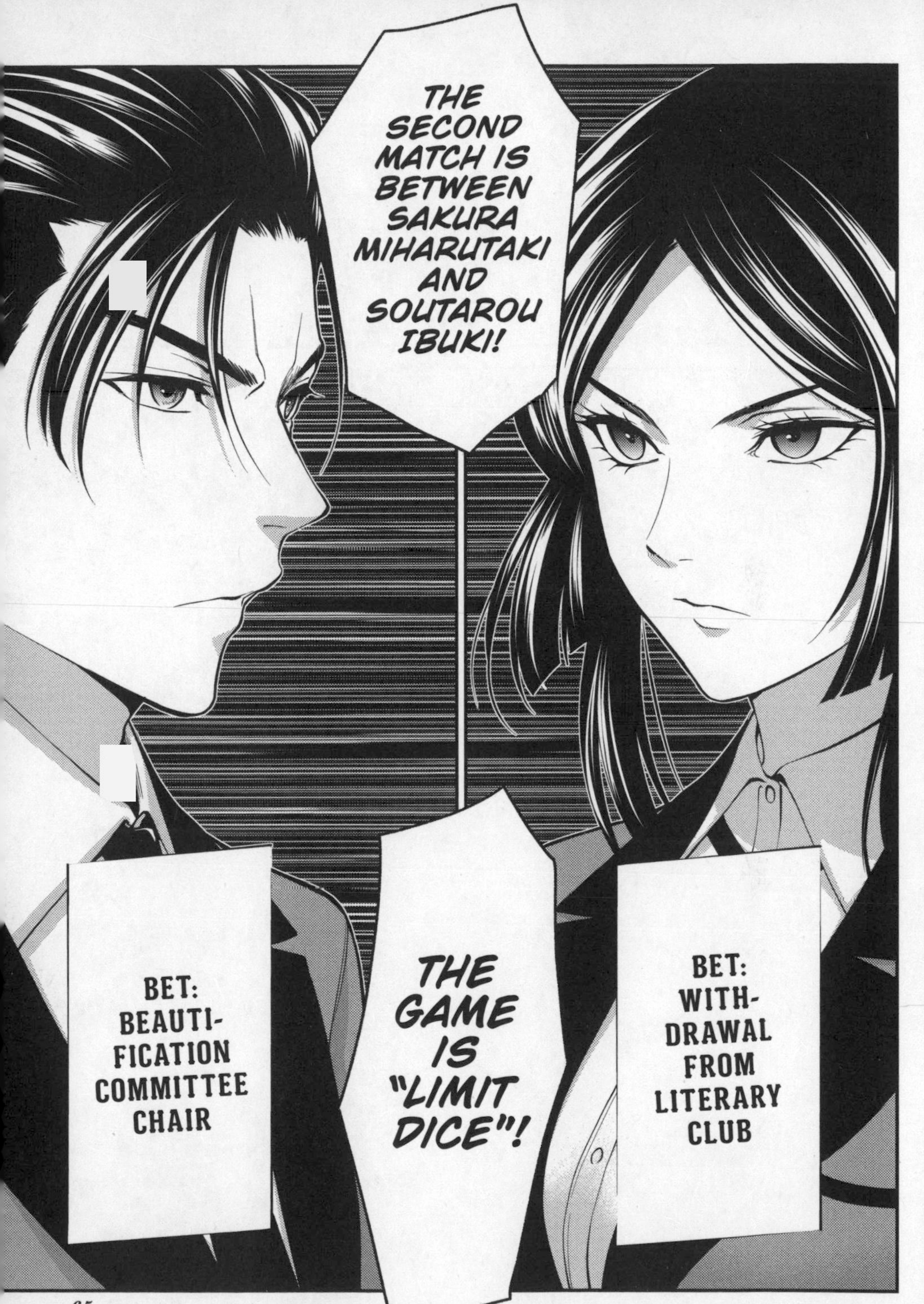
THE SECOND MATCH IS BETWEEN SAKURA MIHARUTAKI AND SOUTAROU IBUKI!
BET: WITH-DRAWAL FROM LITERARY CLUB
THE GAME IS "LIMIT DICE"!
BET: BEAUTI-FICATION COMMITTEE CHAIR

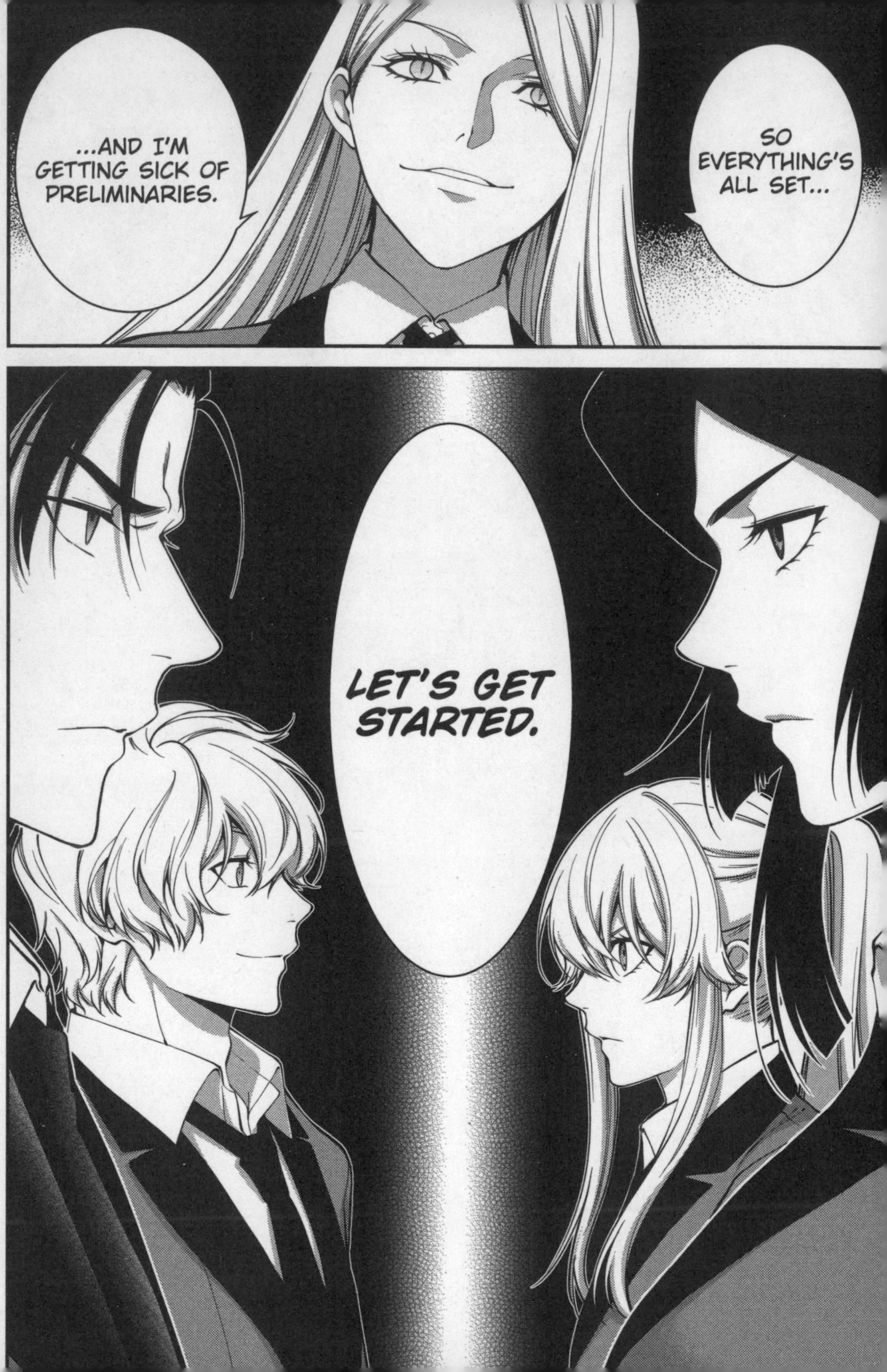
SO EVERYTHING'S ALL SET...
...AND I'M GETTING SICK OF PRELIMINARIES.
LET'S GET STARTED.

Kakegurui Twin

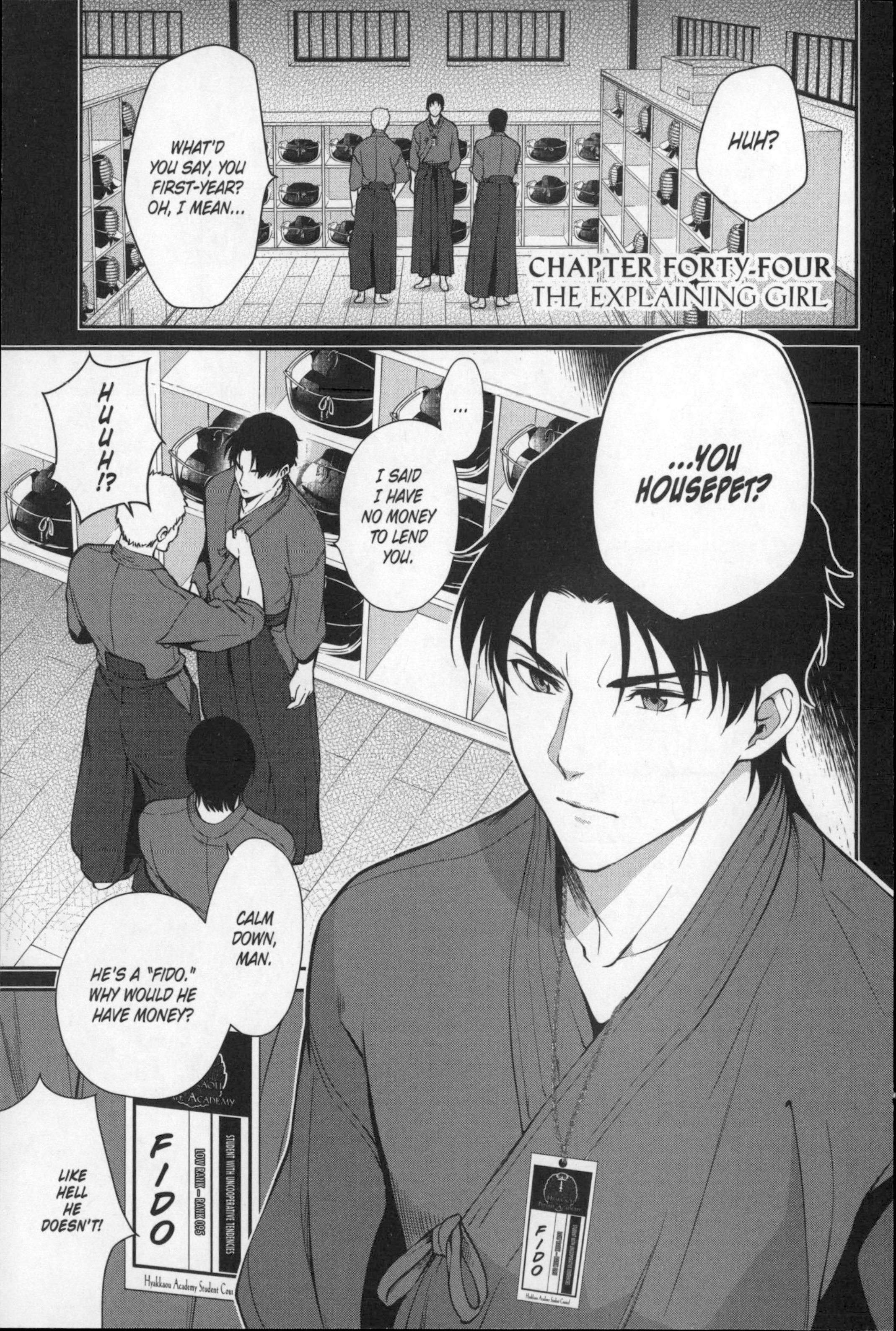
HUH?
WHAT'D YOU SAY, YOU FIRST-YEAR? OH, I MEAN...
CHAPTER FORTY-FOUR
THE EXPLAINING GIRL
...YOU HOUSEPET?
...
I SAID I HAVE NO MONEY TO LEND YOU.
HUUUH!?
CALM DOWN, MAN.
HE'S A "FIDO." WHY WOULD HE HAVE MONEY?
FIDO
STUDENT WITH UNCOOPERATIVE TENDENCIES
LOW RANK – RANK 095
LIKE HELL HE DOESN'T!

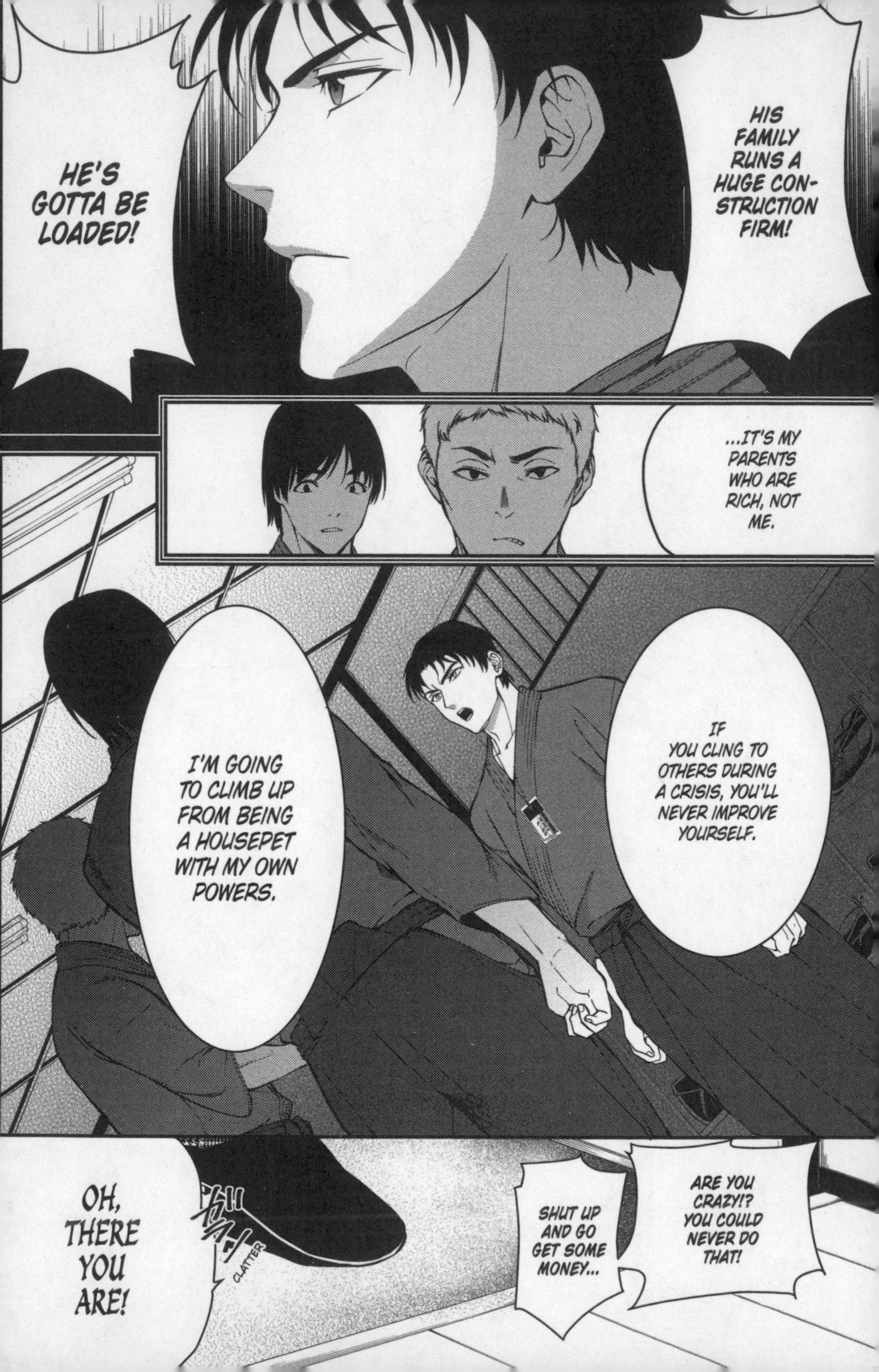
HIS FAMILY RUNS A HUGE CON-STRUCTION FIRM!
HE'S GOTTA BE LOADED!
...IT'S MY PARENTS WHO ARE RICH, NOT ME.
IF YOU CLING TO OTHERS DURING A CRISIS, YOU'LL NEVER IMPROVE YOURSELF.
I'M GOING TO CLIMB UP FROM BEING A HOUSEPET WITH MY OWN POWERS.
ARE YOU CRAZY!? YOU COULD NEVER DO THAT!
SHUT UP AND GO GET SOME MONEY...
CLATTER
OH, THERE YOU ARE!

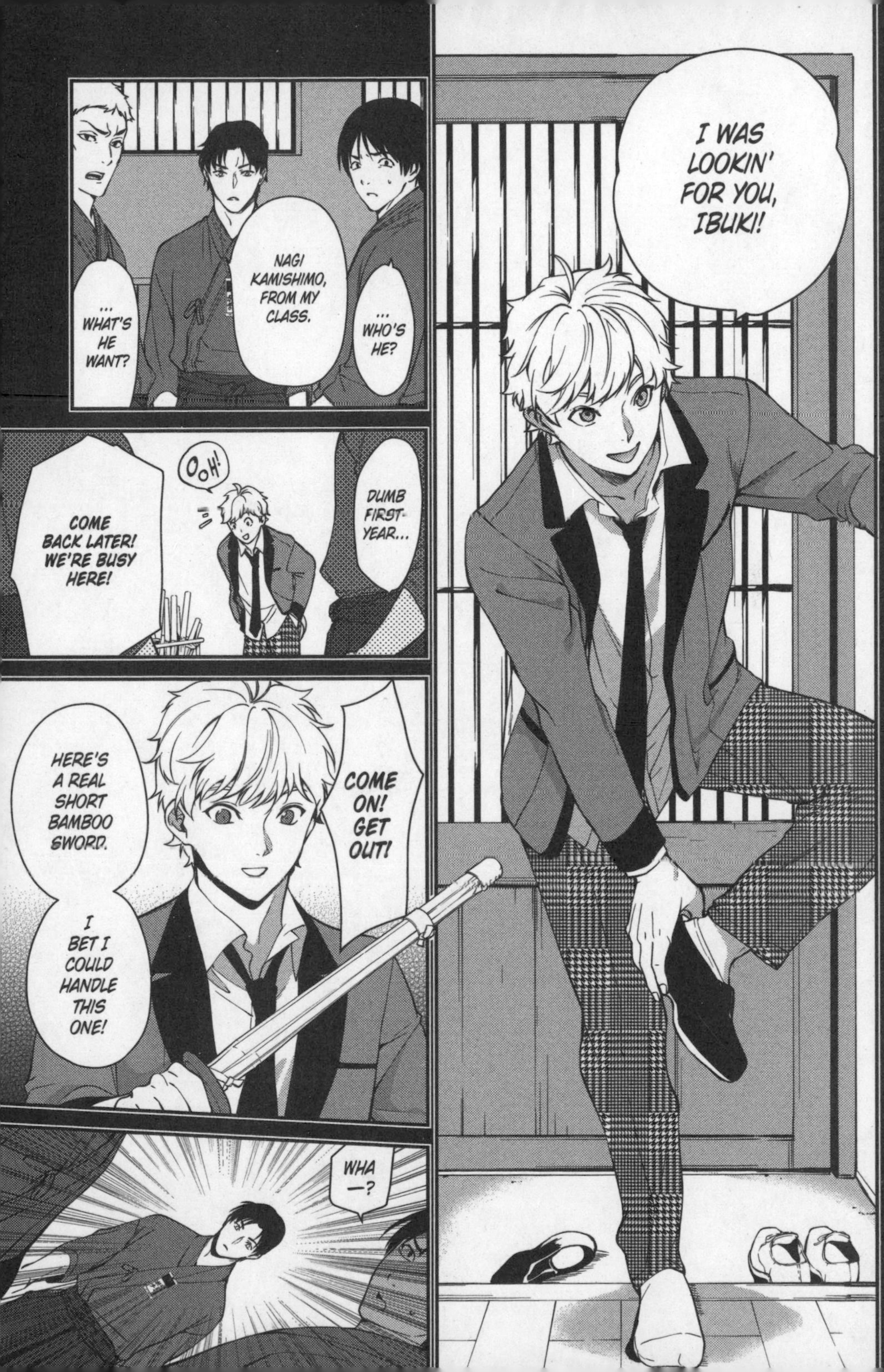
I WAS LOOKIN' FOR YOU, IBUKI!
... WHO'S HE?
NAGI KAMISHIMO, FROM MY CLASS.
... WHAT'S HE WANT?
DUMB FIRST-YEAR...
OOH!
COME BACK LATER! WE'RE BUSY HERE!
COME ON! GET OUT!
HERE'S A REAL SHORT BAMBOO SWORD.
I BET I COULD HANDLE THIS ONE!
WHA—?

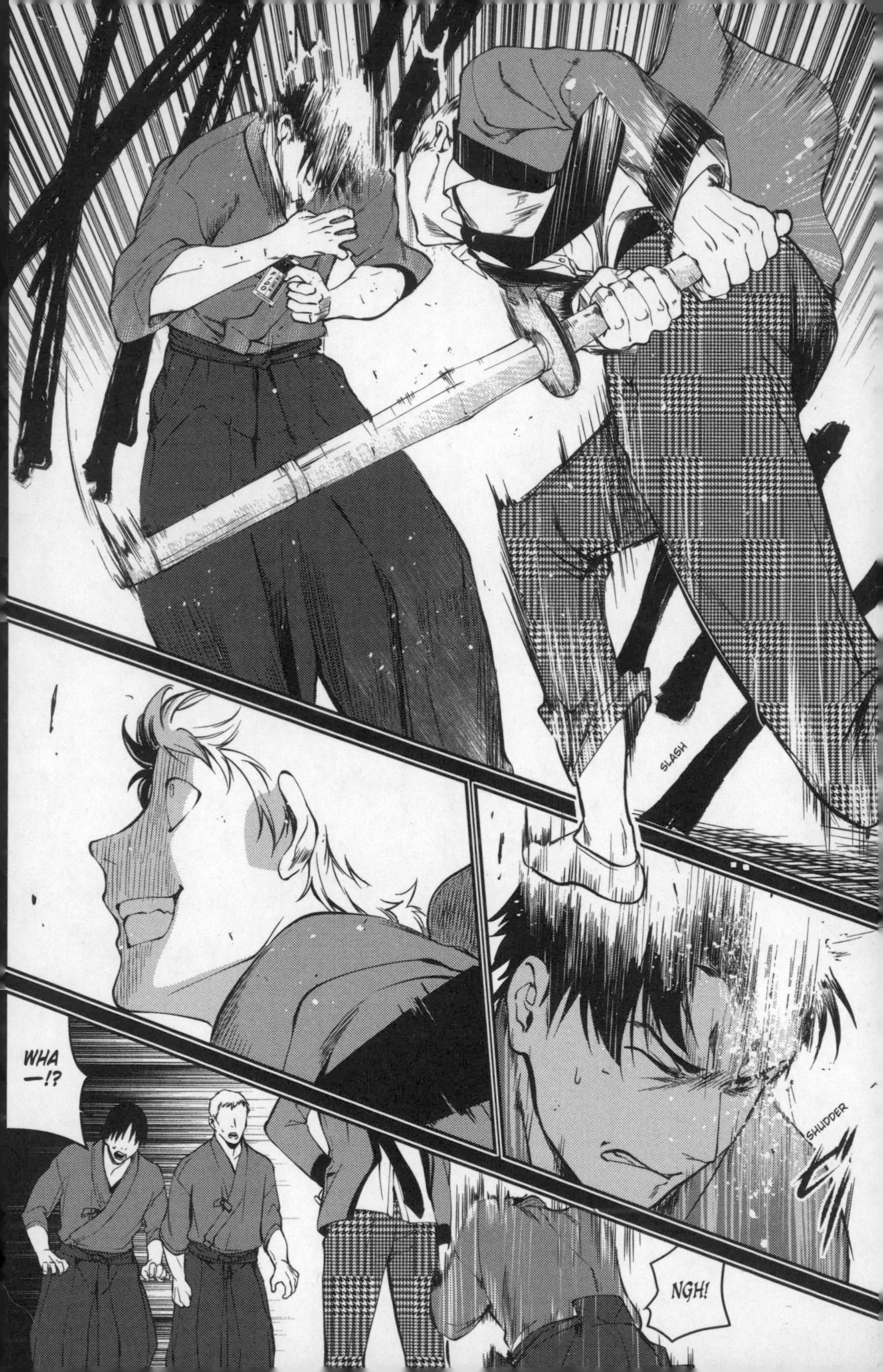
SLASH
SHUDDER
NGH!
WHA—!?

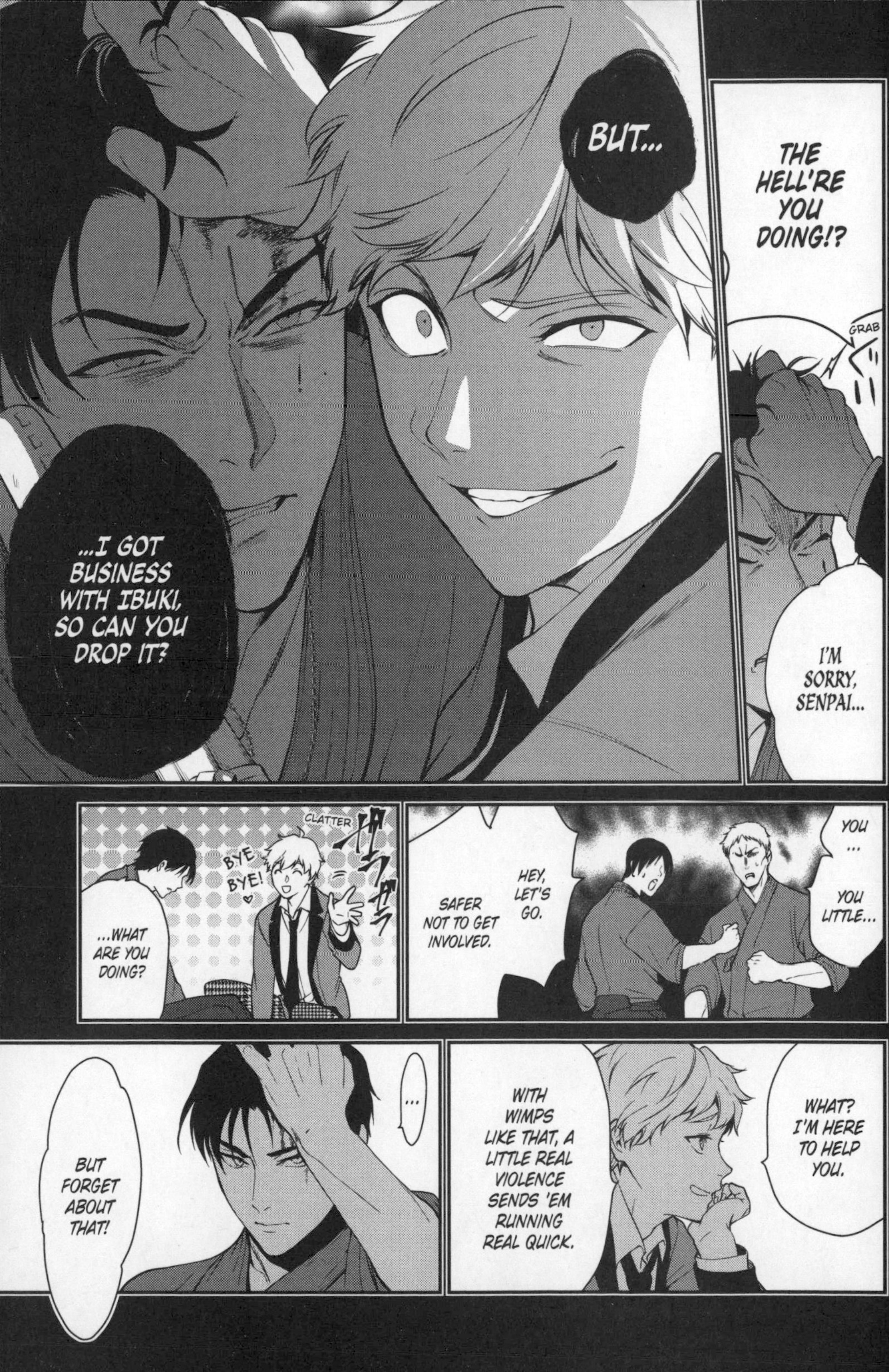
THE HELL'RE YOU DOING!?
GRAB
I'M SORRY, SENPAI...
BUT...
...I GOT BUSINESS WITH IBUKI, SO CAN YOU DROP IT?
YOU ... YOU LITTLE...
HEY, LET'S GO.
SAFER NOT TO GET INVOLVED.
CLATTER
BYE BYE!
...WHAT ARE YOU DOING?
WHAT? I'M HERE TO HELP YOU.
WITH WIMPS LIKE THAT, A LITTLE REAL VIOLENCE SENDS 'EM RUNNING REAL QUICK.
...
BUT FORGET ABOUT THAT!

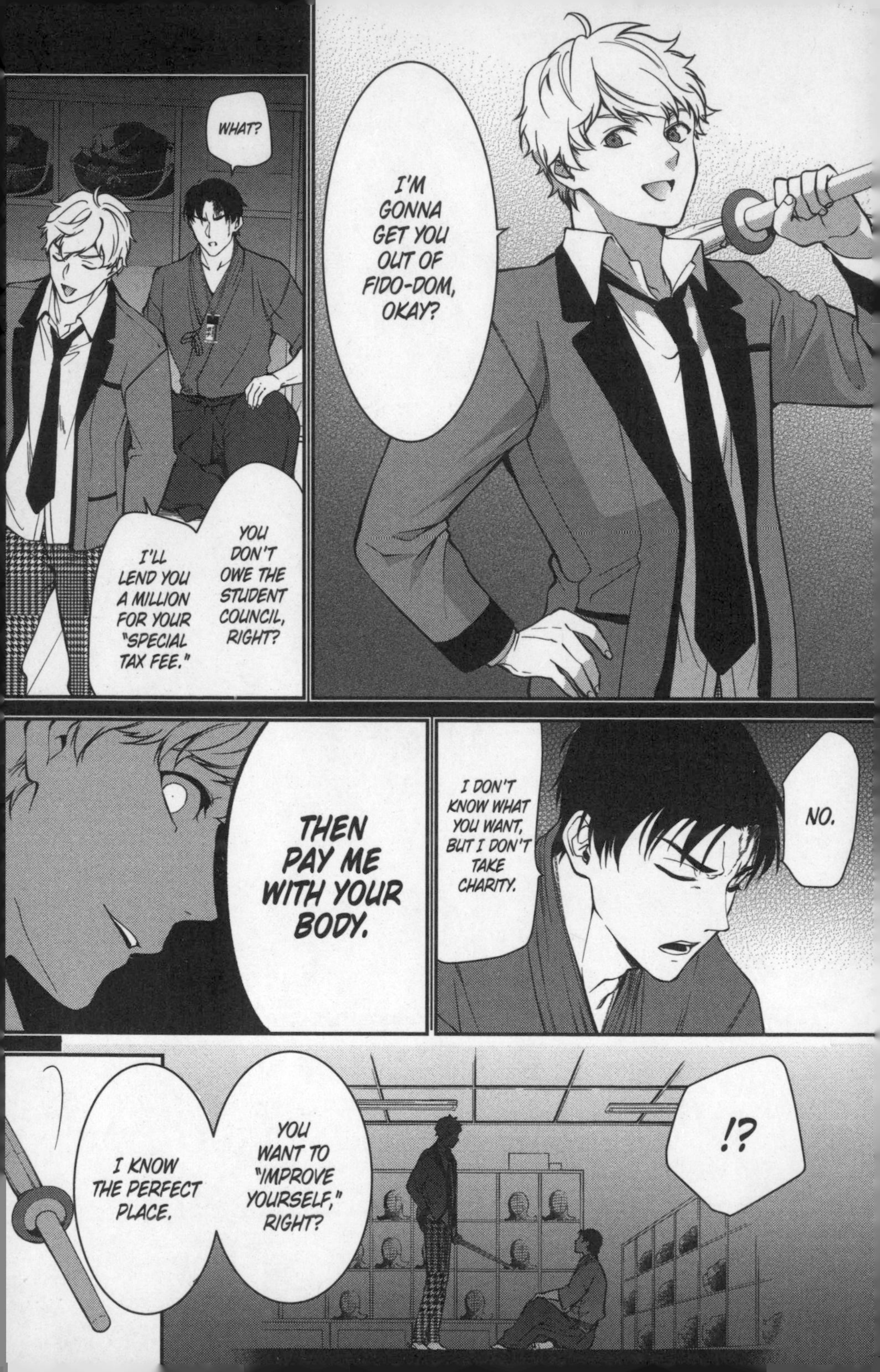
I'M GONNA GET YOU OUT OF FIDO-DOM, OKAY?
WHAT?
YOU DON'T OWE THE STUDENT COUNCIL, RIGHT?
I'LL LEND YOU A MILLION FOR YOUR "SPECIAL TAX FEE."
NO.
I DON'T KNOW WHAT YOU WANT, BUT I DON'T TAKE CHARITY.
THEN PAY ME WITH YOUR BODY.
!?
YOU WANT TO "IMPROVE YOURSELF," RIGHT?
I KNOW THE PERFECT PLACE.

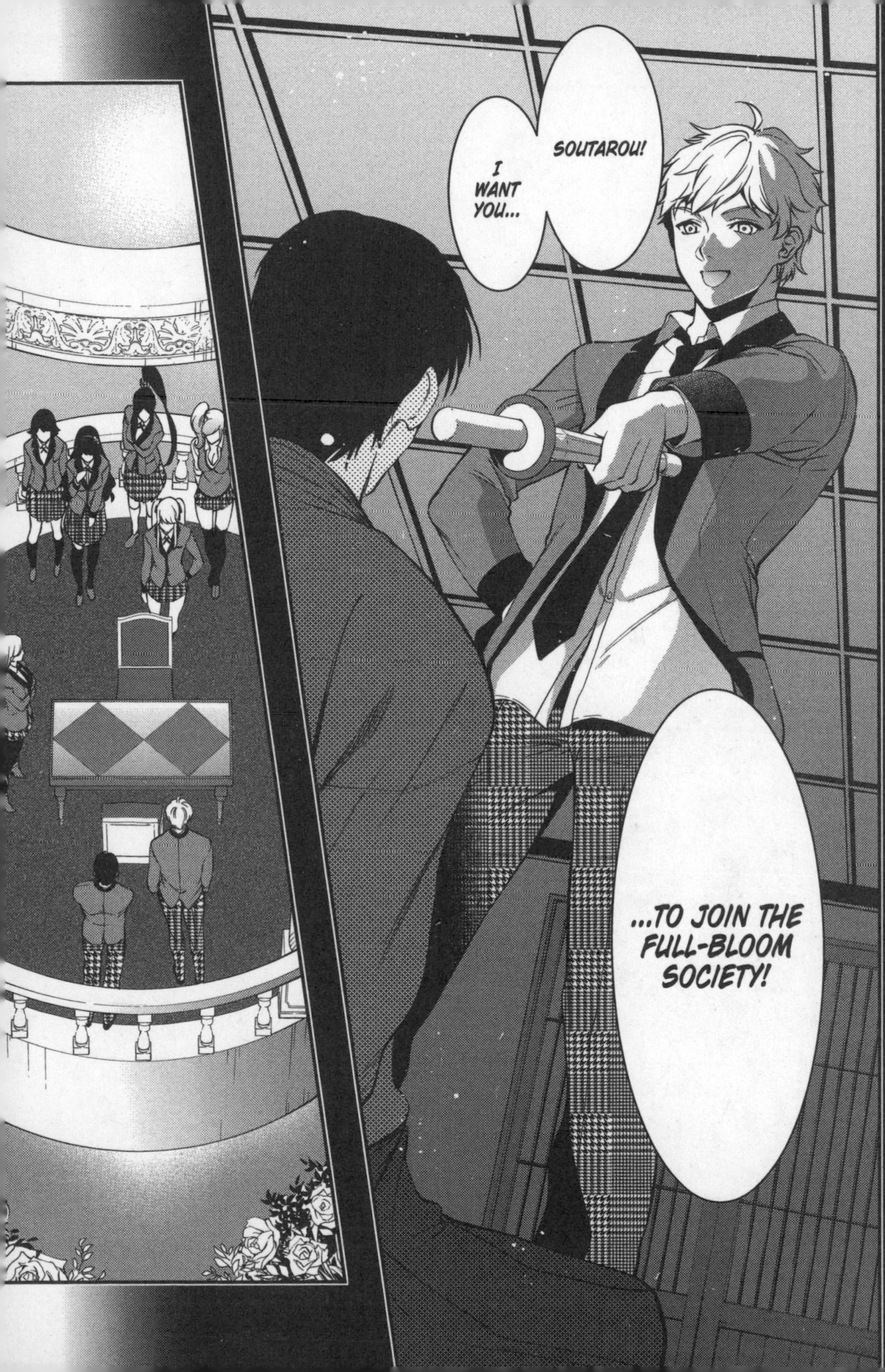
SOUTAROU!
I WANT YOU...
...TO JOIN THE FULL-BLOOM SOCIETY!

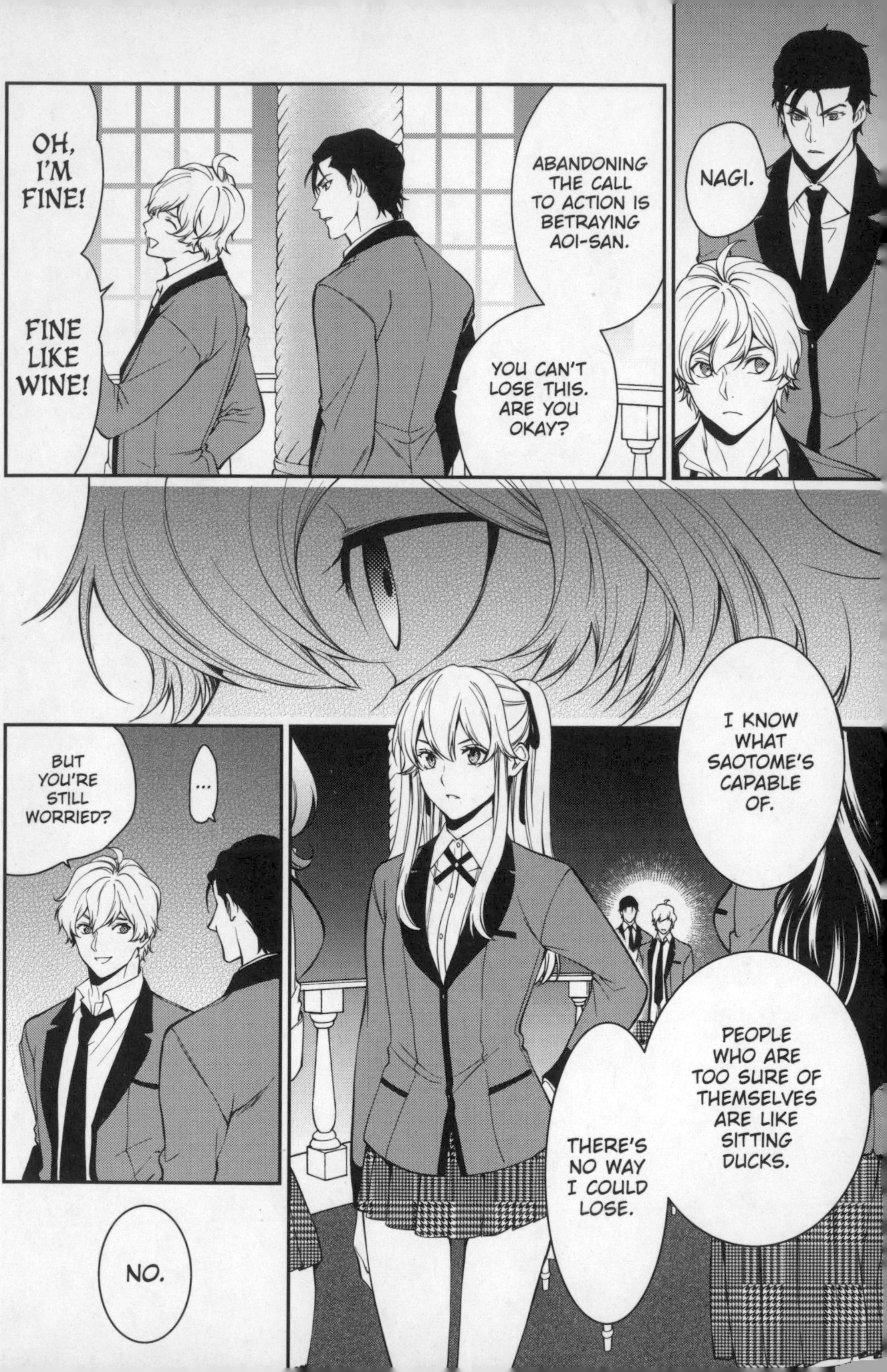
NAGI.
ABANDONING THE CALL TO ACTION IS BETRAYING AOI-SAN.
YOU CAN'T LOSE THIS. ARE YOU OKAY?
OH, I'M FINE!
FINE LIKE WINE!
I KNOW WHAT SAOTOME'S CAPABLE OF.
PEOPLE WHO ARE TOO SURE OF THEMSELVES ARE LIKE SITTING DUCKS.
THERE'S NO WAY I COULD LOSE.
BUT YOU'RE STILL WORRIED?
...
NO.

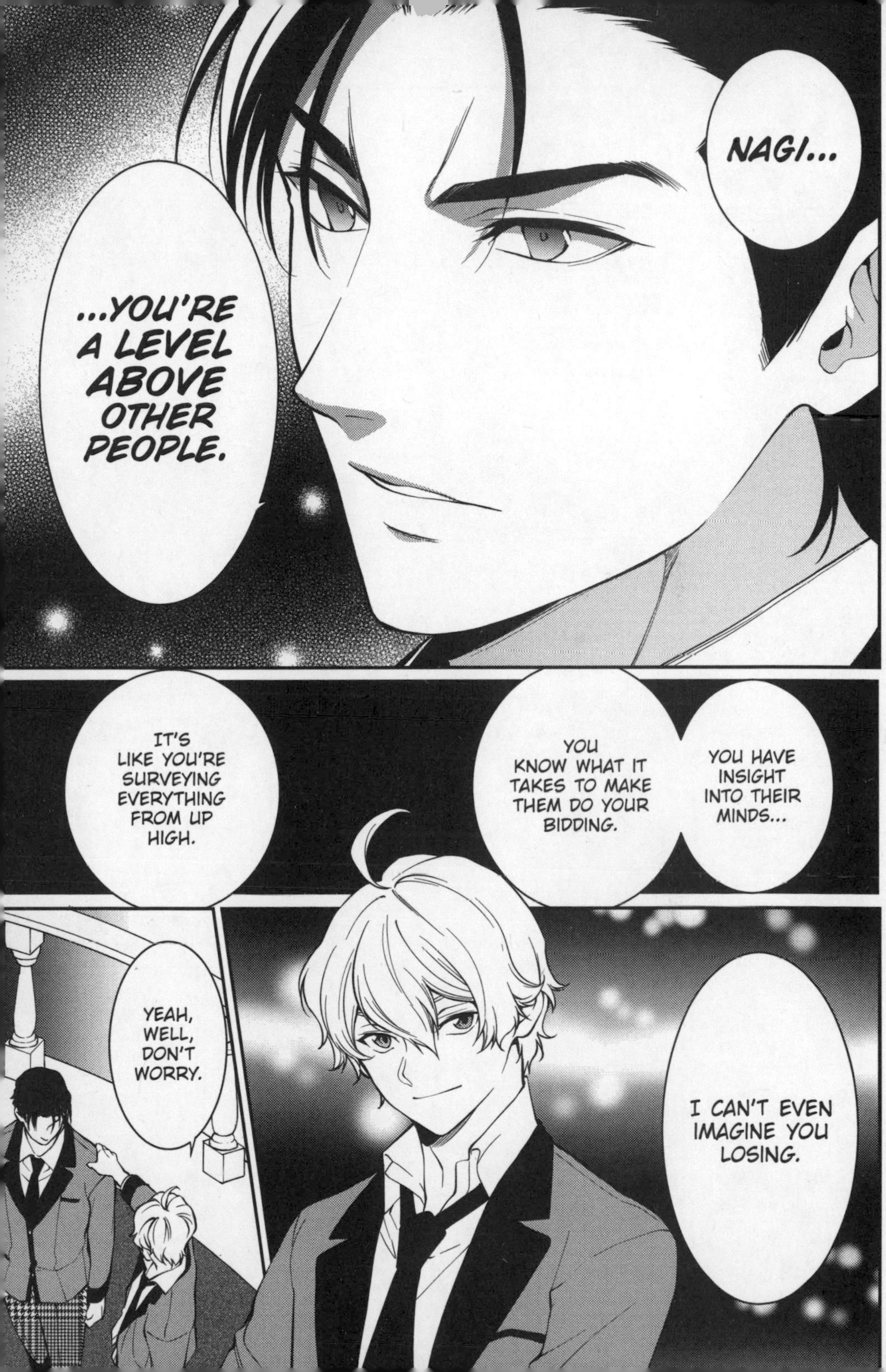
NAGI...
...YOU'RE A LEVEL ABOVE OTHER PEOPLE.
YOU HAVE INSIGHT INTO THEIR MINDS...
YOU KNOW WHAT IT TAKES TO MAKE THEM DO YOUR BIDDING.
IT'S LIKE YOU'RE SURVEYING EVERYTHING FROM UP HIGH.
I CAN'T EVEN IMAGINE YOU LOSING.
YEAH, WELL, DON'T WORRY.

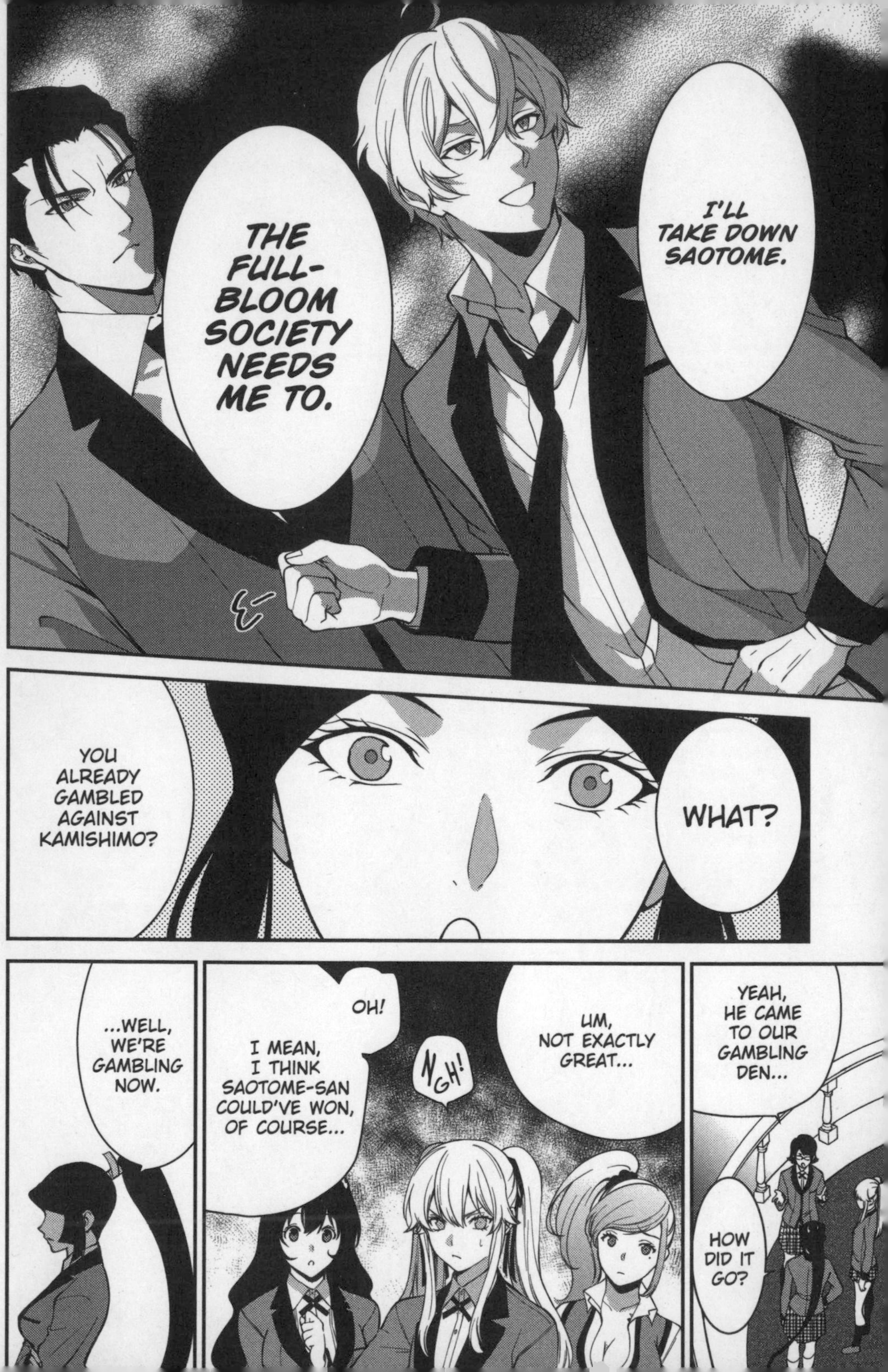

I'LL TAKE DOWN SAOTOME.
THE FULL-BLOOM SOCIETY NEEDS ME TO.
WHAT?
YOU ALREADY GAMBLED AGAINST KAMISHIMO?
YEAH, HE CAME TO OUR GAMBLING DEN...
HOW DID IT GO?
UM, NOT EXACTLY GREAT...
NGH!
OH!
I MEAN, I THINK SAOTOME-SAN COULD'VE WON, OF COURSE...
...WELL, WE'RE GAMBLING NOW.

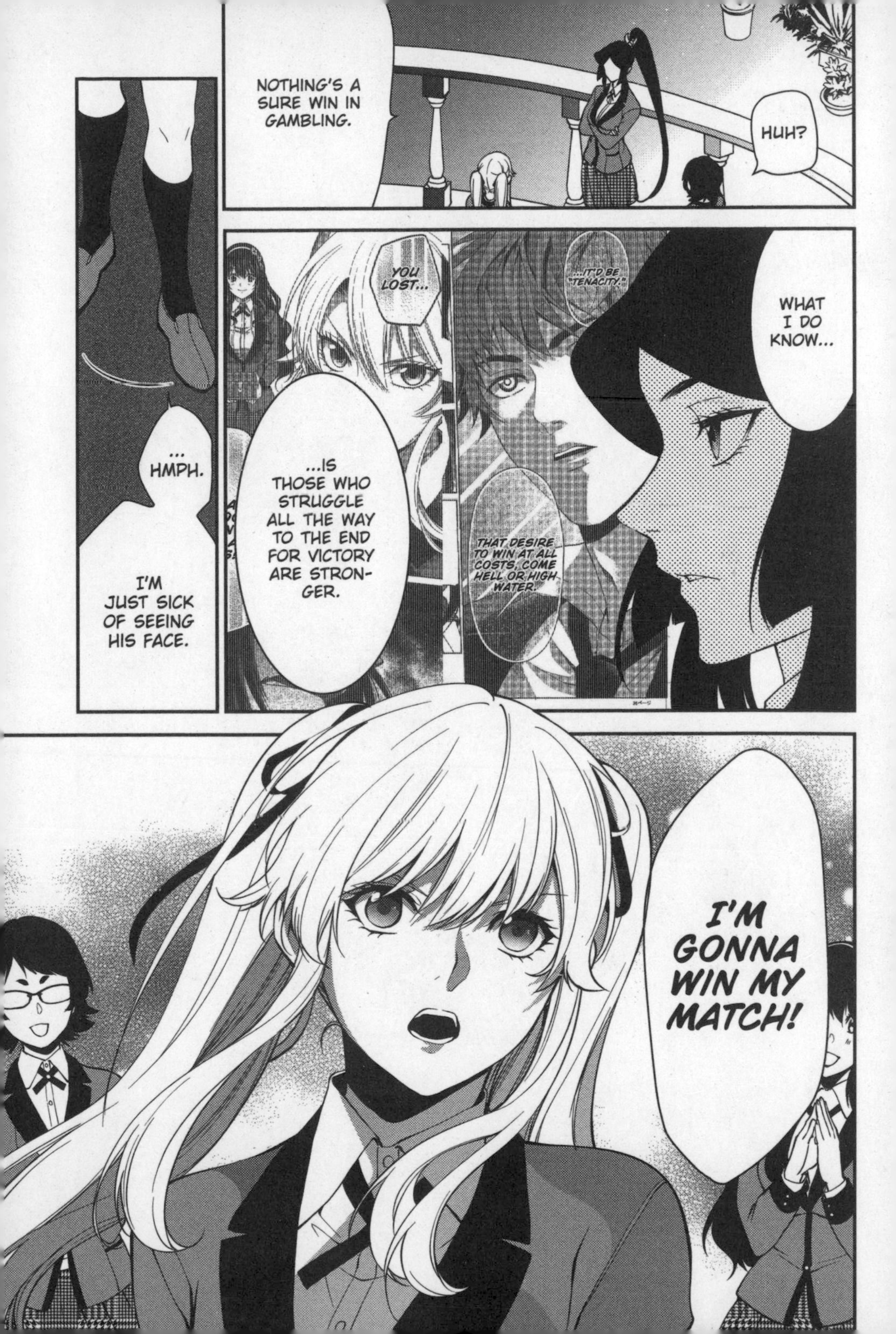
NOTHING'S A SURE WIN IN GAMBLING.
HUH?
WHAT I DO KNOW...
...IT'D BE "TENACITY."
YOU LOST...
THAT DESIRE TO WIN AT ALL COSTS, COME HELL OR HIGH WATER.
...IS THOSE WHO STRUGGLE ALL THE WAY TO THE END FOR VICTORY ARE STRONGER.
...HMPH.
I'M JUST SICK OF SEEING HIS FACE.
I'M GONNA WIN MY MATCH!

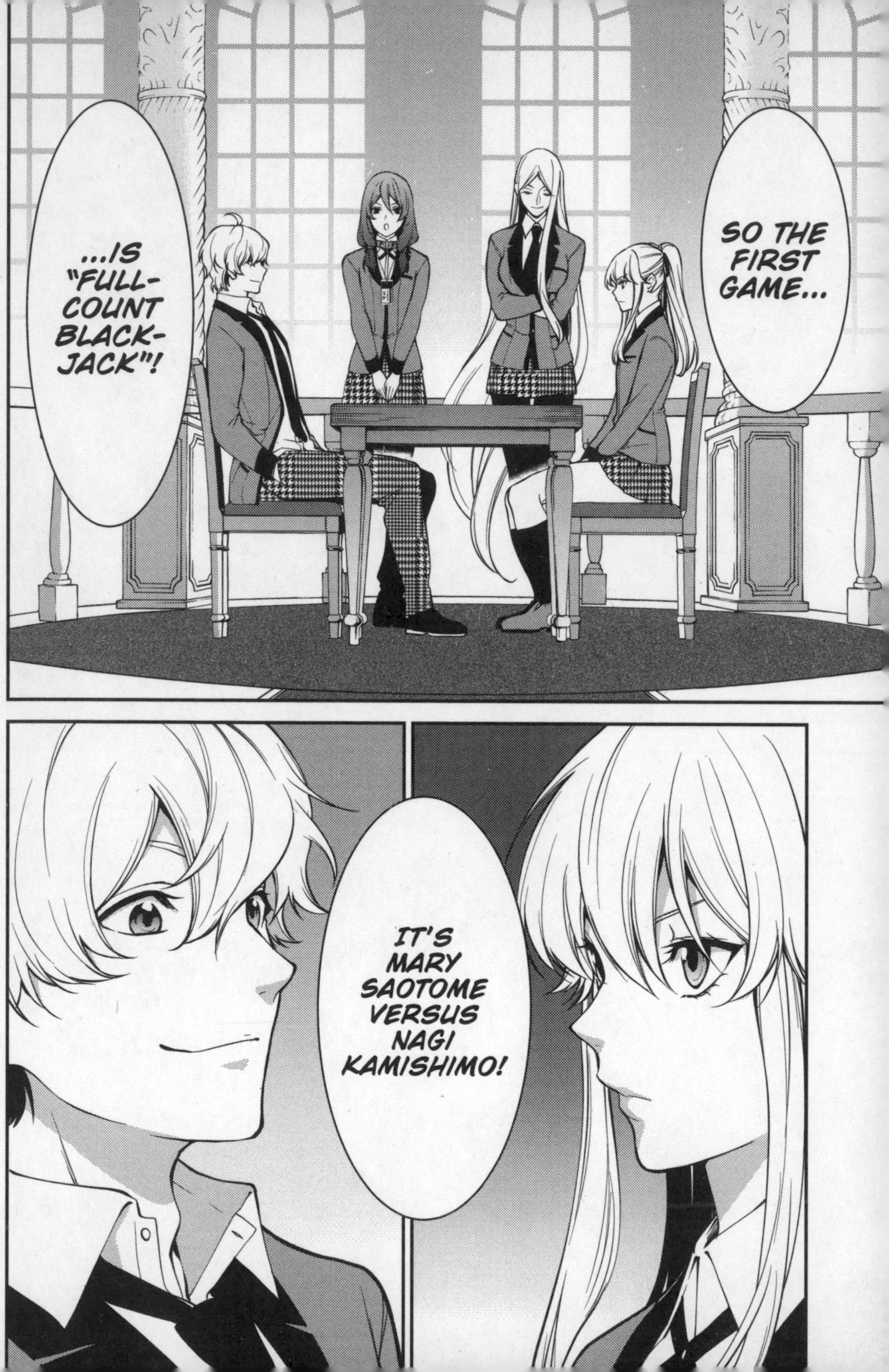
SO THE FIRST GAME...
...IS "FULL-COUNT BLACK-JACK"!
IT'S MARY SAOTOME VERSUS NAGI KAMISHIMO!

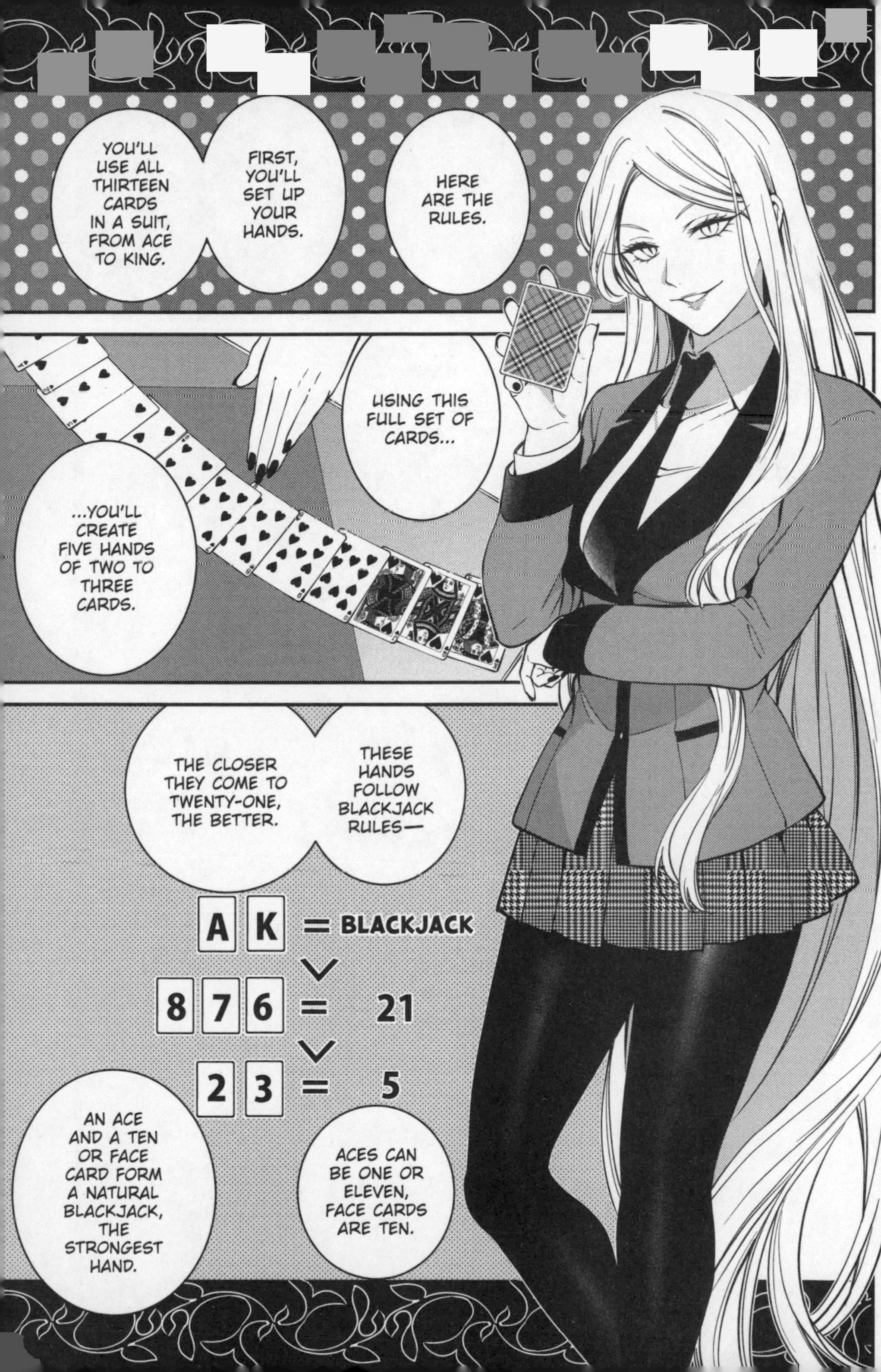
HERE ARE THE RULES.
FIRST, YOU'LL SET UP YOUR HANDS.
YOU'LL USE ALL THIRTEEN CARDS IN A SUIT, FROM ACE TO KING.
USING THIS FULL SET OF CARDS...
...YOU'LL CREATE FIVE HANDS OF TWO TO THREE CARDS.
THESE HANDS FOLLOW BLACKJACK RULES—
THE CLOSER THEY COME TO TWENTY-ONE, THE BETTER.
A K = BLACKJACK
8 7 6 = 21
2 3 = 5
ACES CAN BE ONE OR ELEVEN, FACE CARDS ARE TEN.
AN ACE AND A TEN OR FACE CARD FORM A NATURAL BLACKJACK, THE STRONGEST HAND.

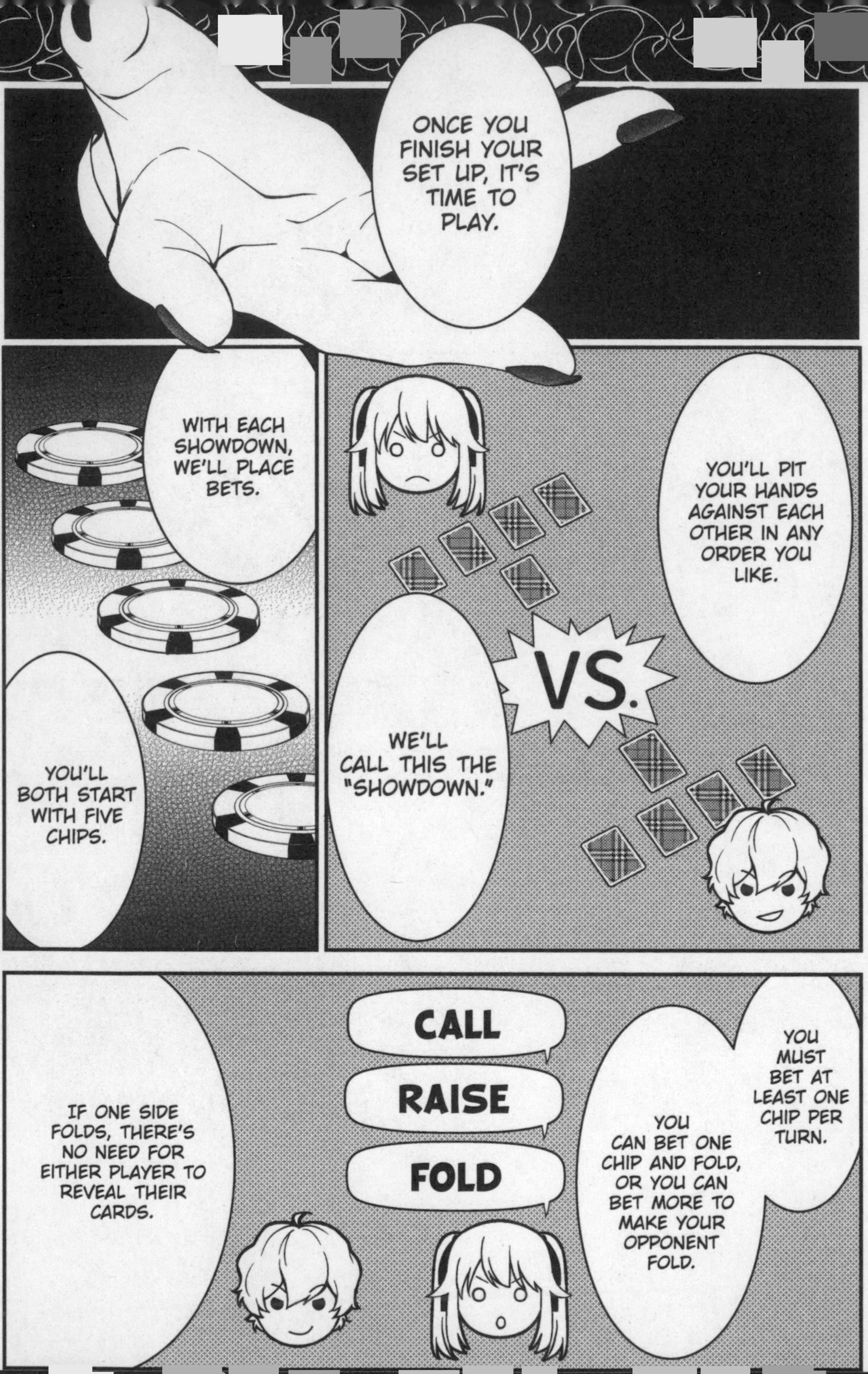
ONCE YOU FINISH YOUR SET UP, IT'S TIME TO PLAY.
YOU'LL PIT YOUR HANDS AGAINST EACH OTHER IN ANY ORDER YOU LIKE.
VS.
WE'LL CALL THIS THE "SHOWDOWN."
WITH EACH SHOWDOWN, WE'LL PLACE BETS.
YOU'LL BOTH START WITH FIVE CHIPS.
YOU MUST BET AT LEAST ONE CHIP PER TURN.
CALL
RAISE
FOLD
YOU CAN BET ONE CHIP AND FOLD, OR YOU CAN BET MORE TO MAKE YOUR OPPONENT FOLD.
IF ONE SIDE FOLDS, THERE'S NO NEED FOR EITHER PLAYER TO REVEAL THEIR CARDS.

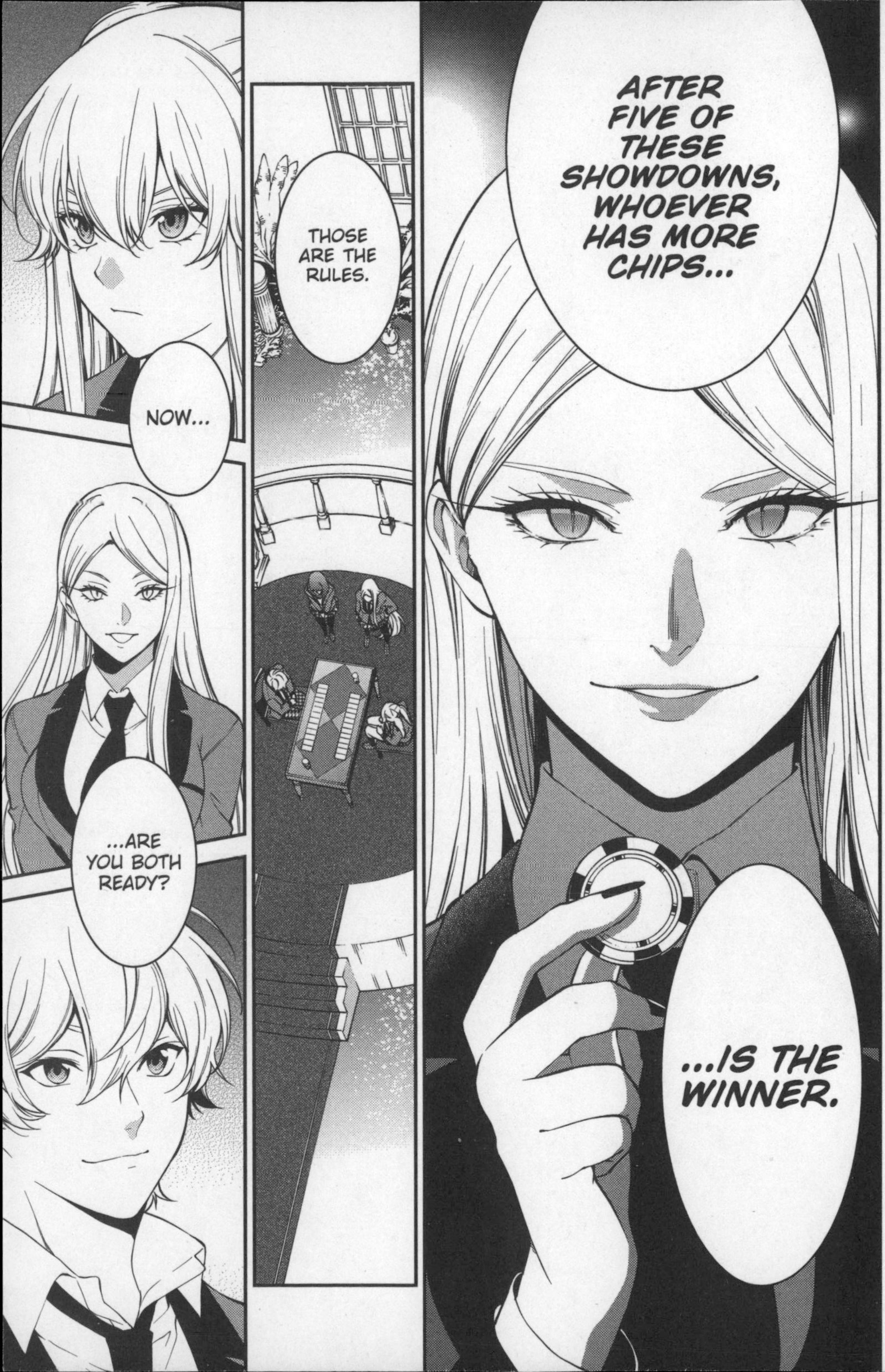
AFTER FIVE OF THESE SHOWDOWNS, WHOEVER HAS MORE CHIPS...
...IS THE WINNER.
THOSE ARE THE RULES.
NOW...
...ARE YOU BOTH READY?

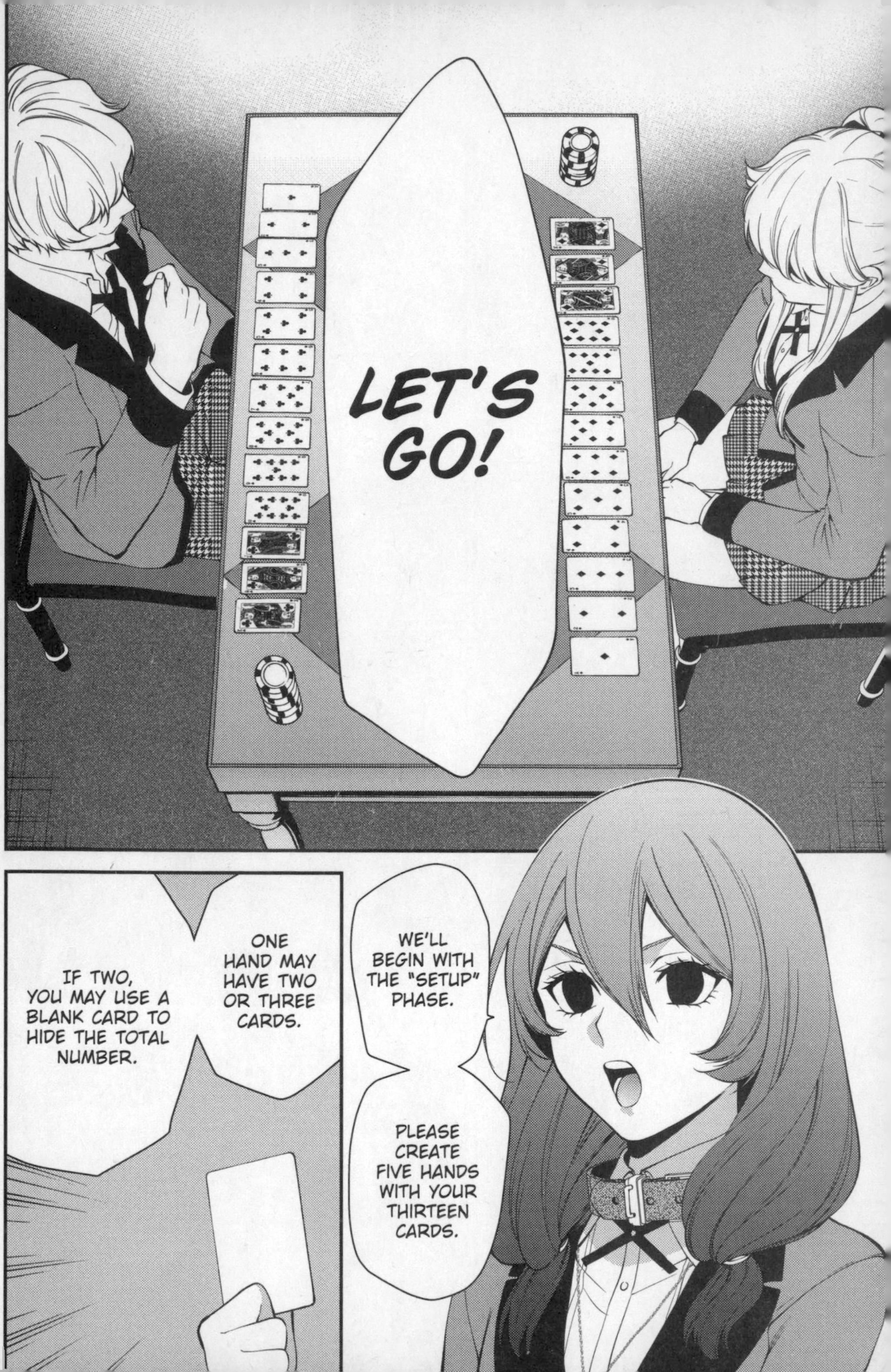
LET'S GO!
WE'LL BEGIN WITH THE "SETUP" PHASE.
PLEASE CREATE FIVE HANDS WITH YOUR THIRTEEN CARDS.
ONE HAND MAY HAVE TWO OR THREE CARDS.
IF TWO, YOU MAY USE A BLANK CARD TO HIDE THE TOTAL NUMBER.

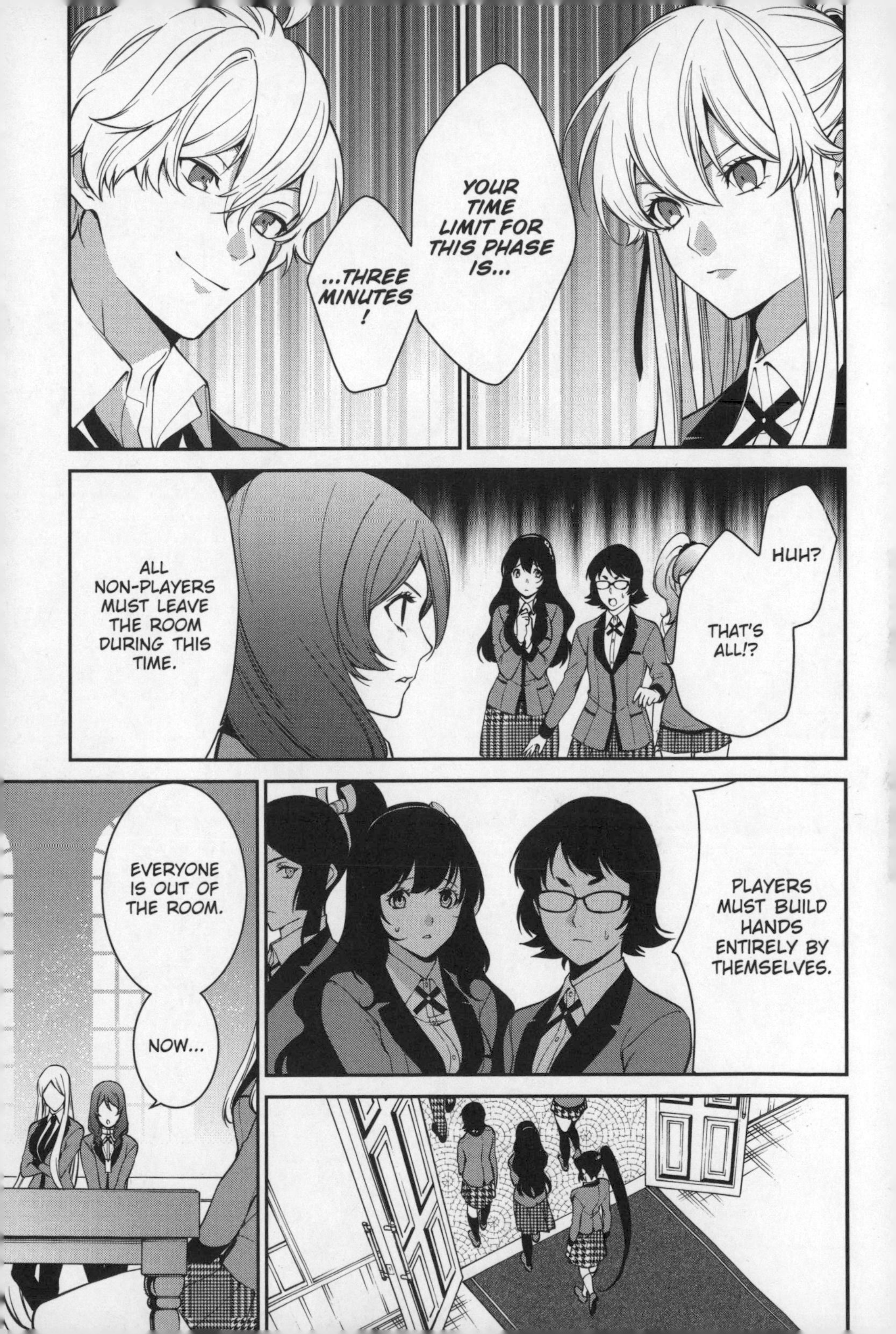
YOUR TIME LIMIT FOR THIS PHASE IS...
...THREE MINUTES!
HUH?
THAT'S ALL!?
ALL NON-PLAYERS MUST LEAVE THE ROOM DURING THIS TIME.
PLAYERS MUST BUILD HANDS ENTIRELY BY THEMSELVES.
EVERYONE IS OUT OF THE ROOM.
NOW...

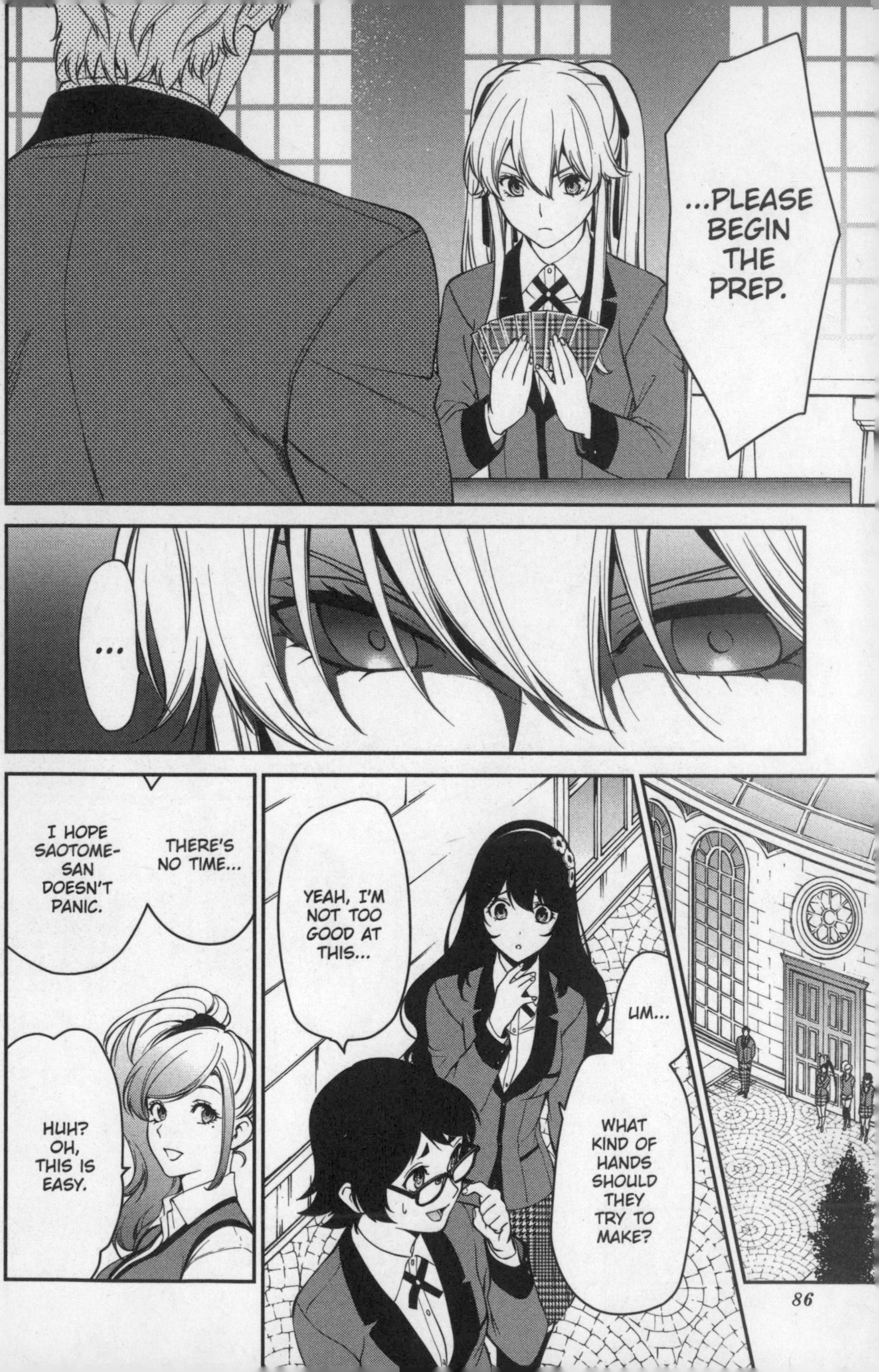
...PLEASE BEGIN THE PREP.
...
UM...
WHAT KIND OF HANDS SHOULD THEY TRY TO MAKE?
YEAH, I'M NOT TOO GOOD AT THIS...
THERE'S NO TIME...
I HOPE SAOTOME-SAN DOESN'T PANIC.
HUH? OH, THIS IS EASY.

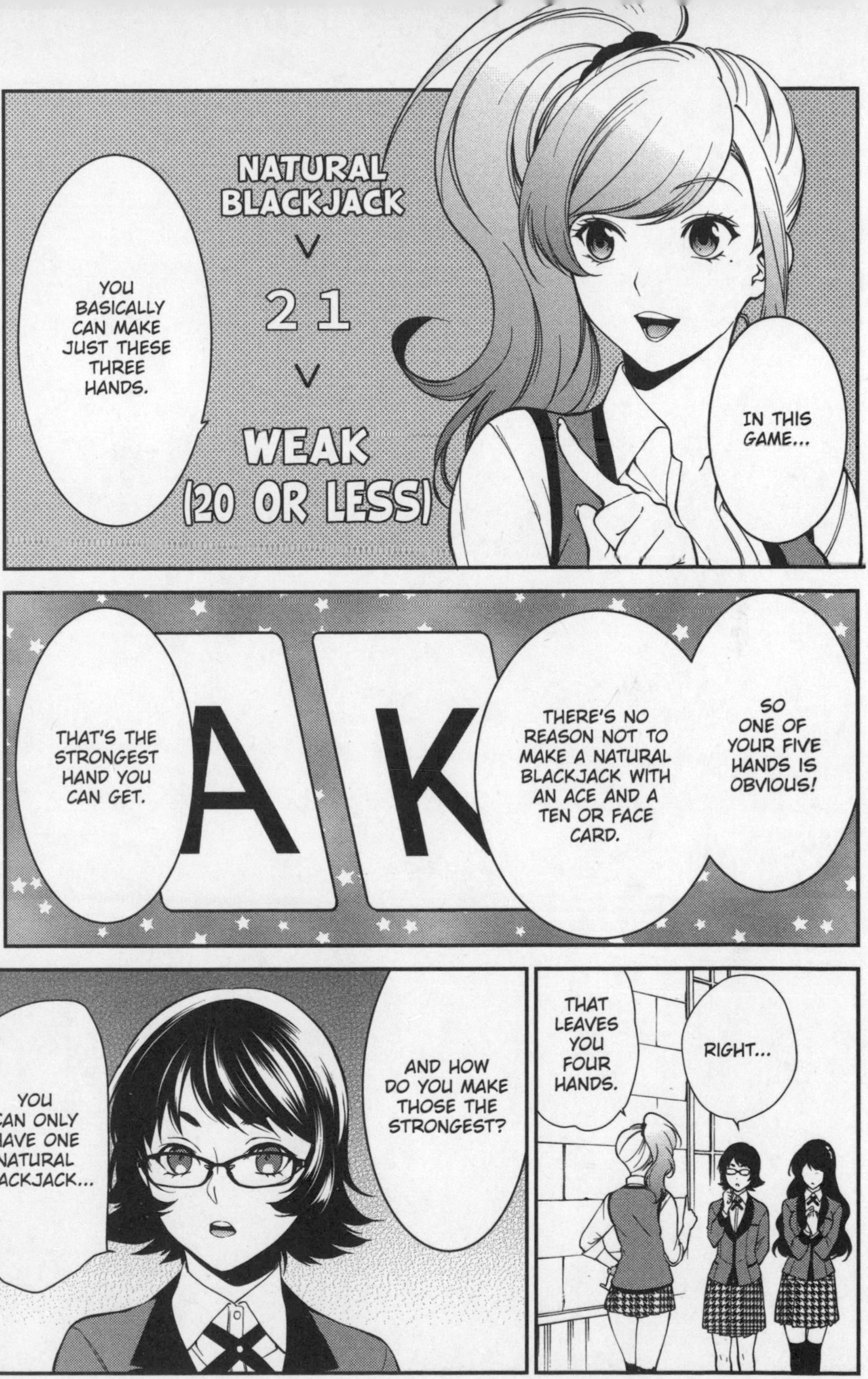
IN THIS GAME...
NATURAL BLACKJACK
>
21
>
WEAK (20 OR LESS)
YOU BASICALLY CAN MAKE JUST THESE THREE HANDS.
SO ONE OF YOUR FIVE HANDS IS OBVIOUS!
THERE'S NO REASON NOT TO MAKE A NATURAL BLACKJACK WITH AN ACE AND A TEN OR FACE CARD.
K
A
THAT'S THE STRONGEST HAND YOU CAN GET.
RIGHT...
THAT LEAVES YOU FOUR HANDS.
AND HOW DO YOU MAKE THOSE THE STRONGEST?
YOU CAN ONLY HAVE ONE NATURAL BLACKJACK...

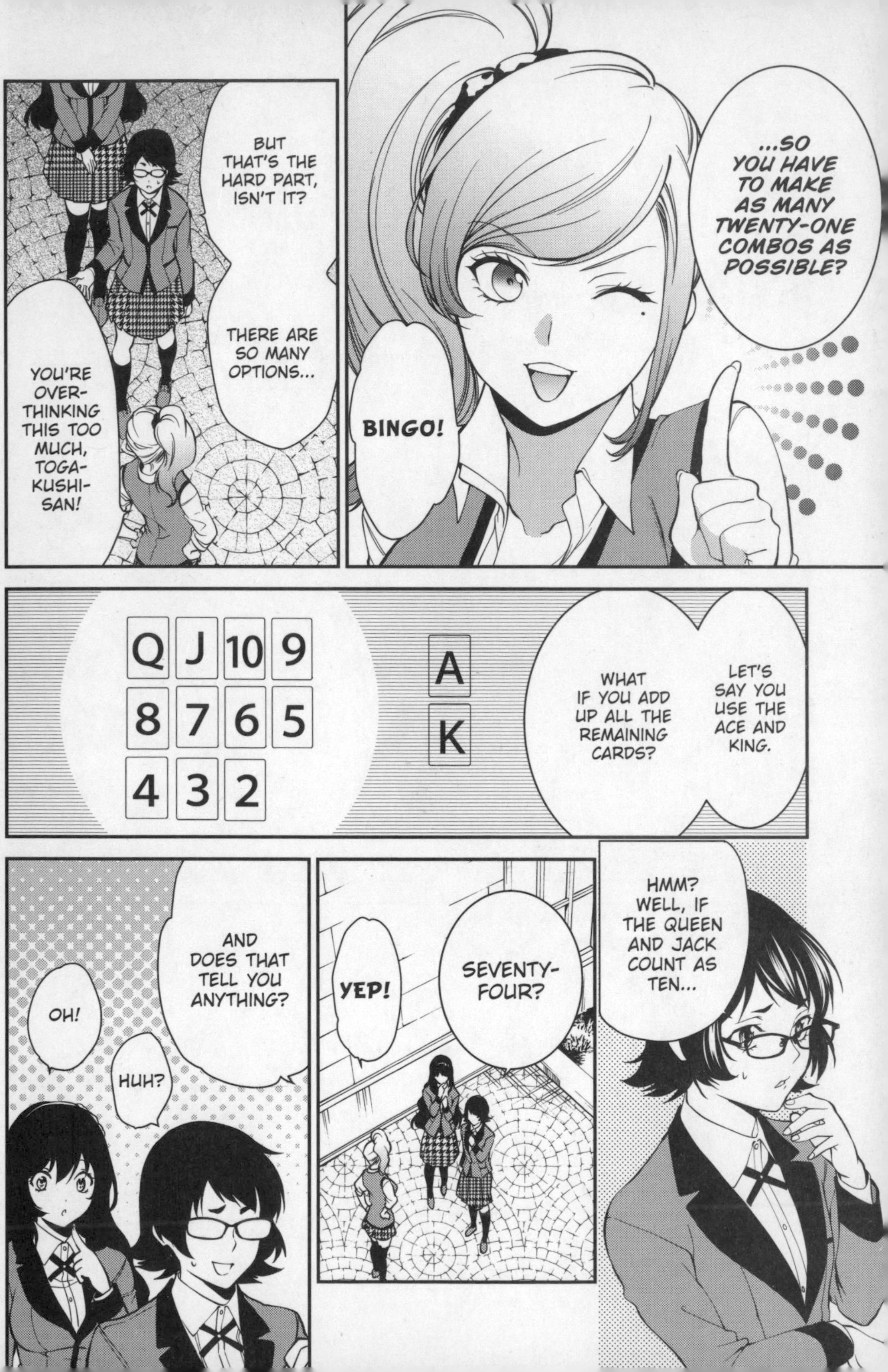
...SO YOU HAVE TO MAKE AS MANY TWENTY-ONE COMBOS AS POSSIBLE?
BINGO!
BUT THAT'S THE HARD PART, ISN'T IT?
THERE ARE SO MANY OPTIONS...
YOU'RE OVER-THINKING THIS TOO MUCH, TOGA-KUSHI-SAN!
LET'S SAY YOU USE THE ACE AND KING.
WHAT IF YOU ADD UP ALL THE REMAINING CARDS?
A K
Q J 10 9
8 7 6 5
4 3 2
HMM? WELL, IF THE QUEEN AND JACK COUNT AS TEN...
SEVENTY-FOUR?
YEP!
AND DOES THAT TELL YOU ANYTHING?
HUH?
OH!

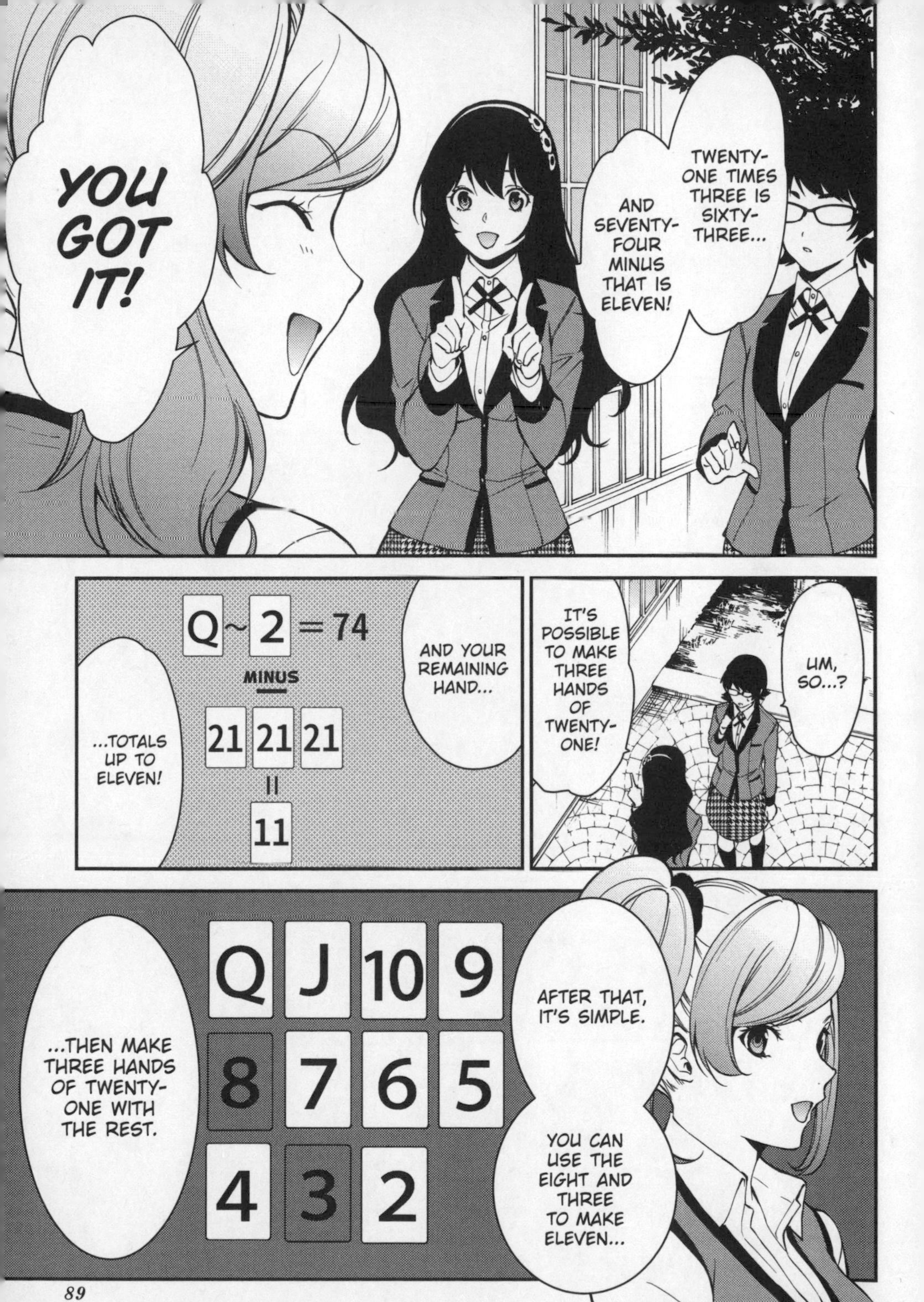
TWENTY-ONE TIMES THREE IS SIXTY-THREE...
AND SEVENTY-FOUR MINUS THAT IS ELEVEN!
YOU GOT IT!
UM, SO...?
IT'S POSSIBLE TO MAKE THREE HANDS OF TWENTY-ONE!
AND YOUR REMAINING HAND...
Q ~ 2 = 74
MINUS
21 21 21
=
11
...TOTALS UP TO ELEVEN!
AFTER THAT, IT'S SIMPLE.
YOU CAN USE THE EIGHT AND THREE TO MAKE ELEVEN...
Q J 10 9
8 7 6 5
4 3 2
...THEN MAKE THREE HANDS OF TWENTY-ONE WITH THE REST.

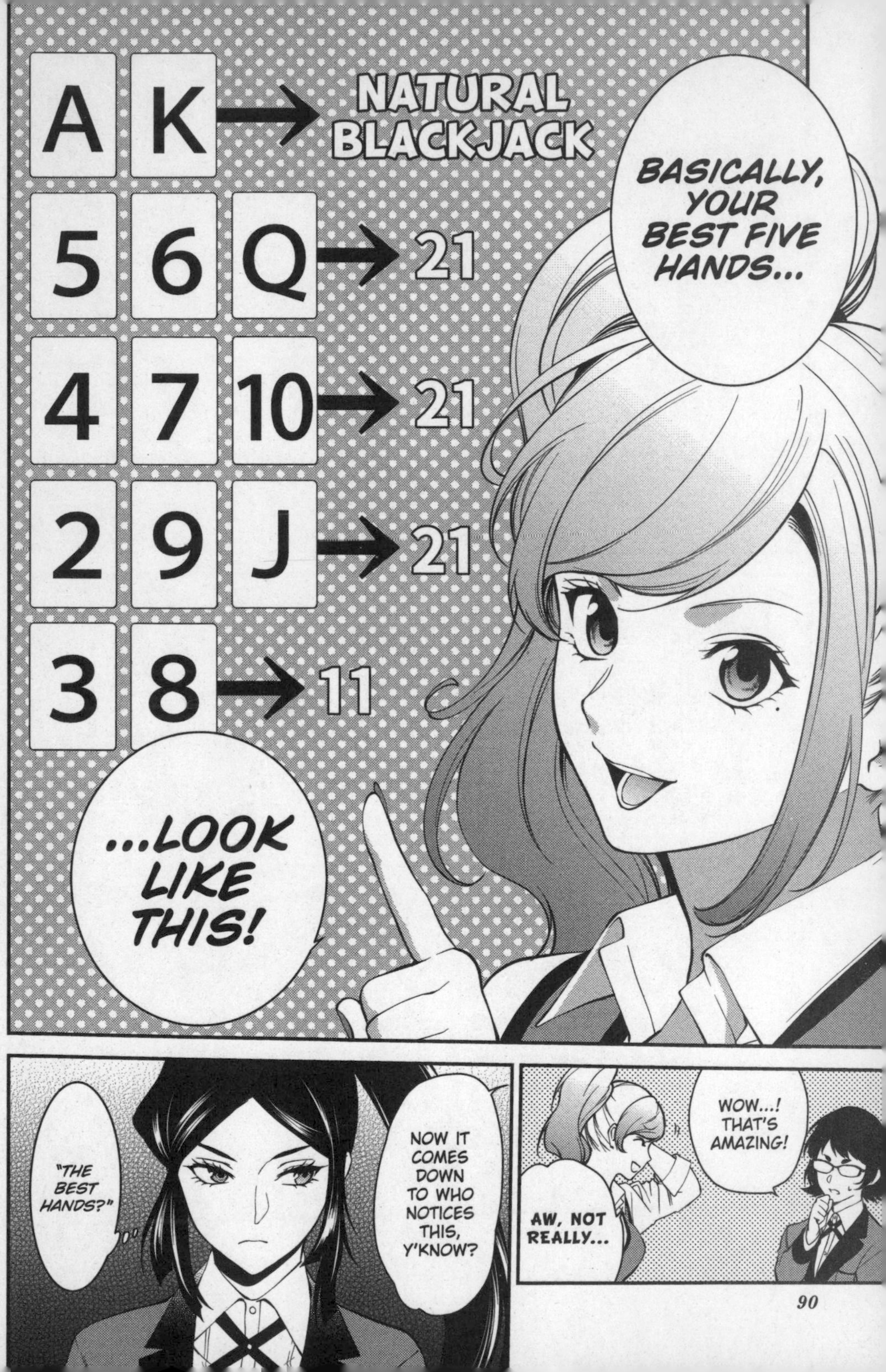
A K → NATURAL BLACKJACK
5 6 Q → 21
4 7 10 → 21
2 9 J → 21
3 8 → 11
BASICALLY, YOUR BEST FIVE HANDS...
...LOOK LIKE THIS!
WOW...! THAT'S AMAZING!
AW, NOT REALLY...
NOW IT COMES DOWN TO WHO NOTICES THIS, Y'KNOW?
"THE BEST HANDS?"

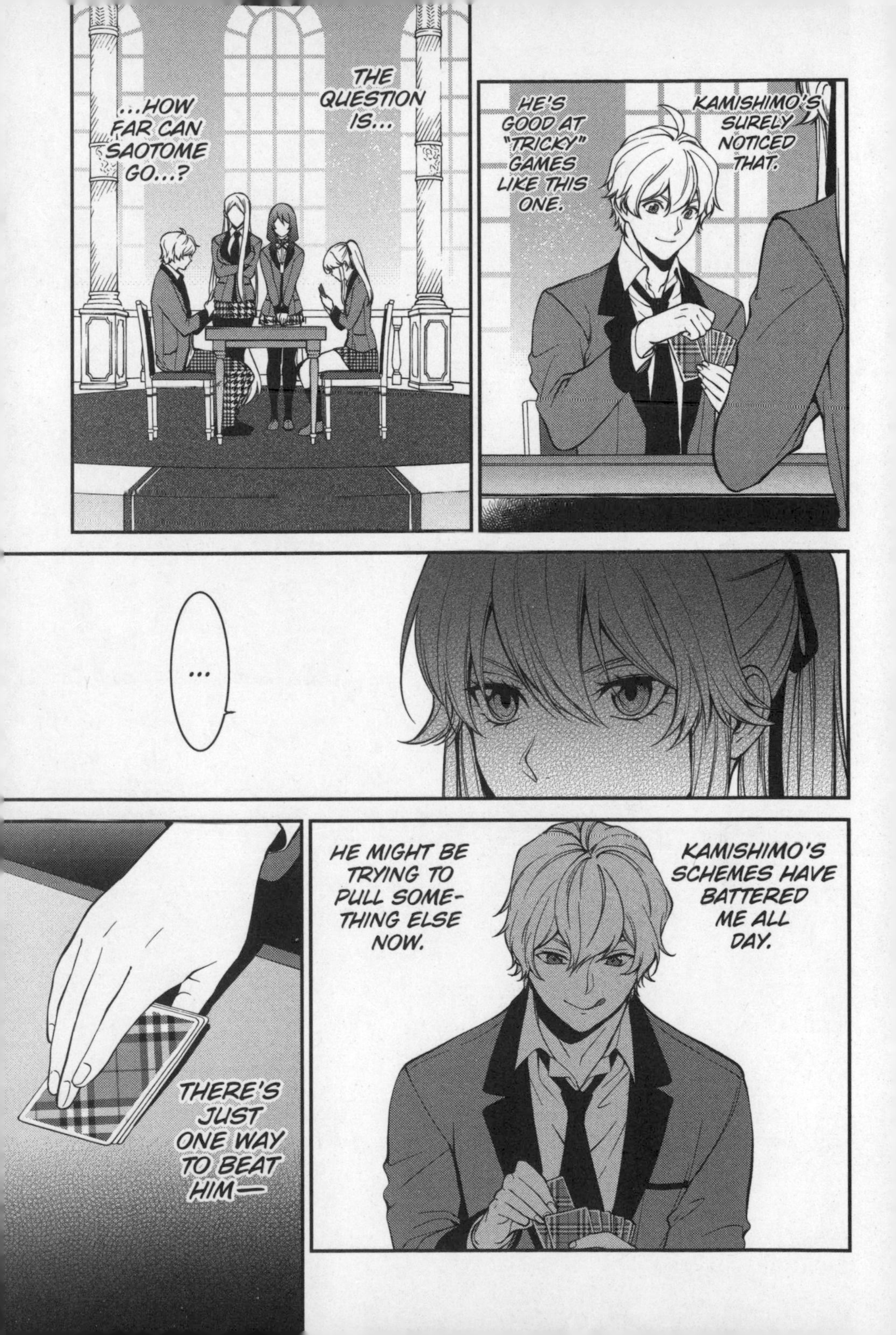
KAMISHIMO'S SURELY NOTICED THAT.
HE'S GOOD AT "TRICKY" GAMES LIKE THIS ONE.
THE QUESTION IS...
...HOW FAR CAN SAOTOME GO...?
...
KAMISHIMO'S SCHEMES HAVE BATTERED ME ALL DAY.
HE MIGHT BE TRYING TO PULL SOME-THING ELSE NOW.
THERE'S JUST ONE WAY TO BEAT HIM—

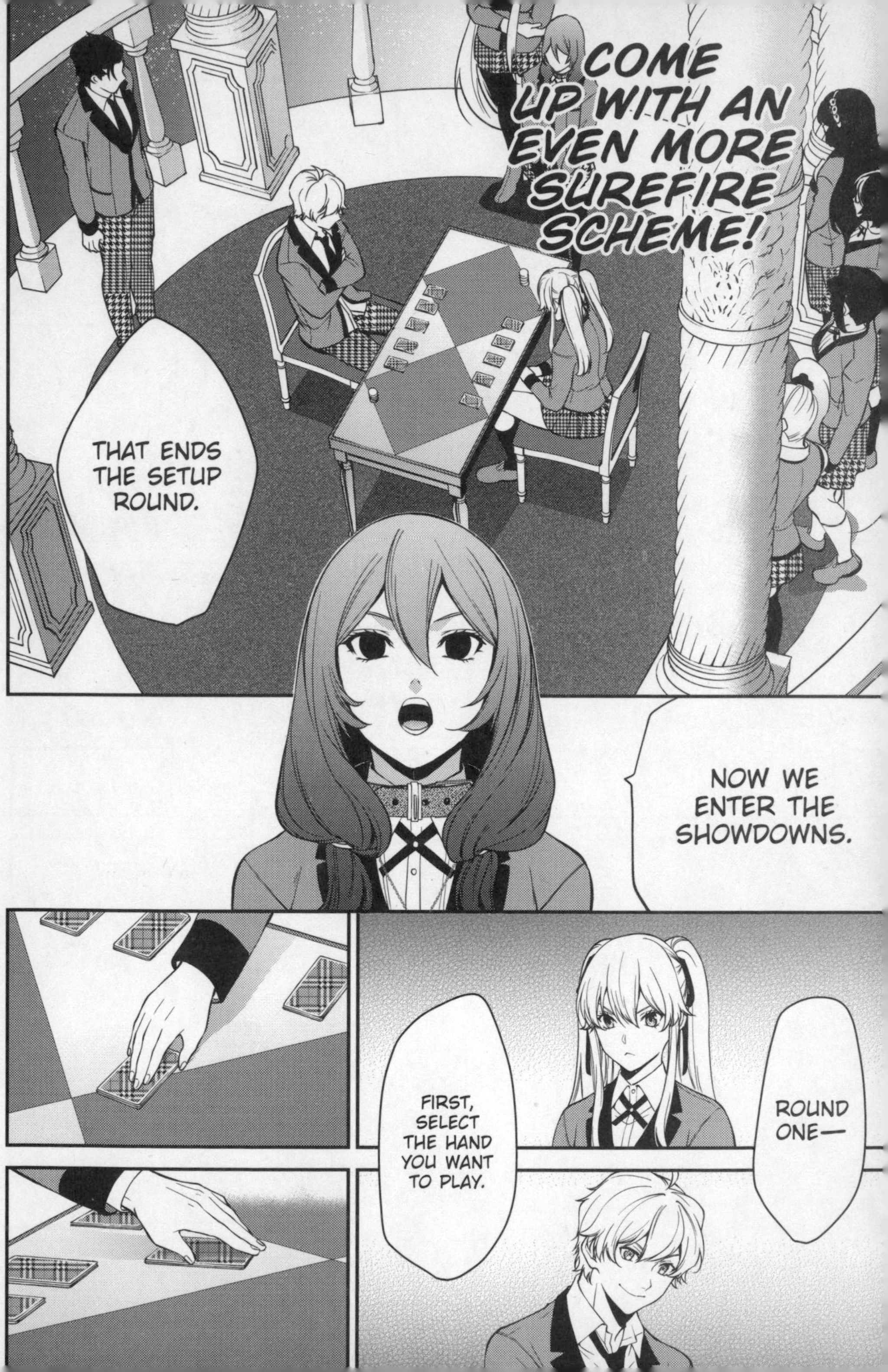
COME UP WITH AN EVEN MORE SUREFIRE SCHEME!
THAT ENDS THE SETUP ROUND.
NOW WE ENTER THE SHOWDOWNS.
ROUND ONE—
FIRST, SELECT THE HAND YOU WANT TO PLAY.

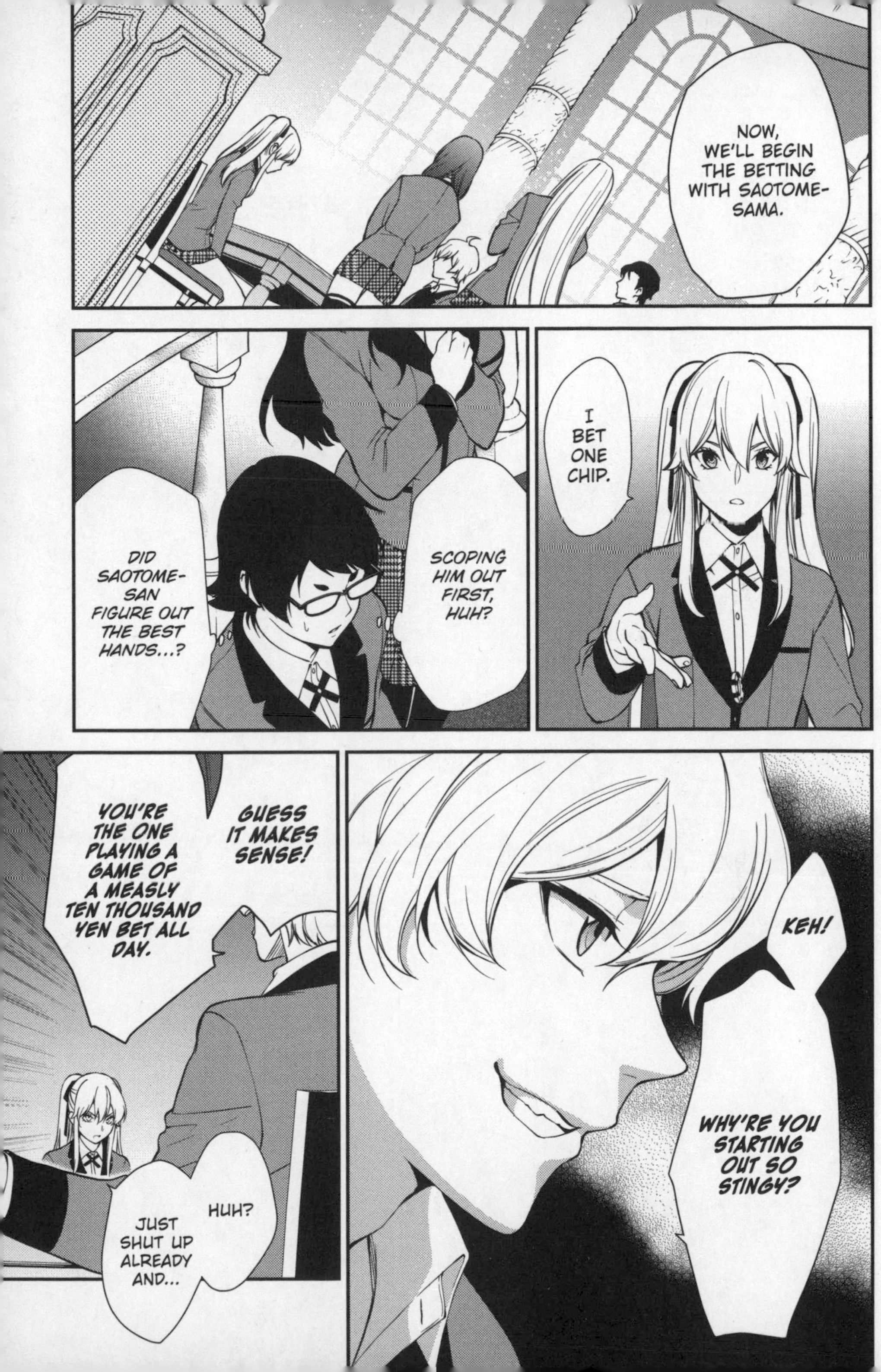
NOW, WE'LL BEGIN THE BETTING WITH SAOTOME-SAMA.
I BET ONE CHIP.
SCOPING HIM OUT FIRST, HUH?
DID SAOTOME-SAN FIGURE OUT THE BEST HANDS...?
KEH!
WHY'RE YOU STARTING OUT SO STINGY?
GUESS IT MAKES SENSE!
YOU'RE THE ONE PLAYING A GAME OF A MEASLY TEN THOUSAND YEN BET ALL DAY.
HUH?
JUST SHUT UP ALREADY AND...

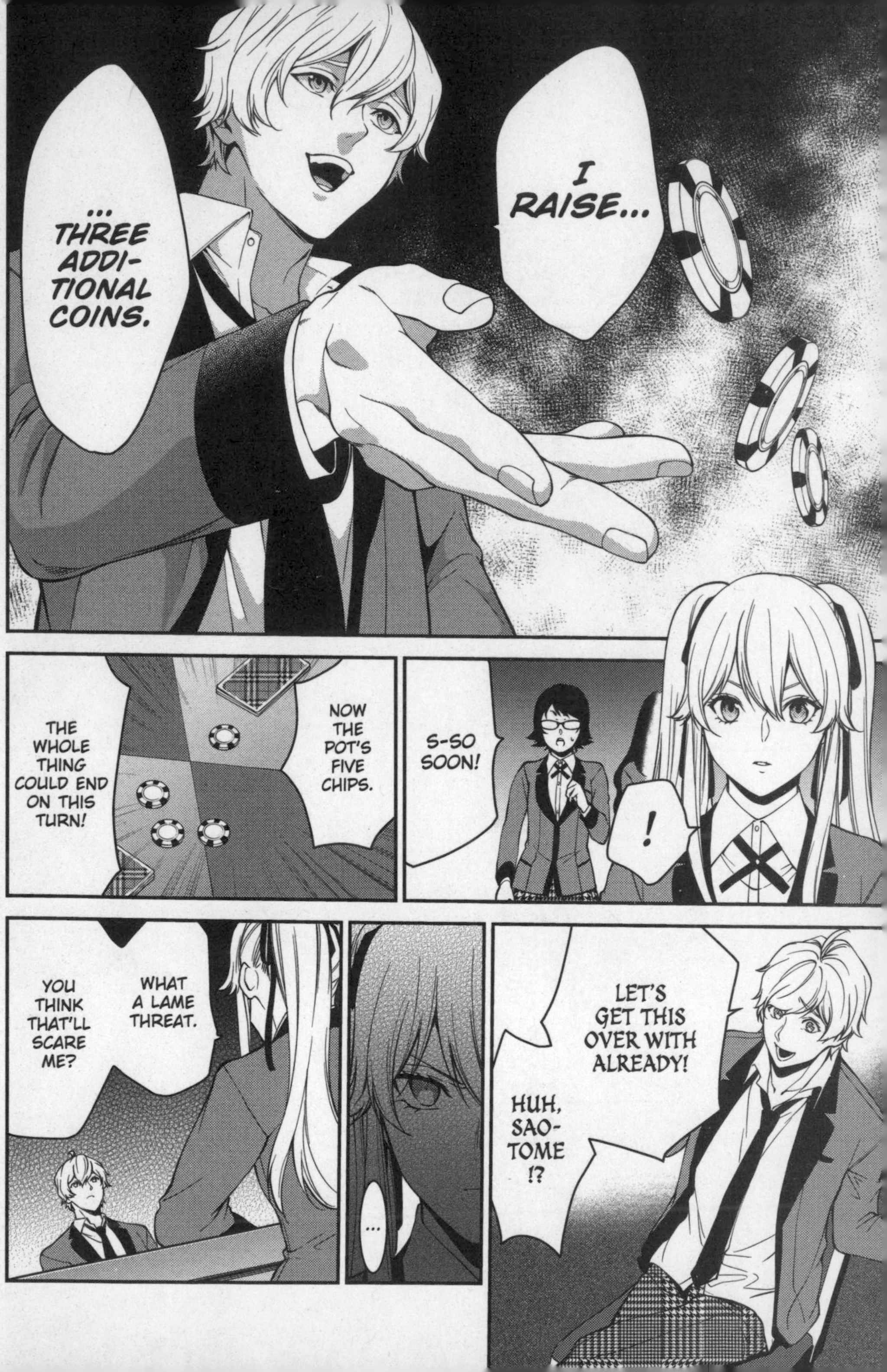
I RAISE...
...THREE ADDITIONAL COINS.
!
S-SO SOON!
NOW THE POT'S FIVE CHIPS.
THE WHOLE THING COULD END ON THIS TURN!
LET'S GET THIS OVER WITH ALREADY!
HUH, SAOTOME!?
...
WHAT A LAME THREAT.
YOU THINK THAT'LL SCARE ME?

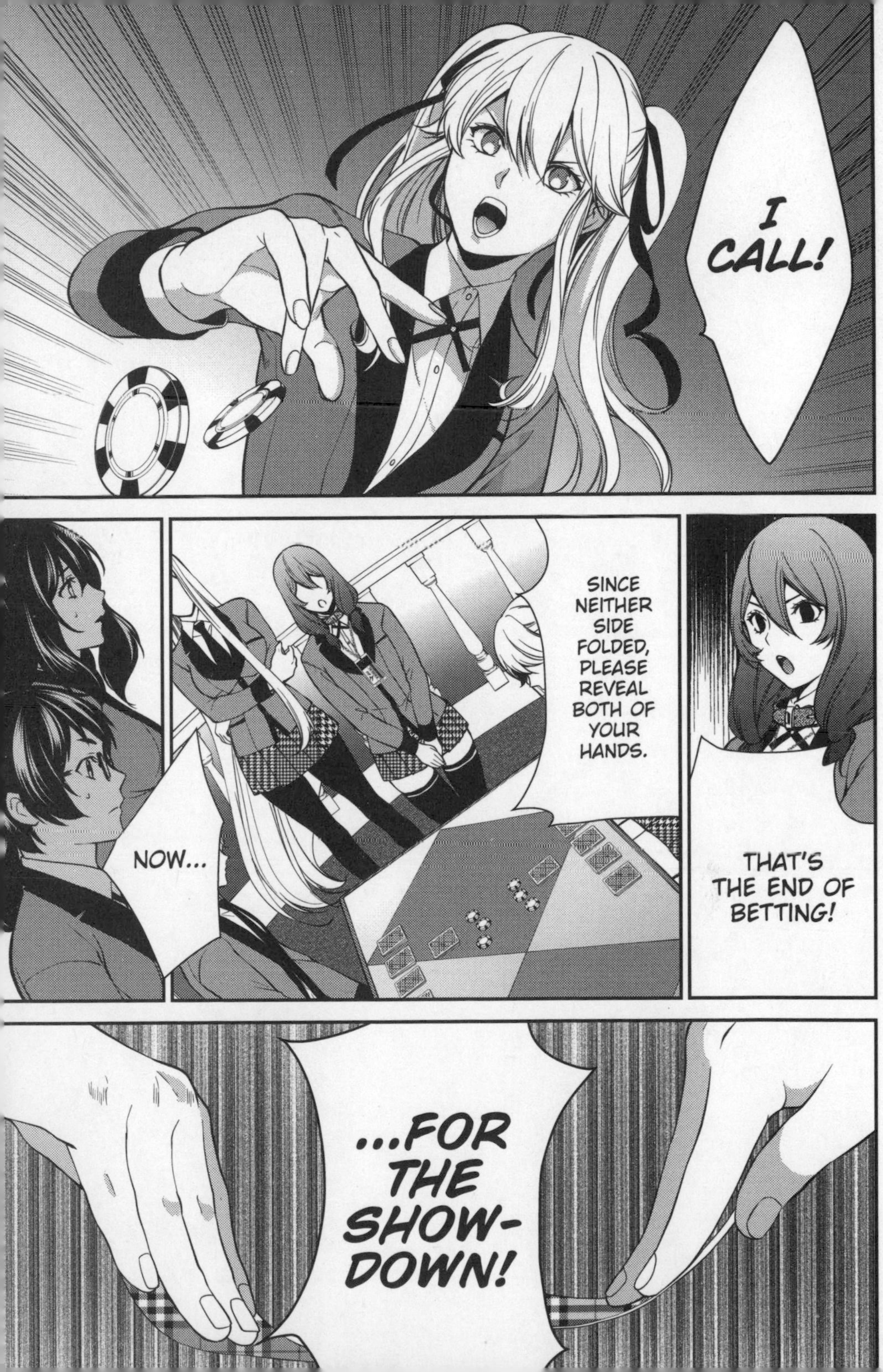
I CALL!
THAT'S THE END OF BETTING!
SINCE NEITHER SIDE FOLDED, PLEASE REVEAL BOTH OF YOUR HANDS.
NOW...
...FOR THE SHOW-DOWN!

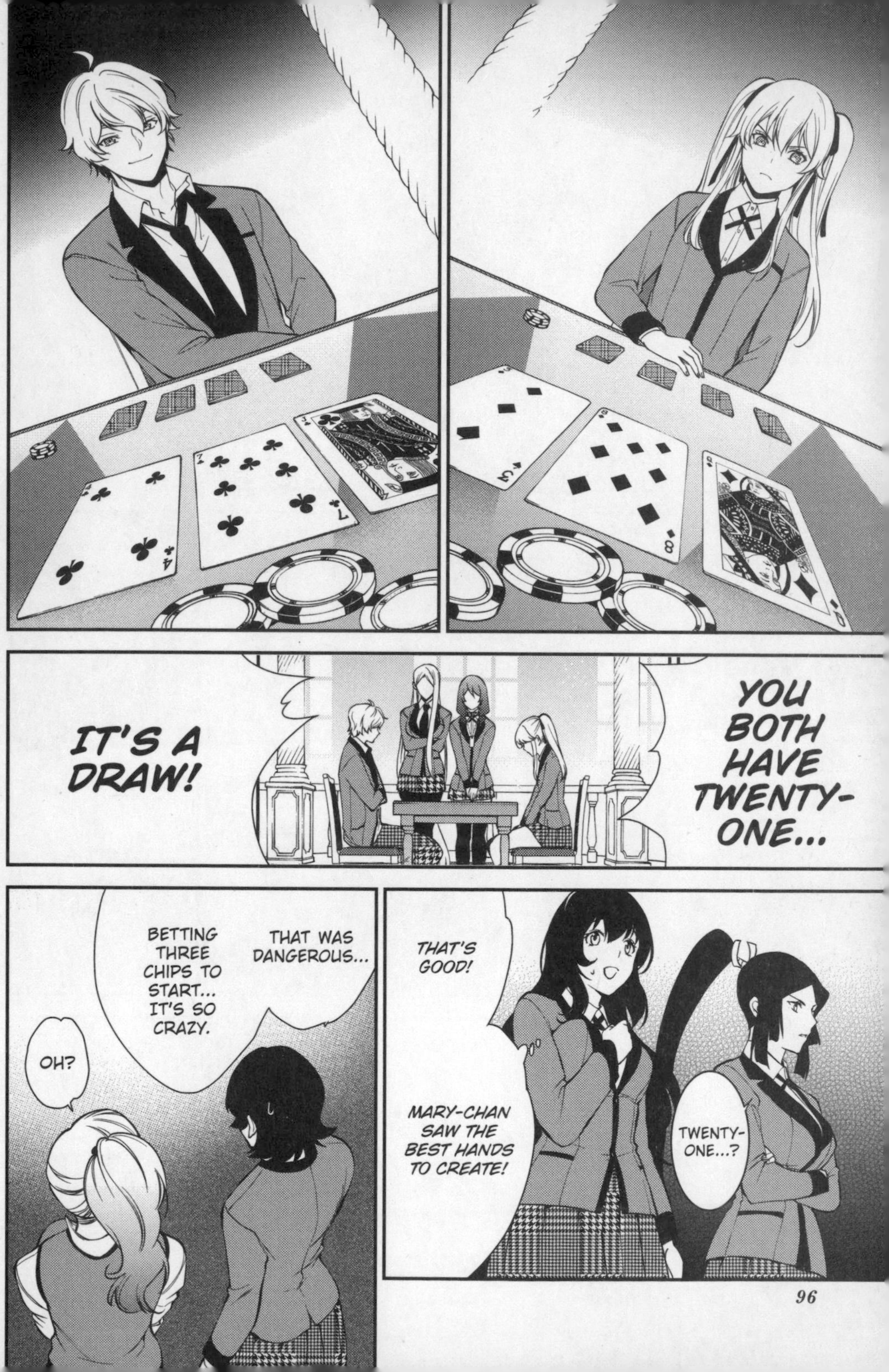
YOU BOTH HAVE TWENTY-ONE...
IT'S A DRAW!
THAT'S GOOD!
MARY-CHAN SAW THE BEST HANDS TO CREATE!
TWENTY-ONE...?
THAT WAS DANGEROUS...
BETTING THREE CHIPS TO START... IT'S SO CRAZY.
OH?

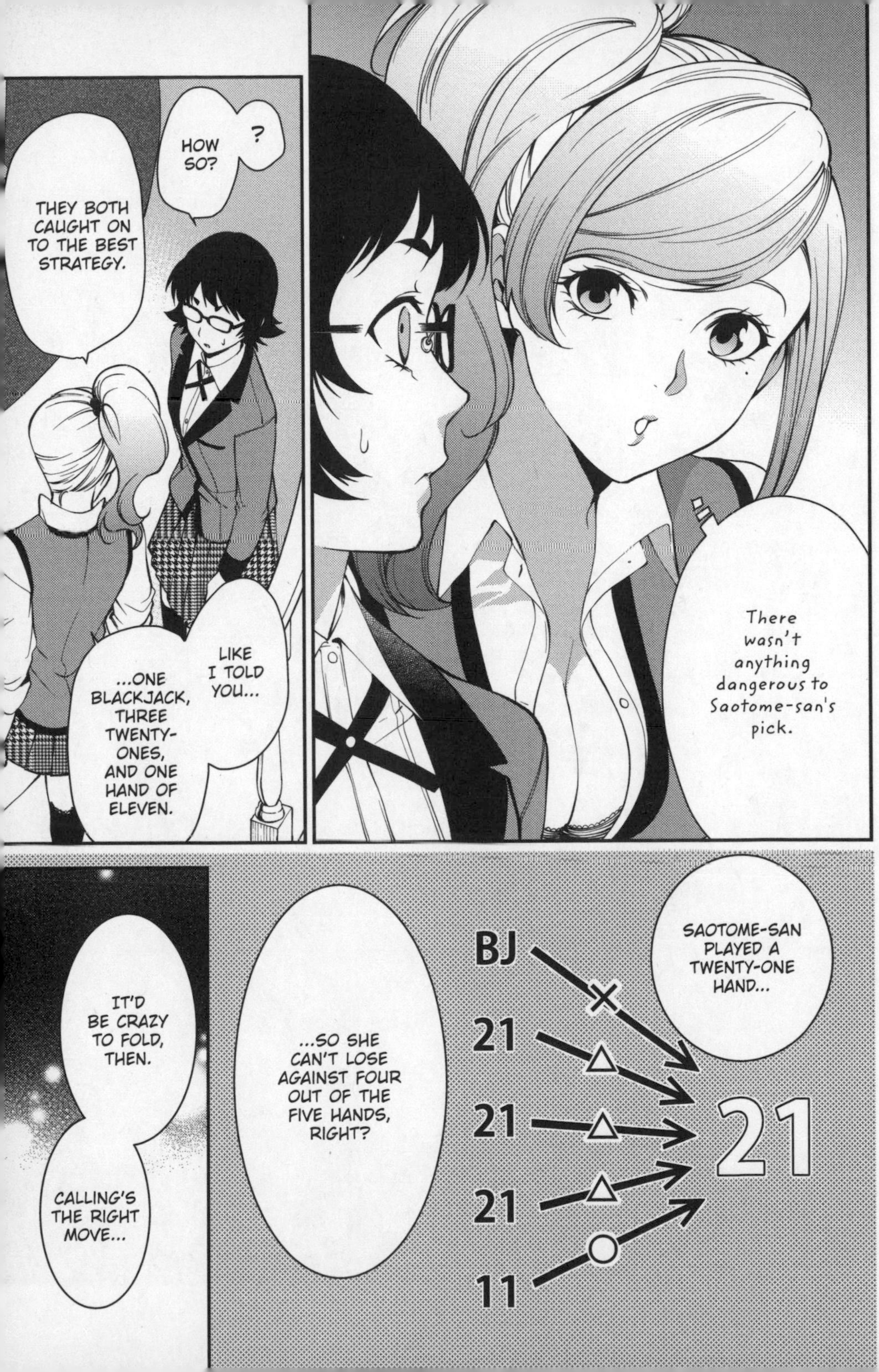
There wasn't anything dangerous to Saotome-san's pick.
?
HOW SO?
THEY BOTH CAUGHT ON TO THE BEST STRATEGY.
LIKE I TOLD YOU...
...ONE BLACKJACK, THREE TWENTY-ONES, AND ONE HAND OF ELEVEN.
SAOTOME-SAN PLAYED A TWENTY-ONE HAND...
BJ
21
21
21
11
21
...SO SHE CAN'T LOSE AGAINST FOUR OUT OF THE FIVE HANDS, RIGHT?
IT'D BE CRAZY TO FOLD, THEN.
CALLING'S THE RIGHT MOVE...

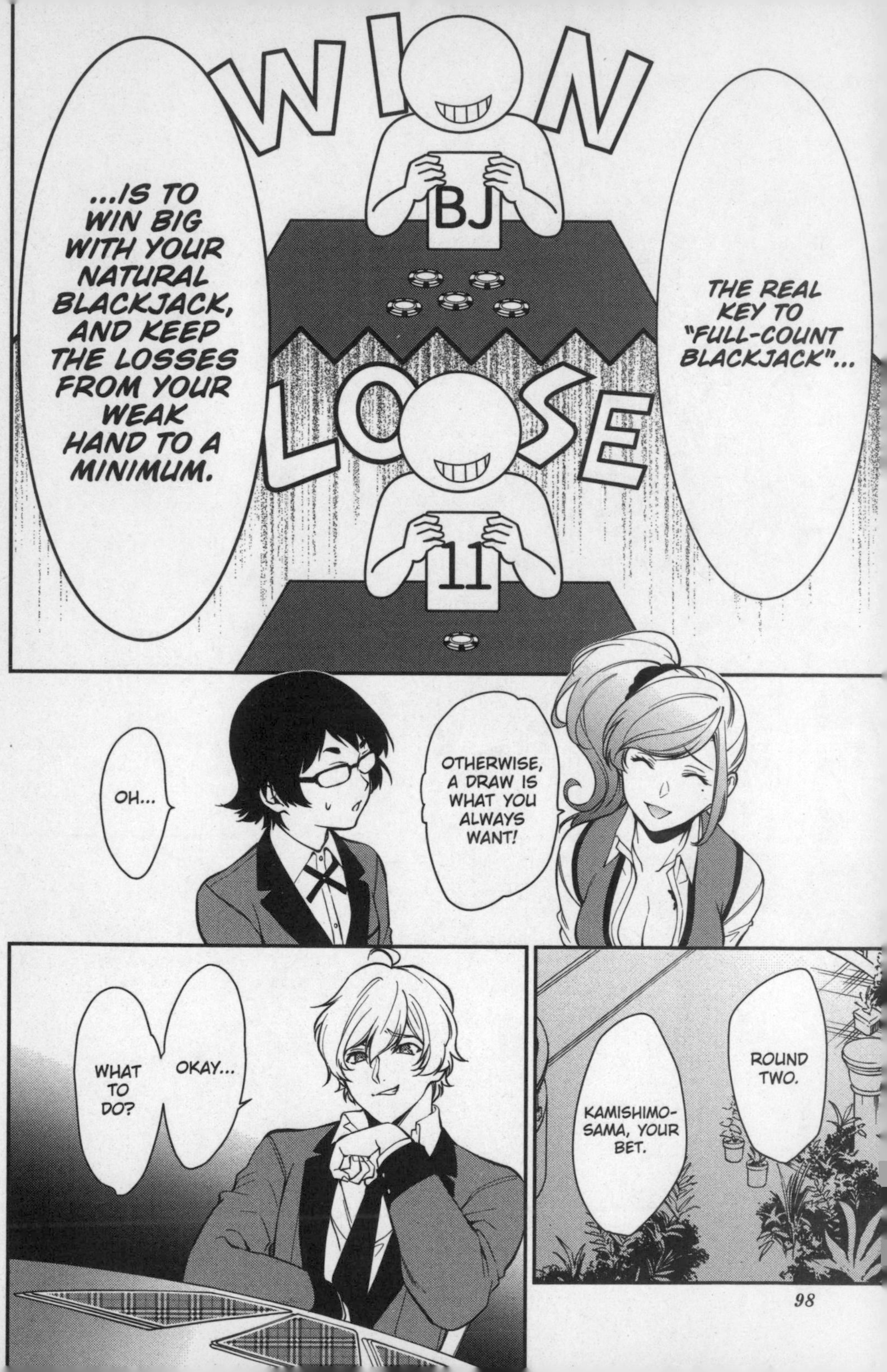
THE REAL KEY TO "FULL-COUNT BLACKJACK"...
WIN
BJ
LOOSE
11
...IS TO WIN BIG WITH YOUR NATURAL BLACKJACK, AND KEEP THE LOSSES FROM YOUR WEAK HAND TO A MINIMUM.
OTHERWISE, A DRAW IS WHAT YOU ALWAYS WANT!
OH...
ROUND TWO.
KAMISHIMO-SAMA, YOUR BET.
OKAY...
WHAT TO DO?

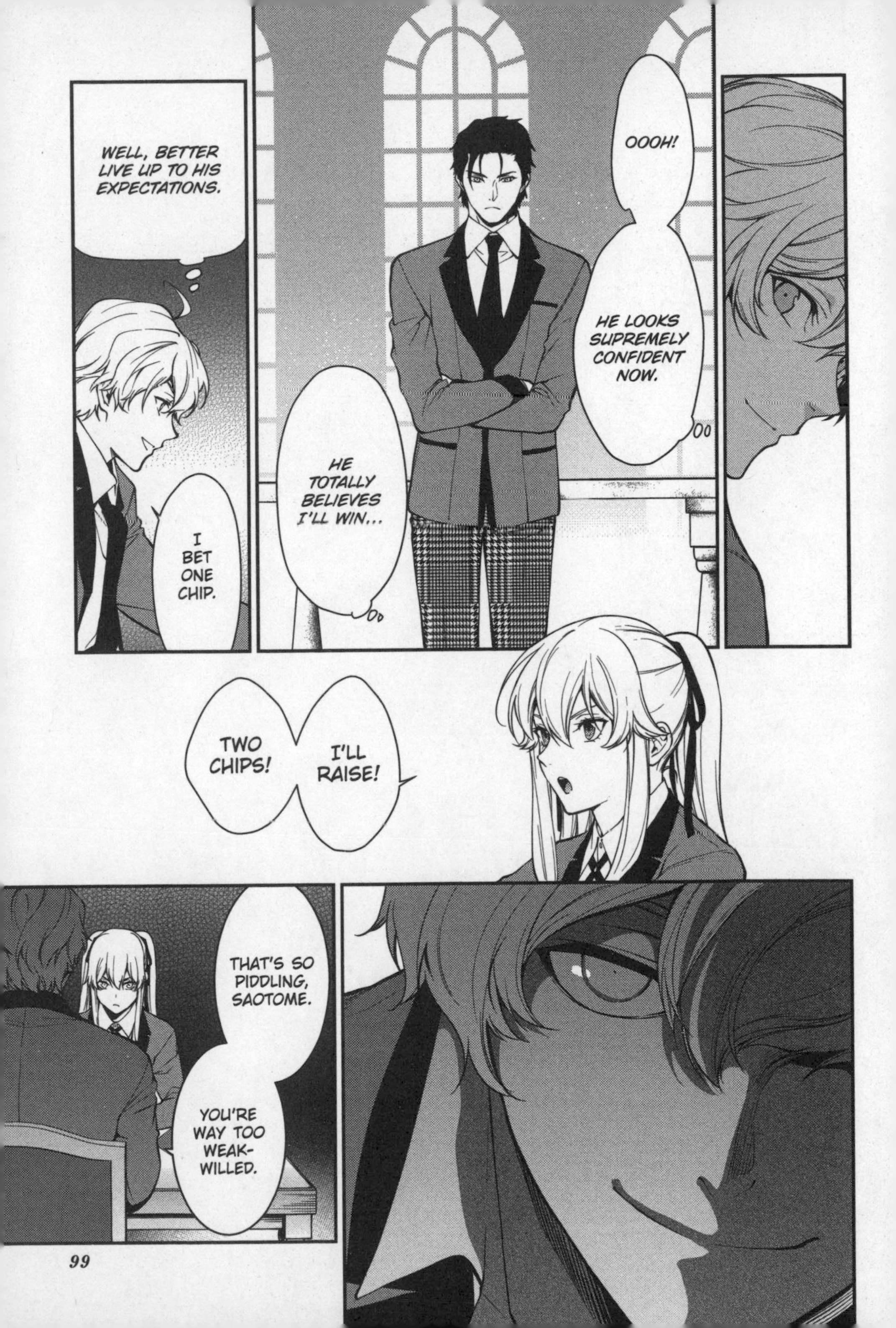

OOOH!
HE LOOKS SUPREMELY CONFIDENT NOW.
HE TOTALLY BELIEVES I'LL WIN...
WELL, BETTER LIVE UP TO HIS EXPECTATIONS.
I BET ONE CHIP.
I'LL RAISE!
TWO CHIPS!
THAT'S SO PIDDLING, SAOTOME.
YOU'RE WAY TOO WEAK-WILLED.

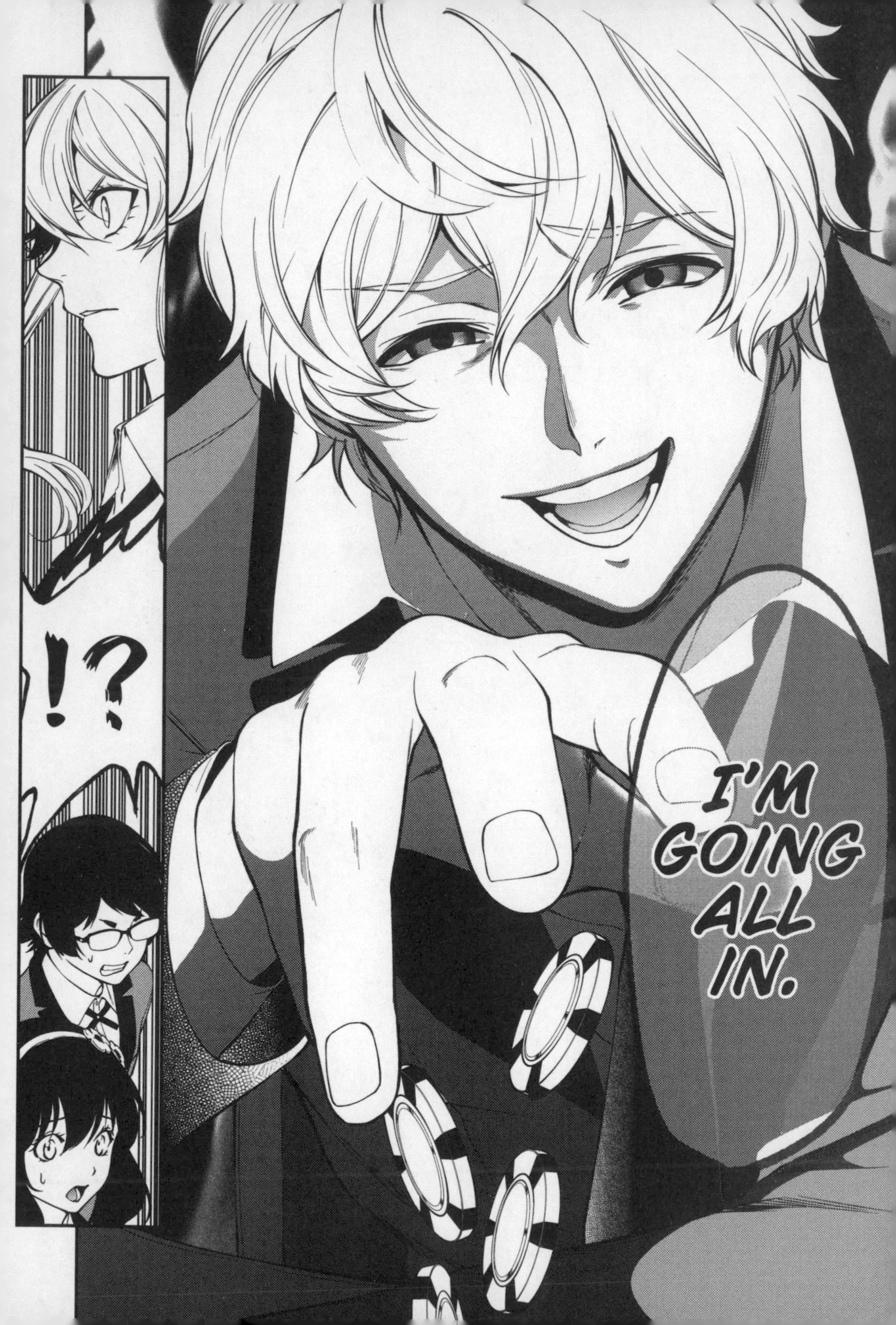
I'M GOING ALL IN.
!?

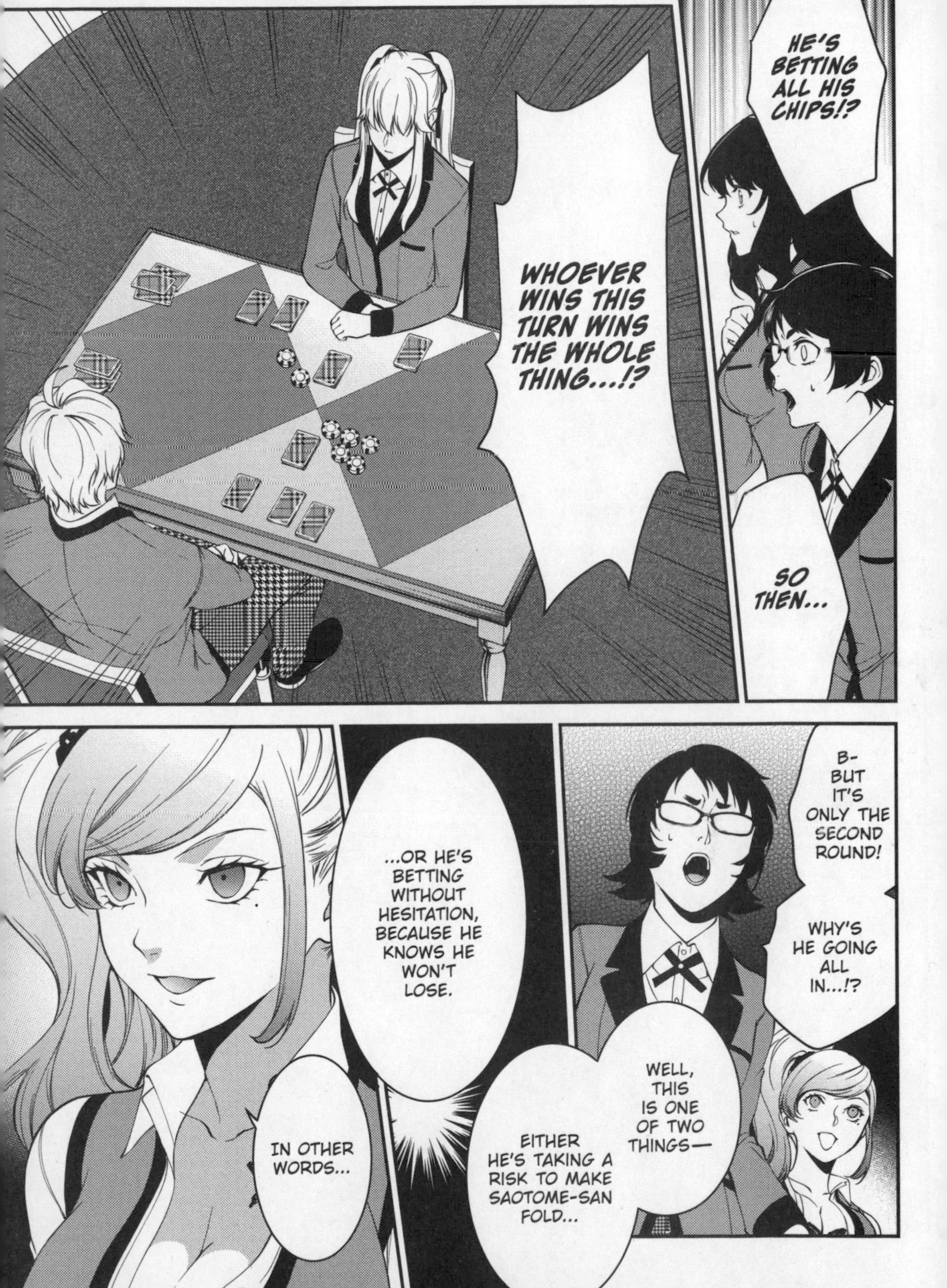
HE'S BETTING ALL HIS CHIPS!?
SO THEN...
WHOEVER WINS THIS TURN WINS THE WHOLE THING...!?
B-BUT IT'S ONLY THE SECOND ROUND!
WHY'S HE GOING ALL IN...!?
WELL, THIS IS ONE OF TWO THINGS—
EITHER HE'S TAKING A RISK TO MAKE SAOTOME-SAN FOLD...
...OR HE'S BETTING WITHOUT HESITATION, BECAUSE HE KNOWS HE WON'T LOSE.
IN OTHER WORDS...

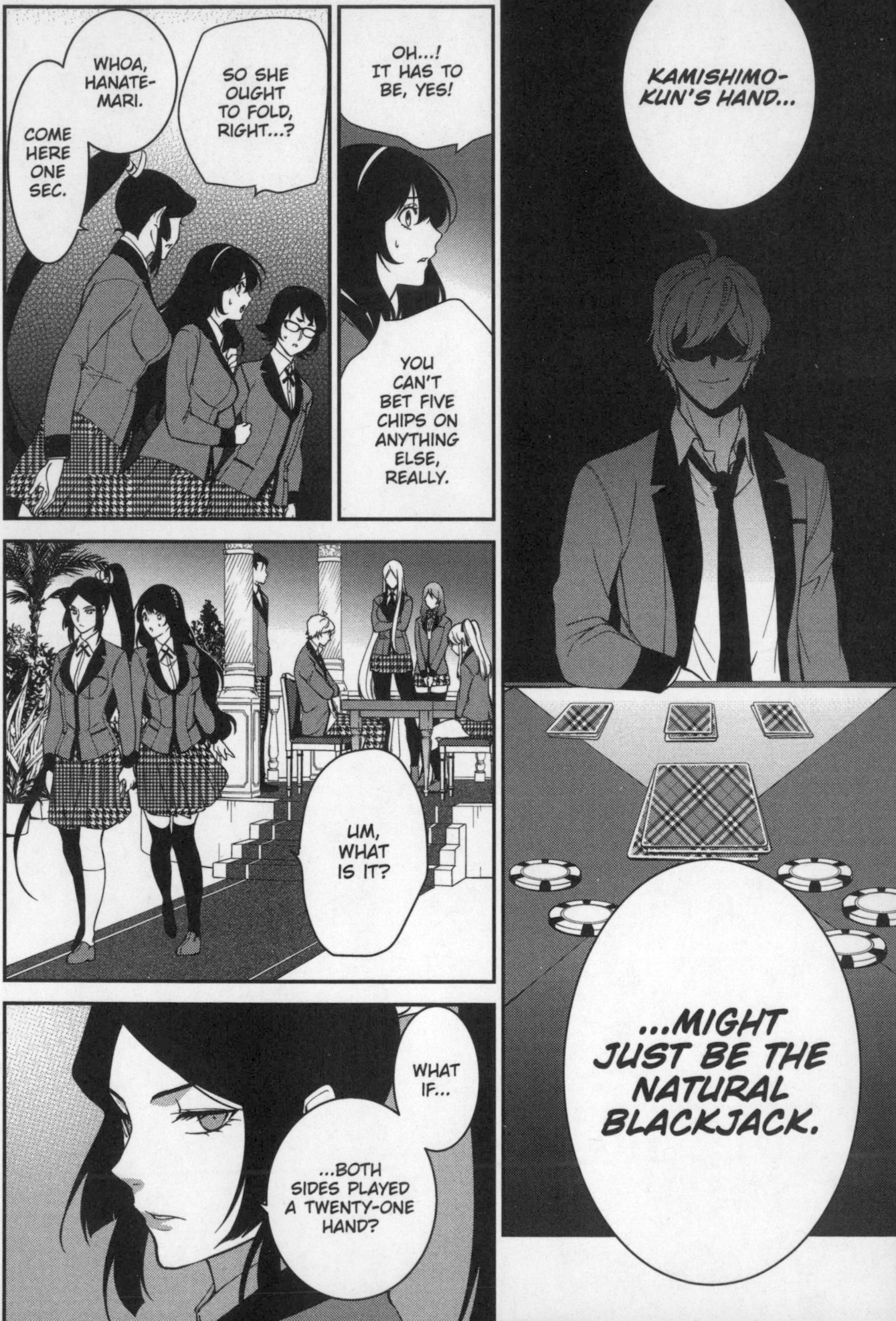
KAMISHIMO-KUN'S HAND...
...MIGHT JUST BE THE NATURAL BLACKJACK.
SO SHE OUGHT TO FOLD, RIGHT...?
OH...! IT HAS TO BE, YES!
YOU CAN'T BET FIVE CHIPS ON ANYTHING ELSE, REALLY.
WHOA, HANATE-MARI.
COME HERE ONE SEC.
UM, WHAT IS IT?
WHAT IF...
...BOTH SIDES PLAYED A TWENTY-ONE HAND?

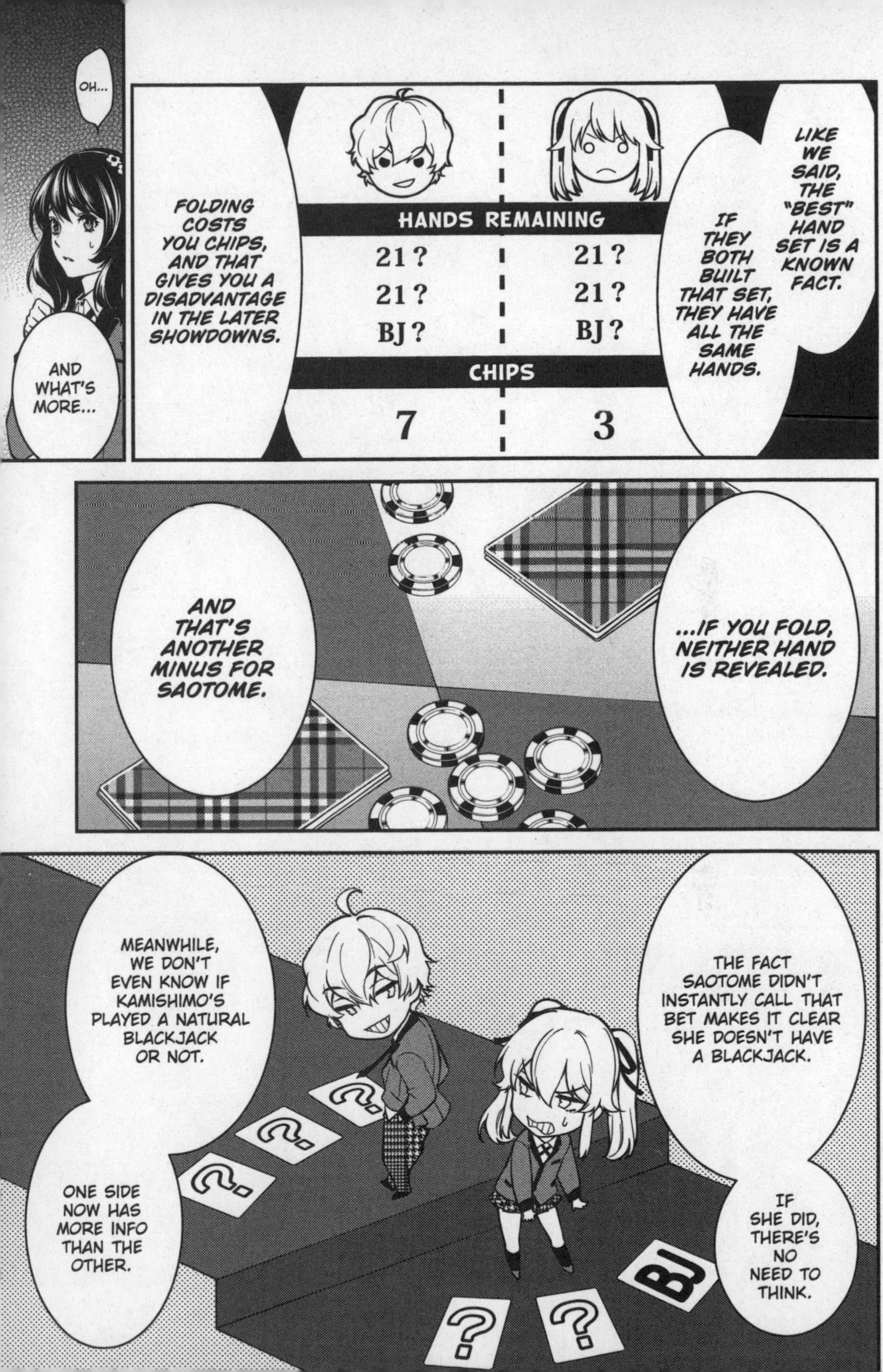
LIKE WE SAID, THE "BEST" HAND SET IS A KNOWN FACT.
IF THEY BOTH BUILT THAT SET, THEY HAVE ALL THE SAME HANDS.
HANDS REMAINING
21? 21?
21? 21?
BJ? BJ?
CHIPS
7 3
FOLDING COSTS YOU CHIPS, AND THAT GIVES YOU A DISADVANTAGE IN THE LATER SHOWDOWNS.
OH...
AND WHAT'S MORE...
...IF YOU FOLD, NEITHER HAND IS REVEALED.
AND THAT'S ANOTHER MINUS FOR SAOTOME.
THE FACT SAOTOME DIDN'T INSTANTLY CALL THAT BET MAKES IT CLEAR SHE DOESN'T HAVE A BLACKJACK.
IF SHE DID, THERE'S NO NEED TO THINK.
BJ
MEANWHILE, WE DON'T EVEN KNOW IF KAMISHIMO'S PLAYED A NATURAL BLACKJACK OR NOT.
ONE SIDE NOW HAS MORE INFO THAN THE OTHER.

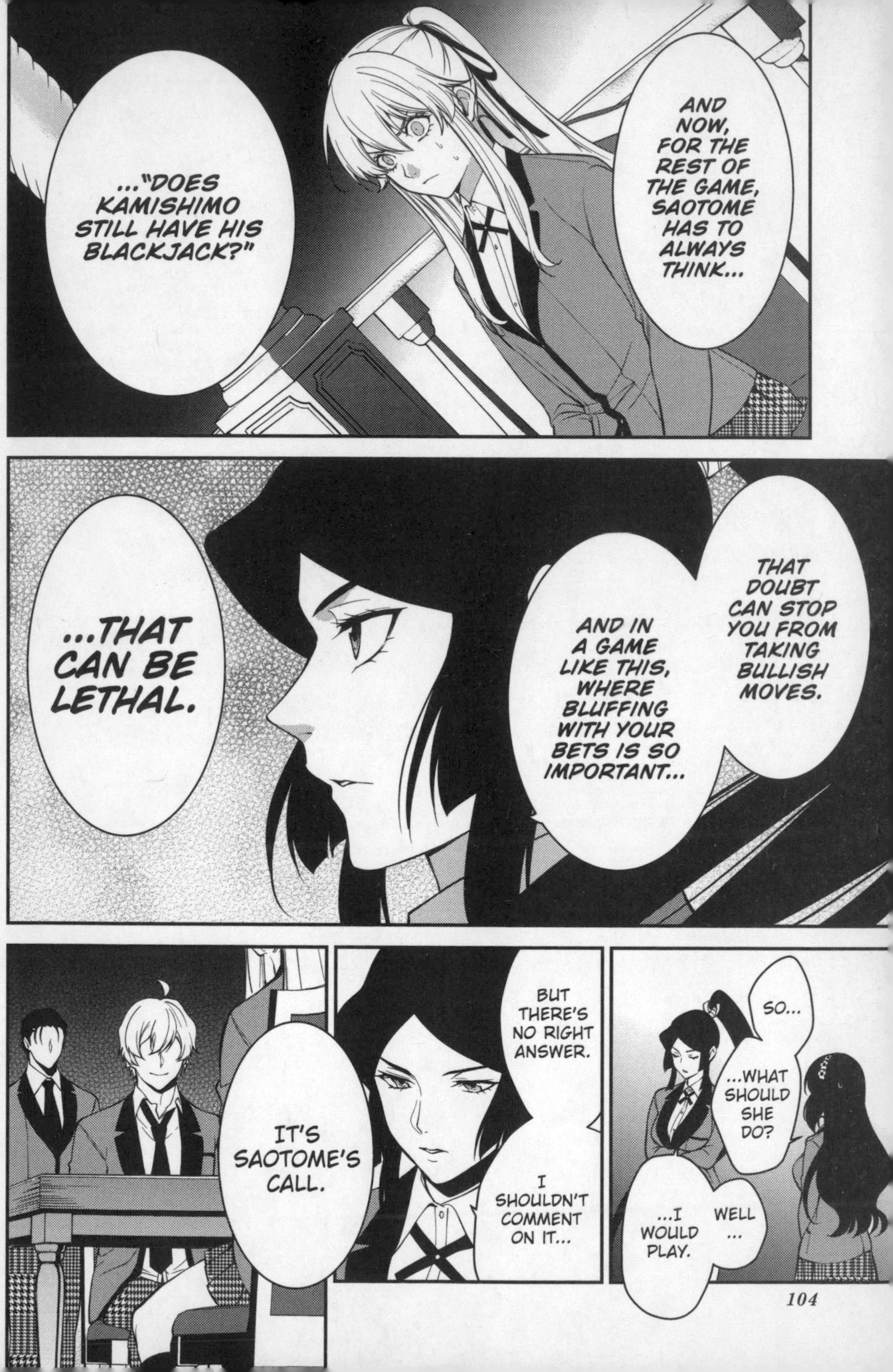
AND NOW, FOR THE REST OF THE GAME, SAOTOME HAS TO ALWAYS THINK...
..."DOES KAMISHIMO STILL HAVE HIS BLACKJACK?"
THAT DOUBT CAN STOP YOU FROM TAKING BULLISH MOVES.
AND IN A GAME LIKE THIS, WHERE BLUFFING WITH YOUR BETS IS SO IMPORTANT...
...THAT CAN BE LETHAL.
SO...
...WHAT SHOULD SHE DO?
WELL ...
...I WOULD PLAY.
BUT THERE'S NO RIGHT ANSWER.
I SHOULDN'T COMMENT ON IT...
IT'S SAOTOME'S CALL.

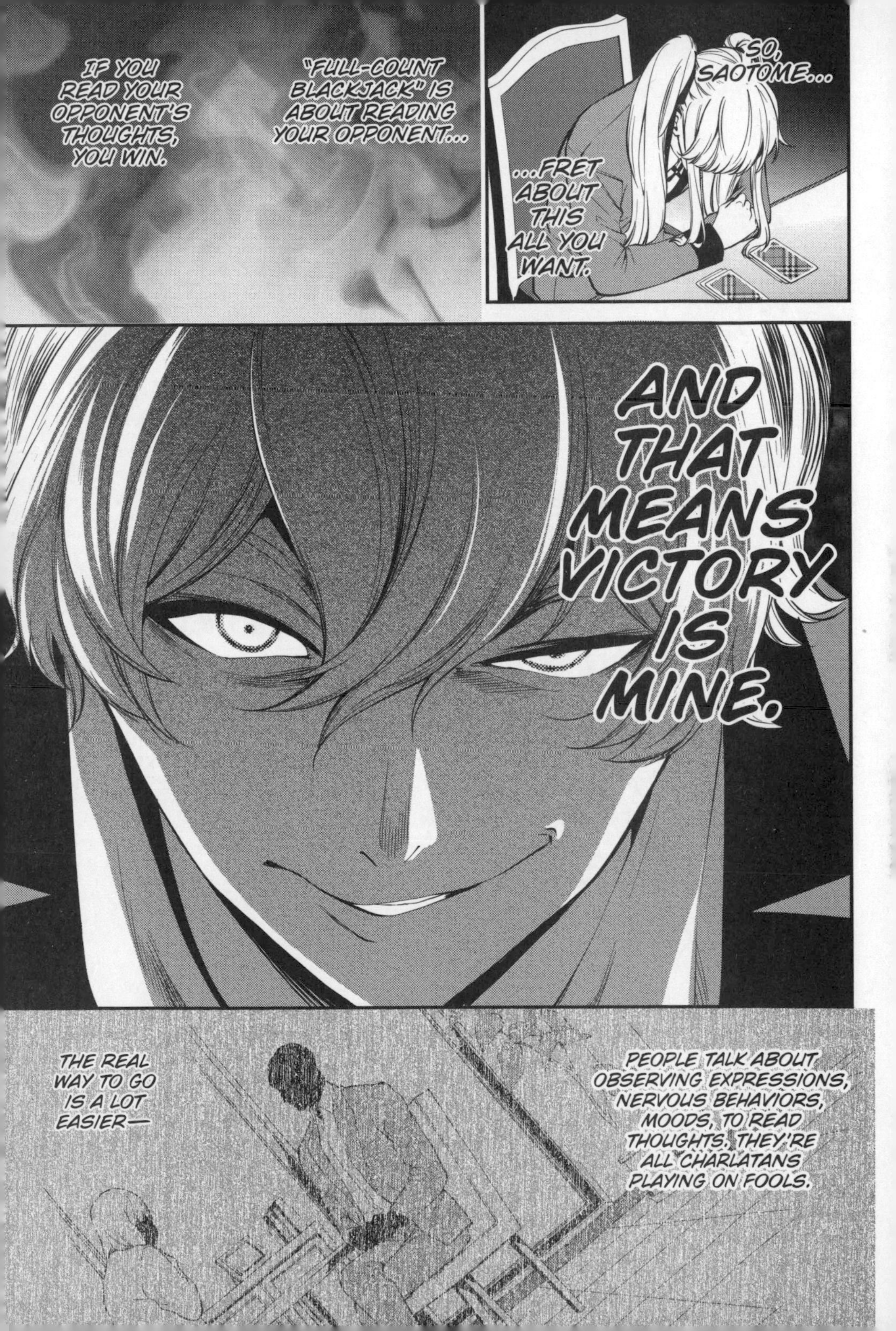
SO, SAOTOME...
...FRET ABOUT THIS ALL YOU WANT.
"FULL-COUNT BLACKJACK" IS ABOUT READING YOUR OPPONENT...
IF YOU READ YOUR OPPONENT'S THOUGHTS, YOU WIN.
AND THAT MEANS VICTORY IS MINE.
PEOPLE TALK ABOUT OBSERVING EXPRESSIONS, NERVOUS BEHAVIORS, MOODS, TO READ THOUGHTS. THEY'RE ALL CHARLATANS PLAYING ON FOOLS.
THE REAL WAY TO GO IS A LOT EASIER—

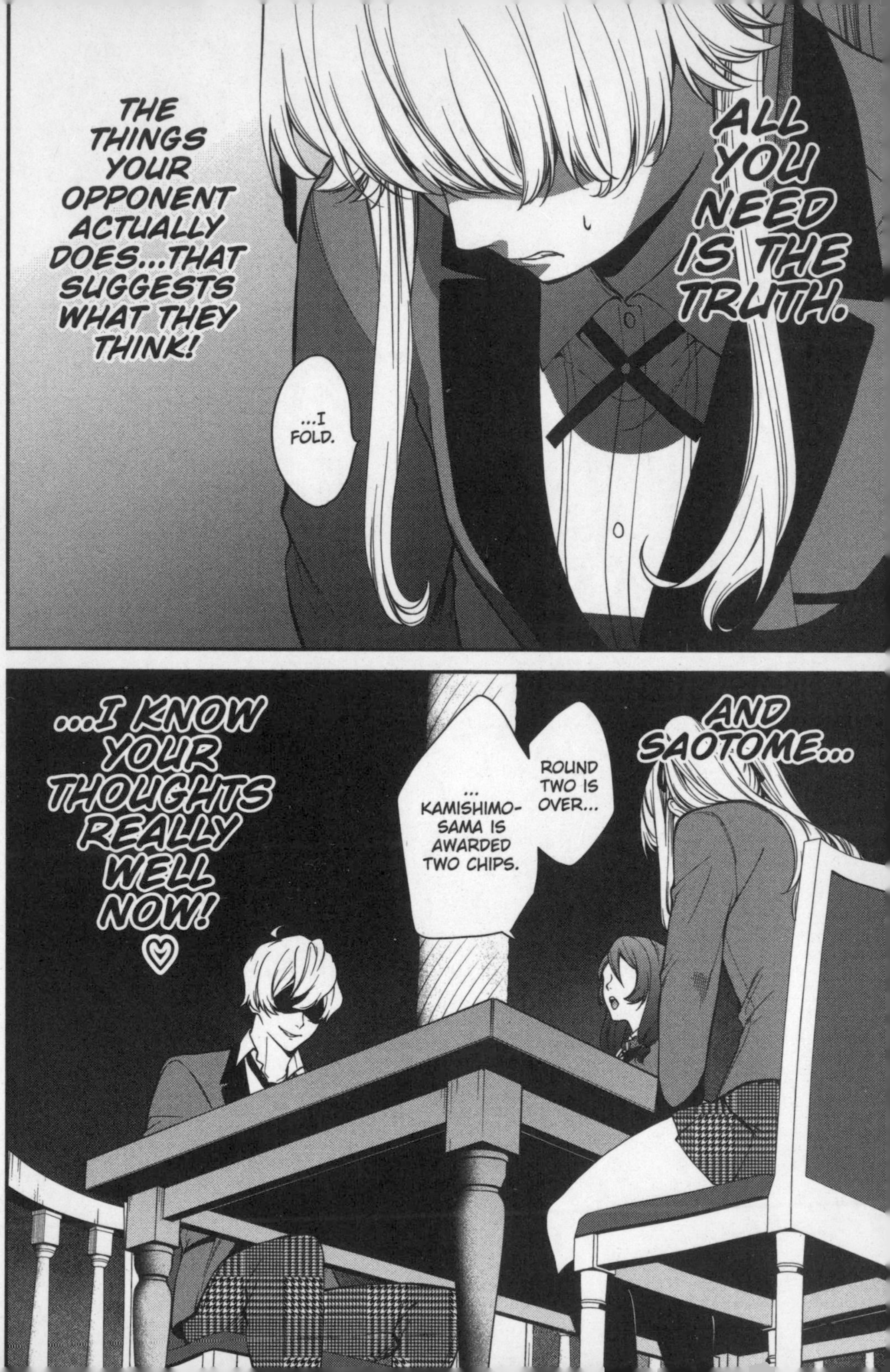
ALL YOU NEED IS THE TRUTH.
THE THINGS YOUR OPPONENT ACTUALLY DOES...THAT SUGGESTS WHAT THEY THINK!
...I FOLD.
AND SAOTOME...
ROUND TWO IS OVER...
...KAMISHIMO-SAMA IS AWARDED TWO CHIPS.
...I KNOW YOUR THOUGHTS REALLY WELL NOW! ♡

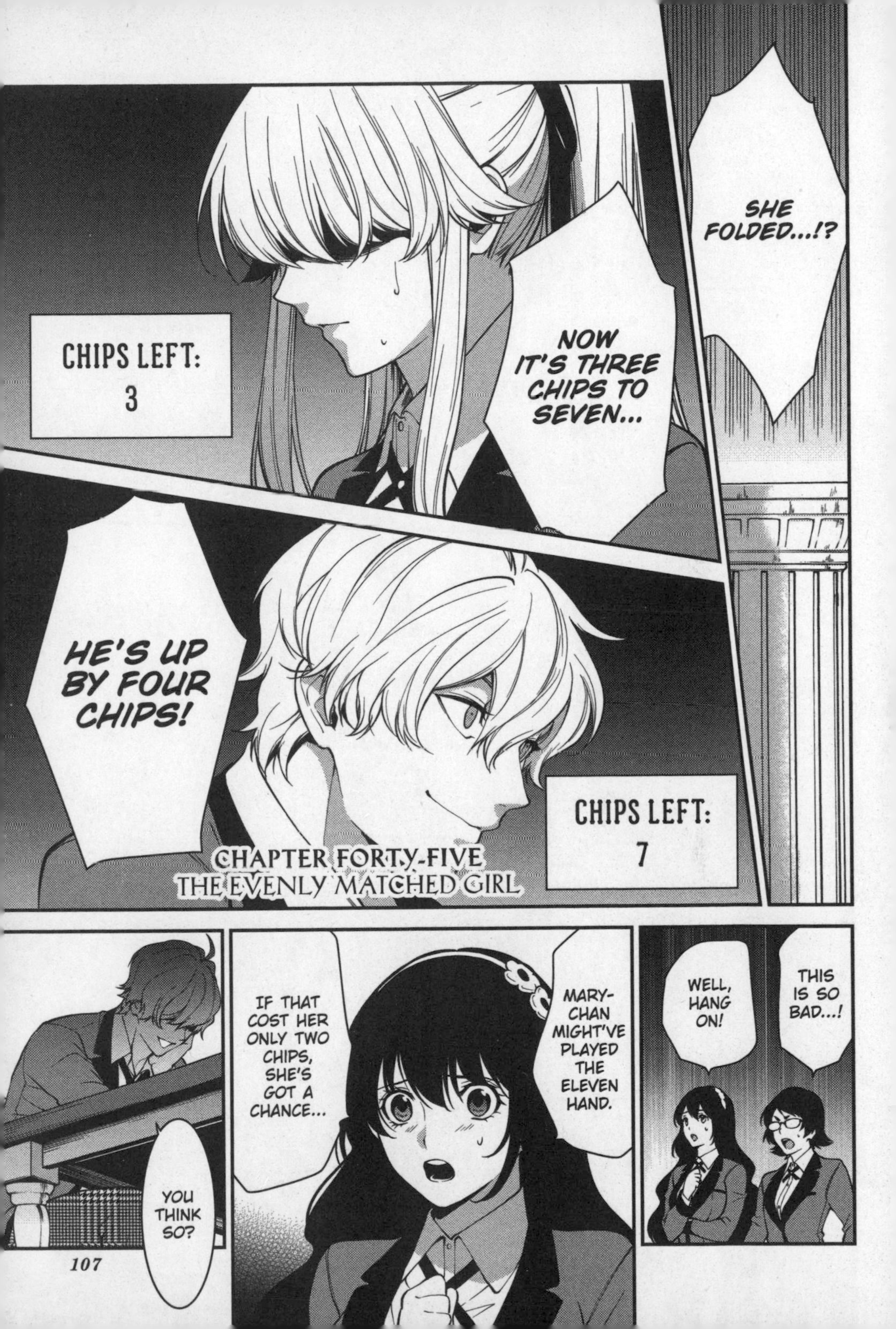
SHE FOLDED...!?
NOW IT'S THREE CHIPS TO SEVEN...
CHIPS LEFT: 3
HE'S UP BY FOUR CHIPS!
CHIPS LEFT: 7
CHAPTER FORTY-FIVE
THE EVENLY MATCHED GIRL
THIS IS SO BAD...!
WELL, HANG ON!
MARY-CHAN MIGHT'VE PLAYED THE ELEVEN HAND.
IF THAT COST HER ONLY TWO CHIPS, SHE'S GOT A CHANCE...
YOU THINK SO?

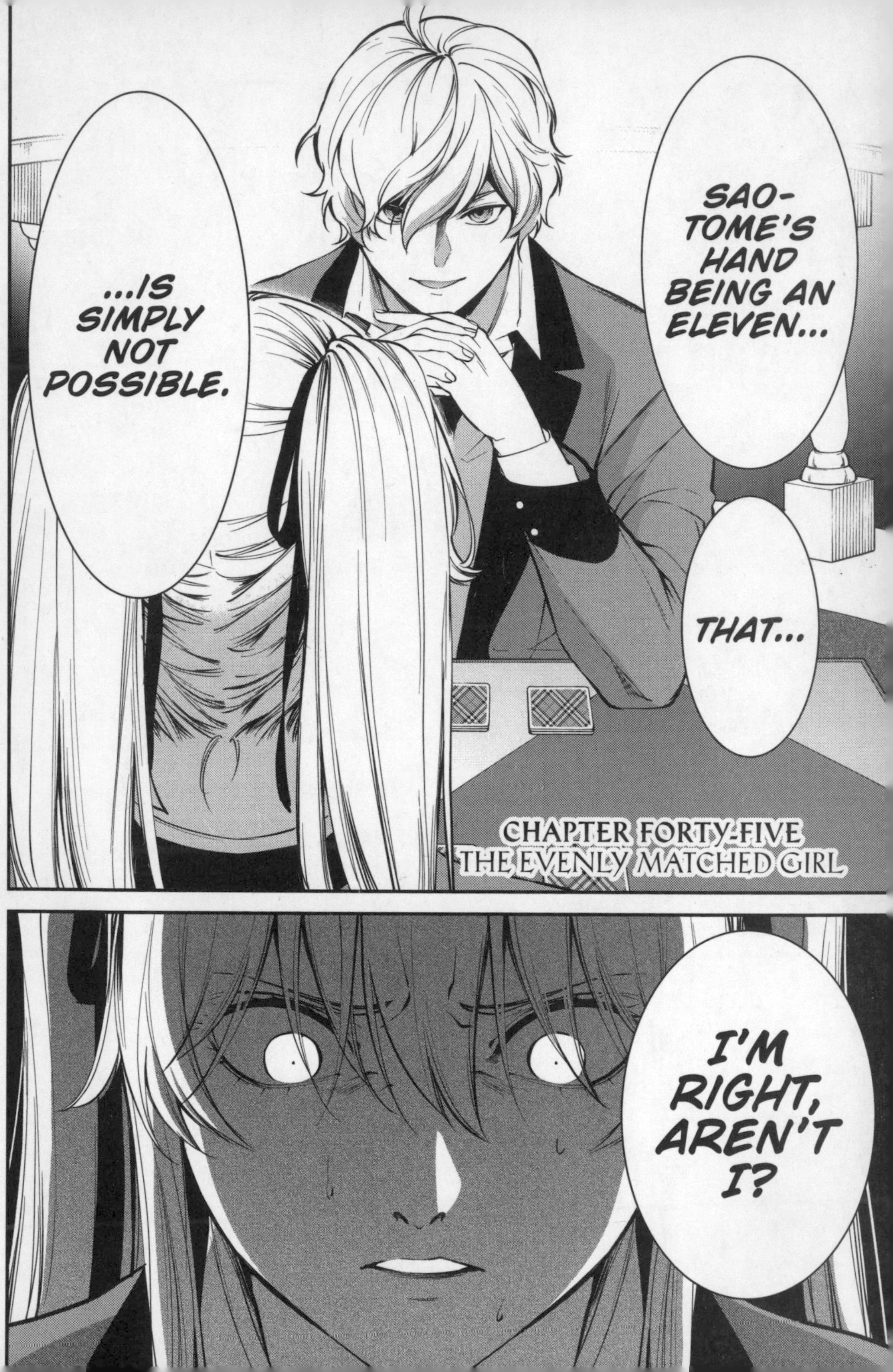
SAO-TOME'S HAND BEING AN ELEVEN...
THAT...
...IS SIMPLY NOT POSSIBLE.
CHAPTER FORTY-FIVE THE EVENLY MATCHED GIRL
I'M RIGHT, AREN'T I?

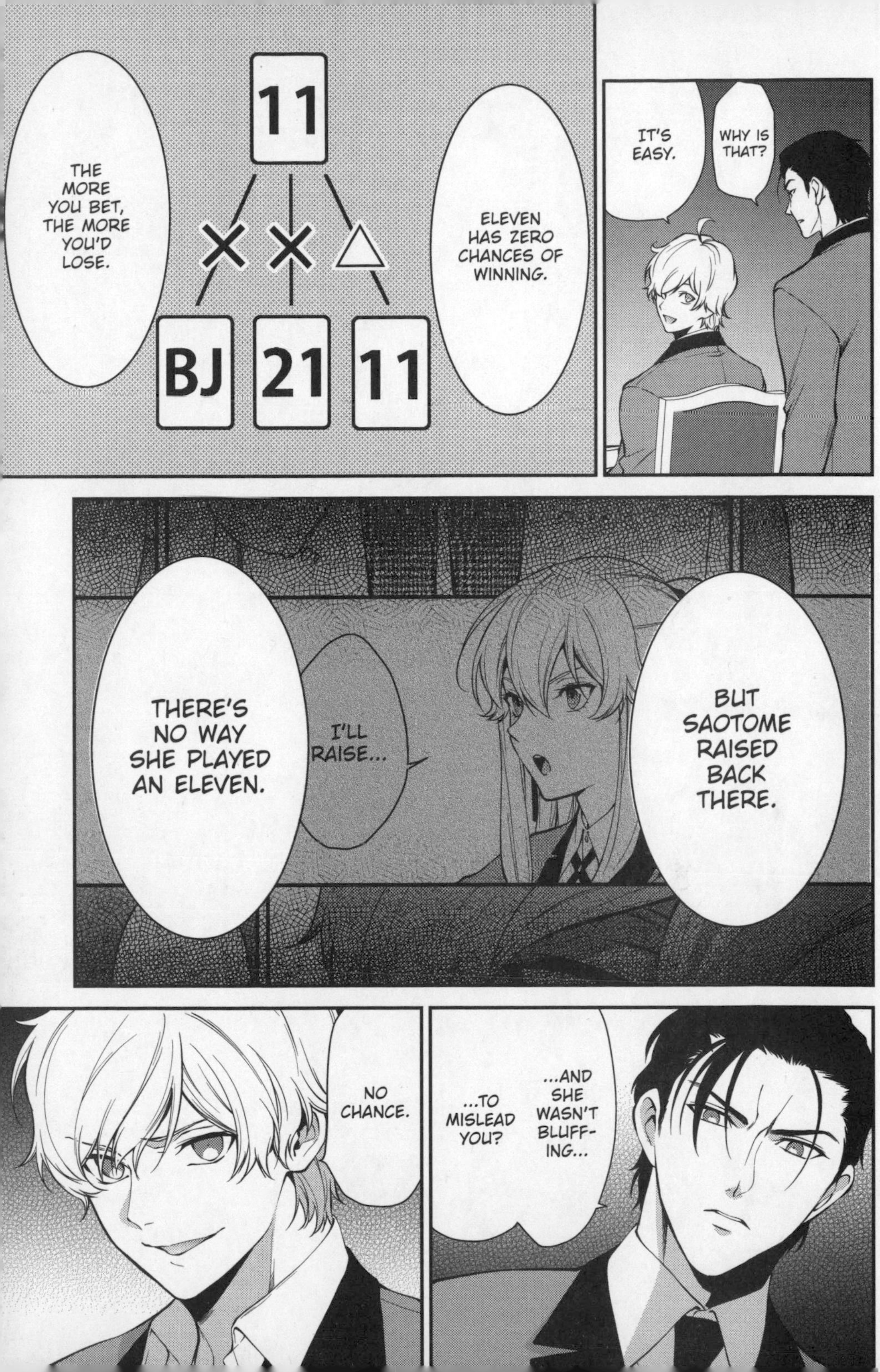
WHY IS THAT?
IT'S EASY.
ELEVEN HAS ZERO CHANCES OF WINNING.
11
×
×
△
BJ
21
11
THE MORE YOU BET, THE MORE YOU'D LOSE.
BUT SAOTOME RAISED BACK THERE.
I'LL RAISE...
THERE'S NO WAY SHE PLAYED AN ELEVEN.
...AND SHE WASN'T BLUFF-ING...
...TO MISLEAD YOU?
NO CHANCE.

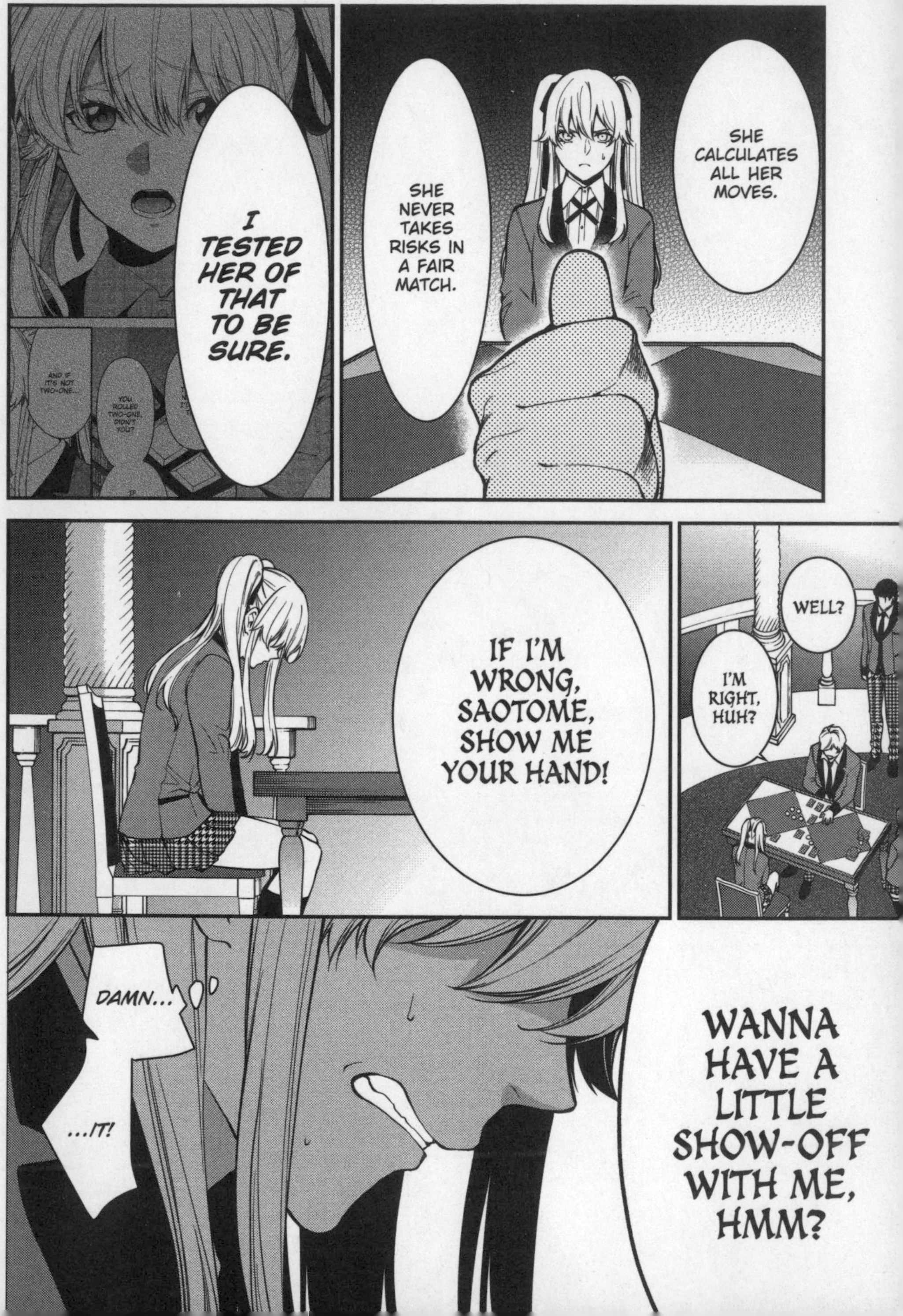
SHE CALCULATES ALL HER MOVES.
SHE NEVER TAKES RISKS IN A FAIR MATCH.
I TESTED HER OF THAT TO BE SURE.
YOU ROLLED TWO-ONE, DIDN'T YOU?
AND IF IT'S NOT TWO-ONE...
WELL?
I'M RIGHT, HUH?
IF I'M WRONG, SAOTOME, SHOW ME YOUR HAND!
WANNA HAVE A LITTLE SHOW-OFF WITH ME, HMM?
DAMN...
...IT!

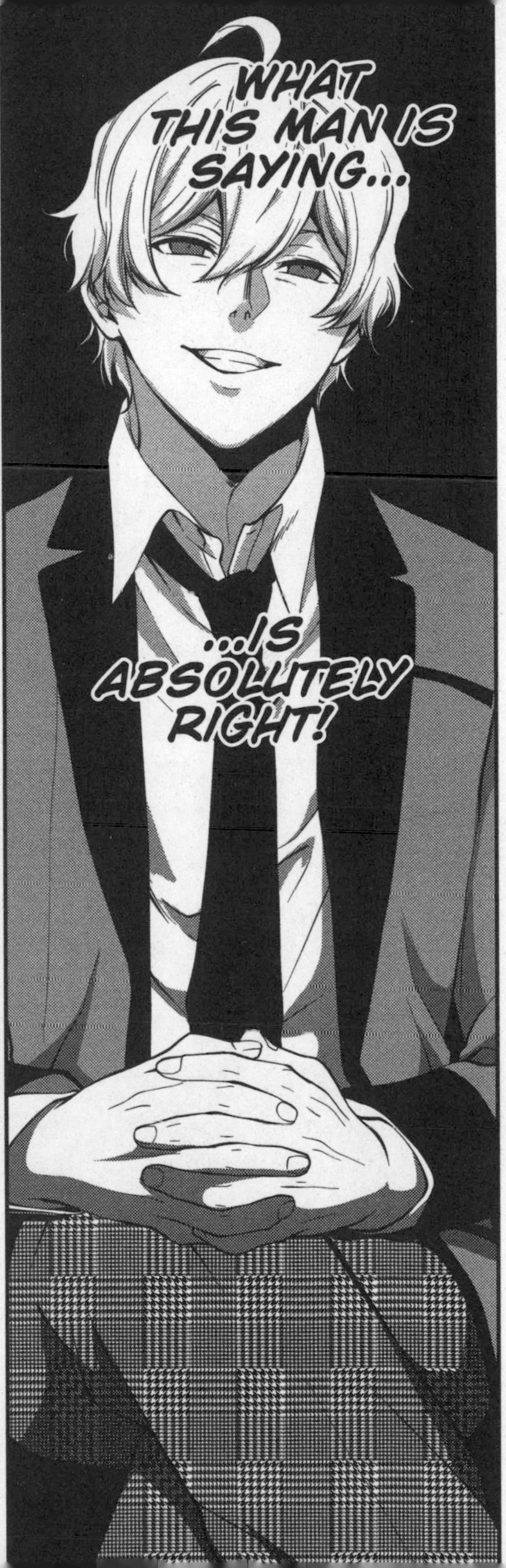
WHAT THIS MAN IS SAYING...
...IS ABSOLUTELY RIGHT!
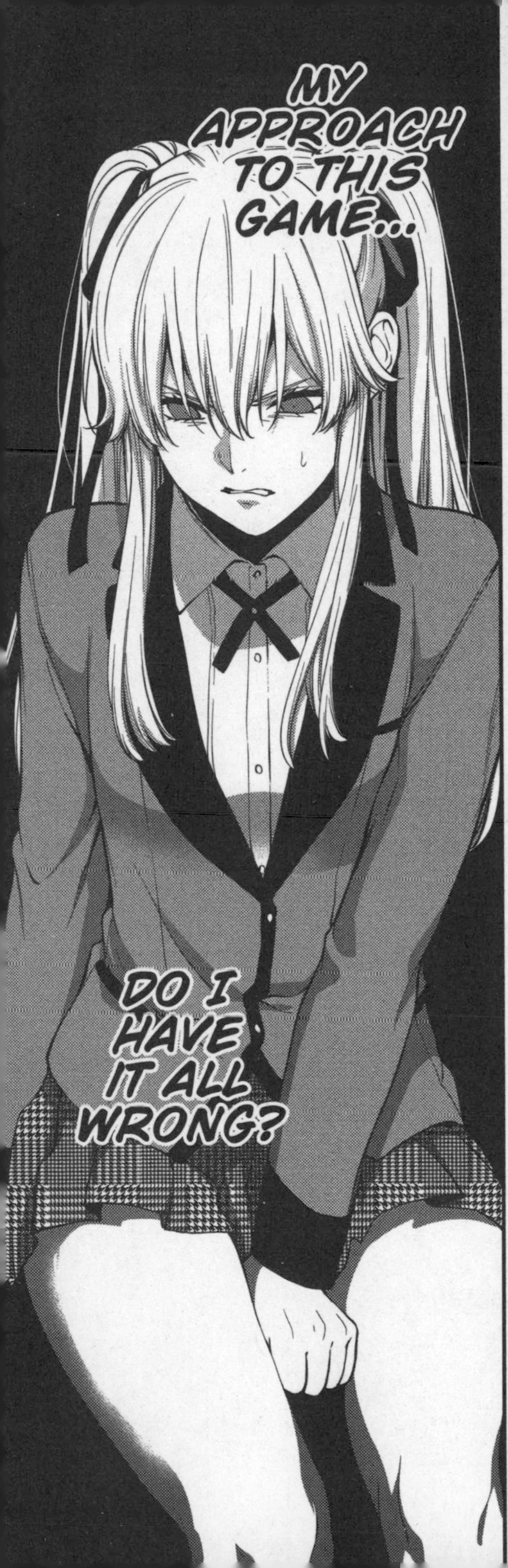
MY APPROACH TO THIS GAME...
DO I HAVE IT ALL WRONG?

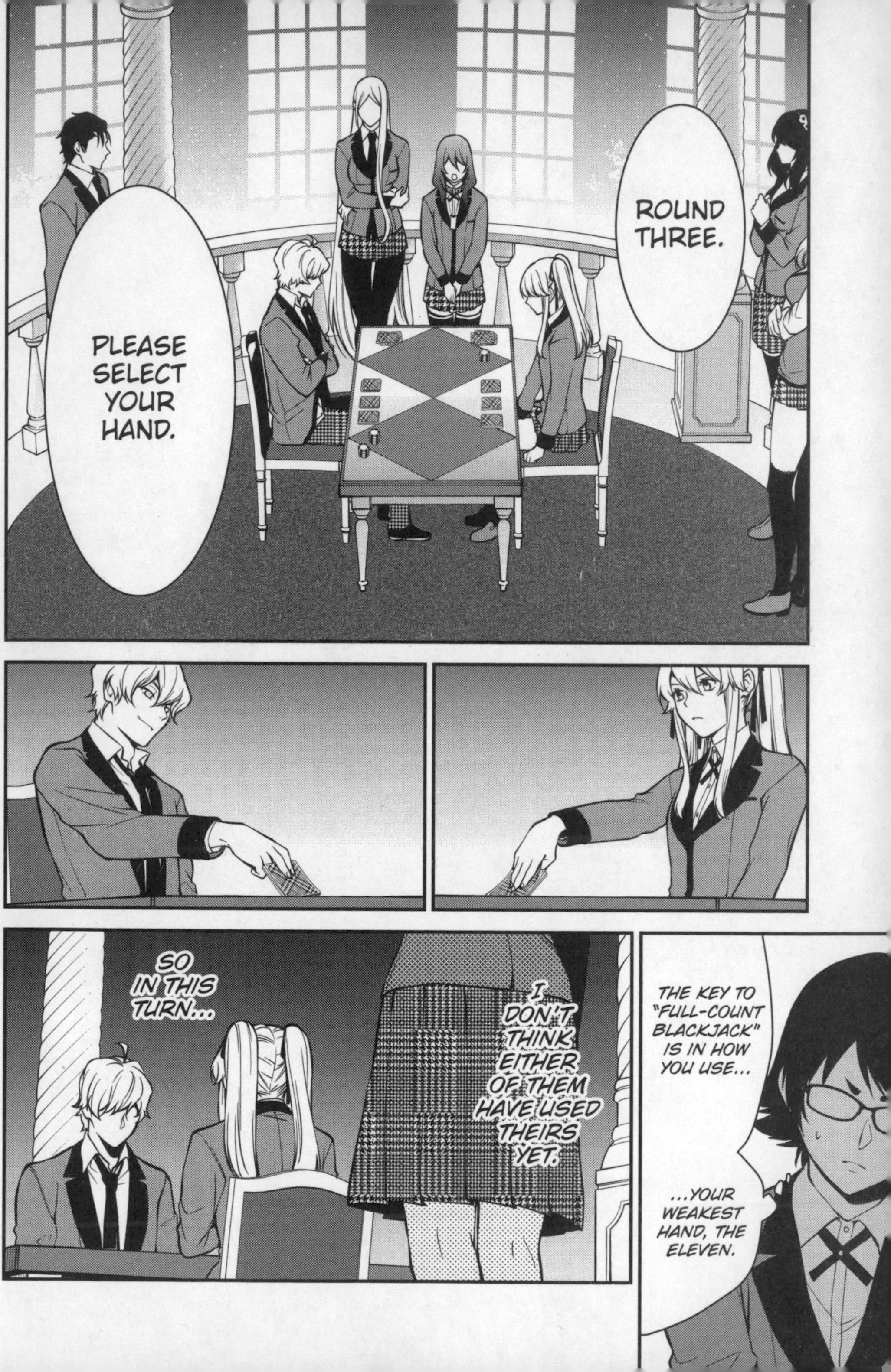
ROUND THREE.
PLEASE SELECT YOUR HAND.
THE KEY TO "FULL-COUNT BLACKJACK" IS IN HOW YOU USE...
...YOUR WEAKEST HAND, THE ELEVEN.
I DON'T THINK EITHER OF THEM HAVE USED THEIRS YET.
SO IN THIS TURN...

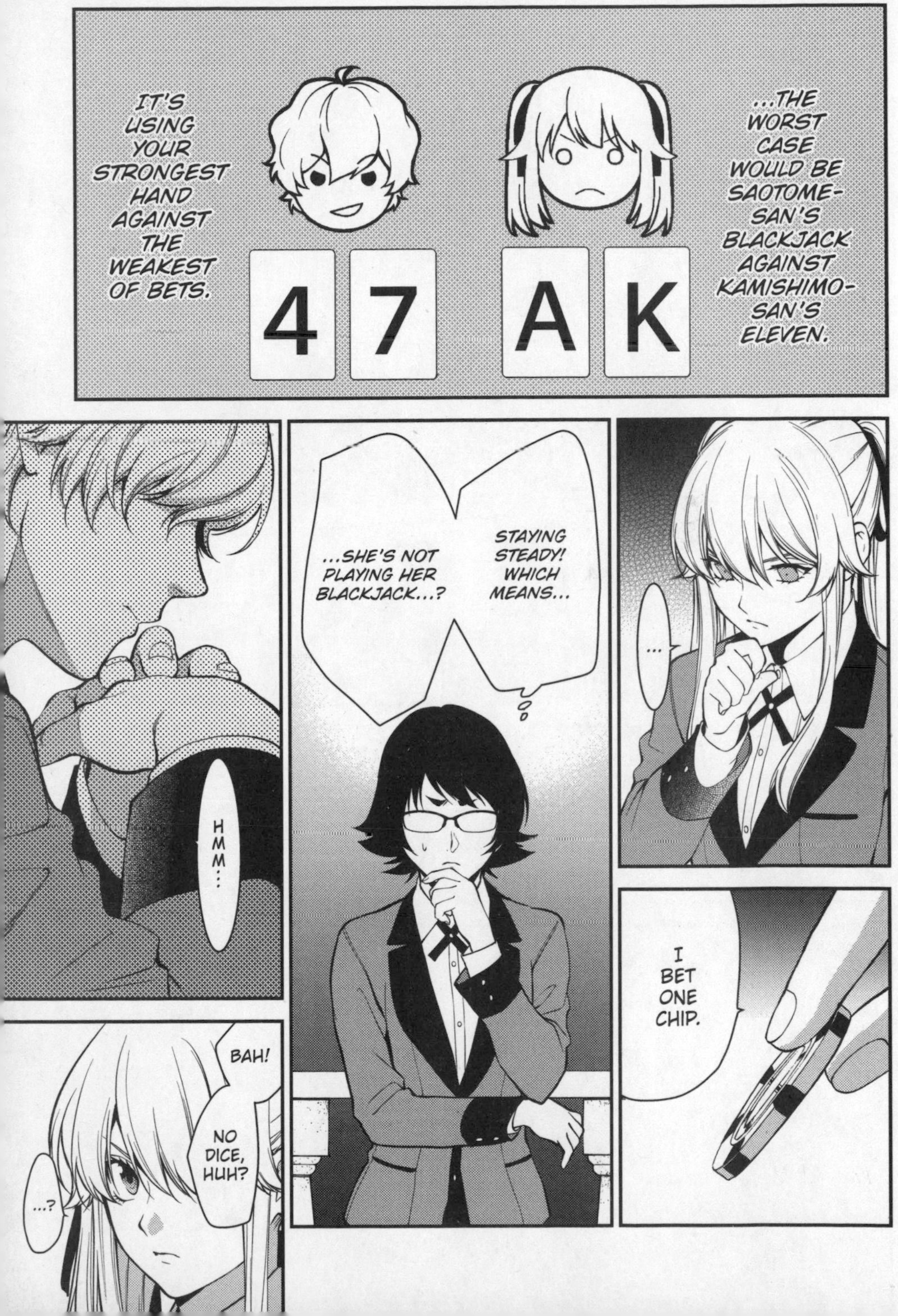
...THE WORST CASE WOULD BE SAOTOME-SAN'S BLACKJACK AGAINST KAMISHIMO-SAN'S ELEVEN.
A K
4 7
IT'S USING YOUR STRONGEST HAND AGAINST THE WEAKEST OF BETS.
...
I BET ONE CHIP.
STAYING STEADY! WHICH MEANS...
...SHE'S NOT PLAYING HER BLACKJACK...?
HMM...
BAH!
NO DICE, HUH?
...?

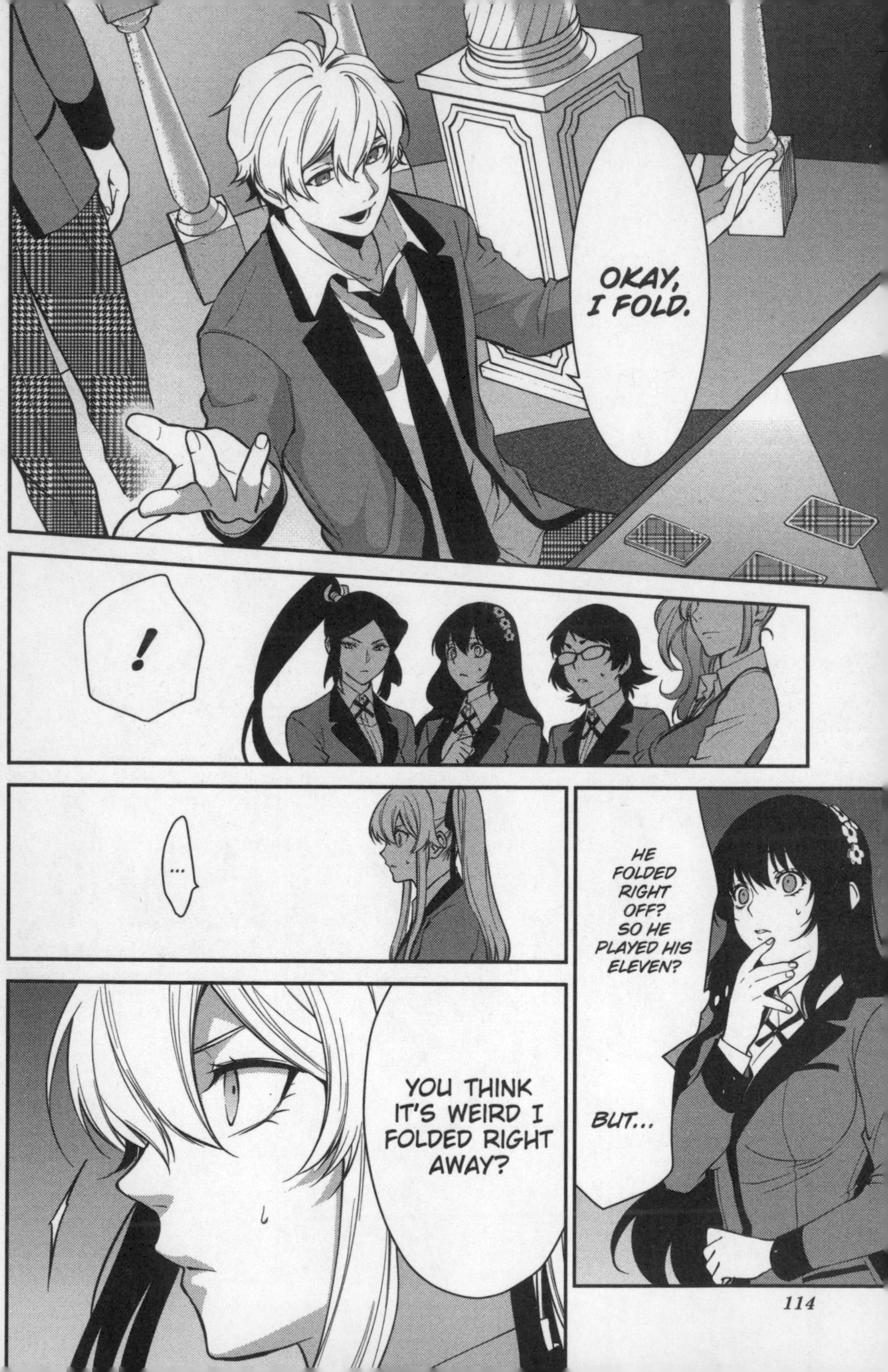
OKAY, I FOLD.
!
HE FOLDED RIGHT OFF? SO HE PLAYED HIS ELEVEN?
BUT...
...
YOU THINK IT'S WEIRD I FOLDED RIGHT AWAY?

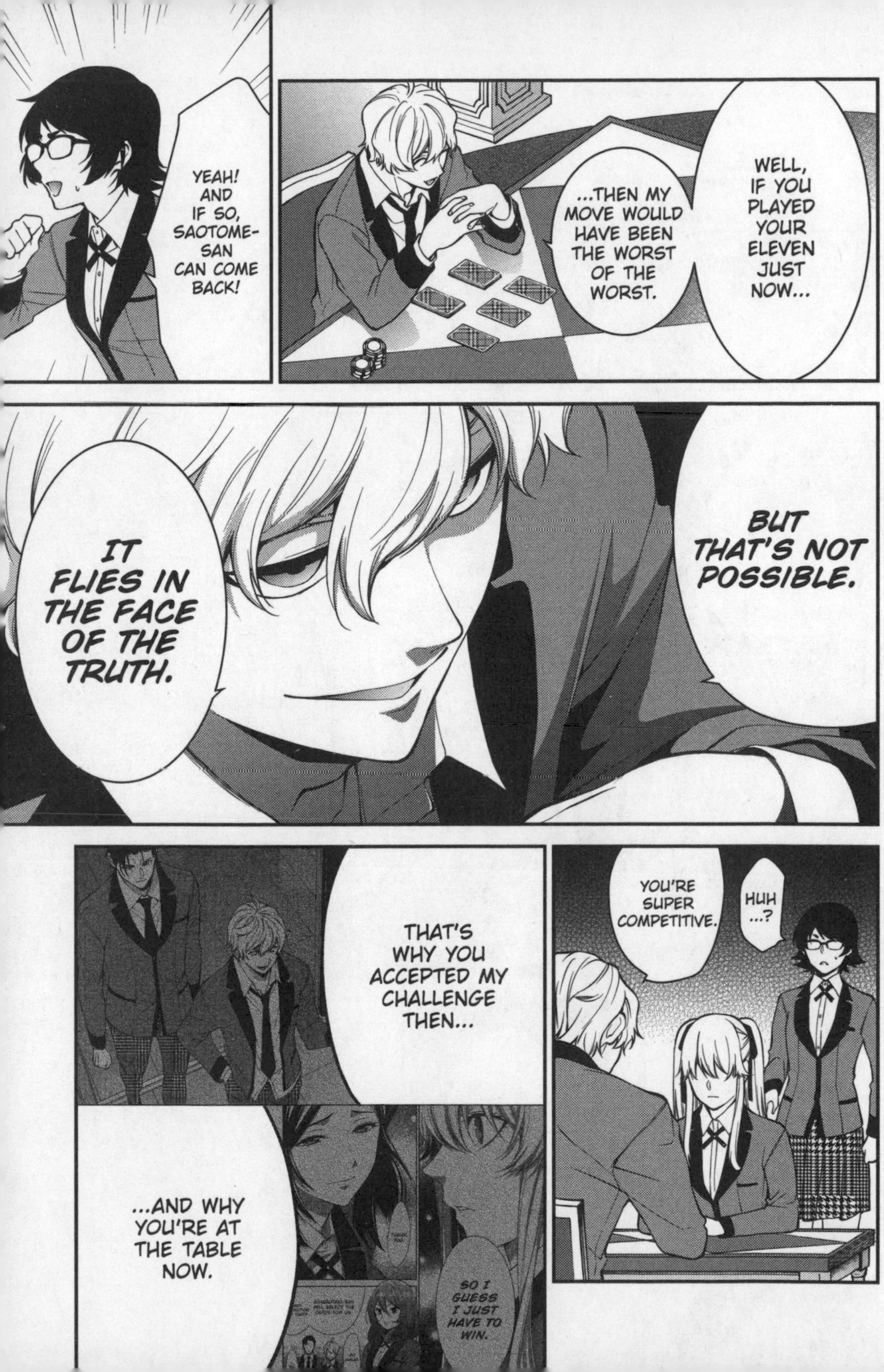
WELL, IF YOU PLAYED YOUR ELEVEN JUST NOW...
...THEN MY MOVE WOULD HAVE BEEN THE WORST OF THE WORST.
YEAH! AND IF SO, SAOTOME-SAN CAN COME BACK!
BUT THAT'S NOT POSSIBLE.
IT FLIES IN THE FACE OF THE TRUTH.
HUH ...?
YOU'RE SUPER COMPETITIVE.
THAT'S WHY YOU ACCEPTED MY CHALLENGE THEN...
...AND WHY YOU'RE AT THE TABLE NOW.
SO I GUESS I JUST HAVE TO WIN.

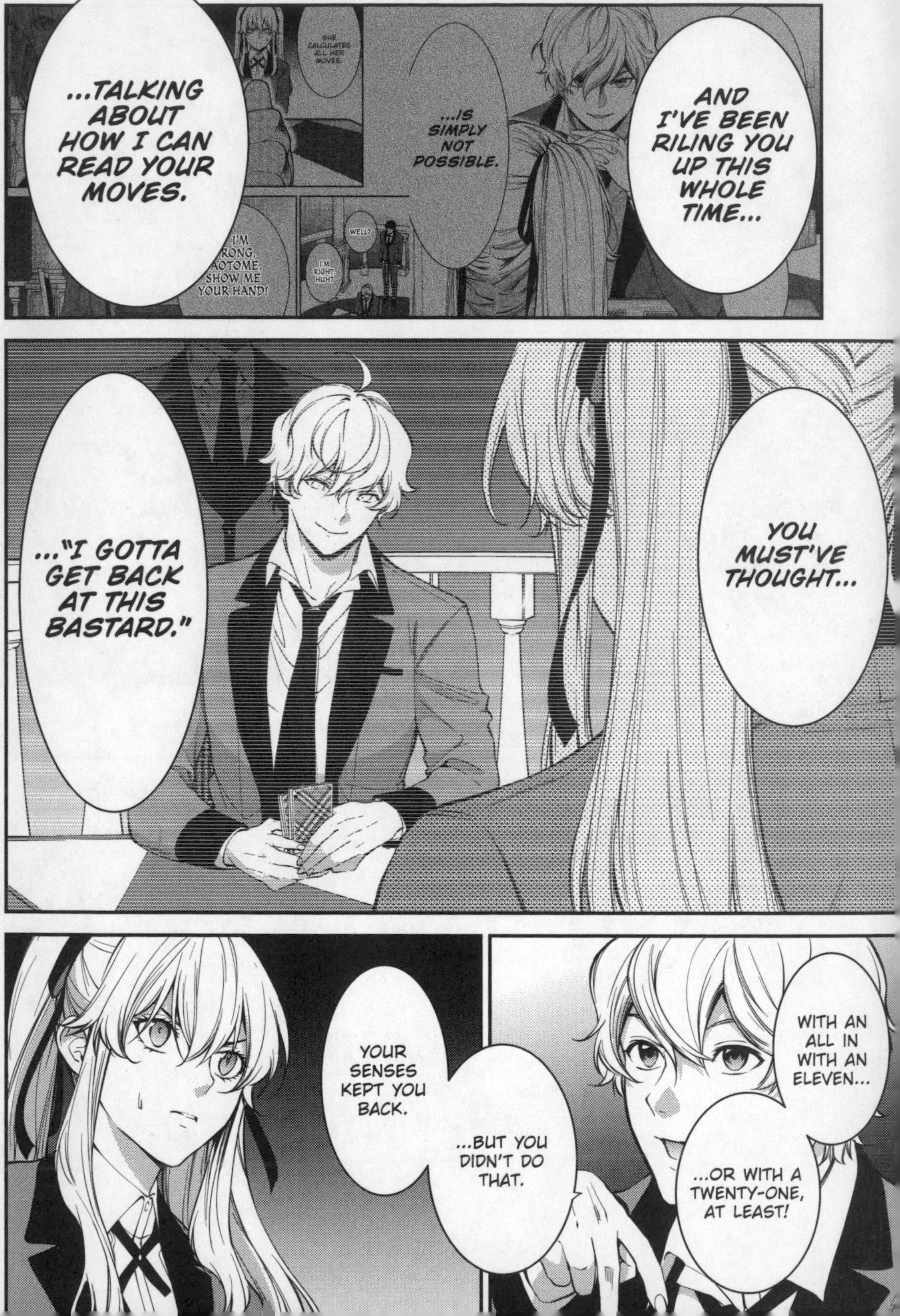
AND I'VE BEEN RILING YOU UP THIS WHOLE TIME...
SHE CALCULATES ALL HER MOVES.
...IS SIMPLY NOT POSSIBLE.
WELL?
I'M RIGHT. HUH?
I'M RONG, AOTOME, SHOW ME YOUR HAND!
...TALKING ABOUT HOW I CAN READ YOUR MOVES.
YOU MUST'VE THOUGHT...
..."I GOTTA GET BACK AT THIS BASTARD."
WITH AN ALL IN WITH AN ELEVEN...
...OR WITH A TWENTY-ONE, AT LEAST!
YOUR SENSES KEPT YOU BACK.
...BUT YOU DIDN'T DO THAT.

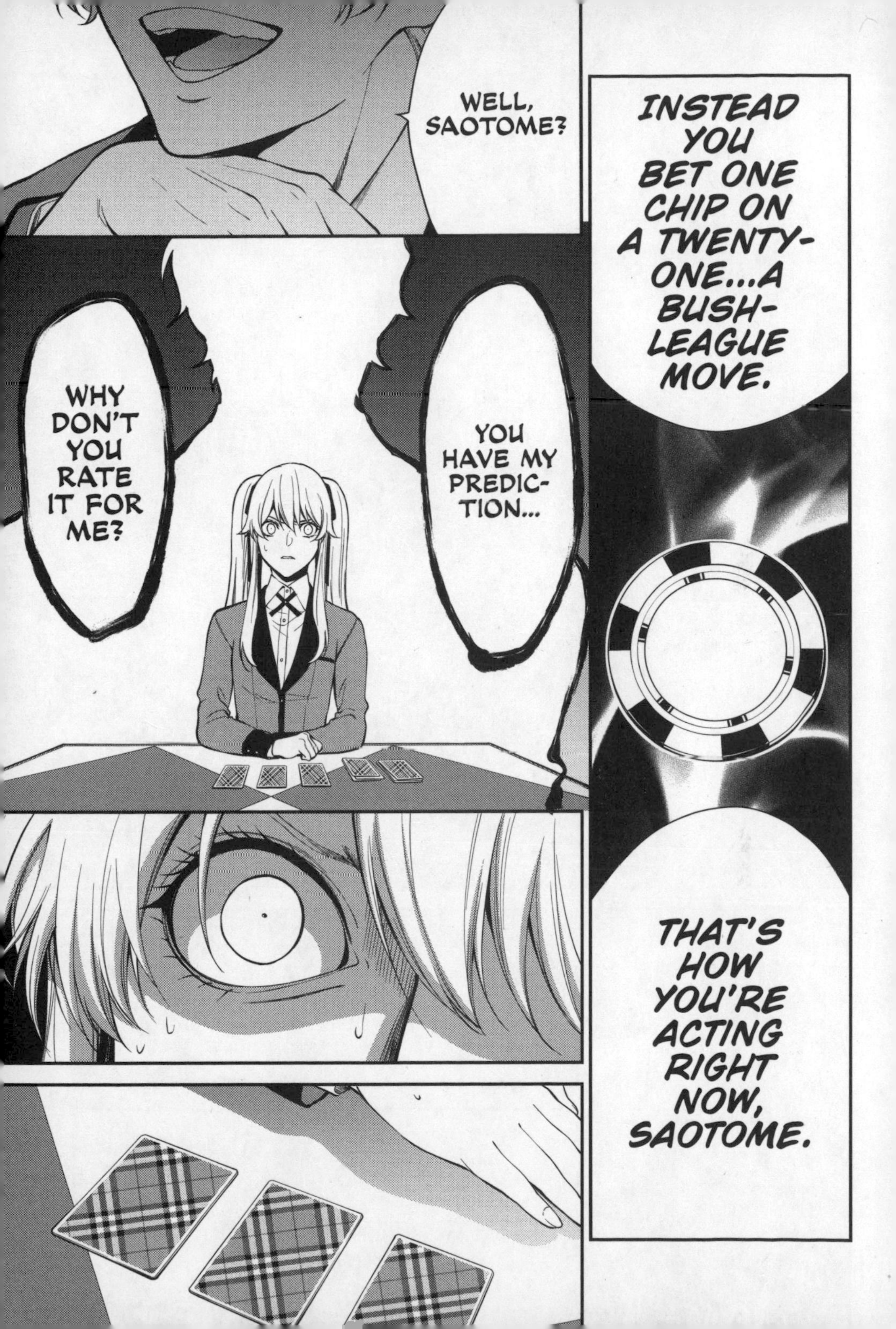
INSTEAD YOU BET ONE CHIP ON A TWENTY-ONE...A BUSH-LEAGUE MOVE.
THAT'S HOW YOU'RE ACTING RIGHT NOW, SAOTOME.
WELL, SAOTOME?
YOU HAVE MY PREDICTION...
WHY DON'T YOU RATE IT FOR ME?

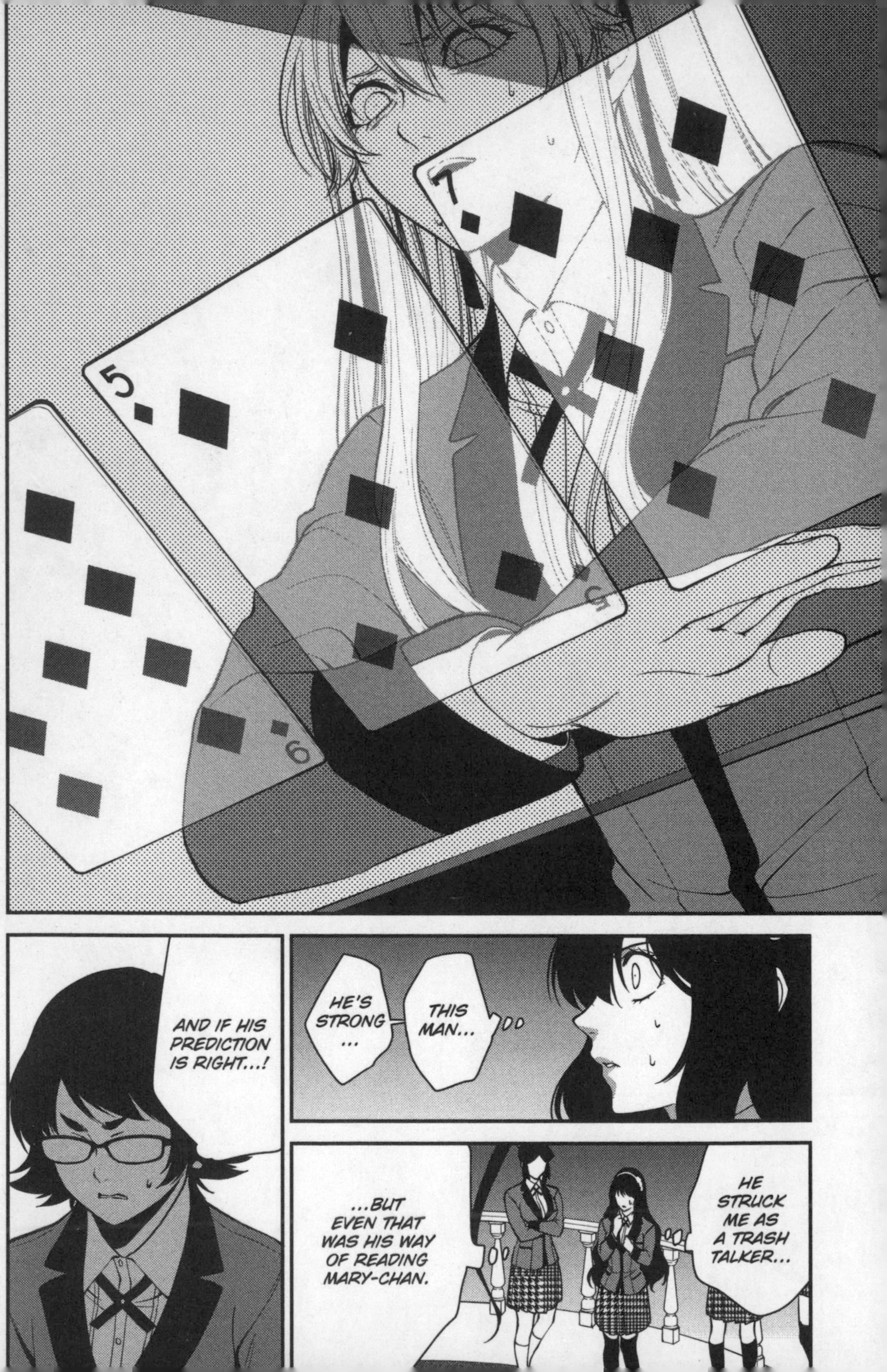
THIS MAN...
HE'S STRONG...
HE STRUCK ME AS A TRASH TALKER...
...BUT EVEN THAT WAS HIS WAY OF READING MARY-CHAN.
AND IF HIS PREDICTION IS RIGHT...!

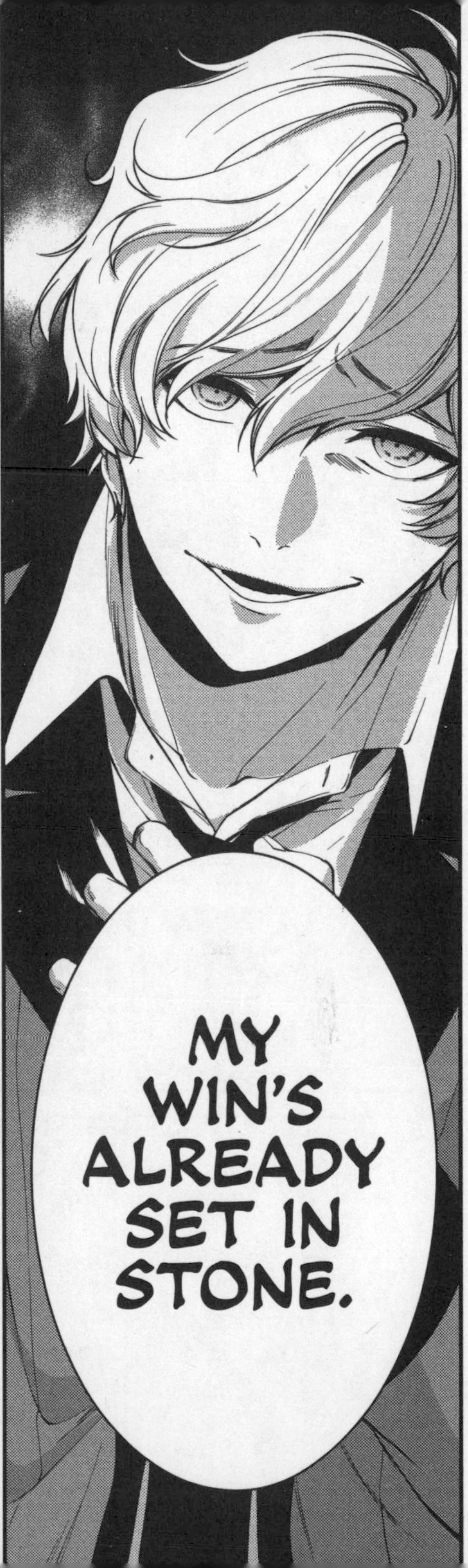
MY WIN'S ALREADY SET IN STONE.

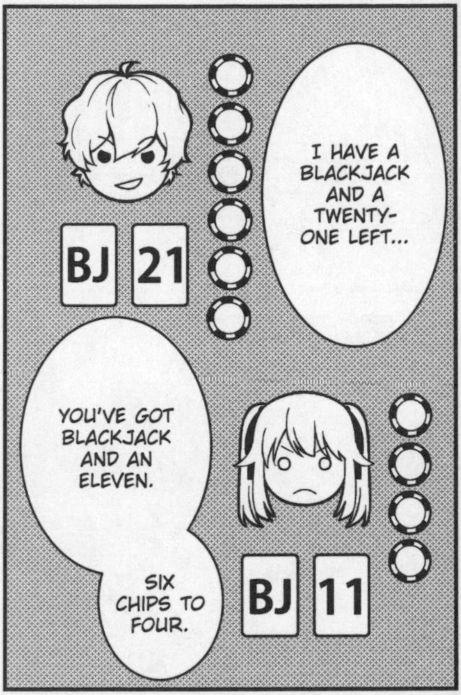
I HAVE A BLACKJACK AND A TWENTY-ONE LEFT...
BJ 21
YOU'VE GOT BLACKJACK AND AN ELEVEN.
SIX CHIPS TO FOUR.
BJ 11

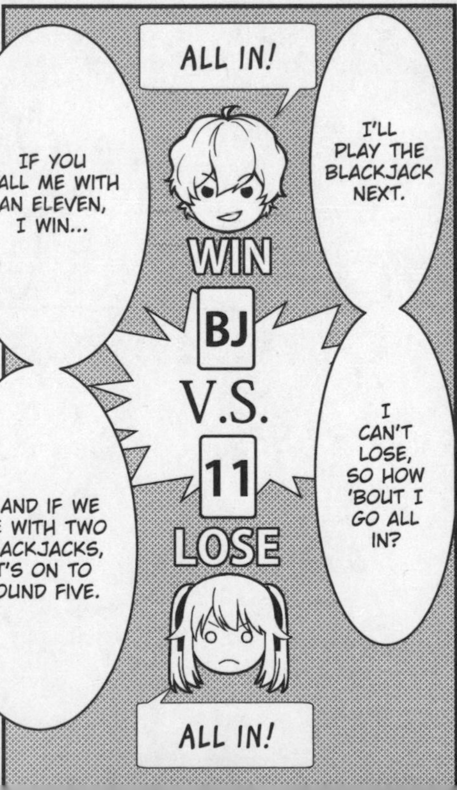
I'LL PLAY THE BLACKJACK NEXT.
ALL IN!
IF YOU CALL ME WITH AN ELEVEN, I WIN...
WIN
BJ
V.S.
11
LOSE
I CAN'T LOSE, SO HOW 'BOUT I GO ALL IN?
...AND IF WE TIE WITH TWO BLACKJACKS, IT'S ON TO ROUND FIVE.
ALL IN!

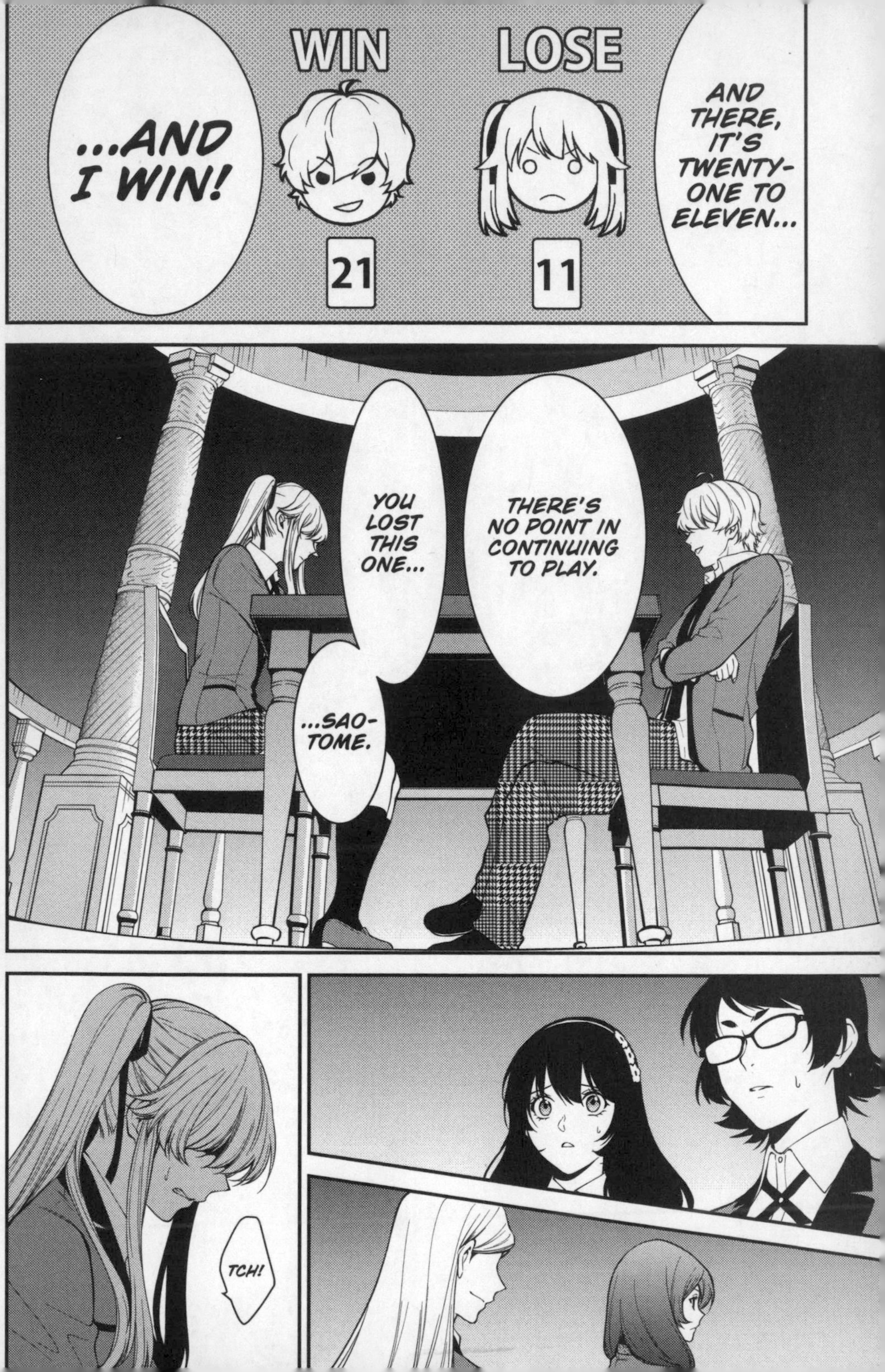
AND THERE, IT'S TWENTY-ONE TO ELEVEN...
LOSE
11
WIN
21
...AND I WIN!
THERE'S NO POINT IN CONTINUING TO PLAY.
YOU LOST THIS ONE...
...SAOTOME.
TCH!

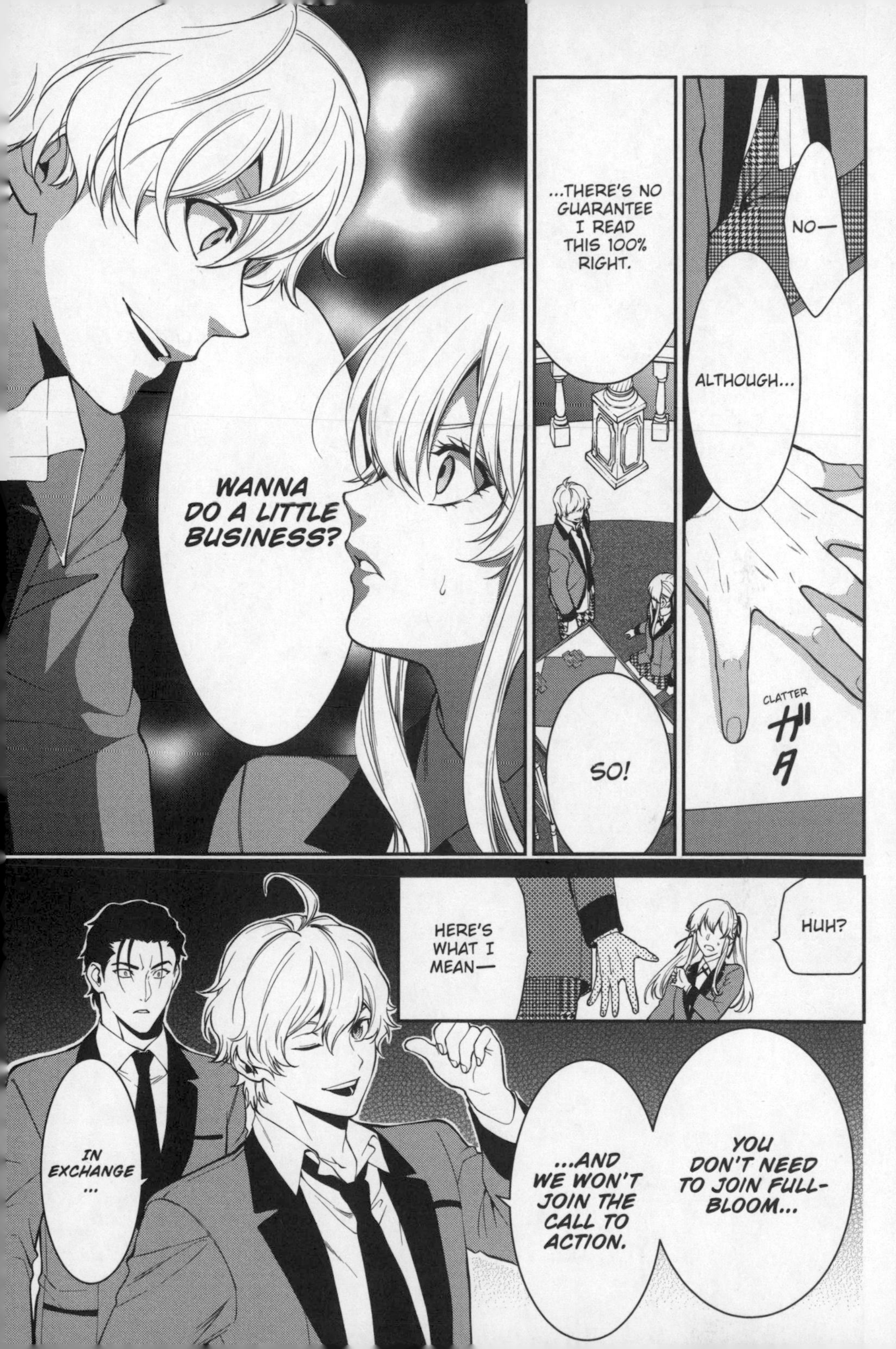
NO—
ALTHOUGH...
CLATTER
ガタ
...THERE'S NO GUARANTEE I READ THIS 100% RIGHT.
SO!
WANNA DO A LITTLE BUSINESS?
HUH?
HERE'S WHAT I MEAN—
YOU DON'T NEED TO JOIN FULL-BLOOM...
...AND WE WON'T JOIN THE CALL TO ACTION.
IN EXCHANGE ...

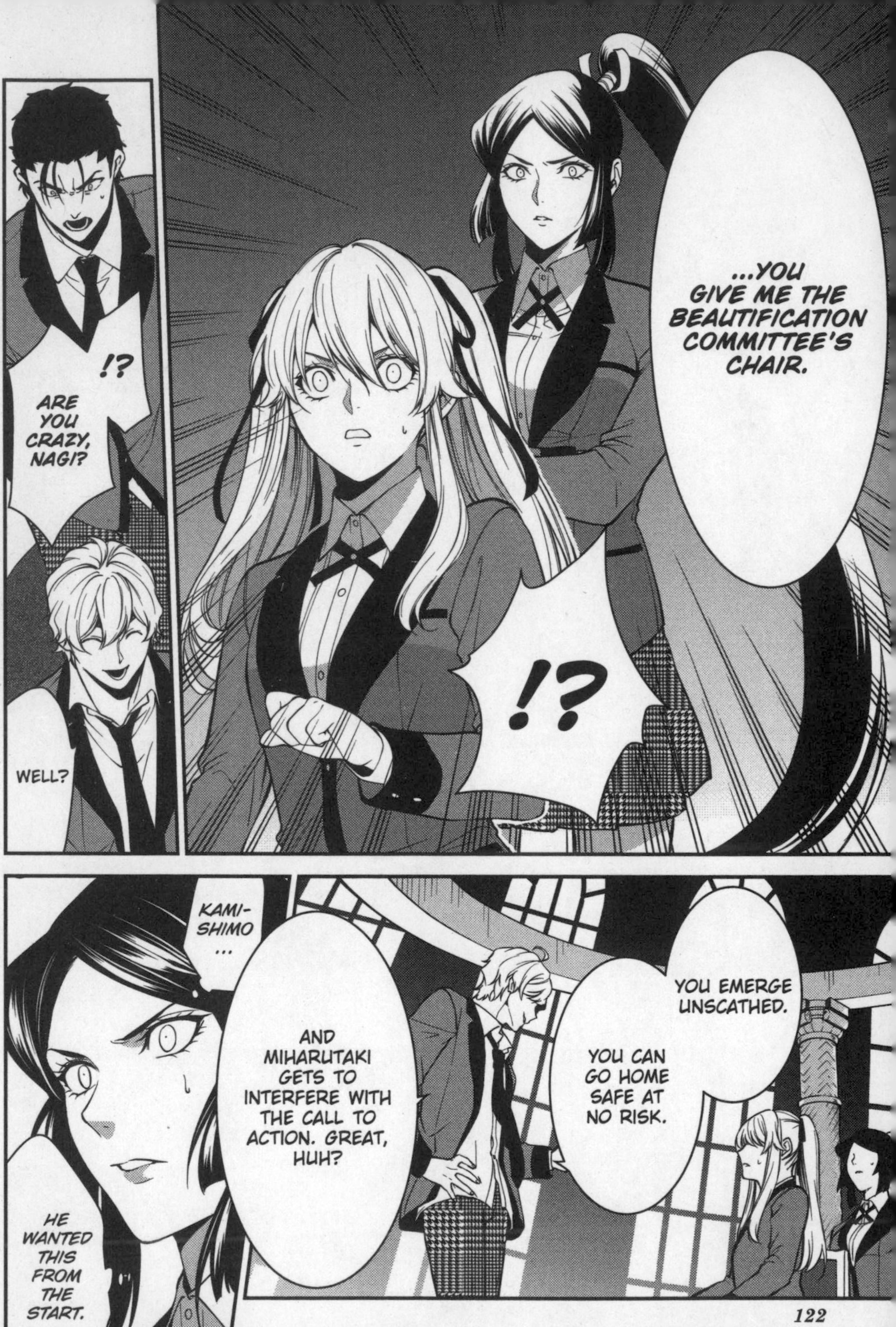
...YOU GIVE ME THE BEAUTIFICATION COMMITTEE'S CHAIR.
!?
!?
ARE YOU CRAZY, NAGI?
WELL?
YOU EMERGE UNSCATHED.
YOU CAN GO HOME SAFE AT NO RISK.
AND MIHARUTAKI GETS TO INTERFERE WITH THE CALL TO ACTION. GREAT, HUH?
KAMI-SHIMO ...
HE WANTED THIS FROM THE START.

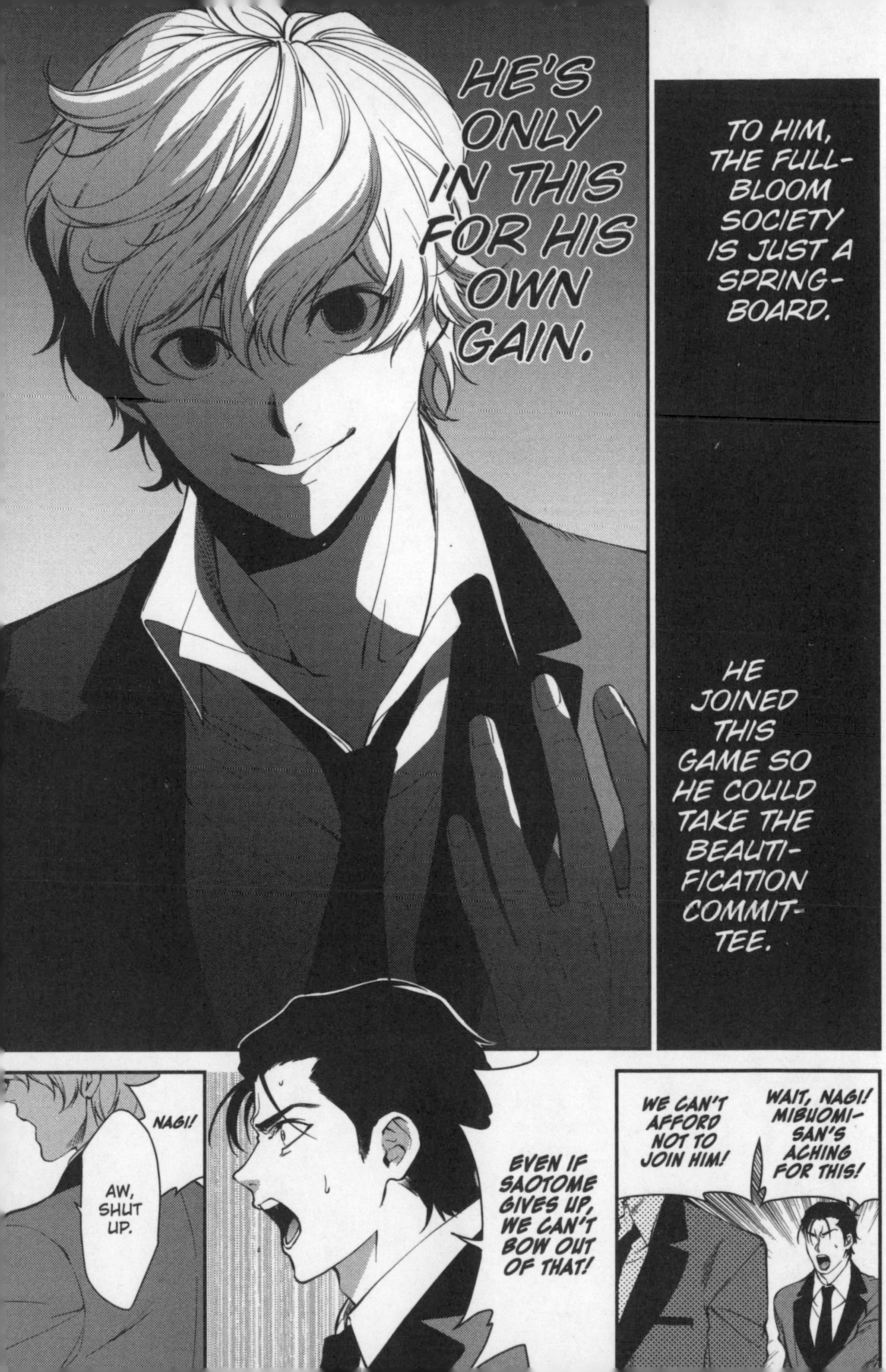
TO HIM, THE FULL-BLOOM SOCIETY IS JUST A SPRING-BOARD.
HE JOINED THIS GAME SO HE COULD TAKE THE BEAUTI-FICATION COMMIT-TEE.
HE'S ONLY IN THIS FOR HIS OWN GAIN.
WAIT, NAGI! MIBUOMI-SAN'S ACHING FOR THIS!
WE CAN'T AFFORD NOT TO JOIN HIM!
EVEN IF SAOTOME GIVES UP, WE CAN'T BOW OUT OF THAT!
NAGI!
AW, SHUT UP.

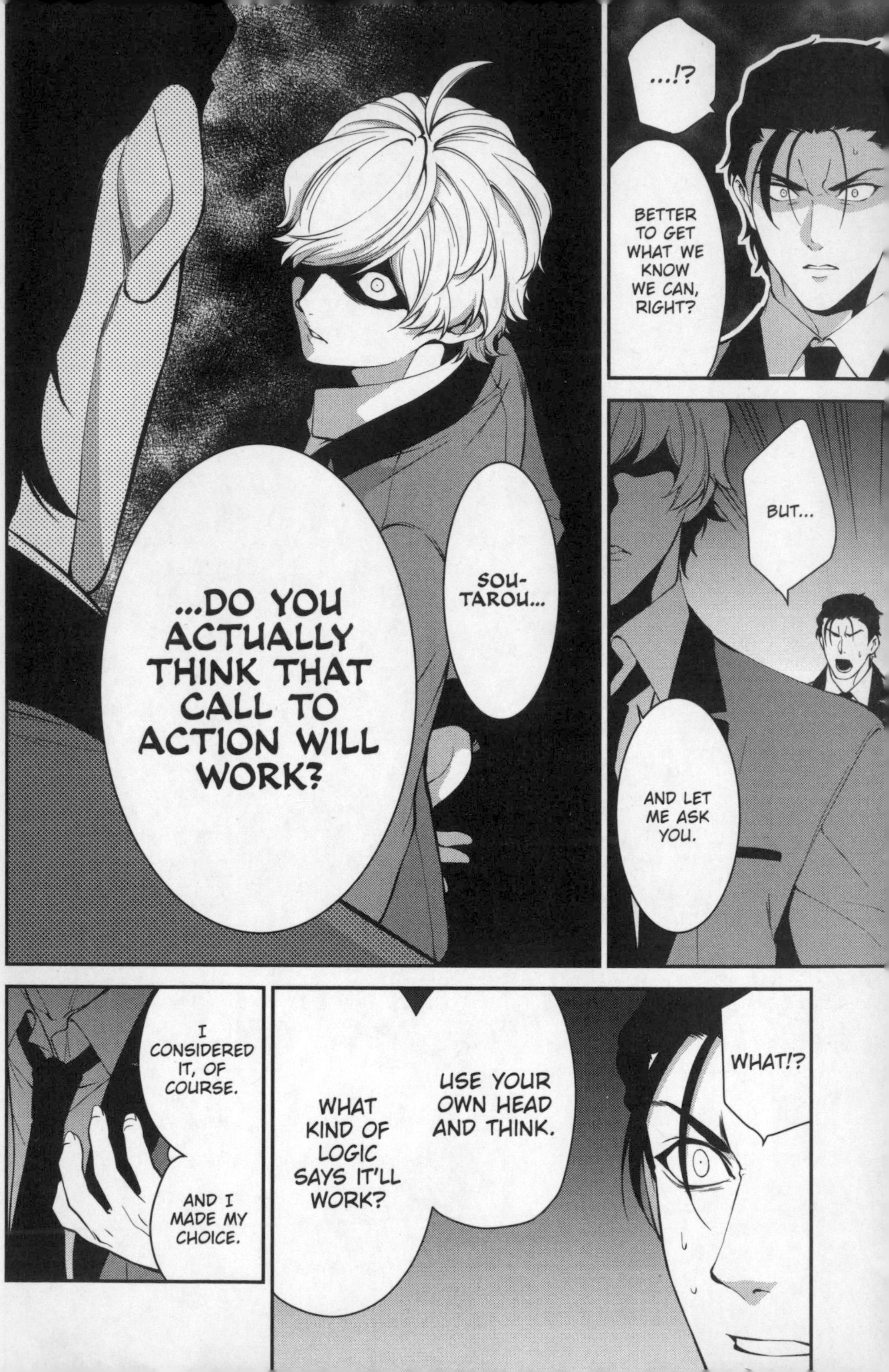
...!?
BETTER TO GET WHAT WE KNOW WE CAN, RIGHT?
BUT...
AND LET ME ASK YOU.
SOU-TAROU...
...DO YOU ACTUALLY THINK THAT CALL TO ACTION WILL WORK?
WHAT!?
USE YOUR OWN HEAD AND THINK.
WHAT KIND OF LOGIC SAYS IT'LL WORK?
I CONSIDERED IT, OF COURSE.
AND I MADE MY CHOICE.

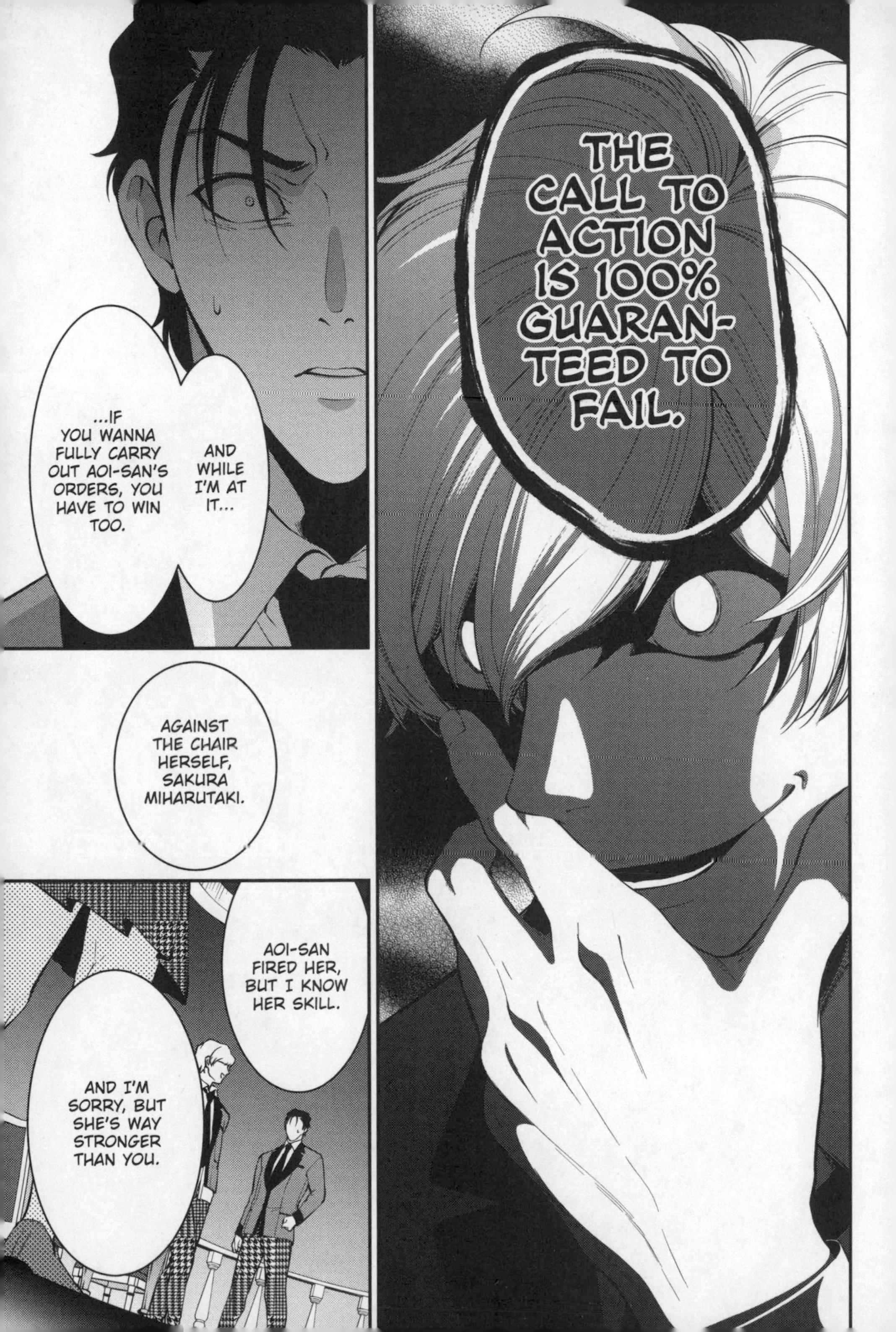
THE CALL TO ACTION IS 100% GUARAN-TEED TO FAIL.
AND WHILE I'M AT IT...
...IF YOU WANNA FULLY CARRY OUT AOI-SAN'S ORDERS, YOU HAVE TO WIN TOO.
AGAINST THE CHAIR HERSELF, SAKURA MIHARUTAKI.
AOI-SAN FIRED HER, BUT I KNOW HER SKILL.
AND I'M SORRY, BUT SHE'S WAY STRONGER THAN YOU.

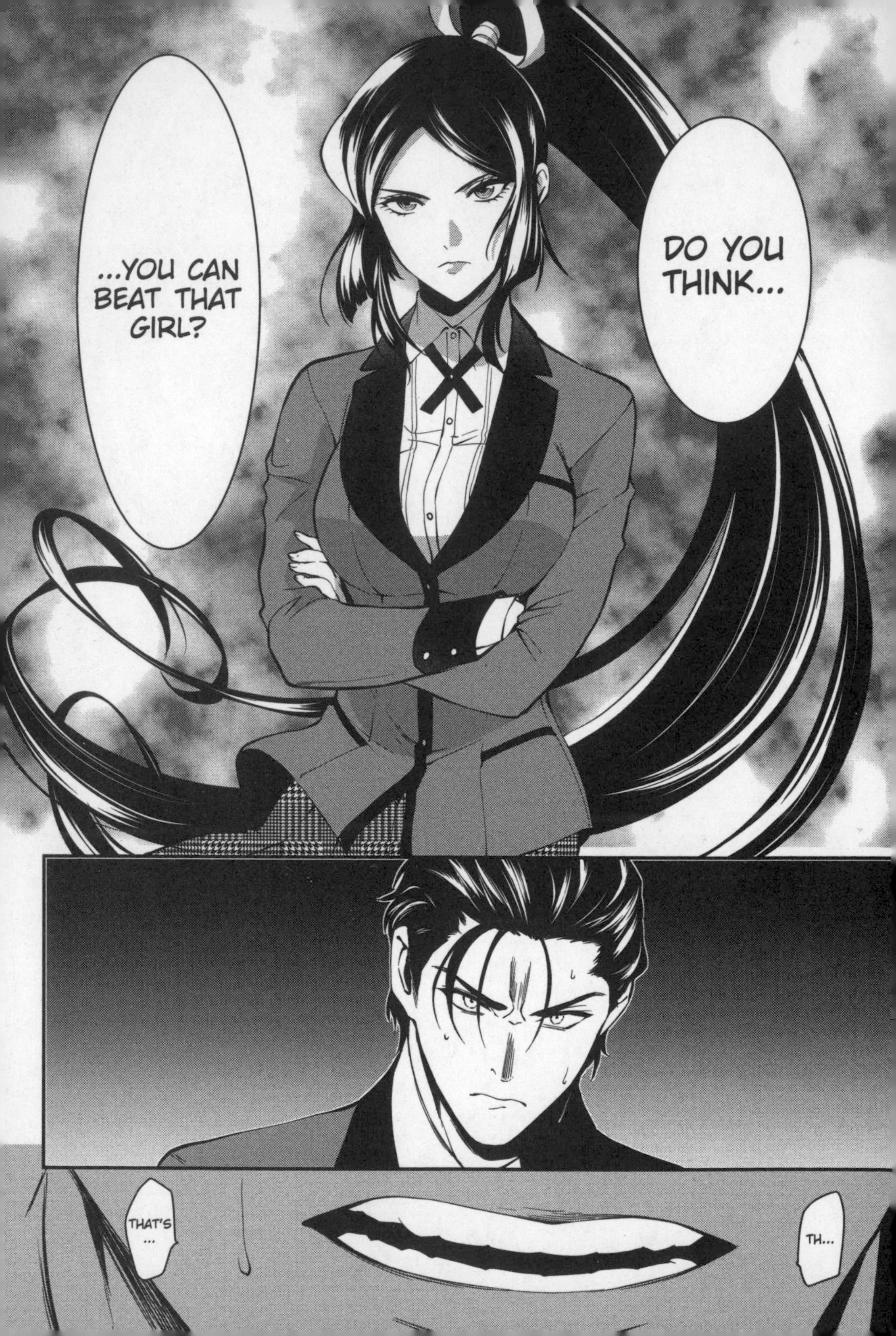
DO YOU THINK...
...YOU CAN BEAT THAT GIRL?
TH...
THAT'S ...

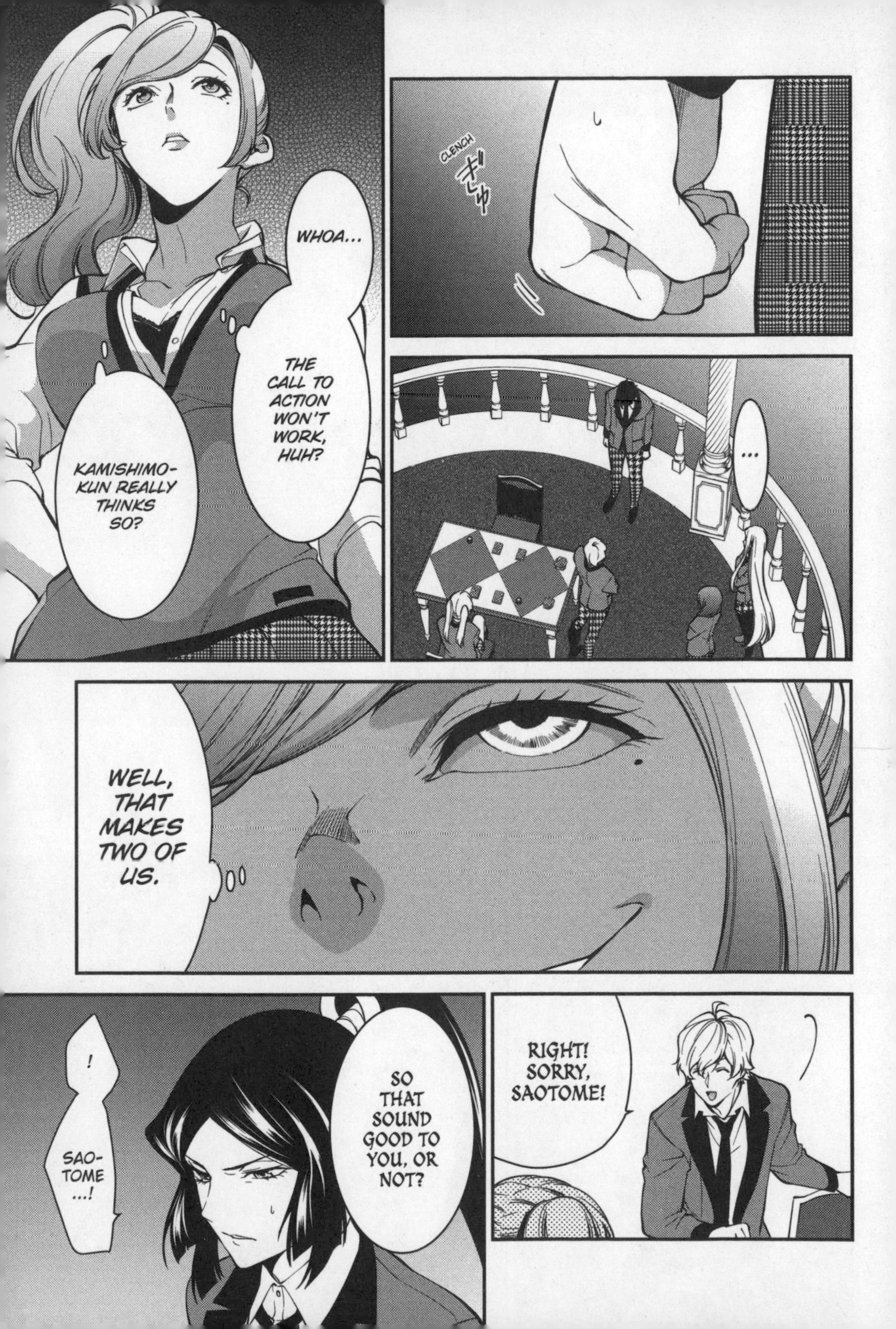
CLENCH
...
WHOA...
THE CALL TO ACTION WON'T WORK, HUH?
KAMISHIMO-KUN REALLY THINKS SO?
WELL, THAT MAKES TWO OF US.
RIGHT! SORRY, SAOTOME!
SO THAT SOUND GOOD TO YOU, OR NOT?
!
SAO-TOME ...!

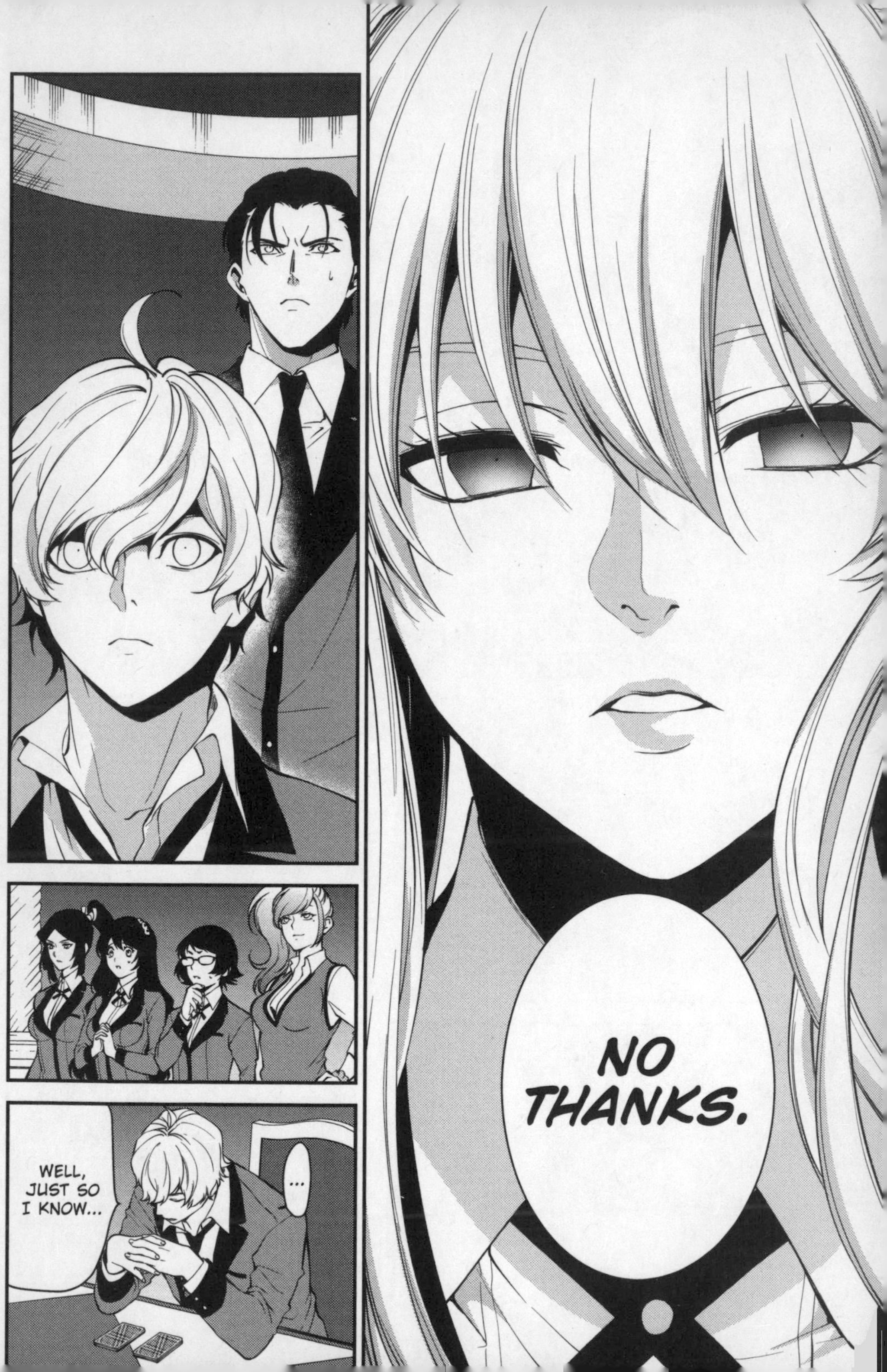
NO THANKS.
...
WELL, JUST SO I KNOW...

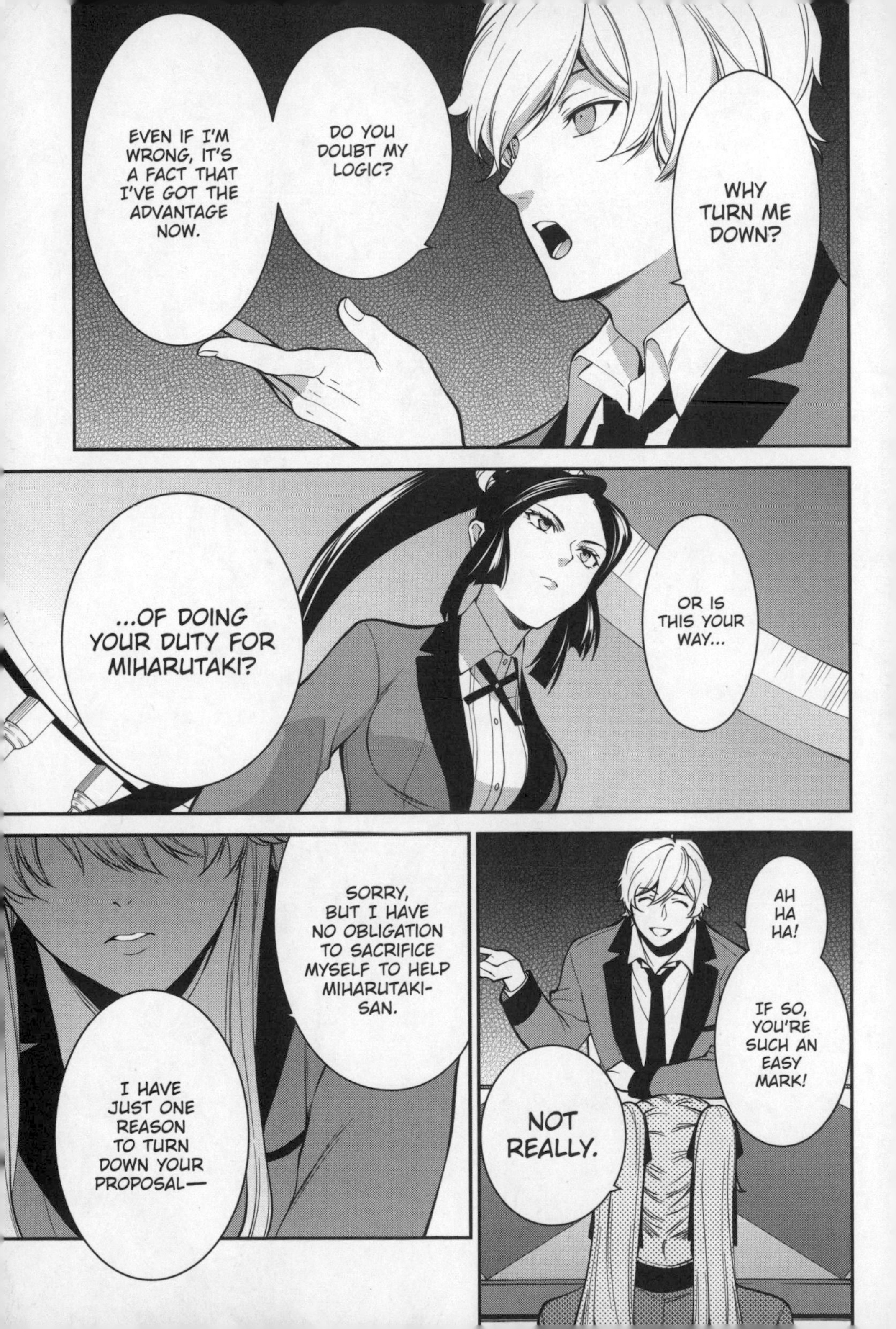
WHY TURN ME DOWN?
DO YOU DOUBT MY LOGIC?
EVEN IF I'M WRONG, IT'S A FACT THAT I'VE GOT THE ADVANTAGE NOW.
OR IS THIS YOUR WAY...
...OF DOING YOUR DUTY FOR MIHARUTAKI?
AH HA HA!
IF SO, YOU'RE SUCH AN EASY MARK!
NOT REALLY.
SORRY, BUT I HAVE NO OBLIGATION TO SACRIFICE MYSELF TO HELP MIHARUTAKI-SAN.
I HAVE JUST ONE REASON TO TURN DOWN YOUR PROPOSAL—

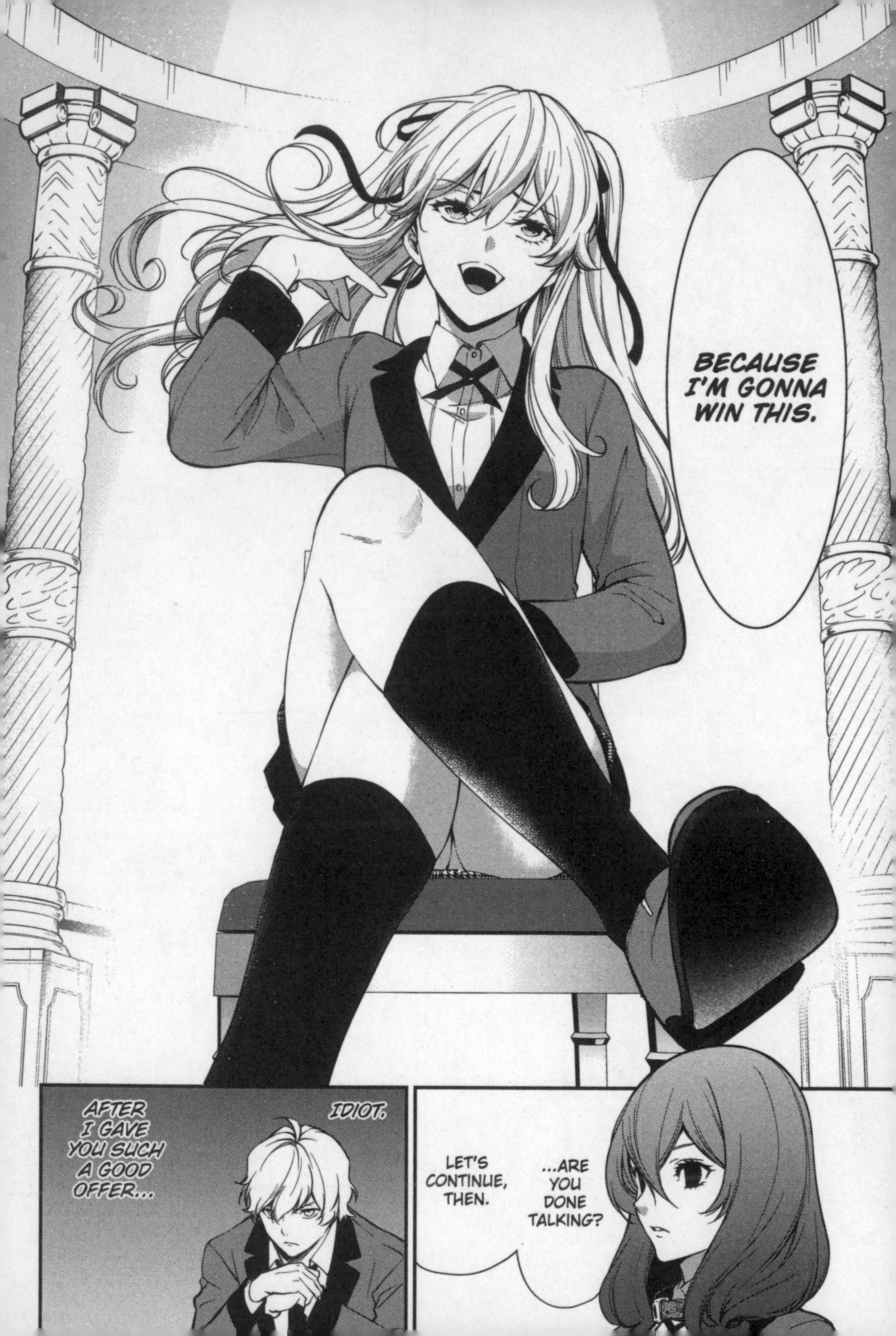
BECAUSE I'M GONNA WIN THIS.
...ARE YOU DONE TALKING?
LET'S CONTINUE, THEN.
IDIOT.
AFTER I GAVE YOU SUCH A GOOD OFFER...

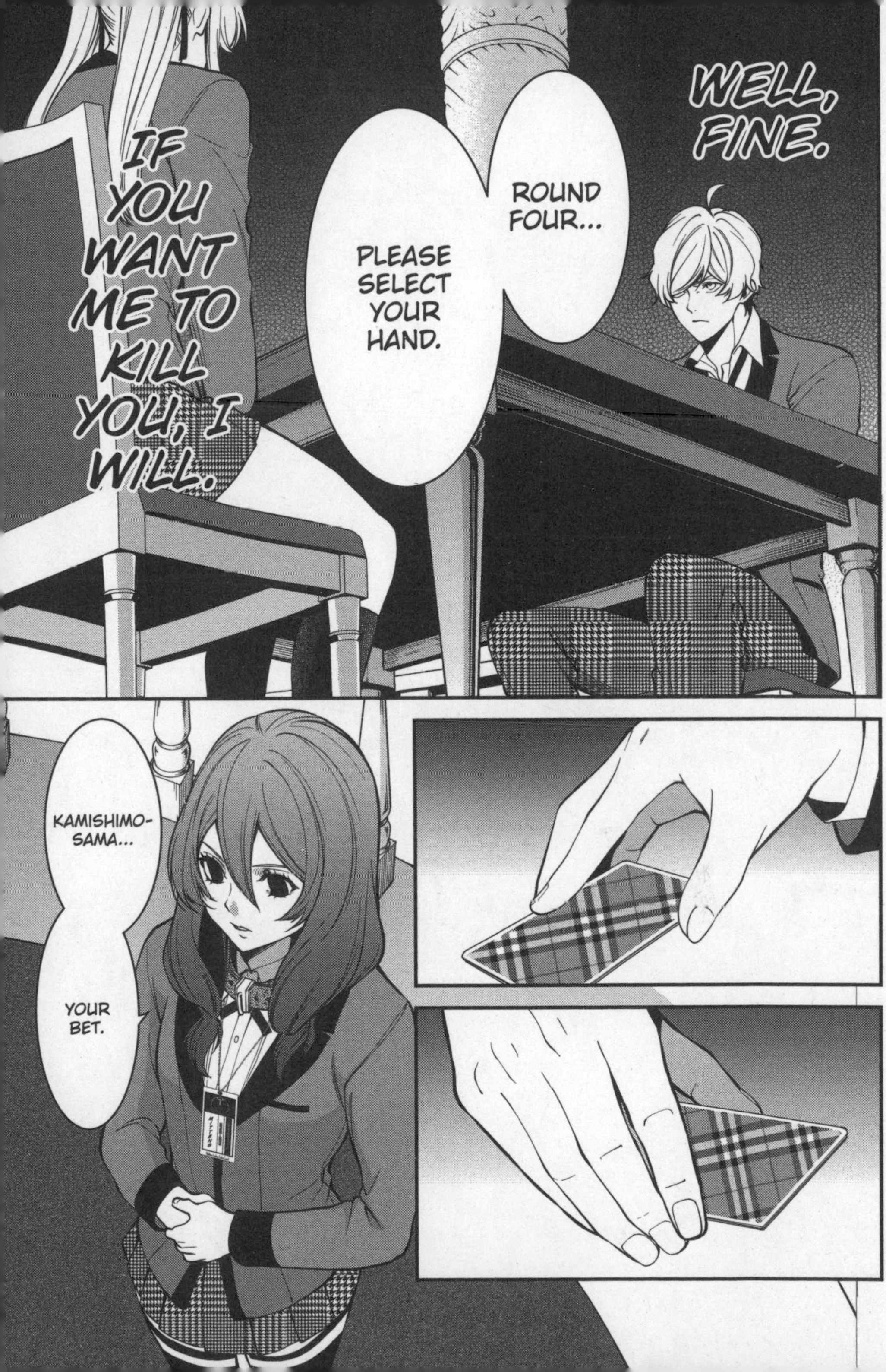
WELL, FINE.
ROUND FOUR...
PLEASE SELECT YOUR HAND.
IF YOU WANT ME TO KILL YOU, I WILL.
KAMISHIMO-SAMA...
YOUR BET.

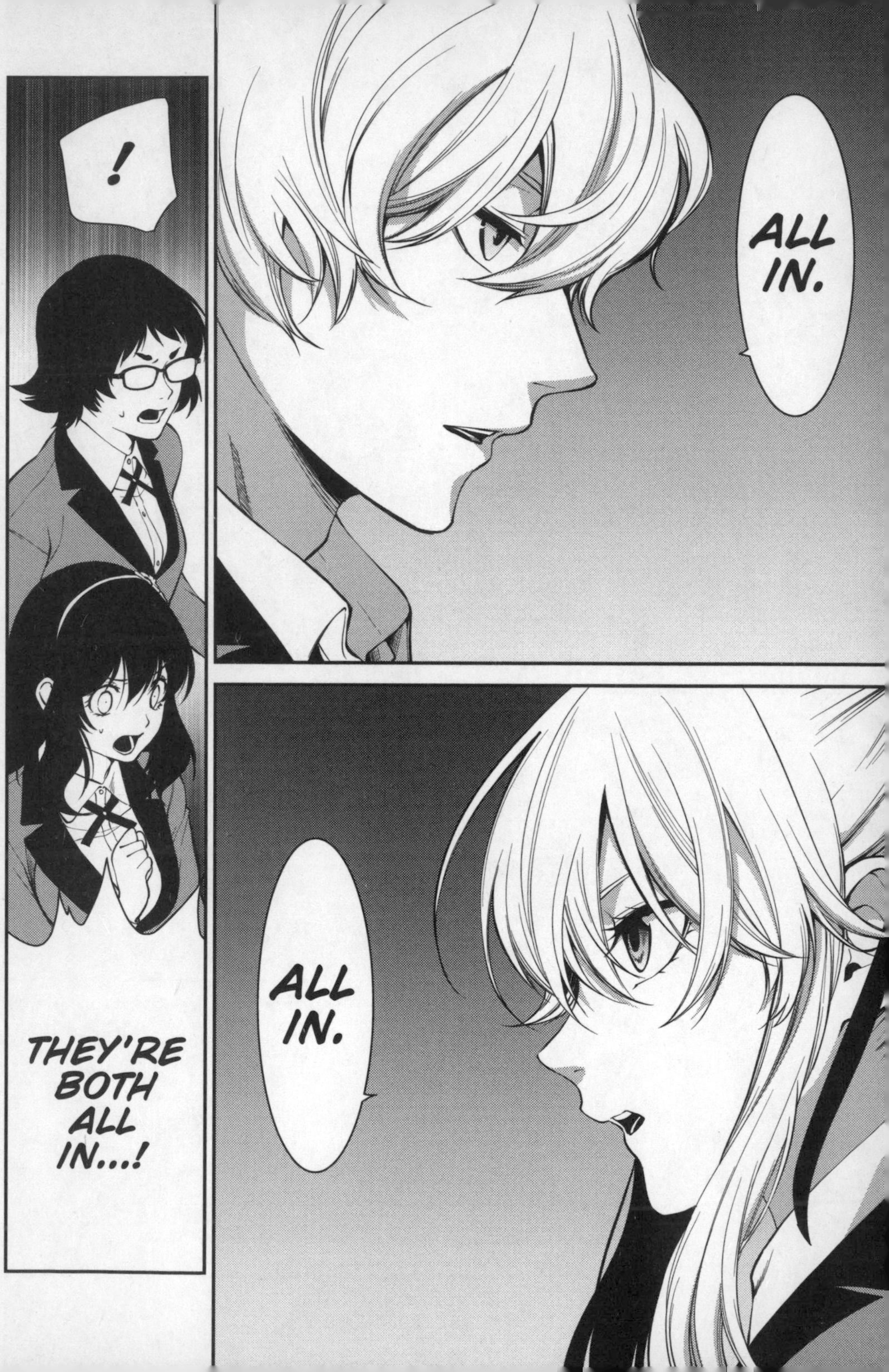
ALL IN.
ALL IN.
!
THEY'RE BOTH ALL IN...!

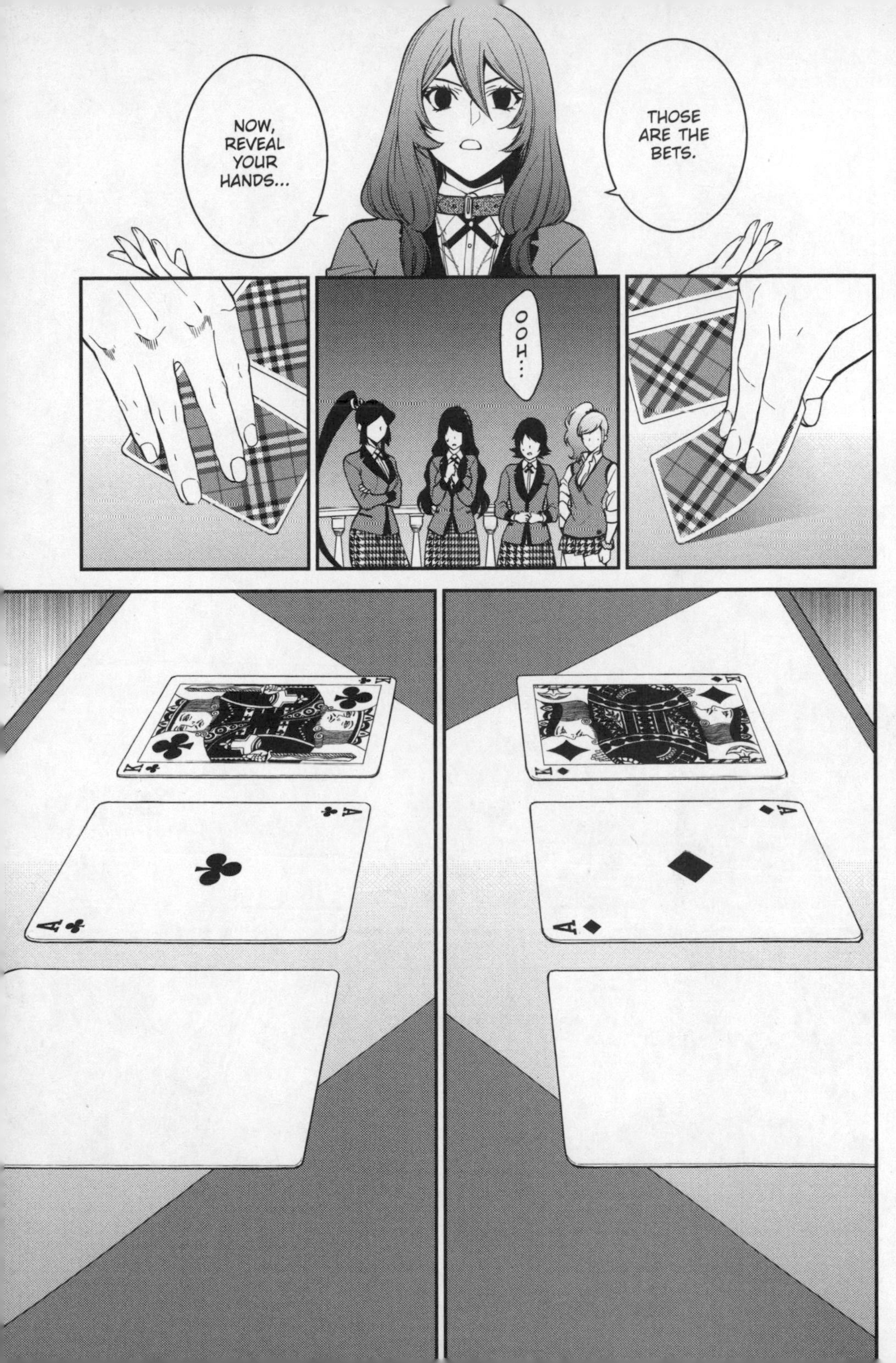
THOSE ARE THE BETS.
NOW, REVEAL YOUR HANDS...
OOH...

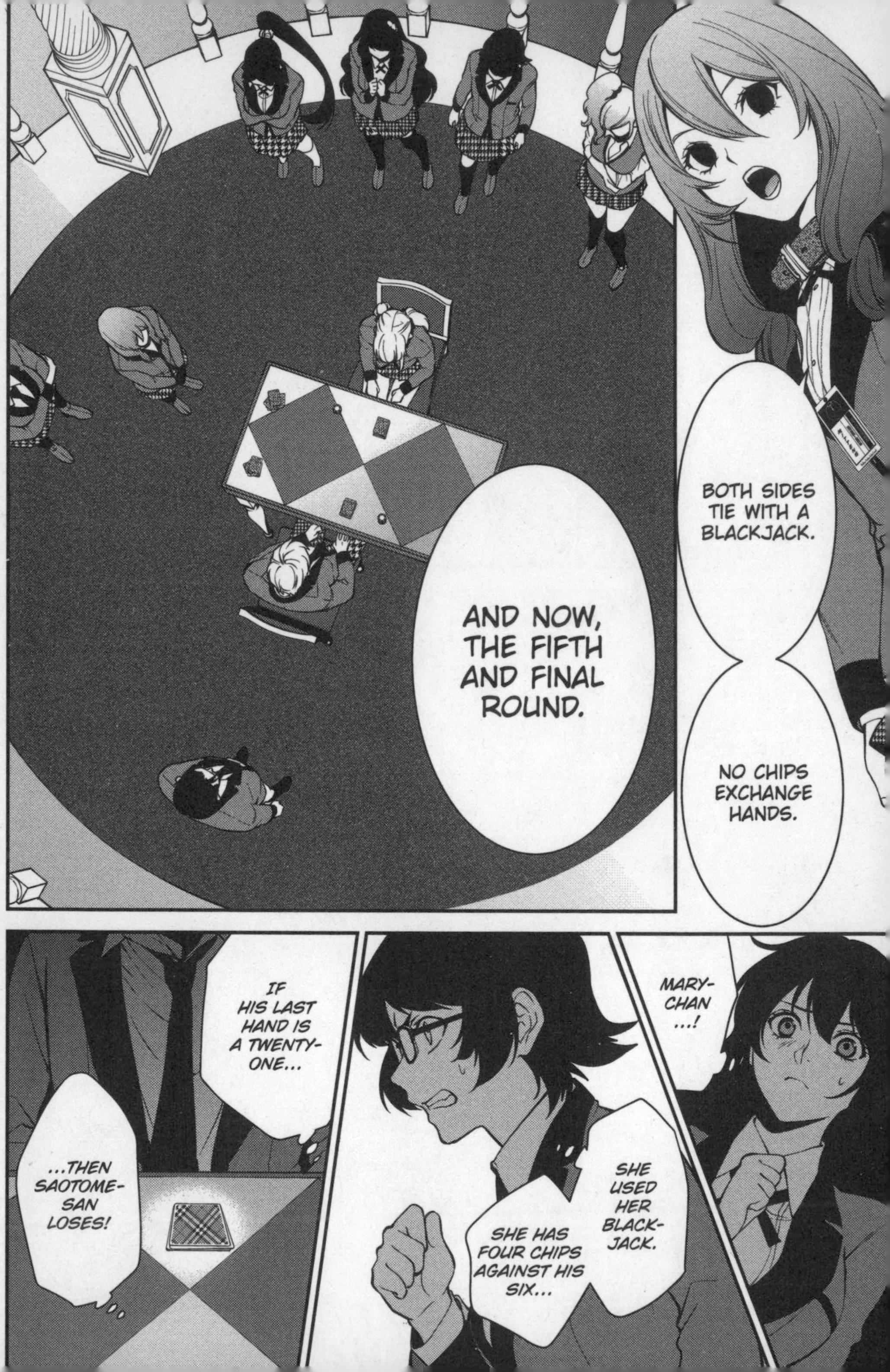
BOTH SIDES TIE WITH A BLACKJACK.
NO CHIPS EXCHANGE HANDS.
AND NOW, THE FIFTH AND FINAL ROUND.
MARY-CHAN ...!
SHE USED HER BLACK-JACK.
SHE HAS FOUR CHIPS AGAINST HIS SIX...
IF HIS LAST HAND IS A TWENTY-ONE...
...THEN SAOTOME-SAN LOSES!

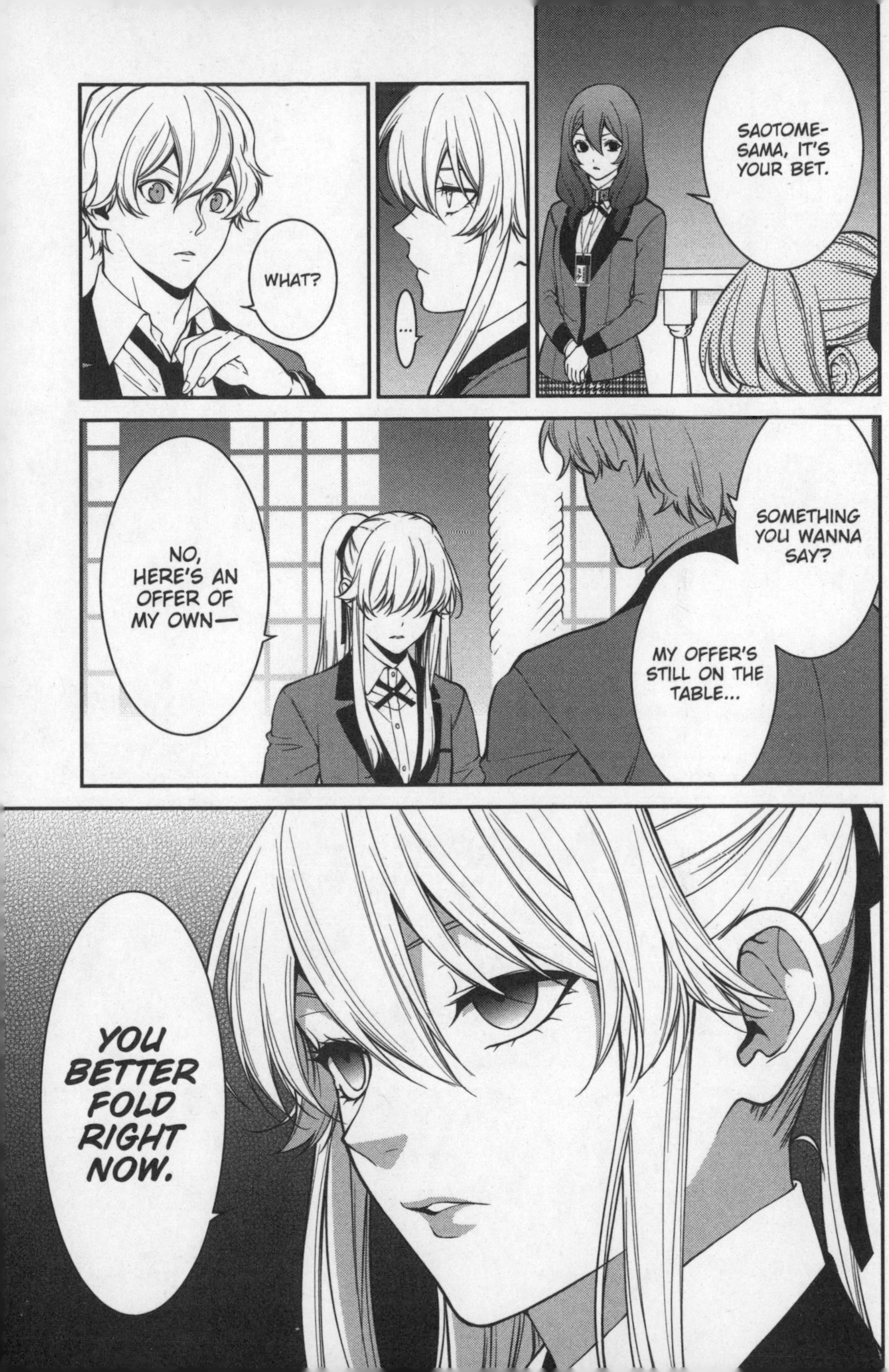
SAOTOME-SAMA, IT'S YOUR BET.
...
WHAT?
SOMETHING YOU WANNA SAY?
MY OFFER'S STILL ON THE TABLE...
NO, HERE'S AN OFFER OF MY OWN—
YOU BETTER FOLD RIGHT NOW.

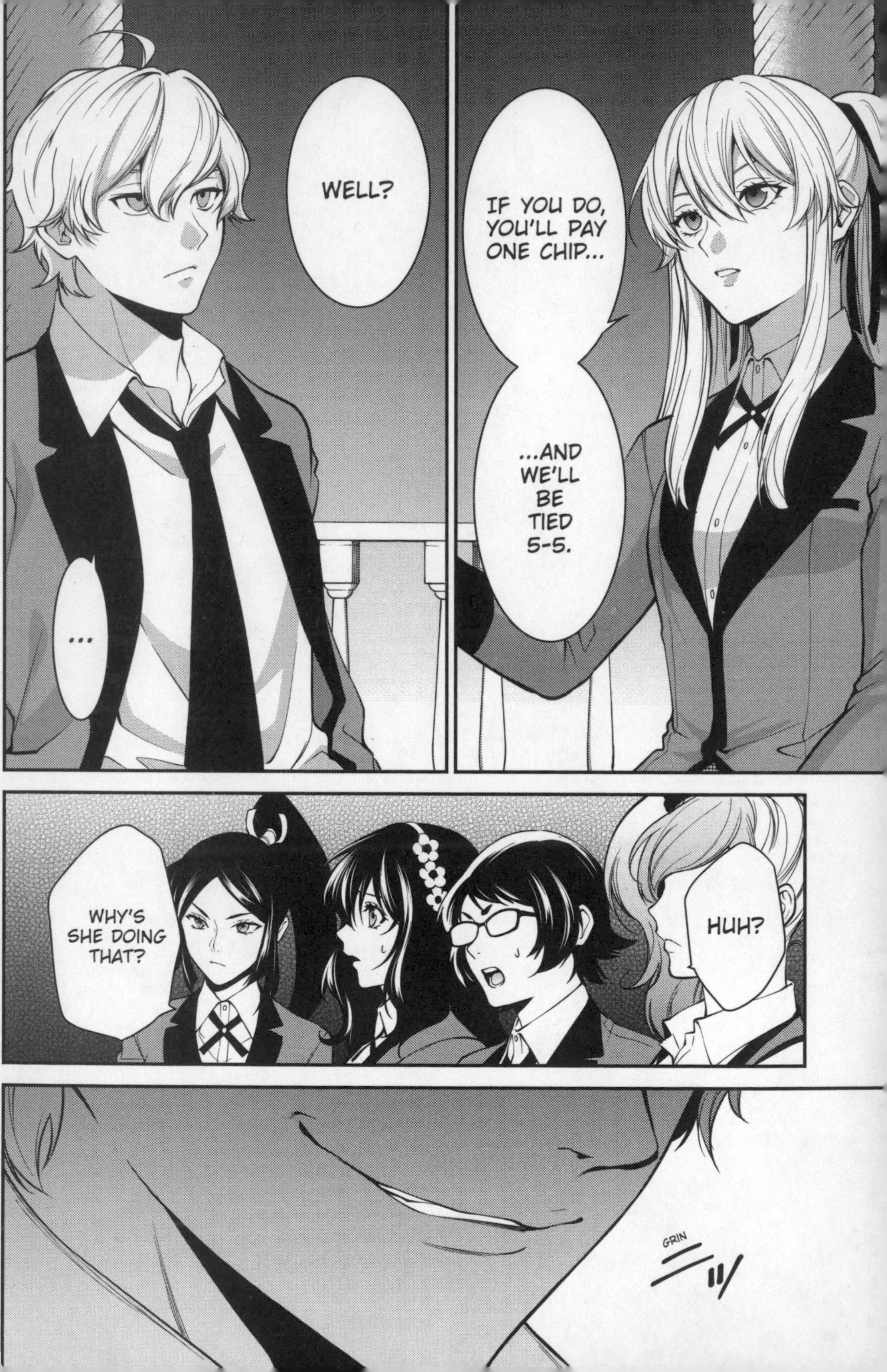
IF YOU DO, YOU'LL PAY ONE CHIP...
...AND WE'LL BE TIED 5-5.
WELL?
...
HUH?
WHY'S SHE DOING THAT?
GRIN

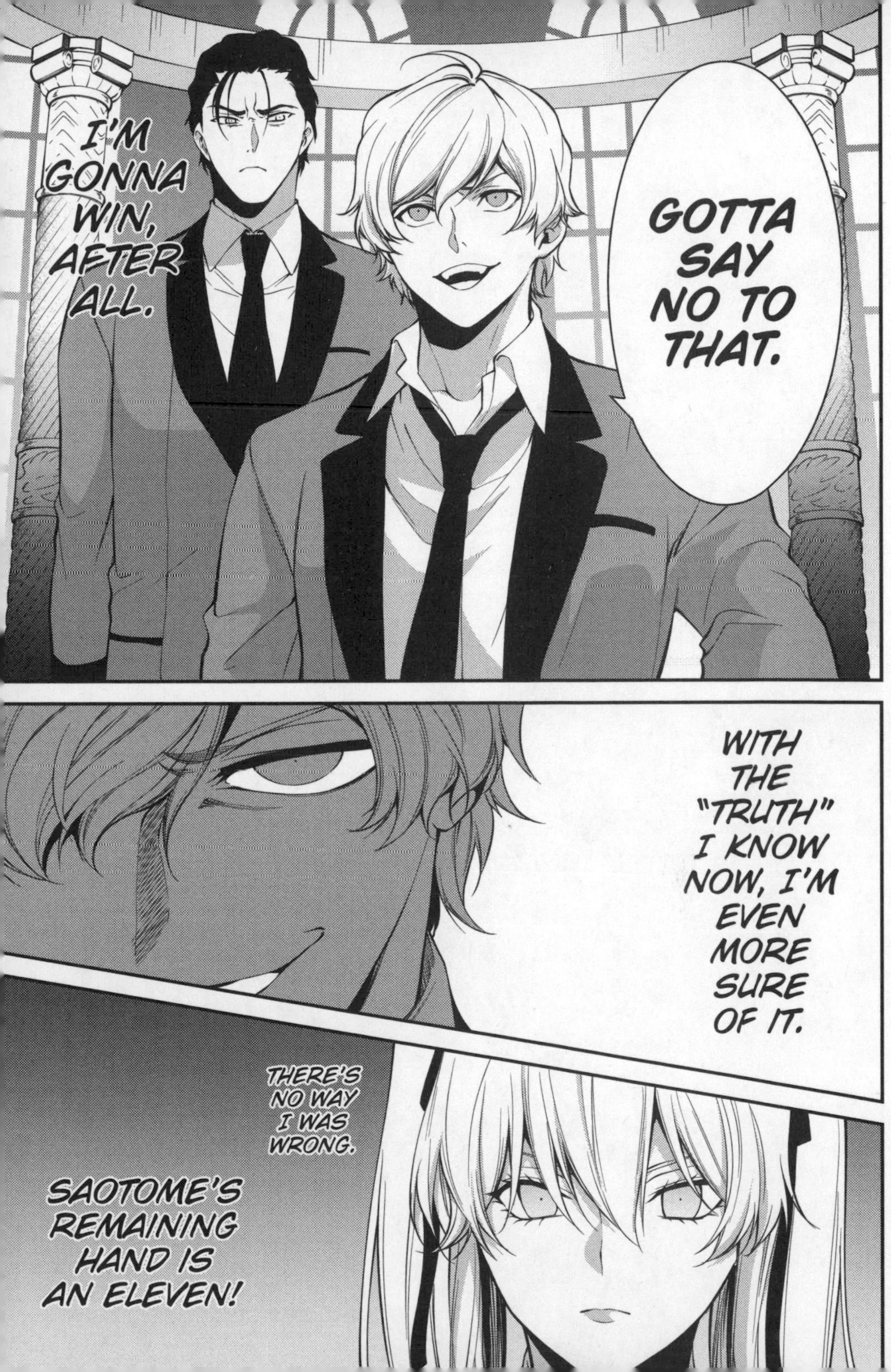
GOTTA SAY NO TO THAT.
I'M GONNA WIN, AFTER ALL.
WITH THE "TRUTH" I KNOW NOW, I'M EVEN MORE SURE OF IT.
THERE'S NO WAY I WAS WRONG.
SAOTOME'S REMAINING HAND IS AN ELEVEN!

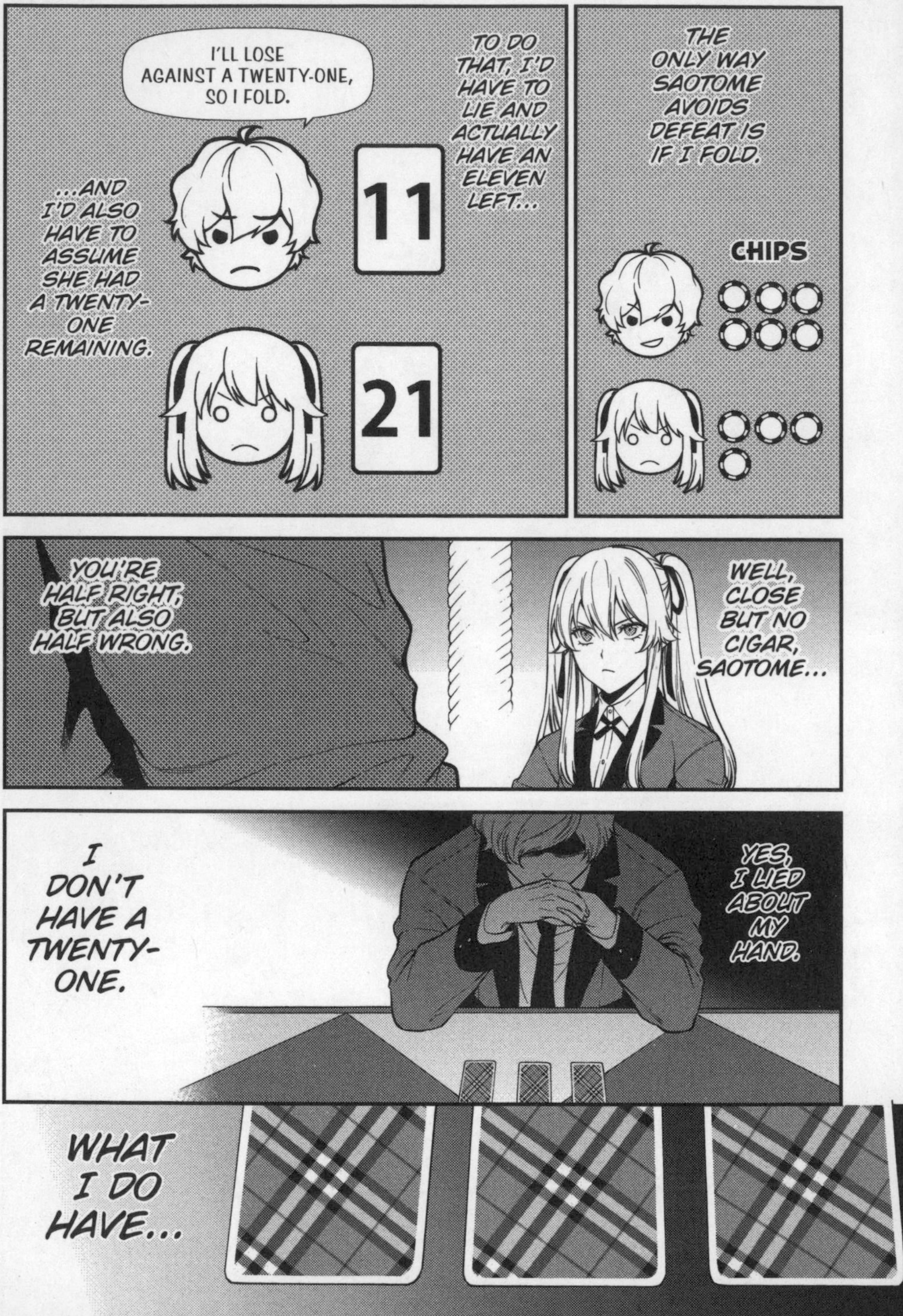
THE ONLY WAY SAOTOME AVOIDS DEFEAT IS IF I FOLD.
CHIPS
I'LL LOSE AGAINST A TWENTY-ONE, SO I FOLD.
TO DO THAT, I'D HAVE TO LIE AND ACTUALLY HAVE AN ELEVEN LEFT...
11
...AND I'D ALSO HAVE TO ASSUME SHE HAD A TWENTY-ONE REMAINING.
21
WELL, CLOSE BUT NO CIGAR, SAOTOME...
YOU'RE HALF RIGHT, BUT ALSO HALF WRONG.
YES, I LIED ABOUT MY HAND.
I DON'T HAVE A TWENTY-ONE.
WHAT I DO HAVE...

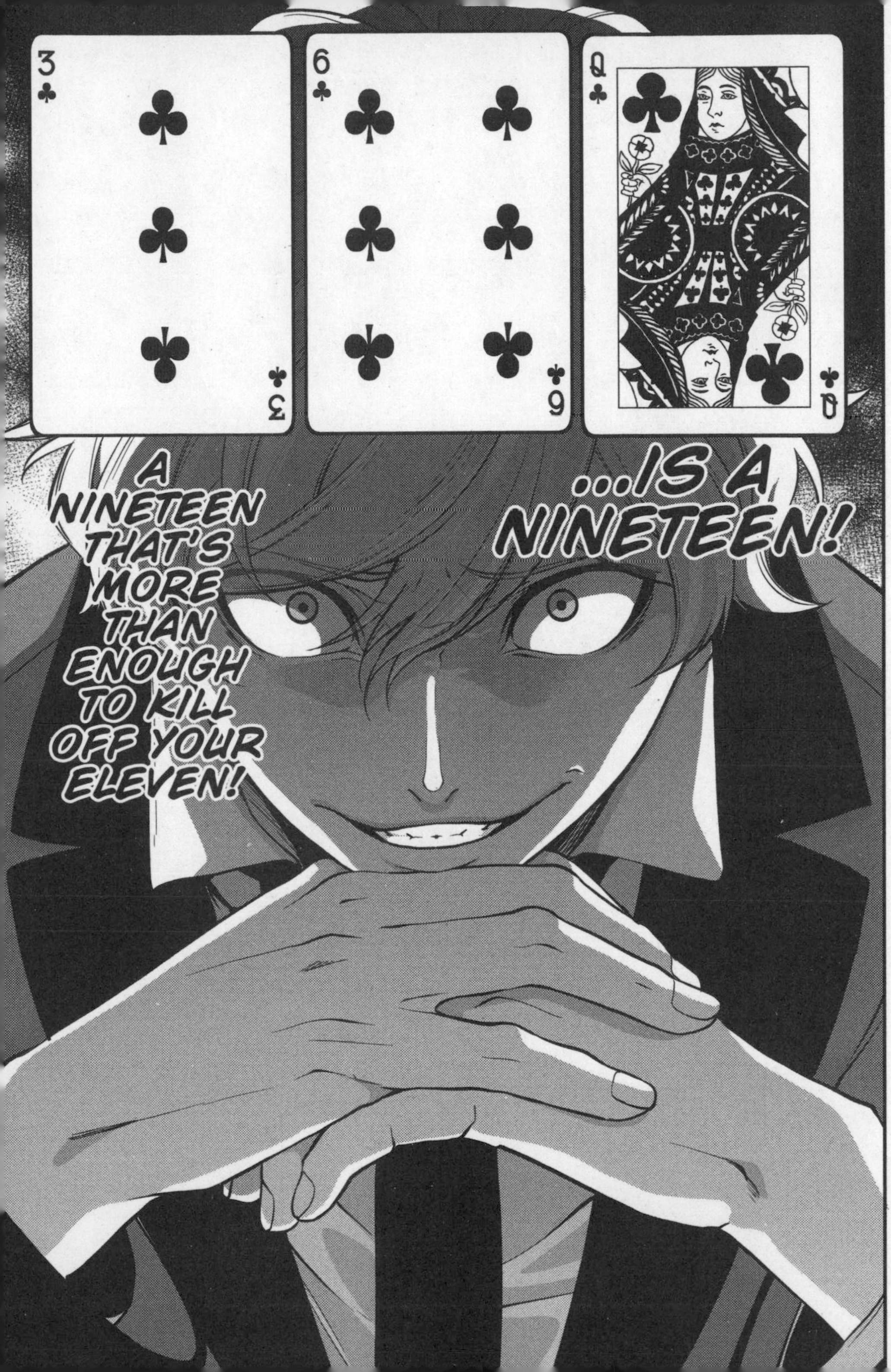
...IS A NINETEEN!
A NINETEEN THAT'S MORE THAN ENOUGH TO KILL OFF YOUR ELEVEN!

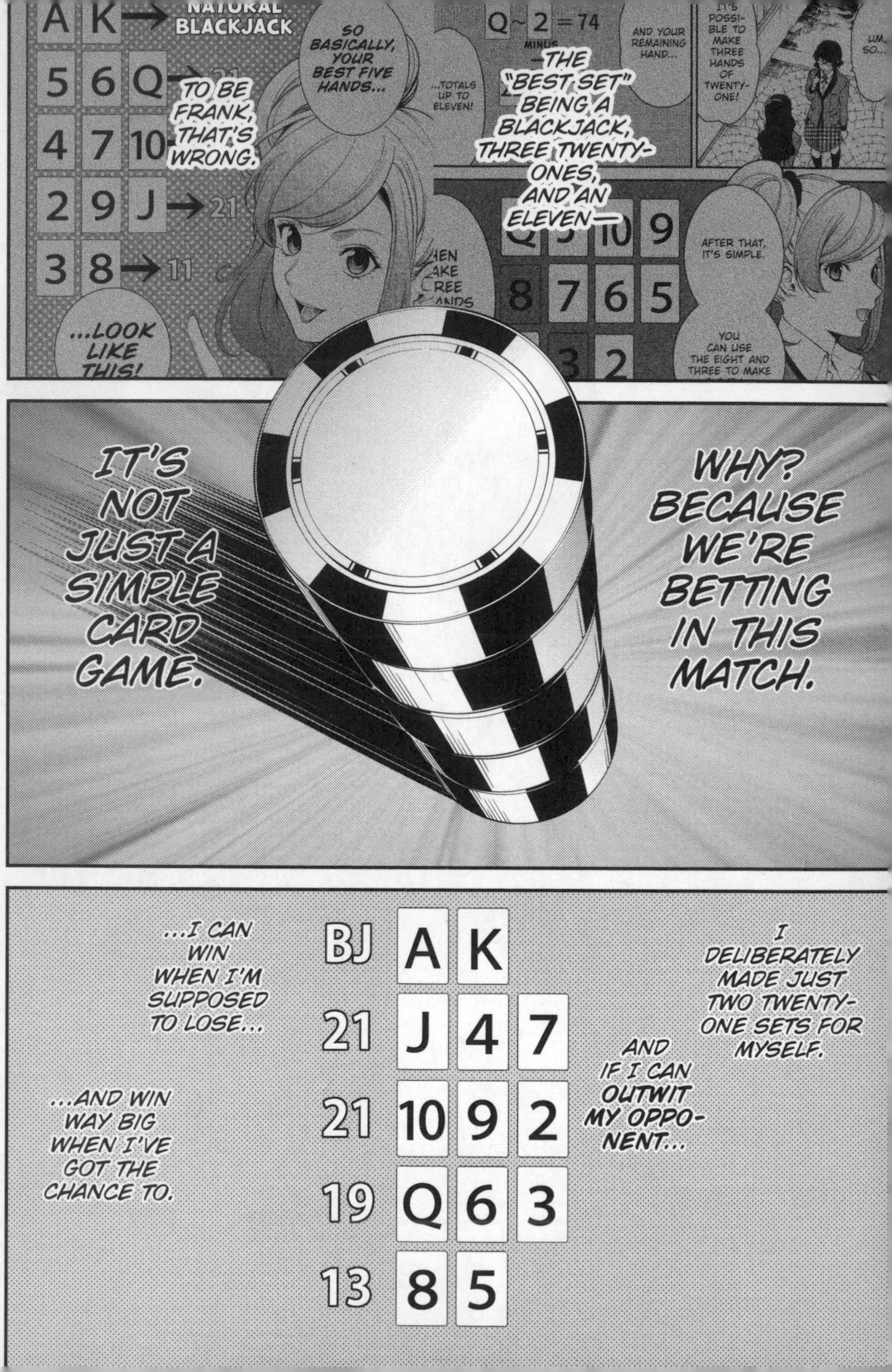
UM, SO...
IT'S POSSIBLE TO MAKE THREE HANDS OF TWENTY-ONE!
AND YOUR REMAINING HAND...
...TOTALS UP TO ELEVEN!
AFTER THAT, IT'S SIMPLE.
YOU CAN USE THE EIGHT AND THREE TO MAKE
Q~2 = 74
MINUS
Q 5 10 9
8 7 6 5
3 2
—THE "BEST SET" BEING A BLACKJACK, THREE TWENTY-ONES, AND AN ELEVEN—
SO BASICALLY, YOUR BEST FIVE HANDS...
...LOOK LIKE THIS!
A K → NATURAL BLACKJACK
5 6 Q → 21
4 7 10
2 9 J → 21
3 8 → 11
TO BE FRANK, THAT'S WRONG.
WHY? BECAUSE WE'RE BETTING IN THIS MATCH.
IT'S NOT JUST A SIMPLE CARD GAME.
I DELIBERATELY MADE JUST TWO TWENTY-ONE SETS FOR MYSELF.
AND IF I CAN OUTWIT MY OPPONENT...
...I CAN WIN WHEN I'M SUPPOSED TO LOSE...
...AND WIN WAY BIG WHEN I'VE GOT THE CHANCE TO.
BJ A K
21 J 4 7
21 10 9 2
19 Q 6 3
13 8 5

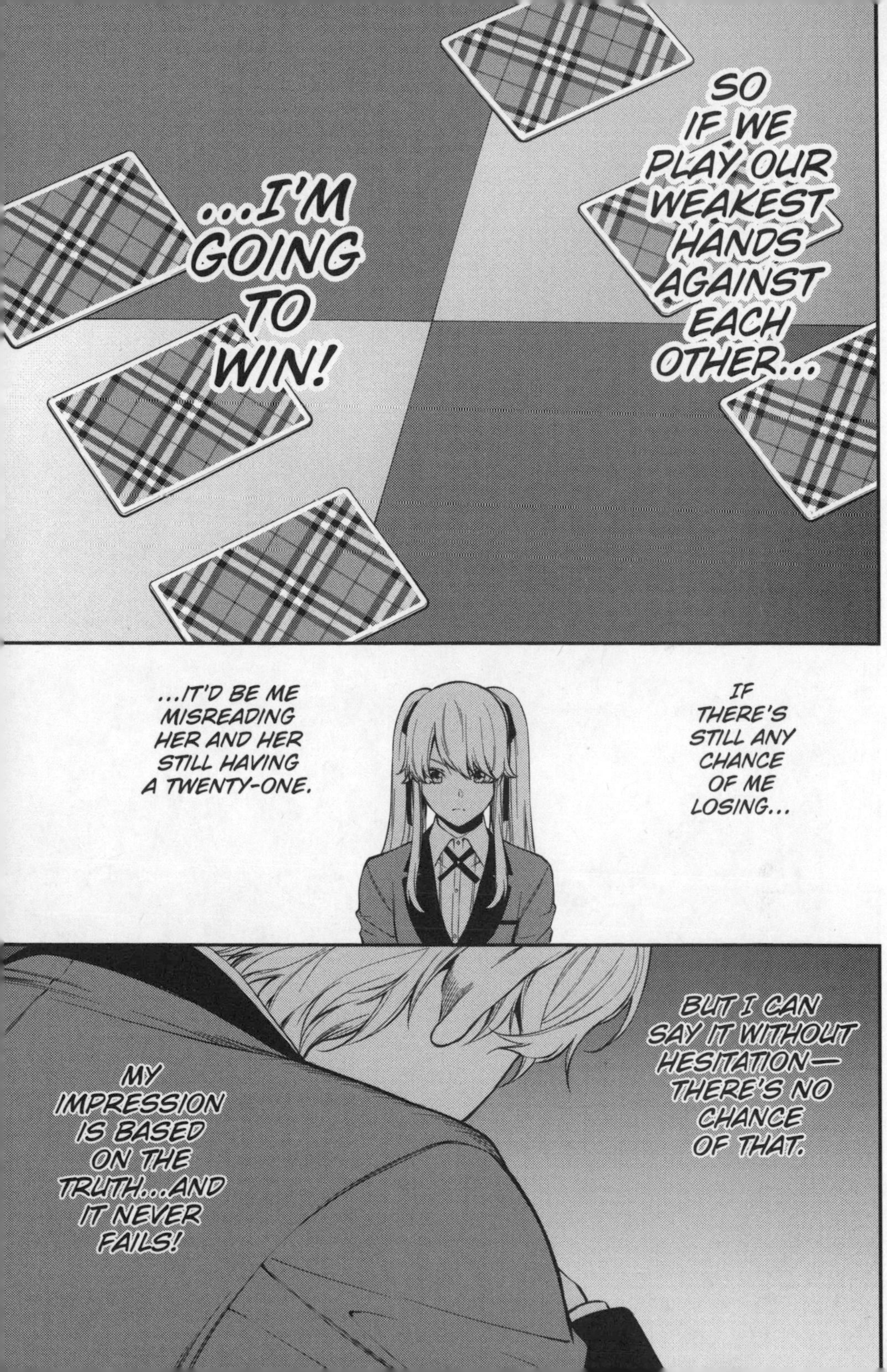
SO IF WE PLAY OUR WEAKEST HANDS AGAINST EACH OTHER...
...I'M GOING TO WIN!
IF THERE'S STILL ANY CHANCE OF ME LOSING...
...IT'D BE ME MISREADING HER AND HER STILL HAVING A TWENTY-ONE.
BUT I CAN SAY IT WITHOUT HESITATION—THERE'S NO CHANCE OF THAT.
MY IMPRESSION IS BASED ON THE TRUTH...AND IT NEVER FAILS!

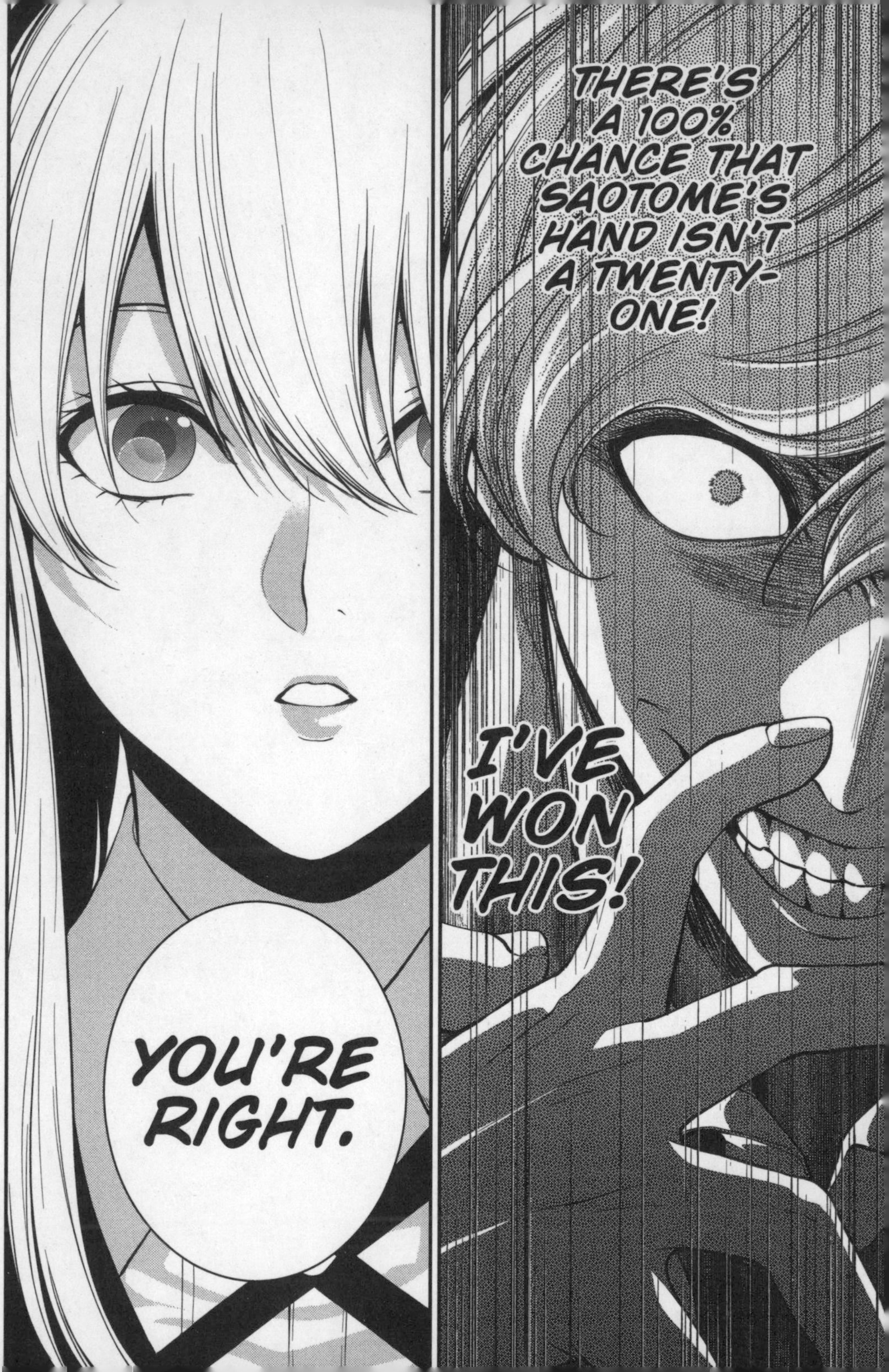
THERE'S A 100% CHANCE THAT SAOTOME'S HAND ISN'T A TWENTY-ONE!
I'VE WON THIS!
YOU'RE RIGHT.

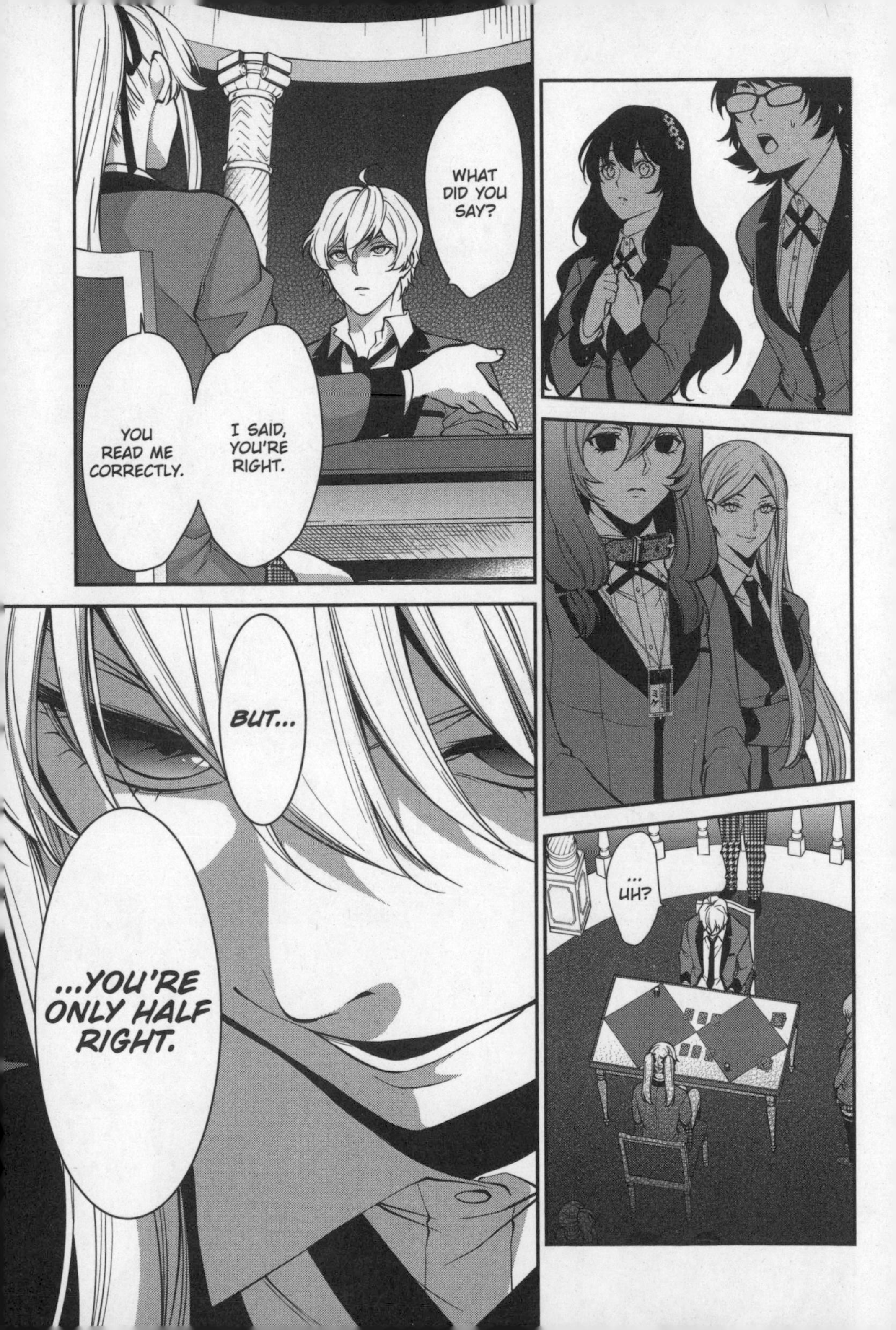
WHAT DID YOU SAY?
I SAID, YOU'RE RIGHT.
YOU READ ME CORRECTLY.
...UH?
BUT...
...YOU'RE ONLY HALF RIGHT.

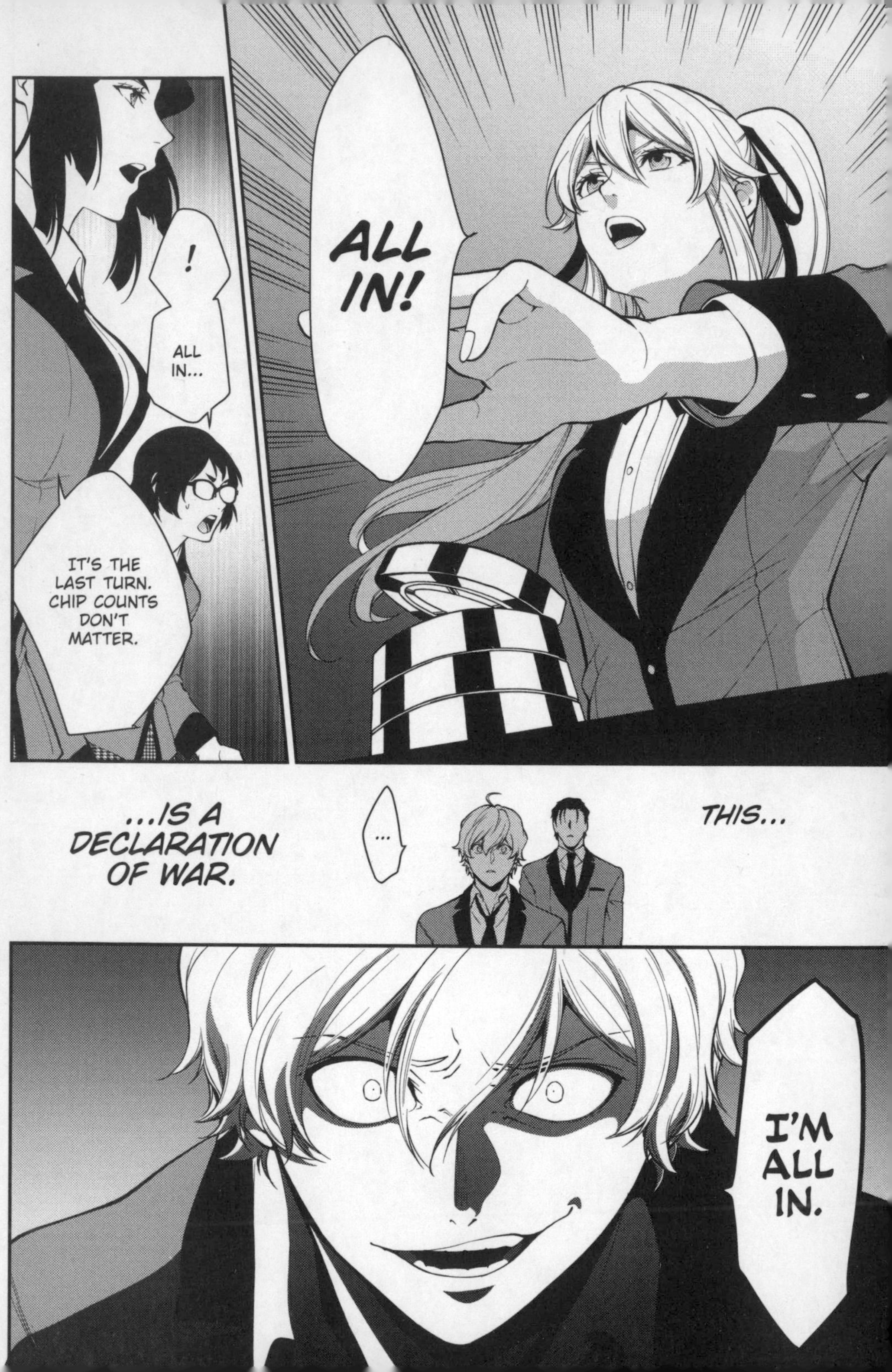
ALL IN!
!
ALL IN...
IT'S THE LAST TURN. CHIP COUNTS DON'T MATTER.
THIS...
...
...IS A DECLARATION OF WAR.
I'M ALL IN.

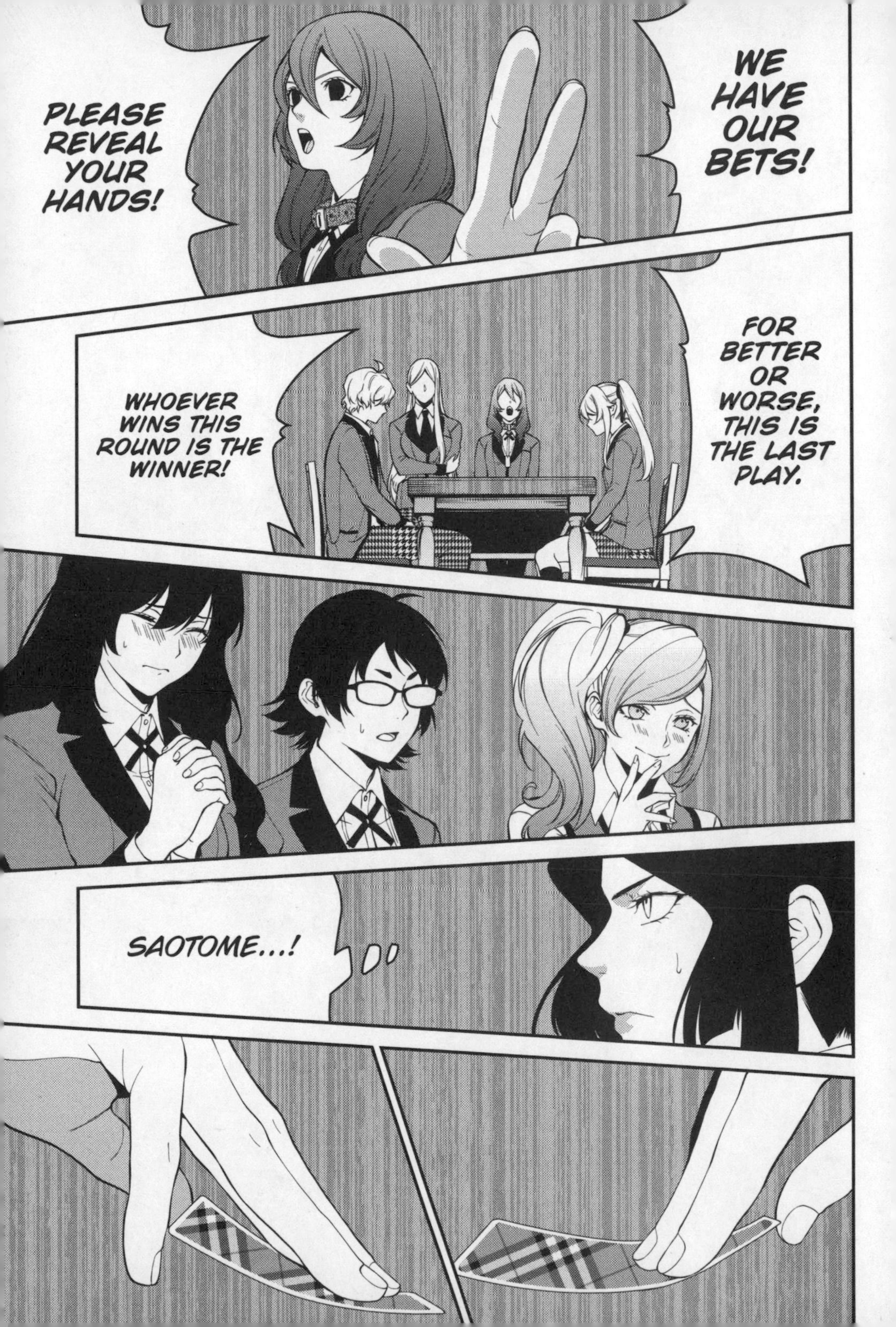
WE HAVE OUR BETS!
PLEASE REVEAL YOUR HANDS!
FOR BETTER OR WORSE, THIS IS THE LAST PLAY.
WHOEVER WINS THIS ROUND IS THE WINNER!
SAOTOME...!

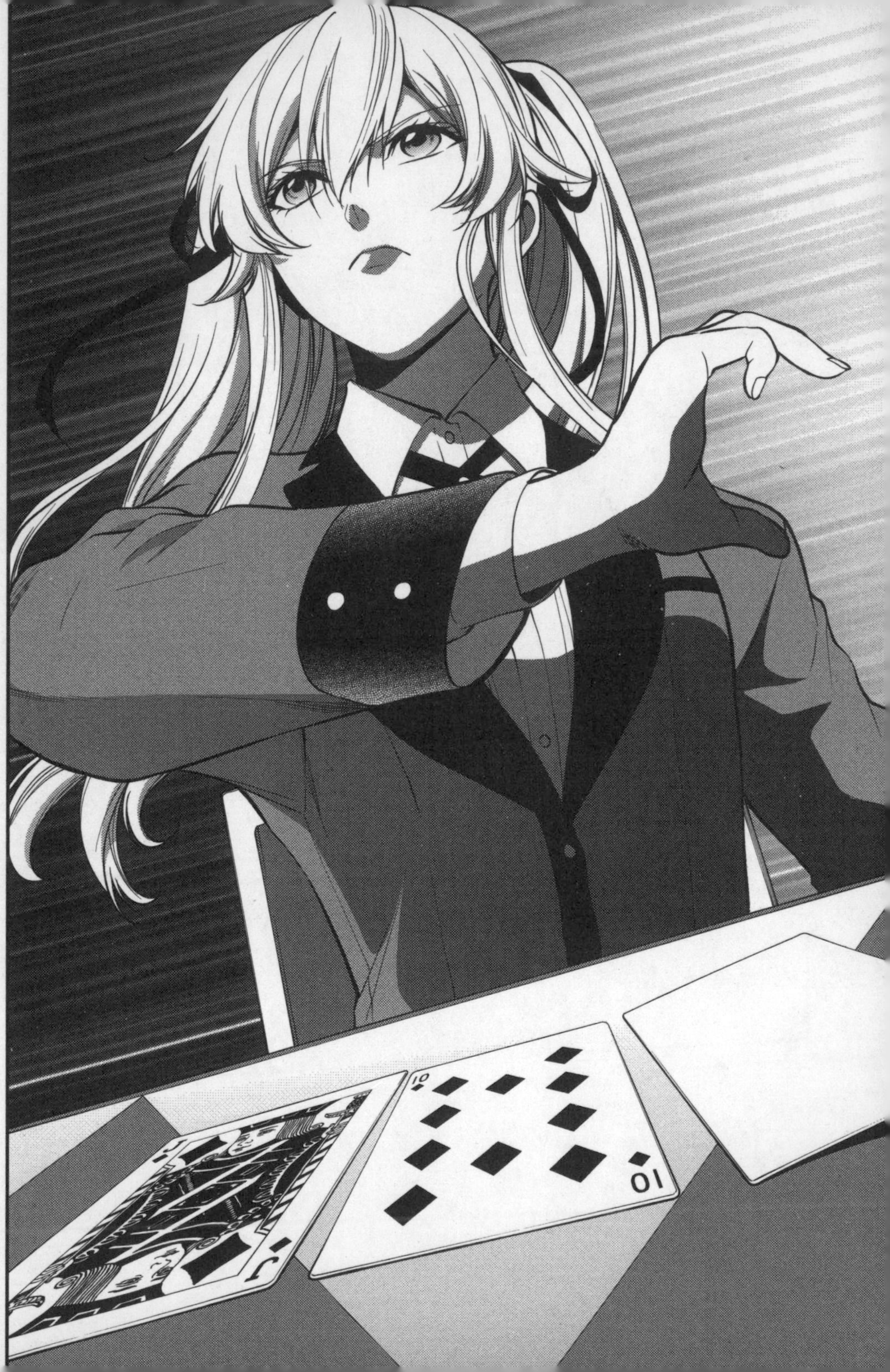

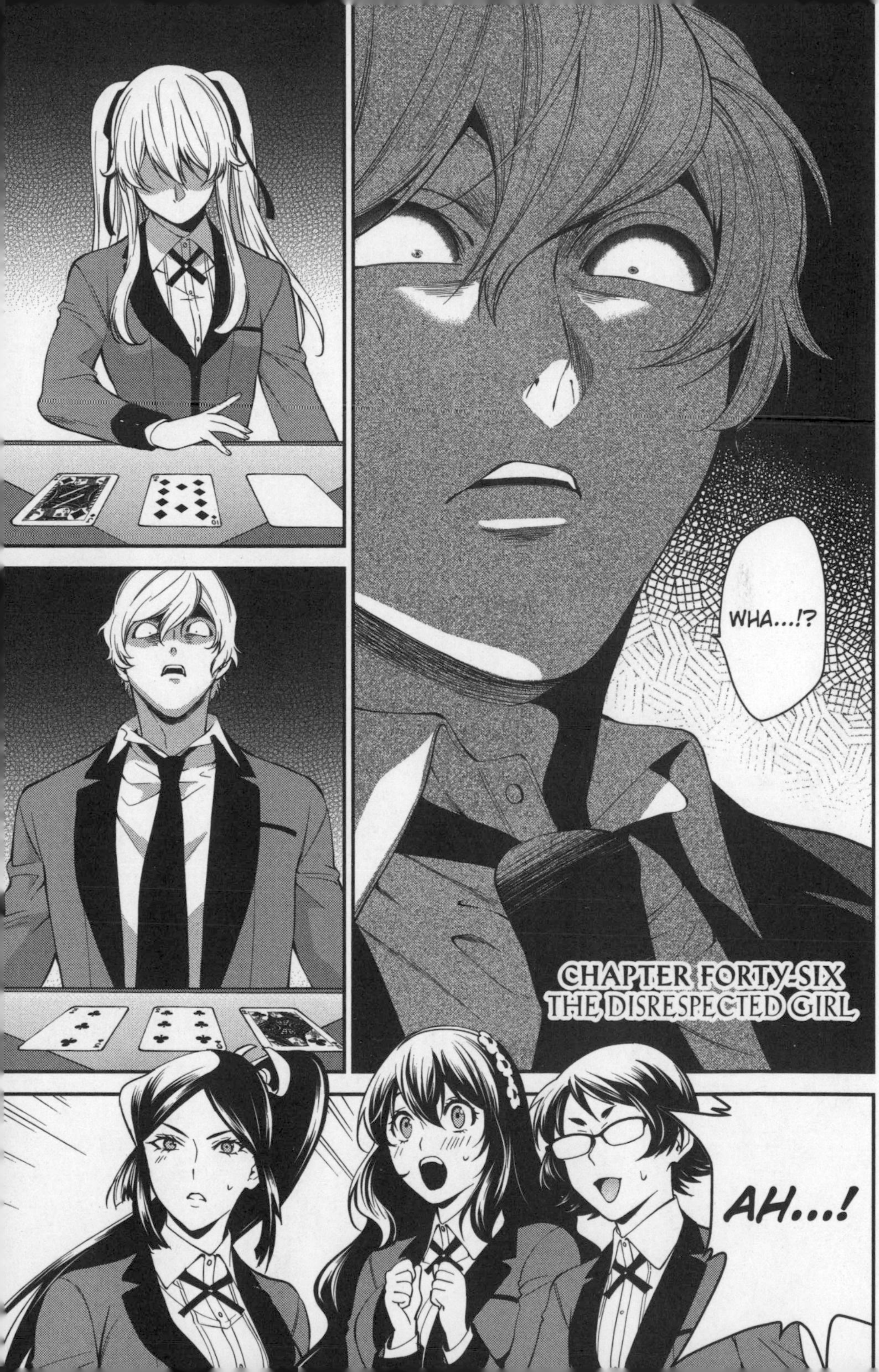
WHA...!?
CHAPTER FORTY-SIX
THE DISRESPECTED GIRL
AH...!

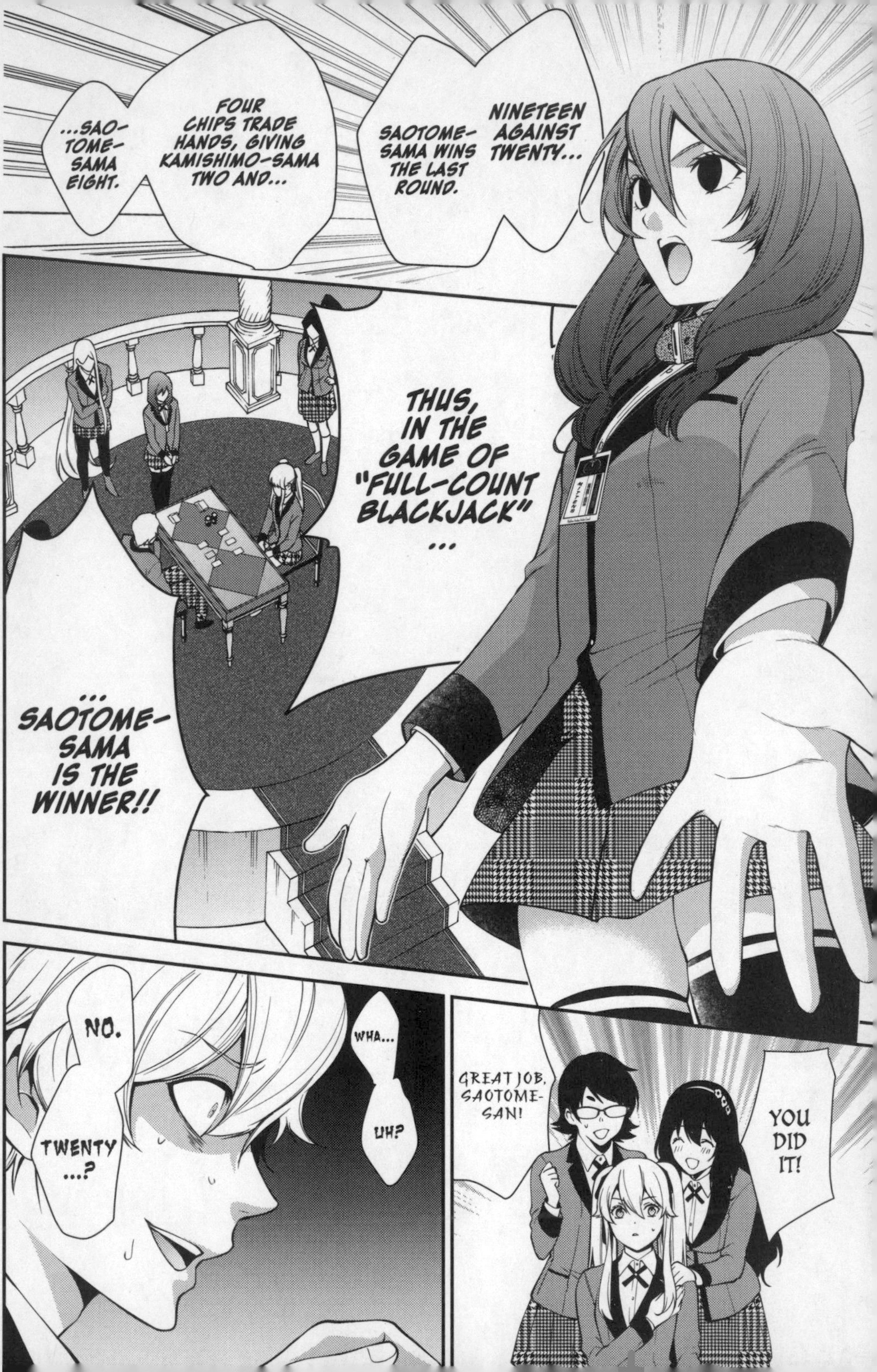
NINETEEN AGAINST TWENTY...
SAOTOME-SAMA WINS THE LAST ROUND.
FOUR CHIPS TRADE HANDS, GIVING KAMISHIMO-SAMA TWO AND...
...SAOTOME-SAMA EIGHT.
THUS, IN THE GAME OF "FULL-COUNT BLACKJACK"...
...SAOTOME-SAMA IS THE WINNER!!
YOU DID IT!
GREAT JOB, SAOTOME-SAN!
WHA...
NO.
UH?
TWENTY...?

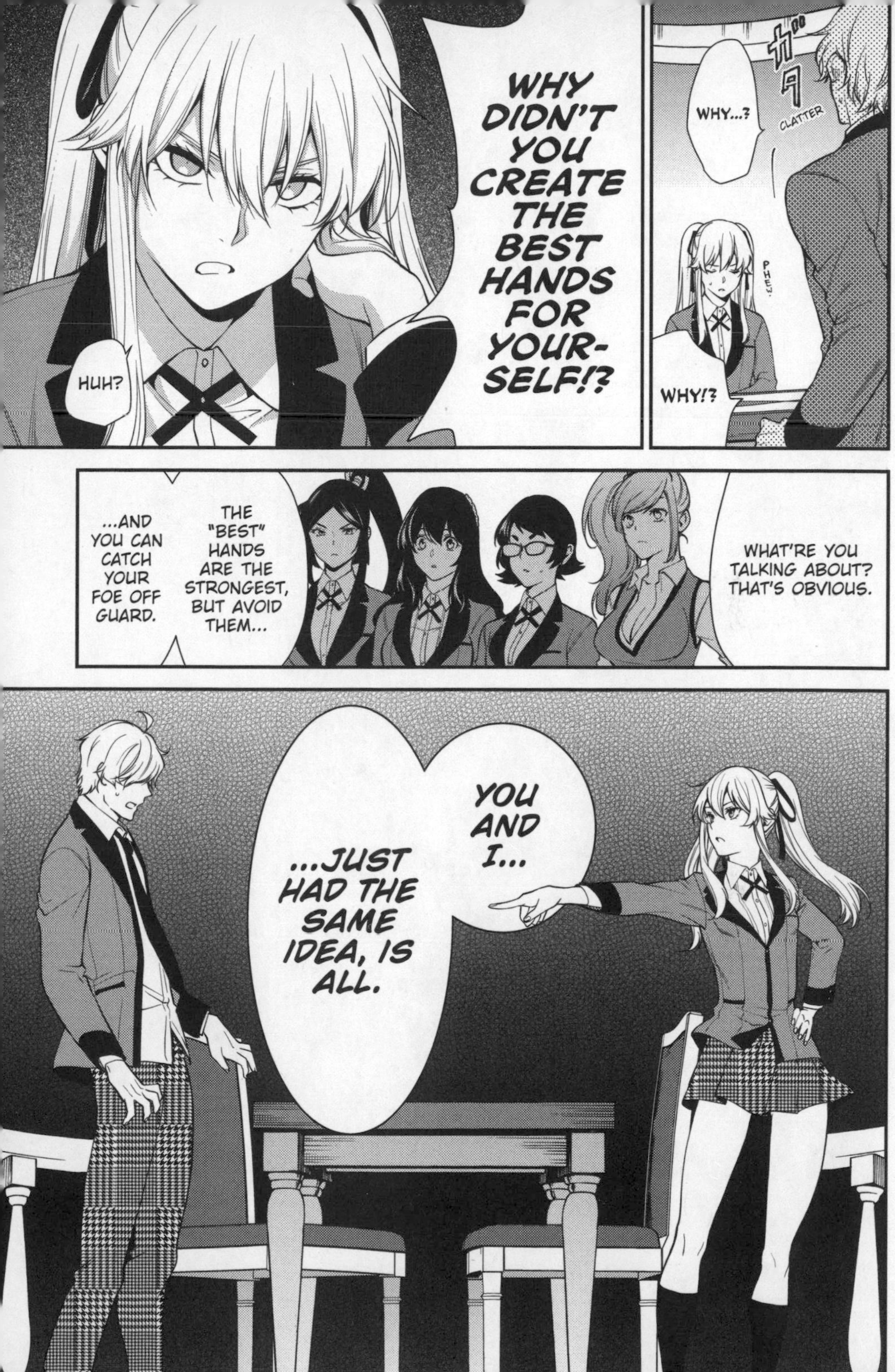
ガタ
CLATTER
WHY...?
PHEW
WHY!?
WHY DIDN'T YOU CREATE THE BEST HANDS FOR YOUR-SELF!?
HUH?
WHAT'RE YOU TALKING ABOUT? THAT'S OBVIOUS.
THE "BEST" HANDS ARE THE STRONGEST, BUT AVOID THEM...
...AND YOU CAN CATCH YOUR FOE OFF GUARD.
YOU AND I...
...JUST HAD THE SAME IDEA, IS ALL.

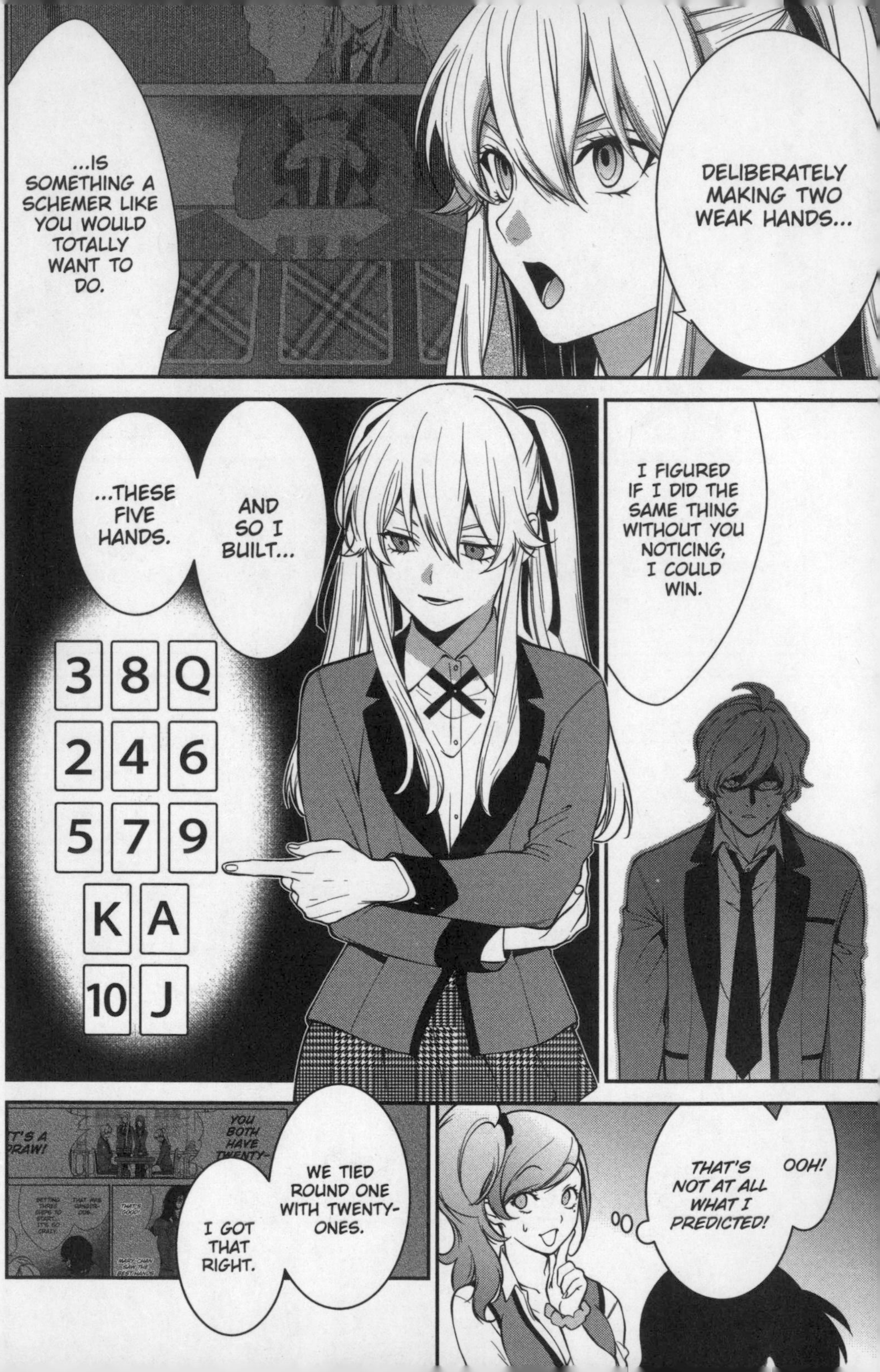
DELIBERATELY MAKING TWO WEAK HANDS...
...IS SOMETHING A SCHEMER LIKE YOU WOULD TOTALLY WANT TO DO.
I FIGURED IF I DID THE SAME THING WITHOUT YOU NOTICING, I COULD WIN.
AND SO I BUILT...
...THESE FIVE HANDS.
3 8 Q
2 4 6
5 7 9
K A
10 J
OOH!
THAT'S NOT AT ALL WHAT I PREDICTED!
WE TIED ROUND ONE WITH TWENTY-ONES.
I GOT THAT RIGHT.
YOU BOTH HAVE TWENTY-

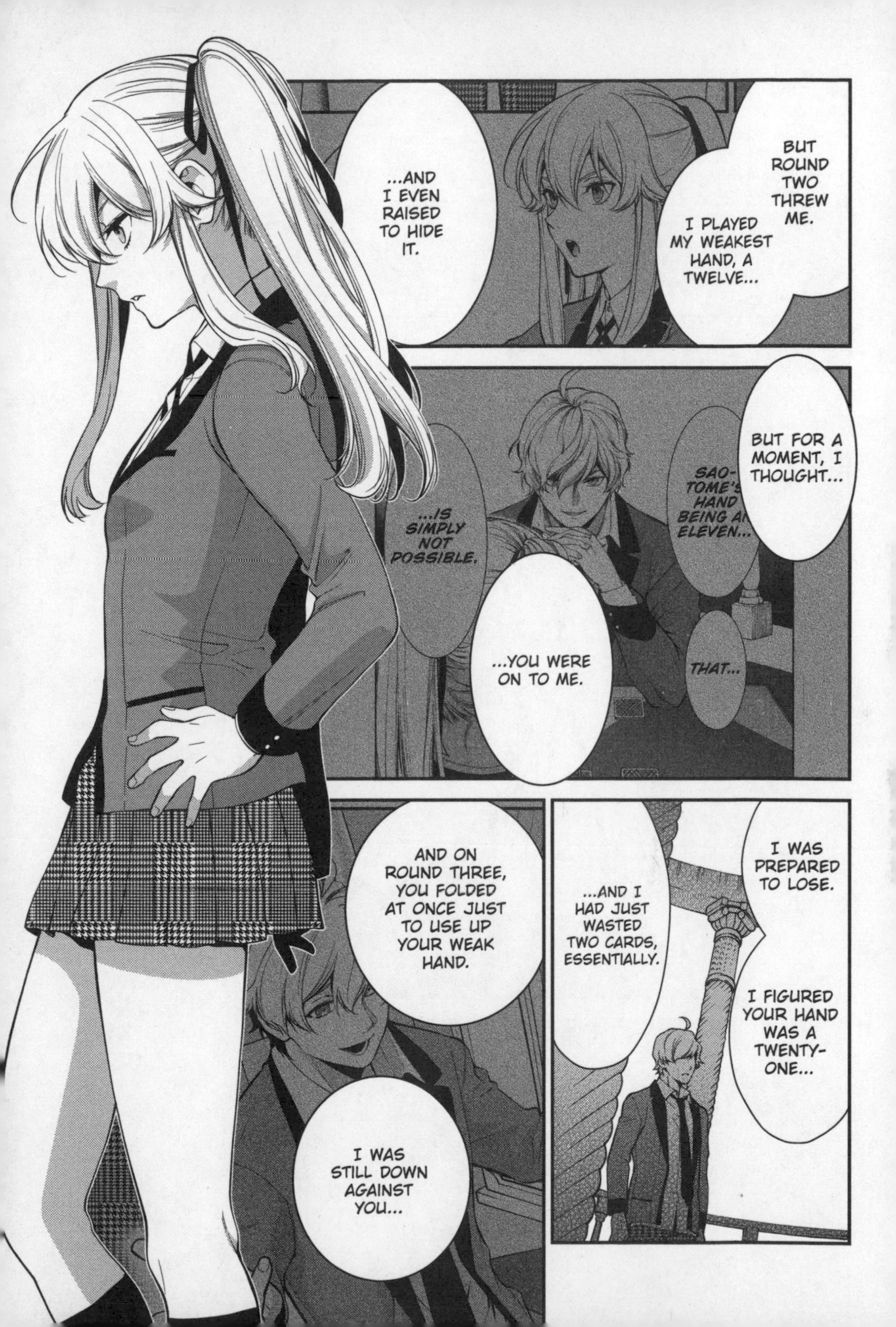
BUT ROUND TWO THREW ME.
I PLAYED MY WEAKEST HAND, A TWELVE...
...AND I EVEN RAISED TO HIDE IT.
BUT FOR A MOMENT, I THOUGHT...
SAO-TOME'S HAND BEING AN ELEVEN...
...IS SIMPLY NOT POSSIBLE.
THAT...
...YOU WERE ON TO ME.
I WAS PREPARED TO LOSE.
...AND I HAD JUST WASTED TWO CARDS, ESSENTIALLY.
I FIGURED YOUR HAND WAS A TWENTY-ONE...
AND ON ROUND THREE, YOU FOLDED AT ONCE JUST TO USE UP YOUR WEAK HAND.
I WAS STILL DOWN AGAINST YOU...

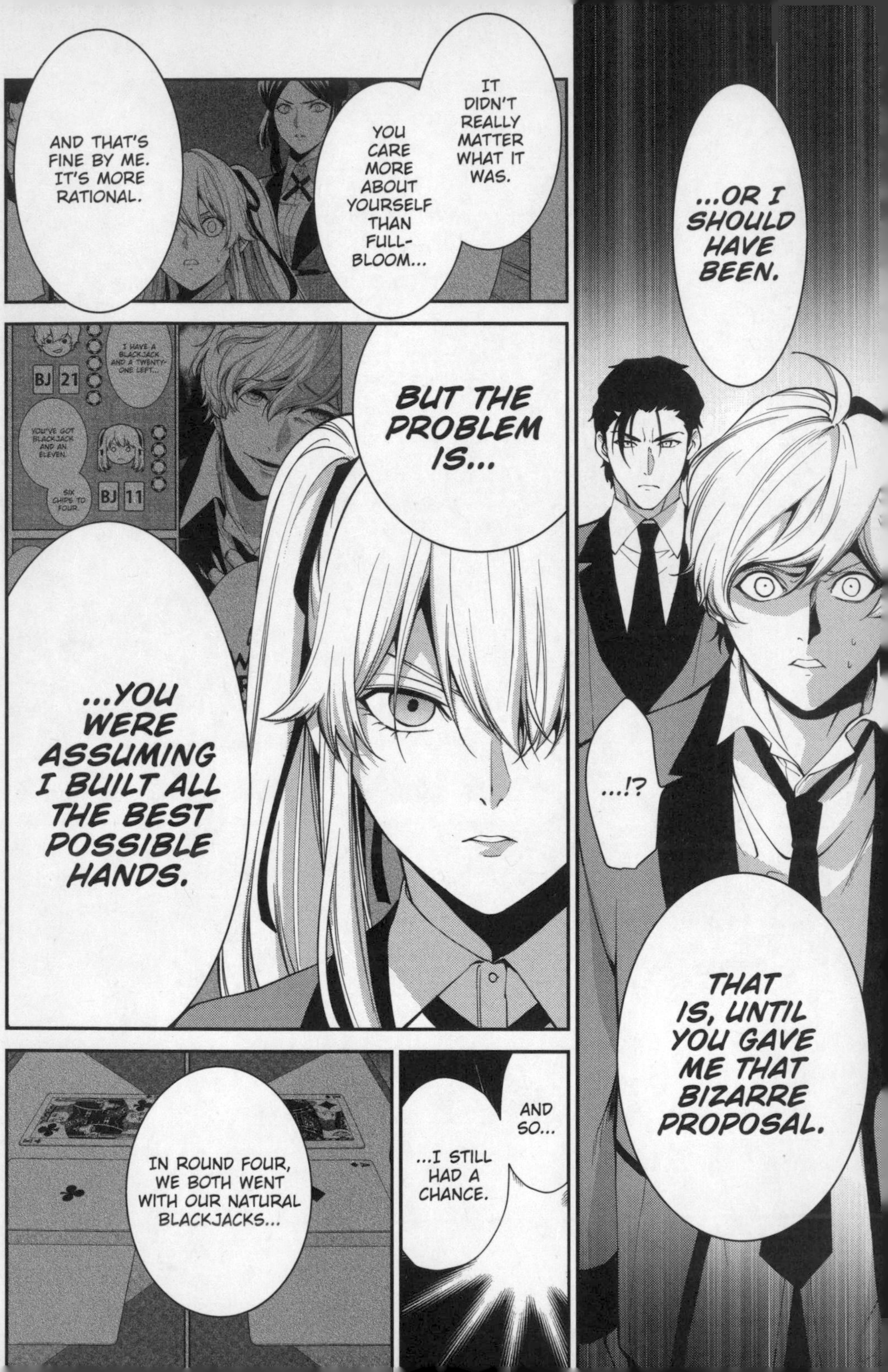
...OR I SHOULD HAVE BEEN.
...!?
THAT IS, UNTIL YOU GAVE ME THAT BIZARRE PROPOSAL.
IT DIDN'T REALLY MATTER WHAT IT WAS.
YOU CARE MORE ABOUT YOURSELF THAN FULL-BLOOM...
AND THAT'S FINE BY ME. IT'S MORE RATIONAL.
BUT THE PROBLEM IS...
I HAVE A BLACKJACK AND A TWENTY-ONE LEFT...
BJ 21
YOU'VE GOT BLACKJACK AND AN ELEVEN.
SIX CHIPS TO FOUR.
BJ 11
...YOU WERE ASSUMING I BUILT ALL THE BEST POSSIBLE HANDS.
AND SO...
...I STILL HAD A CHANCE.
IN ROUND FOUR, WE BOTH WENT WITH OUR NATURAL BLACKJACKS...

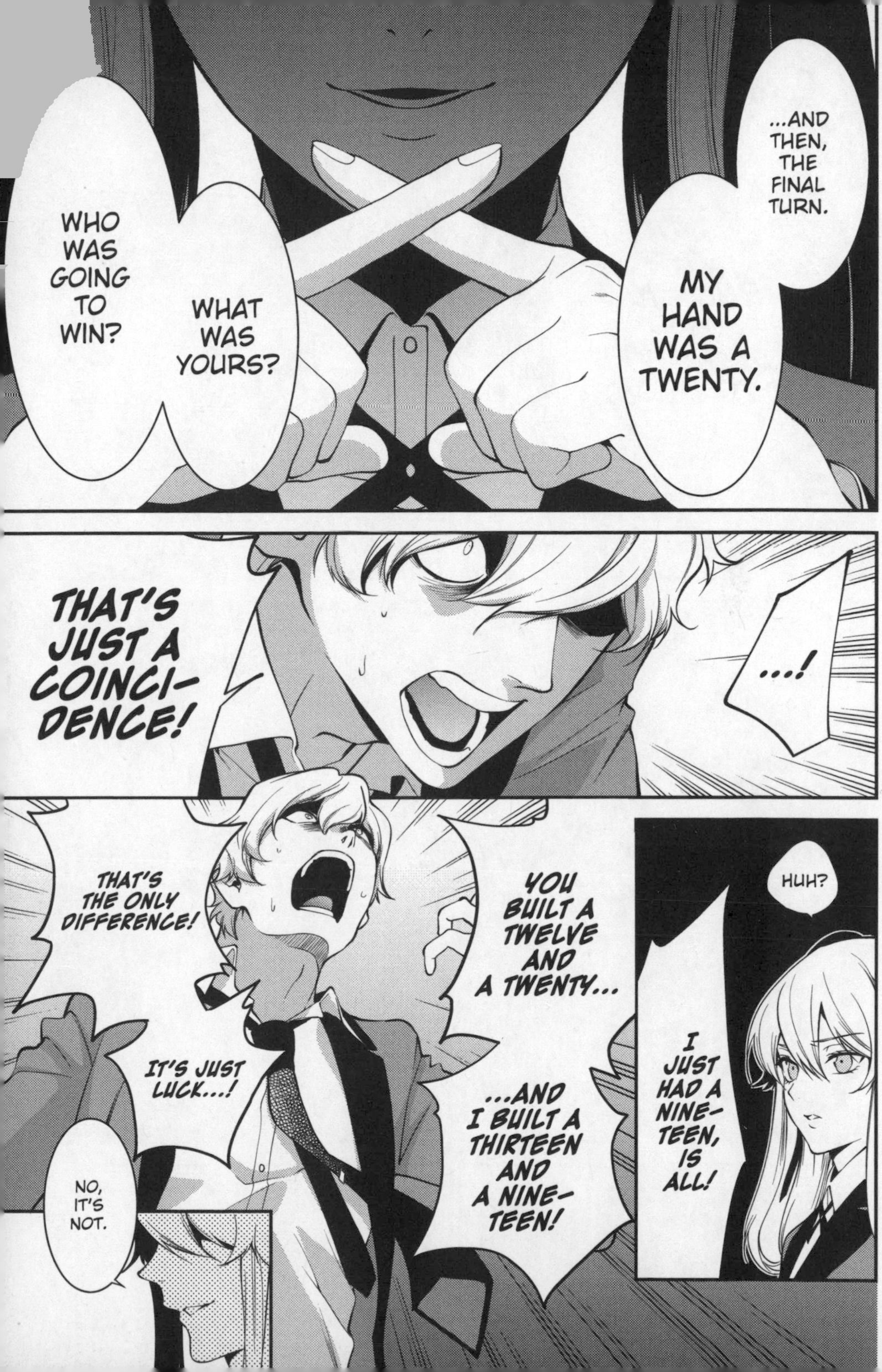

...AND THEN, THE FINAL TURN.
MY HAND WAS A TWENTY.
WHAT WAS YOURS?
WHO WAS GOING TO WIN?
...!
THAT'S JUST A COINCI-DENCE!
HUH?
I JUST HAD A NINE-TEEN, IS ALL!
YOU BUILT A TWELVE AND A TWENTY...
...AND I BUILT A THIRTEEN AND A NINE-TEEN!
THAT'S THE ONLY DIFFERENCE!
IT'S JUST LUCK...!
NO, IT'S NOT.

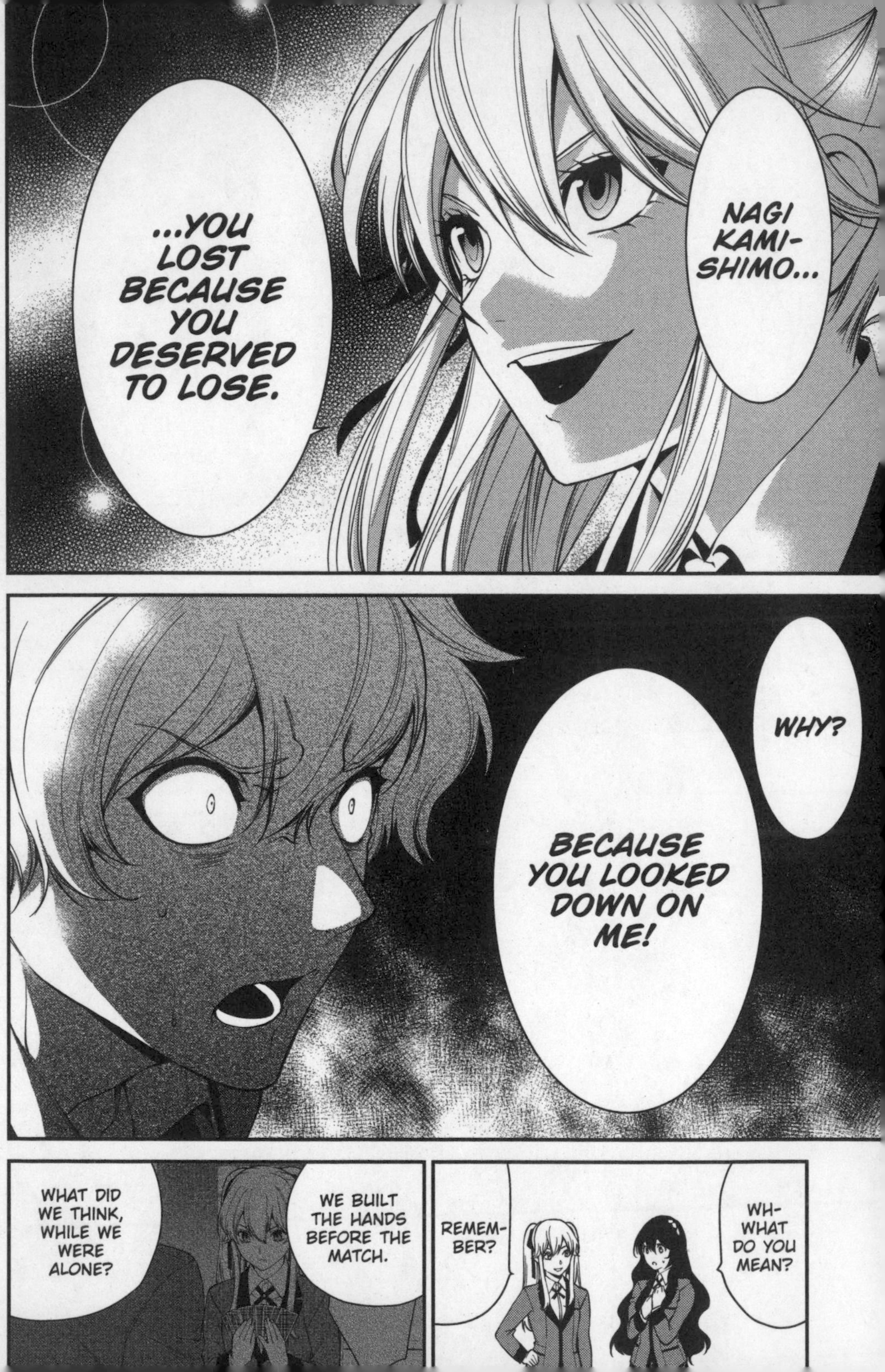
NAGI KAMI-SHIMO...
...YOU LOST BECAUSE YOU DESERVED TO LOSE.
WHY?
BECAUSE YOU LOOKED DOWN ON ME!
WH- WHAT DO YOU MEAN?
REMEMBER?
WE BUILT THE HANDS BEFORE THE MATCH.
WHAT DID WE THINK, WHILE WE WERE ALONE?

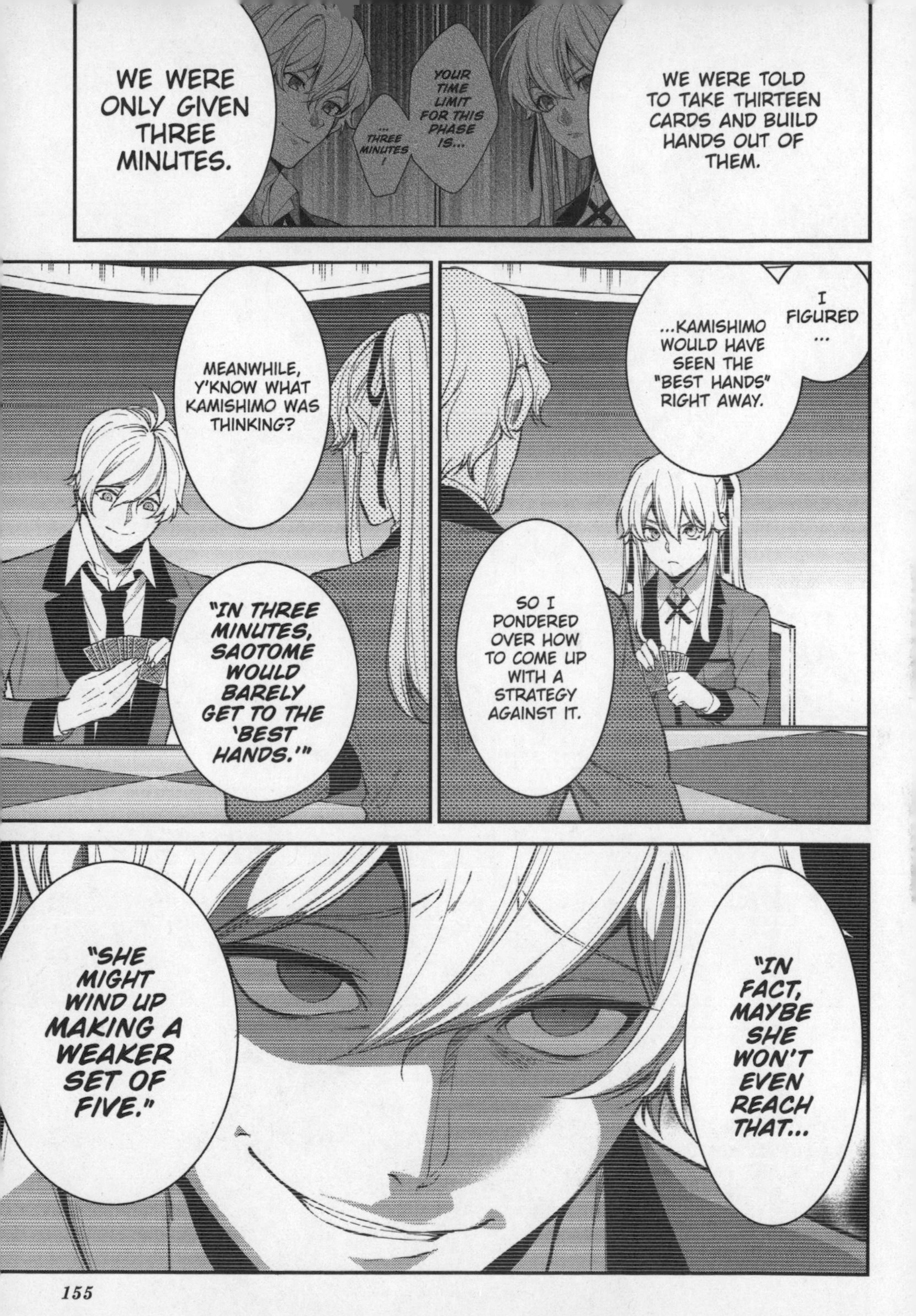
WE WERE TOLD TO TAKE THIRTEEN CARDS AND BUILD HANDS OUT OF THEM.
YOUR TIME LIMIT FOR THIS PHASE IS...
...THREE MINUTES!
WE WERE ONLY GIVEN THREE MINUTES.
I FIGURED...
...KAMISHIMO WOULD HAVE SEEN THE "BEST HANDS" RIGHT AWAY.
SO I PONDERED OVER HOW TO COME UP WITH A STRATEGY AGAINST IT.
MEANWHILE, Y'KNOW WHAT KAMISHIMO WAS THINKING?
"IN THREE MINUTES, SAOTOME WOULD BARELY GET TO THE 'BEST HANDS.'"
"IN FACT, MAYBE SHE WON'T EVEN REACH THAT...
"SHE MIGHT WIND UP MAKING A WEAKER SET OF FIVE."

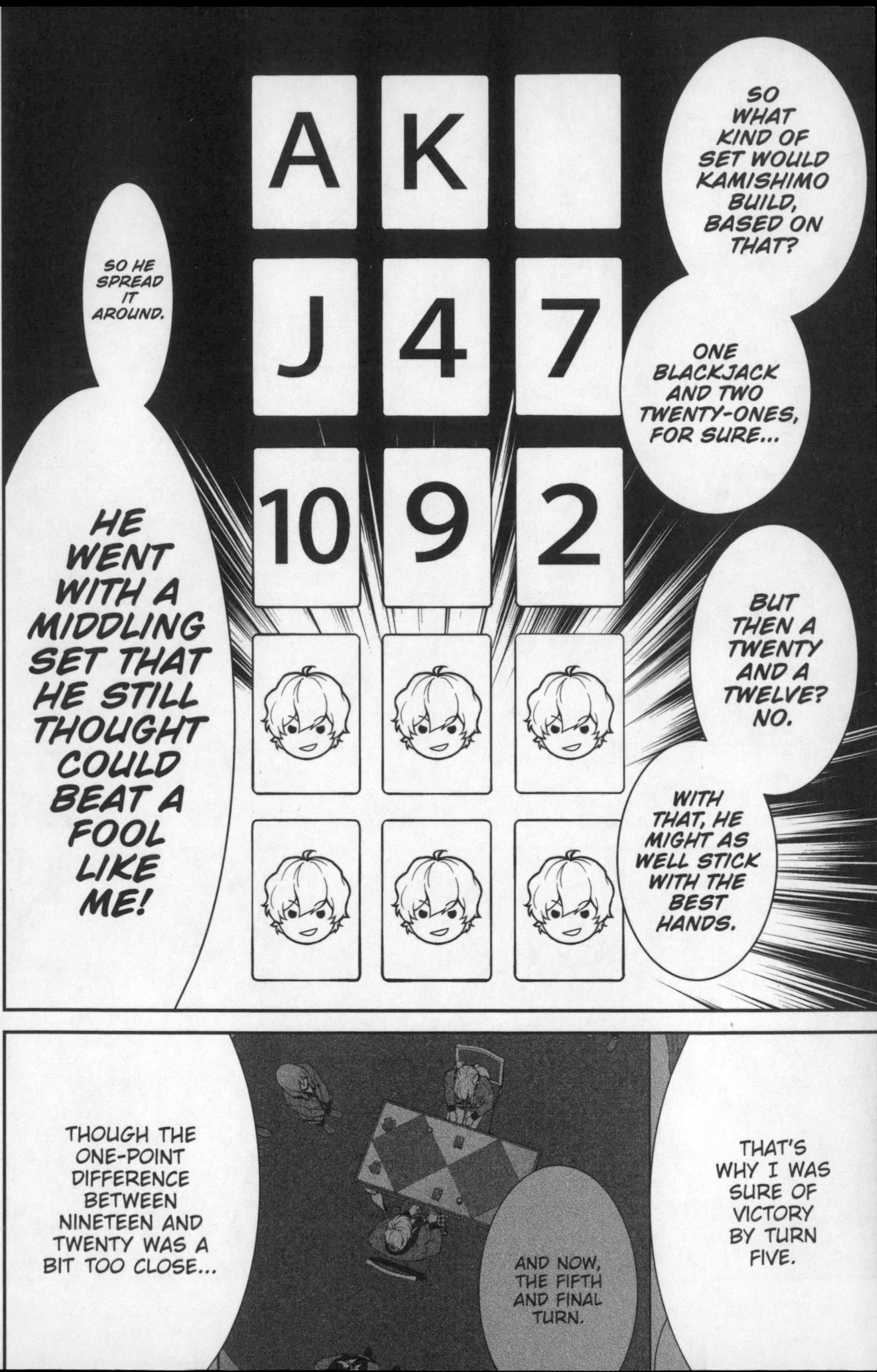
SO WHAT KIND OF SET WOULD KAMISHIMO BUILD, BASED ON THAT?
ONE BLACKJACK AND TWO TWENTY-ONES, FOR SURE...
BUT THEN A TWENTY AND A TWELVE? NO.
WITH THAT, HE MIGHT AS WELL STICK WITH THE BEST HANDS.
SO HE SPREAD IT AROUND.
HE WENT WITH A MIDDLING SET THAT HE STILL THOUGHT COULD BEAT A FOOL LIKE ME!
THAT'S WHY I WAS SURE OF VICTORY BY TURN FIVE.
AND NOW, THE FIFTH AND FINAL TURN.
THOUGH THE ONE-POINT DIFFERENCE BETWEEN NINETEEN AND TWENTY WAS A BIT TOO CLOSE...

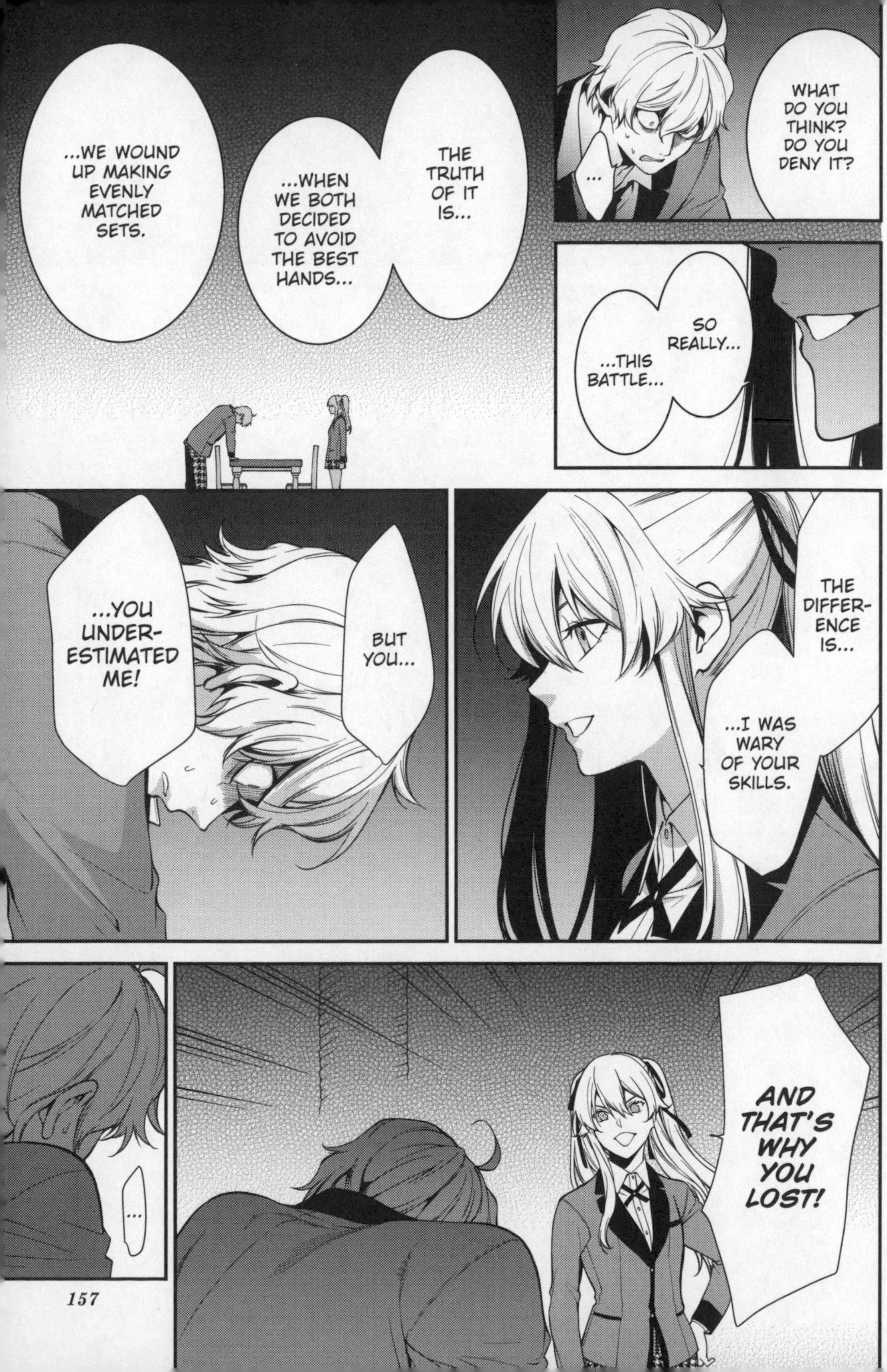
WHAT DO YOU THINK? DO YOU DENY IT?
...
SO REALLY...
...THIS BATTLE...
THE TRUTH OF IT IS...
...WHEN WE BOTH DECIDED TO AVOID THE BEST HANDS...
...WE WOUND UP MAKING EVENLY MATCHED SETS.
THE DIFFERENCE IS...
...I WAS WARY OF YOUR SKILLS.
BUT YOU...
...YOU UNDERESTIMATED ME!
AND THAT'S WHY YOU LOST!
...

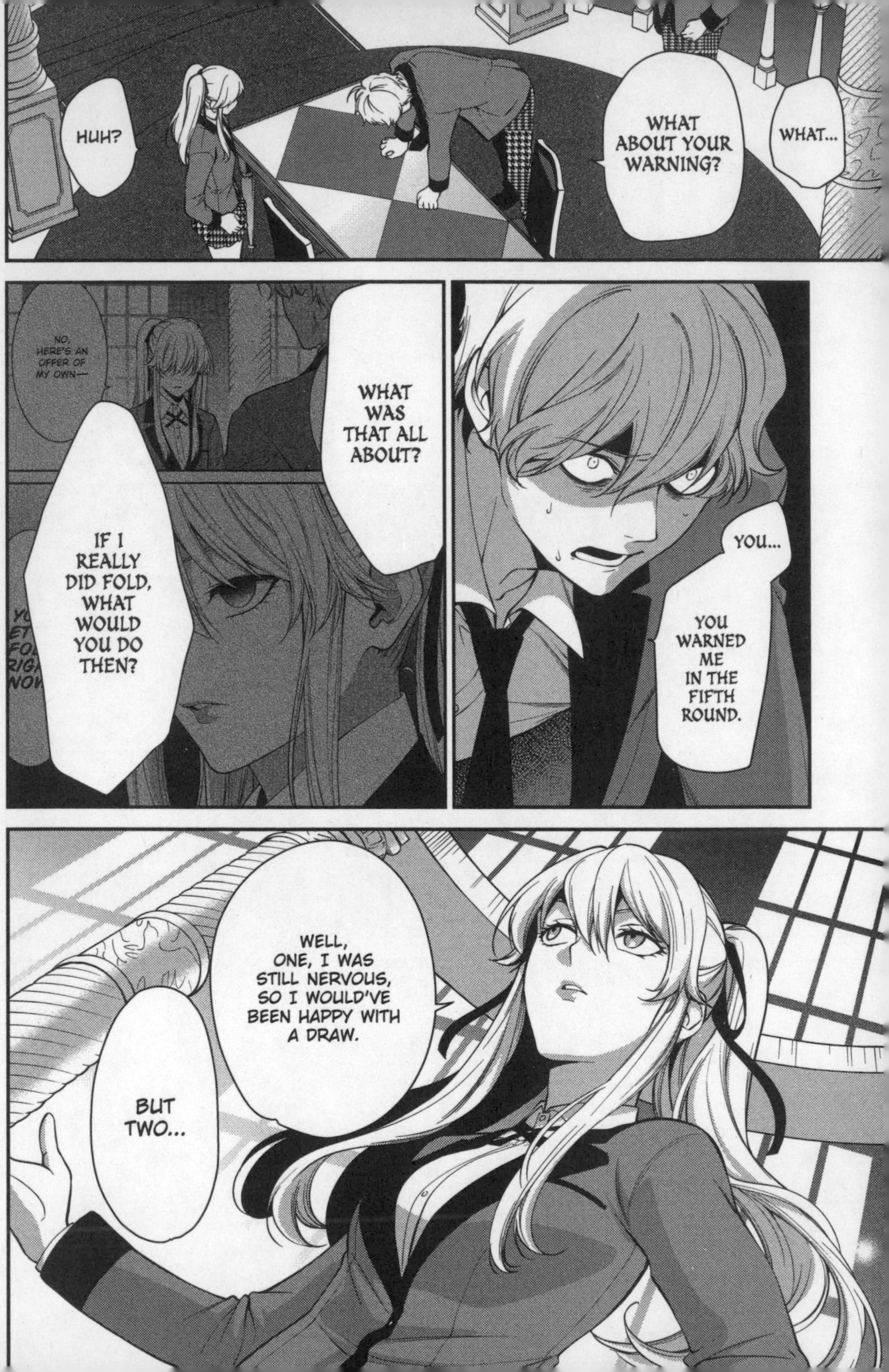
WHAT...
WHAT ABOUT YOUR WARNING?
HUH?
YOU...
YOU WARNED ME IN THE FIFTH ROUND.
WHAT WAS THAT ALL ABOUT?
NO, HERE'S AN OFFER OF MY OWN—
IF I REALLY DID FOLD, WHAT WOULD YOU DO THEN?
WELL, ONE, I WAS STILL NERVOUS, SO I WOULD'VE BEEN HAPPY WITH A DRAW.
BUT TWO...

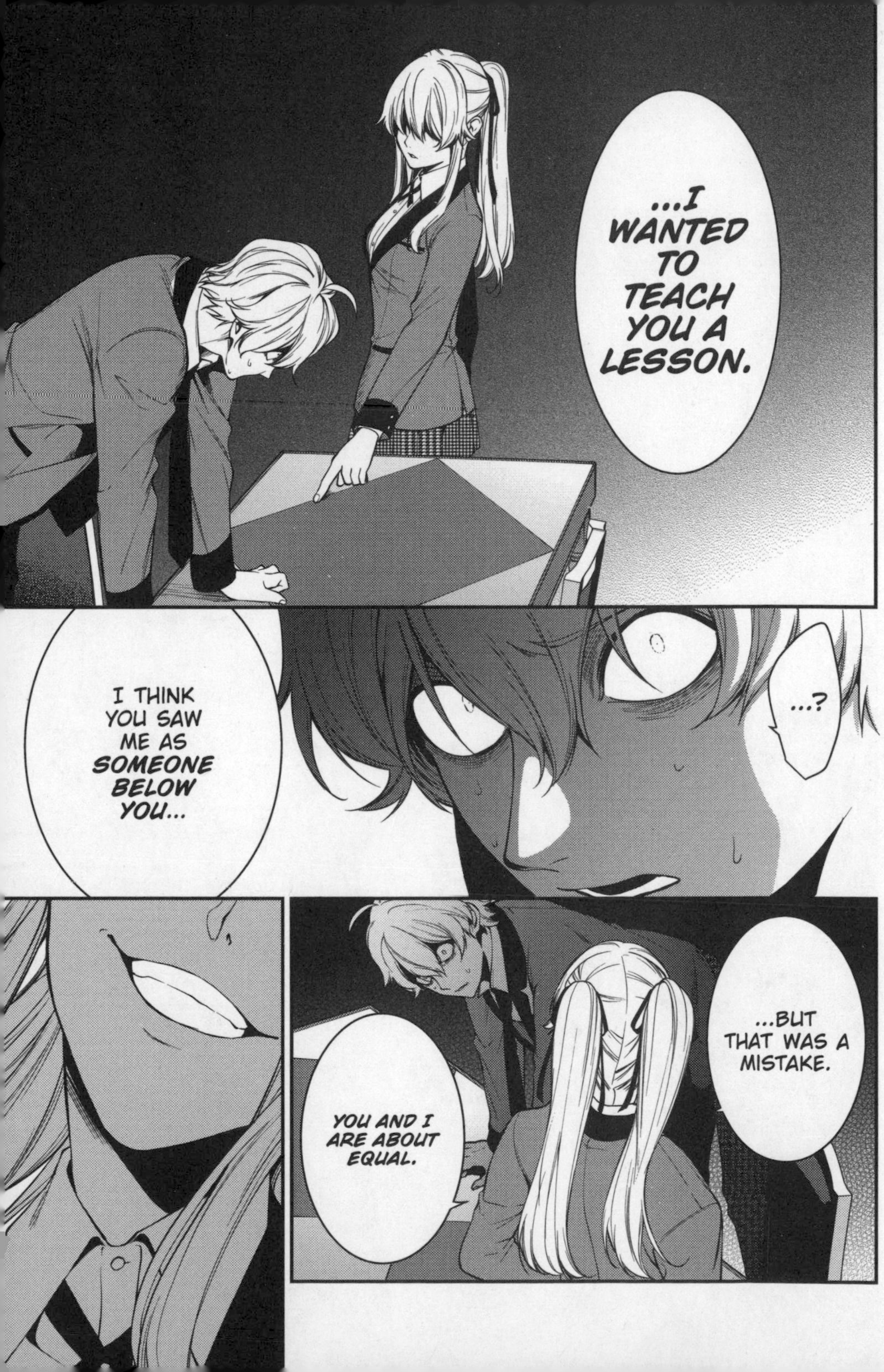
...I WANTED TO TEACH YOU A LESSON.
...?
I THINK YOU SAW ME AS SOMEONE BELOW YOU...
...BUT THAT WAS A MISTAKE.
YOU AND I ARE ABOUT EQUAL.

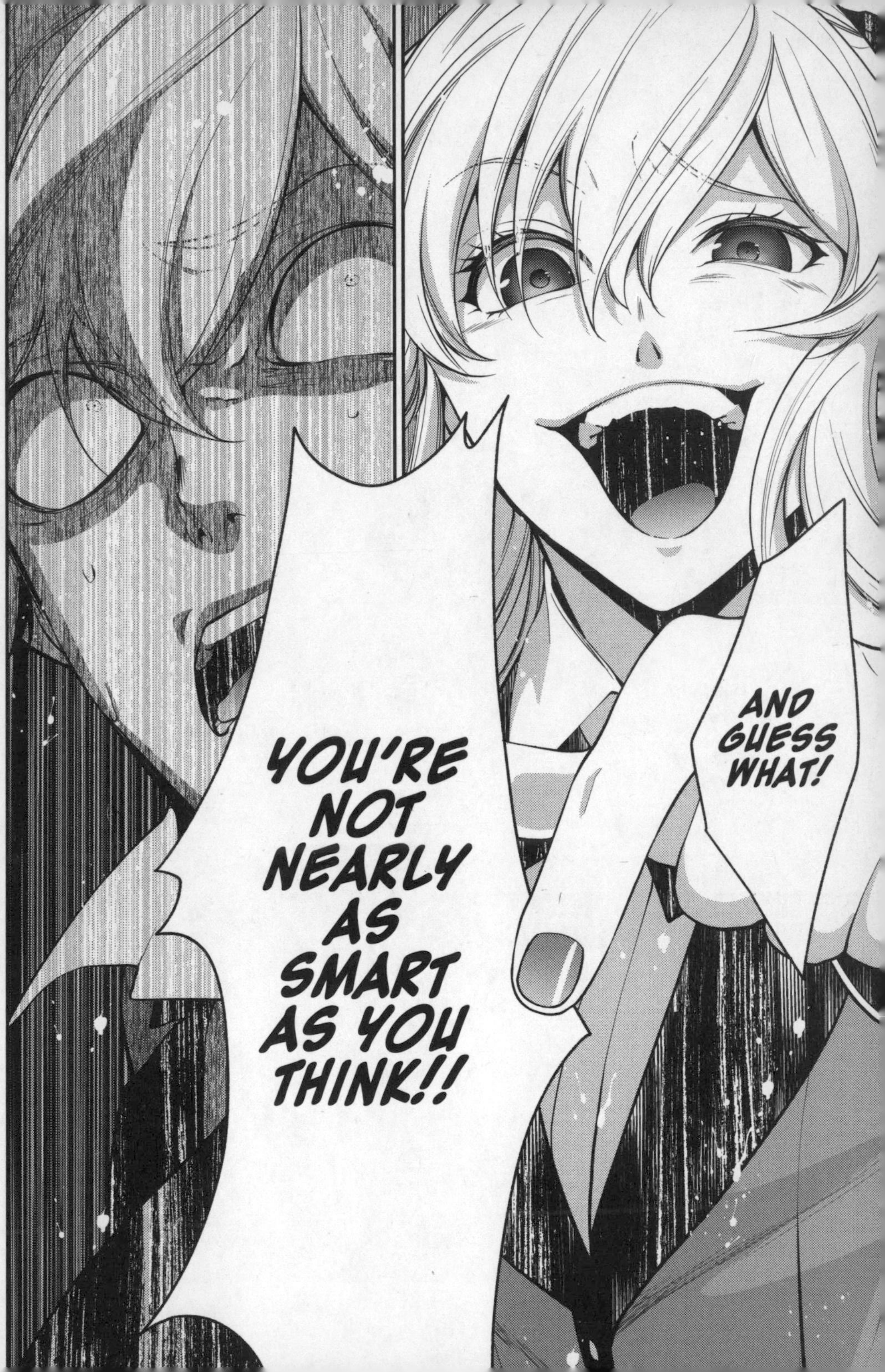
AND GUESS WHAT!
YOU'RE NOT NEARLY AS SMART AS YOU THINK!!

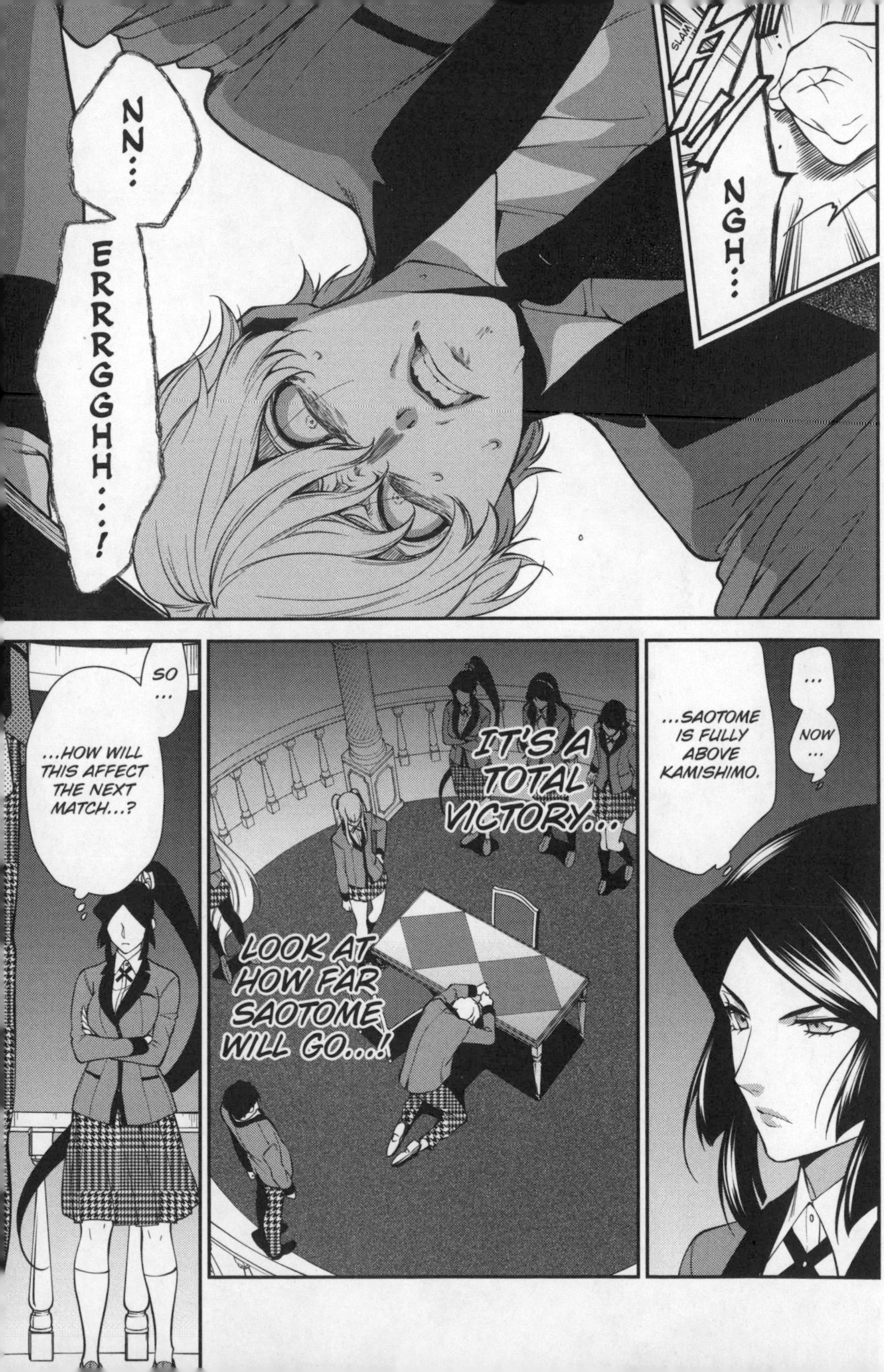
SLAM
NGH...
NN... ERRRGGHH...!
... NOW ...
...SAOTOME IS FULLY ABOVE KAMISHIMO.
IT'S A TOTAL VICTORY...
LOOK AT HOW FAR SAOTOME WILL GO...!
SO ...
...HOW WILL THIS AFFECT THE NEXT MATCH...?

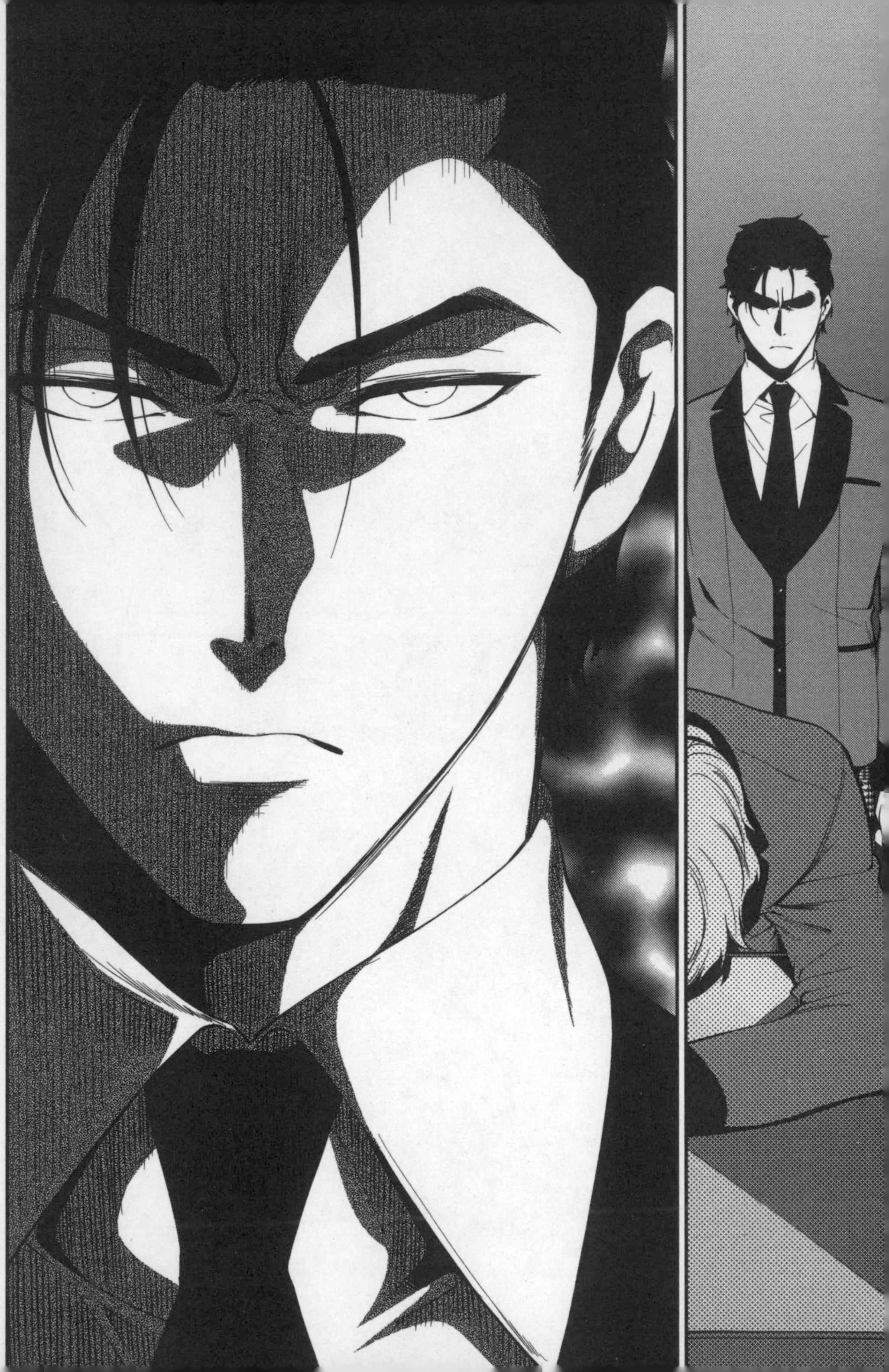

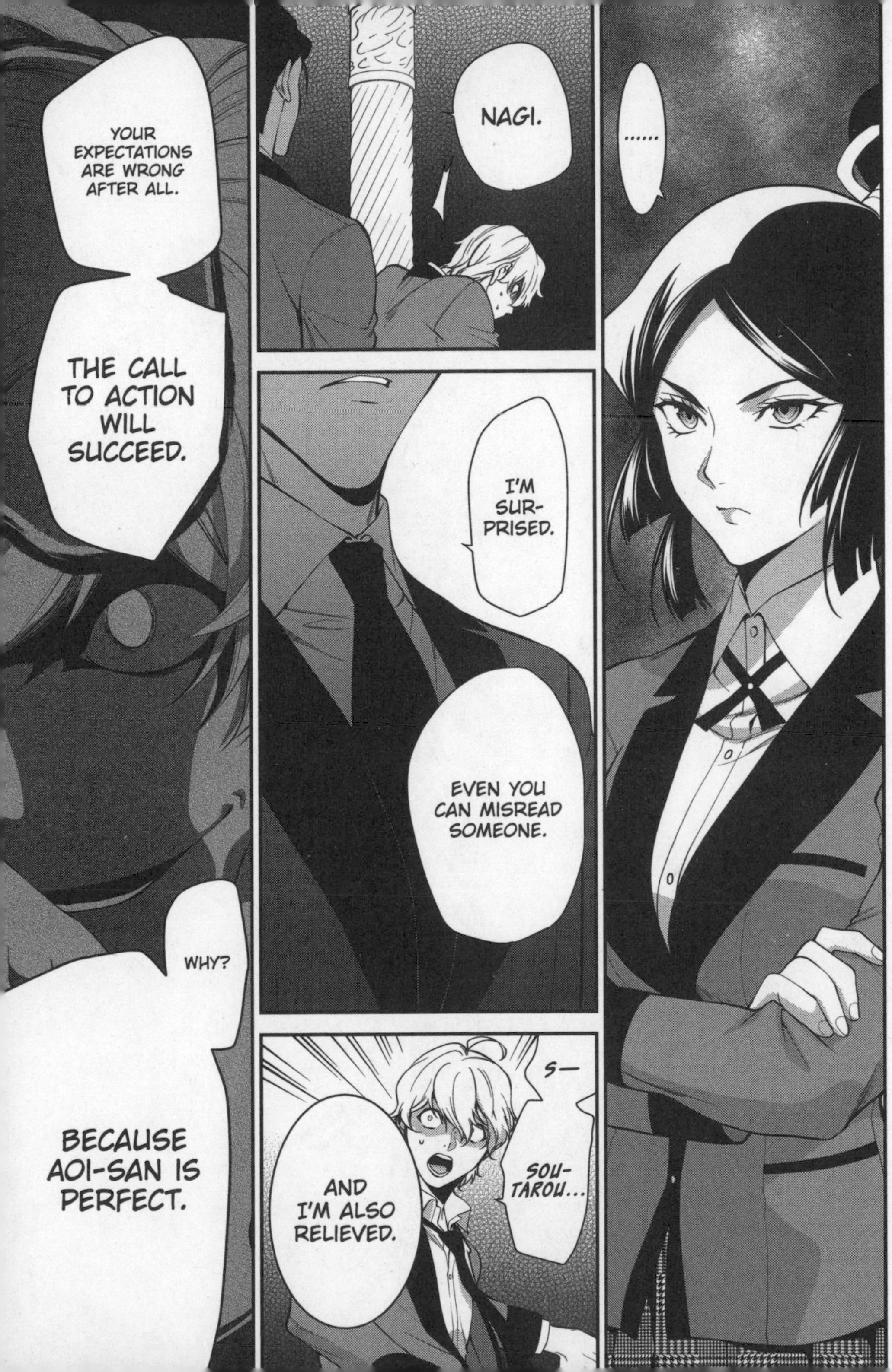
......
NAGI.
I'M SUR-PRISED.
EVEN YOU CAN MISREAD SOMEONE.
S—
SOU-TAROU...
AND I'M ALSO RELIEVED.
YOUR EXPECTATIONS ARE WRONG AFTER ALL.
THE CALL TO ACTION WILL SUCCEED.
WHY?
BECAUSE AOI-SAN IS PERFECT.

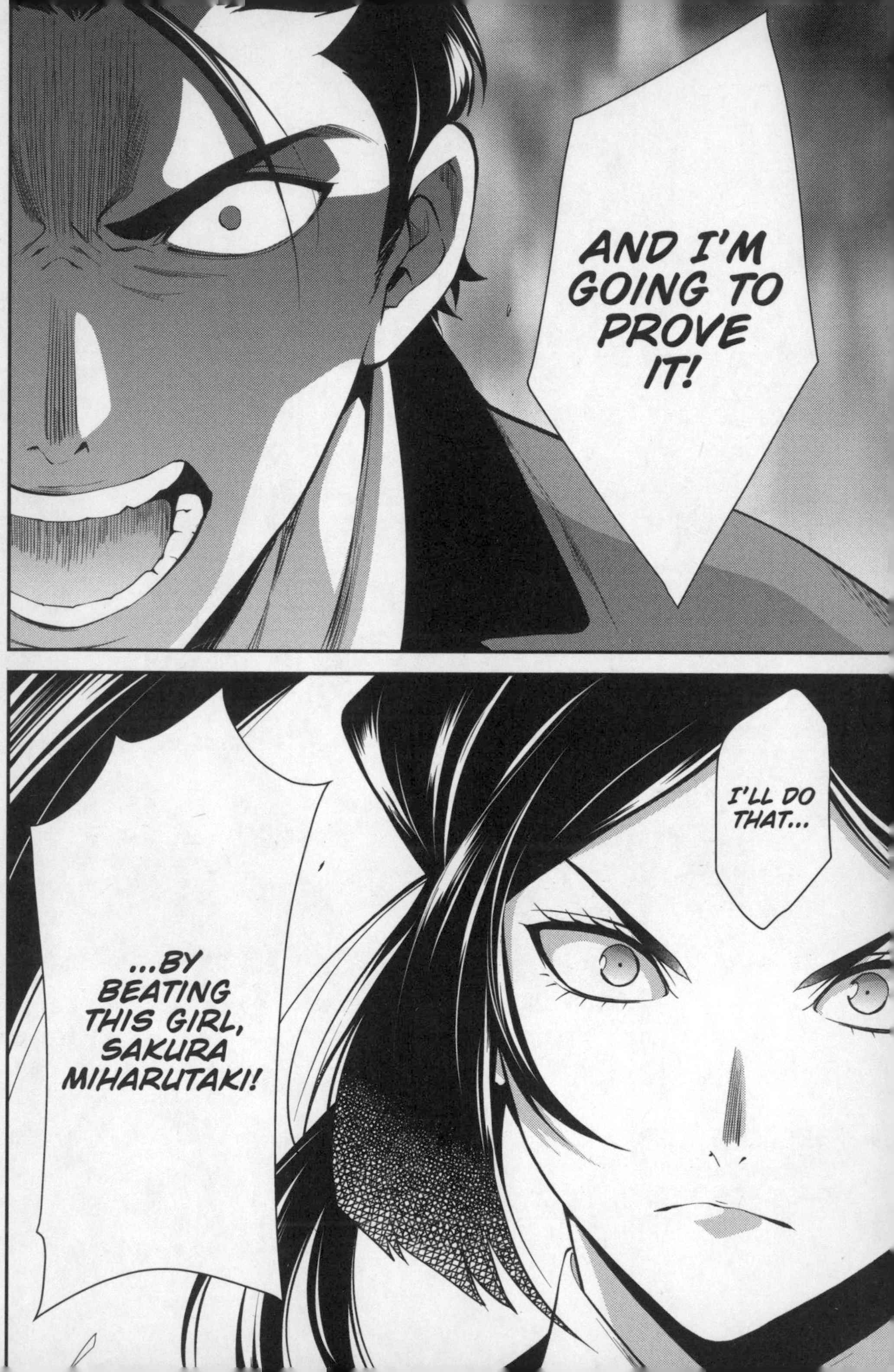
AND I'M GOING TO PROVE IT!
I'LL DO THAT...
...BY BEATING THIS GIRL, SAKURA MIHARUTAKI!

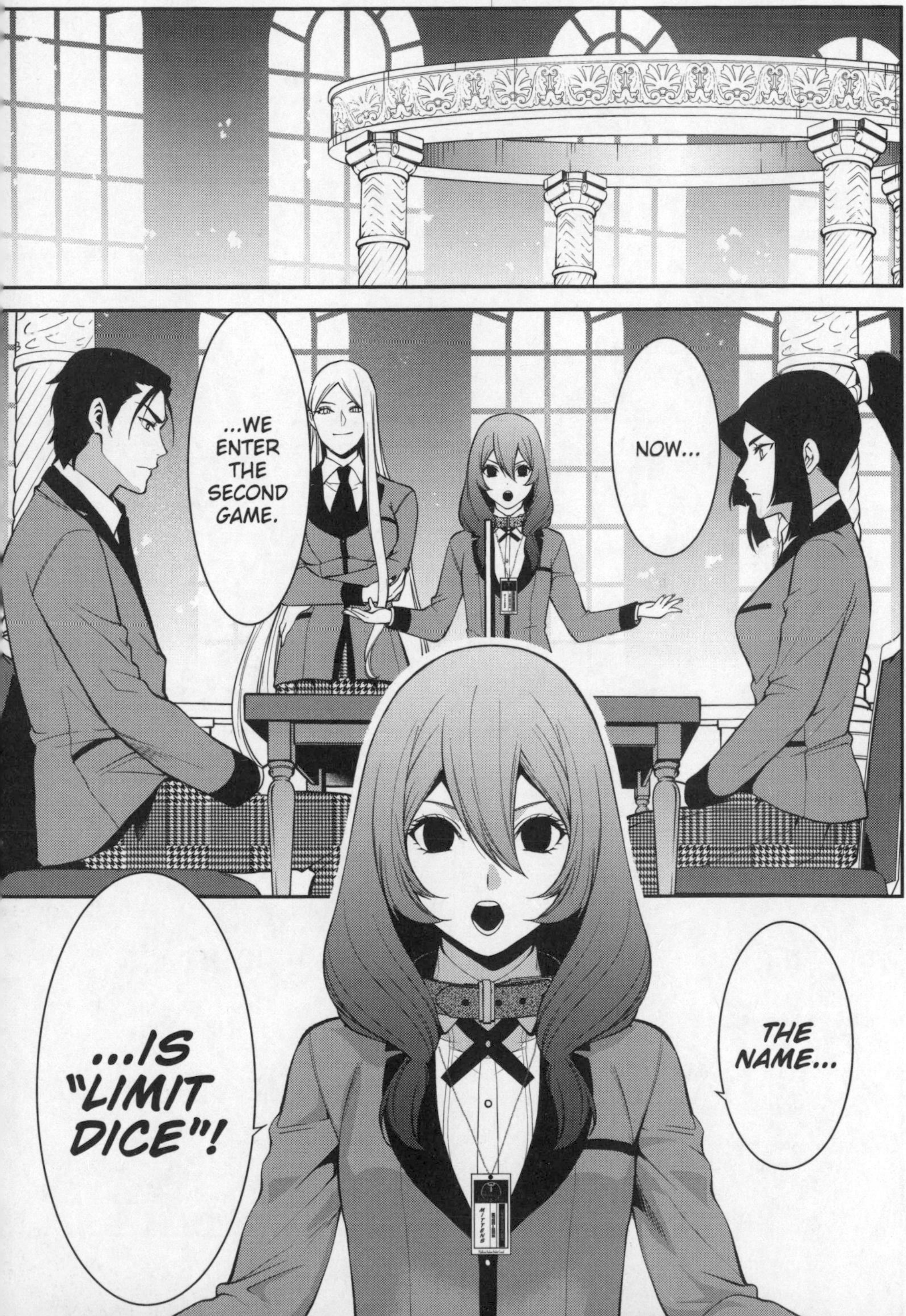
NOW...
...WE ENTER THE SECOND GAME.
THE NAME...
...IS "LIMIT DICE"!

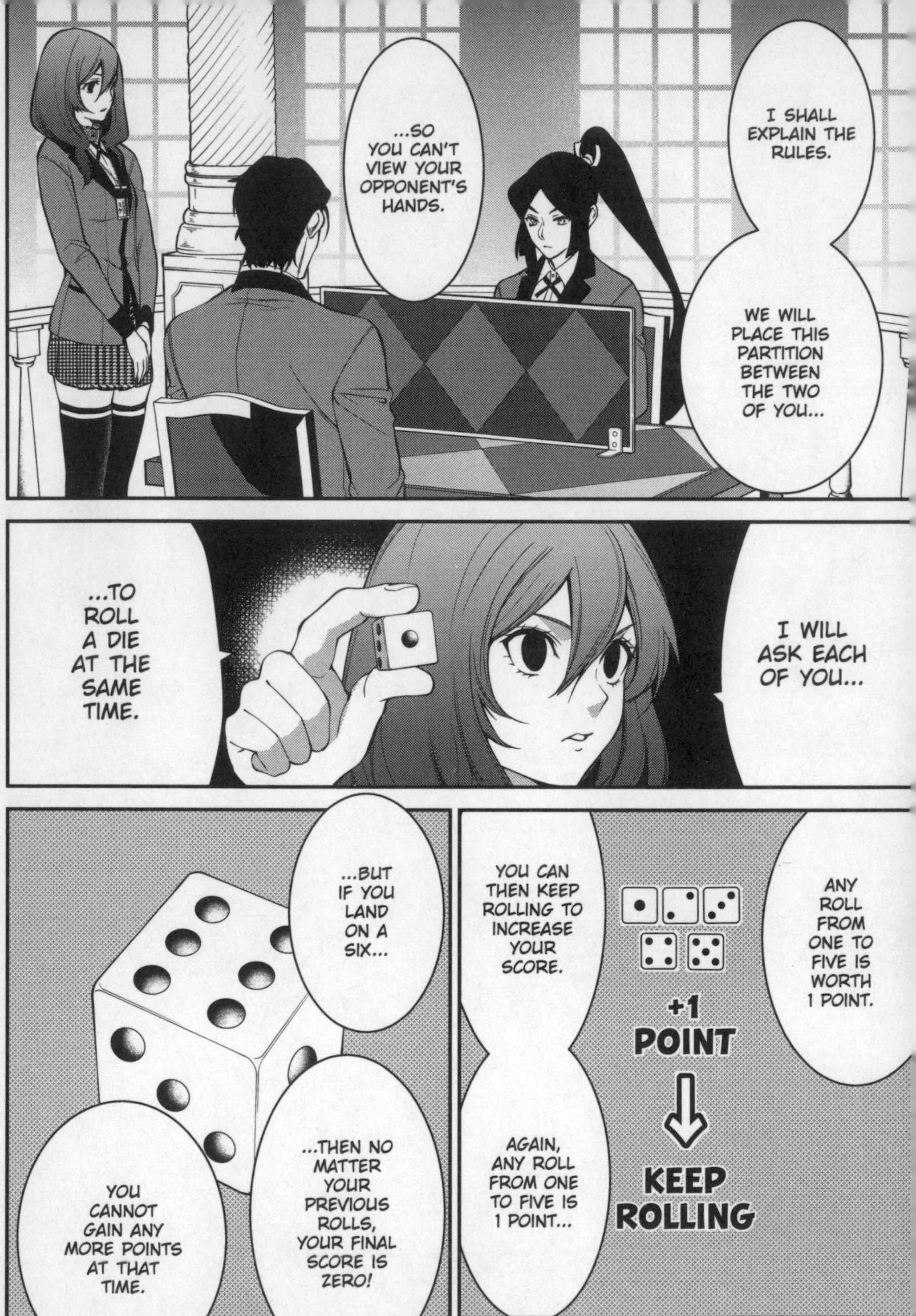
I SHALL EXPLAIN THE RULES.
WE WILL PLACE THIS PARTITION BETWEEN THE TWO OF YOU...
...SO YOU CAN'T VIEW YOUR OPPONENT'S HANDS.
I WILL ASK EACH OF YOU...
...TO ROLL A DIE AT THE SAME TIME.
ANY ROLL FROM ONE TO FIVE IS WORTH 1 POINT.
+1 POINT
KEEP ROLLING
YOU CAN THEN KEEP ROLLING TO INCREASE YOUR SCORE.
AGAIN, ANY ROLL FROM ONE TO FIVE IS 1 POINT...
...BUT IF YOU LAND ON A SIX...
...THEN NO MATTER YOUR PREVIOUS ROLLS, YOUR FINAL SCORE IS ZERO!
YOU CANNOT GAIN ANY MORE POINTS AT THAT TIME.

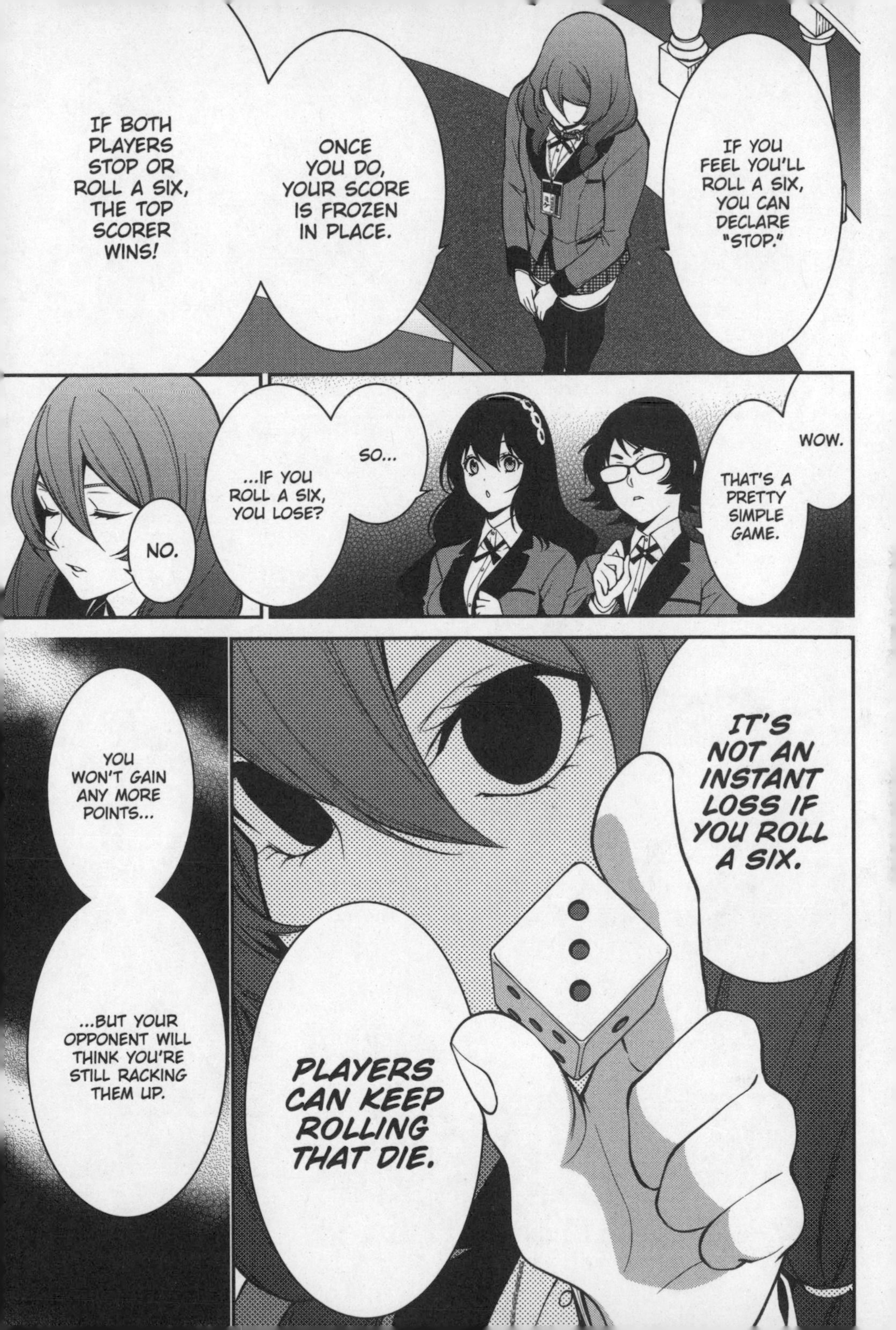
IF YOU FEEL YOU'LL ROLL A SIX, YOU CAN DECLARE "STOP."
ONCE YOU DO, YOUR SCORE IS FROZEN IN PLACE.
IF BOTH PLAYERS STOP OR ROLL A SIX, THE TOP SCORER WINS!
WOW.
THAT'S A PRETTY SIMPLE GAME.
SO...
...IF YOU ROLL A SIX, YOU LOSE?
NO.
IT'S NOT AN INSTANT LOSS IF YOU ROLL A SIX.
PLAYERS CAN KEEP ROLLING THAT DIE.
YOU WON'T GAIN ANY MORE POINTS...
...BUT YOUR OPPONENT WILL THINK YOU'RE STILL RACKING THEM UP.

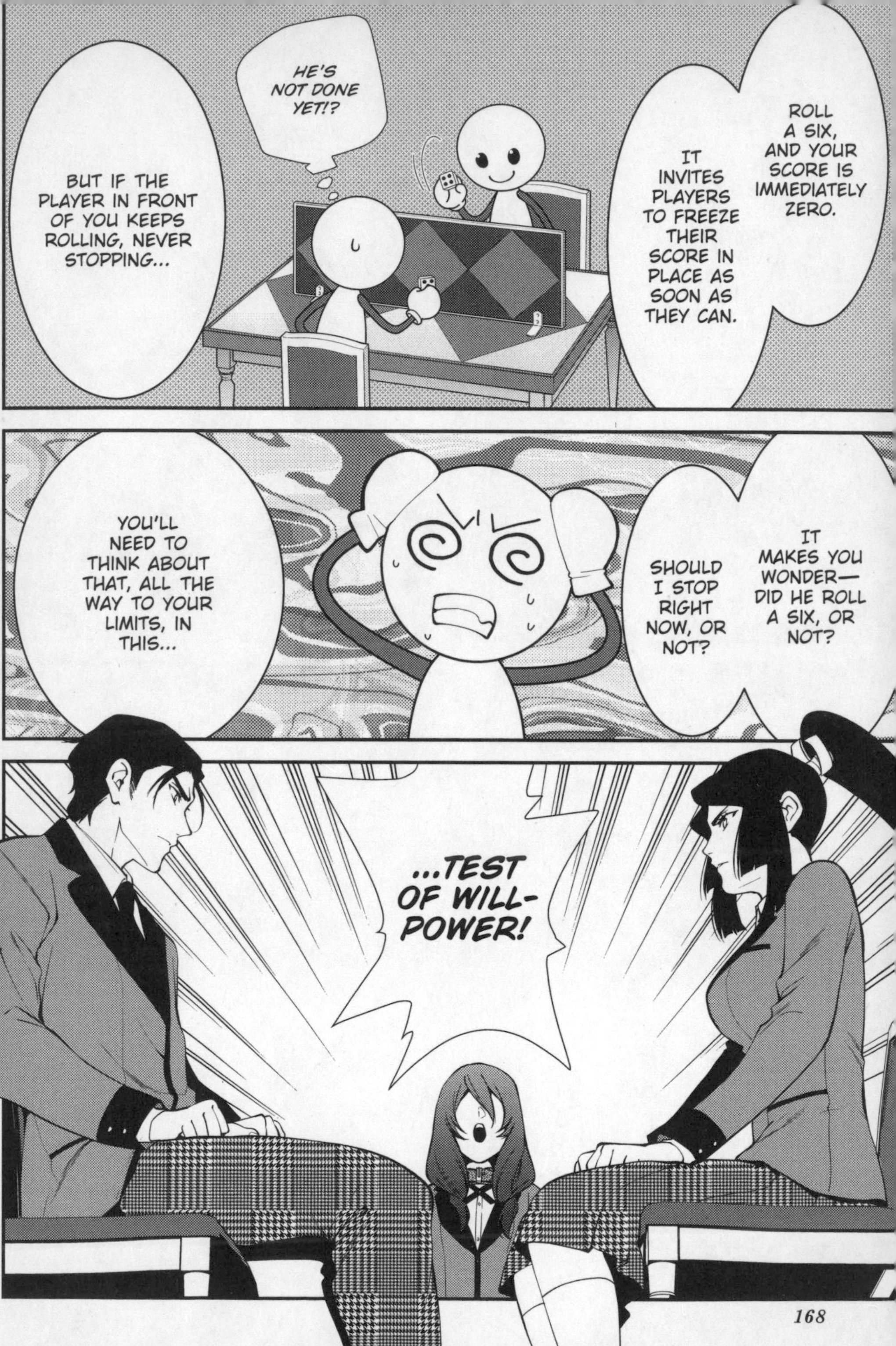
ROLL A SIX, AND YOUR SCORE IS IMMEDIATELY ZERO.
IT INVITES PLAYERS TO FREEZE THEIR SCORE IN PLACE AS SOON AS THEY CAN.
HE'S NOT DONE YET!?
BUT IF THE PLAYER IN FRONT OF YOU KEEPS ROLLING, NEVER STOPPING...
IT MAKES YOU WONDER—DID HE ROLL A SIX, OR NOT?
SHOULD I STOP RIGHT NOW, OR NOT?
YOU'LL NEED TO THINK ABOUT THAT, ALL THE WAY TO YOUR LIMITS, IN THIS...
...TEST OF WILL-POWER!

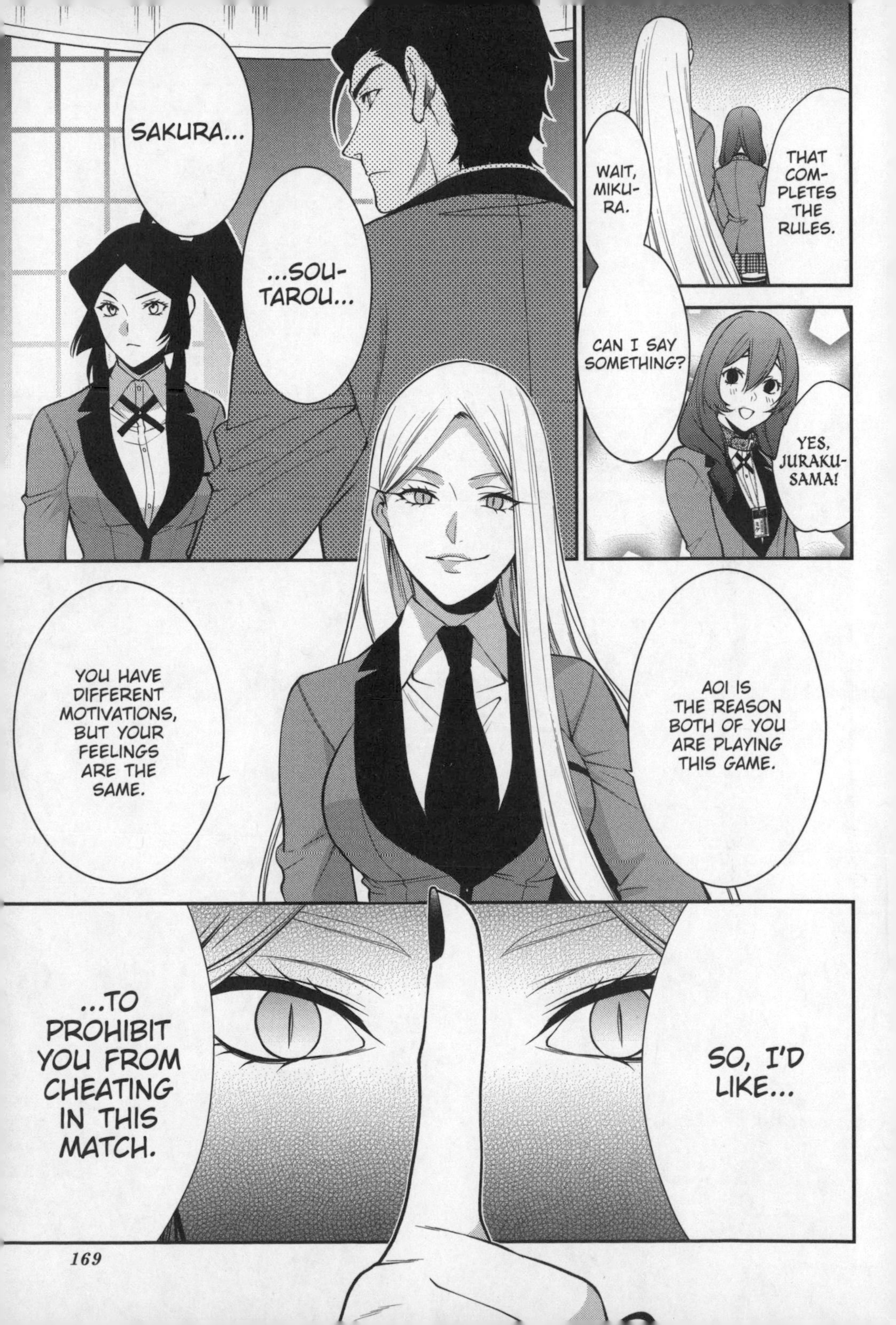
THAT COMPLETES THE RULES.
WAIT, MIKURA.
CAN I SAY SOMETHING?
YES, JURAKU-SAMA!
SAKURA...
...SOUTAROU...
AOI IS THE REASON BOTH OF YOU ARE PLAYING THIS GAME.
YOU HAVE DIFFERENT MOTIVATIONS, BUT YOUR FEELINGS ARE THE SAME.
SO, I'D LIKE...
...TO PROHIBIT YOU FROM CHEATING IN THIS MATCH.

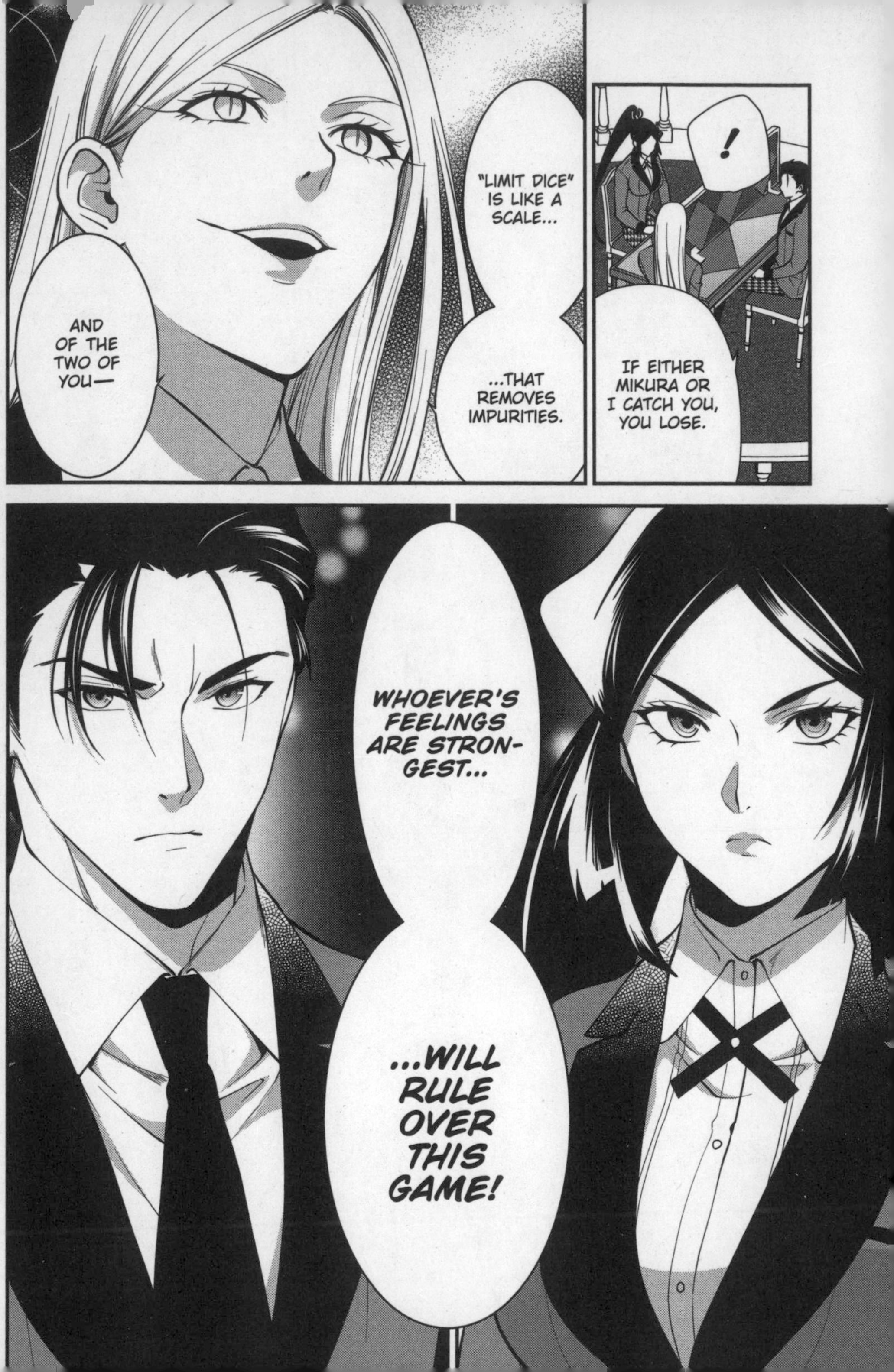
!
IF EITHER MIKURA OR I CATCH YOU, YOU LOSE.
"LIMIT DICE" IS LIKE A SCALE...
...THAT REMOVES IMPURITIES.
AND OF THE TWO OF YOU—
WHOEVER'S FEELINGS ARE STRON-GEST...
...WILL RULE OVER THIS GAME!

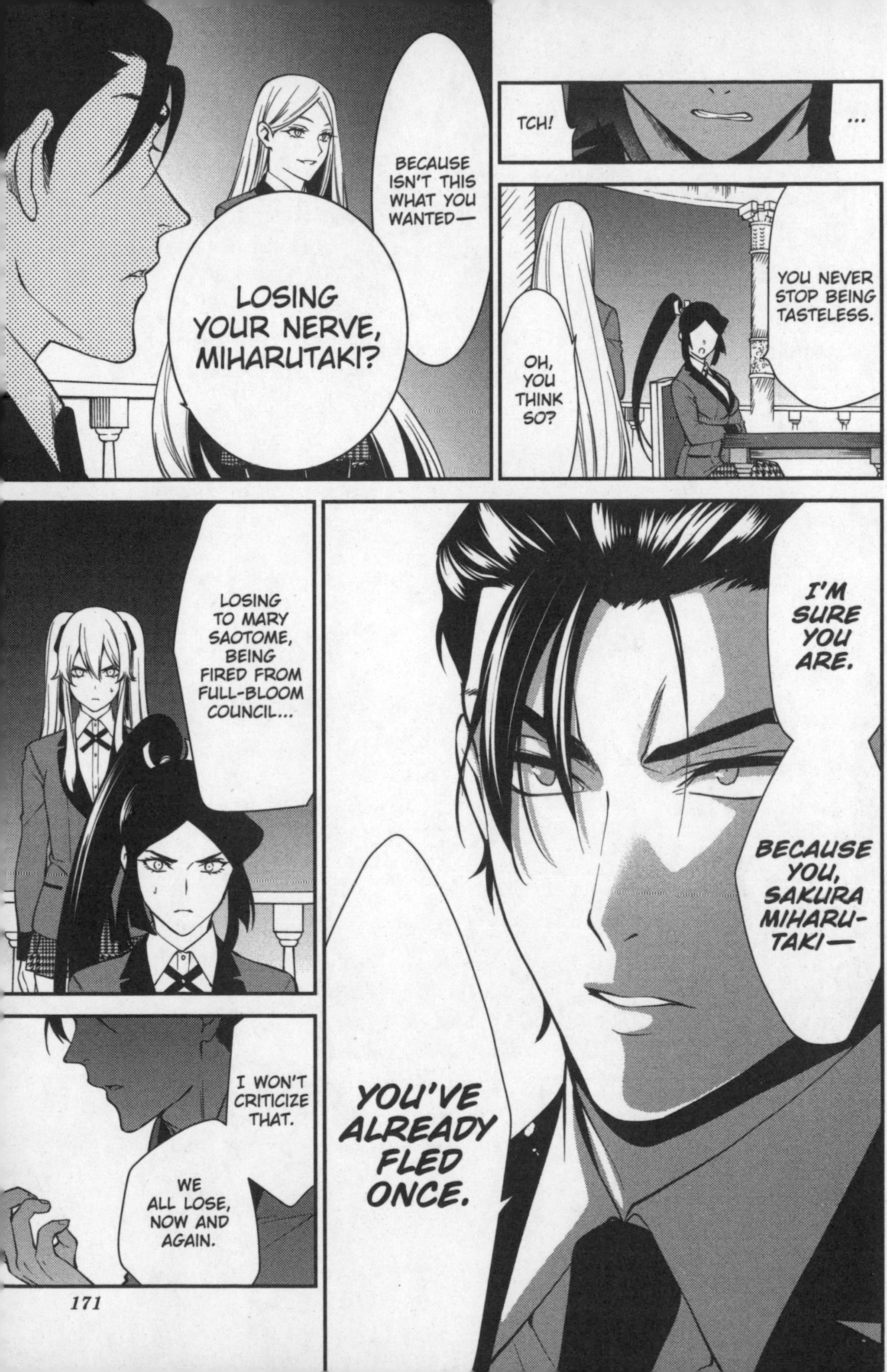
...
TCH!
YOU NEVER STOP BEING TASTELESS.
OH, YOU THINK SO?
BECAUSE ISN'T THIS WHAT YOU WANTED—
LOSING YOUR NERVE, MIHARUTAKI?
I'M SURE YOU ARE.
BECAUSE YOU, SAKURA MIHARU-TAKI—
YOU'VE ALREADY FLED ONCE.
LOSING TO MARY SAOTOME, BEING FIRED FROM FULL-BLOOM COUNCIL...
I WON'T CRITICIZE THAT.
WE ALL LOSE, NOW AND AGAIN.

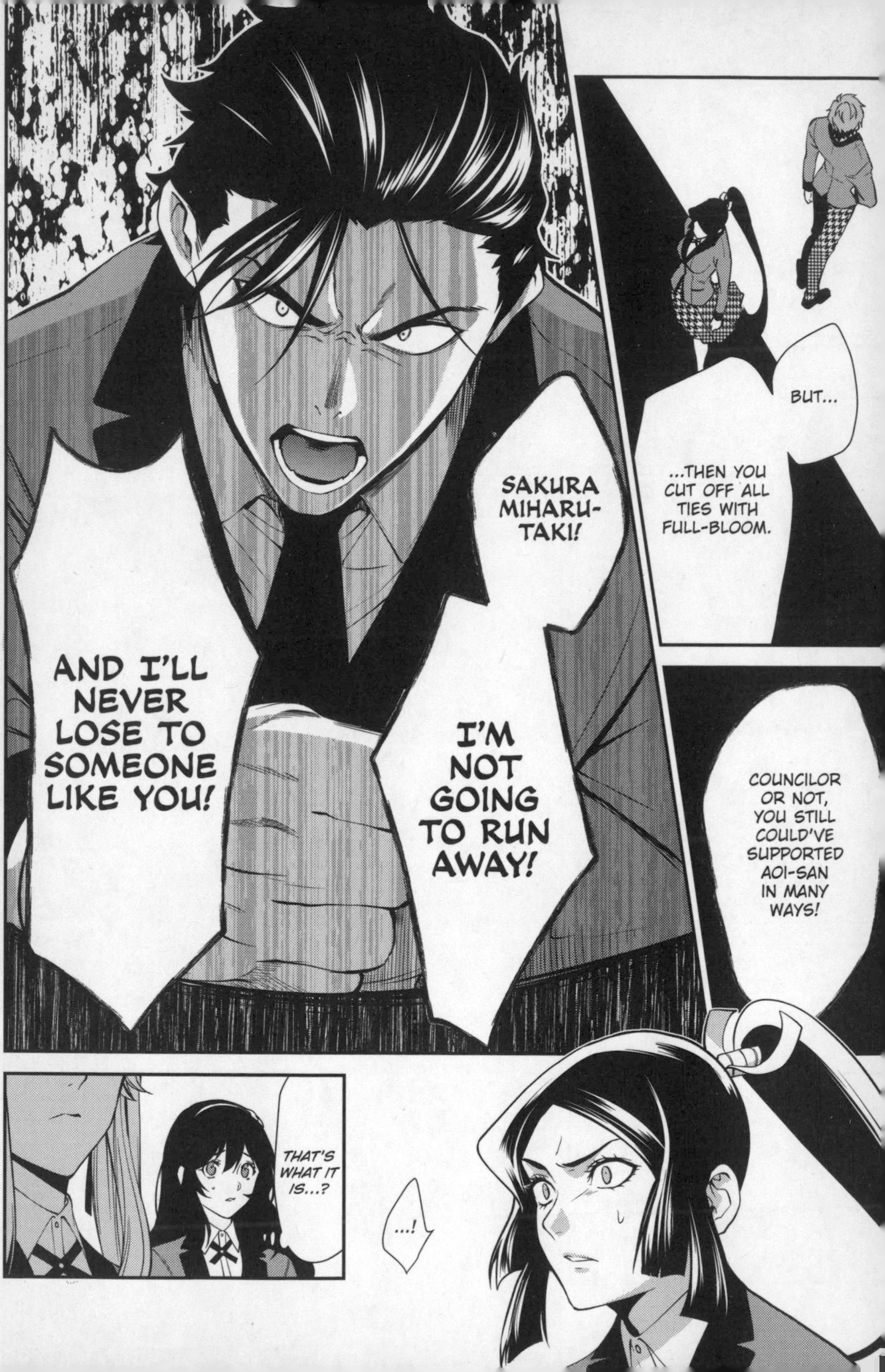
BUT...
...THEN YOU CUT OFF ALL TIES WITH FULL-BLOOM.
COUNCILOR OR NOT, YOU STILL COULD'VE SUPPORTED AOI-SAN IN MANY WAYS!
...!
SAKURA MIHARU-TAKI!
I'M NOT GOING TO RUN AWAY!
AND I'LL NEVER LOSE TO SOMEONE LIKE YOU!
THAT'S WHAT IT IS...?

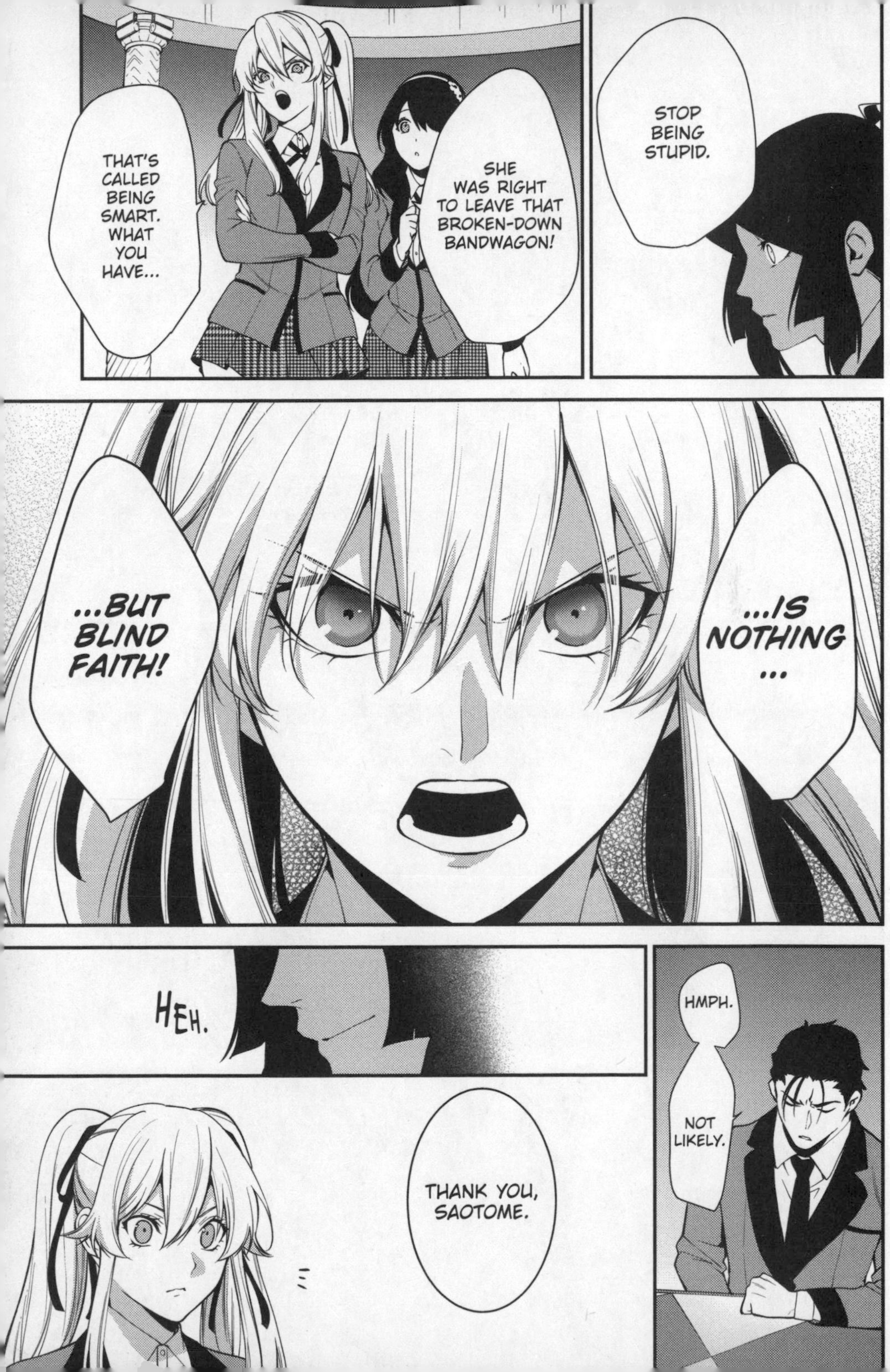
STOP BEING STUPID.
SHE WAS RIGHT TO LEAVE THAT BROKEN-DOWN BANDWAGON!
THAT'S CALLED BEING SMART. WHAT YOU HAVE...
...IS NOTHING ...
...BUT BLIND FAITH!
HMPH.
NOT LIKELY.
HEH.
THANK YOU, SAOTOME.

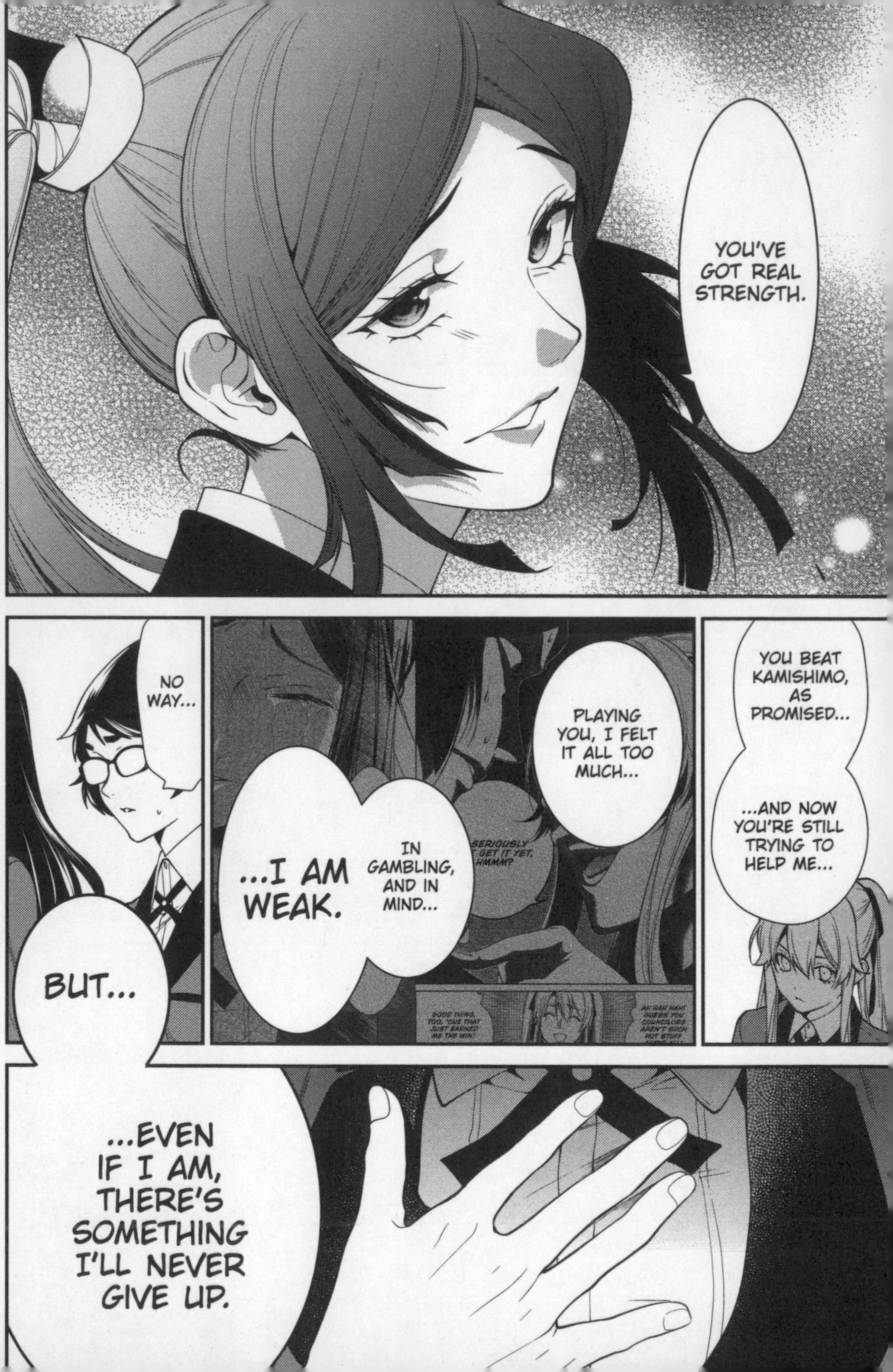
YOU'VE GOT REAL STRENGTH.
YOU BEAT KAMISHIMO, AS PROMISED...
...AND NOW YOU'RE STILL TRYING TO HELP ME...
PLAYING YOU, I FELT IT ALL TOO MUCH...
IN GAMBLING, AND IN MIND...
...I AM WEAK.
NO WAY...
BUT...
...EVEN IF I AM, THERE'S SOMETHING I'LL NEVER GIVE UP.

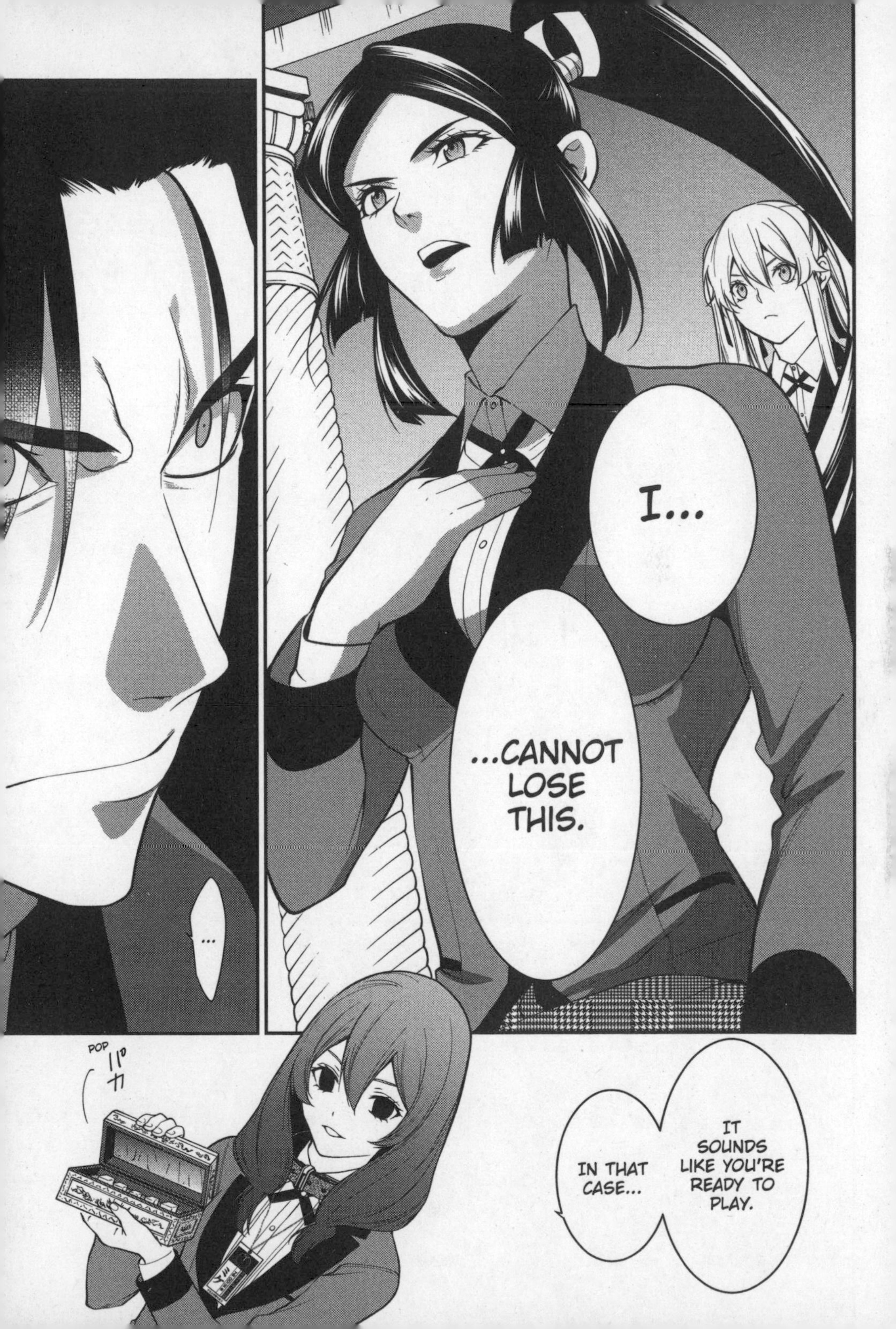
I...
...CANNOT LOSE THIS.
...
POP
パカ
IT SOUNDS LIKE YOU'RE READY TO PLAY.
IN THAT CASE...

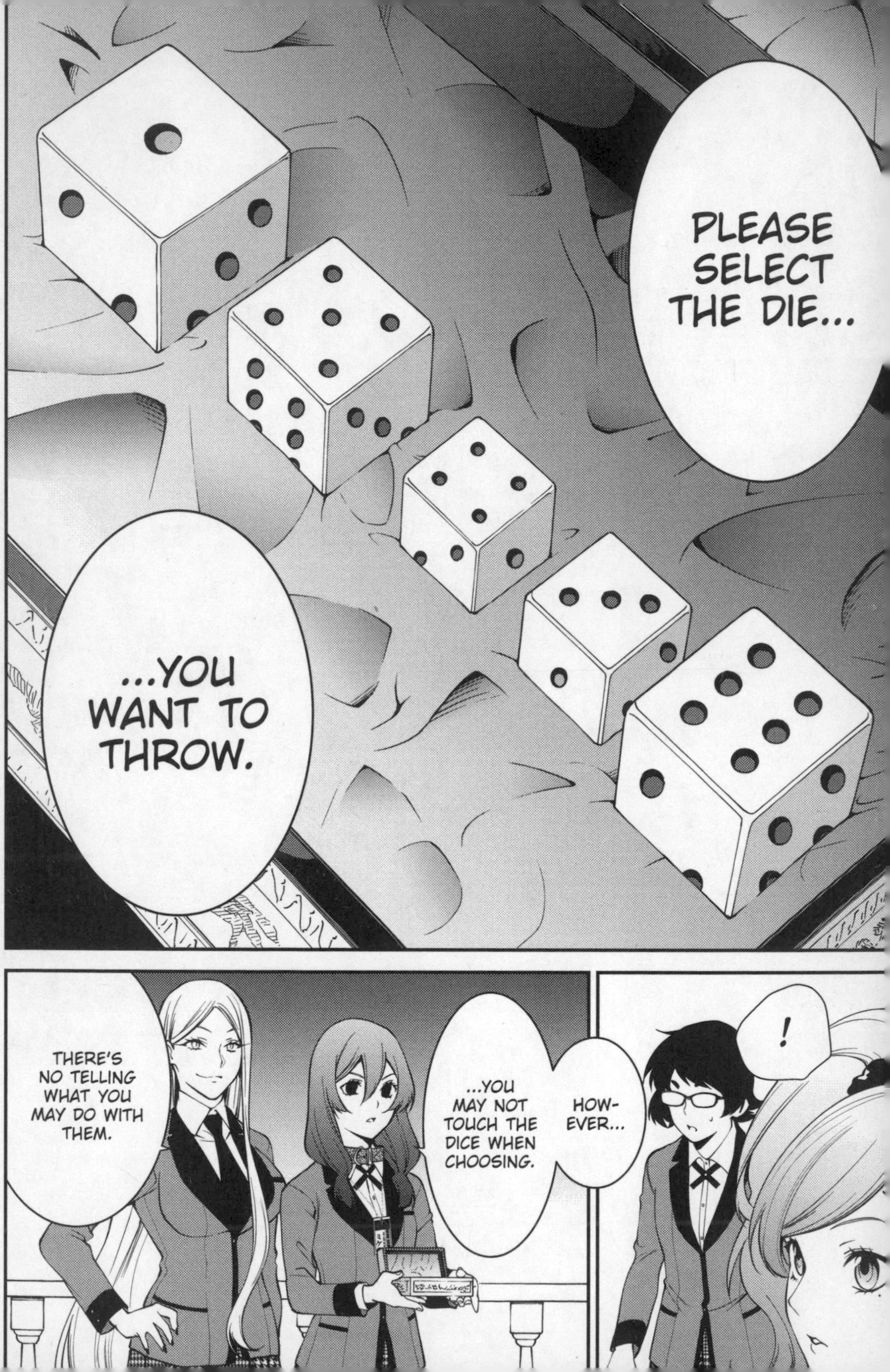
PLEASE SELECT THE DIE...
...YOU WANT TO THROW.
!
HOW-EVER...
...YOU MAY NOT TOUCH THE DICE WHEN CHOOSING.
THERE'S NO TELLING WHAT YOU MAY DO WITH THEM.

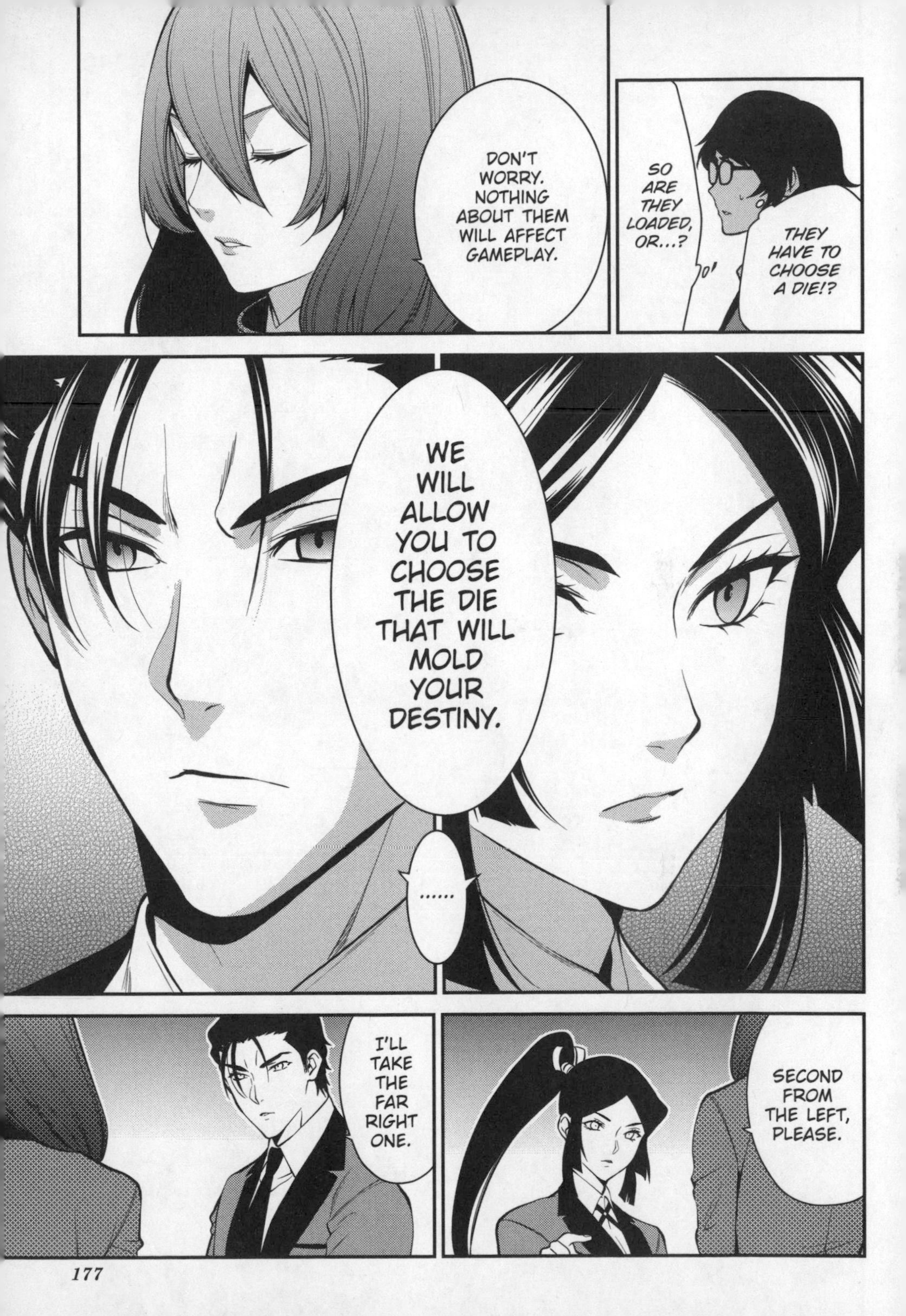
THEY HAVE TO CHOOSE A DIE!?
SO ARE THEY LOADED, OR...?
DON'T WORRY. NOTHING ABOUT THEM WILL AFFECT GAMEPLAY.
WE WILL ALLOW YOU TO CHOOSE THE DIE THAT WILL MOLD YOUR DESTINY.
......
SECOND FROM THE LEFT, PLEASE.
I'LL TAKE THE FAR RIGHT ONE.

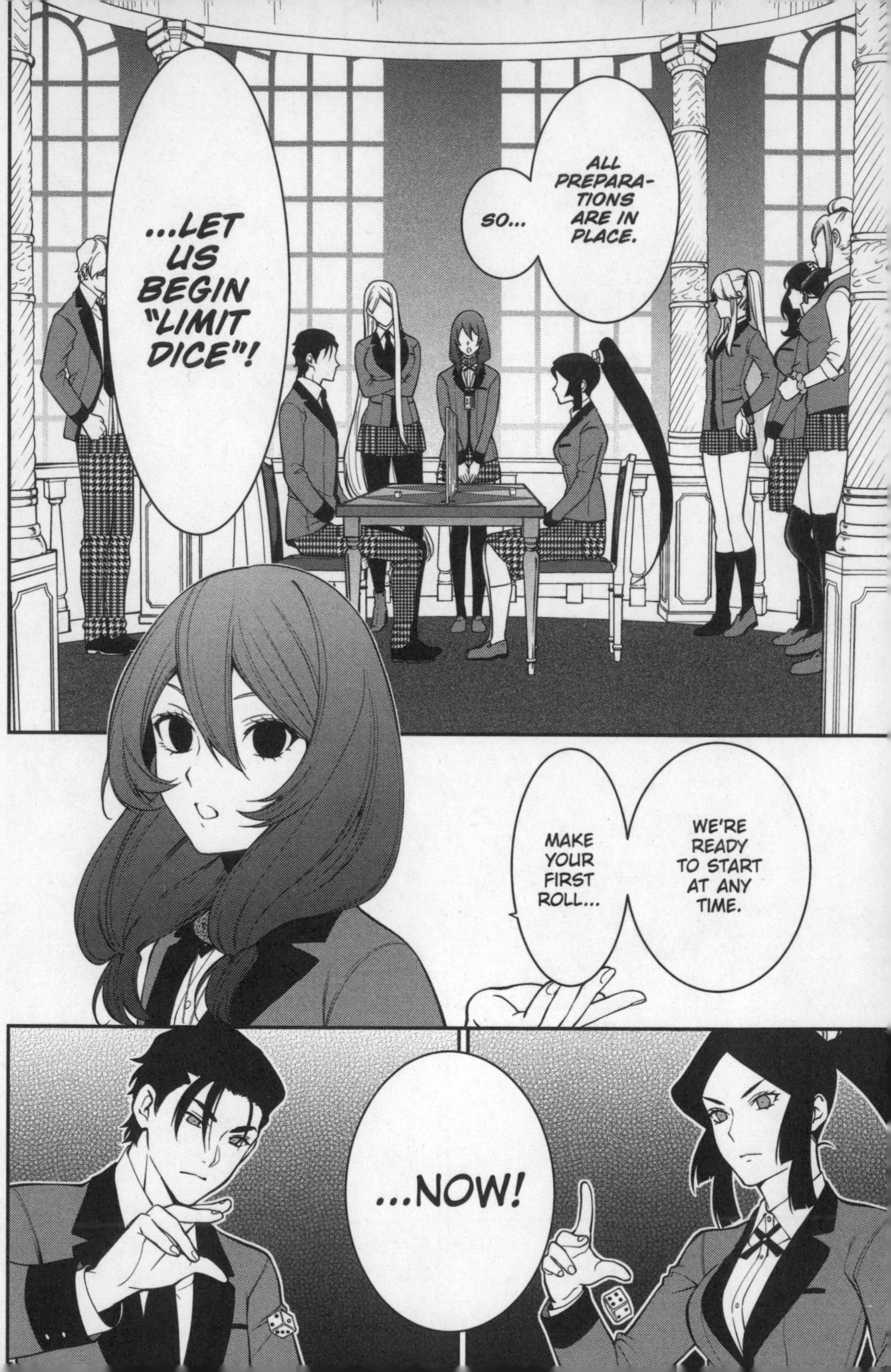
ALL PREPARATIONS ARE IN PLACE.
SO...
...LET US BEGIN "LIMIT DICE"!
WE'RE READY TO START AT ANY TIME.
MAKE YOUR FIRST ROLL...
...NOW!

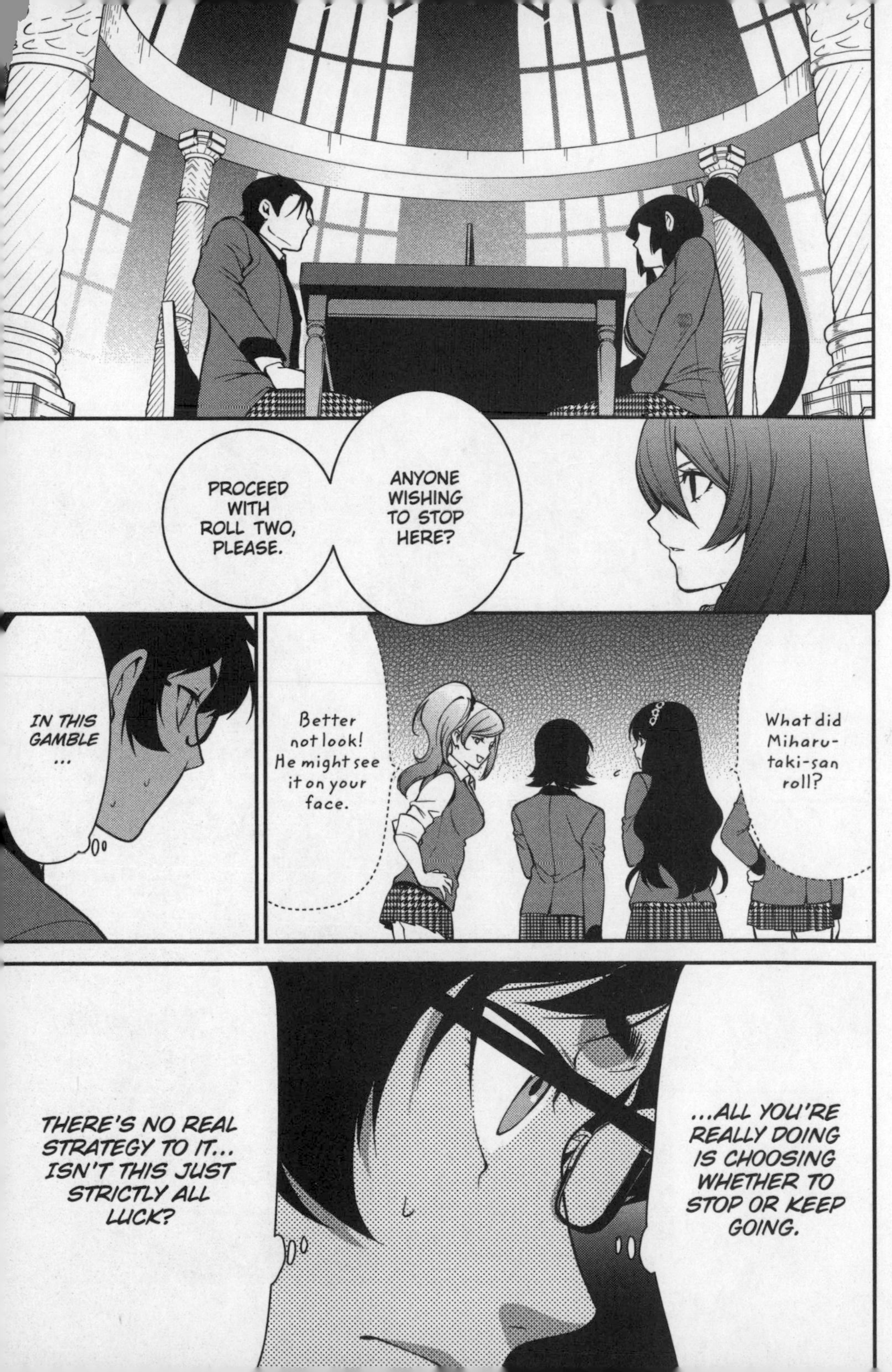
ANYONE WISHING TO STOP HERE?
PROCEED WITH ROLL TWO, PLEASE.
What did Miharu-taki-san roll?
Better not look! He might see it on your face.
IN THIS GAMBLE...
...ALL YOU'RE REALLY DOING IS CHOOSING WHETHER TO STOP OR KEEP GOING.
THERE'S NO REAL STRATEGY TO IT... ISN'T THIS JUST STRICTLY ALL LUCK?

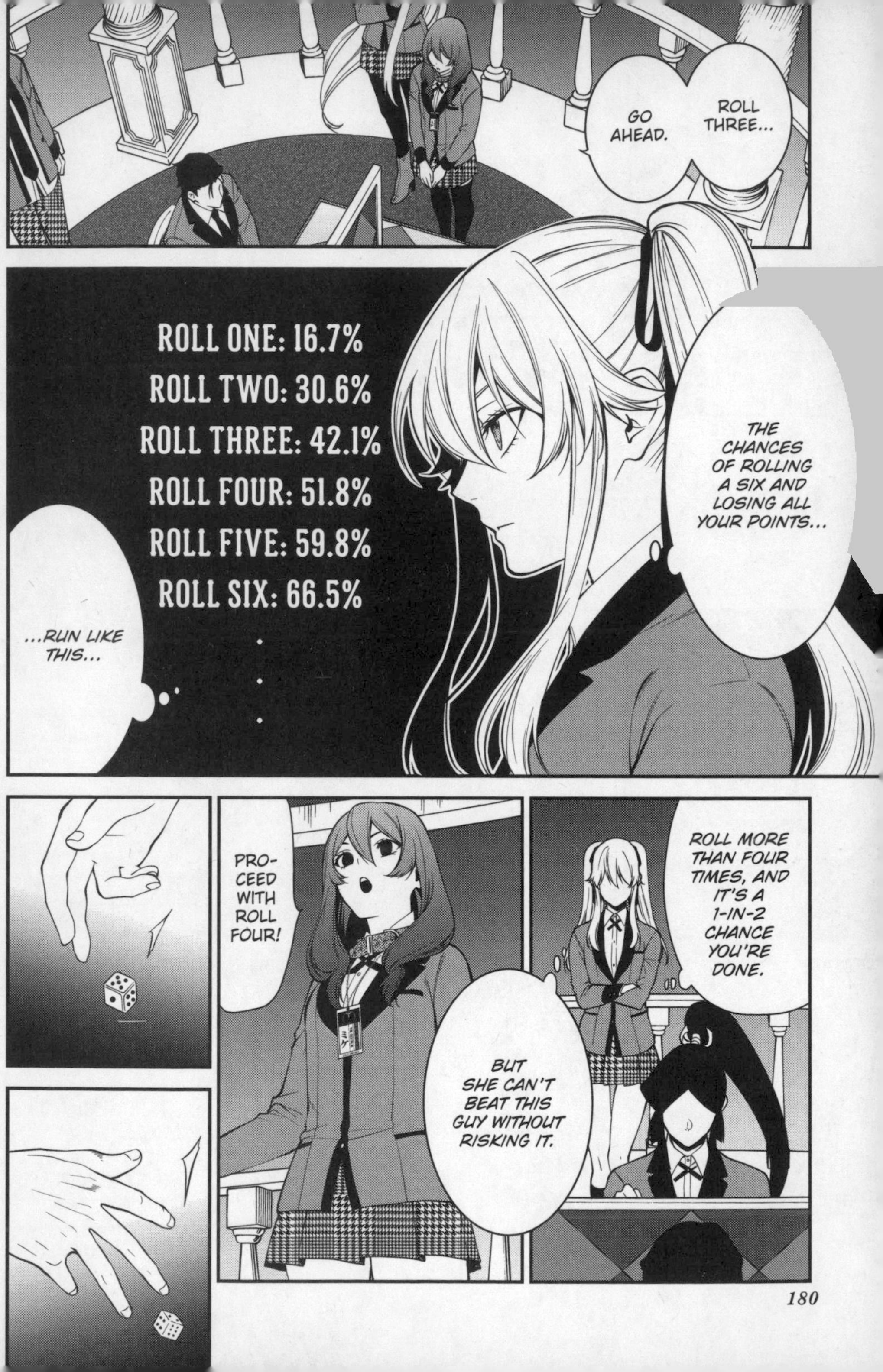
ROLL THREE... GO AHEAD.
THE CHANCES OF ROLLING A SIX AND LOSING ALL YOUR POINTS...
ROLL ONE: 16.7%
ROLL TWO: 30.6%
ROLL THREE: 42.1%
ROLL FOUR: 51.8%
ROLL FIVE: 59.8%
ROLL SIX: 66.5%
...RUN LIKE THIS...
ROLL MORE THAN FOUR TIMES, AND IT'S A 1-IN-2 CHANCE YOU'RE DONE.
BUT SHE CAN'T BEAT THIS GUY WITHOUT RISKING IT.
PROCEED WITH ROLL FOUR!

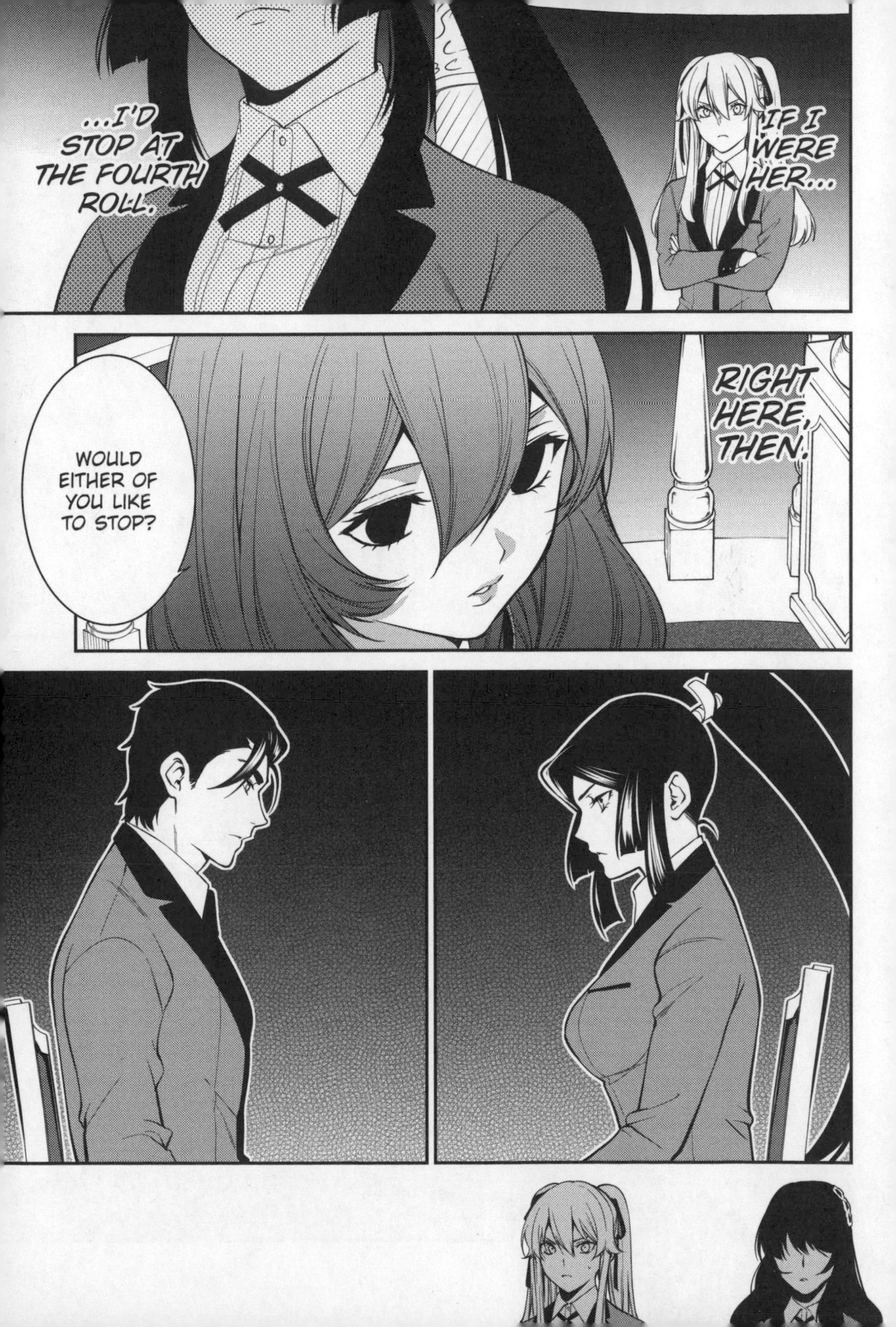
IF I WERE HER...
...I'D STOP AT THE FOURTH ROLL.
RIGHT HERE, THEN.
WOULD EITHER OF YOU LIKE TO STOP?

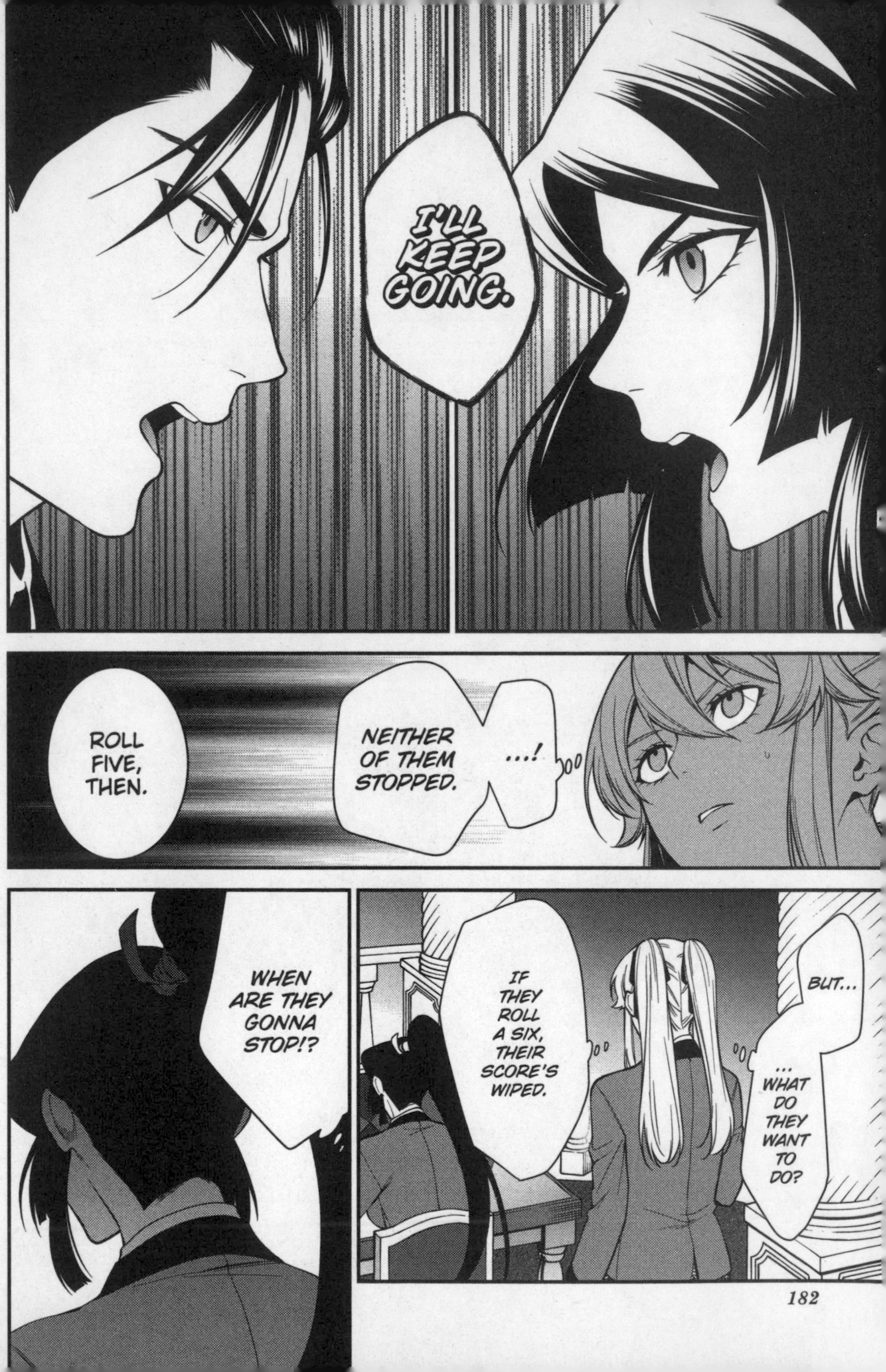
I'LL KEEP GOING.
...!
NEITHER OF THEM STOPPED.
ROLL FIVE, THEN.
BUT...
...WHAT DO THEY WANT TO DO?
IF THEY ROLL A SIX, THEIR SCORE'S WIPED.
WHEN ARE THEY GONNA STOP!?

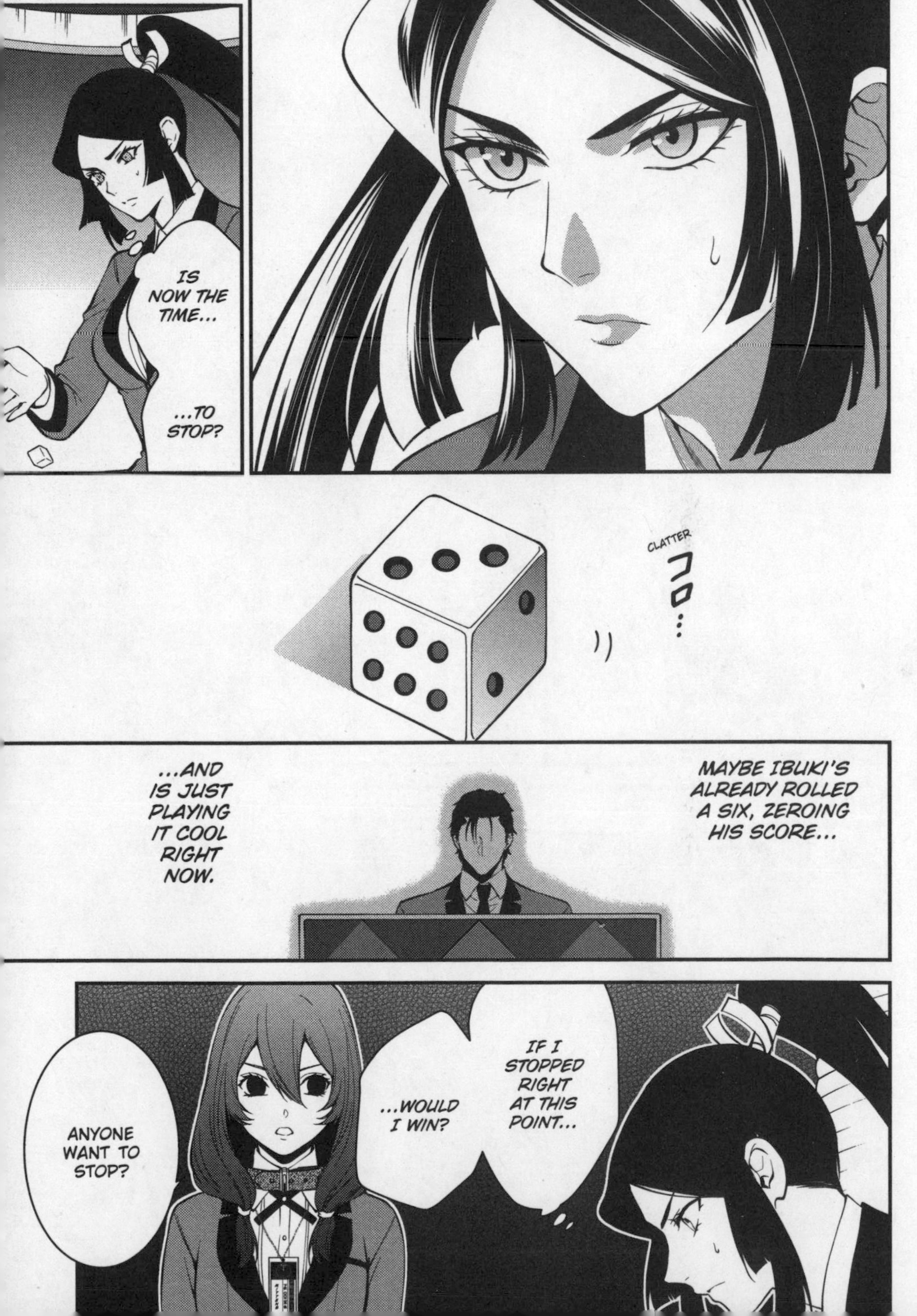
IS NOW THE TIME...
...TO STOP?
CLATTER
コロ...
MAYBE IBUKI'S ALREADY ROLLED A SIX, ZEROING HIS SCORE...
...AND IS JUST PLAYING IT COOL RIGHT NOW.
IF I STOPPED RIGHT AT THIS POINT...
...WOULD I WIN?
ANYONE WANT TO STOP?

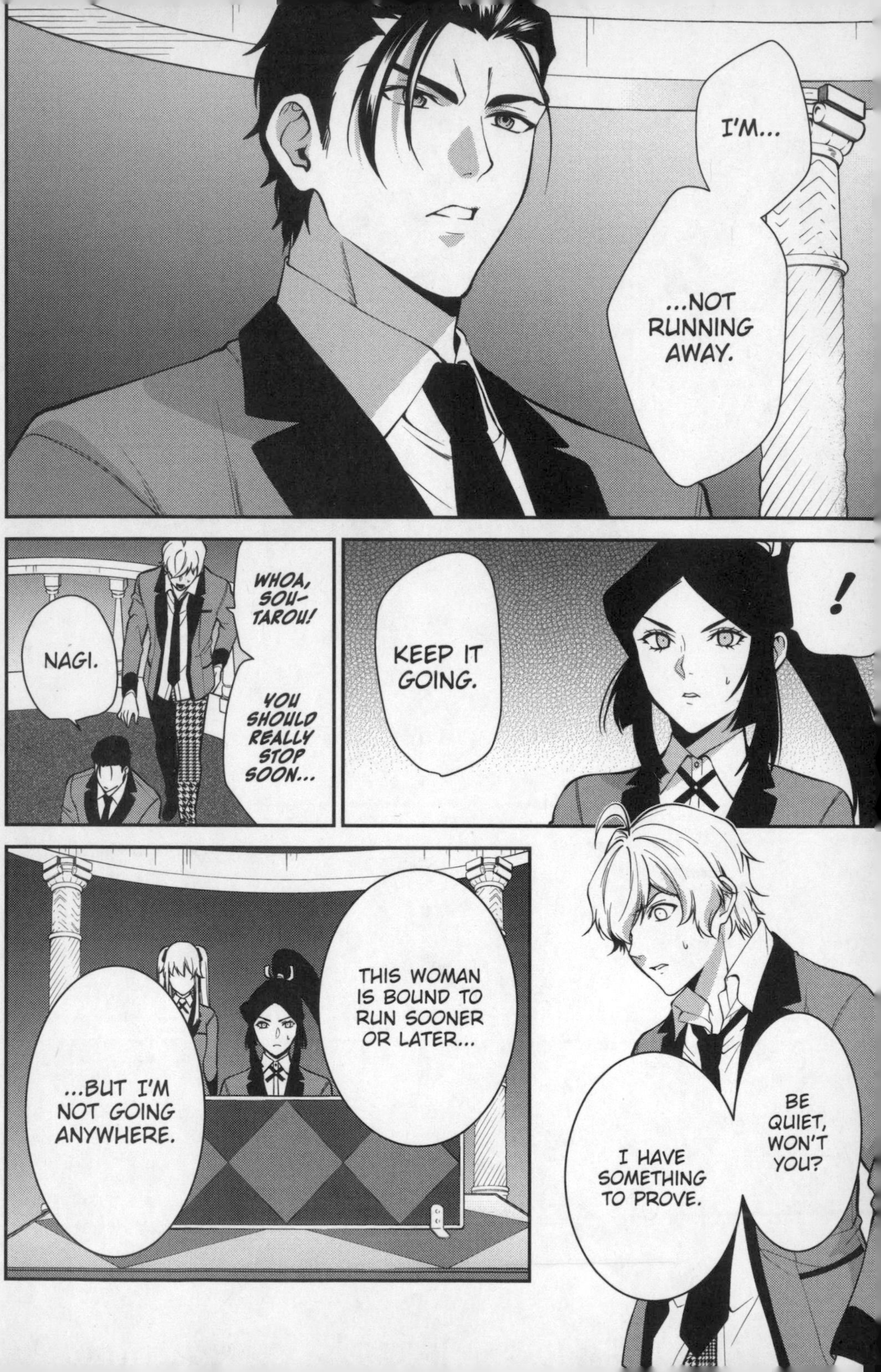
I'M...
...NOT RUNNING AWAY.
!
KEEP IT GOING.
WHOA, SOU-TAROU!
YOU SHOULD REALLY STOP SOON...
NAGI.
BE QUIET, WON'T YOU?
I HAVE SOMETHING TO PROVE.
THIS WOMAN IS BOUND TO RUN SOONER OR LATER...
...BUT I'M NOT GOING ANYWHERE.

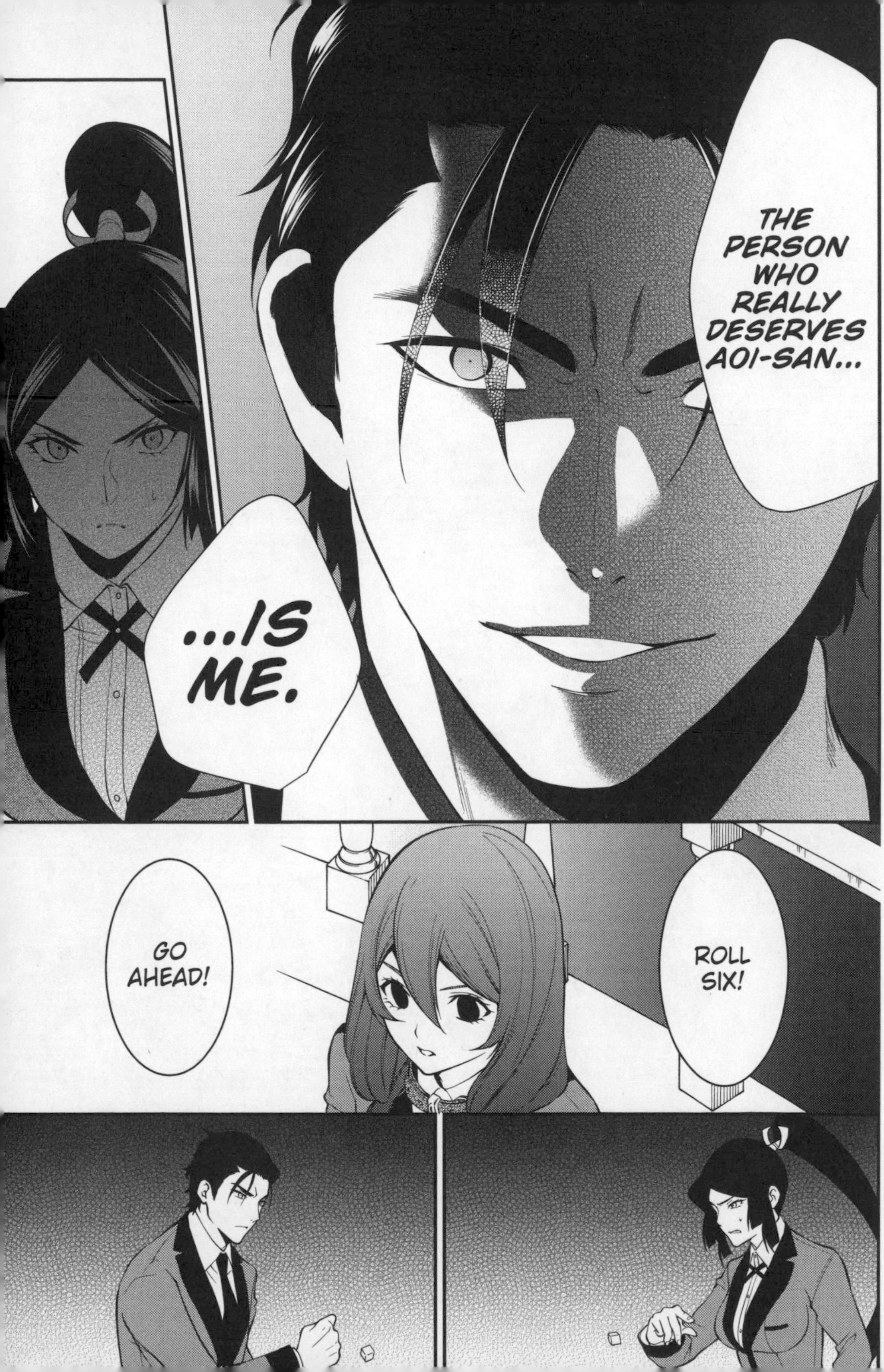
THE PERSON WHO REALLY DESERVES AOI-SAN...
...IS ME.
ROLL SIX!
GO AHEAD!

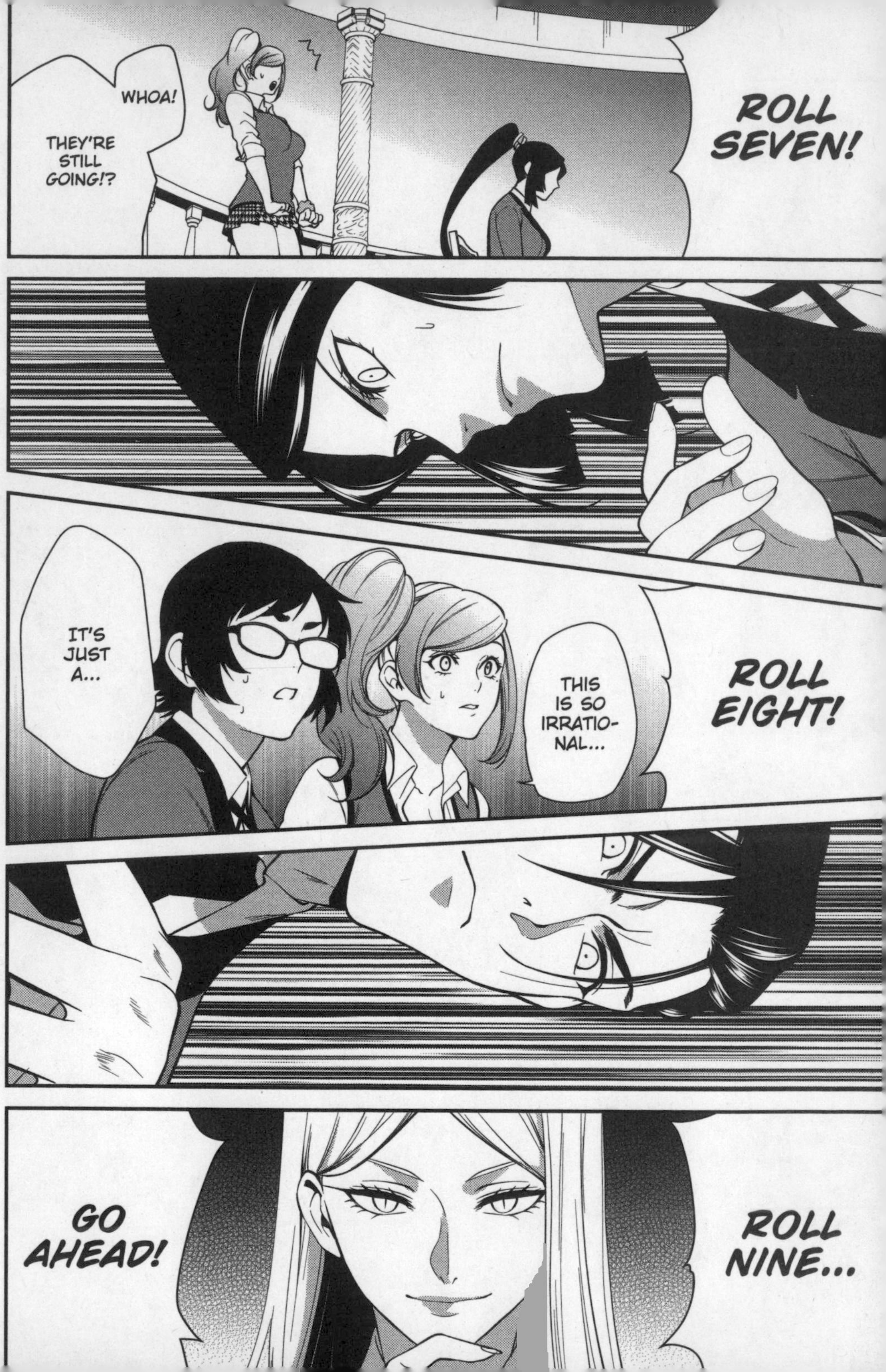
ROLL SEVEN!
WHOA!
THEY'RE STILL GOING!?
ROLL EIGHT!
THIS IS SO IRRATIO-NAL...
IT'S JUST A...
ROLL NINE...
GO AHEAD!

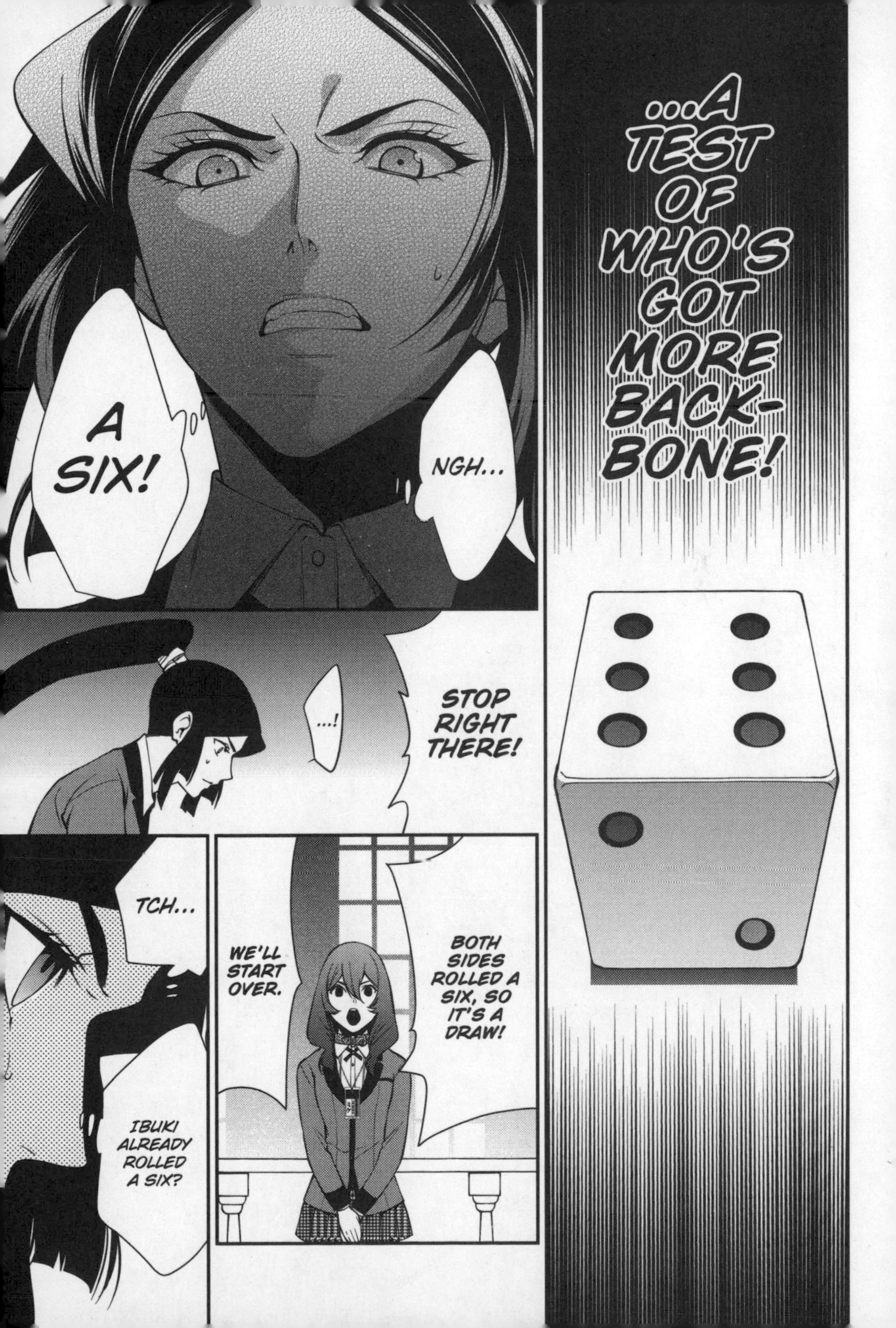
...A TEST OF WHO'S GOT MORE BACK-BONE!
NGH...
A SIX!
STOP RIGHT THERE!
...!
BOTH SIDES ROLLED A SIX, SO IT'S A DRAW!
WE'LL START OVER.
TCH...
IBUKI ALREADY ROLLED A SIX?

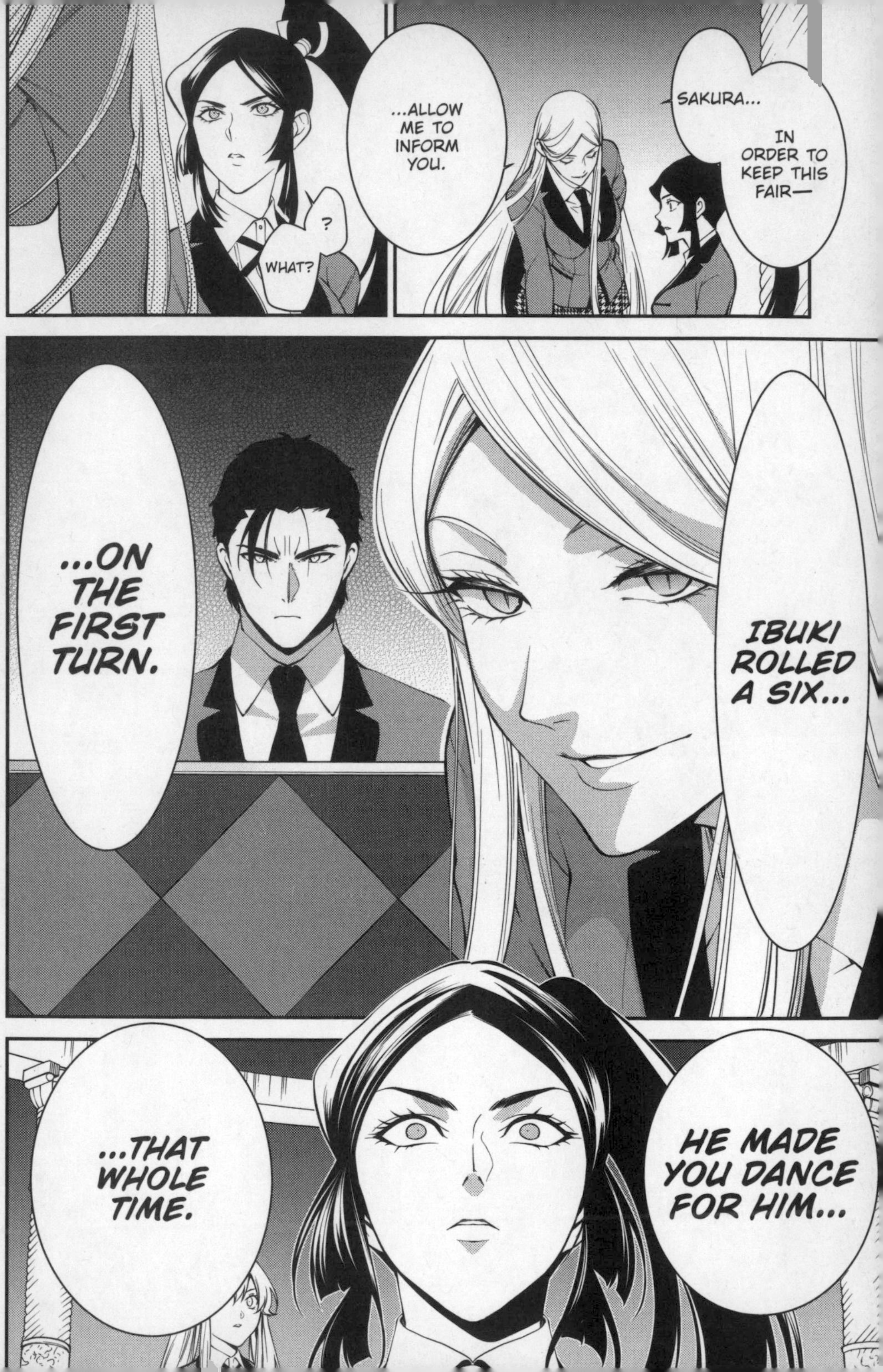
SAKURA...
IN ORDER TO KEEP THIS FAIR—
...ALLOW ME TO INFORM YOU.
?
WHAT?
IBUKI ROLLED A SIX...
...ON THE FIRST TURN.
HE MADE YOU DANCE FOR HIM...
...THAT WHOLE TIME.

Kakegurui Twin

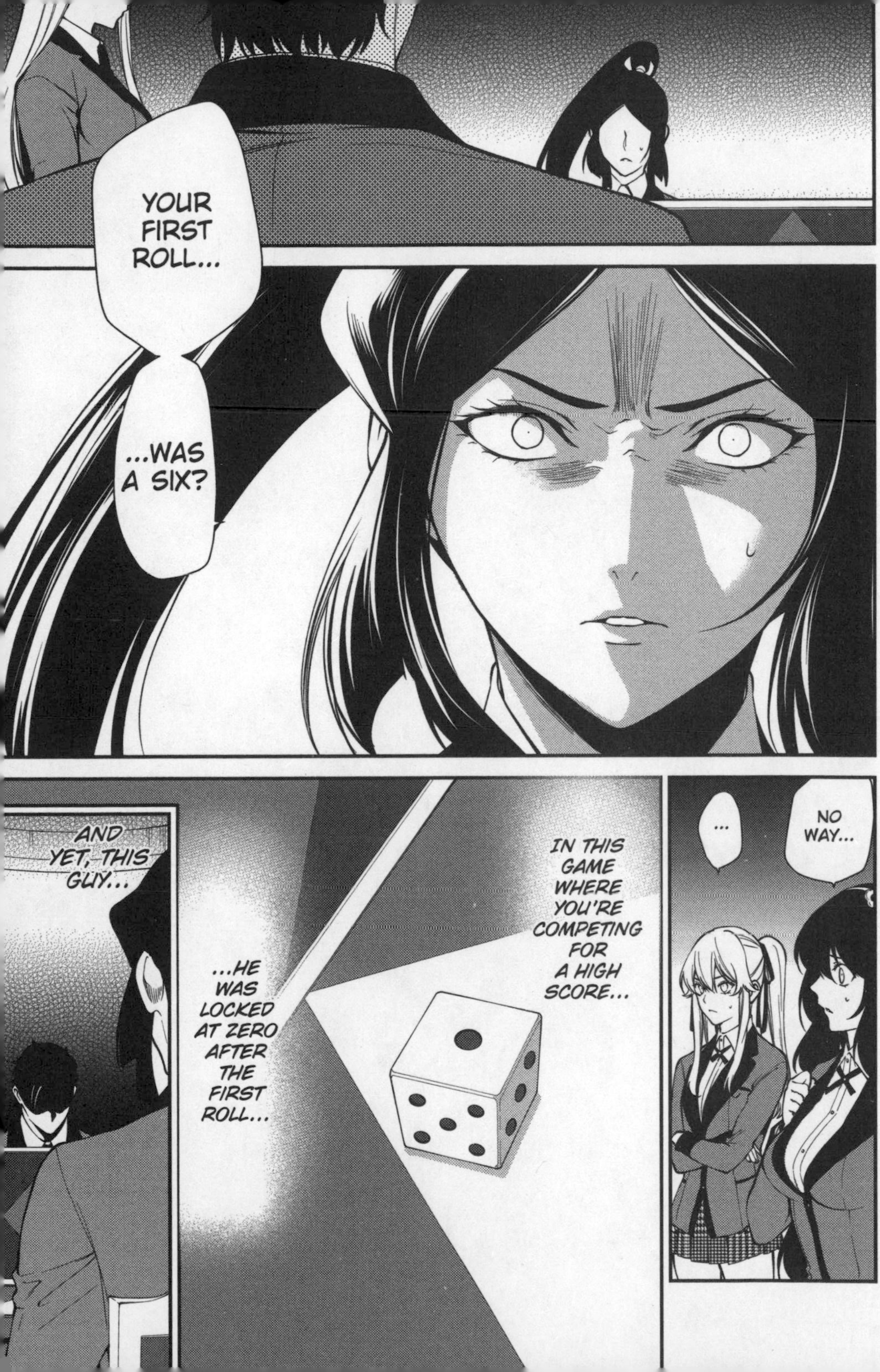
YOUR FIRST ROLL...
...WAS A SIX?
NO WAY...
...
AND YET, THIS GUY...
IN THIS GAME WHERE YOU'RE COMPETING FOR A HIGH SCORE...
...HE WAS LOCKED AT ZERO AFTER THE FIRST ROLL...

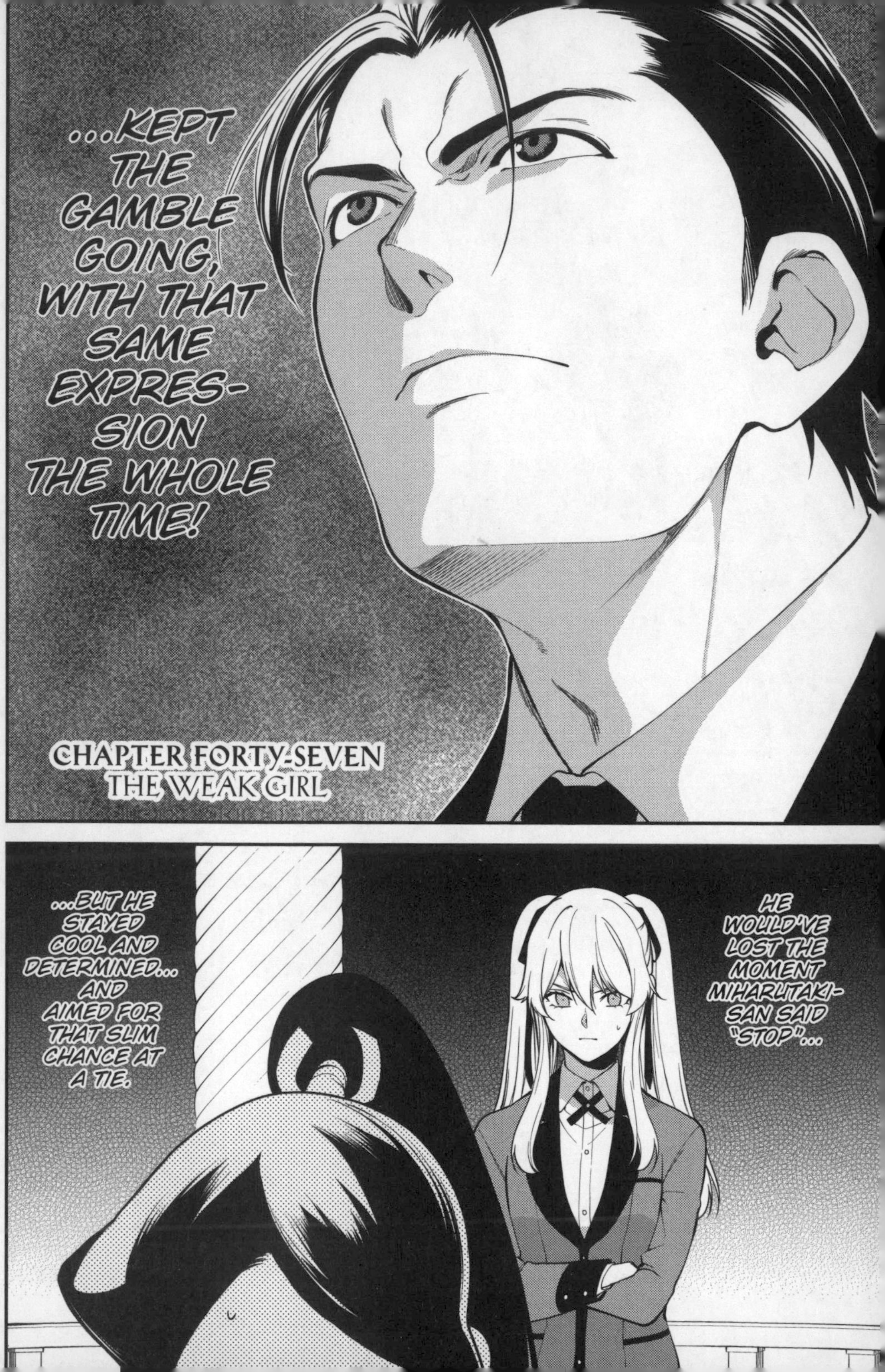
...KEPT THE GAMBLE GOING, WITH THAT SAME EXPRES-SION THE WHOLE TIME!
CHAPTER FORTY-SEVEN
THE WEAK GIRL
HE WOULD'VE LOST THE MOMENT MIHARUTAKI-SAN SAID "STOP"...
...BUT HE STAYED COOL AND DETERMINED... AND AIMED FOR THAT SLIM CHANCE AT A TIE.

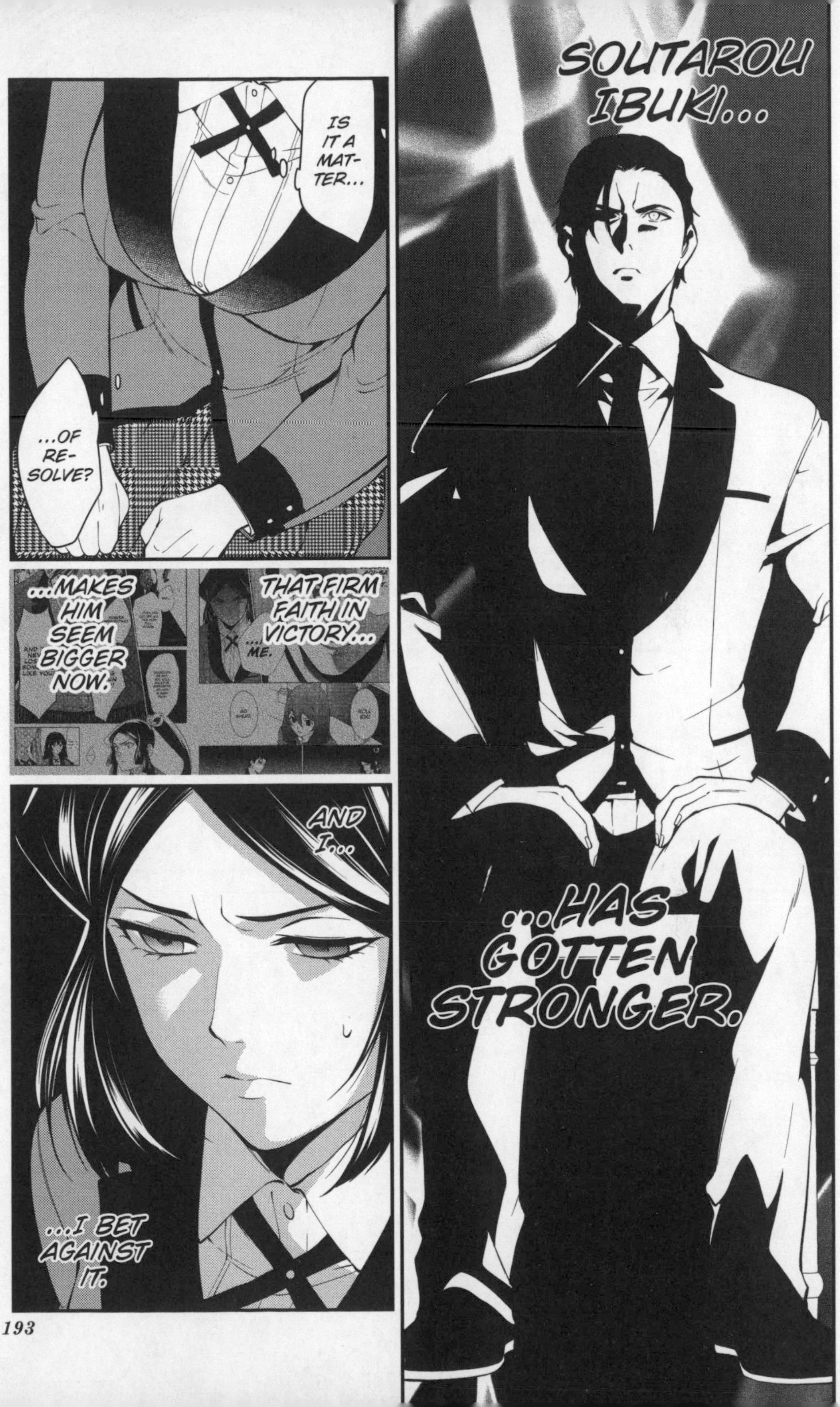
SOUTAROU IBUKI...
...HAS GOTTEN STRONGER.
IS IT A MAT-TER...
...OF RE-SOLVE?
THAT FIRM FAITH IN VICTORY...
...MAKES HIM SEEM BIGGER NOW.
AND I...
...I BET AGAINST IT.

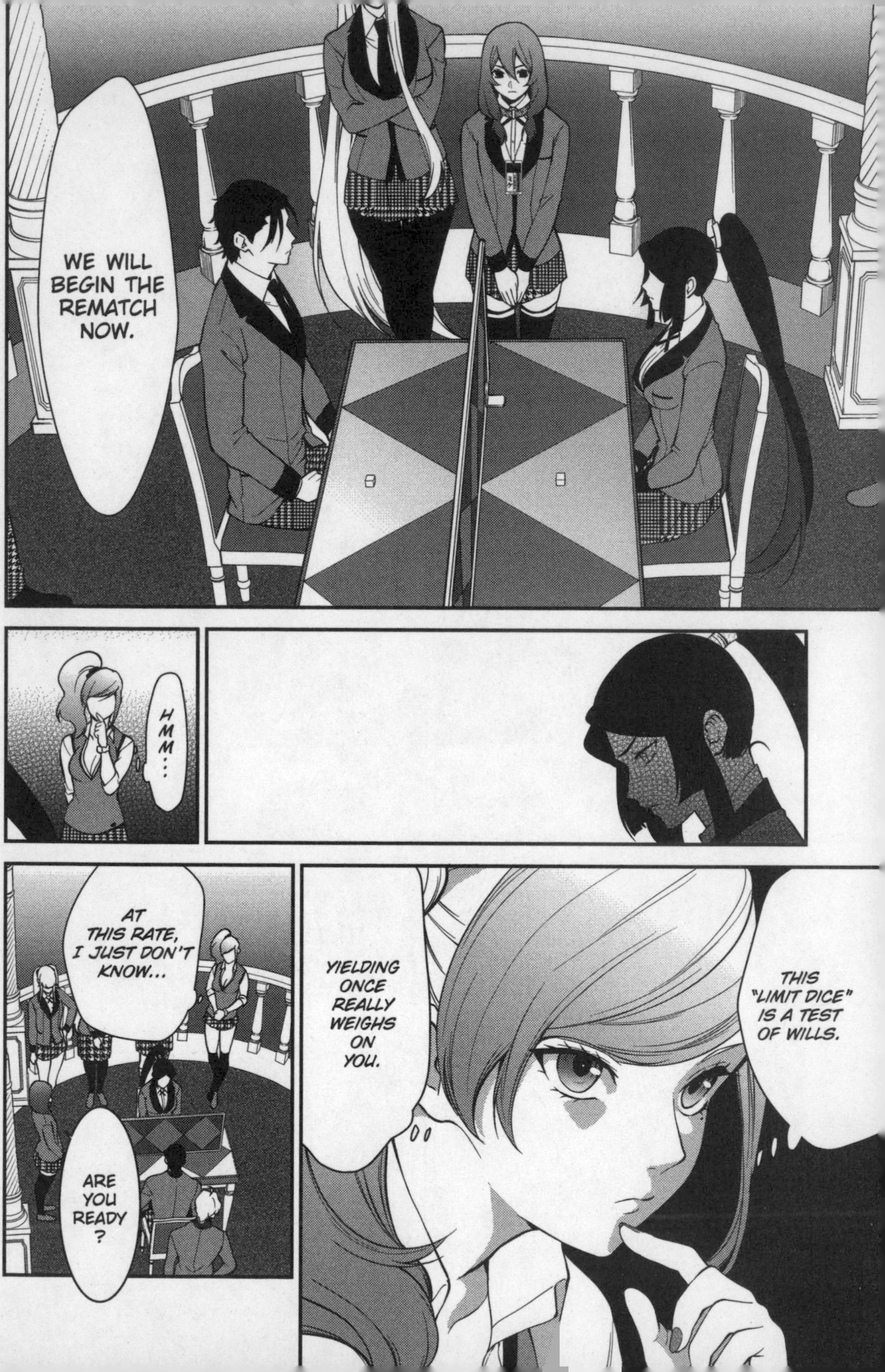
WE WILL BEGIN THE REMATCH NOW.
HMM...
THIS "LIMIT DICE" IS A TEST OF WILLS.
YIELDING ONCE REALLY WEIGHS ON YOU.
AT THIS RATE, I JUST DON'T KNOW...
ARE YOU READY?

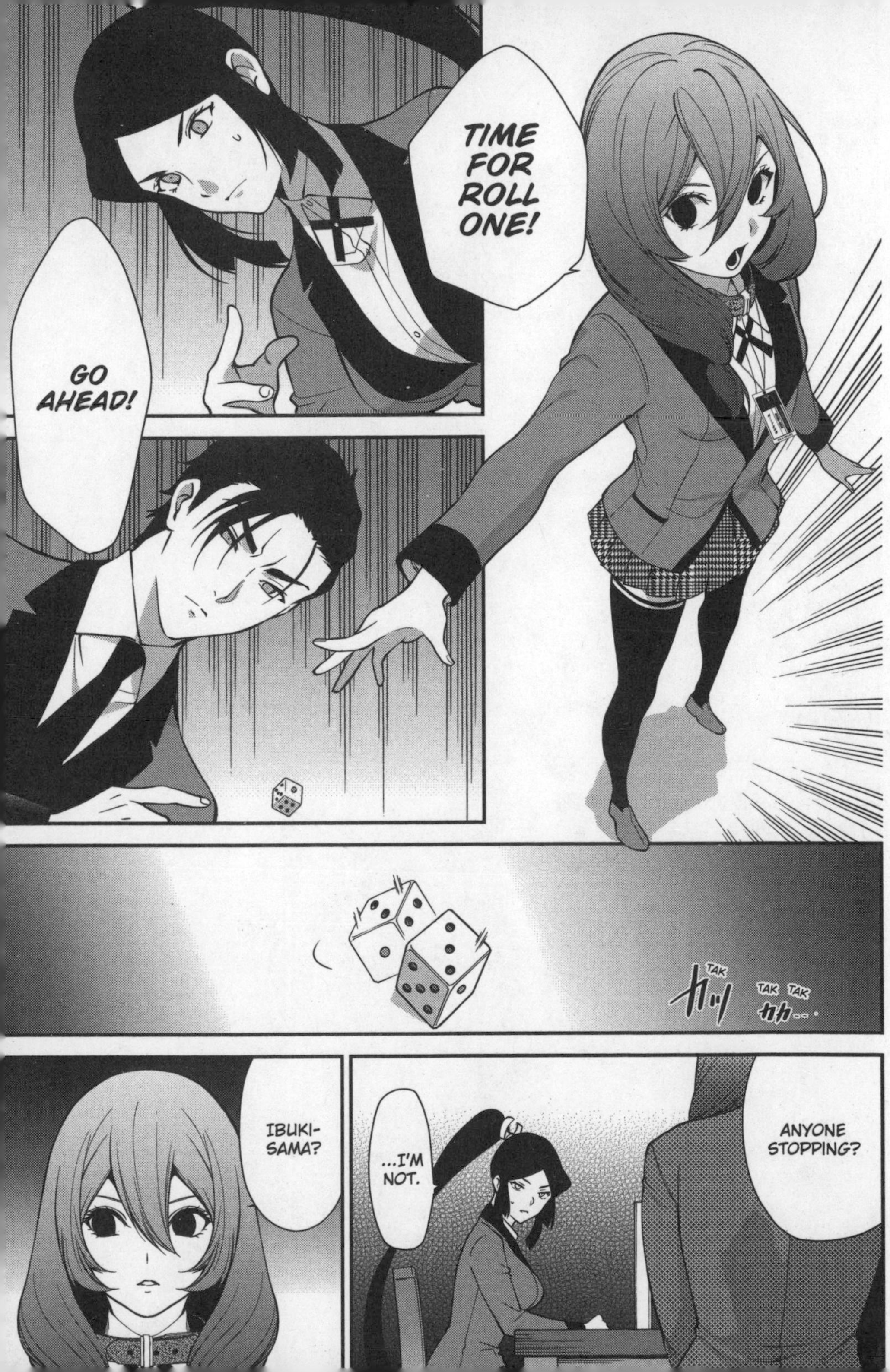
TIME FOR ROLL ONE!
GO AHEAD!
カッ TAK
カカ… TAK TAK
ANYONE STOPPING?
...I'M NOT.
IBUKI-SAMA?

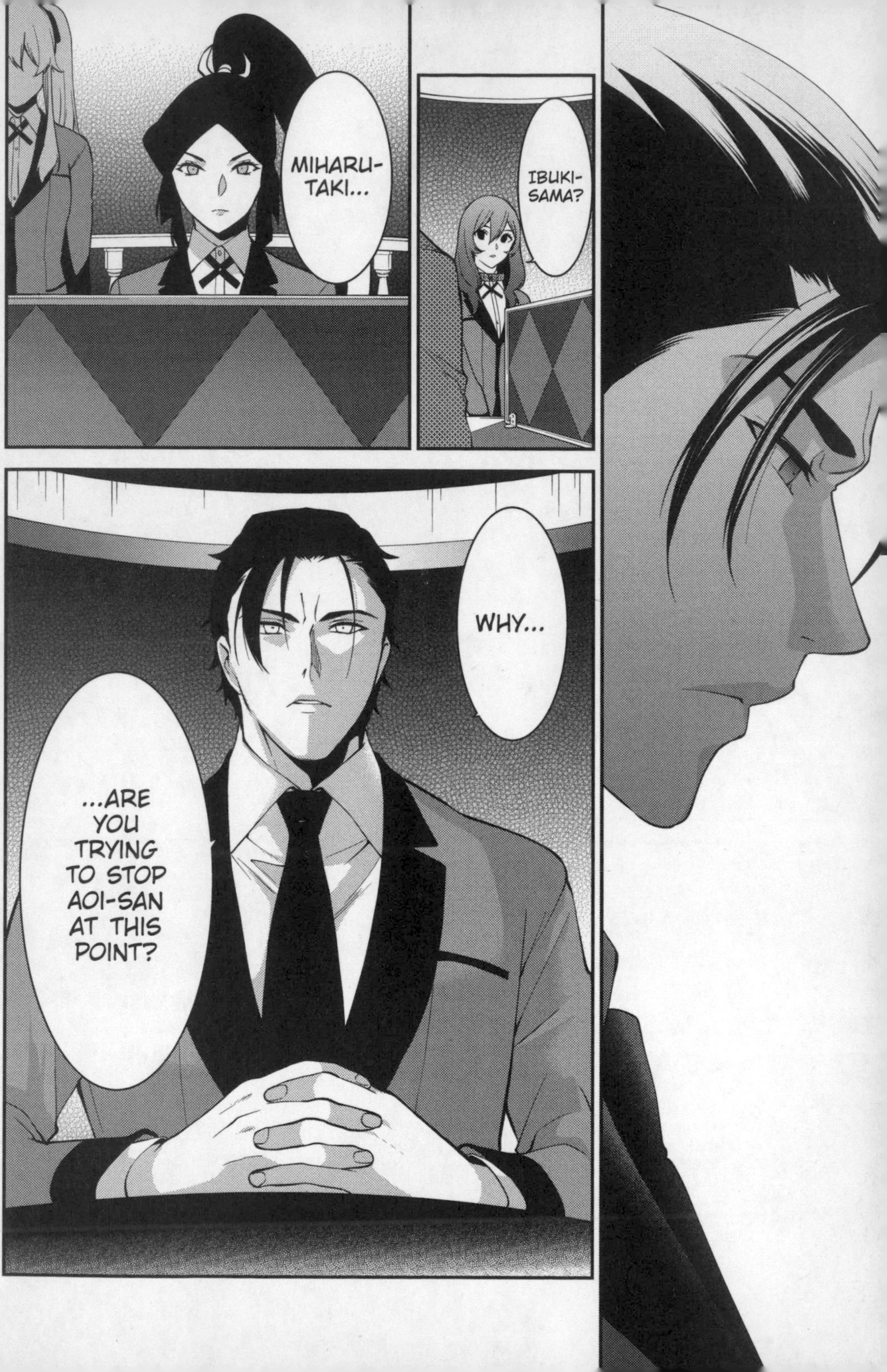
IBUKI-SAMA?
MIHARU-TAKI...
WHY...
...ARE YOU TRYING TO STOP AOI-SAN AT THIS POINT?

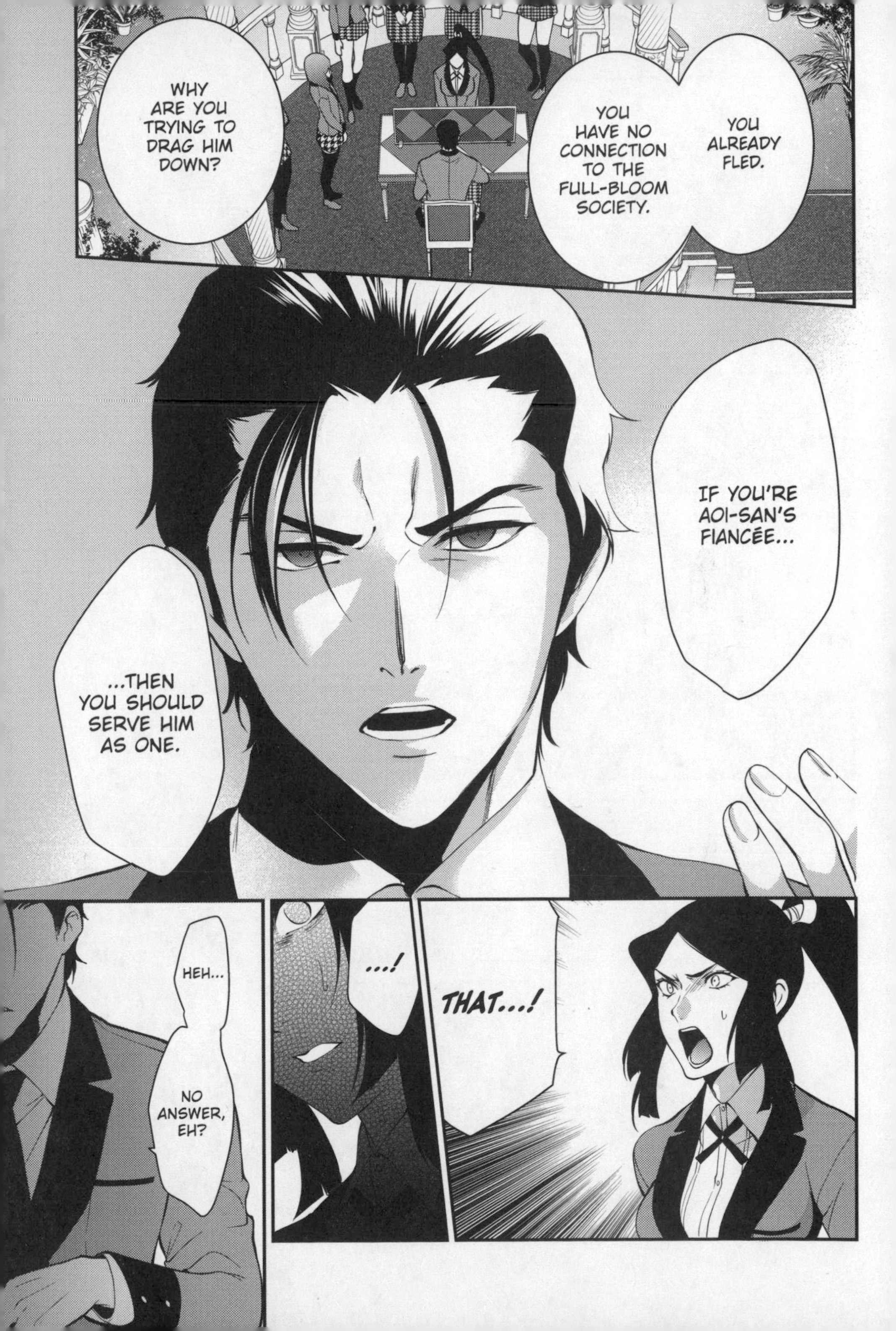
YOU ALREADY FLED.
YOU HAVE NO CONNECTION TO THE FULL-BLOOM SOCIETY.
WHY ARE YOU TRYING TO DRAG HIM DOWN?
IF YOU'RE AOI-SAN'S FIANCÉE...
...THEN YOU SHOULD SERVE HIM AS ONE.
THAT...!
...!
HEH...
NO ANSWER, EH?

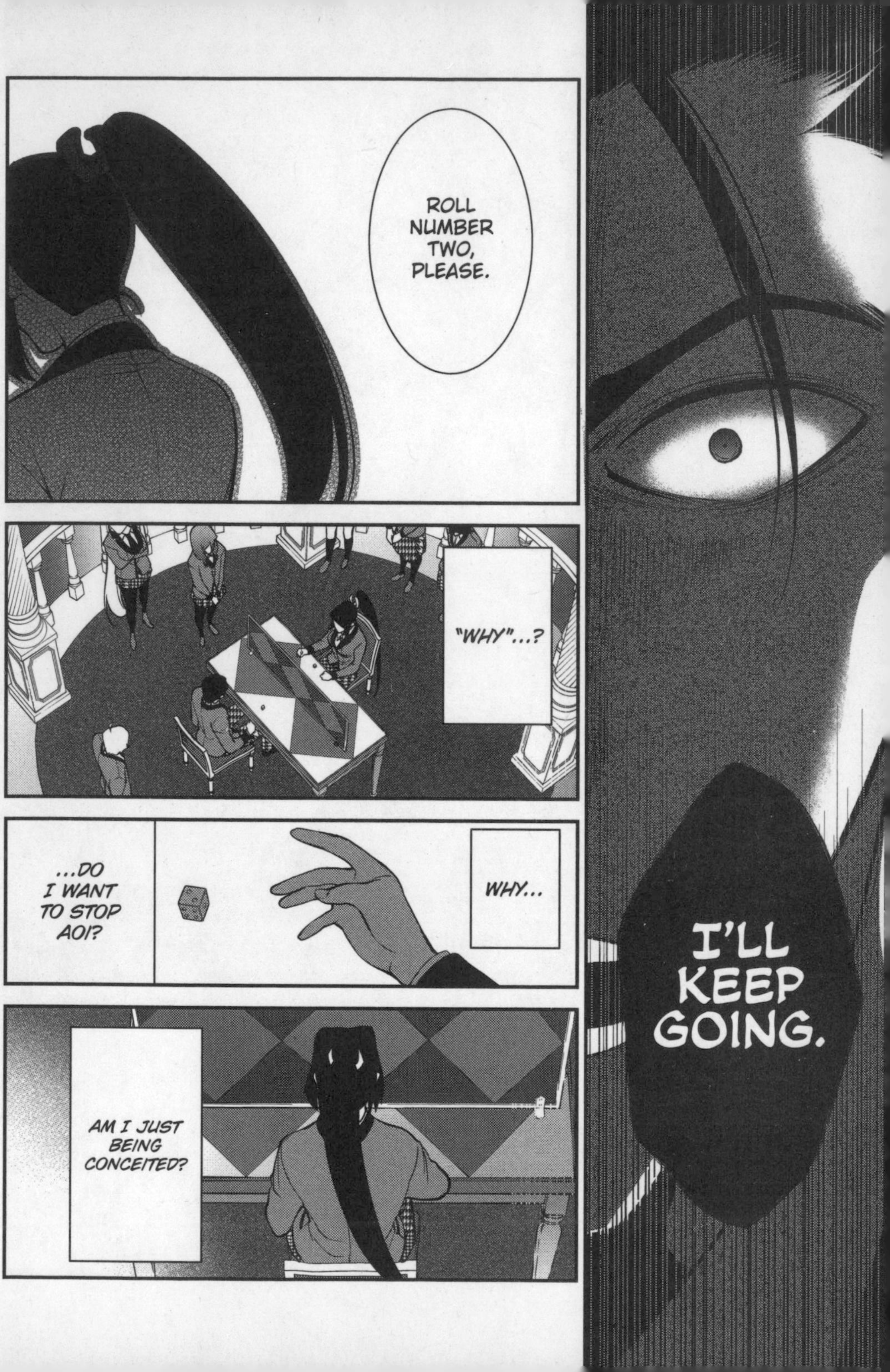
I'LL KEEP GOING.
ROLL NUMBER TWO, PLEASE.
"WHY"...?
WHY...
...DO I WANT TO STOP AOI?
AM I JUST BEING CONCEITED?

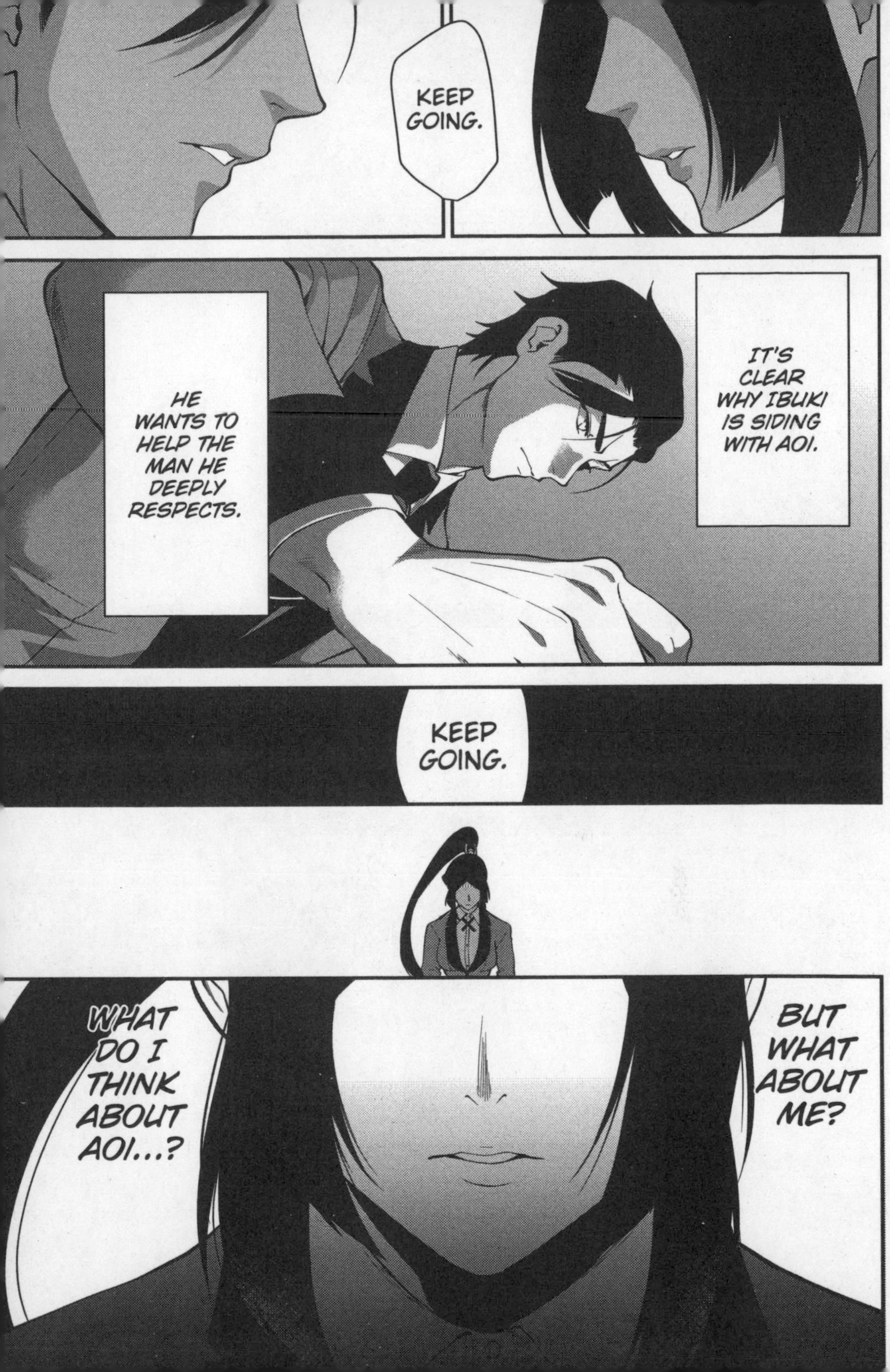
KEEP GOING.
IT'S CLEAR WHY IBUKI IS SIDING WITH AOI.
HE WANTS TO HELP THE MAN HE DEEPLY RESPECTS.
KEEP GOING.
BUT WHAT ABOUT ME?
WHAT DO I THINK ABOUT AOI...?

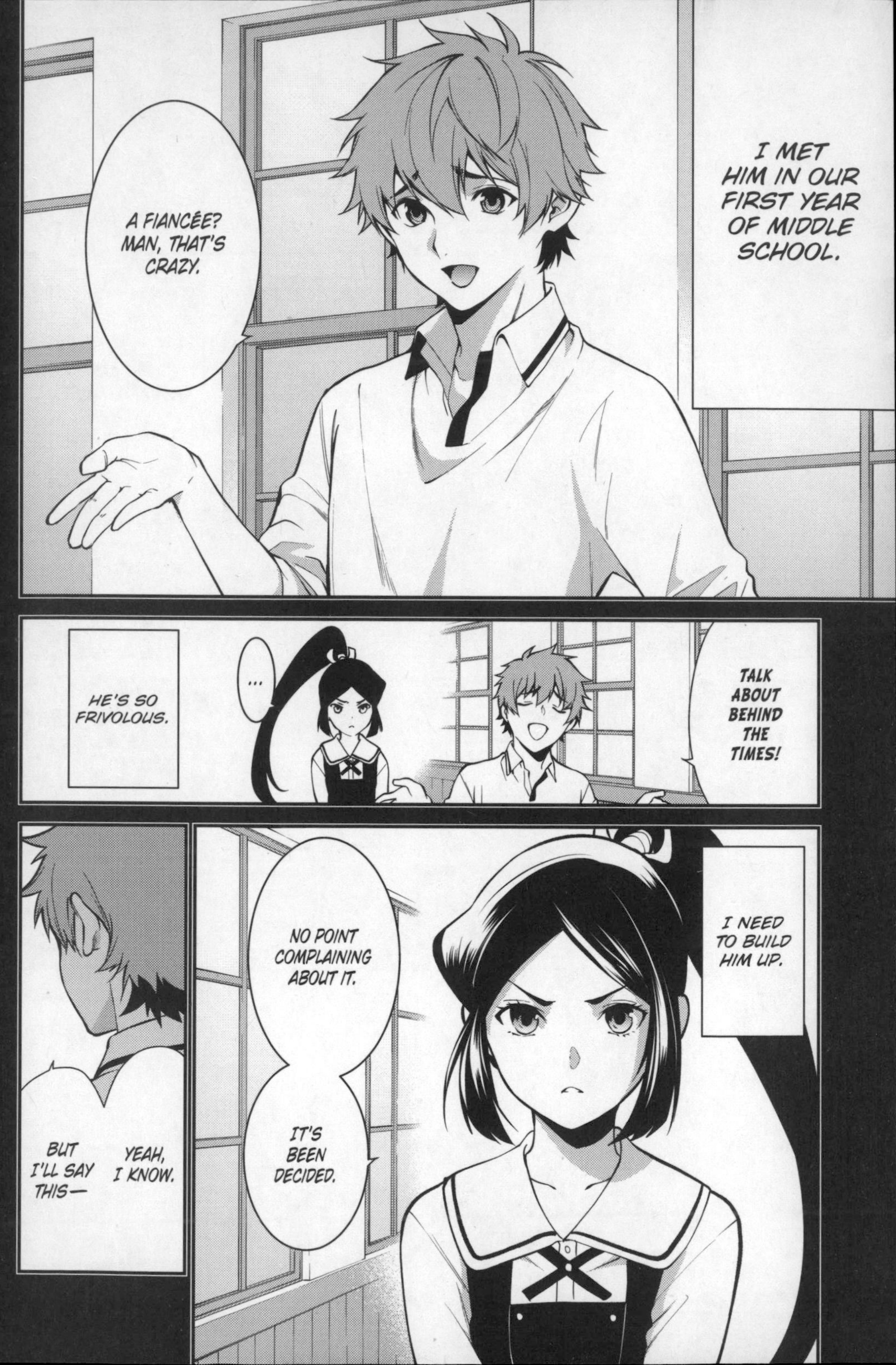
I MET HIM IN OUR FIRST YEAR OF MIDDLE SCHOOL.
A FIANCÉE? MAN, THAT'S CRAZY.
TALK ABOUT BEHIND THE TIMES!
...
HE'S SO FRIVOLOUS.
I NEED TO BUILD HIM UP.
NO POINT COMPLAINING ABOUT IT.
IT'S BEEN DECIDED.
YEAH, I KNOW.
BUT I'LL SAY THIS—

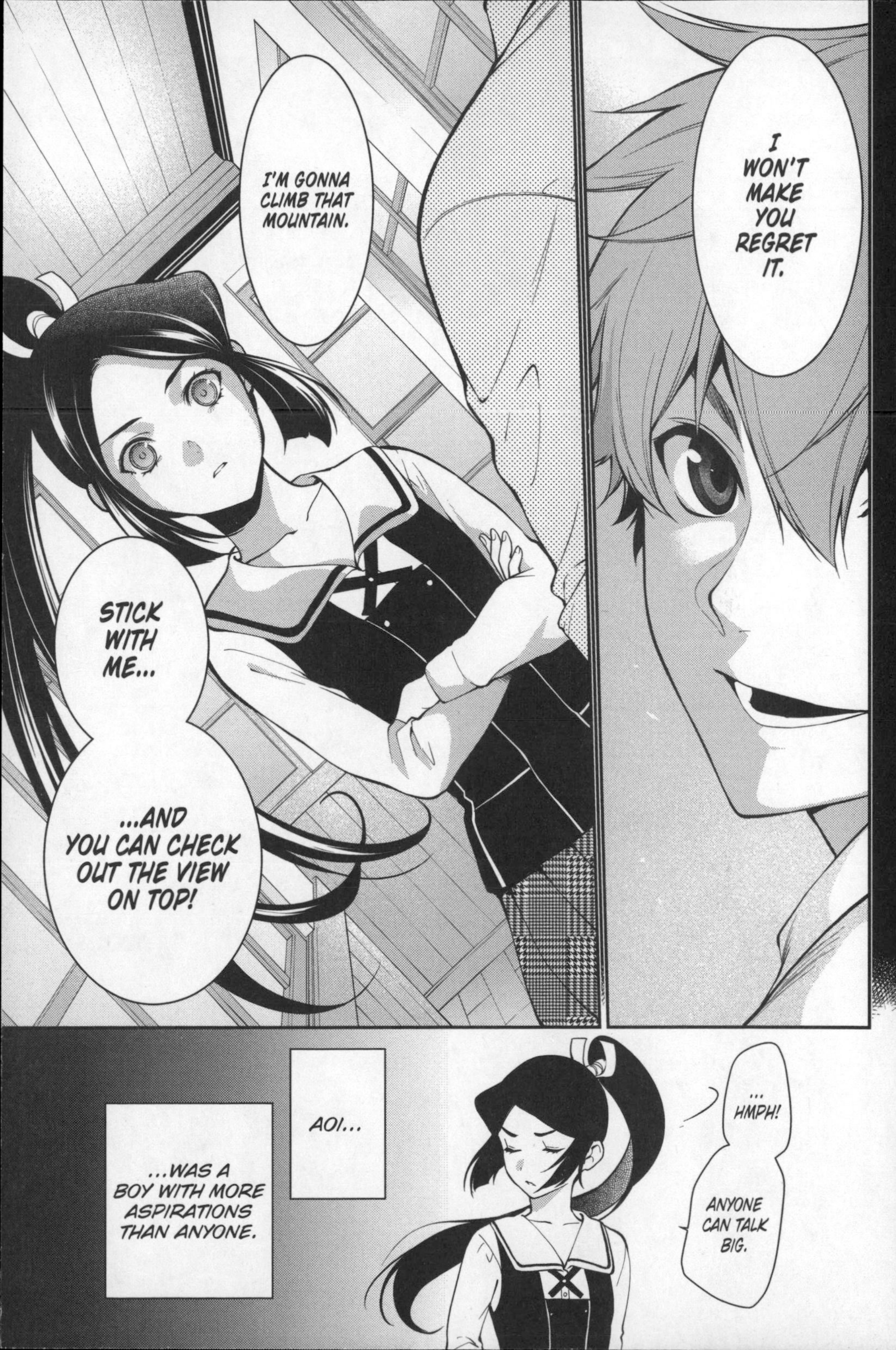
I WON'T MAKE YOU REGRET IT.
I'M GONNA CLIMB THAT MOUNTAIN.
STICK WITH ME...
...AND YOU CAN CHECK OUT THE VIEW ON TOP!
... HMPH!
ANYONE CAN TALK BIG.
AOI...
...WAS A BOY WITH MORE ASPIRATIONS THAN ANYONE.

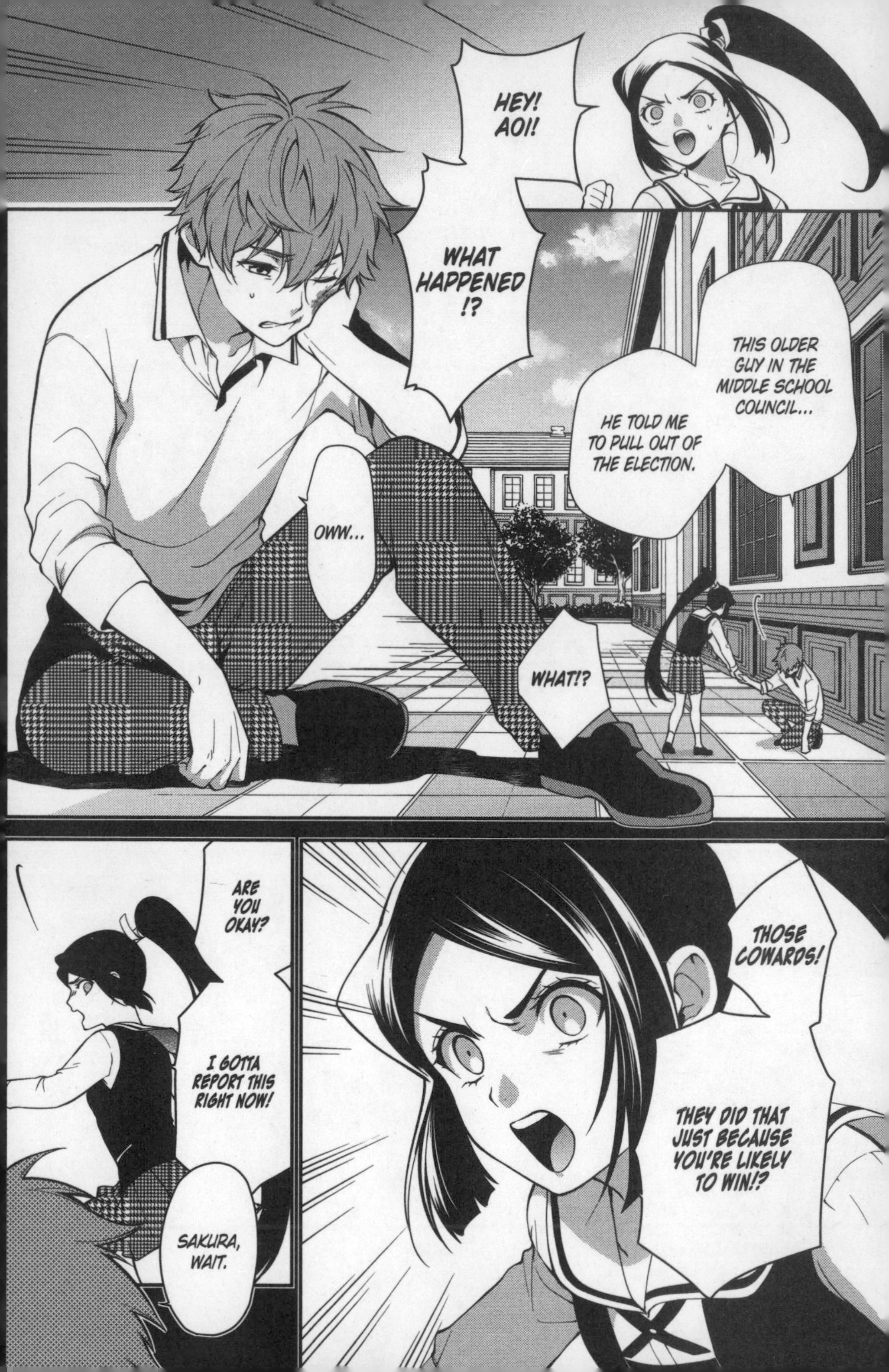
HEY! AOI!
WHAT HAPPENED!?
THIS OLDER GUY IN THE MIDDLE SCHOOL COUNCIL...
HE TOLD ME TO PULL OUT OF THE ELECTION.
OWW...
WHAT!?
THOSE COWARDS!
THEY DID THAT JUST BECAUSE YOU'RE LIKELY TO WIN!?
ARE YOU OKAY?
I GOTTA REPORT THIS RIGHT NOW!
SAKURA, WAIT.

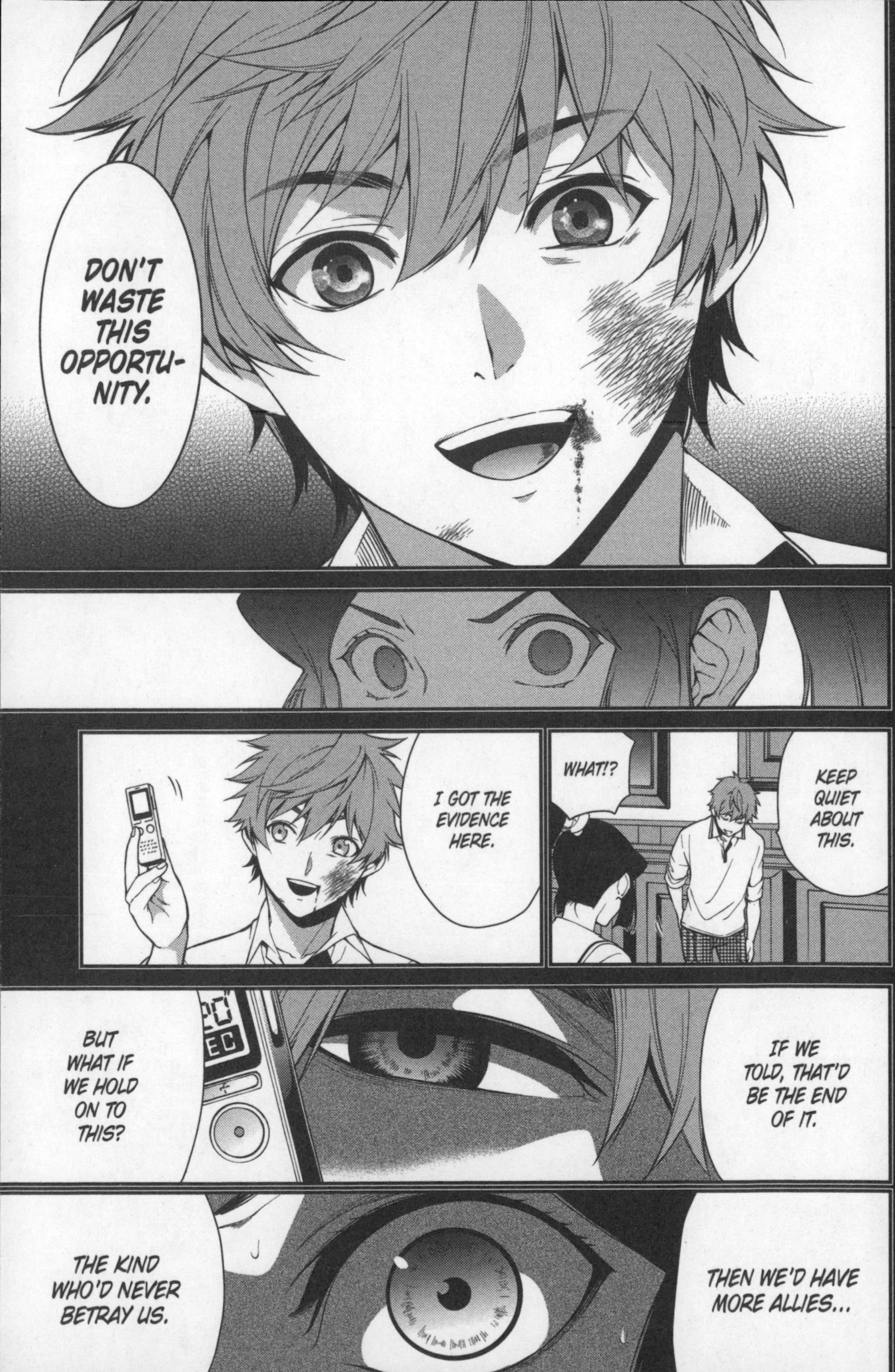
DON'T WASTE THIS OPPORTU-NITY.
KEEP QUIET ABOUT THIS.
WHAT!?
I GOT THE EVIDENCE HERE.
IF WE TOLD, THAT'D BE THE END OF IT.
BUT WHAT IF WE HOLD ON TO THIS?
THEN WE'D HAVE MORE ALLIES...
THE KIND WHO'D NEVER BETRAY US.

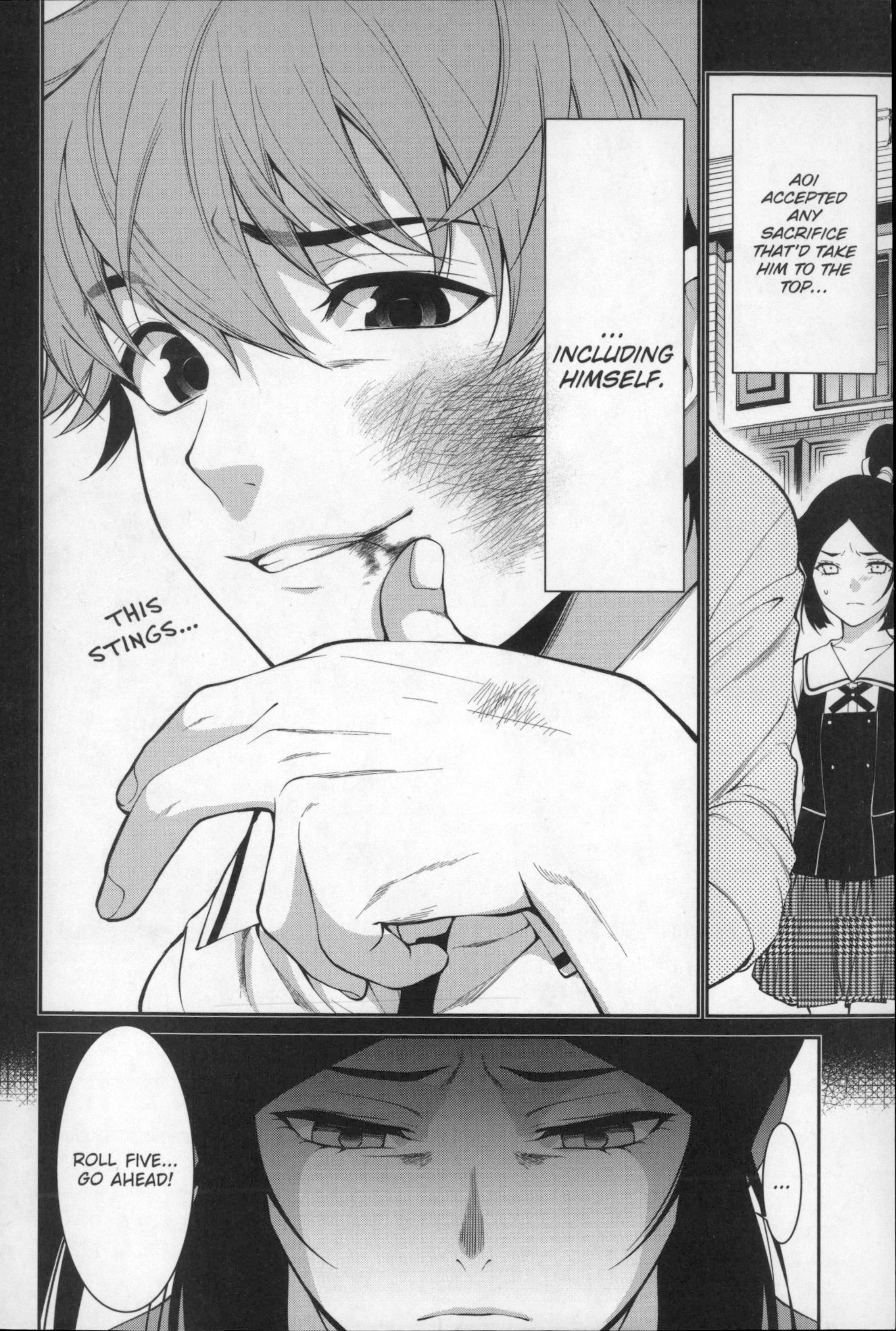
AOI ACCEPTED ANY SACRIFICE THAT'D TAKE HIM TO THE TOP...
...INCLUDING HIMSELF.
THIS STINGS...
...
ROLL FIVE... GO AHEAD!

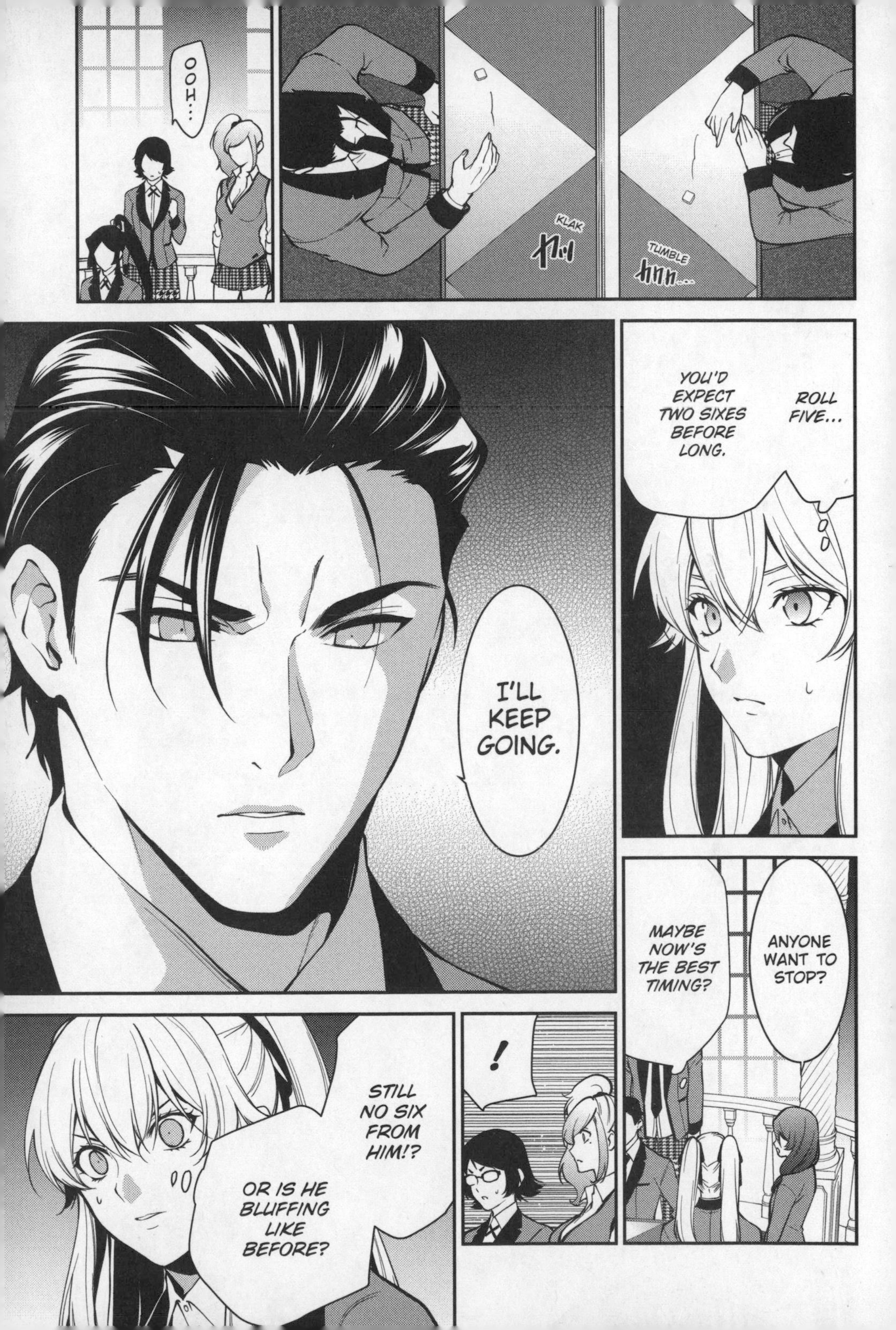
TUMBLE
KLAK
OOH...
ROLL FIVE...
YOU'D EXPECT TWO SIXES BEFORE LONG.
I'LL KEEP GOING.
ANYONE WANT TO STOP?
MAYBE NOW'S THE BEST TIMING?
!
STILL NO SIX FROM HIM!?
OR IS HE BLUFFING LIKE BEFORE?

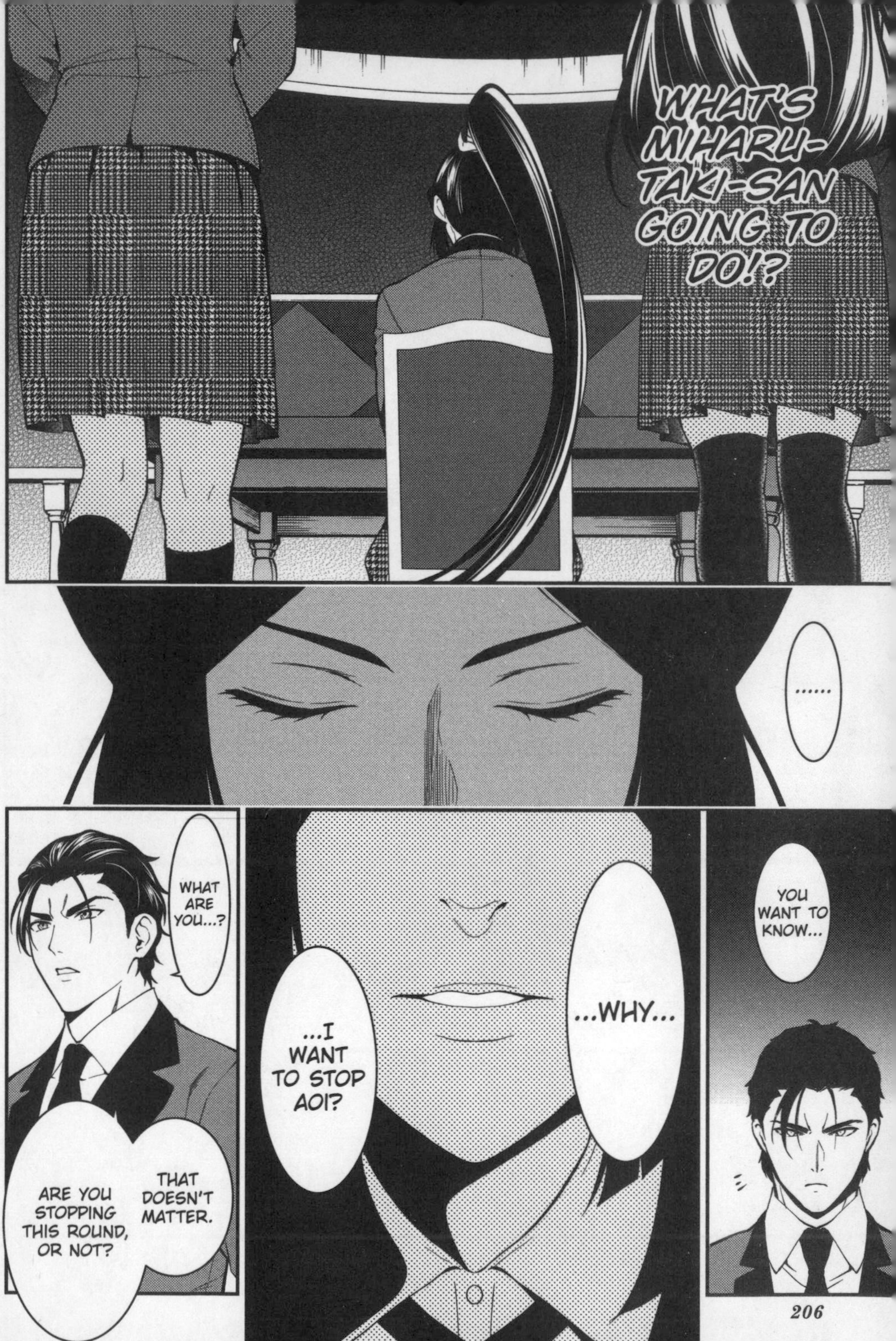
WHAT'S MIHARU-TAKI-SAN GOING TO DO!?
......
YOU WANT TO KNOW...
...WHY...
...I WANT TO STOP AOI?
WHAT ARE YOU...?
THAT DOESN'T MATTER.
ARE YOU STOPPING THIS ROUND, OR NOT?

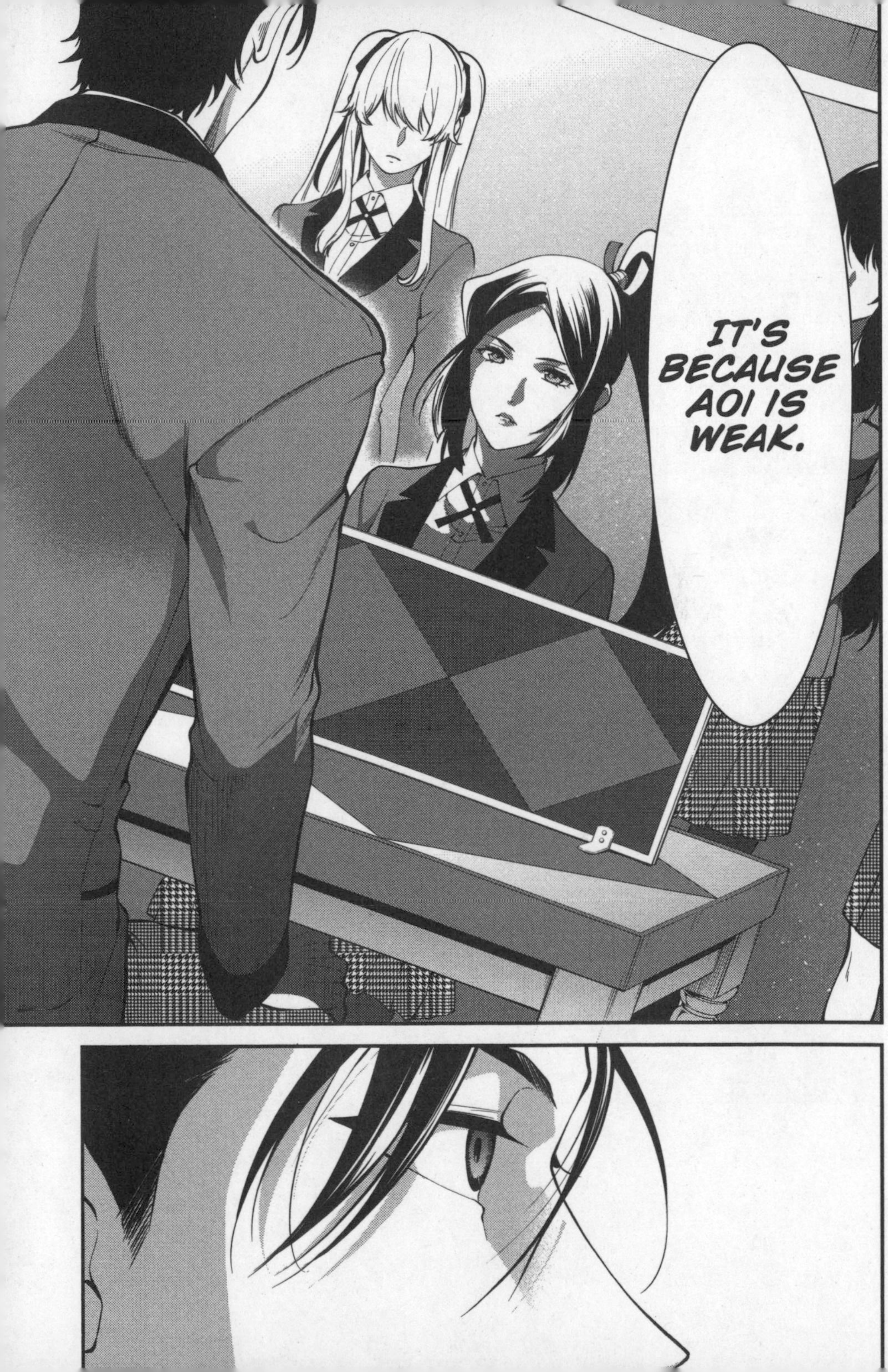
IT'S BECAUSE AOI IS WEAK.

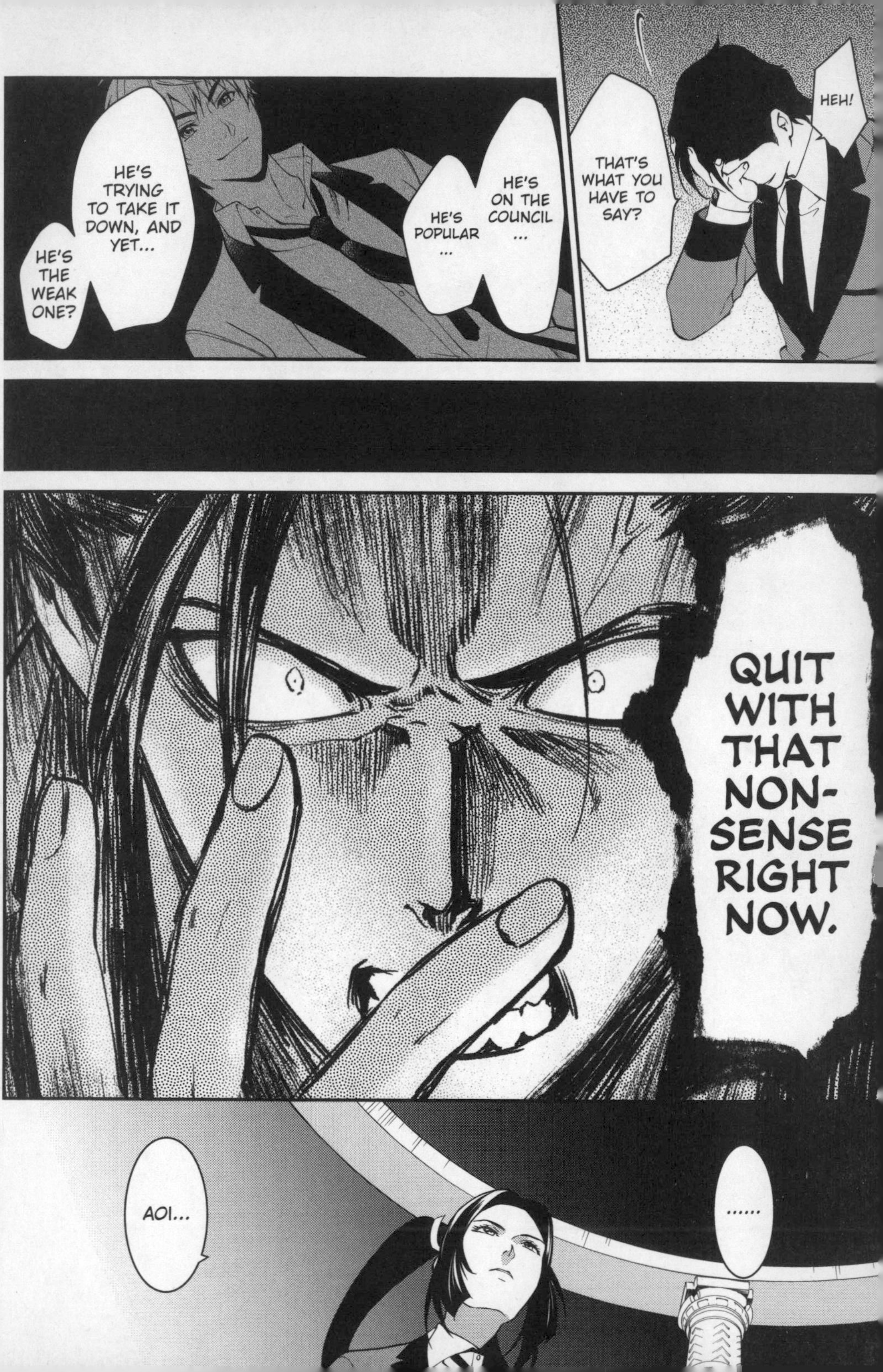
HEH!
THAT'S WHAT YOU HAVE TO SAY?
HE'S ON THE COUNCIL ...
HE'S POPULAR ...
HE'S TRYING TO TAKE IT DOWN, AND YET...
HE'S THE WEAK ONE?
QUIT WITH THAT NON-SENSE RIGHT NOW.
......
AOI...

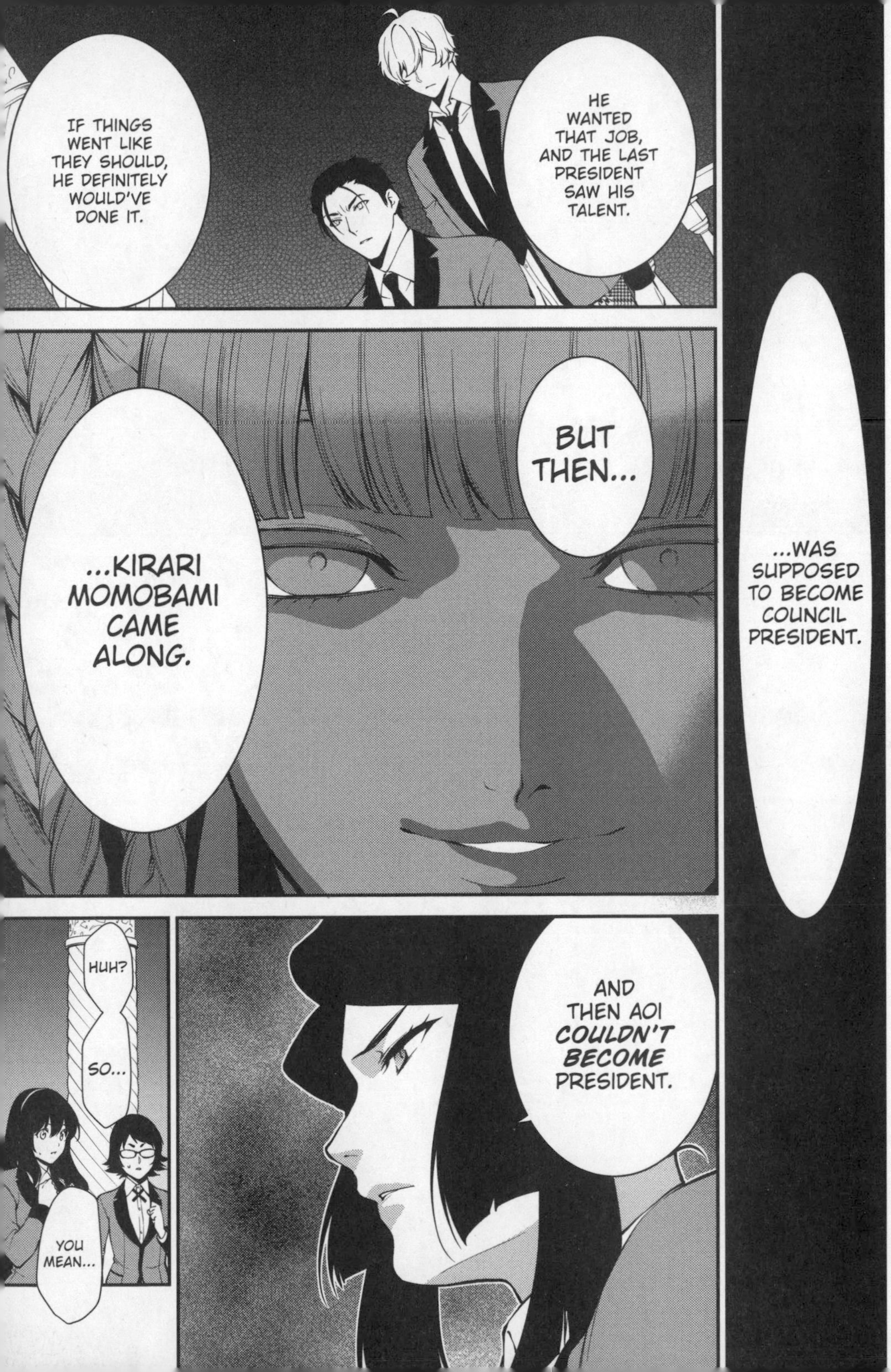

...WAS SUPPOSED TO BECOME COUNCIL PRESIDENT.
HE WANTED THAT JOB, AND THE LAST PRESIDENT SAW HIS TALENT.
IF THINGS WENT LIKE THEY SHOULD, HE DEFINITELY WOULD'VE DONE IT.
BUT THEN...
...KIRARI MOMOBAMI CAME ALONG.
AND THEN AOI *COULDN'T BECOME* PRESIDENT.
HUH?
SO...
YOU MEAN...

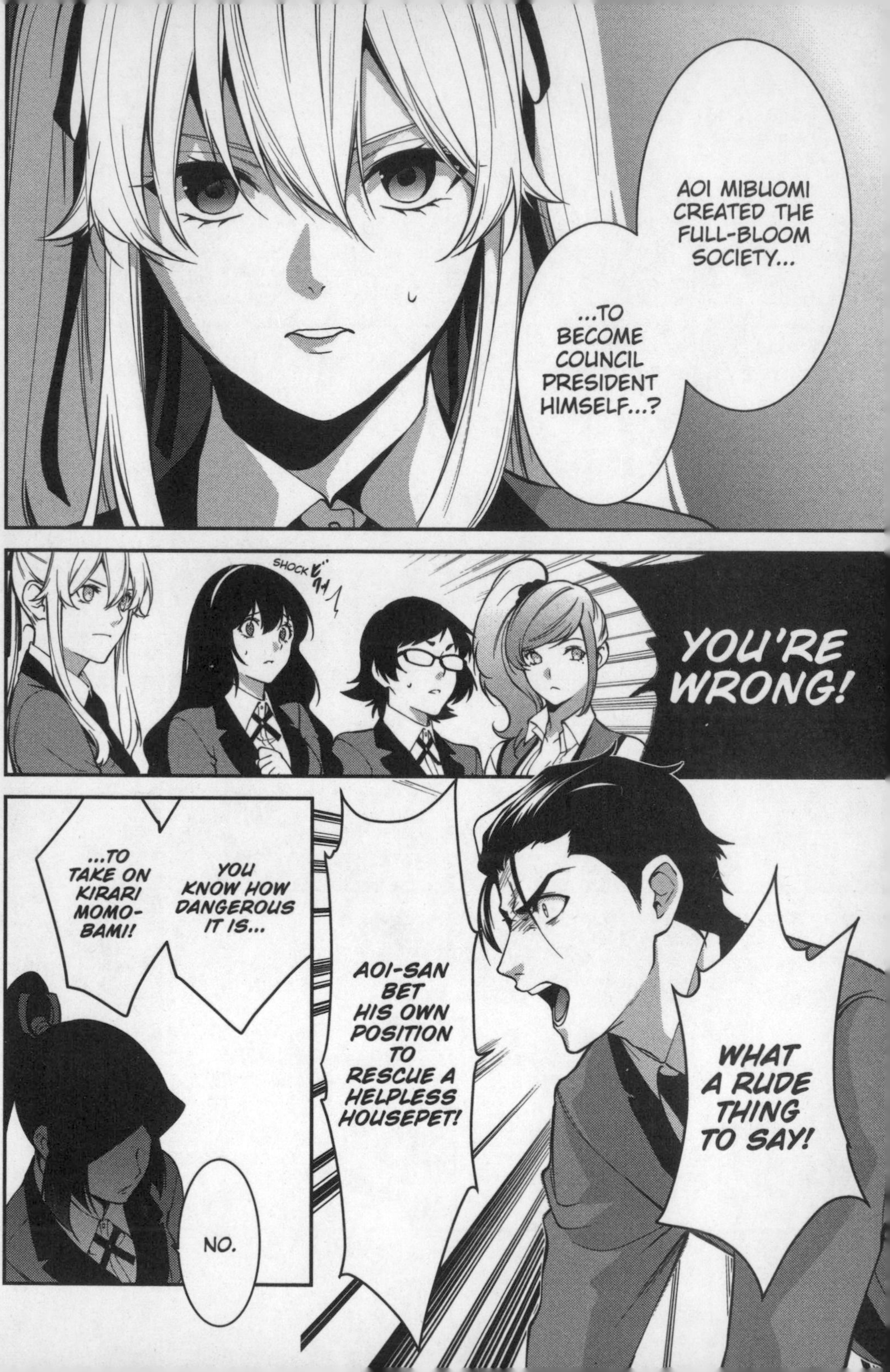
AOI MIBUOMI CREATED THE FULL-BLOOM SOCIETY...
...TO BECOME COUNCIL PRESIDENT HIMSELF...?
YOU'RE WRONG!
SHOCK
WHAT A RUDE THING TO SAY!
AOI-SAN BET HIS OWN POSITION TO RESCUE A HELPLESS HOUSEPET!
YOU KNOW HOW DANGEROUS IT IS...
...TO TAKE ON KIRARI MOMO-BAMI!
NO.

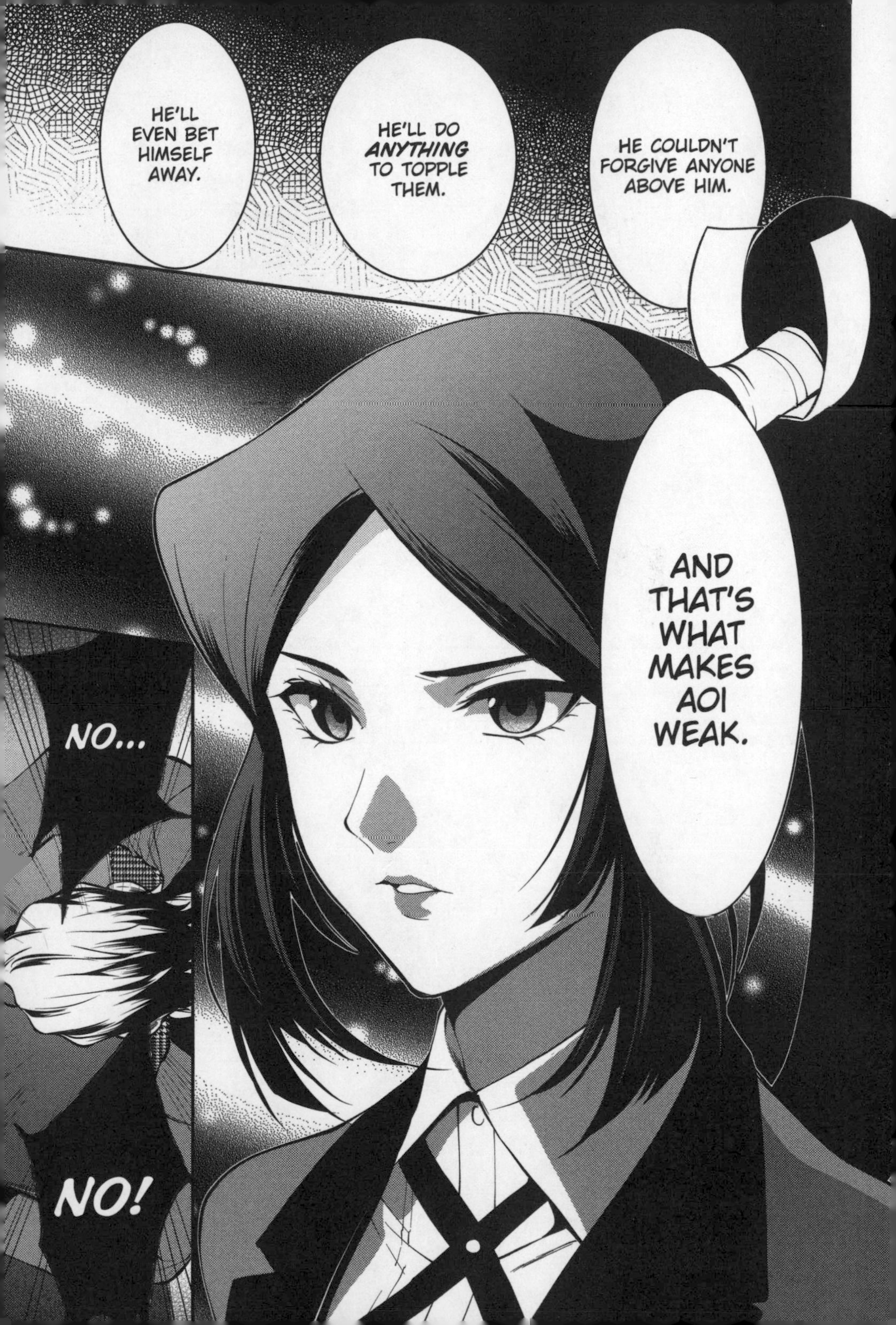
HE COULDN'T FORGIVE ANYONE ABOVE HIM.
HE'LL DO *ANYTHING* TO TOPPLE THEM.
HE'LL EVEN BET HIMSELF AWAY.
AND THAT'S WHAT MAKES AOI WEAK.
NO...
NO!

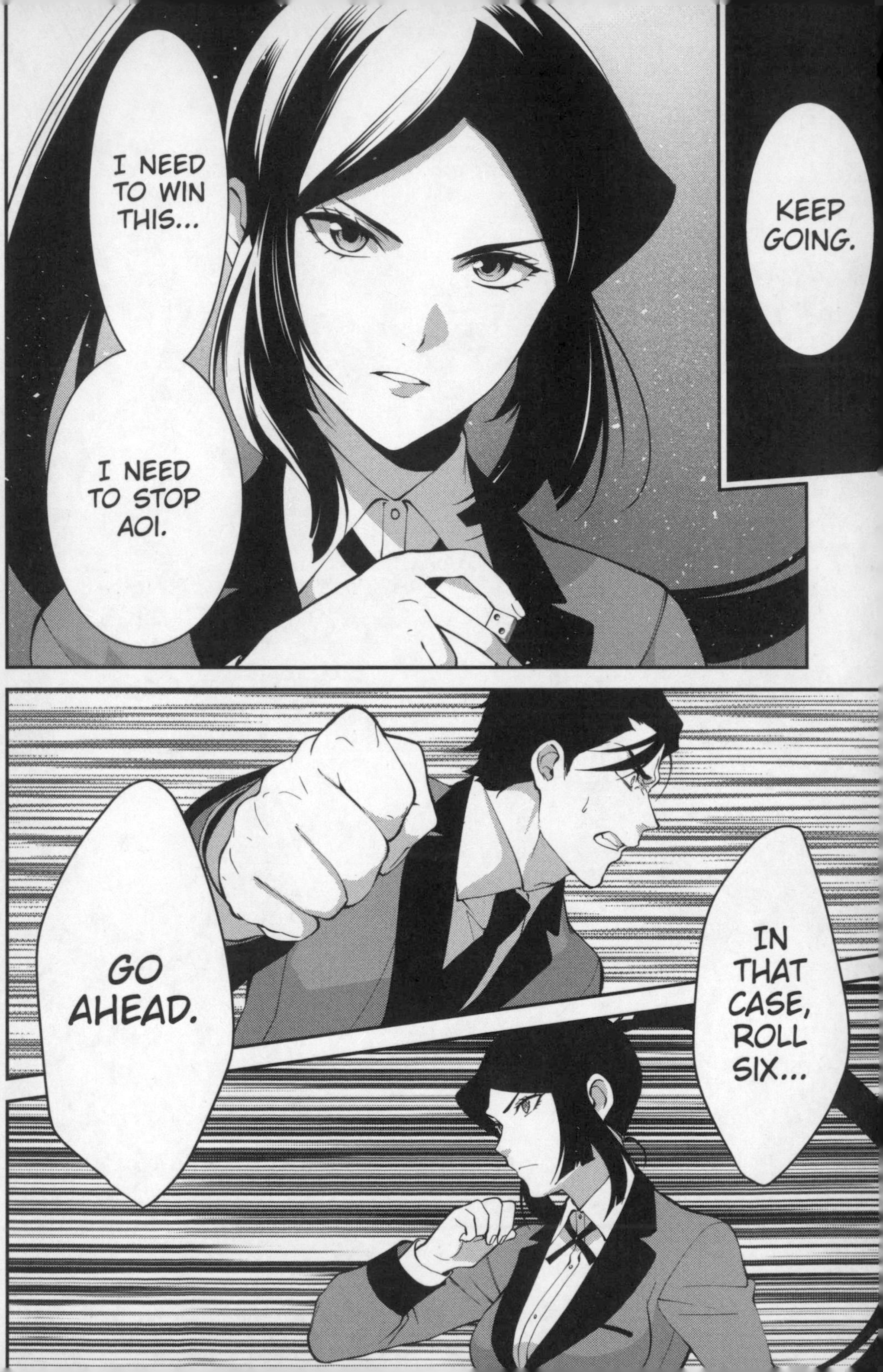
KEEP GOING.
I NEED TO WIN THIS...
I NEED TO STOP AOI.
IN THAT CASE, ROLL SIX...
GO AHEAD.

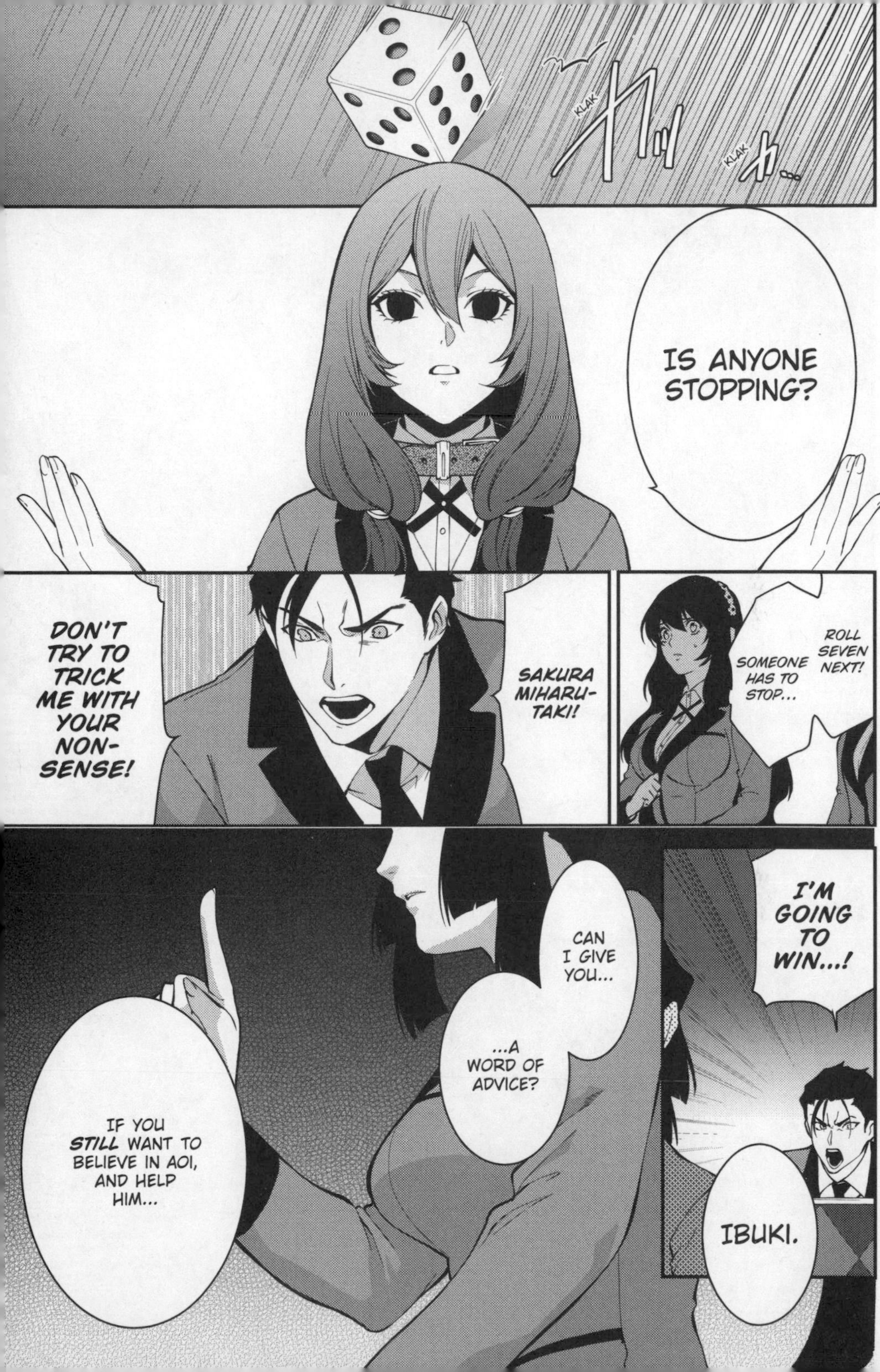
KLAK
KLAK
IS ANYONE STOPPING?
ROLL SEVEN NEXT!
SOMEONE HAS TO STOP...
SAKURA MIHARU-TAKI!
DON'T TRY TO TRICK ME WITH YOUR NON-SENSE!
I'M GOING TO WIN...!
IBUKI.
CAN I GIVE YOU...
...A WORD OF ADVICE?
IF YOU *STILL* WANT TO BELIEVE IN AOI, AND HELP HIM...

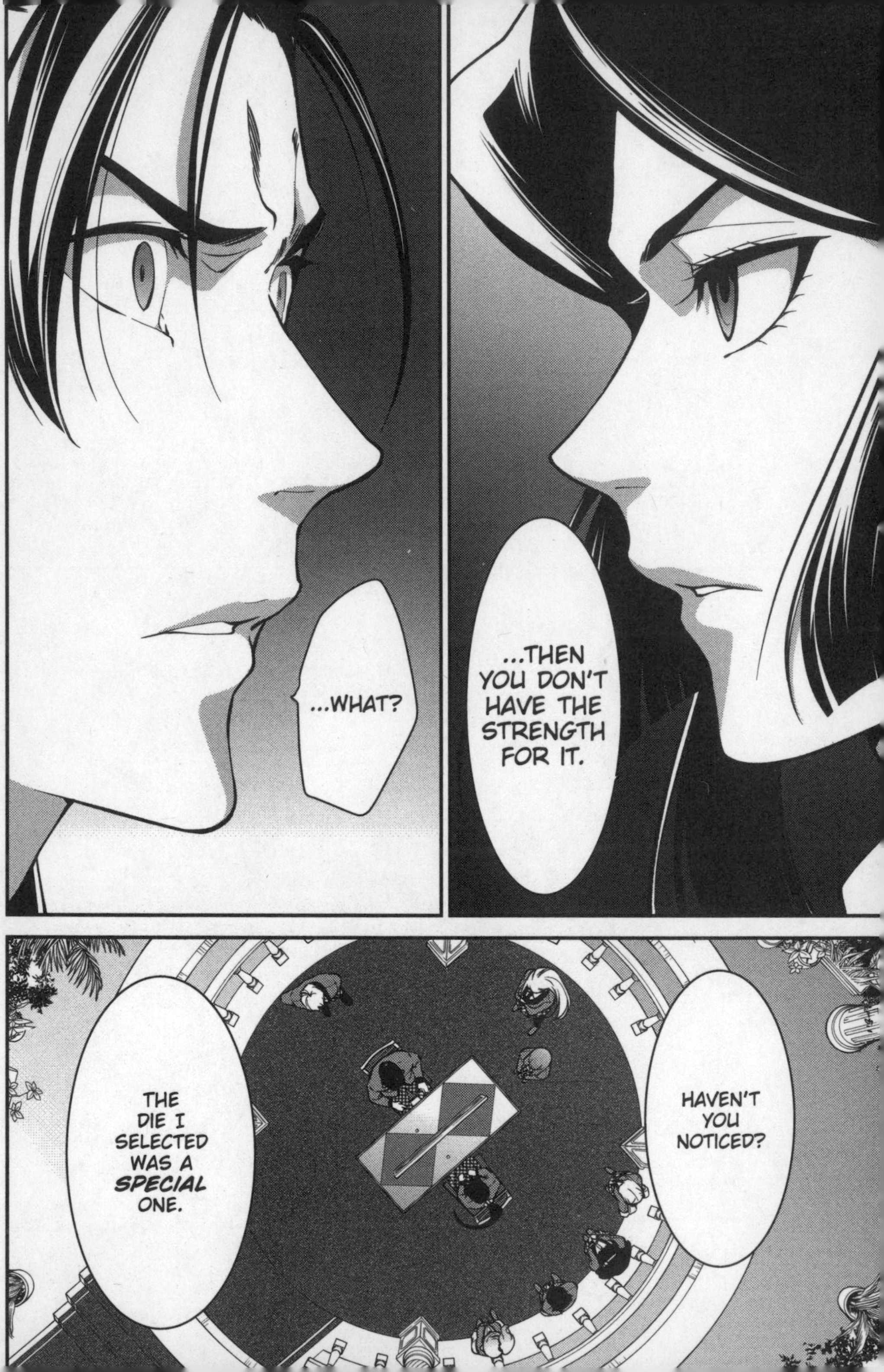
...THEN YOU DON'T HAVE THE STRENGTH FOR IT.
...WHAT?
HAVEN'T YOU NOTICED?
THE DIE I SELECTED WAS A ***SPECIAL*** ONE.

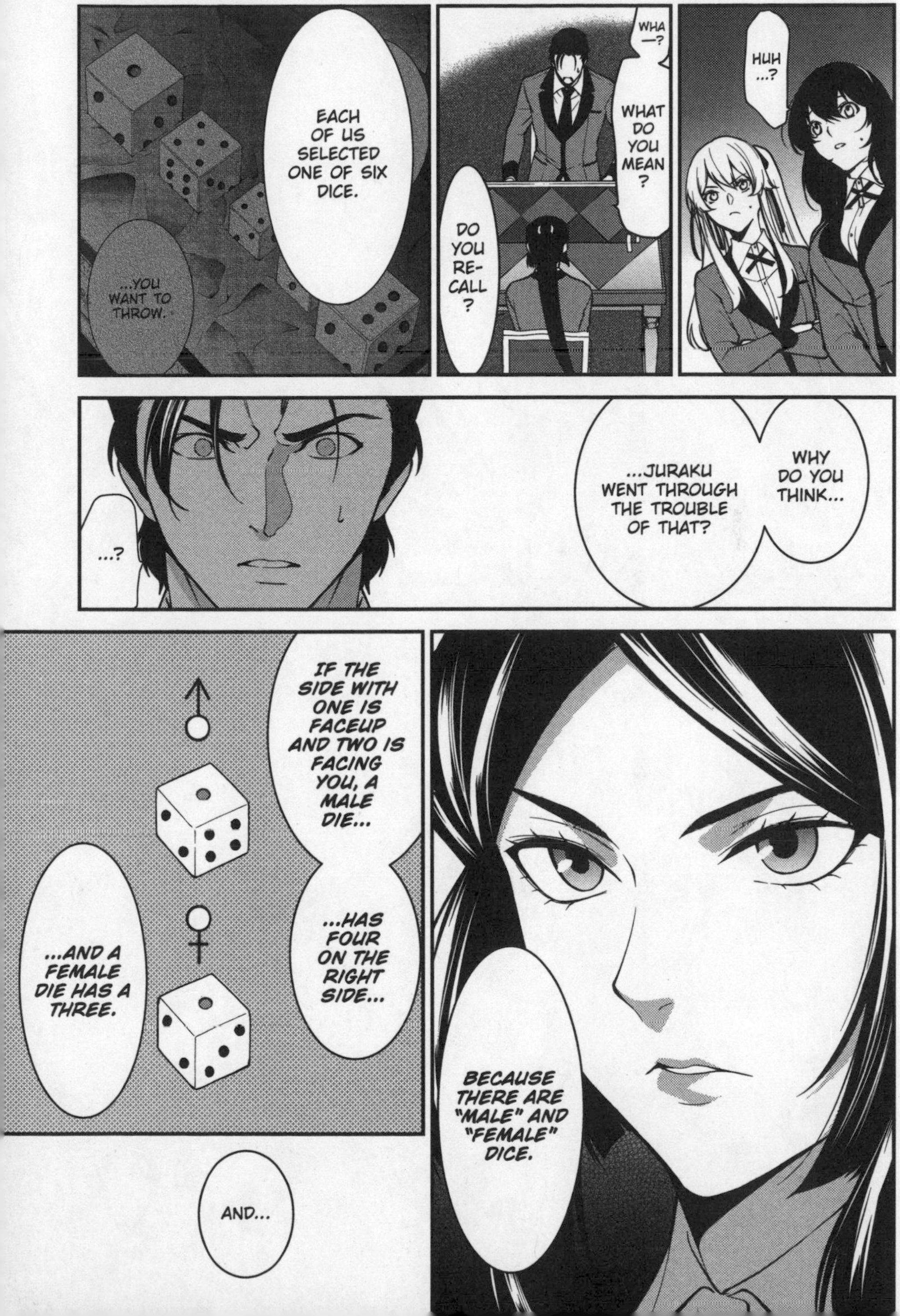
HUH ...?
WHA—?
WHAT DO YOU MEAN?
DO YOU RE-CALL?
EACH OF US SELECTED ONE OF SIX DICE.
...YOU WANT TO THROW.
WHY DO YOU THINK...
...JURAKU WENT THROUGH THE TROUBLE OF THAT?
...?
BECAUSE THERE ARE "MALE" AND "FEMALE" DICE.
IF THE SIDE WITH ONE IS FACEUP AND TWO IS FACING YOU, A MALE DIE...
...HAS FOUR ON THE RIGHT SIDE...
...AND A FEMALE DIE HAS A THREE.
AND...

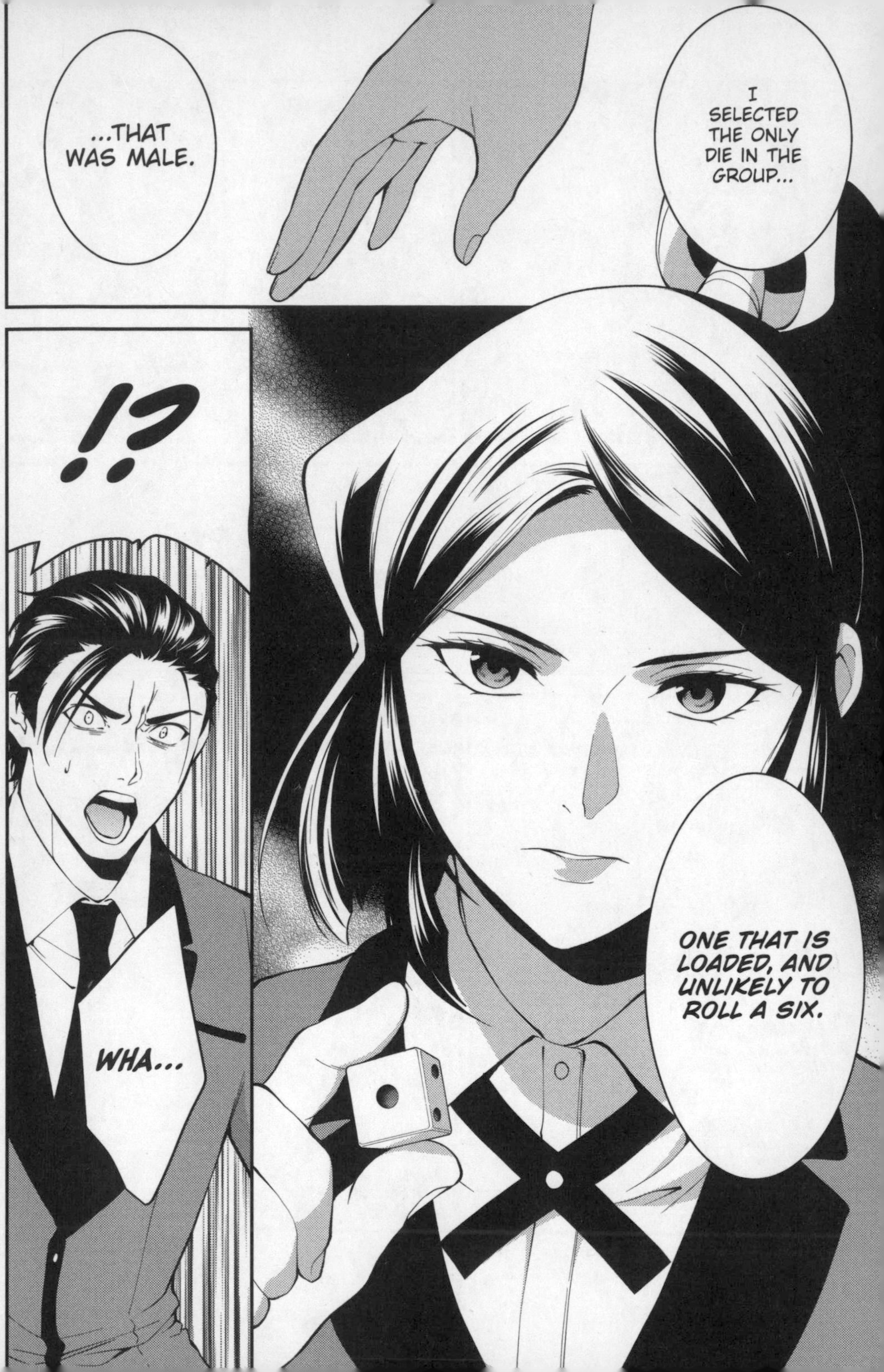
I SELECTED THE ONLY DIE IN THE GROUP...
...THAT WAS MALE.
ONE THAT IS LOADED, AND UNLIKELY TO ROLL A SIX.
!?
WHA...

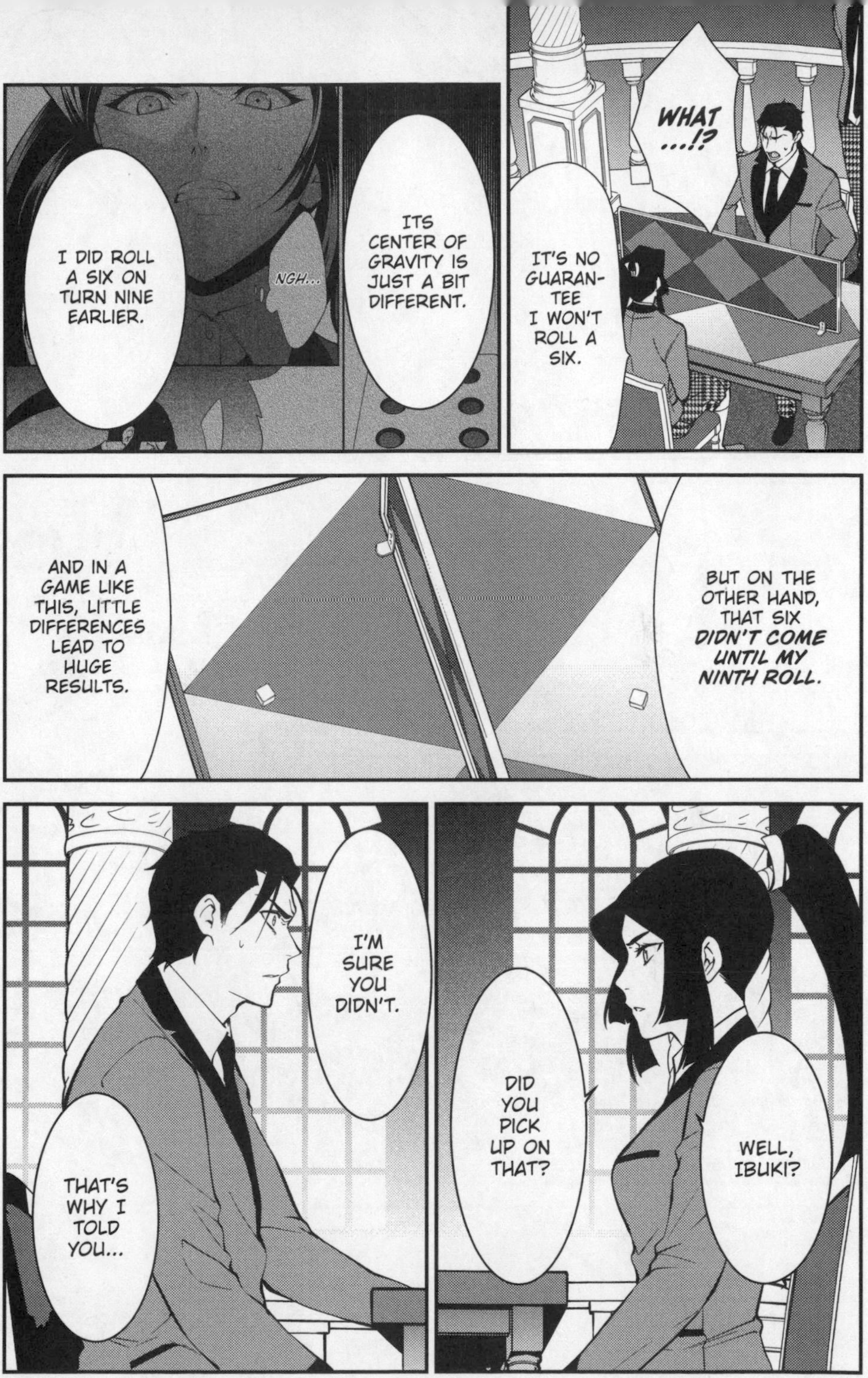

WHAT ...!?
IT'S NO GUARANTEE I WON'T ROLL A SIX.
ITS CENTER OF GRAVITY IS JUST A BIT DIFFERENT.
NGH...
I DID ROLL A SIX ON TURN NINE EARLIER.
BUT ON THE OTHER HAND, THAT SIX DIDN'T COME UNTIL MY NINTH ROLL.
AND IN A GAME LIKE THIS, LITTLE DIFFERENCES LEAD TO HUGE RESULTS.
WELL, IBUKI?
DID YOU PICK UP ON THAT?
I'M SURE YOU DIDN'T.
THAT'S WHY I TOLD YOU...

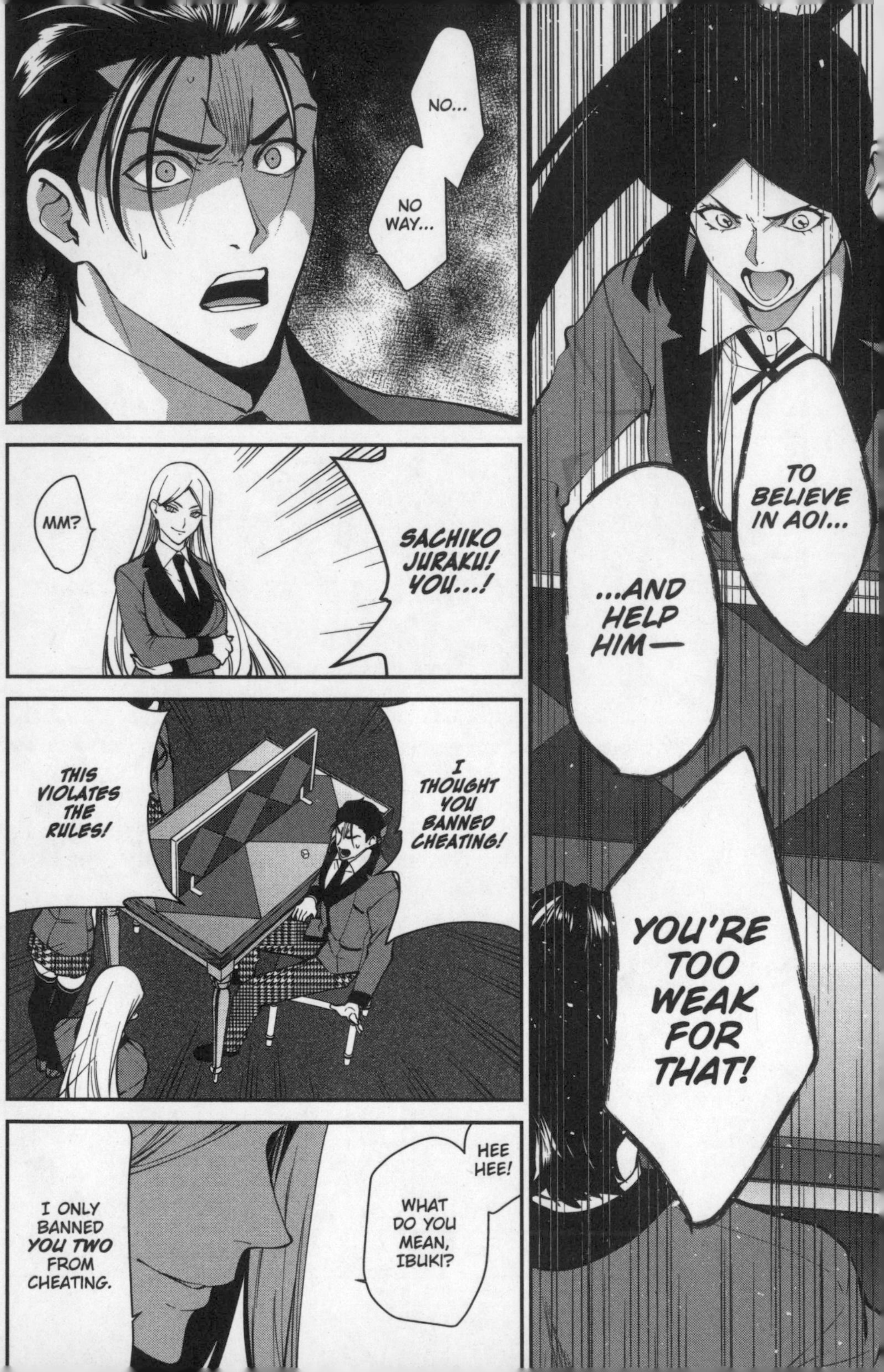
TO BELIEVE IN AOI...
...AND HELP HIM—
YOU'RE TOO WEAK FOR THAT!
NO...
NO WAY...
SACHIKO JURAKU! YOU...!
MM?
I THOUGHT YOU BANNED CHEATING!
THIS VIOLATES THE RULES!
HEE HEE!
WHAT DO YOU MEAN, IBUKI?
I ONLY BANNED YOU TWO FROM CHEATING.

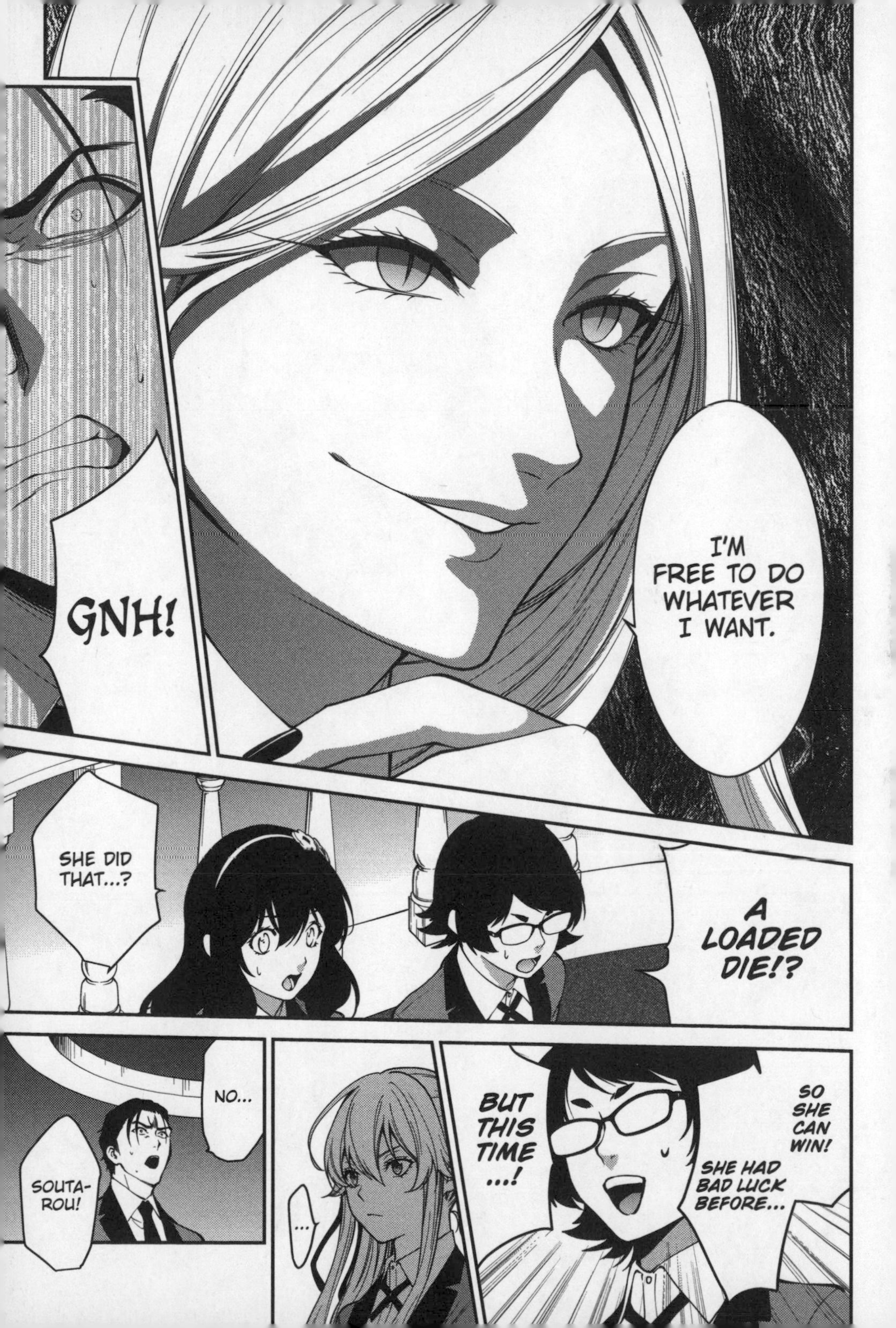
I'M FREE TO DO WHATEVER I WANT.
GNH!
A LOADED DIE!?
SHE DID THAT...?
SO SHE CAN WIN!
SHE HAD BAD LUCK BEFORE...
BUT THIS TIME...!
...
NO...
SOUTA-ROU!

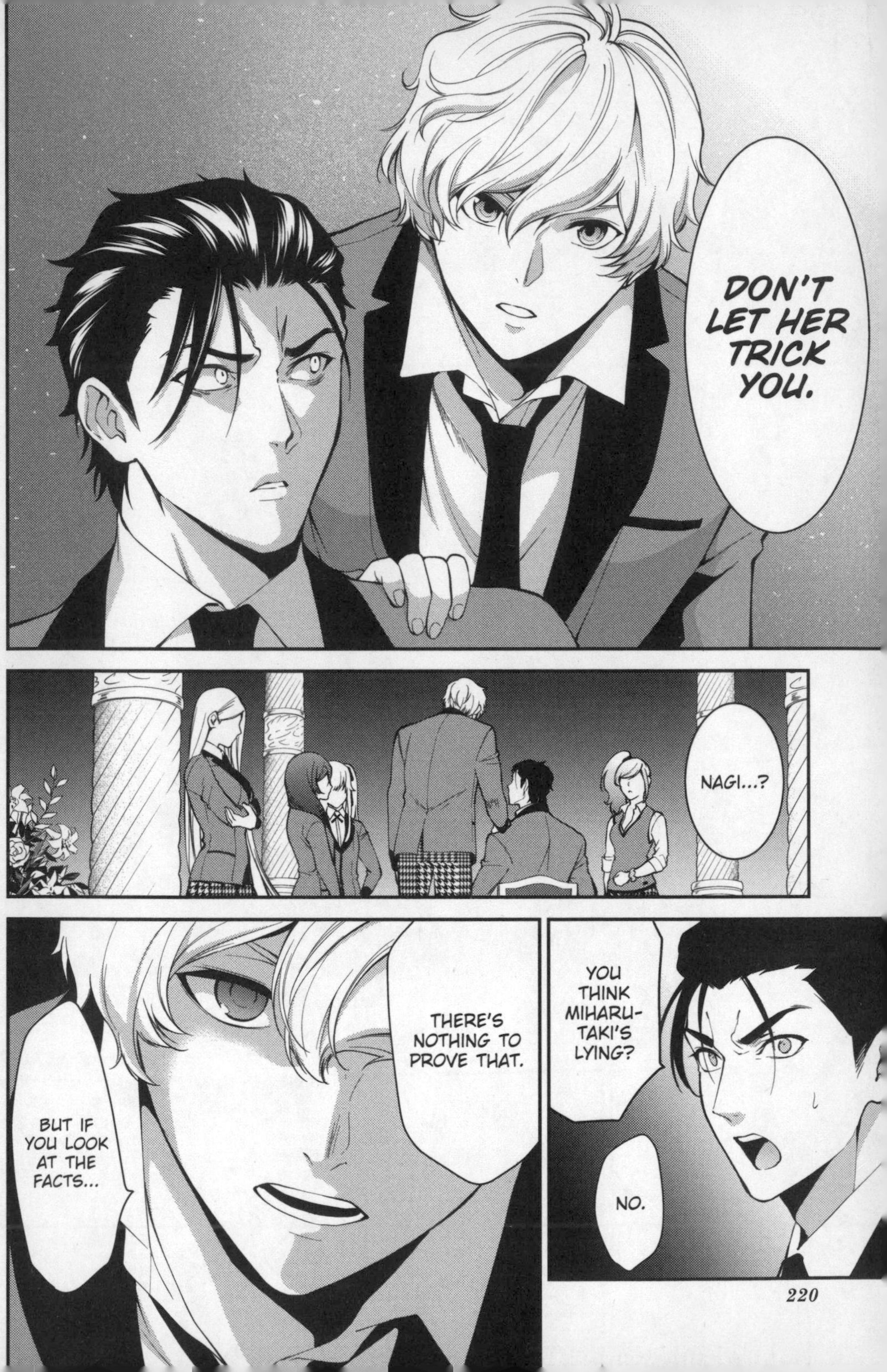
DON'T LET HER TRICK YOU.
NAGI...?
YOU THINK MIHARU-TAKI'S LYING?
NO.
THERE'S NOTHING TO PROVE THAT.
BUT IF YOU LOOK AT THE FACTS...

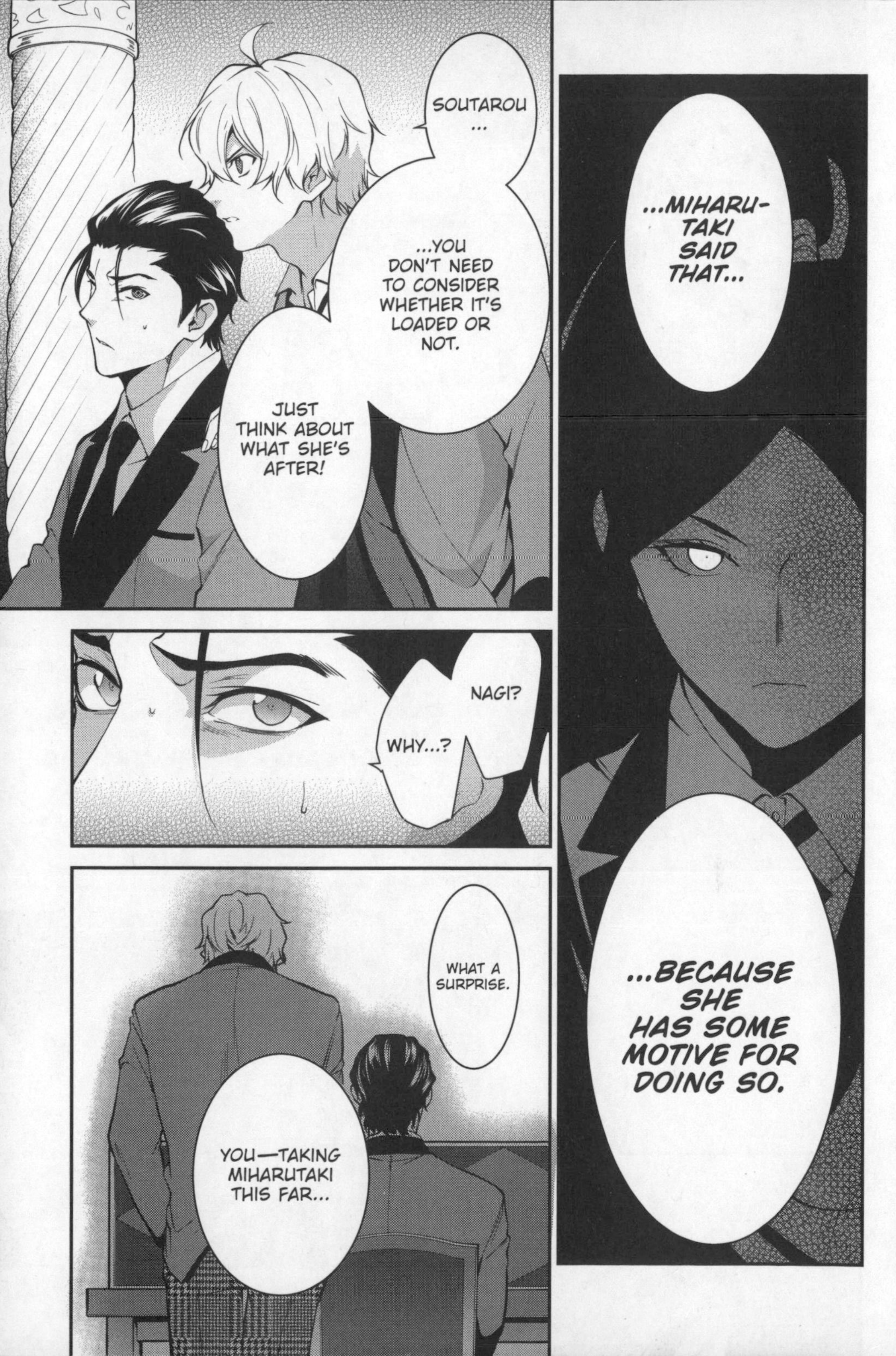
...MIHARUTAKI SAID THAT...
...BECAUSE SHE HAS SOME MOTIVE FOR DOING SO.
SOUTAROU...
...YOU DON'T NEED TO CONSIDER WHETHER IT'S LOADED OR NOT.
JUST THINK ABOUT WHAT SHE'S AFTER!
NAGI?
WHY...?
WHAT A SURPRISE.
YOU—TAKING MIHARUTAKI THIS FAR...

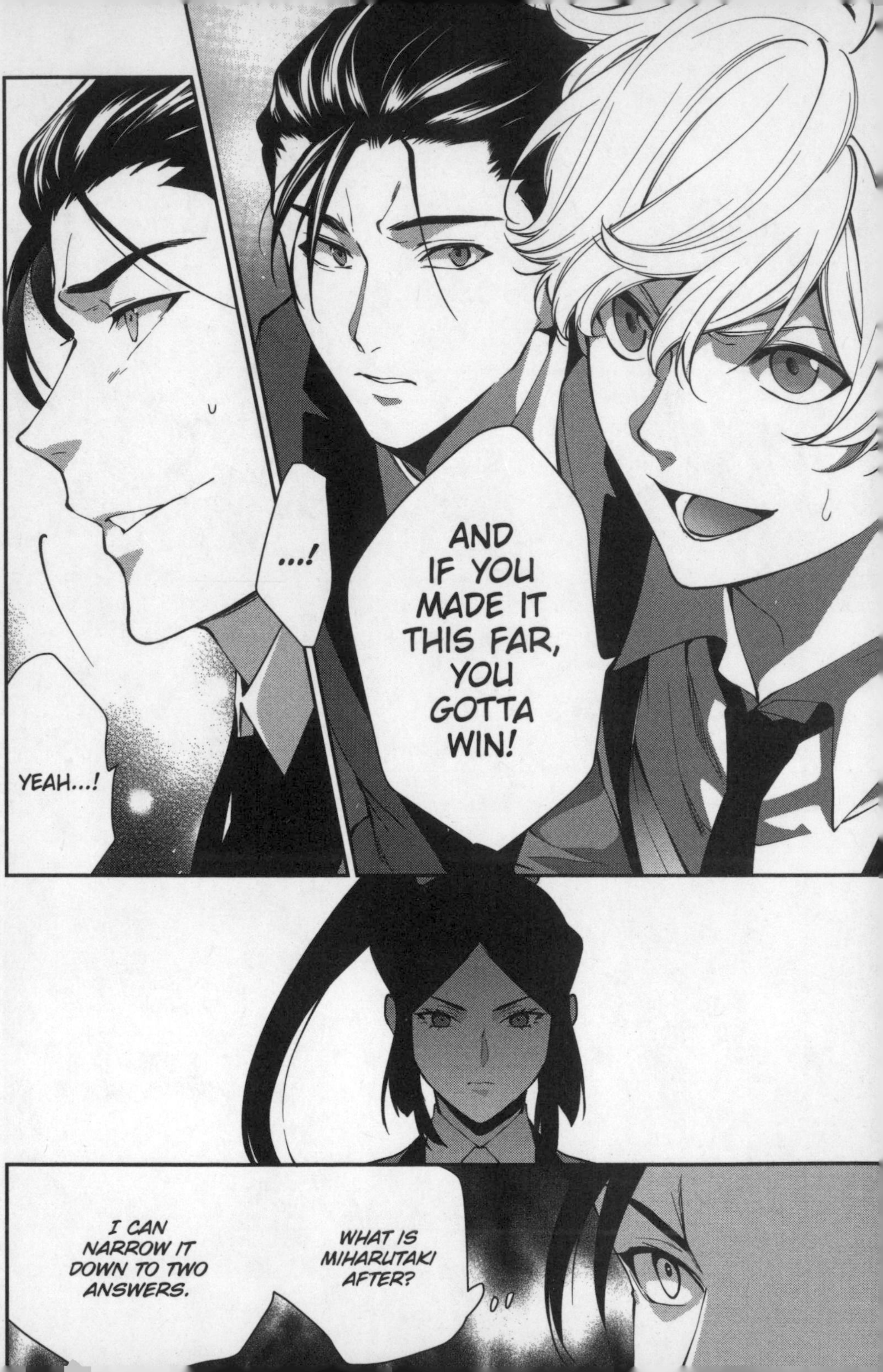
AND IF YOU MADE IT THIS FAR, YOU GOTTA WIN!
...!
YEAH...!
WHAT IS MIHARUTAKI AFTER?
I CAN NARROW IT DOWN TO TWO ANSWERS.

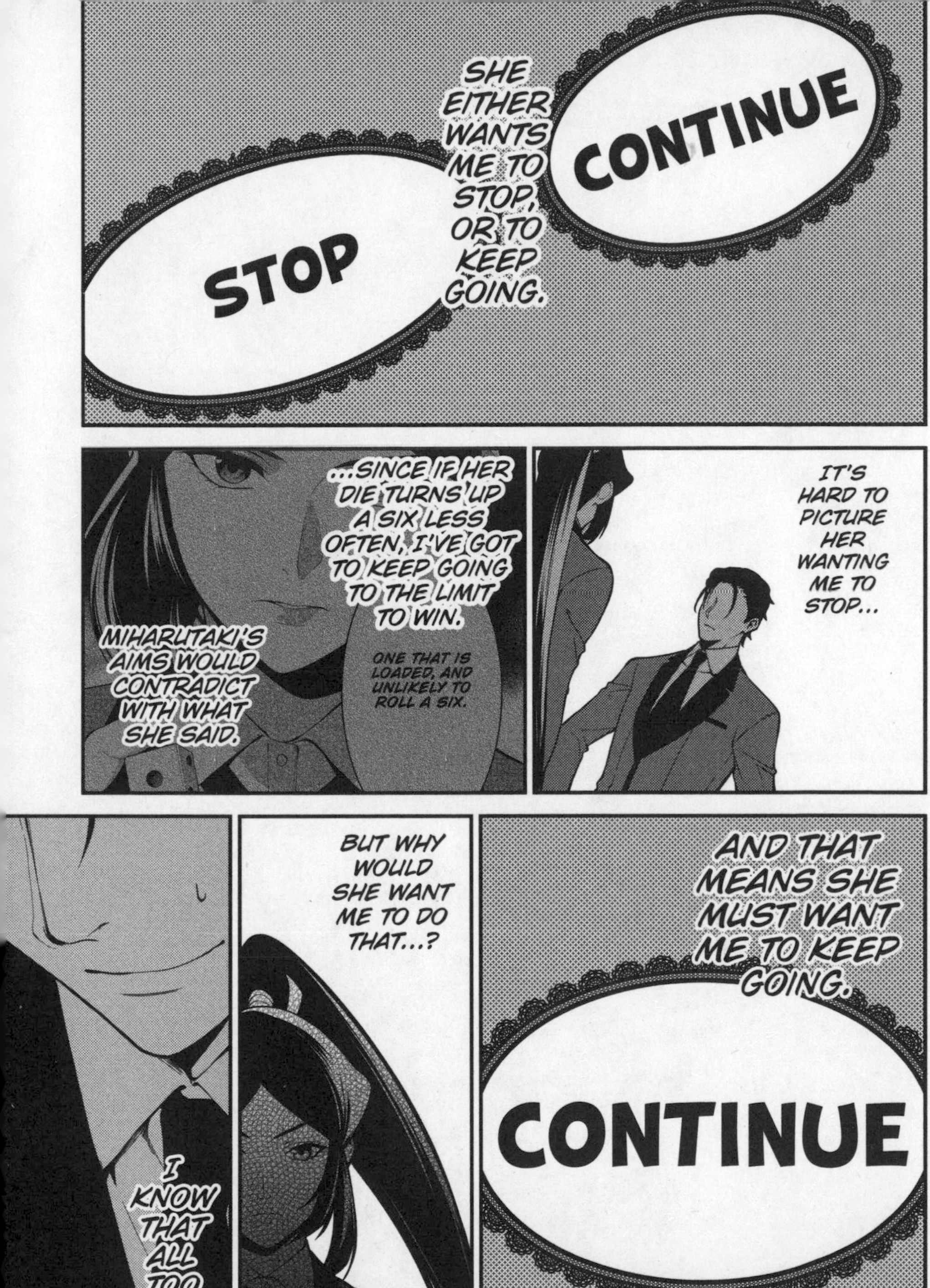
CONTINUE
SHE EITHER WANTS ME TO STOP, OR TO KEEP GOING.
STOP
IT'S HARD TO PICTURE HER WANTING ME TO STOP...
...SINCE IF HER DIE TURNS UP A SIX LESS OFTEN, I'VE GOT TO KEEP GOING TO THE LIMIT TO WIN.
ONE THAT IS LOADED, AND UNLIKELY TO ROLL A SIX.
MIHARUTAKI'S AIMS WOULD CONTRADICT WITH WHAT SHE SAID.
AND THAT MEANS SHE MUST WANT ME TO KEEP GOING.
CONTINUE
BUT WHY WOULD SHE WANT ME TO DO THAT...?
I KNOW THAT ALL TOO WELL.

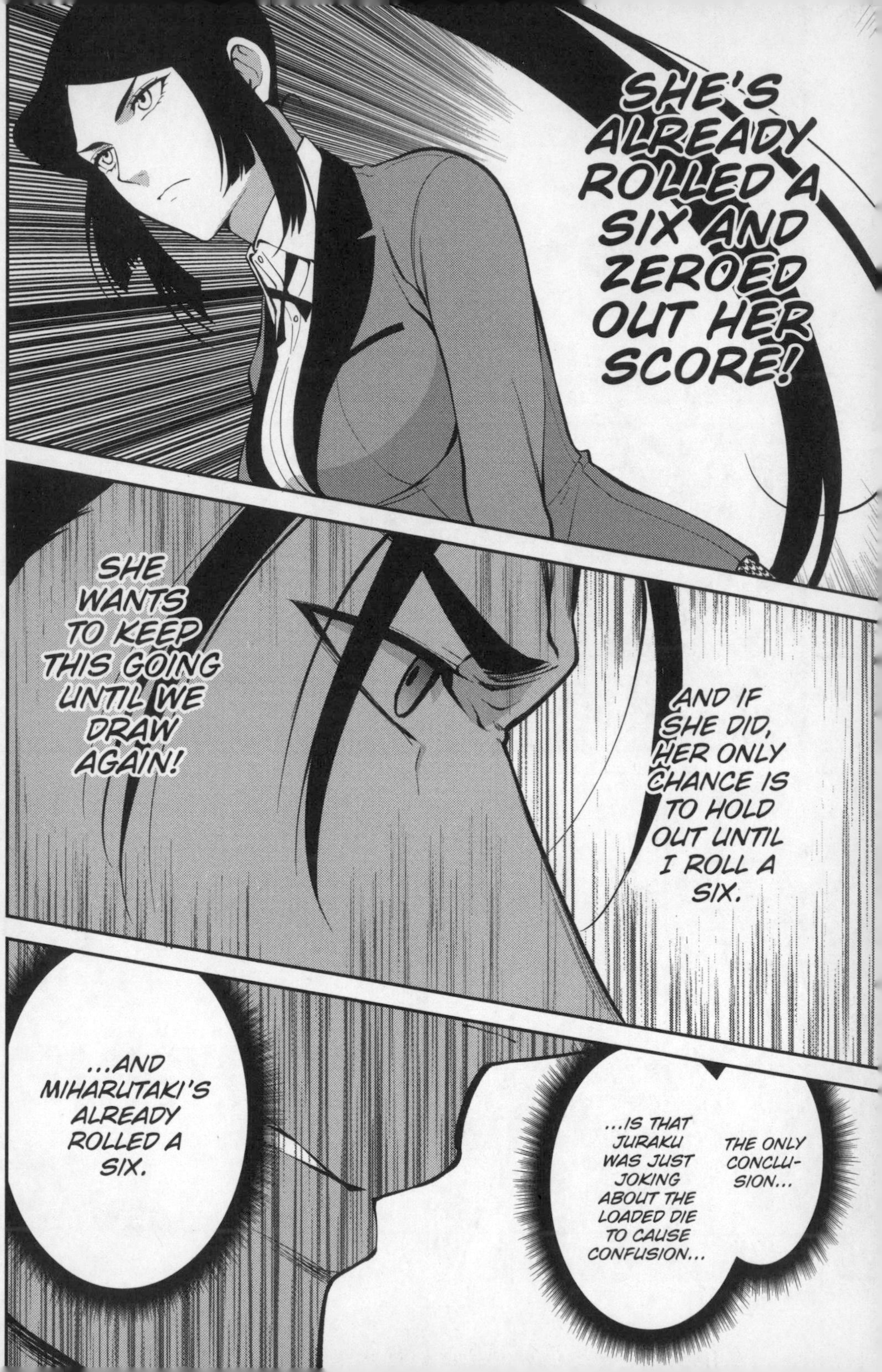
SHE'S ALREADY ROLLED A SIX AND ZEROED OUT HER SCORE!
AND IF SHE DID, HER ONLY CHANCE IS TO HOLD OUT UNTIL I ROLL A SIX.
SHE WANTS TO KEEP THIS GOING UNTIL WE DRAW AGAIN!
THE ONLY CONCLUSION...
...IS THAT JURAKU WAS JUST JOKING ABOUT THE LOADED DIE TO CAUSE CONFUSION...
...AND MIHARUTAKI'S ALREADY ROLLED A SIX.

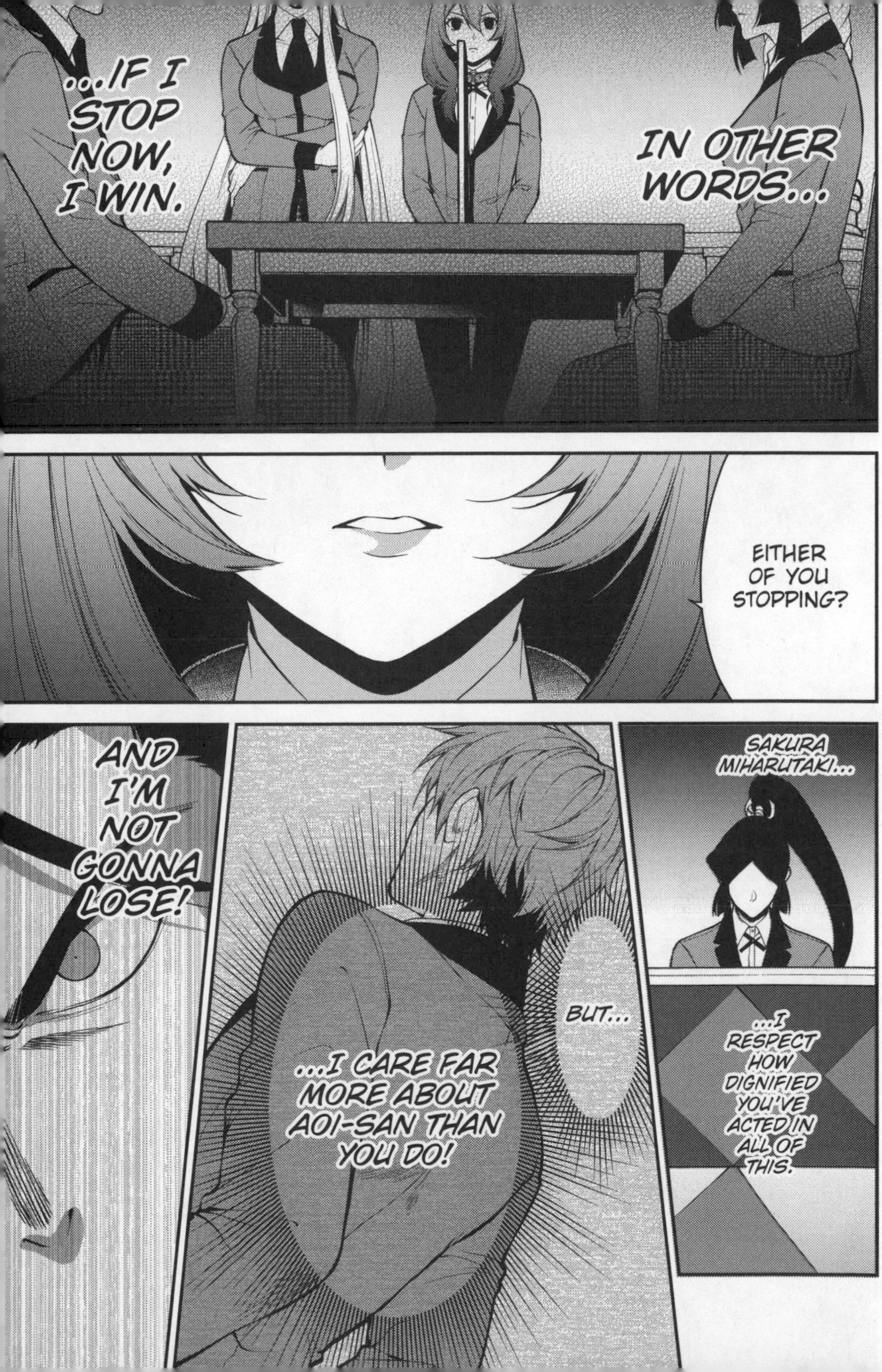
IN OTHER WORDS...
...IF I STOP NOW, I WIN.
EITHER OF YOU STOPPING?
SAKURA MIHARUTAKI...
...I RESPECT HOW DIGNIFIED YOU'VE ACTED IN ALL OF THIS.
BUT...
...I CARE FAR MORE ABOUT AOI-SAN THAN YOU DO!
AND I'M NOT GONNA LOSE!

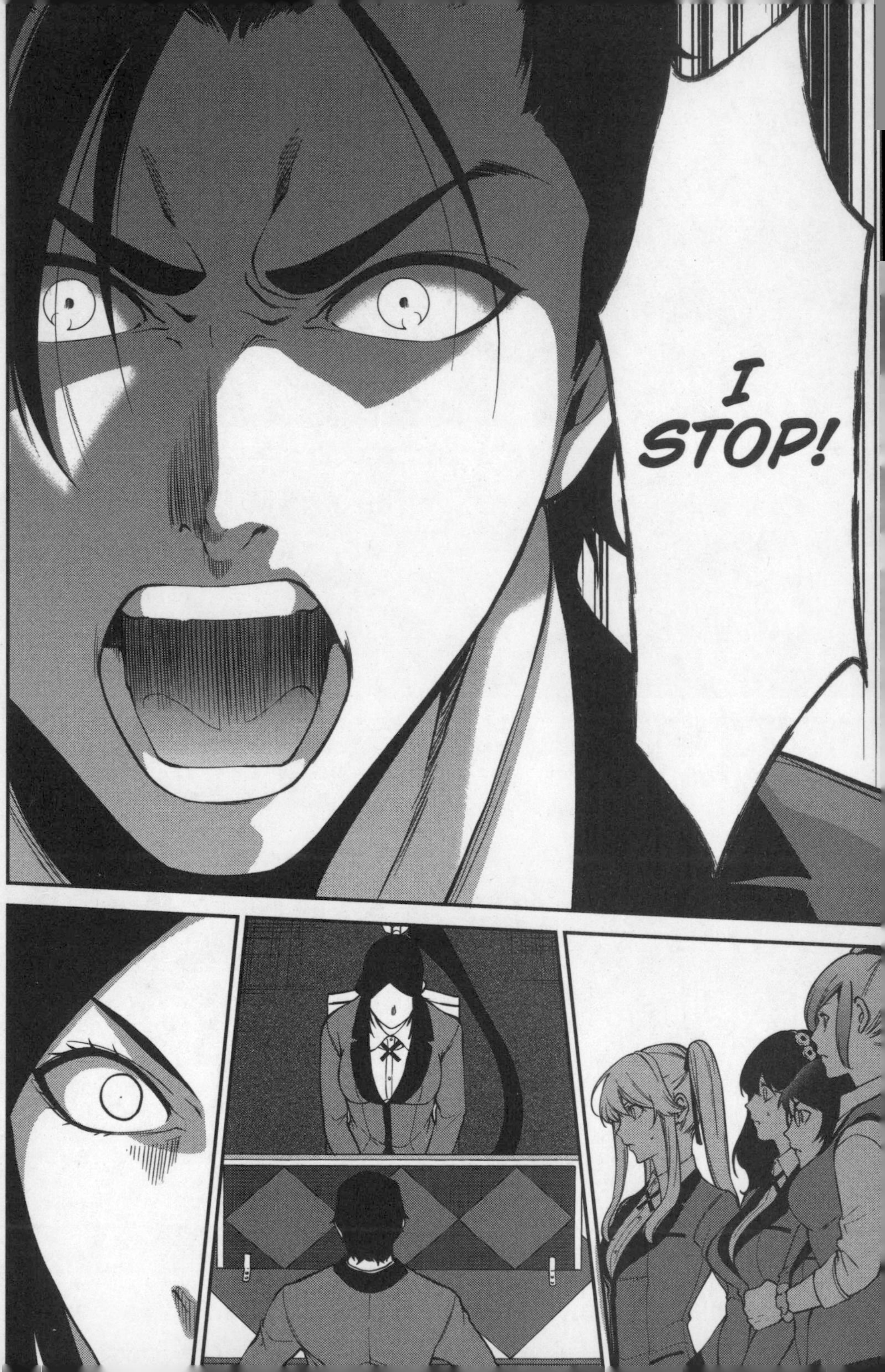
I STOP!

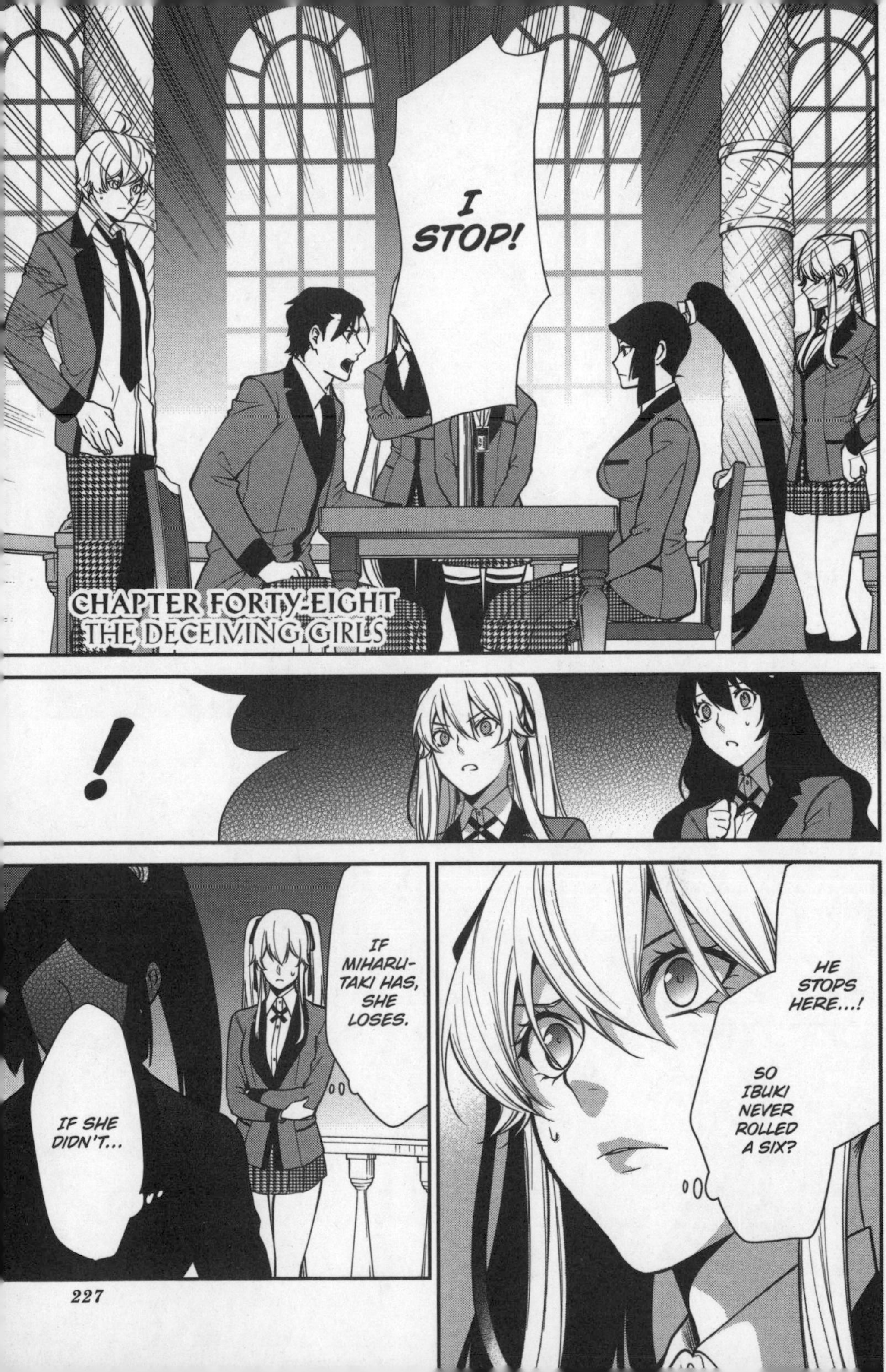

I STOP!
CHAPTER FORTY-EIGHT THE DECEIVING GIRLS
!
HE STOPS HERE...!
SO IBUKI NEVER ROLLED A SIX?
IF MIHARU-TAKI HAS, SHE LOSES.
IF SHE DIDN'T...

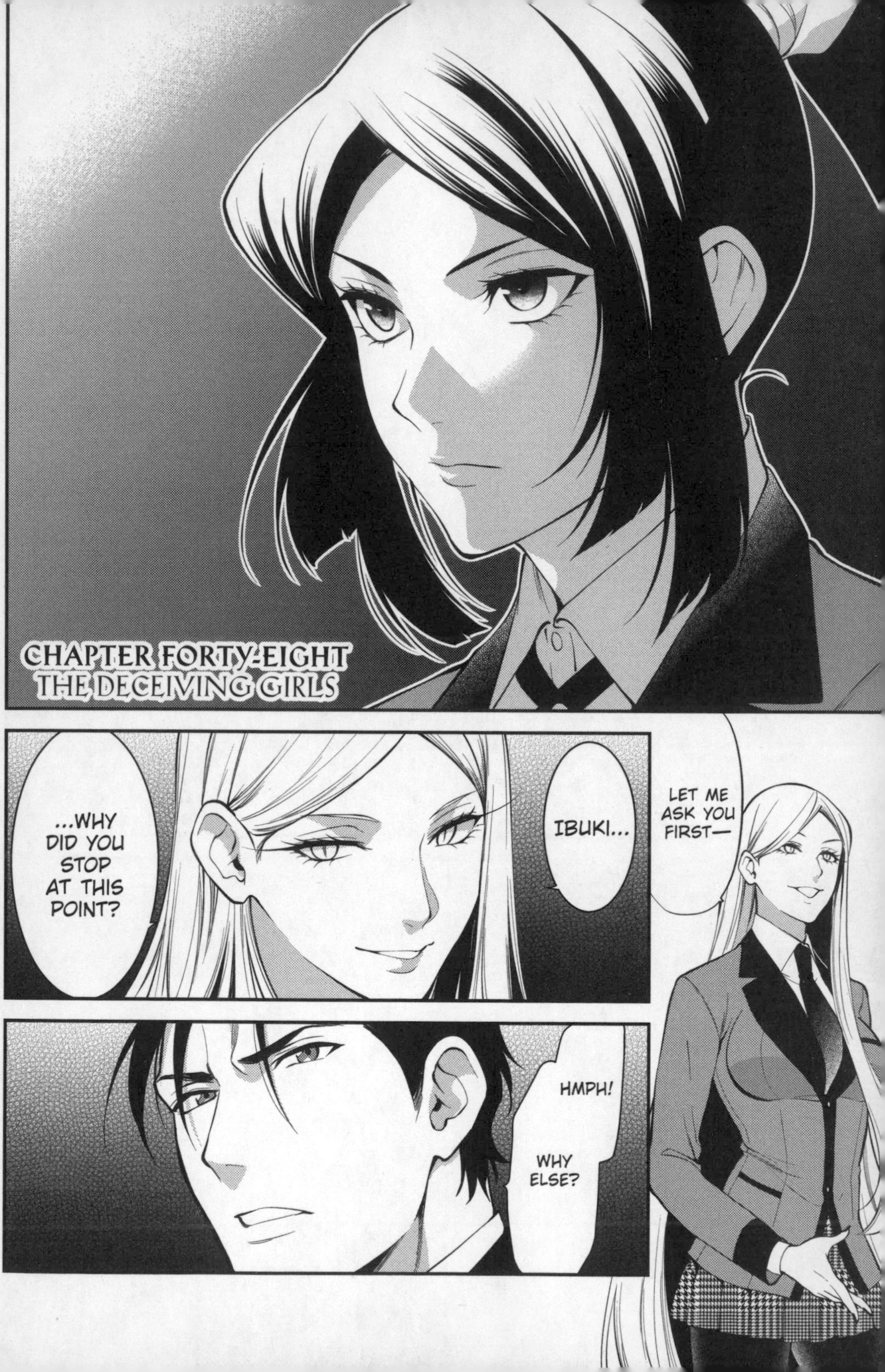
CHAPTER FORTY-EIGHT
THE DECEIVING GIRLS
LET ME ASK YOU FIRST—
IBUKI...
...WHY DID YOU STOP AT THIS POINT?
HMPH!
WHY ELSE?

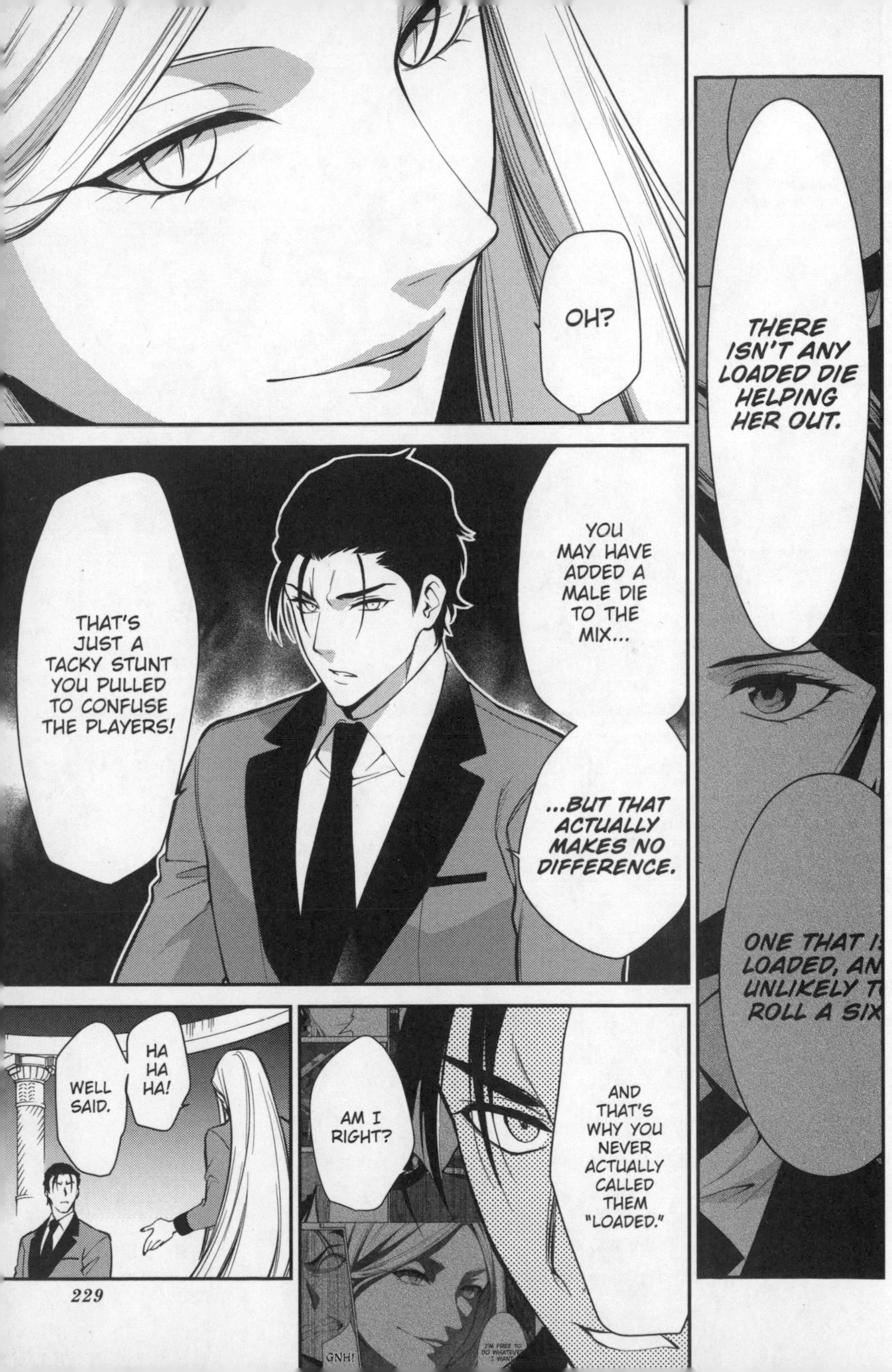
THERE ISN'T ANY LOADED DIE HELPING HER OUT.
ONE THAT IS LOADED, AN UNLIKELY T ROLL A SIX
OH?
YOU MAY HAVE ADDED A MALE DIE TO THE MIX...
...BUT THAT ACTUALLY MAKES NO DIFFERENCE.
THAT'S JUST A TACKY STUNT YOU PULLED TO CONFUSE THE PLAYERS!
AND THAT'S WHY YOU NEVER ACTUALLY CALLED THEM "LOADED."
AM I RIGHT?
I'M FREE TO DO WHATEVER I WANT.
GNH!
HA HA HA!
WELL SAID.

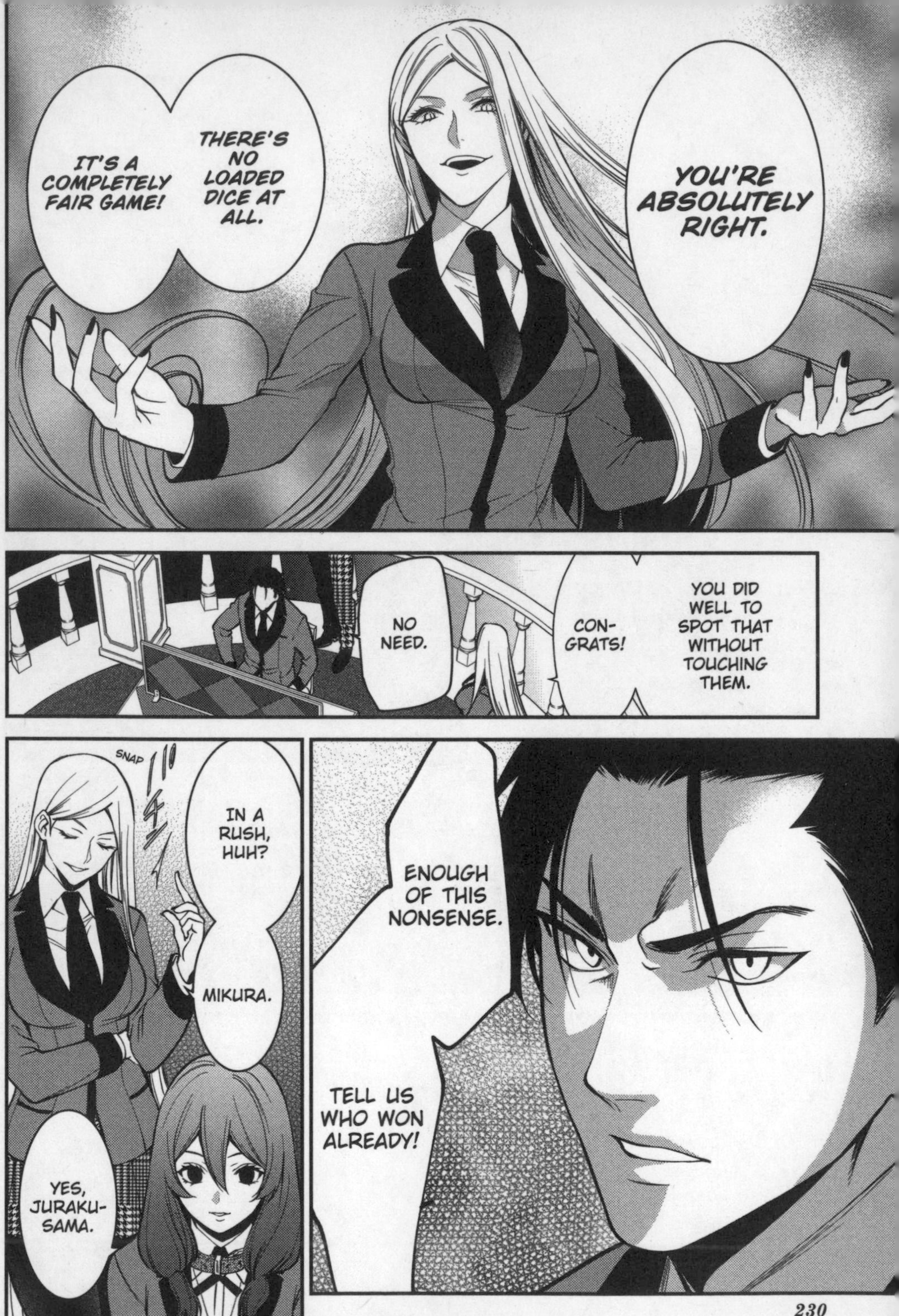
YOU'RE ABSOLUTELY RIGHT.
THERE'S NO LOADED DICE AT ALL.
IT'S A COMPLETELY FAIR GAME!
YOU DID WELL TO SPOT THAT WITHOUT TOUCHING THEM.
CON-GRATS!
NO NEED.
ENOUGH OF THIS NONSENSE.
TELL US WHO WON ALREADY!
SNAP
IN A RUSH, HUH?
MIKURA.
YES, JURAKU-SAMA.

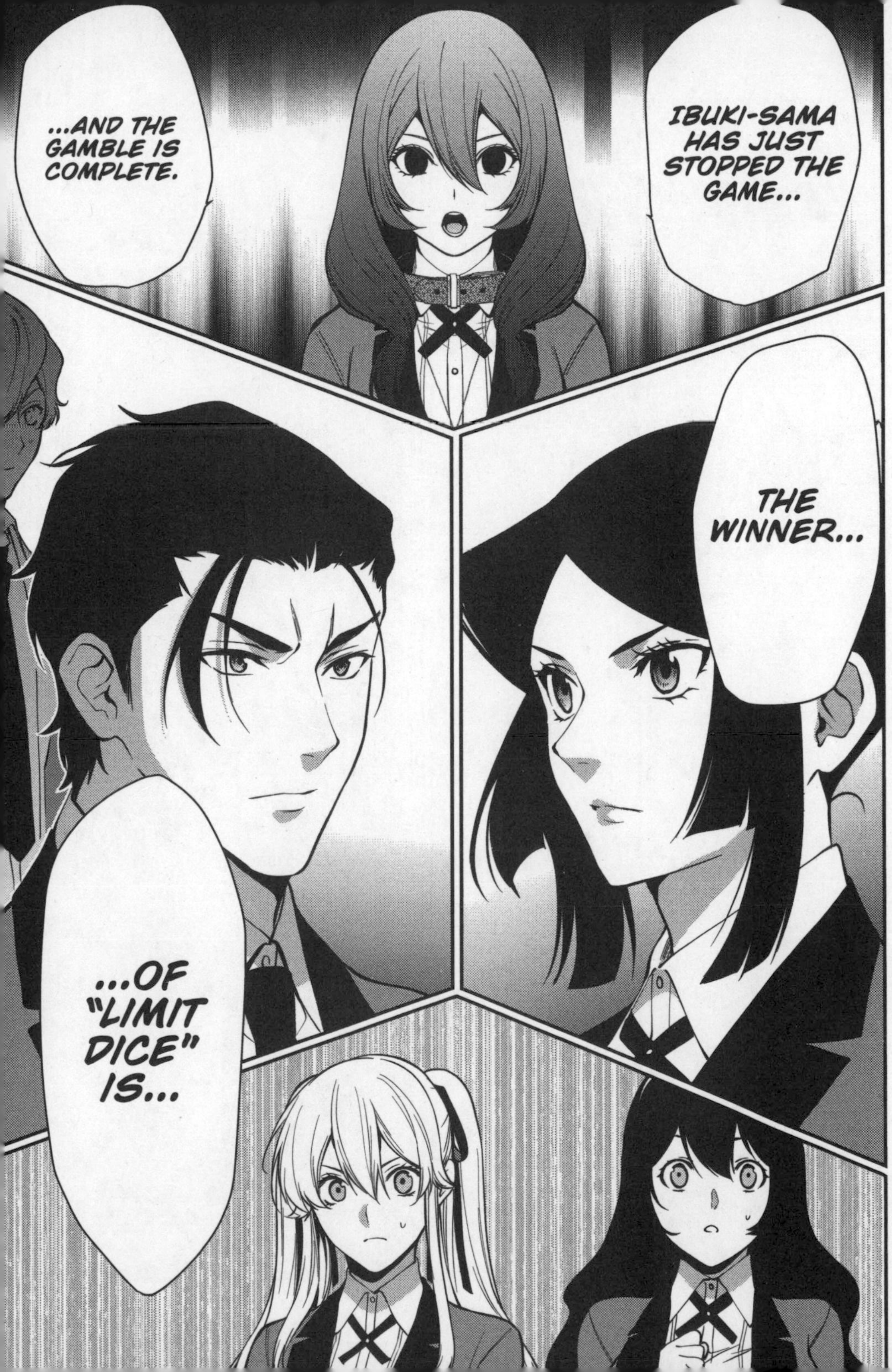
IBUKI-SAMA HAS JUST STOPPED THE GAME...
...AND THE GAMBLE IS COMPLETE.
THE WINNER...
...OF "LIMIT DICE" IS...

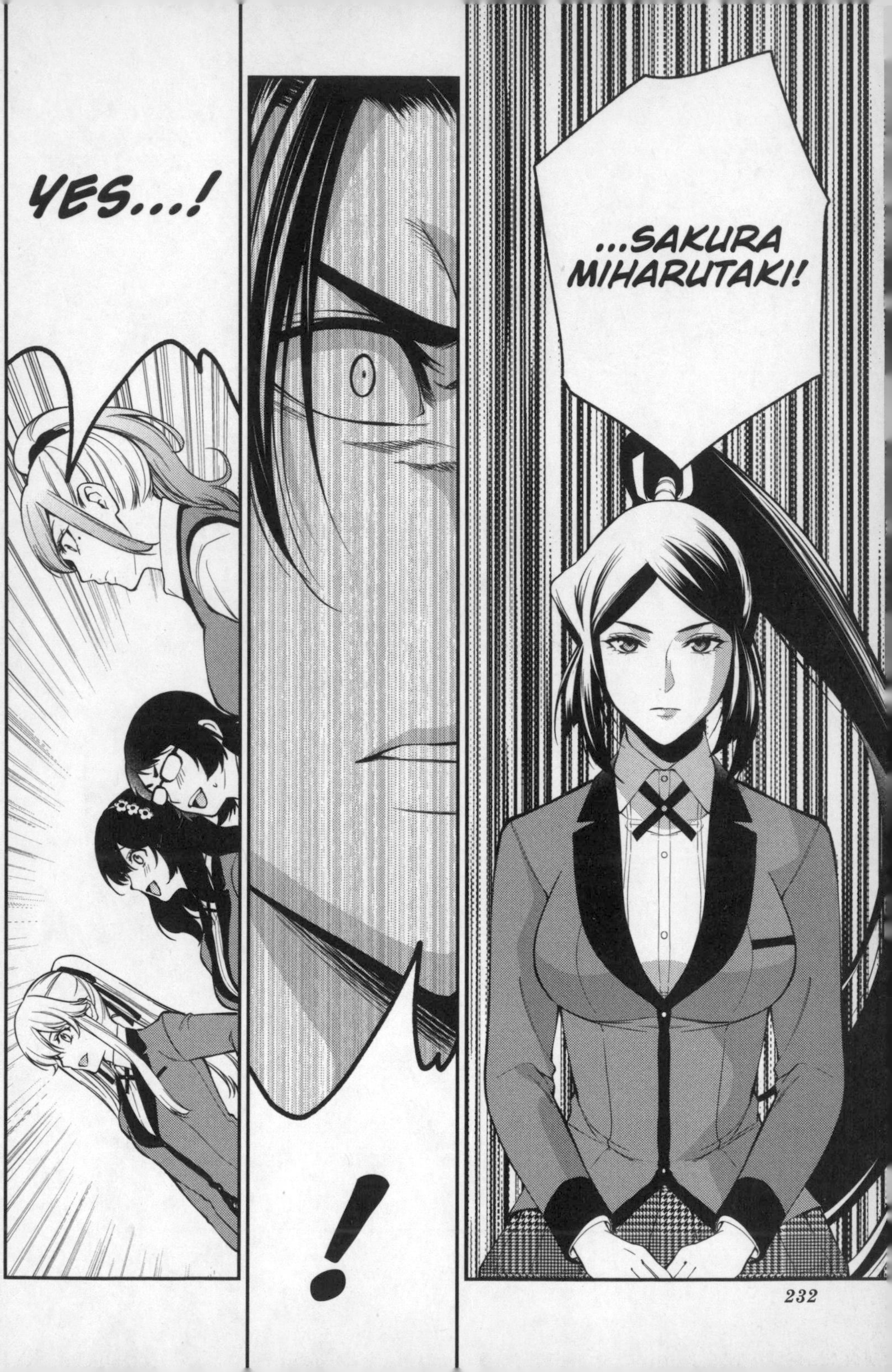
...SAKURA MIHARUTAKI!
!
YES...!

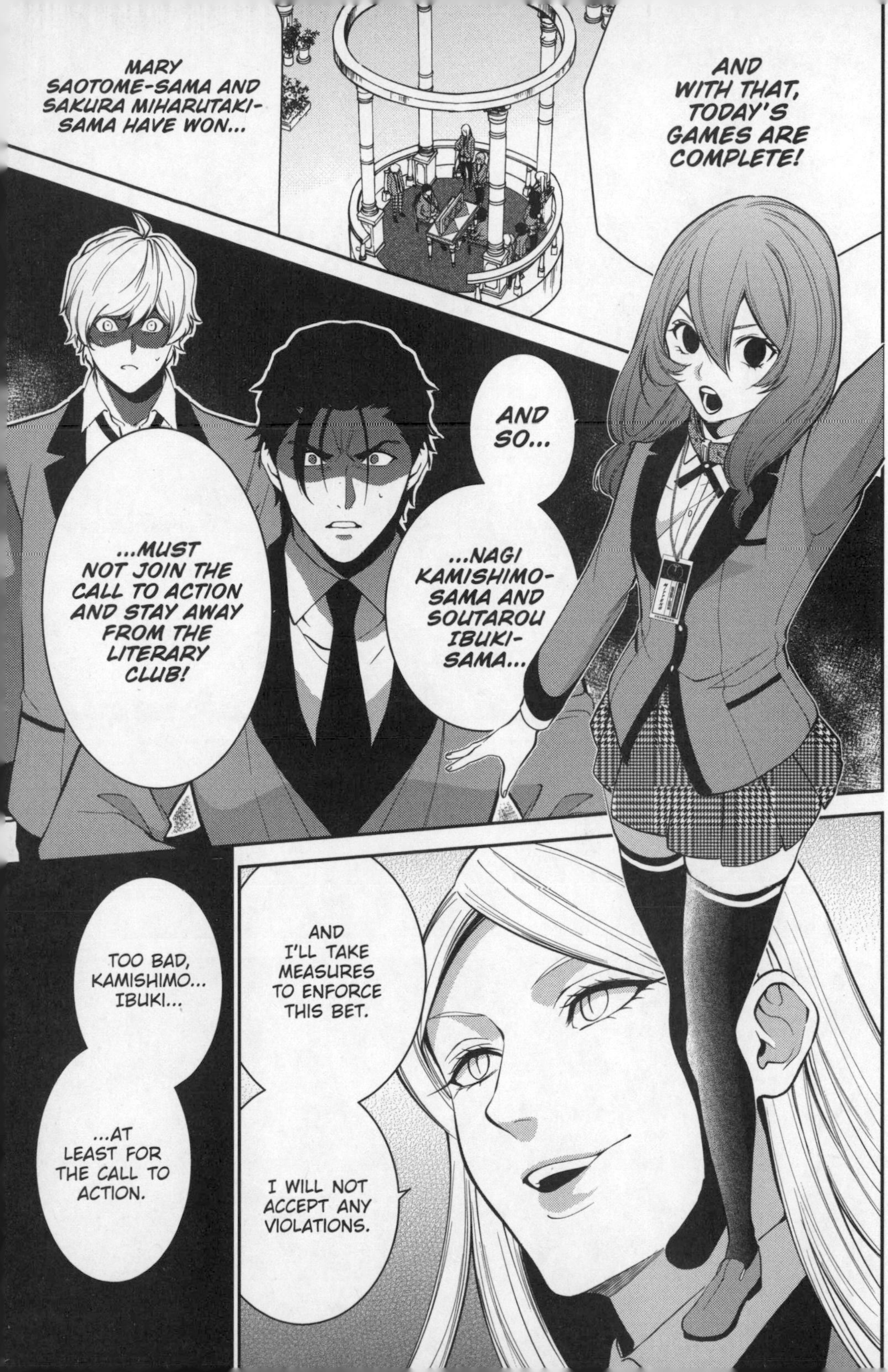
AND WITH THAT, TODAY'S GAMES ARE COMPLETE!
MARY SAOTOME-SAMA AND SAKURA MIHARUTAKI-SAMA HAVE WON...
AND SO...
...NAGI KAMISHIMO-SAMA AND SOUTAROU IBUKI-SAMA...
...MUST NOT JOIN THE CALL TO ACTION AND STAY AWAY FROM THE LITERARY CLUB!
AND I'LL TAKE MEASURES TO ENFORCE THIS BET.
I WILL NOT ACCEPT ANY VIOLATIONS.
TOO BAD, KAMISHIMO... IBUKI...
...AT LEAST FOR THE CALL TO ACTION.

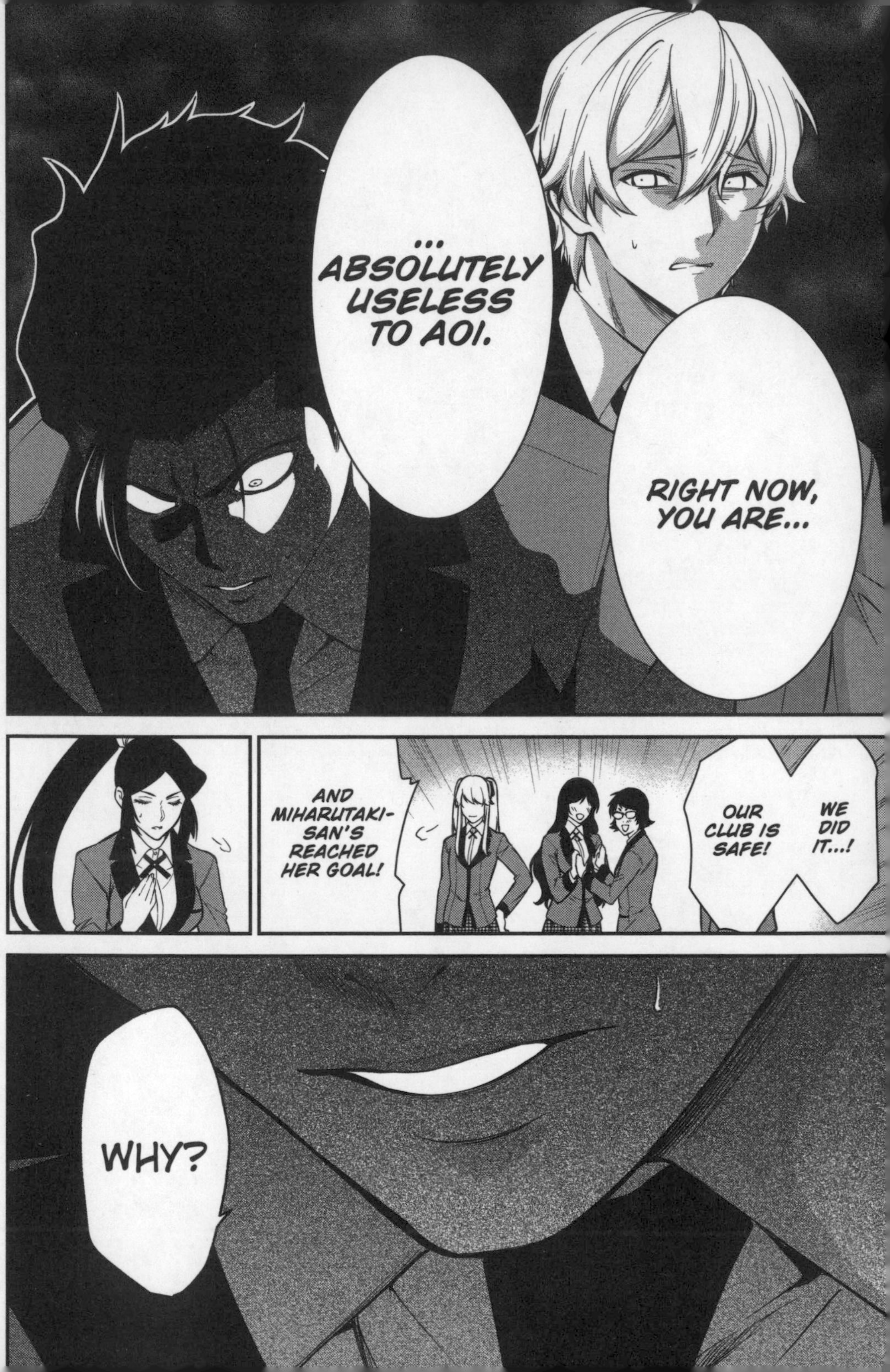
RIGHT NOW, YOU ARE...
...ABSOLUTELY USELESS TO AOI.
WE DID IT...!
OUR CLUB IS SAFE!
AND MIHARUTAKI-SAN'S REACHED HER GOAL!
WHY?

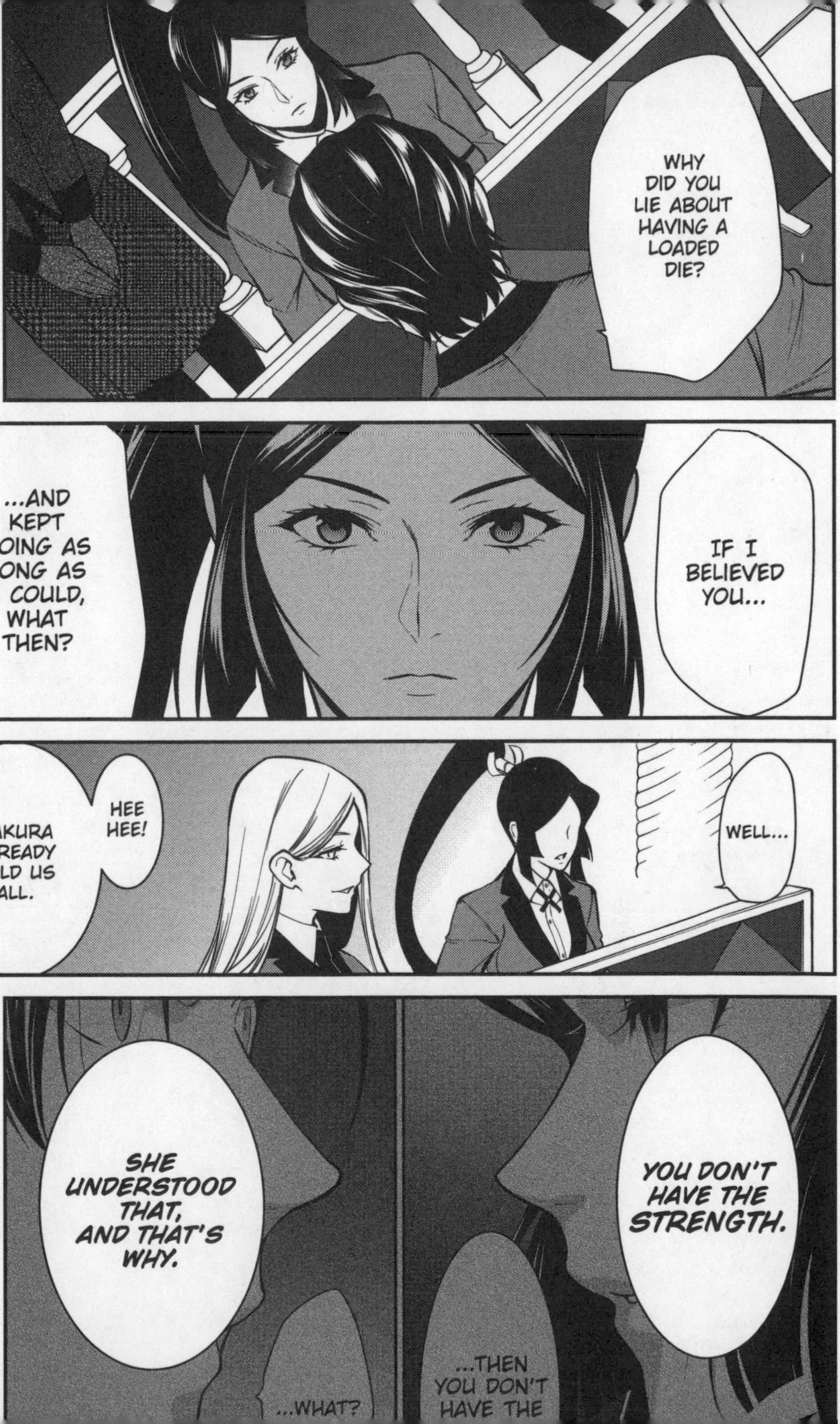
WHY DID YOU LIE ABOUT HAVING A LOADED DIE?
IF I BELIEVED YOU...
...AND KEPT GOING AS LONG AS I COULD, WHAT THEN?
WELL...
HEE HEE!
SAKURA ALREADY TOLD US ALL.
YOU DON'T HAVE THE STRENGTH.
...THEN YOU DON'T HAVE THE
SHE UNDERSTOOD THAT, AND THAT'S WHY.
...WHAT?

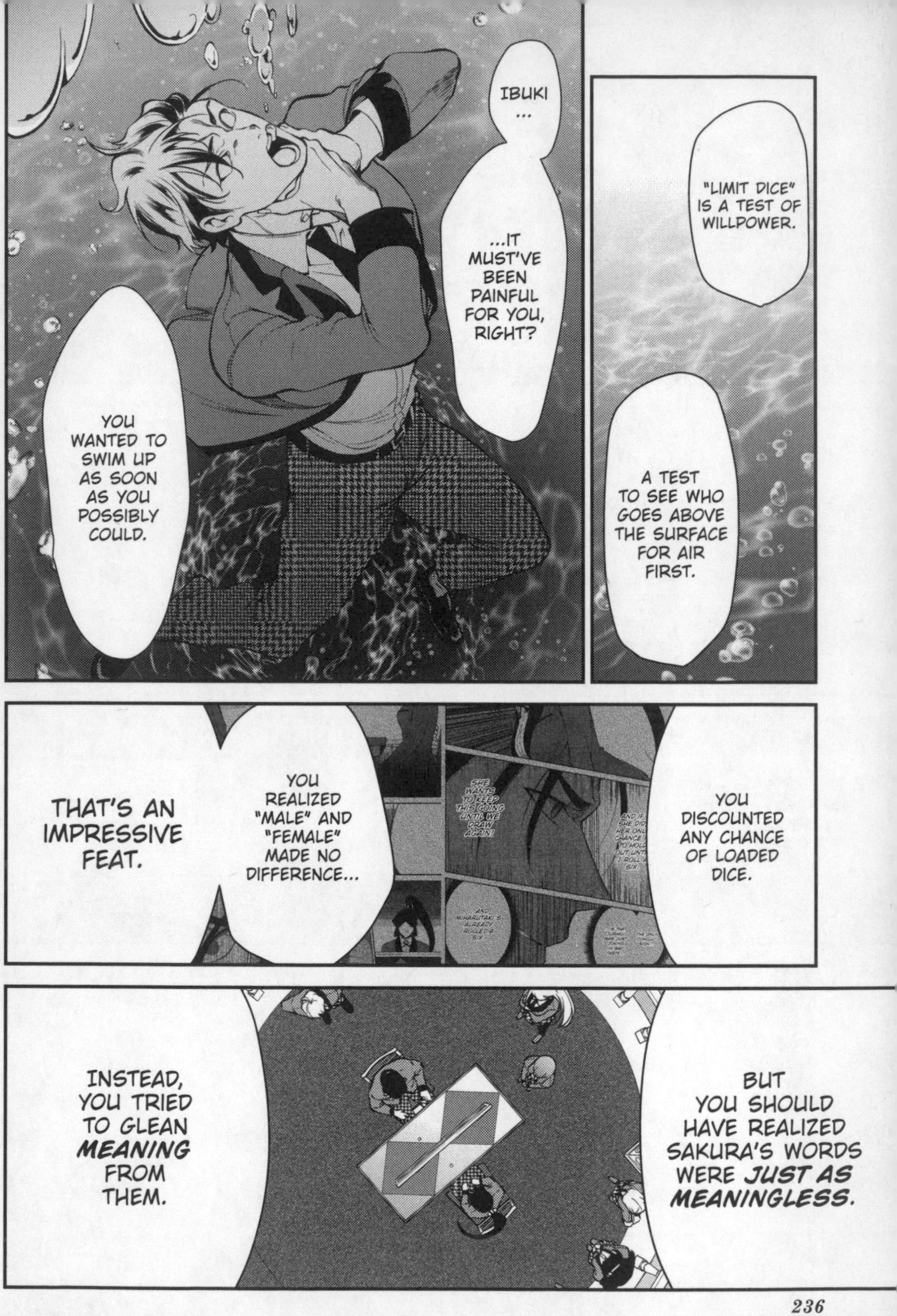
"LIMIT DICE" IS A TEST OF WILLPOWER.
A TEST TO SEE WHO GOES ABOVE THE SURFACE FOR AIR FIRST.
IBUKI...
...IT MUST'VE BEEN PAINFUL FOR YOU, RIGHT?
YOU WANTED TO SWIM UP AS SOON AS YOU POSSIBLY COULD.
YOU DISCOUNTED ANY CHANCE OF LOADED DICE.
SHE WANTS TO KEEP THIS GOING UNTIL WE DRAW AGAIN!
AND MIHARUTAKI'S ALREADY ROLLED A SIX.
YOU REALIZED "MALE" AND "FEMALE" MADE NO DIFFERENCE...
THAT'S AN IMPRESSIVE FEAT.
BUT YOU SHOULD HAVE REALIZED SAKURA'S WORDS WERE ***JUST AS MEANINGLESS***.
INSTEAD, YOU TRIED TO GLEAN ***MEANING*** FROM THEM.

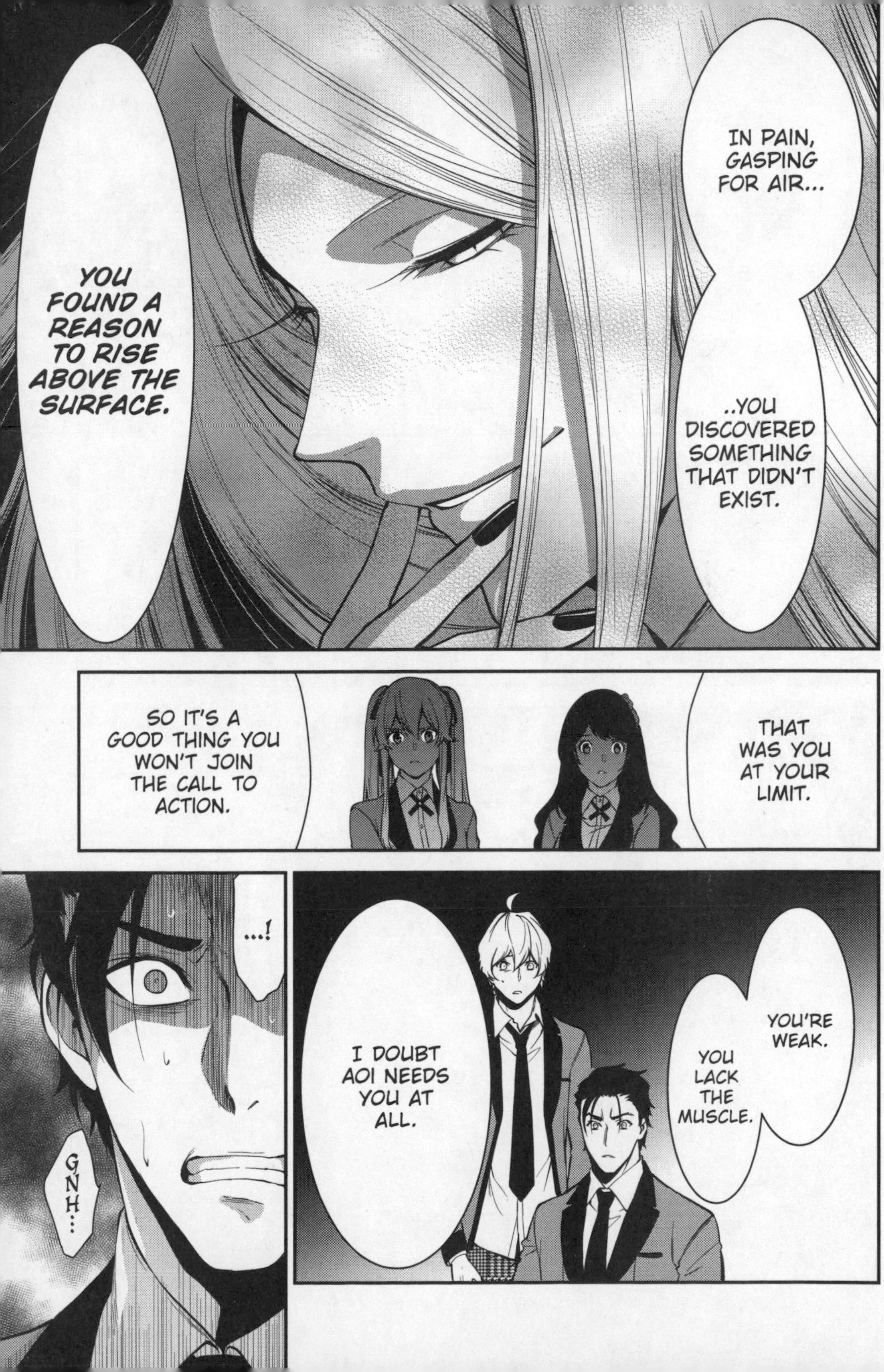

IN PAIN, GASPING FOR AIR...
..YOU DISCOVERED SOMETHING THAT DIDN'T EXIST.
YOU FOUND A REASON TO RISE ABOVE THE SURFACE.
THAT WAS YOU AT YOUR LIMIT.
SO IT'S A GOOD THING YOU WON'T JOIN THE CALL TO ACTION.
YOU'RE WEAK.
YOU LACK THE MUSCLE.
I DOUBT AOI NEEDS YOU AT ALL.
...!
GNH...

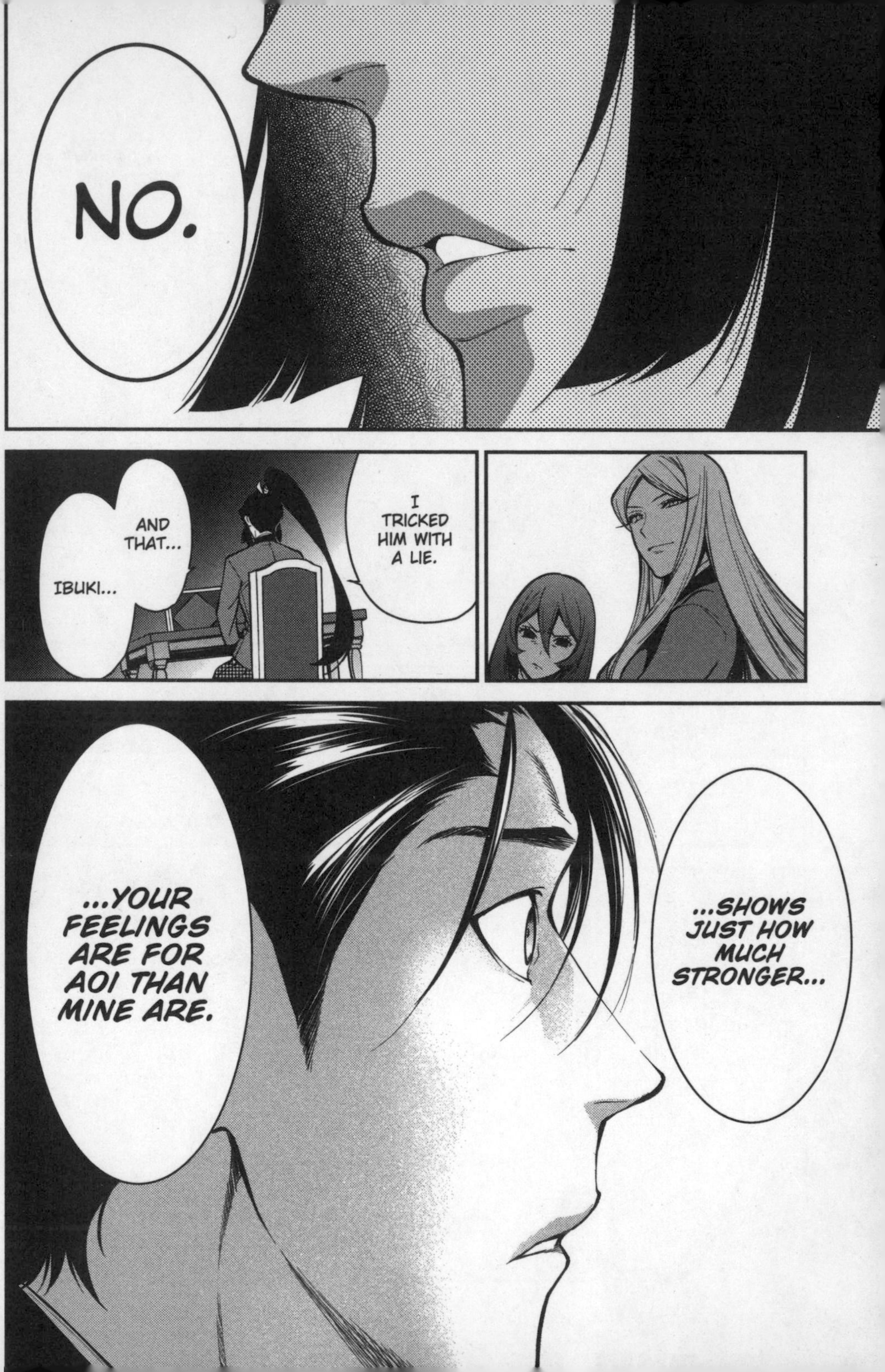
NO.
I TRICKED HIM WITH A LIE.
AND THAT... IBUKI...
...SHOWS JUST HOW MUCH STRONGER...
...YOUR FEELINGS ARE FOR AOI THAN MINE ARE.

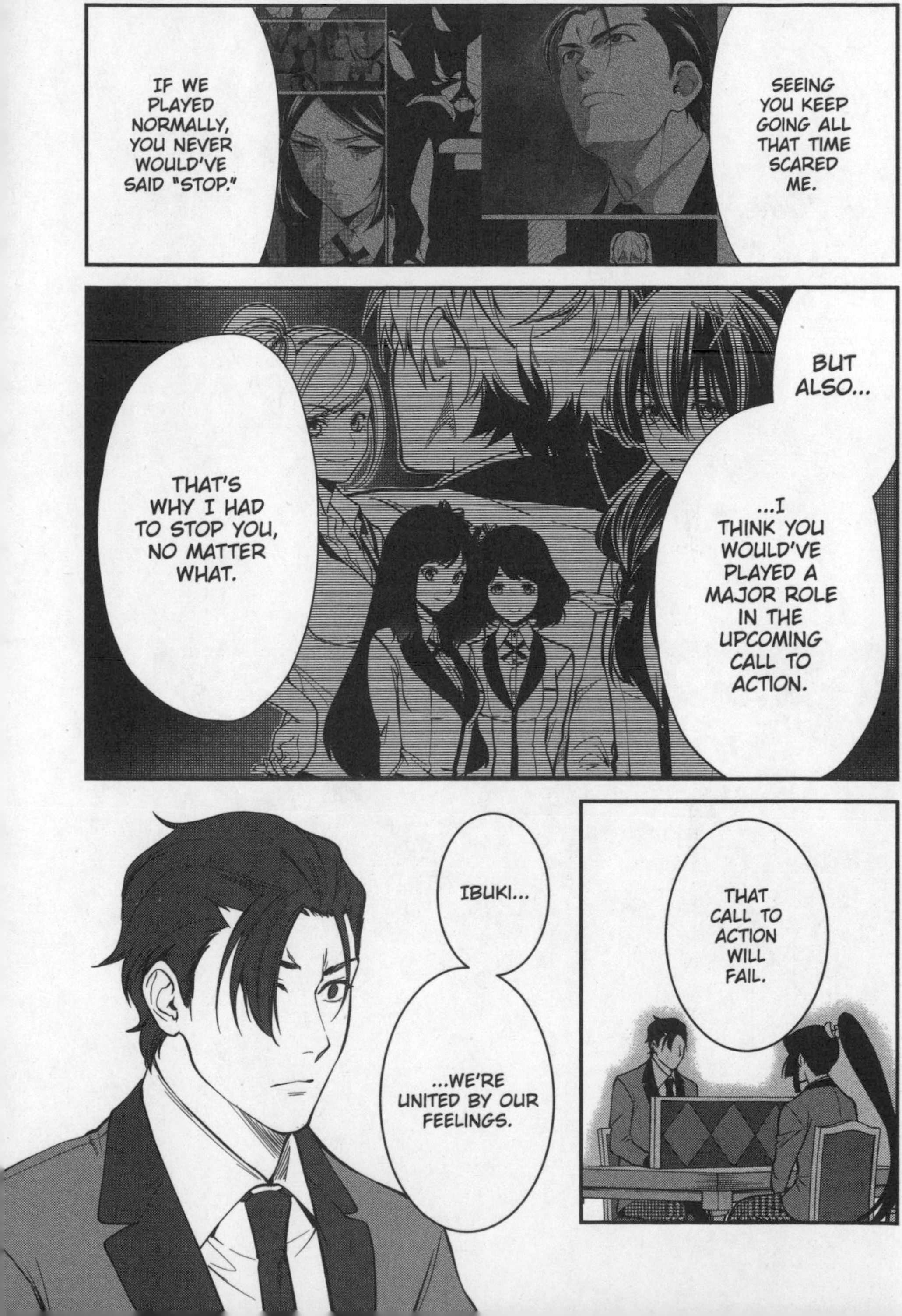
SEEING YOU KEEP GOING ALL THAT TIME SCARED ME.
IF WE PLAYED NORMALLY, YOU NEVER WOULD'VE SAID "STOP."
BUT ALSO...
...I THINK YOU WOULD'VE PLAYED A MAJOR ROLE IN THE UPCOMING CALL TO ACTION.
THAT'S WHY I HAD TO STOP YOU, NO MATTER WHAT.
THAT CALL TO ACTION WILL FAIL.
IBUKI...
...WE'RE UNITED BY OUR FEELINGS.

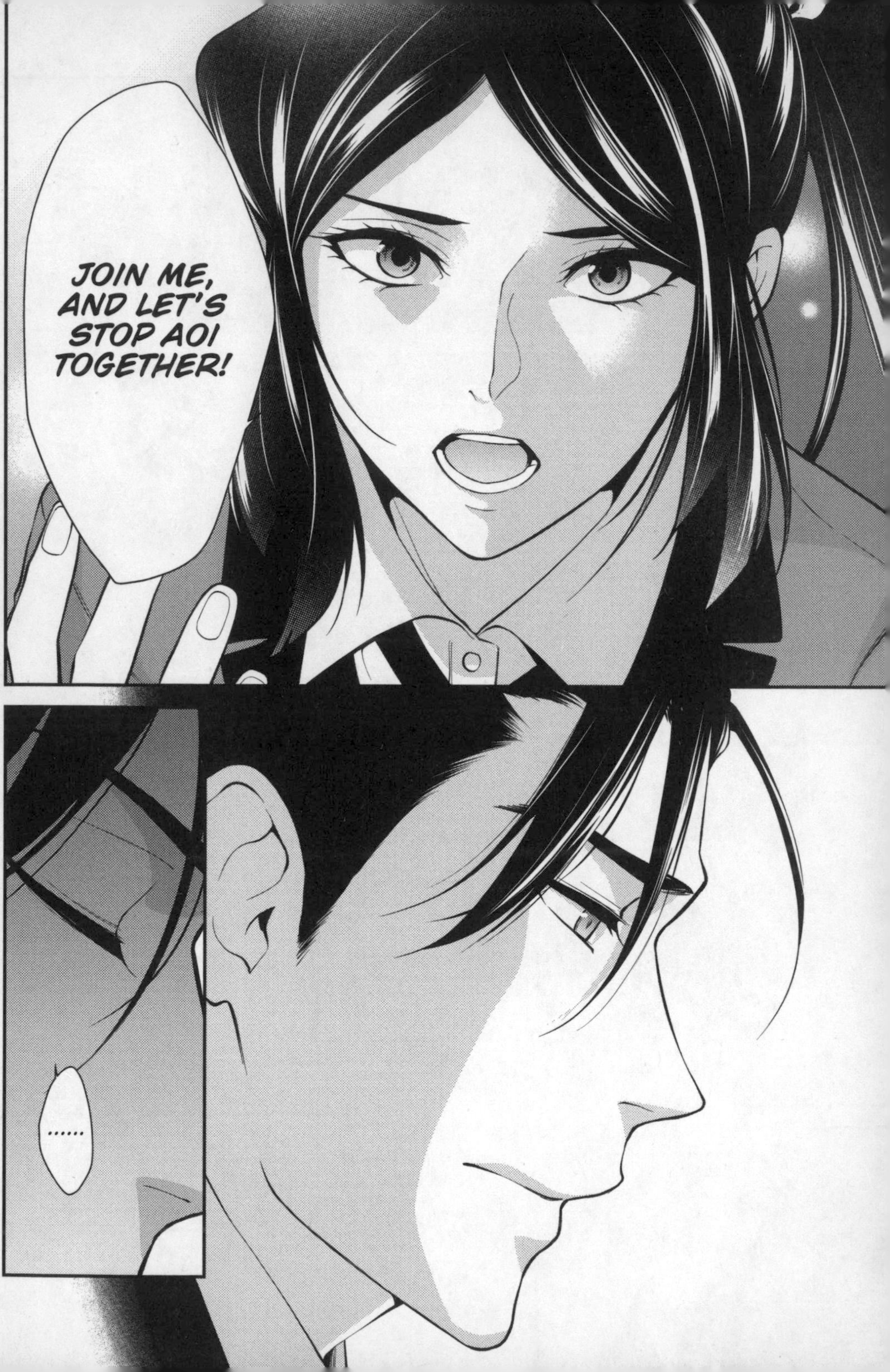
JOIN ME, AND LET'S STOP AOI TOGETHER!
......

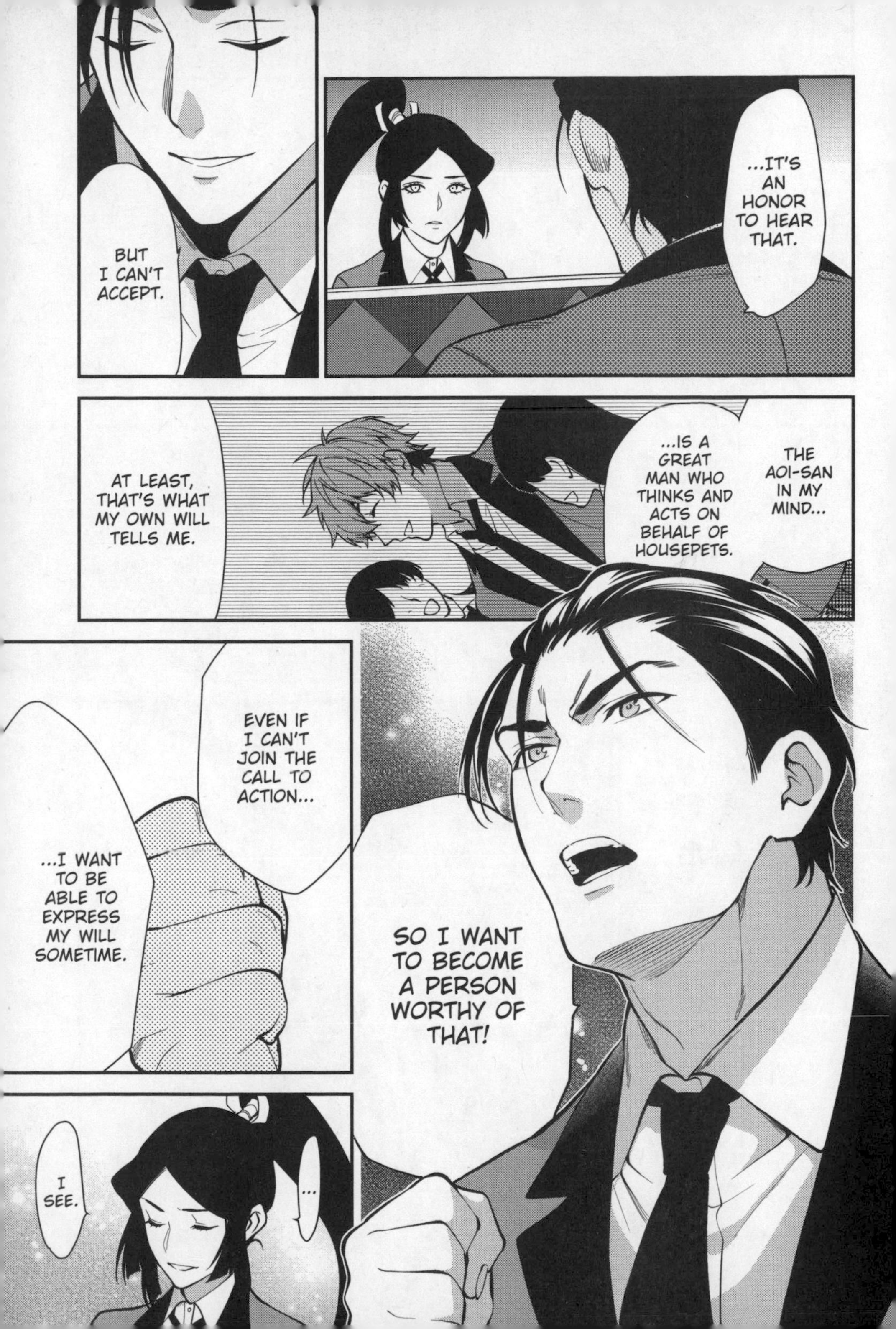
...IT'S AN HONOR TO HEAR THAT.
BUT I CAN'T ACCEPT.
THE AOI-SAN IN MY MIND...
...IS A GREAT MAN WHO THINKS AND ACTS ON BEHALF OF HOUSEPETS.
AT LEAST, THAT'S WHAT MY OWN WILL TELLS ME.
SO I WANT TO BECOME A PERSON WORTHY OF THAT!
EVEN IF I CAN'T JOIN THE CALL TO ACTION...
...I WANT TO BE ABLE TO EXPRESS MY WILL SOMETIME.
...
I SEE.

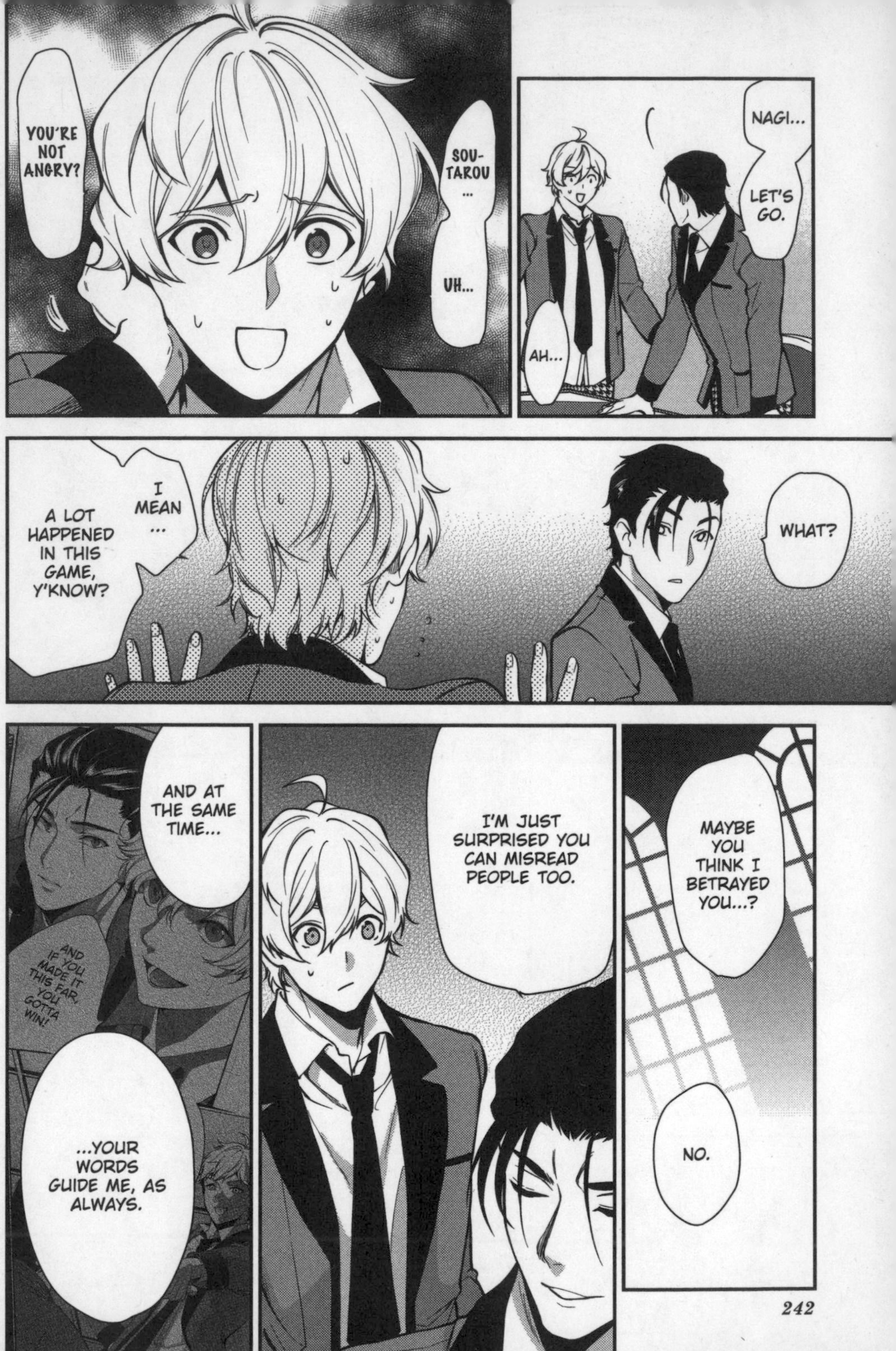
NAGI...
LET'S GO.
AH...
SOU-TAROU ...
UH...
YOU'RE NOT ANGRY?
WHAT?
I MEAN ...
A LOT HAPPENED IN THIS GAME, Y'KNOW?
MAYBE YOU THINK I BETRAYED YOU...?
NO.
I'M JUST SURPRISED YOU CAN MISREAD PEOPLE TOO.
AND AT THE SAME TIME...
AND IF YOU MADE IT THIS FAR, YOU GOTTA WIN!
...YOUR WORDS GUIDE ME, AS ALWAYS.

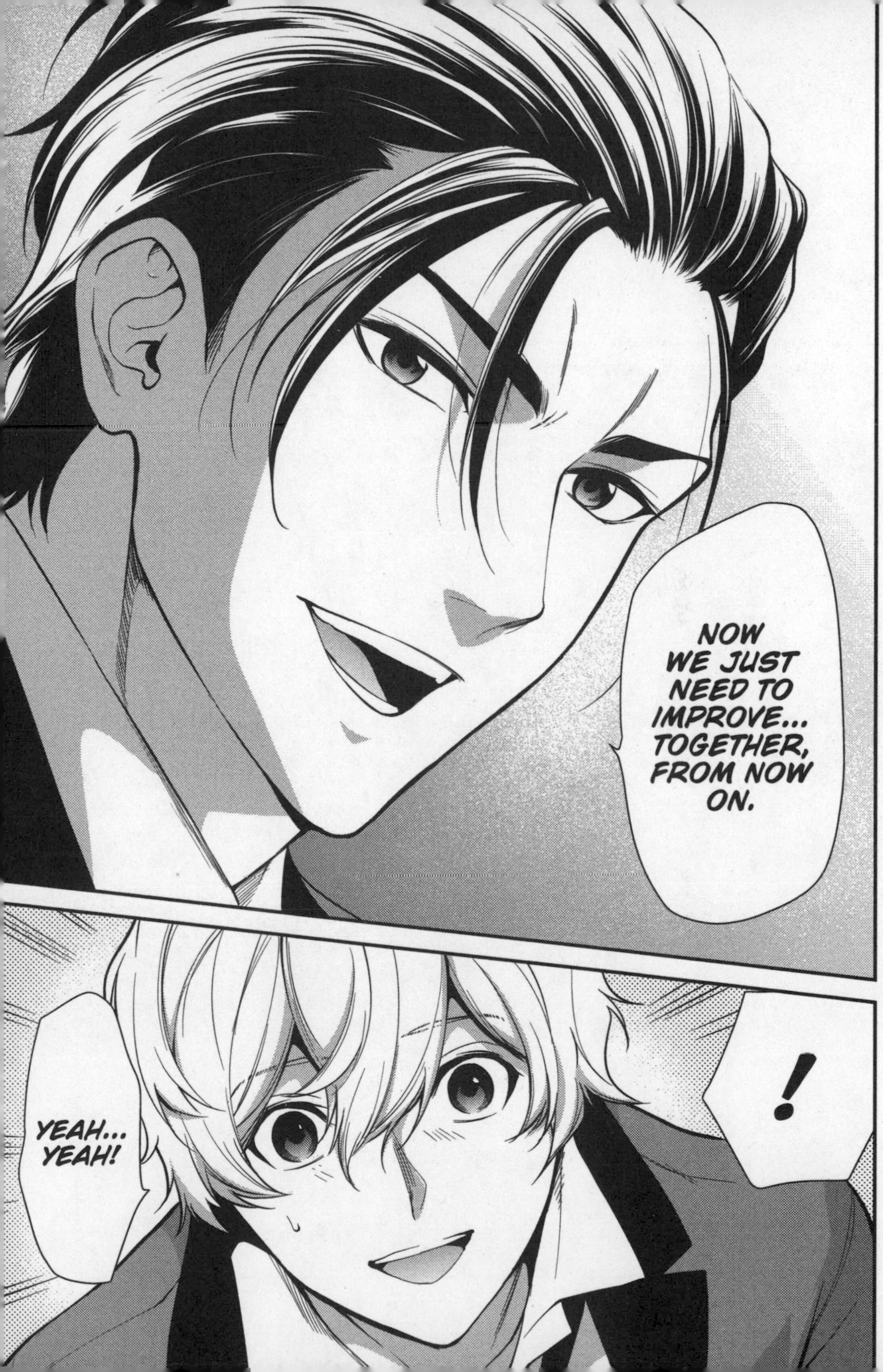
NOW WE JUST NEED TO IMPROVE... TOGETHER, FROM NOW ON.
!
YEAH... YEAH!

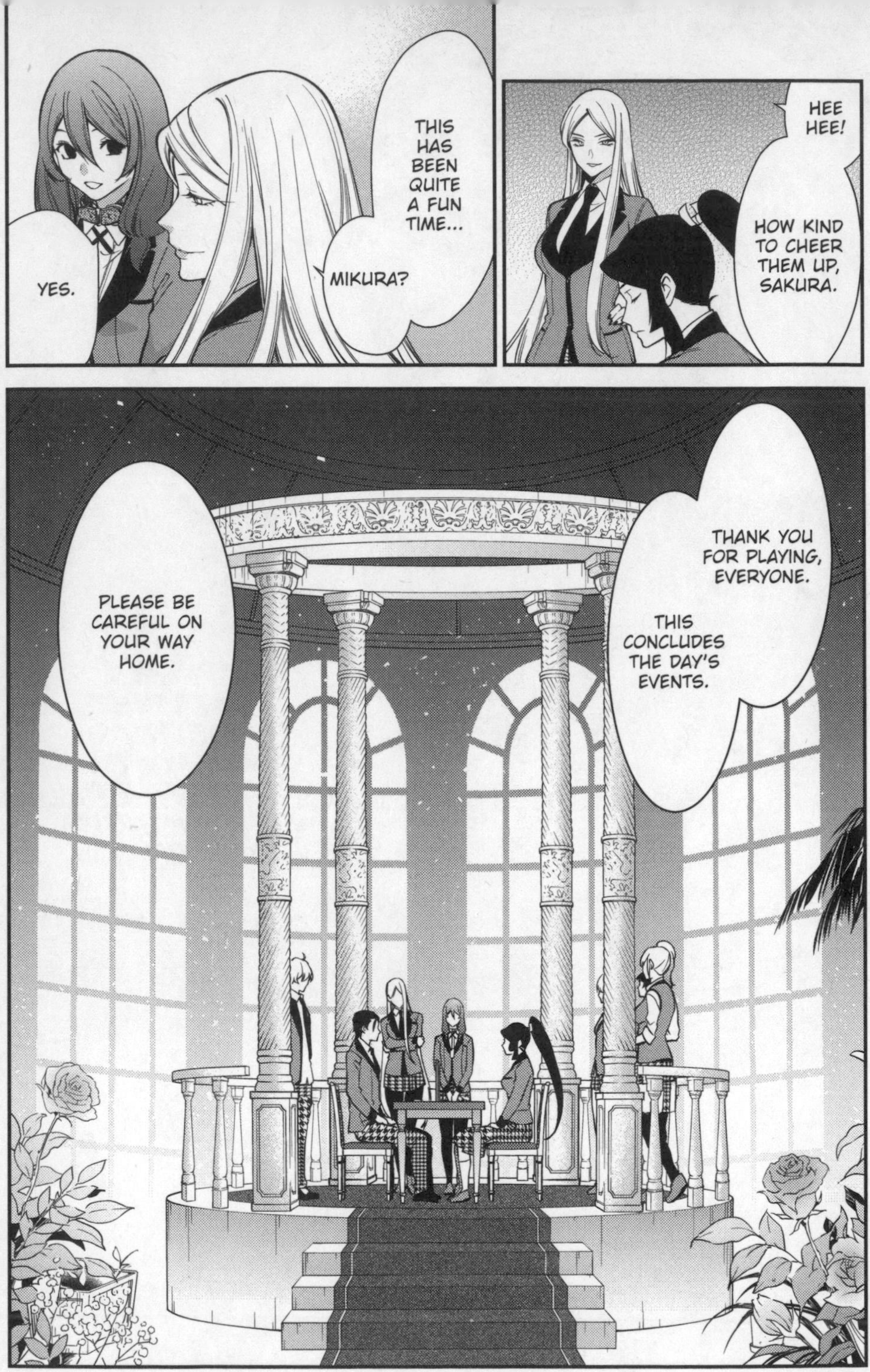
HEE HEE!
HOW KIND TO CHEER THEM UP, SAKURA.
THIS HAS BEEN QUITE A FUN TIME...
MIKURA?
YES.
THANK YOU FOR PLAYING, EVERYONE.
THIS CONCLUDES THE DAY'S EVENTS.
PLEASE BE CAREFUL ON YOUR WAY HOME.

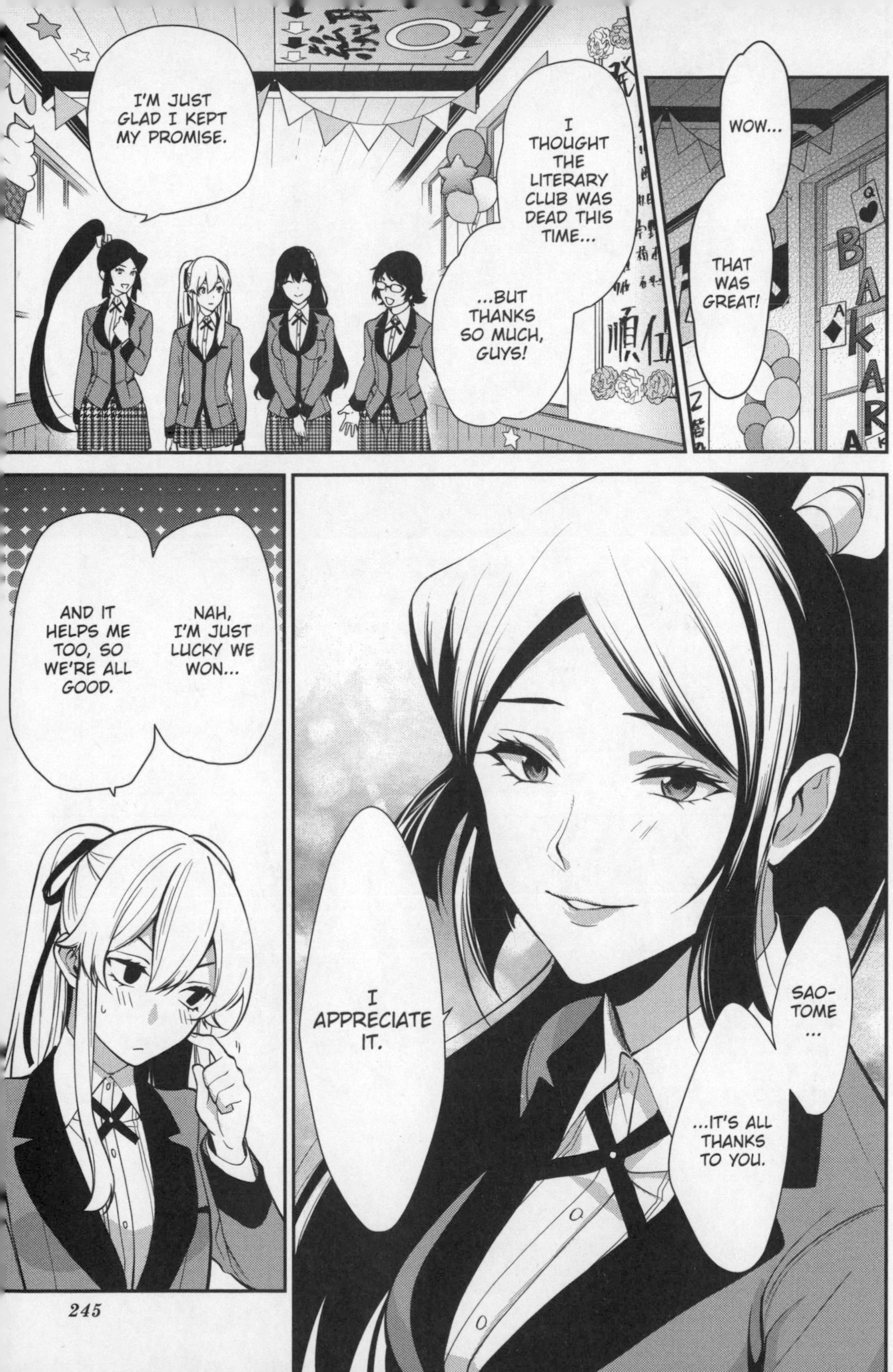

WOW...
THAT WAS GREAT!
I THOUGHT THE LITERARY CLUB WAS DEAD THIS TIME...
...BUT THANKS SO MUCH, GUYS!
I'M JUST GLAD I KEPT MY PROMISE.
SAO-TOME...
...IT'S ALL THANKS TO YOU.
I APPRECIATE IT.
NAH, I'M JUST LUCKY WE WON...
AND IT HELPS ME TOO, SO WE'RE ALL GOOD.

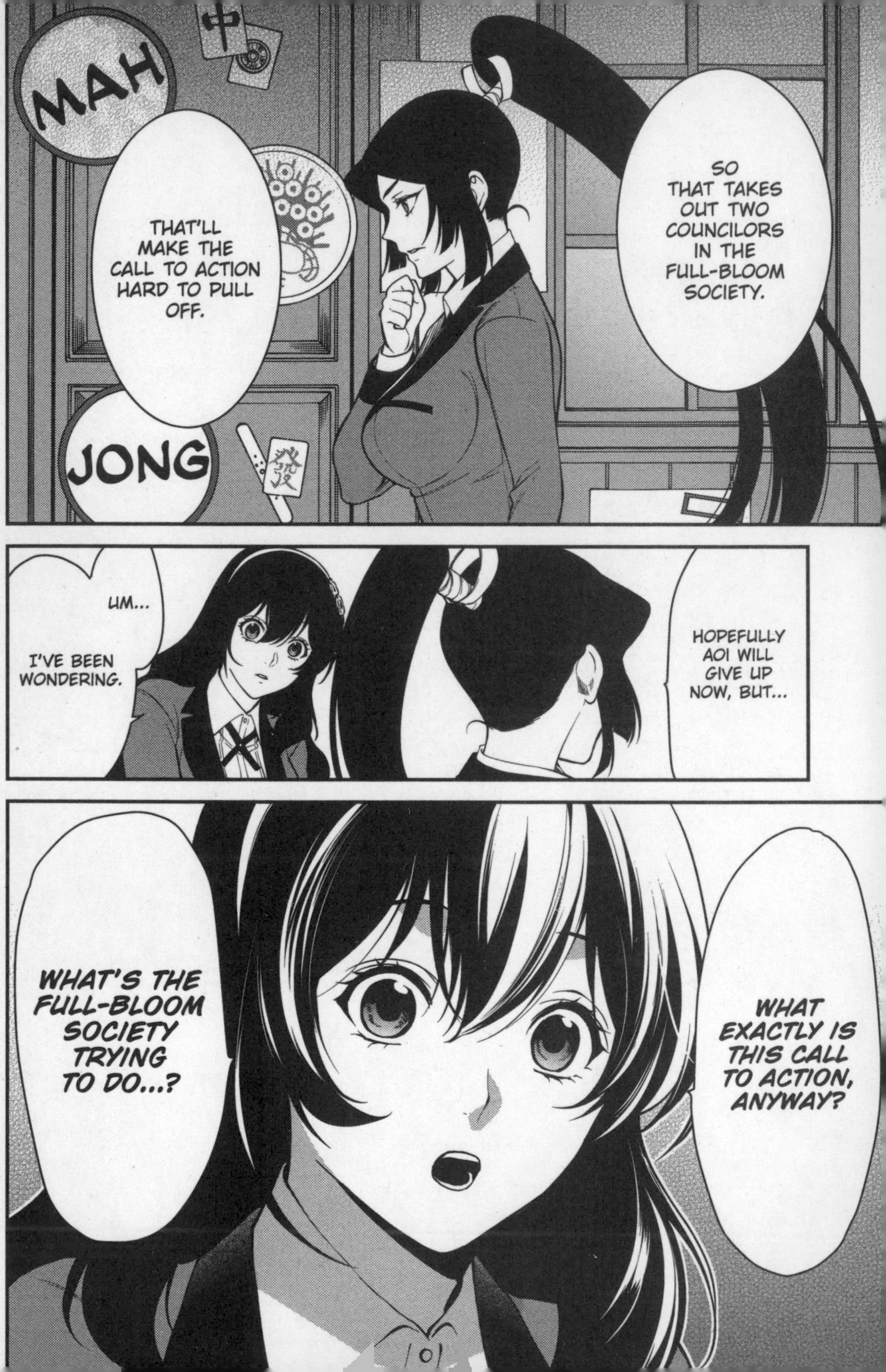
SO THAT TAKES OUT TWO COUNCILORS IN THE FULL-BLOOM SOCIETY.
MAH
THAT'LL MAKE THE CALL TO ACTION HARD TO PULL OFF.
JONG
HOPEFULLY AOI WILL GIVE UP NOW, BUT...
UM...
I'VE BEEN WONDERING.
WHAT EXACTLY IS THIS CALL TO ACTION, ANYWAY?
WHAT'S THE FULL-BLOOM SOCIETY TRYING TO DO...?

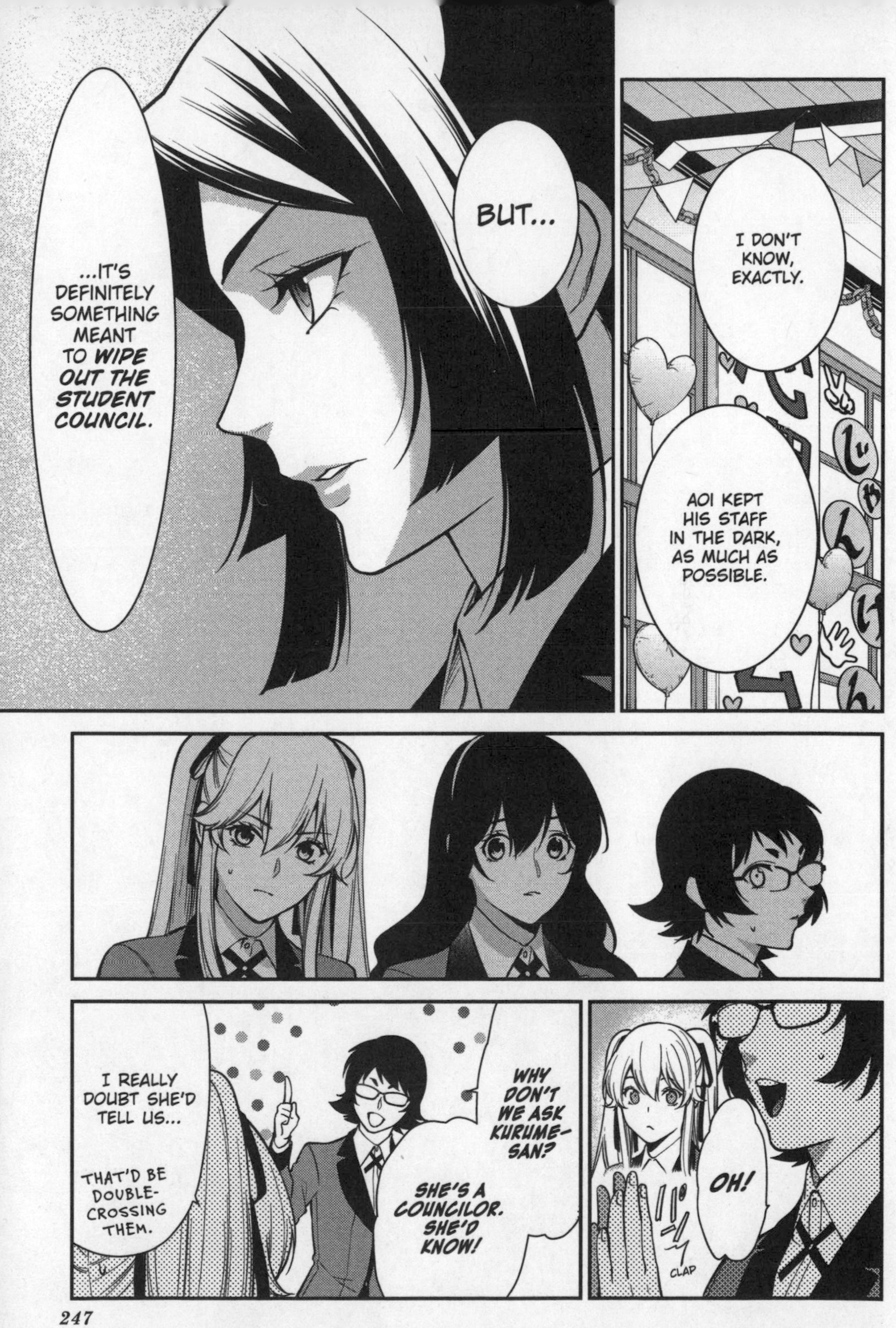
I DON'T KNOW, EXACTLY.
AOI KEPT HIS STAFF IN THE DARK, AS MUCH AS POSSIBLE.
BUT...
...IT'S DEFINITELY SOMETHING MEANT TO *WIPE OUT THE STUDENT COUNCIL*.
OH!
CLAP
WHY DON'T WE ASK KURUME-SAN?
SHE'S A COUNCILOR. SHE'D KNOW!
I REALLY DOUBT SHE'D TELL US...
THAT'D BE DOUBLE-CROSSING THEM.

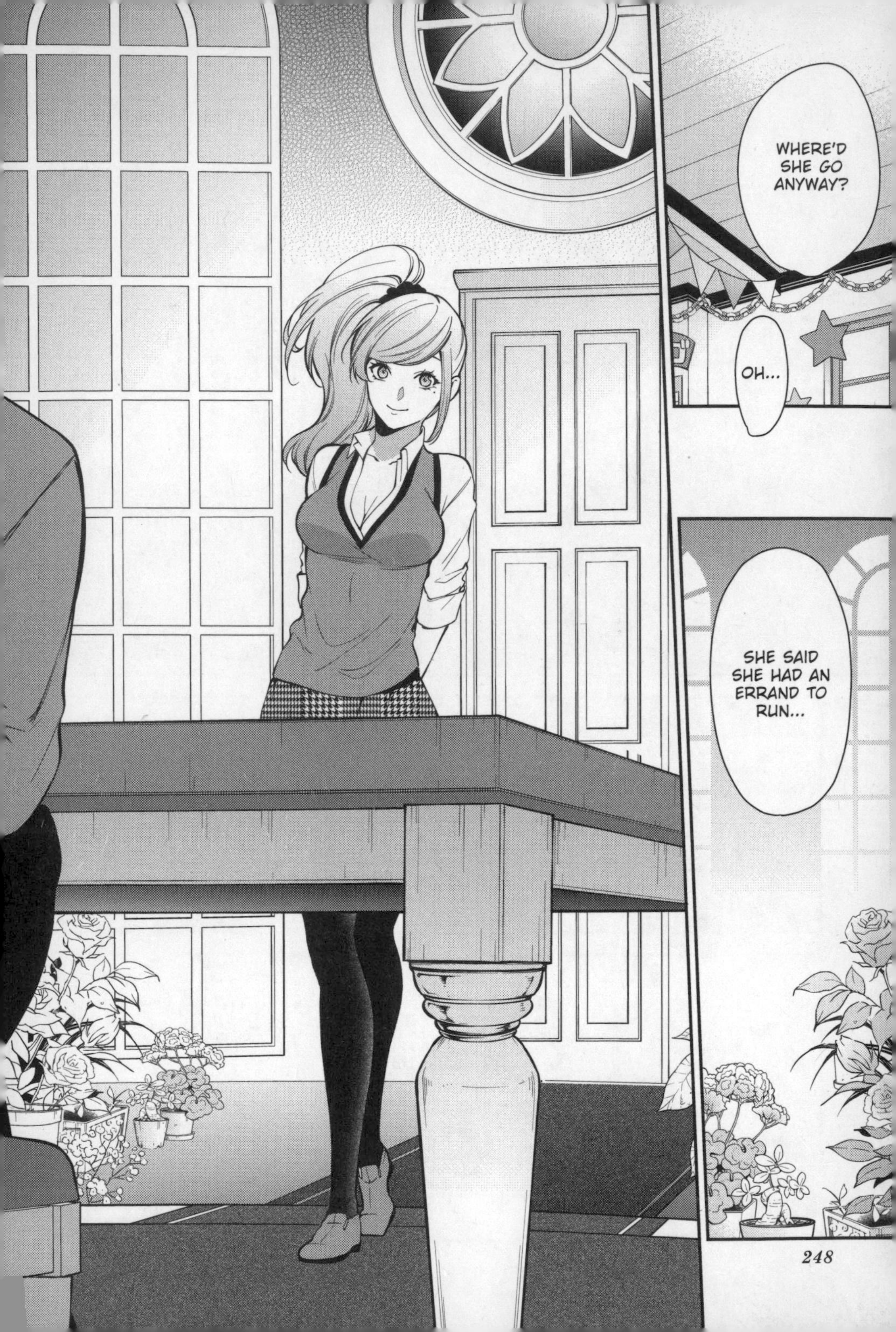
WHERE'D SHE GO ANYWAY?
OH...
SHE SAID SHE HAD AN ERRAND TO RUN...

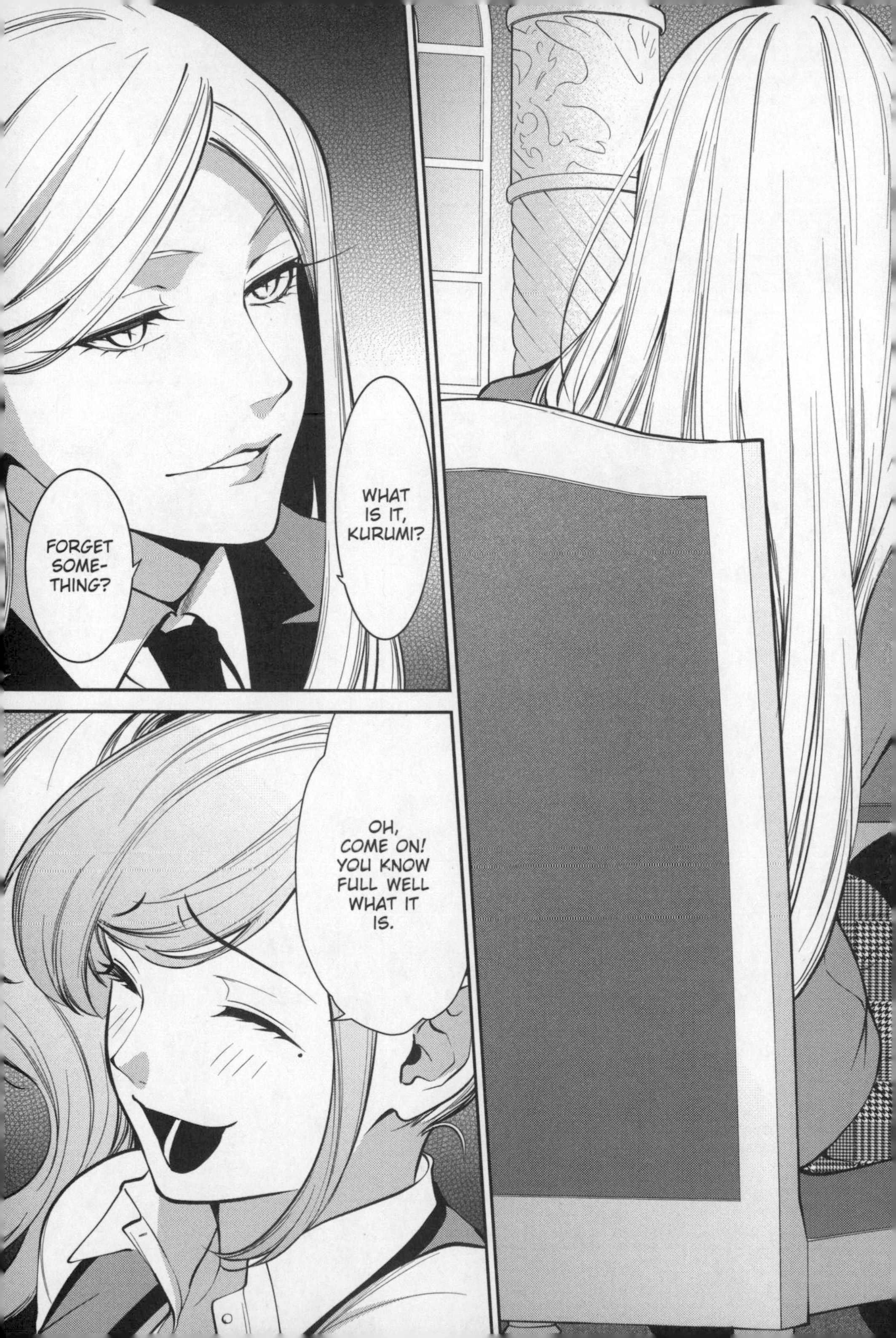
WHAT IS IT, KURUMI?
FORGET SOME-THING?
OH, COME ON! YOU KNOW FULL WELL WHAT IT IS.

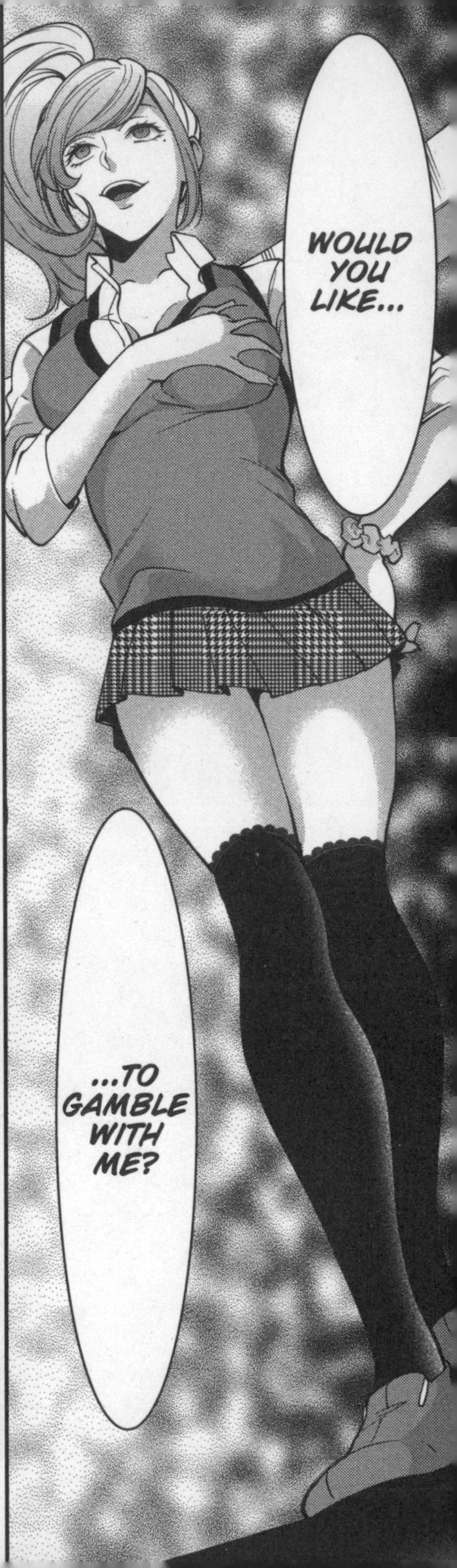
WOULD YOU LIKE...
...TO GAMBLE WITH ME?
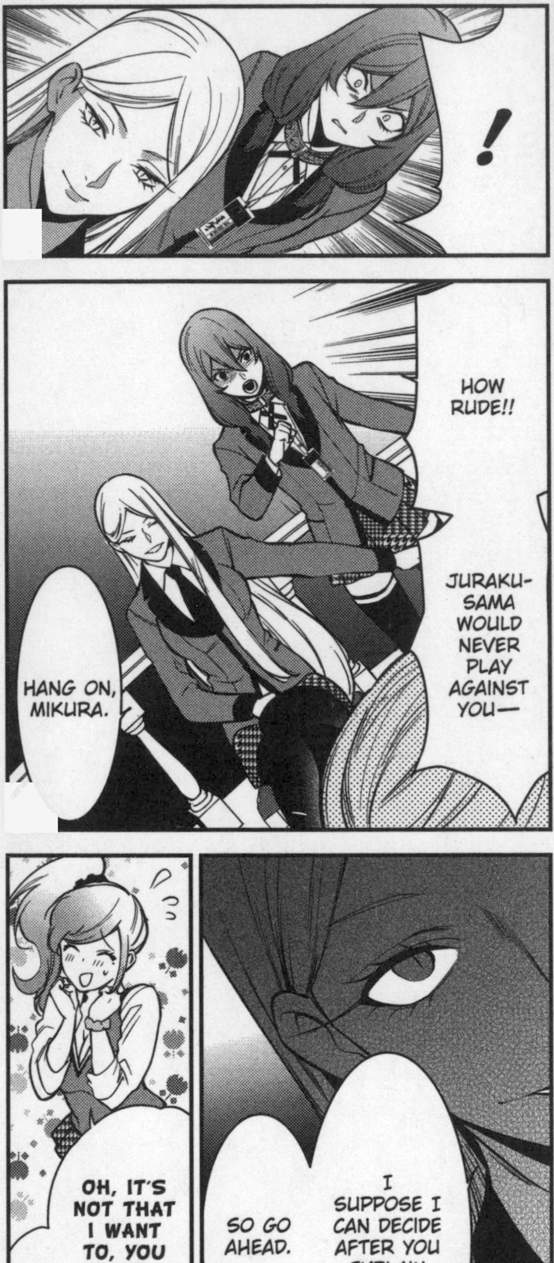
!
HOW RUDE!!
JURAKU-SAMA WOULD NEVER PLAY AGAINST YOU—
HANG ON, MIKURA.
I SUPPOSE I CAN DECIDE AFTER YOU EXPLAIN WHY.
SO GO AHEAD.
OH, IT'S NOT THAT I WANT TO, YOU KNOW!
IT'S SCARY!

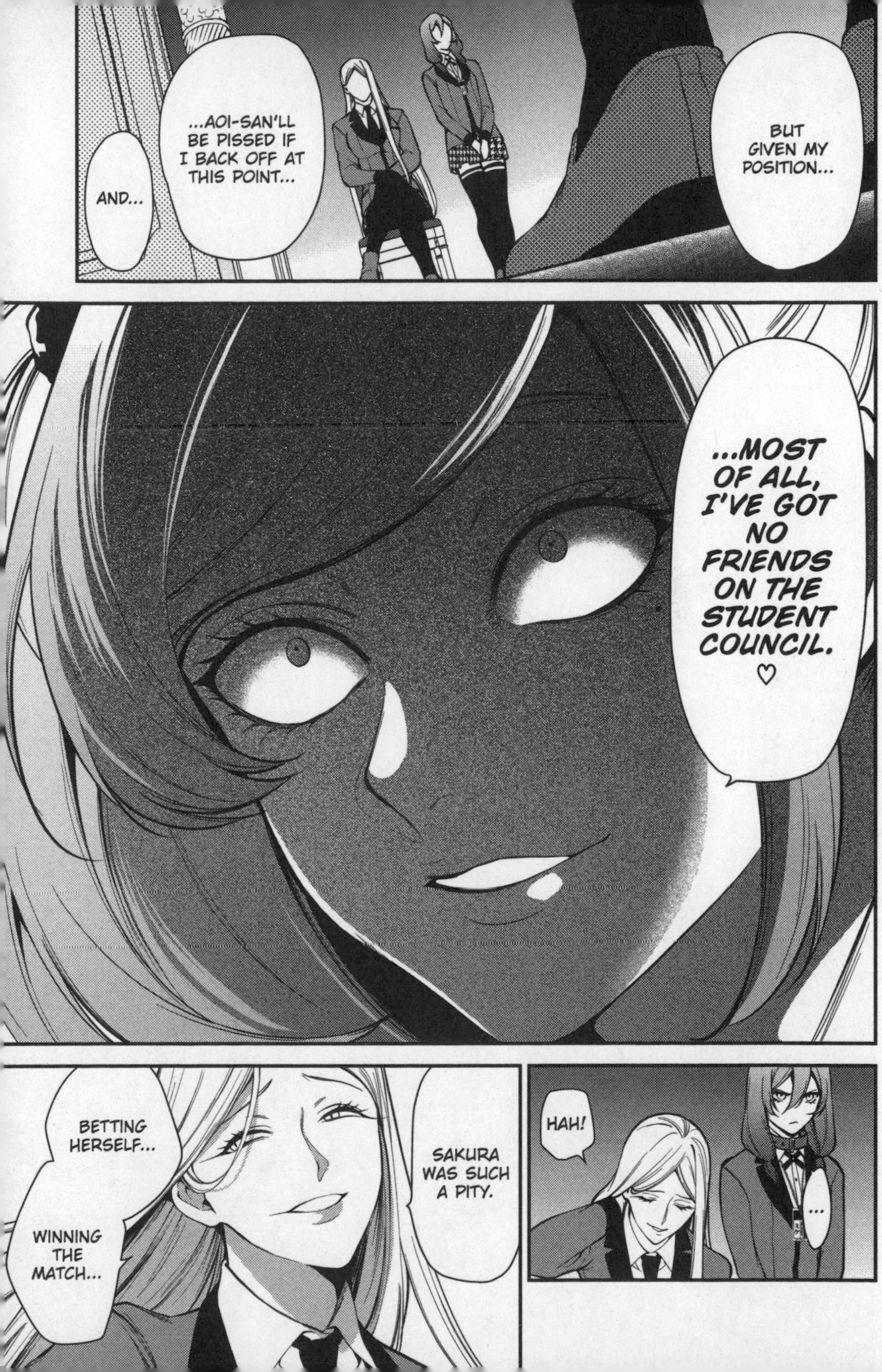
BUT GIVEN MY POSITION...
...AOI-SAN'LL BE PISSED IF I BACK OFF AT THIS POINT...
AND...
...MOST OF ALL, I'VE GOT NO FRIENDS ON THE STUDENT COUNCIL. ♡
HAH!
...
SAKURA WAS SUCH A PITY.
BETTING HERSELF...
WINNING THE MATCH...

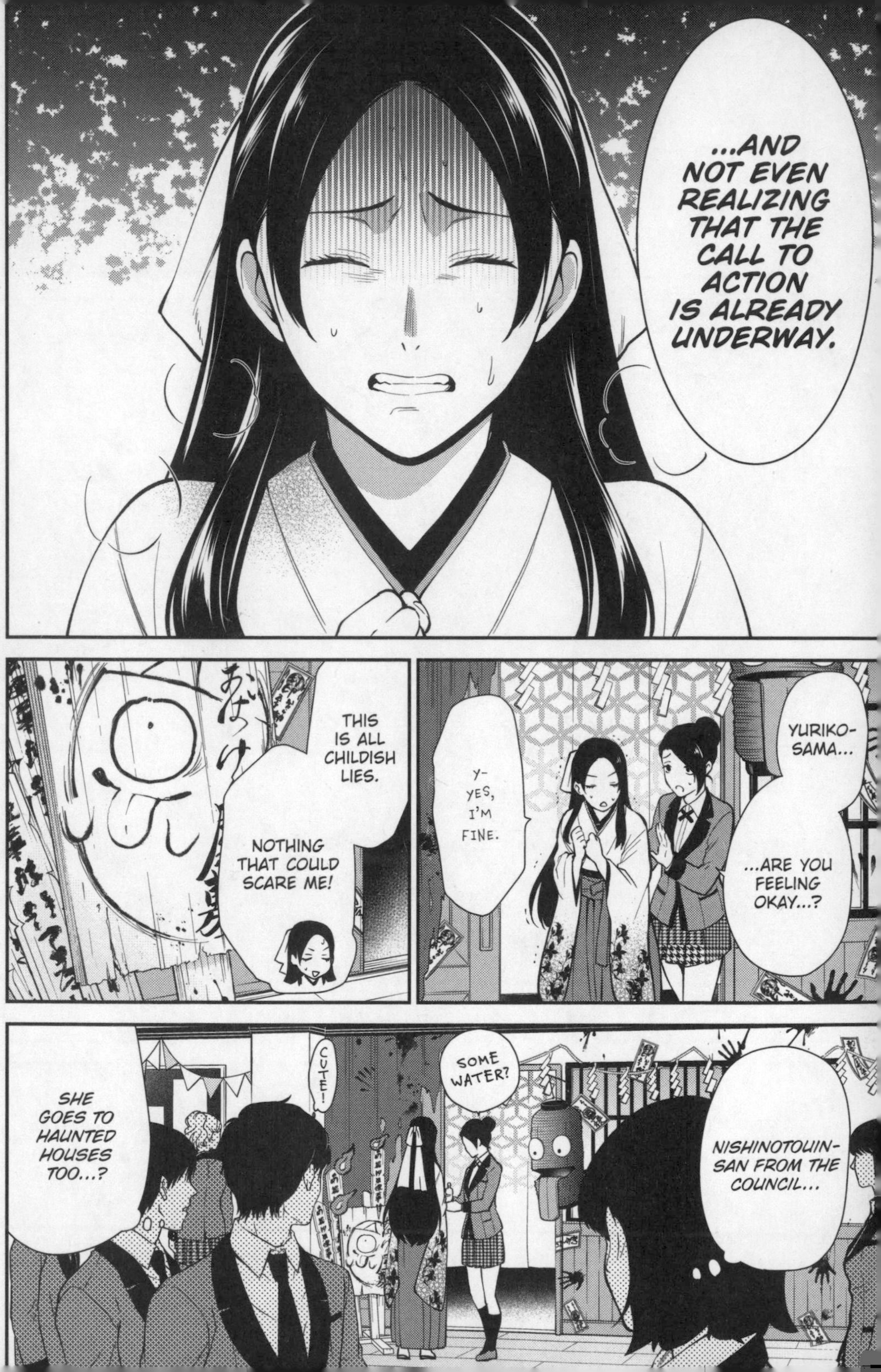
...AND NOT EVEN REALIZING THAT THE CALL TO ACTION IS ALREADY UNDERWAY.
YURIKO-SAMA...
...ARE YOU FEELING OKAY...?
Y-YES, I'M FINE.
THIS IS ALL CHILDISH LIES.
NOTHING THAT COULD SCARE ME!
NISHINOTOUIN-SAN FROM THE COUNCIL...
SOME WATER?
CUTE!
SHE GOES TO HAUNTED HOUSES TOO...?

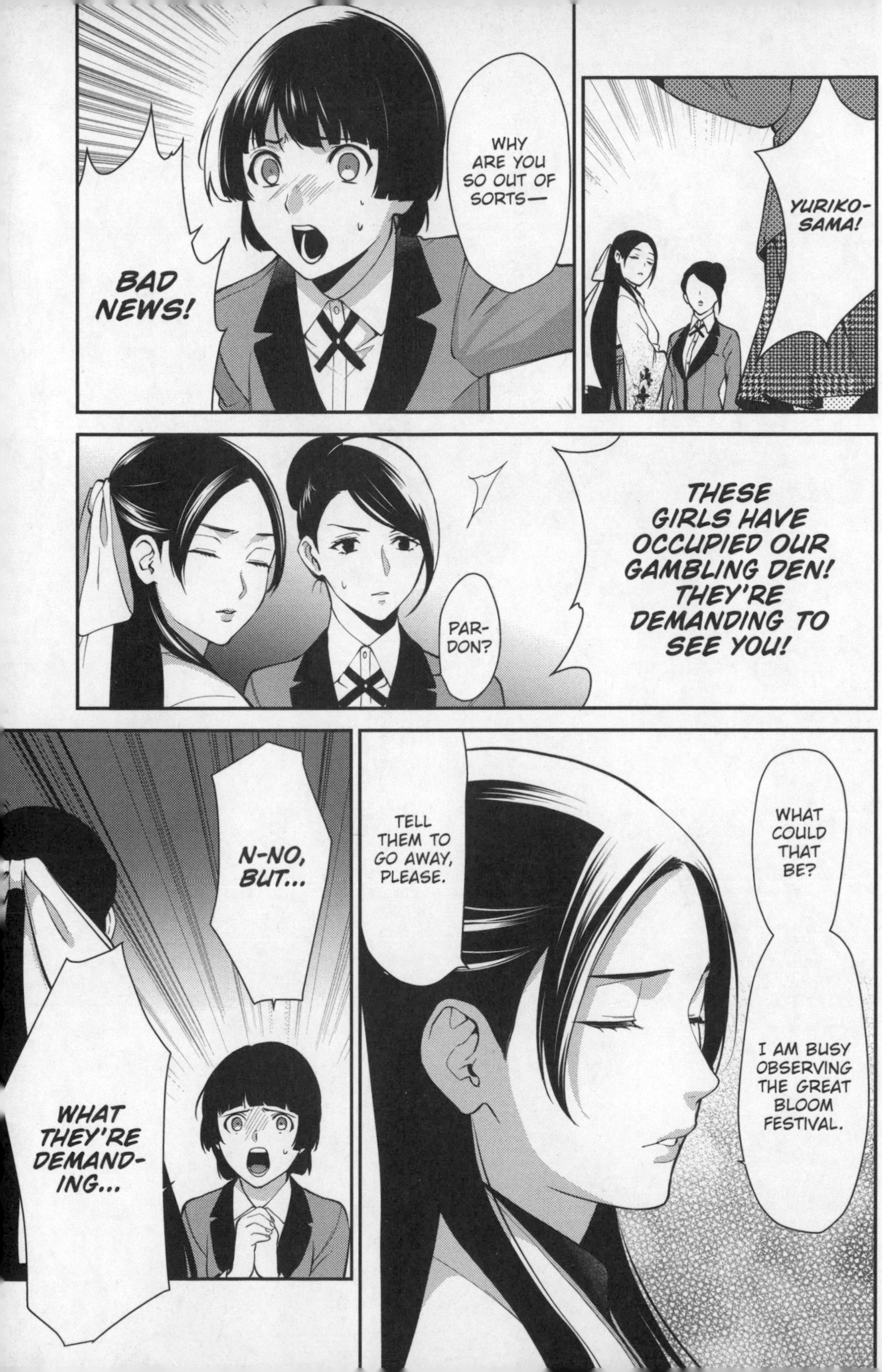
YURIKO-SAMA!
WHY ARE YOU SO OUT OF SORTS—
BAD NEWS!
THESE GIRLS HAVE OCCUPIED OUR GAMBLING DEN! THEY'RE DEMANDING TO SEE YOU!
PAR-DON?
WHAT COULD THAT BE?
TELL THEM TO GO AWAY, PLEASE.
I AM BUSY OBSERVING THE GREAT BLOOM FESTIVAL.
N-NO, BUT...
WHAT THEY'RE DEMAND-ING...

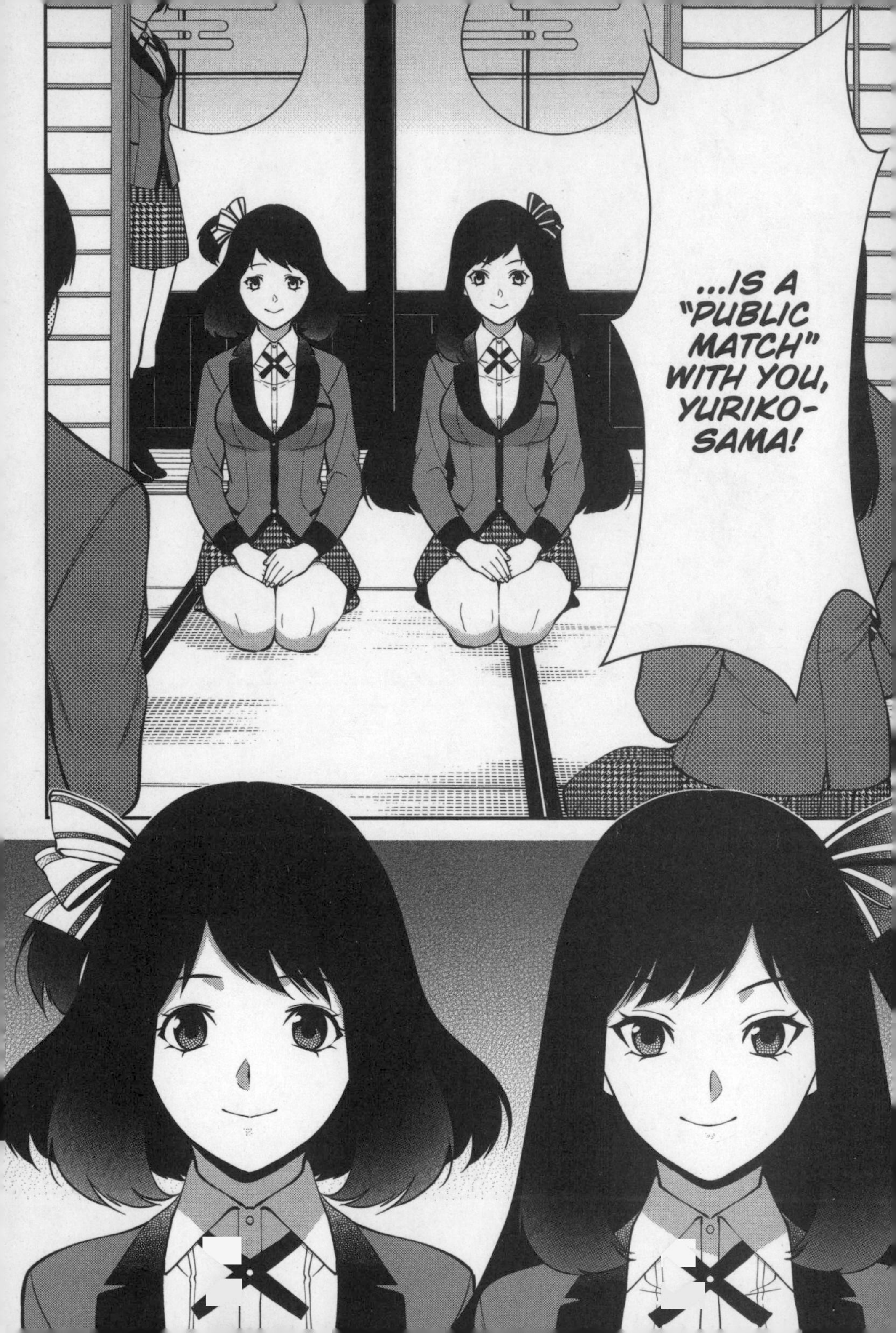
...IS A "PUBLIC MATCH" WITH YOU, YURIKO-SAMA!

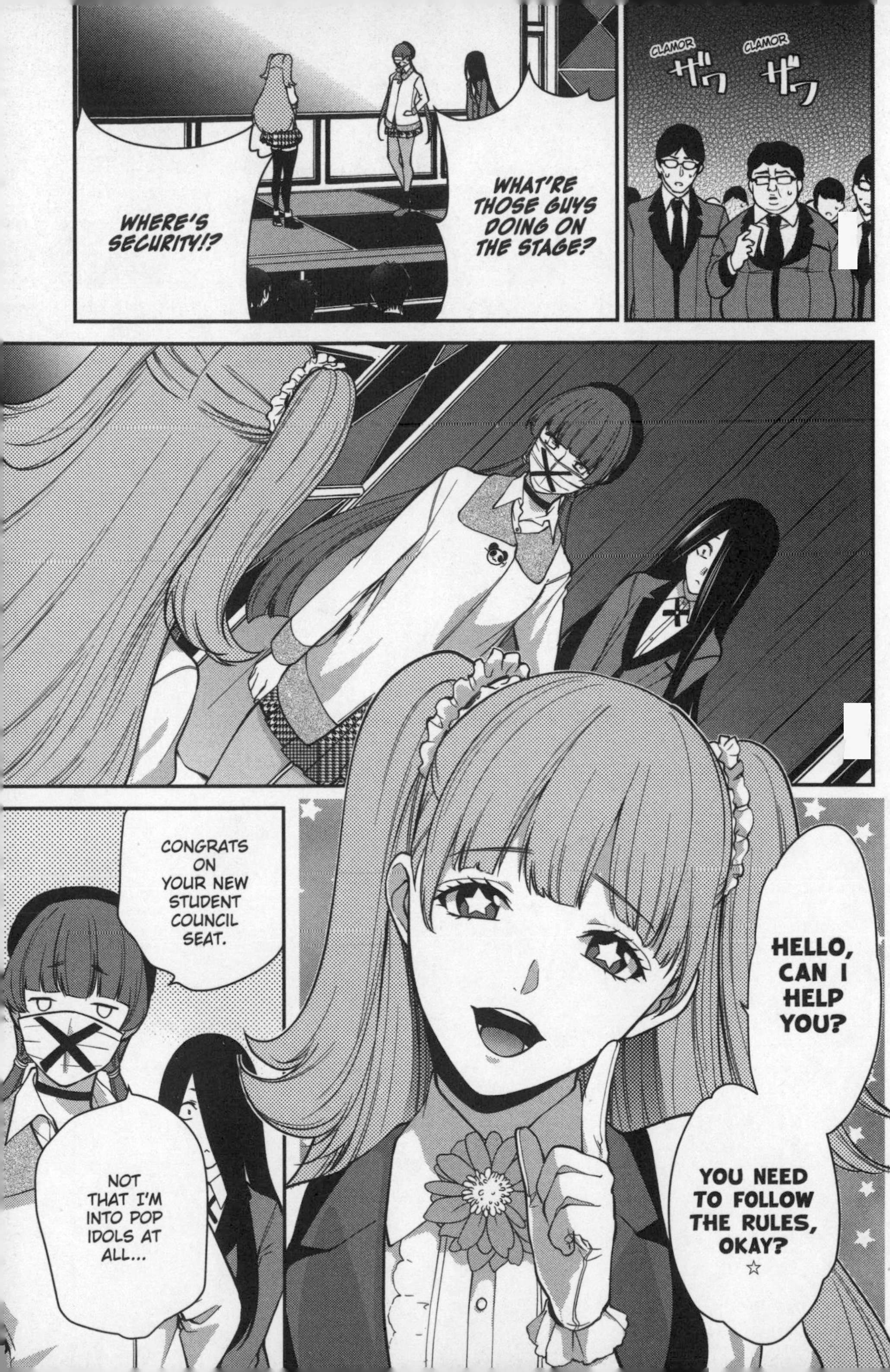
CLAMOR
ザワ
CLAMOR
ザワ
WHAT'RE THOSE GUYS DOING ON THE STAGE?
WHERE'S SECURITY!?
HELLO, CAN I HELP YOU?
YOU NEED TO FOLLOW THE RULES, OKAY? ☆
CONGRATS ON YOUR NEW STUDENT COUNCIL SEAT.
NOT THAT I'M INTO POP IDOLS AT ALL...

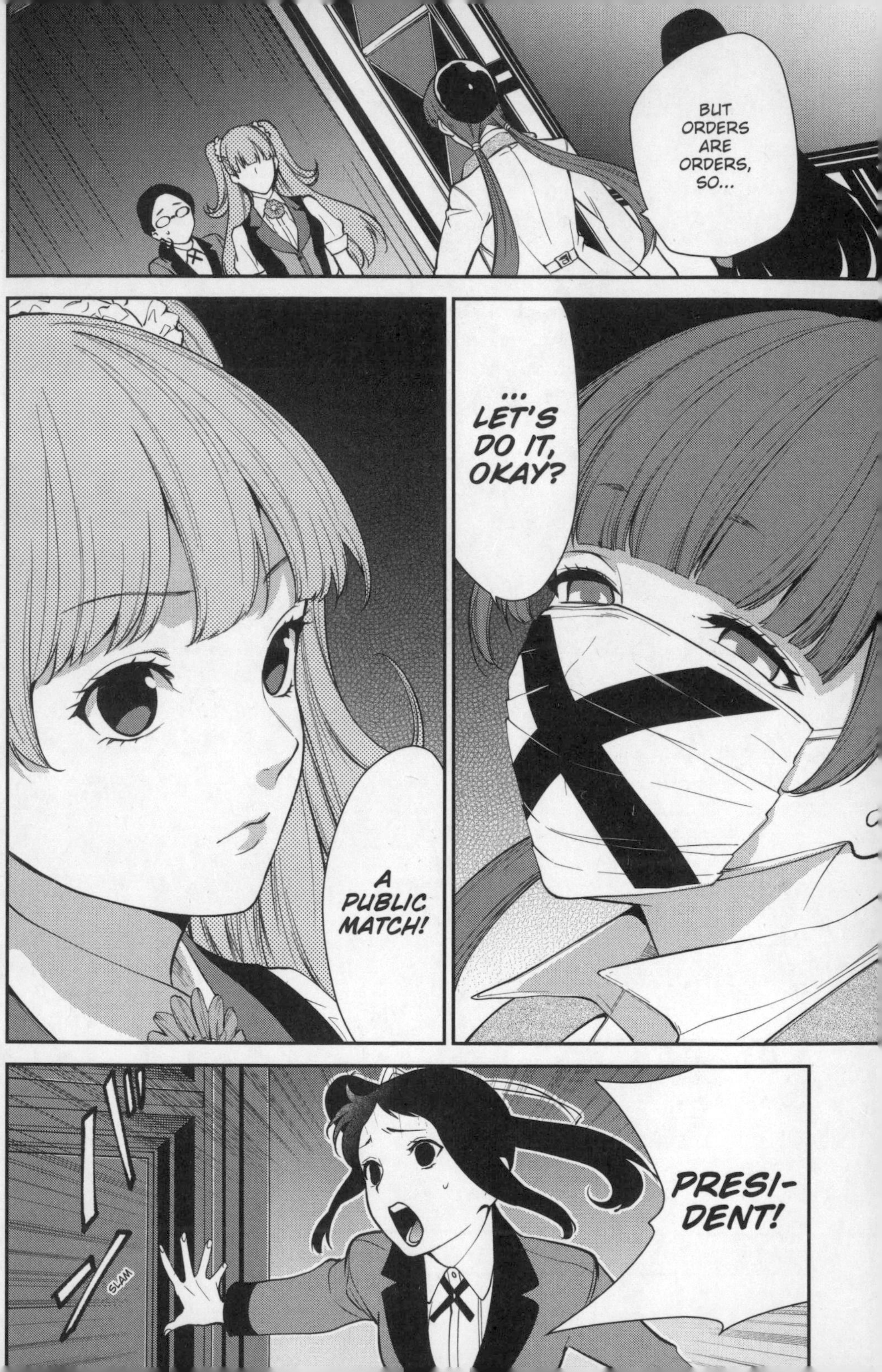
BUT ORDERS ARE ORDERS, SO...
... LET'S DO IT, OKAY?
A PUBLIC MATCH!
PRESI-DENT!
SLAM

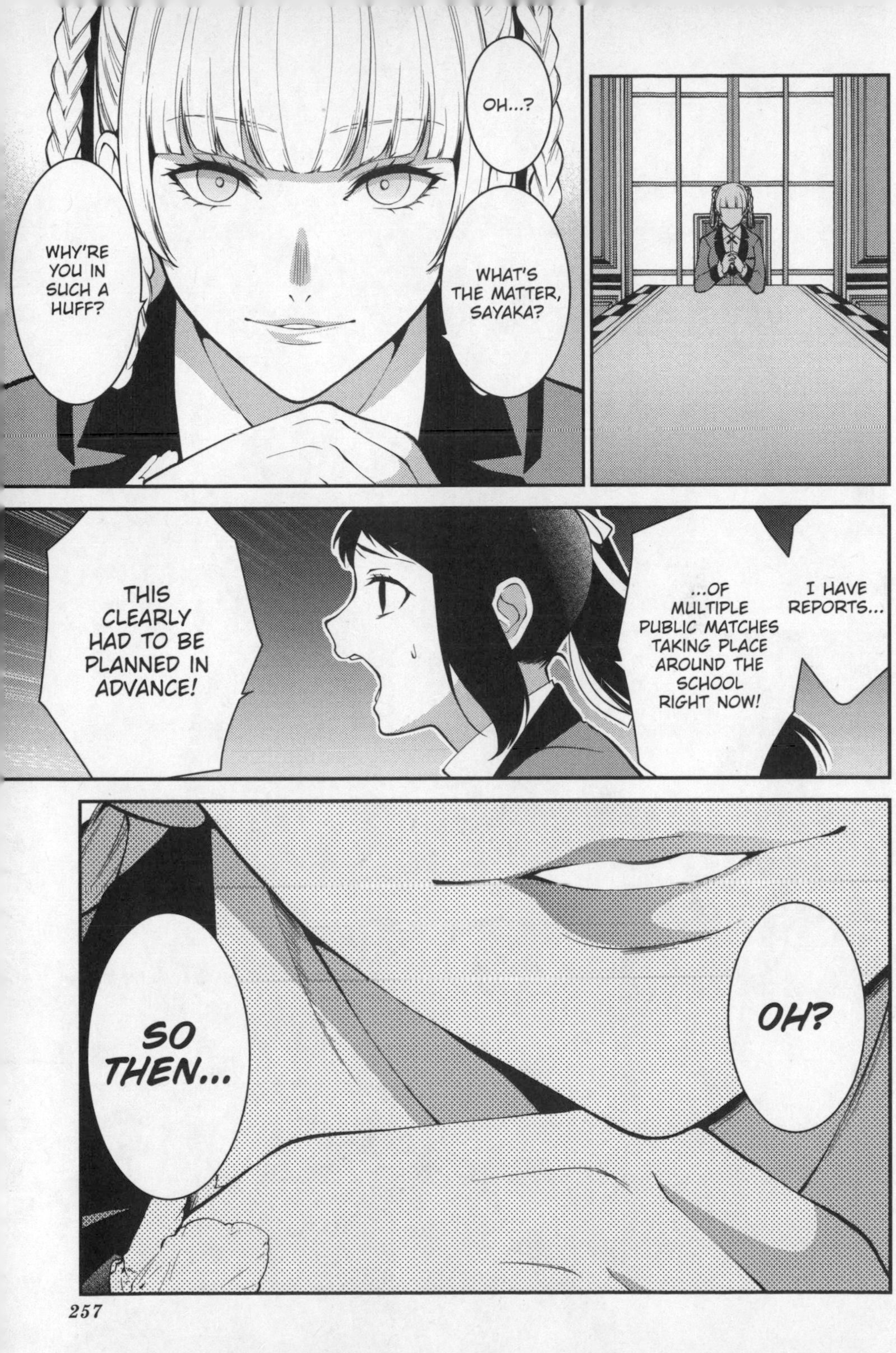

OH...?
WHAT'S THE MATTER, SAYAKA?
WHY'RE YOU IN SUCH A HUFF?
I HAVE REPORTS...
...OF MULTIPLE PUBLIC MATCHES TAKING PLACE AROUND THE SCHOOL RIGHT NOW!
THIS CLEARLY HAD TO BE PLANNED IN ADVANCE!
OH?
SO THEN...

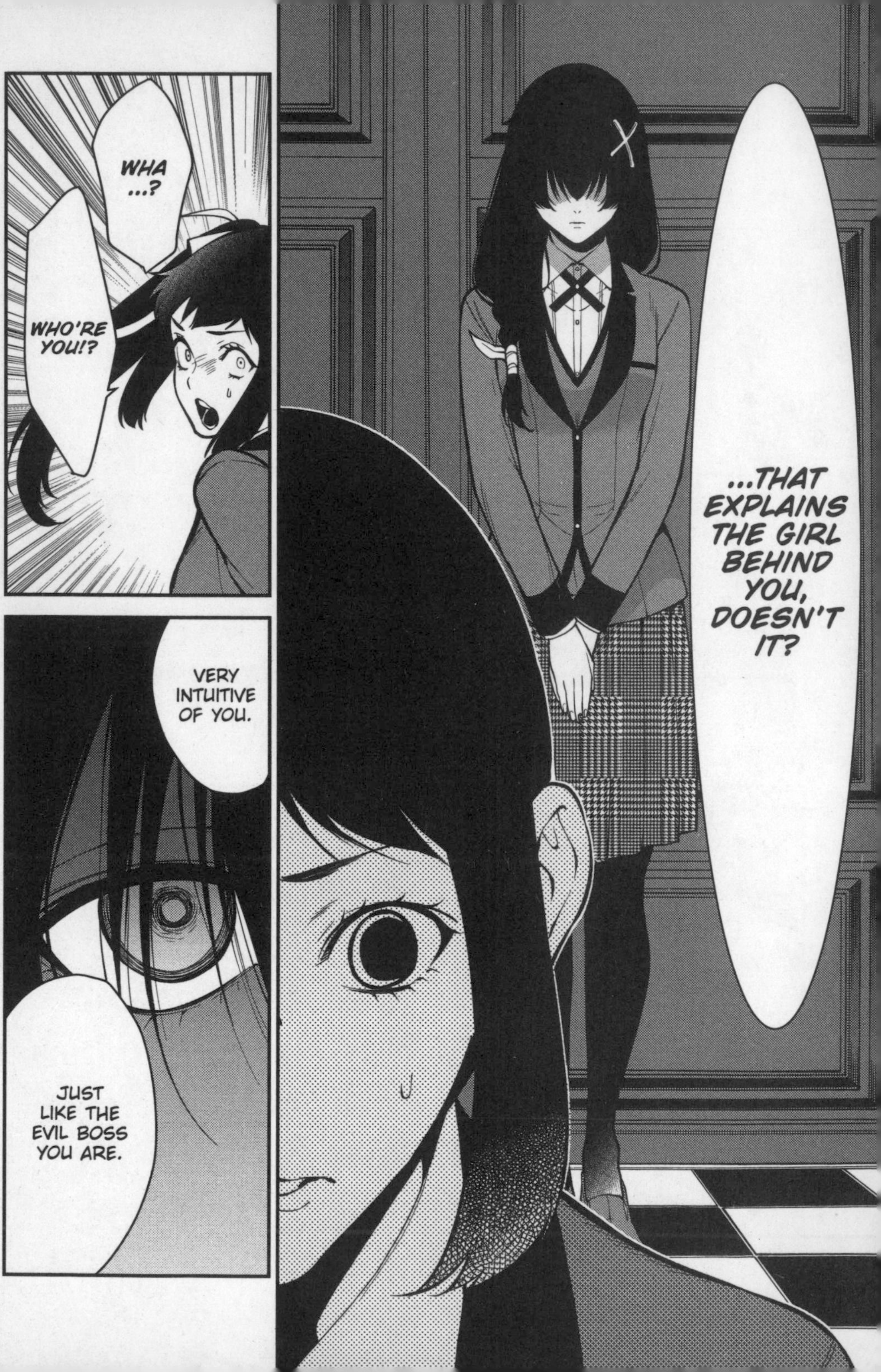
...THAT EXPLAINS THE GIRL BEHIND YOU, DOESN'T IT?
WHA ...?
WHO'RE YOU!?
VERY INTUITIVE OF YOU.
JUST LIKE THE EVIL BOSS YOU ARE.

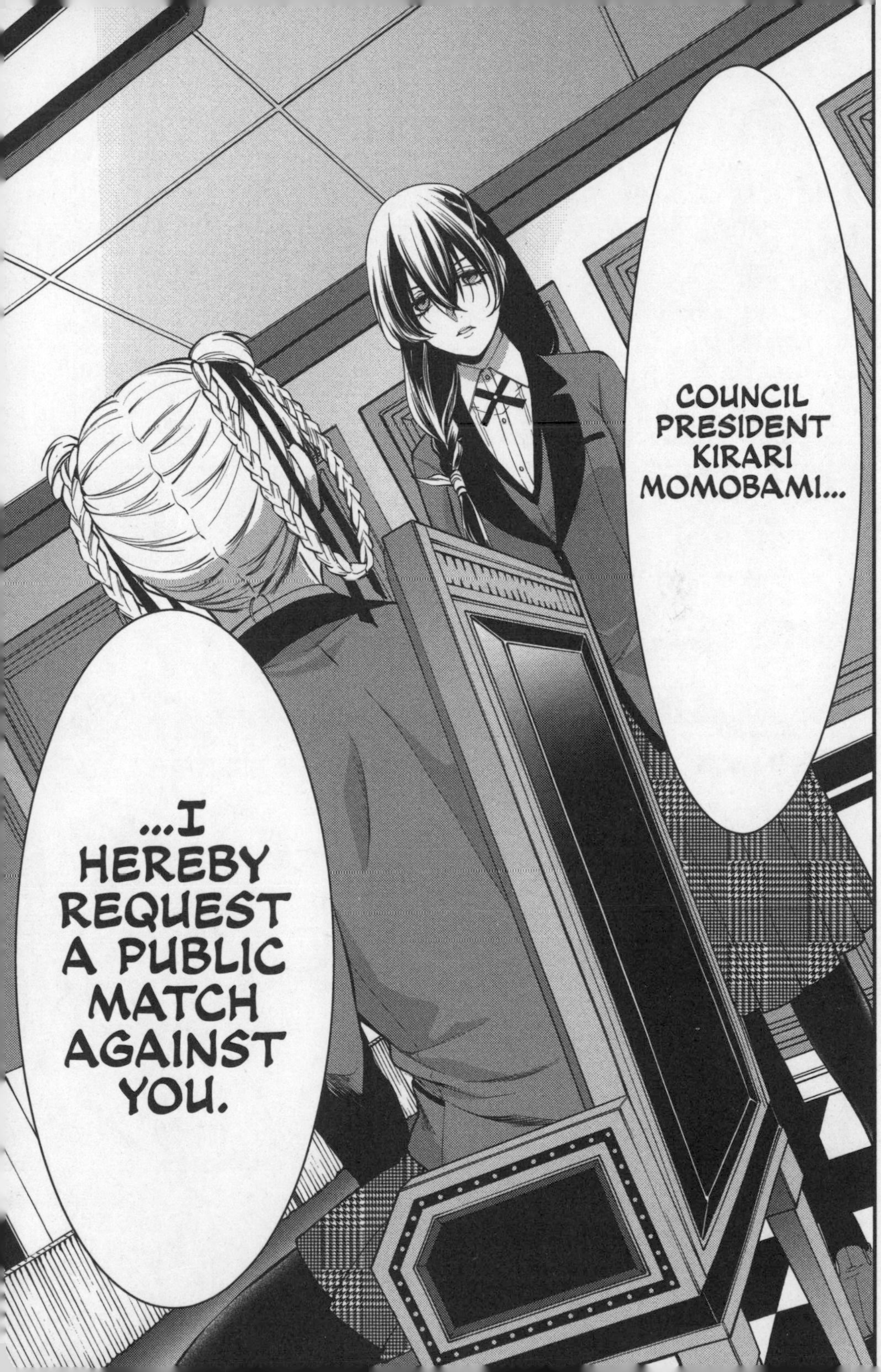
COUNCIL PRESIDENT KIRARI MOMOBAMI...
...I HEREBY REQUEST A PUBLIC MATCH AGAINST YOU.

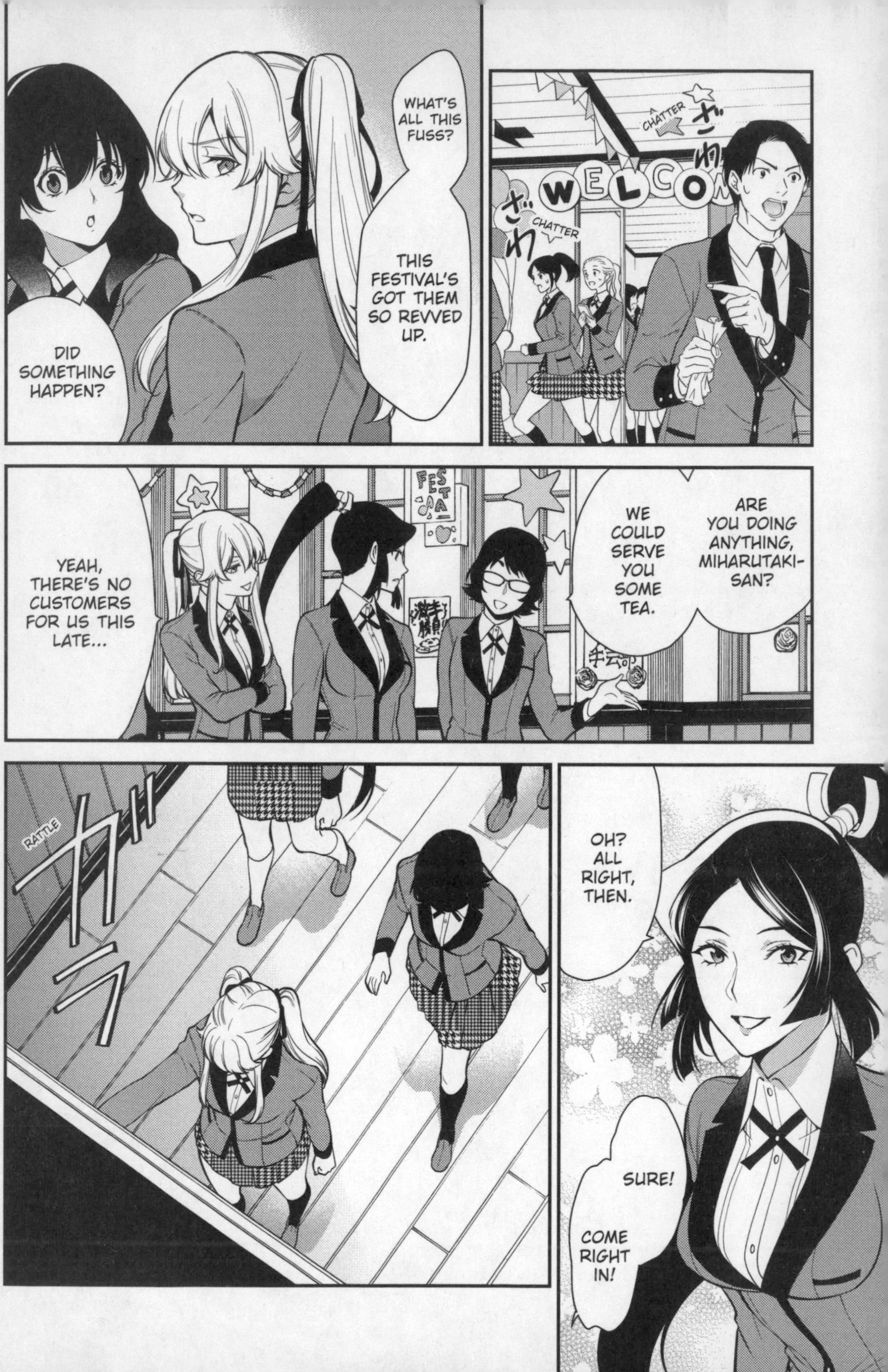
CHATTER
ざわ
CHATTER
ざわ
WHAT'S ALL THIS FUSS?
THIS FESTIVAL'S GOT THEM SO REVVED UP.
DID SOMETHING HAPPEN?
ARE YOU DOING ANYTHING, MIHARUTAKI-SAN?
WE COULD SERVE YOU SOME TEA.
YEAH, THERE'S NO CUSTOMERS FOR US THIS LATE...
OH? ALL RIGHT, THEN.
SURE!
COME RIGHT IN!
RATTLE

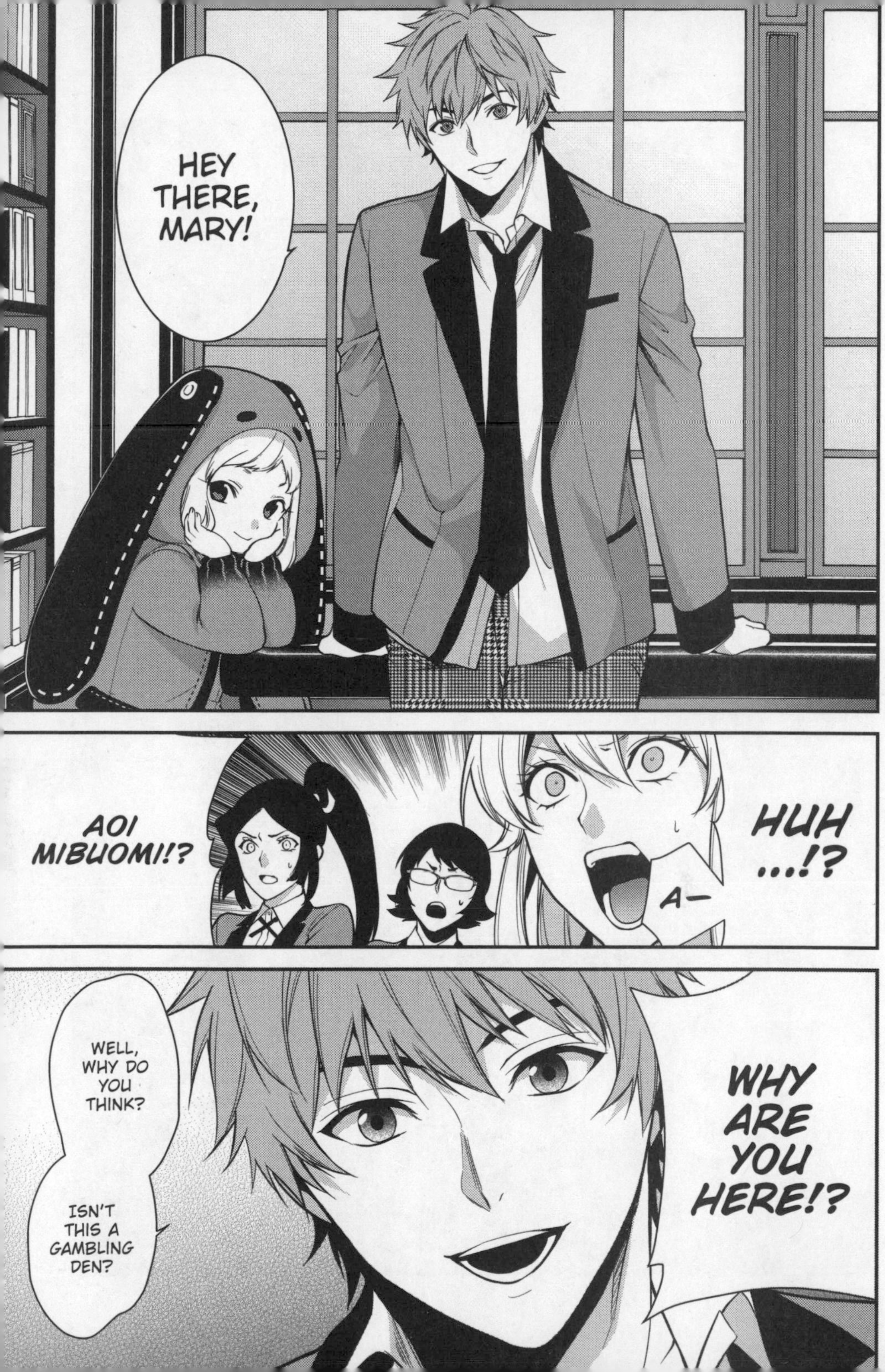
HEY THERE, MARY!
HUH ...!?
A—
AOI MIBUOMI!?
WHY ARE YOU HERE!?
WELL, WHY DO YOU THINK?
ISN'T THIS A GAMBLING DEN?

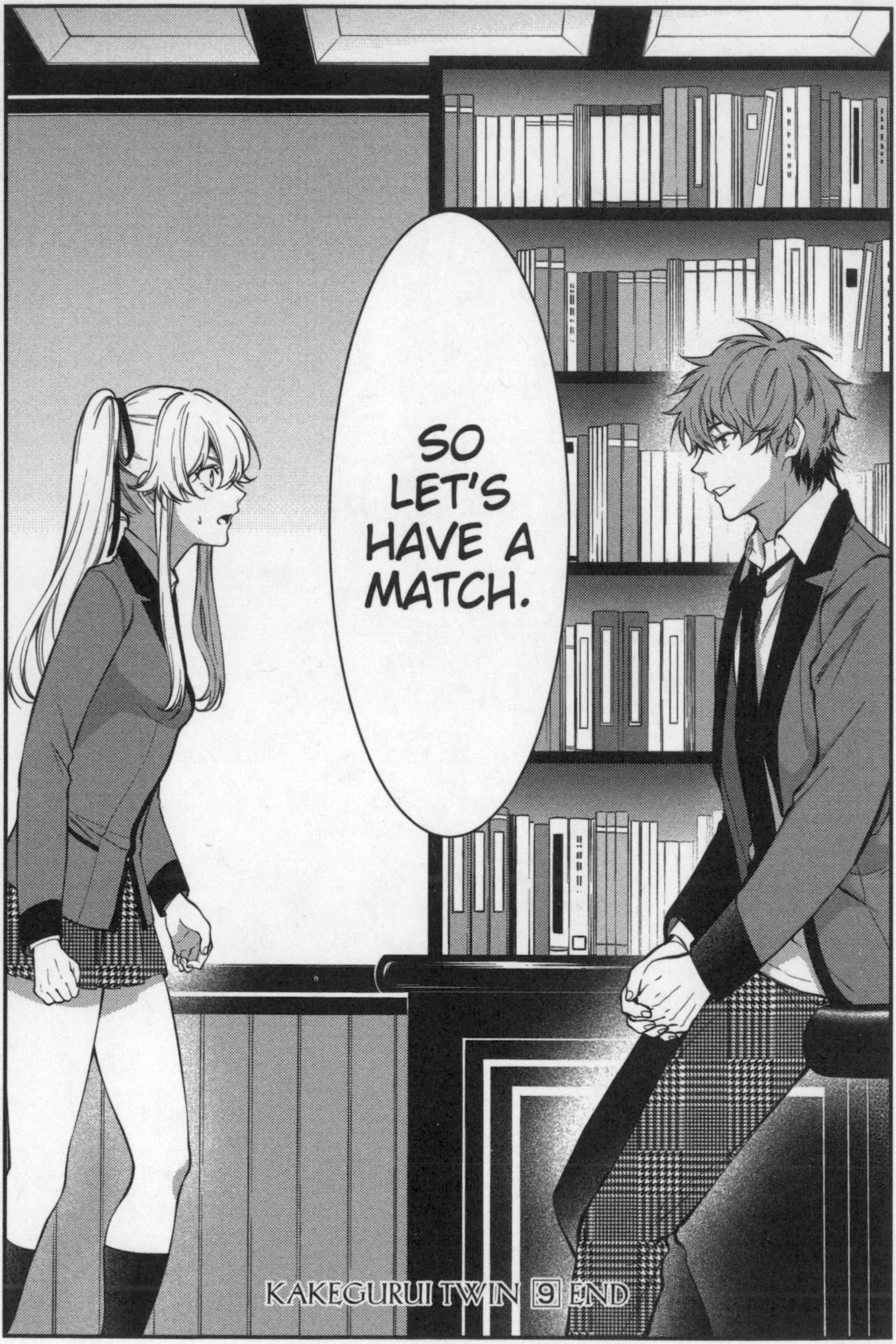
SO LET'S HAVE A MATCH.
KAKEGURUI TWIN 9 END

TIME FOR SOME END-OF-THE-VOLUME BONUS COMICS!

NAGI-KUN AND SOUTAROU-KUN'S DAILY LIFE

* This has no relation to the actual story.

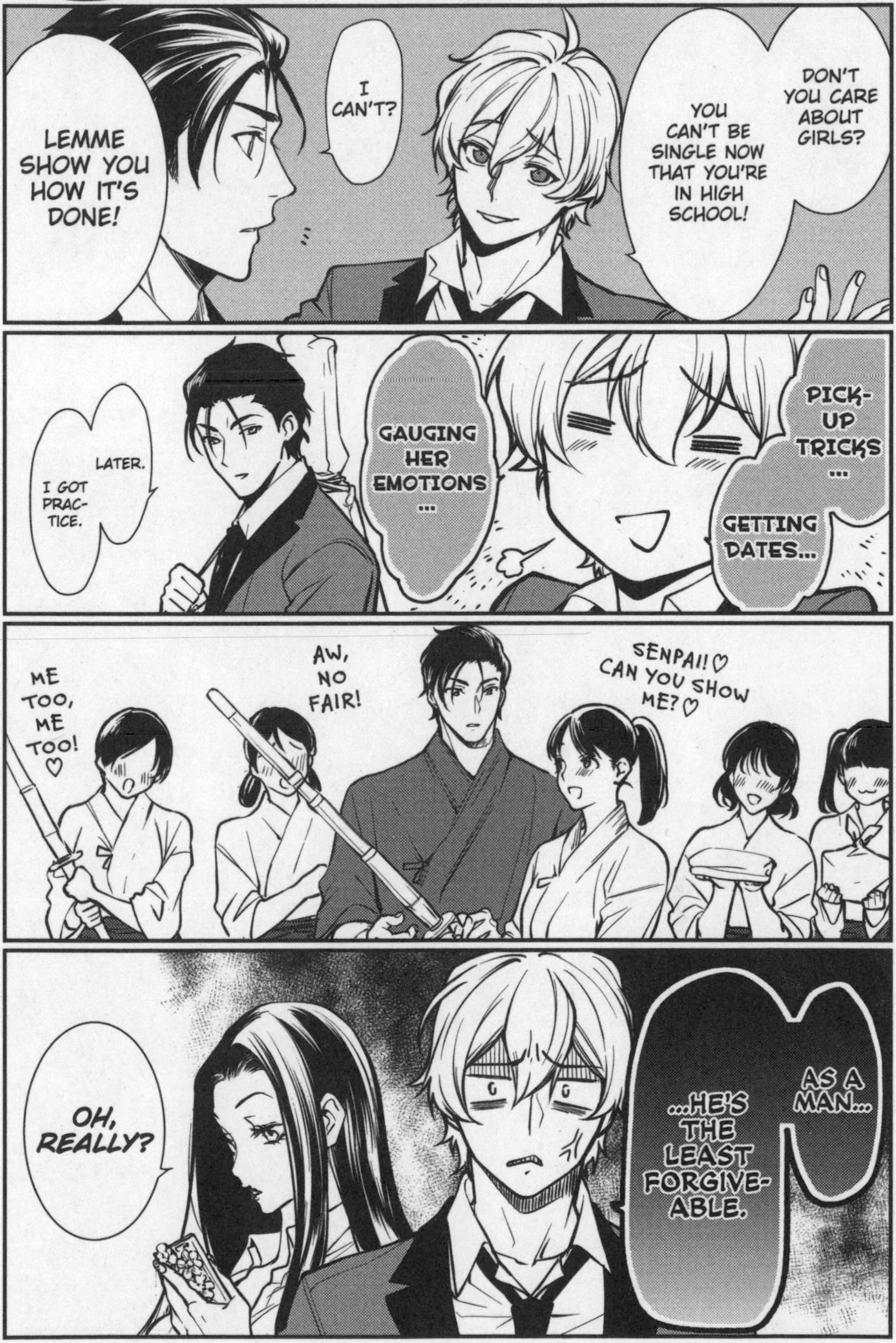
DON'T YOU CARE ABOUT GIRLS?
YOU CAN'T BE SINGLE NOW THAT YOU'RE IN HIGH SCHOOL!
I CAN'T?
LEMME SHOW YOU HOW IT'S DONE!
PICK-UP TRICKS...
GETTING DATES...
GAUGING HER EMOTIONS...
LATER.
I GOT PRAC-TICE.
SENPAI!♡ CAN YOU SHOW ME?♡
AW, NO FAIR!
ME TOO, ME TOO! ♡
AS A MAN...
...HE'S THE LEAST FORGIVE-ABLE.
OH, REALLY?

GAMBLING, THAT IS MY RAISON D'ÊTRE.

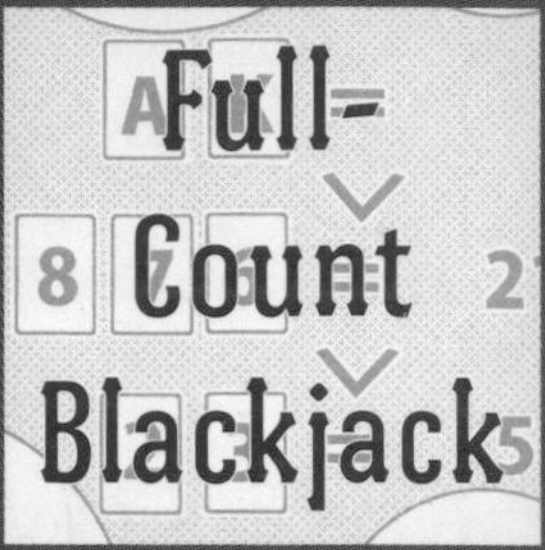
Full-Count Blackjack

This game seems to offer a lot of freedom, but it actually has an optimum solution. It's likely that your ability to see this optimum solution dictates whether you'll win or lose. In a way, if you can't, you won't even be able to step into the ring.
If both sides play optimally, however, the game comes down to how you bet chips—making it a gamble in the real meaning of the term.

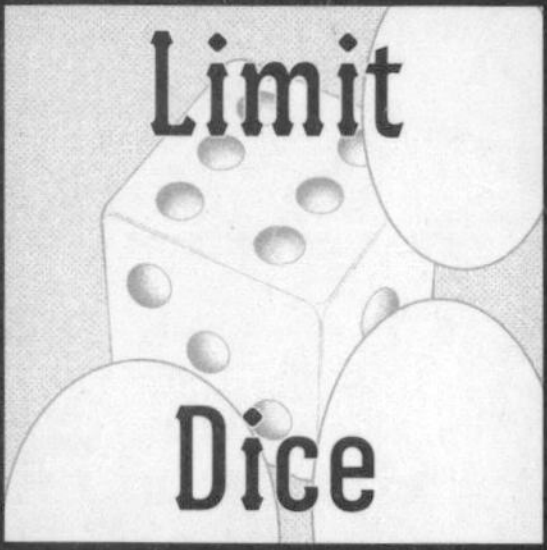
Limit Dice

As mentioned in the story, this is a test of willpower. You have a 1-in-6 chance of rolling a six at any time. What about if you roll ten times, don't get a six, then roll again? Well, it's still 1-in-6, of course. In other words, if you keep rolling without stopping, you always have more of a chance to score points than not. However, keep rolling, and you're going to get a six eventually. So when do you stop? It's hard to decide mathematically—you need to reason with your emotions and gauge your opponent as you choose. That's the kind of game it is.

Thank you for picking up Volume 9 of *Kakegurui Twin*! With Nagi and Soutarou making their real debut, Miharutaki-san reentering the scene, and the two full-on gambles, I think we've really stuffed this volume full of neat stuff. It'd make me very happy if you enjoyed it.
The other day, I joined my artist Saiki-sensei on a trip to Barcelona to attend the Salón del Manga comic event. Interacting with local fans—and learning that there are *Twin* aficionados in places it takes half a day to fly to—made me happier than ever before.

Now for some thanks. Thanks for Saiki-sensei and his assistants, who always produce perfect art for me (the Mary sketch he drew on Casa Batlló's guestbook was super cute). Thanks to our editors, Sasaki-sama and Yumoto-sama, and everyone else involved with the production of this book. Finally, to all our readers. Thanks to the support from so many of you, we managed to release Volume 9 of this series. Thank you all very, very much. Let's keep it going!
See all of you in Volume 10.

Homura Kawamoto

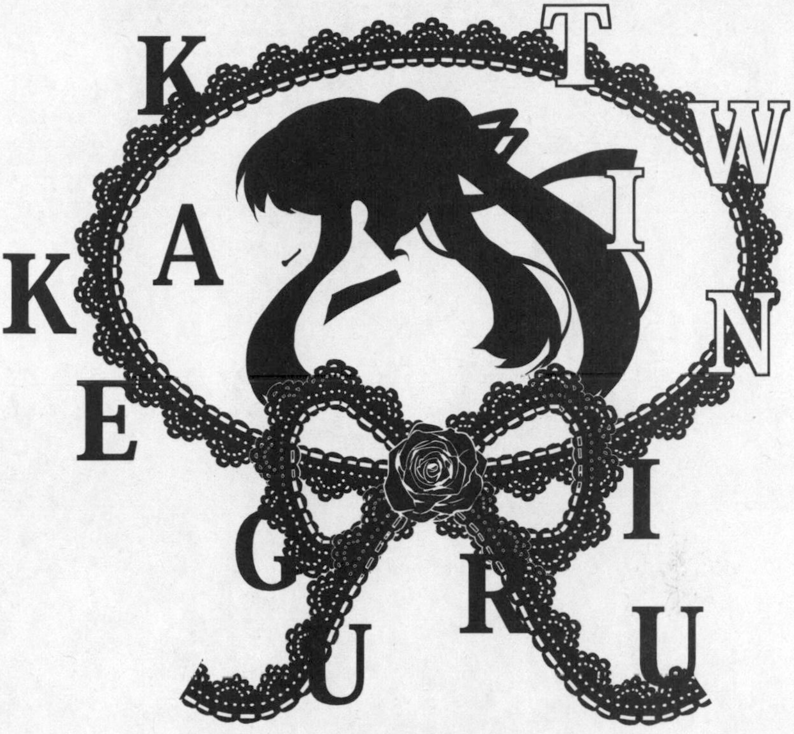
KAKEGURUI TWIN

IX

Special Thanks

My editors
Kawamoto-sama

Ken'ichi Sato-sama
Kozue Tachikawa-sama

Thank you for purchasing Volume 9.

With Full-Bloom's "call to action" beginning, I personally can't wait to see how Ouri's bout with the president will work out. And will Mary and Aoi work out their respective fates in their next match? It seems like we're approaching the final stages, but I wonder how things will turn out? I couldn't predict it at all, so I'm always way too excited to receive Kawamoto-sensei's storyboards every month.
Hang in there, Mary...!

Kei Saiki

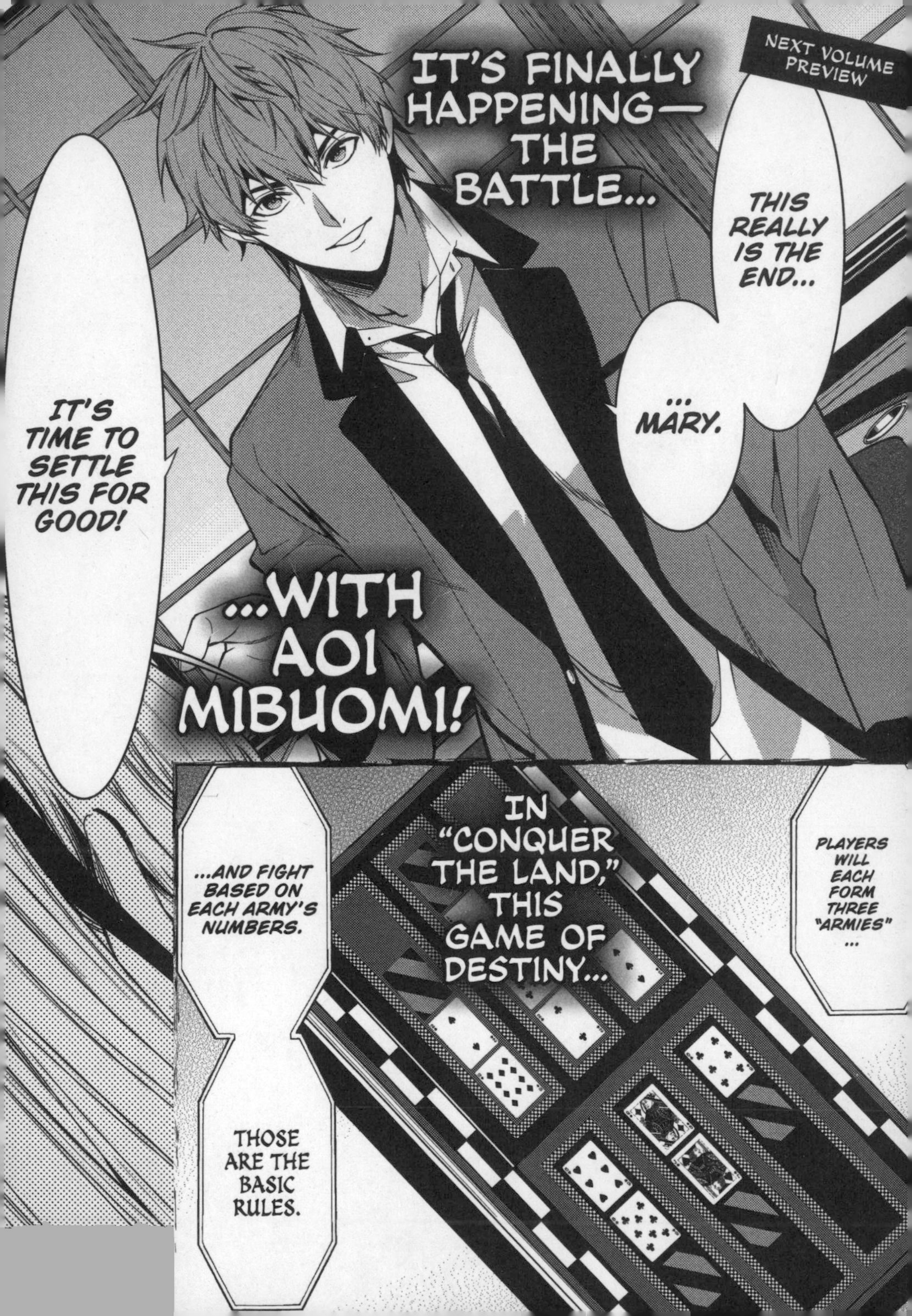
NEXT VOLUME PREVIEW
THIS REALLY IS THE END...
IT'S FINALLY HAPPENING—THE BATTLE...
... MARY.
IT'S TIME TO SETTLE THIS FOR GOOD!
...WITH AOI MIBUOMI!
PLAYERS WILL EACH FORM THREE "ARMIES" ...
IN "CONQUER THE LAND," THIS GAME OF DESTINY...
...AND FIGHT BASED ON EACH ARMY'S NUMBERS.
THOSE ARE THE BASIC RULES.

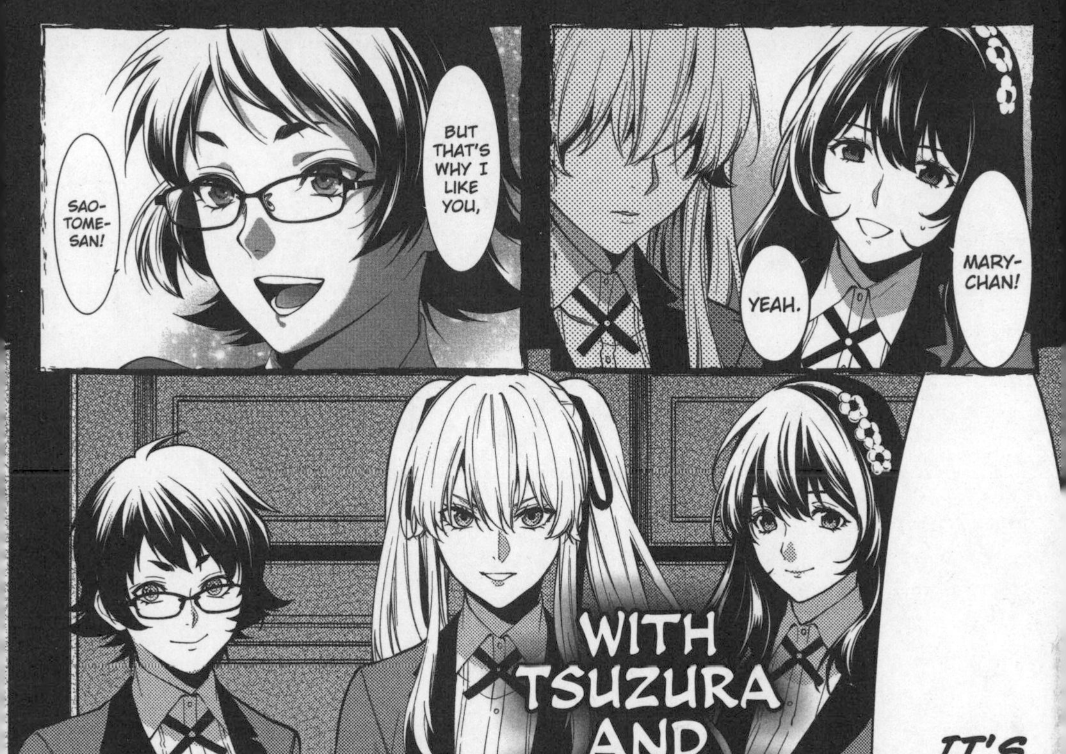

KAKEGURUI TWIN
VOLUME 10

COMING SOON!!

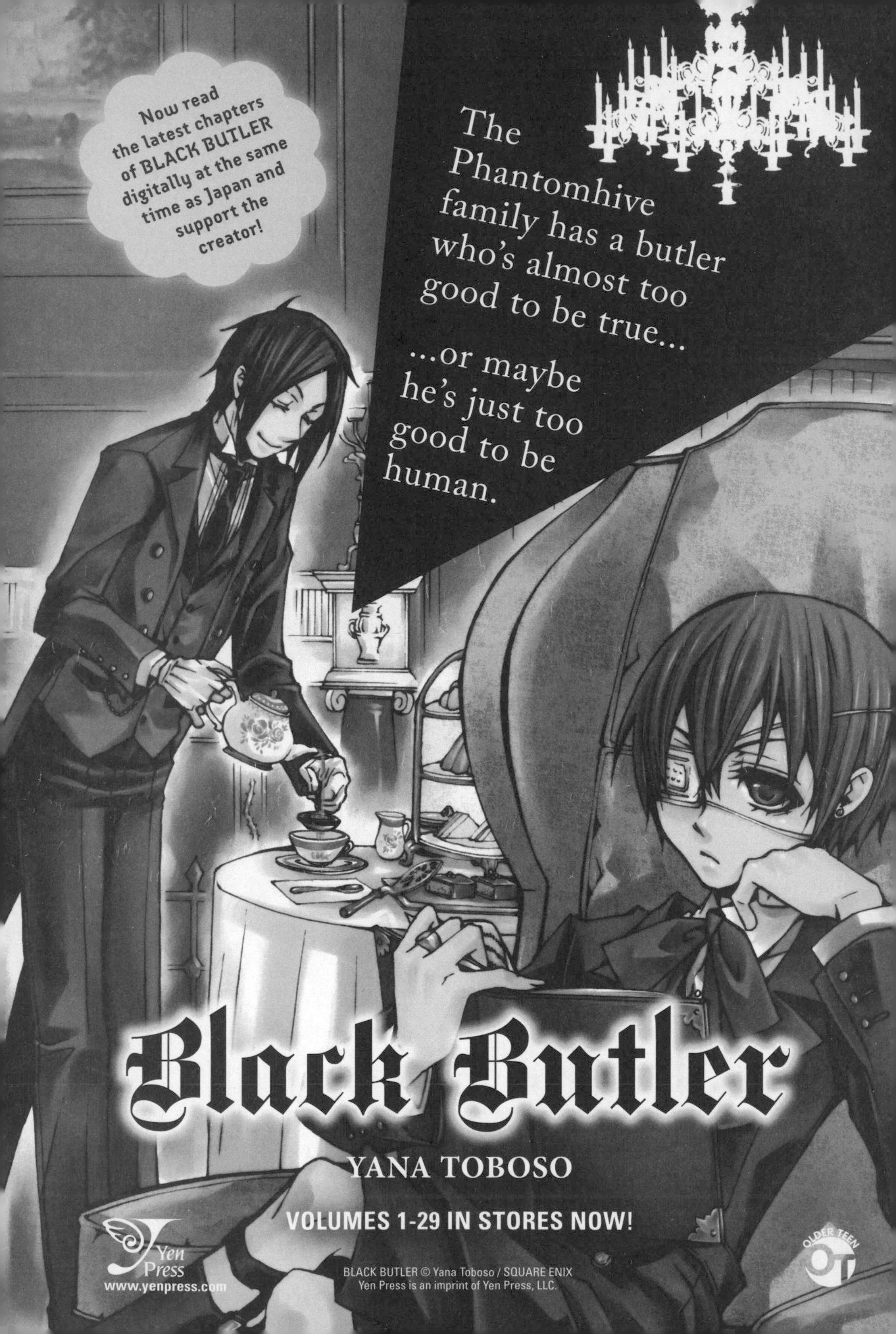
Now read the latest chapters of BLACK BUTLER digitally at the same time as Japan and support the creator!
The Phantomhive family has a butler who's almost too good to be true...
...or maybe he's just too good to be human.
Black Butler
YANA TOBOSO
VOLUMES 1-29 IN STORES NOW!
Yen Press
www.yenpress.com
BLACK BUTLER © Yana Toboso / SQUARE ENIX
Yen Press is an imprint of Yen Press, LLC.
OLDER TEEN
OT

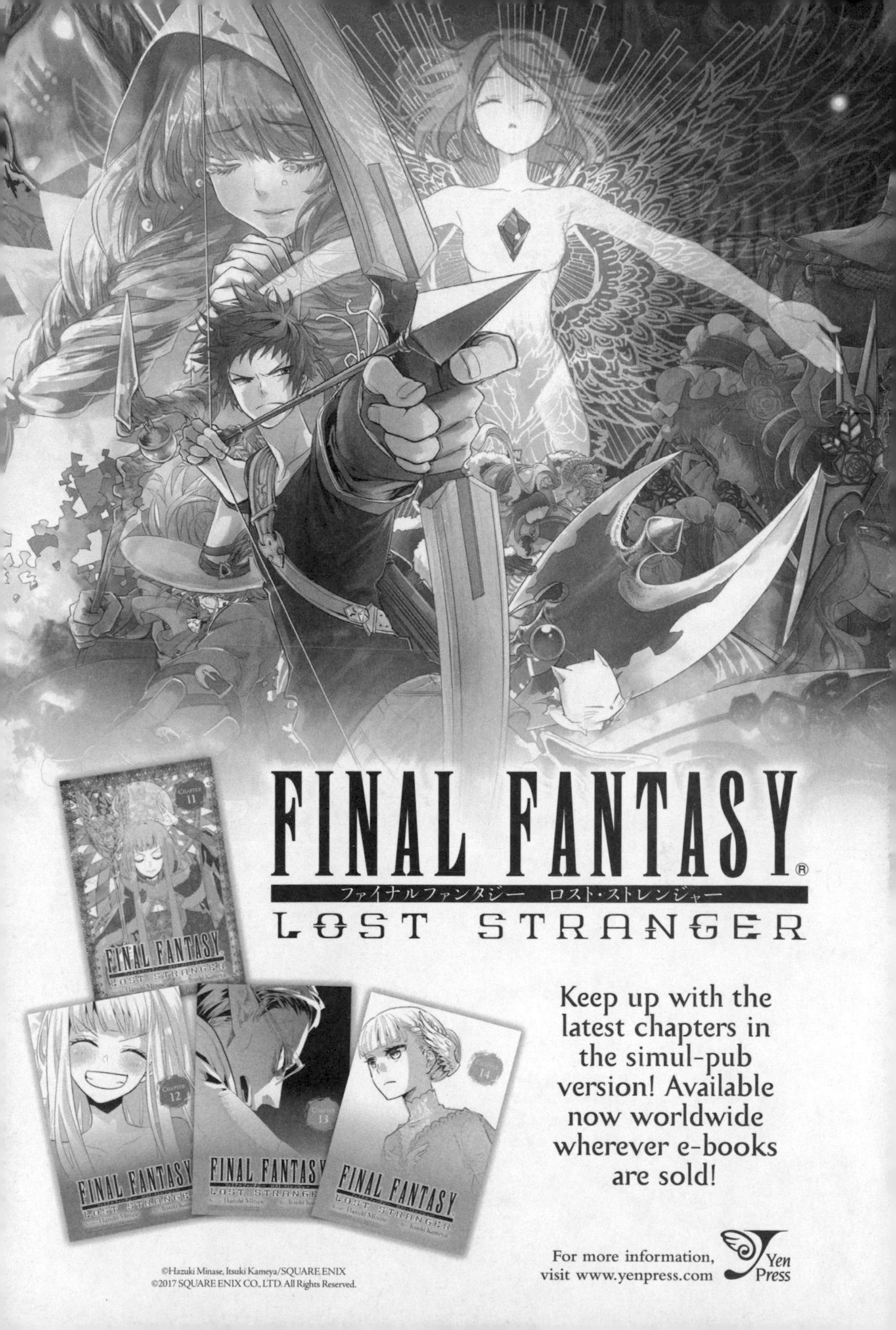
FINAL FANTASY®
ファイナルファンタジー　ロスト・ストレンジャー
LOST STRANGER
Keep up with the latest chapters in the simul-pub version! Available now worldwide wherever e-books are sold!
For more information, visit www.yenpress.com
Yen Press
©Hazuki Minase, Itsuki Kameya/SQUARE ENIX
©2017 SQUARE ENIX CO., LTD. All Rights Reserved.

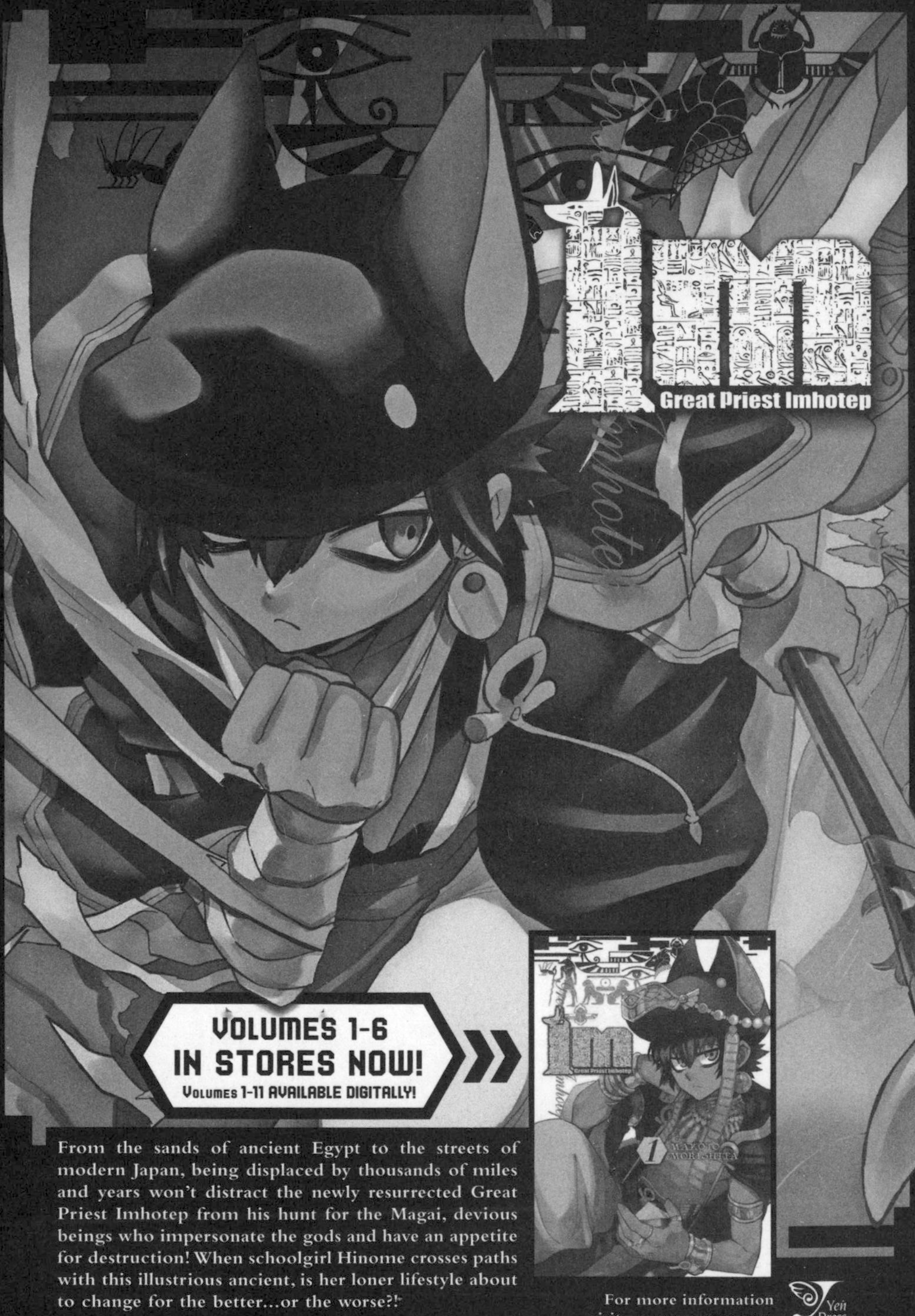
Im
Great Priest Imhotep
VOLUMES 1-6
IN STORES NOW!
VOLUMES 1-11 AVAILABLE DIGITALLY!

Toilet-bound Hanako-Kun

At Kamome Academy, rumors abound about the school's Seven Mysteries, one of which is Hanako-san. Said to occupy the third stall of the third floor girls' bathroom in the old school building, Hanako-san grants any wish when summoned. Nene Yashiro, an occult-loving high school girl who dreams of romance, ventures into this haunted bathroom...but the Hanako-san she meets there is nothing like she imagined! Kamome Academy's Hanako-san...is a boy!

Yen Press

For more information
visit www.yenpress.com

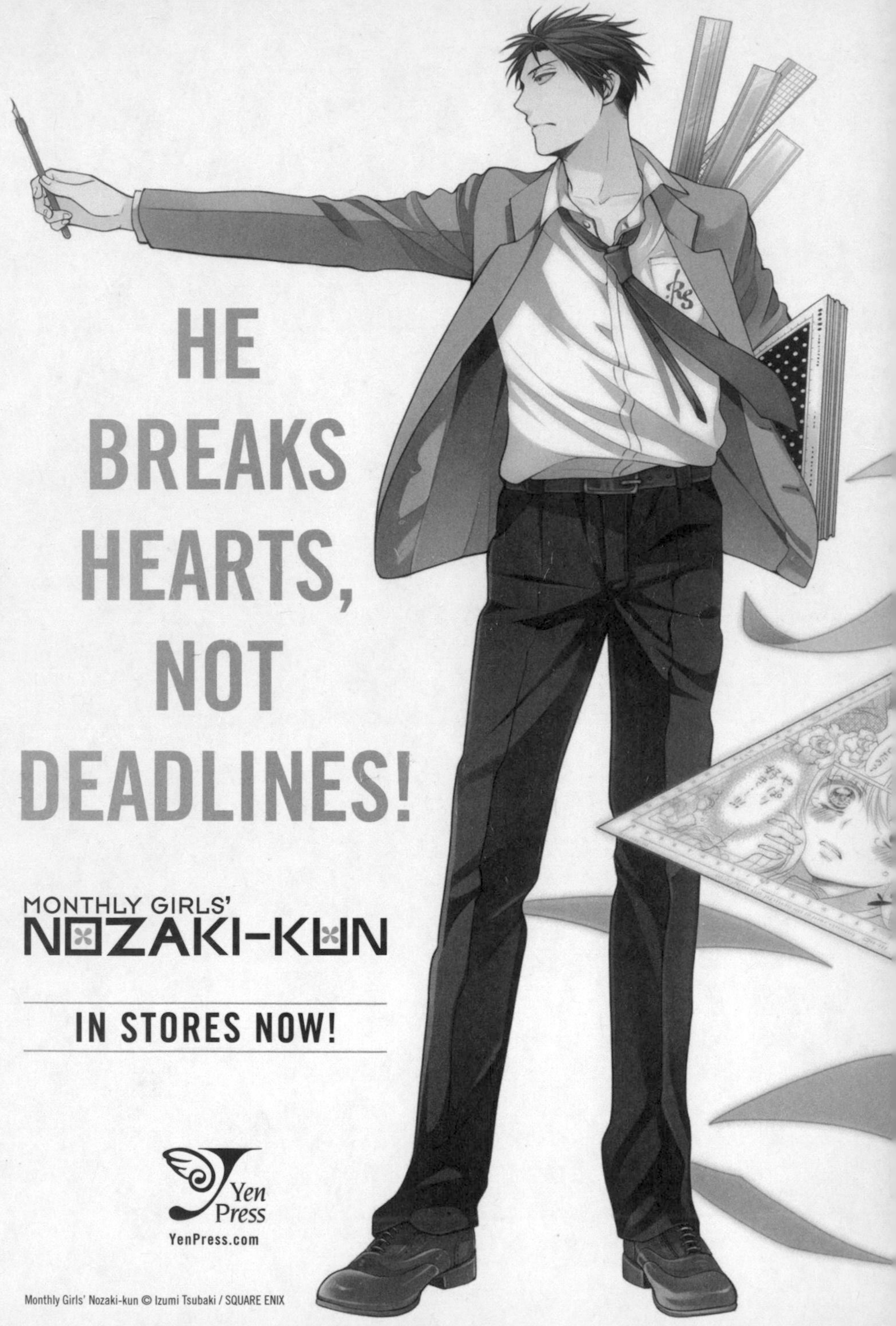
HE BREAKS HEARTS, NOT DEADLINES!
MONTHLY GIRLS'
NOZAKI-KUN
IN STORES NOW!
Yen Press
YenPress.com
Monthly Girls' Nozaki-kun © Izumi Tsubaki / SQUARE ENIX

Karino Takatsu, creator of
SERVANT × SERVICE, presents:

My Monster Girl's Too Cool For You

Burning adoration melts her heart...literally!

Karino Takatsu

In a world where *youkai* and
humans attend school together,
a boy named Atsushi Fukuzumi
falls for snow *youkai* Muku Shiroishi. Fukuzumi's passionate feelings
melt Muku's heart...and the rest of her?! The first volume of an
interspecies romantic comedy you're sure to fall head over heels for
is now available!!

Read new installments of this series every month at the same time as Japan!

CHAPTERS AVAILABLE NOW AT E-TAILERS EVERYWHERE!

STORY: **Homura Kawamoto**   ART: **Kei Saiki**

Translation: Kevin Gifford   Lettering: Anthony Quintessenza

This book is a work of fiction. Names, characters, places, and incidents are the product of the author's imagination or are used fictitiously. Any resemblance to actual events, locales, or persons, living or dead, is coincidental.

KAKEGURUI TWIN Vol. 9 ©2019 Homura Kawamoto, Kei Saiki/ SQUARE ENIX CO., LTD.
First published in Japan in 2019 by SQUARE ENIX CO., LTD.
English translation rights arranged with SQUARE ENIX CO., LTD. and Yen Press, LLC through Tuttle-Mori Agency, Inc.

English translation ©2021 by SQUARE ENIX CO., LTD.

Yen Press
150 West 30th Street, 19th Floor
New York, NY 10001

Visit us at yenpress.com
facebook.com/yenpress
twitter.com/yenpress
yenpress.tumblr.com
instagram.com/yenpress

First Yen Press Edition: February 2021

The Yen Press name and logo are trademarks of Yen Press, LLC.

Yen Press is an imprint of Yen Press, LLC.
The publisher is not responsible for websites (or their content) that are not owned by the publisher.

Library of Congress Control Number: 2018961911

ISBNs: 978-1-9753-1389-0 (paperback)
       978-1-9753-1388-3 (ebook)

10 9 8 7 6 5 4 3 2 1

WOR

Printed in the United States of America